Praise for *The Persian Puzzle*

"If you're looking for one book to read about Iran with both a history and a prescription—a history from the beginning of ancient Iran and a prescription for what U.S. policy toward Iran should be—*The Persian Puzzle* is it."
—*Los Angeles Times*

"Important and groundbreaking . . . By combining detailed history with rigorous policy analysis, and writing with refreshing clarity and zip, Pollack has given us the single best book on the U.S.-Iran relationship to date."
—*The Washington Monthly*

"What *The Persian Puzzle* does most effectively is put America's relationship with Iran into historical perspective." —*The New York Times*

"*The Persian Puzzle* is a meticulous and important analysis of how American-Iranian relations have failed consistently since 1953, the year the CIA stumbled into Iran's postcolonial mess and engineered a coup." —Salon.com

"Pollack has done a good job of describing the issues that make the U.S.-Iranian relationship a troubled one. . . . *The Persian Puzzle* is a valuable reference as the United States seeks a solution to Iran's latest nuclear challenge."
—*New York Post*

"Part history lesson, part current affairs primer and part party policy memo . . . For anyone wanting to understand the stark choices the U.S. faces concerning Iran, and how to respond to them, this is the place to start."
—*Publishers Weekly*

"Superbly written." —*Booklist*

THE
PERSIAN
PUZZLE

Kenneth M. Pollack

THE
PERSIAN
PUZZLE

---

*The Conflict Between
Iran and America*

RANDOM HOUSE TRADE PAPERBACKS

NEW YORK

2005 Random House Trade Paperback Edition

Published in the United States by Random House Trade Paperbacks,
an imprint of The Random House Publishing Group,
a division of Random House, Inc., New York.

RANDOM HOUSE TRADE PAPERBACKS and colophon are trademarks of Random House, Inc.

Originally published in hardcover in the United States by Random House,
an imprint of The Random House Publishing Group,
a division of Random House, Inc., in 2004.

Grateful acknowledgment is made to the University of Nebraska Press for
permission to reprint four maps from *Arabs at War: Military Effectiveness,
1948–1991* by Kenneth M. Pollack, © 2002 by the University of Nebraska
Press. Reprinted by permission of the University of Nebraska Press.

Library of Congress Cataloging-in-Publication Data
Pollack, Kenneth M. (Kenneth Michael).
The Persian puzzle : the conflict between Iran
and America / Kenneth M. Pollack.
p.   cm.
Includes index.
ISBN 0-8129-7336-4
1. United States—Foreign relations—Iran.
2. Iran—Foreign relations—United States.   I. Title.
E183.8.I55P58 2004
327.7305—dc22
2004054153

Printed in the United States of America

www.atrandom.com

8 9

Book design by Victoria Wong

For Aidan,
my brand-new reason for caring about
what the world is like tomorrow

Foreword

STROBE TALBOTT

This book is the latest evidence of Ken Pollack's impeccable sense of timing. Two years ago, in October 2002, as the Bush administration was focusing the world's attention on the dangers posed by Saddam Hussein, Ken's best-selling *The Threatening Storm: The Case for Invading Iraq* appeared. It argued both for decisive use of force and for a strategy to win the peace that would follow a military victory.

Now Iran is increasingly the focus of international attention—and, with *The Persian Puzzle,* of Ken's incisive analysis and hardheaded policy prescription as well. He brings to the task his own twelve-year experience at the CIA and the National Security Council and a year of scholarly research. With nearly four times the territory and three times the population of Iraq, Iran has two and a half millennia of distinctive culture. "Contained in that history," Ken writes, "are all of the elements of our current impasse. Most Iranians know that history—or some warped version of it—too well. Most Americans know it too little."

The memory of centuries of foreign manipulation and interference is a constant factor in the foreign and domestic policy of modern Iran—and part of the reason that modernity itself is a source of deep ambivalence. The "Great Game" that Russia and Britain played for control over Central Asia in the nineteenth century left scars on generations of Iranian leaders and deeply instilled a determination to insulate Iran against foreign influence. When America came into its own as a global power after World War II, Iranians, for a brief moment, saw the United States as a protector against Soviet and British infringements. But when the CIA masterminded a coup against a nationalist prime minister and reinstated the shah on the Peacock Throne, Iranians, writes Ken, went back to "believing that the United States had the ability (and the desire) to control their destinies even when we did not."

American interest in Iran during the Cold War was episodic. Washington looked at the country through two lenses: competition with the Soviet Union and the economics of oil. Both were important considerations, but neither induced the United States to give priority to the study of Iran as such. The American desire for a strong and oil-rich partner in the Middle East led a series of U.S. administrations largely to look the other way while the opulence and corruption of the shah's rule fed popular resentments that would eventually lead to an explosion.

The backlash came with the Islamist Revolution led by Ayatollah Khomeini in 1979. Besides overthrowing the U.S.-friendly shah, the ayatollah's followers promptly took American diplomats in Tehran hostage for fourteen months, but with consequences for the U.S.-Iran relationship that would last much longer. Khomeini and the mullahs went on to impose a radical ideology on the population and sponsored terrorism against Israel and the United States. It was one of the many ironies of the period that after the revolution Saddam Hussein became, as Franklin Roosevelt might have put it, "our son of a bitch" in the Gulf region. The Reagan administration backed him in the long and brutal war he fought against Iran—including the use of poison gas against Kurdish villages and Iranian troops.

Ken argues that the long-standing Iranian fear of the outside world may have lessened somewhat over the past twenty-five years. One reason is that the population has come to blame the obscurantist Islamic clerics who rule them, not foreign powers, for failing to fix the country's economic woes and for imposing political oppression and creating social ills.

But while the people of Iran, especially the younger generation, may want to see their country open up to the world, the hard-liners who are still very much in charge continue to harbor al-Qa'eda operatives and pursue a clandestine nuclear program. Ken shuns simple answers and sifts the evidence in search of the grittier truth that will be useful to policy makers and an informed public. He offers a diplomatic way forward. It features a coordinated U.S.-European pursuit of a deal with Iran on its nuclear ambitions.

In its timeliness, its trenchancy, and its solid grounding in nonpartisan, objective research, Ken's book is a model of what we try to do at Brookings and how we do it. It is also typical of the work that goes on week in and week out at our Saban Center for Middle East Policy, established through the generosity of our trustee, Haim Saban, and led by its director, Martin Indyk. Ken is director of research at the Saban Center. He and Martin have made it, over the past two years since its founding, the go-to source for members of the policy community, the press, and the public interested in the best analysis of the Middle East.

Having made this contribution to making sense of *The Persian Puzzle,* Ken has thrown himself into helping solve the even larger one of the greater Middle East.

Contents

Maps

Iran and Neighboring States

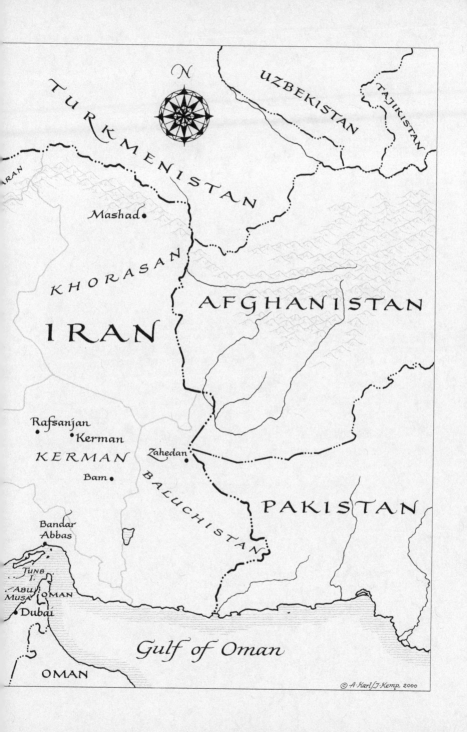

N

TURKMENISTAN

UZBEKISTAN

TAJIKISTAN

Mashad

KHORASAN

AFGHANISTAN

IRAN

Rafsanjan
Kerman

KERMAN

Zahedan

Bam

BALUCHISTAN

PAKISTAN

Bandar
Abbas

TUNB I.

ABU
MUSA   OMAN

Dubai

Gulf of Oman

OMAN

© A·Karl/J·Kemp, 2000

Introduction:
The Persistence of Memory

Persia. The name alone conjures images of the exotic. Veiled women. Strange spices. Labyrinthine bazaars. Men selling ornate carpets. For some, the name may still evoke an antique land. The great kings Darius and Xerxes, or Cyrus before them. The battles of Salamis and Marathon, where our Greek forebears (or so we describe them) faced down the vast armies of Asia marching under the banners of the king of kings of Persia.

Iran. For Americans, that name brings to mind very different images. Mad ayatollahs blaming all of the ills of the world on the "Great Satan." Hostage takers. Terrorists. Our prime adversary in the Persian Gulf for the past twenty-five years. It is also a name that, for many Americans, symbolizes frustration. The familiar refrain "Why do they hate us so much?" was being asked by Americans about Iranians long before the tragedy of September 11, 2001. Iran's motives, its politics, and its policies are often a source of utter confusion for many Americans.

Let me add two points that might ease some of that anguished perplexity: first, although they often refuse to acknowledge it, most Iranians are equally confused and ignorant about the United States. Second, Iranians themselves are often hard pressed to explain their country's actions.

The only way to understand the twenty-five-year confrontation between Iran and the United States is to know the history of the relationship. Contained in that history are all of the elements of our current impasse. Most Iranians know that history—or some warped version of it—too well. Most Americans know it too little. To a certain extent, that is the first of many profound differences that lie at the heart of our belligerent stand-off.

Although the recent past is of greatest relevance to the near future, when dealing with a nation such as Iran, there is no escaping its more distant past. Nor is it possible to understand the roots of Iran's rage at the United States without knowing a bit about the origins of our affiliation, and the ups and downs it followed during the latter half of the twentieth century. Much of the ferocious hatred each side reserves for the other was born from the pain each has felt at different times when they believed they had been betrayed—jilted may be a more appropriate term—by the other.

The importance of unraveling that history lies at the heart of understanding the choices that we, the United States, have to move forward with Iran—whether in friendship or in continued anger. Anyone who cannot master that history, cannot understand how to move beyond it.

Problems and Possibilities

Over the past twenty-five years it has become something of a commonplace for Americans writing about Iran to begin their books by arguing that Iran is an important country in an important part of the world and therefore critical to American trade and diplomacy; that the history of Iranian-American animosity was a tragedy that could have and should have been avoided; and that the continuing confrontation was mostly the doing of small groups of benighted extremists on both sides.

That is not my starting point. While I do not disagree that Iran is an important country in an important part of the world, and I believe that it would be nice if the two countries had better relations, I approach the topic of Iranian-American relations from the perspective that there are fundamental differences that lie at the root of our confrontation. The United States has some very important problems with the Iranians (and they have some very important problems with us). My reason for writing this book is not to plead for greater compassion for either side but to explain the origins of these problems and examine how best to address them. I like most of the Iranians I have met, I think that most Iranians want a better relationship with the United States, and I think that we would benefit from a warmer relationship with their country. But I will say very bluntly that I don't think the United States "needs" Iran; we have been isolated from Iran for twenty-five years and in that time have experienced the most extraordinary economic prosperity in our history, coupled with strategic developments that have made the United States the most powerful nation the world has ever seen. Clearly, the lack of a warm relationship with Iran has not exactly held us back.

The same cannot be said for the Iranians. They have not fared particularly well over the past twenty-five years. They are not destitute, but their economy is hobbled. They are not quite international pariahs, but they have an unsavory reputation that follows them wherever they go. In her most recent book on Iran, Robin Wright quotes an Iranian shoe salesman turned bus driver lamenting, "Now we're treated as outcasts. Few foreigners come here anymore, and it's almost impossible for ordinary Iranians to get visas to go abroad. We'd probably be all alone if it weren't for our oil."[1] Nor have Iranians been able to realize anything like the kind of prosperity or status that their geostrategic position, natural resources, and national endowments ought to afford them. In part for that reason, many (probably most) Iranians are eager for improved ties with the United States—at least in the abstract. What stands between us and them is a sea of troubles.

It is not necessarily that this sea is wide, but it is very deep and it seems to be forever storm-swept. One can tick off America's problems with Iran on one hand: support for terrorism, pursuit of nuclear weapons, opposition to the Middle East peace process, undermining of regional stability, and a poor human rights record. But none of these issues is easily dismissed and each one is a tangle. That tangle consists of decades of accumulated psychological scar tissue. The United States and Iran have a relatively brief (as historians tend to measure things) but terribly involved history. Like former lovers who went through a messy divorce, we have a lot of "issues."

One of the principal themes of this book is not just that understanding the history of U.S.-Iranian relations is absolutely essential to appreciate the nature of the problems we currently confront, but that the imbalance in historical knowledge is also part of the problem. Americans are serial amnesiacs; as a nation, we forget what we have done almost immediately after doing it. We often hold grudges, but we just as often can't remember why. We are mostly a forward-thinking and future-oriented people, and we tend to ignore the past for the sake of concentrating on the future—"let's not dwell on the past" and "water under the bridge" are characteristically American expressions. Many Americans know almost nothing about the sources of Iranian grievance against the United States, where our own grudge against Tehran came from, and why the two sides have found it so difficult to overcome their differences.

Unfortunately, that very ignorance contributes to the difficulty of addressing our current problems with Iran. It allows extremists on both sides of the political spectrum to suggest that easy solutions are available to our problems if we would just embrace them. And because most Americans do not understand the complexities of the relationship and the depths of the confrontation, they can be easily swayed by these siren songs.

This raises the second principal theme of this book: there are no easy answers to our problems with Tehran. It may sound strange to say this given the problems the United States has faced in both Iraq and Afghanistan, but in both of those cases there was a simple and straightforward option to address the problems created by Saddam Hussein and the Taliban. In the case of Iran, that same option is all but impossible short of a direct, unprovoked Iranian act of war against the United States. All of the other options on the table are much harder to make work than they may seem at first blush. It is worth remembering that in the twenty-five years since the taking of the U.S. Embassy in Tehran, the United States has tried every policy imaginable, from undeclared warfare to unilateral concessions, and none of them has solved our problems with Iran (although some were more successful than others in accomplishing secondary American goals).

If Americans know the history of Iran and U.S.-Iranian relations too little, then Iranians know it too well. For Iranians, the history is a constant stumbling block, made much worse by the fact that what they know as history is, in most cases, a distorted concoction of their own nationalist, religious, and even Marxist zealots. This too makes it crucial that Americans understand both the truth of that history and the version of it known by most Iranians. Our history must be a source of lessons for the future, but we must also understand the lessons that Iranians have (mis)learned in the past.

For all of these reasons, if we are ever to ameliorate, let alone eliminate, our problems with Iran, we must start with an appreciation of their history and ours together. And now is a good time to be thinking about how we are going to handle our differences.

Why Iran, Why Now?

I chose to write this book now because there are signs of important developments coming in Iran in the not too distant future. These developments could be positive or negative—a transition to real democracy or the solidification of Islamist autocracy, the acquisition of nuclear weapons or the embrace of collective security, a greater openness to the outside world or a greater effort to shut it out. All are possible. These changes hold out a series of challenges and opportunities for the United States. We may be able to open the path to a much better relationship with Iran in the future, or we may face a much more dangerous threat. But the one truth that has emerged over the past two or three years is that it is increasingly important that the United States begin to make some fundamental decisions about Iran and fashion a policy to achieve our goals.

As anyone who has served in government knows, it is easiest to redirect the ship of state if changes are made well in advance of dramatic events—and hardest when forced to react to sudden, unforeseen developments. By the same token, it is very difficult to find the political willingness to make far-reaching change as long as problems seem distant. Unable to turn away from the problems it created in Iraq and unable to reconcile the deep internal divisions over policy toward Iran, the Bush administration has adopted a policy of "kicking the can down the road" where Iran is concerned. It has left Iran policy mostly in the hands of the International Atomic Energy Agency and our European allies—none of whom are terribly interested in looking out for America's best interests. Thus, difficult as it is to tear our attention away from the all-consuming problems of Iraq, Afghanistan, Saudi Arabia, Gaza, and the West Bank, it is time to think long and hard about Iran. If we do not, I fear that in a few years' time we will wish that we had.

Today, the United States is waist deep in a war against terror. With the demise of the Taliban regime in Afghanistan, Iran is probably the world's worst state sponsor of terrorism. If the goal of the United States is to eliminate terrorism as a legitimate method of expressing political grievance, then Iran's policies must surely be addressed. However, the worst mistake we could make would be to approach Iran through the prism of the war on terrorism. Getting Iran out of the terrorism business will be very difficult and the approach we have used with Afghanistan and Iraq would likely be a grave mistake with Iran. Dealing with Iranian sponsorship of terrorism means dealing with Iran on its own terms, and that takes us back to the tangle of U.S.-Iranian relations.

The same can be said for Iran's nuclear program. Like a bad dream, Iran's nuclear program continues to plague us night after night. While no one really knows how close Iran is to acquiring a workable weapon—and our various experiences with Iraq over the past fifteen years should make us very cautious about all such predictions—there does seem to be a consensus among even the most dovish that Iran is further along in acquiring a nuclear weapons capability than was believed even a few years ago.

Iran's nuclear program in particular makes the present an important moment to consider policy toward Iran. There is no way of knowing how Iran will behave if they acquire nuclear weapons. Their past behavior certainly gives reasons for concern. If possession of a nuclear deterrent prompts Iran to revert to an aggressive, anti-American foreign policy of destabilizing regional regimes, as it tried in the 1980s and early 1990s, it could cause great harm to U.S. interests in the region. However, because Iran is still probably some way off from acquiring nuclear weapons, there is reason to believe that the United States could take actions in the near term that might delay or even preclude such an event altogether. Moreover, at least for the moment, our leading allies have shown some concern regarding Iran's nuclear weapons program, and this too suggests that the United States might have options for dealing with this problem that were not available even five years ago. If we do not take advantage of this window of opportunity to deal with Iran's nuclear program in particular, someday we doubtless will regret not having done so.

The issue of Iraq raises another Iran-related problem. The reconstruction of Iraq was always going to be a long, hard process, but we have made it much harder than it ever needed to be thanks to our many mistakes during the first year after the fall of Baghdad. Iran has considerable assets it can bring to bear in Iraq. If we can somehow convince them to be helpful there, it potentially might mean the difference between success and failure. On the other hand, if they decide to try to undermine our efforts there, they could create the kind of hellish conditions for American forces that they eventually did for us in Lebanon in the early 1980s.

Finally, we must recognize that there has been an important change in Iran since 2004 that requires a fresh look at our policy. After the stunning victory of Mohammad Khatami in the presidential election of 1997, it became a commonplace to assume that Iran was changing for the better—democratization at home, moderation abroad seemed the inevitable path for the country. To a considerable extent, that gave American policy makers an out when contemplating Iran. The certainty that Iran was changing for the better, even if no one knew how quickly, relieved a lot of pressure to deal with Iran's troubling behavior since it was assumed that time would eventually solve all of our problems.

Since the disastrous Majles (the Iranian Parliament) elections of February 2004, however, this can no longer be taken for granted. As chapter 12 explains, the successful emasculation of Khatami's reform movement and the development of a modified "China model" by Iran's hard-liners suggests that while the vast majority of Iranians still want that change, they may not get it anytime soon. If Iranian hard-liners have found a way to hold on to power for the foreseeable future, then the United States must confront a much harder range of choices than we realized even a few years ago. Iran's hard-liners may have lost the edge and the unrealistic ambitions of Ayatollah Khomeini, but it is still less than certain that they can be trusted to pursue a policy of moderation and engagement with the Western world—let alone the United States. In those circumstances, Iran's determination to acquire nuclear weapons and continued support for terrorism become even more disquieting.

A St. Patrick's Day Lesson

On March 17, 2000, I stood in a packed room at the Omni Shoreham Hotel in Washington, watching from the wings while Secretary of State Madeleine Albright gave a speech I knew practically by heart. I had not written that speech, but as the director for Persian Gulf affairs at the National Security Council, I had spent weeks wrestling with the text—and the people who wrote it. It was not a perfect speech (a topic to which I return in chapter 11), but it was pretty good. At one dramatic moment, Secretary Albright announced, "In 1953, the United States played a significant role in orchestrating the overthrow of Iran's popular Prime Minister, Mohammad Mosaddeq. The Eisenhower administration believed its actions were justified for strategic reasons; but the coup was clearly a setback for Iran's political development. And it is easy to see now why many Iranians continue to resent this intervention by America in their internal affairs. Moreover, during the next quarter century, the United States and the West gave sustained backing to the Shah's regime. Although it did much to develop the country economically, the Shah's government also brutally repressed political dissent. As President Clinton has said, the United States must bear its fair share of responsibility for the problems that have arisen in U.S.-Iranian relations. Even in more recent years, aspects of U.S. policy towards Iraq during its conflict with Iran appear now to have been regrettably short-sighted, especially in light of our subsequent experiences with Saddam Hussein."

Iranians had angrily demanded such an admission from the United States for two decades. The 1953 coup in particular was central to their anger at the United States and their conception of America's manipulation of Iran for the twenty-five years that followed. Now they finally had the acknowledgment and apology that they had wanted. What was their response? Ayatollah Khamene'i, Iran's supreme leader himself, gave Tehran's answer to the assembled masses at Mashhad:

> Just a few days ago an American minister delivered a speech. After half a century, or over 40 years, the Americans have now confessed that they staged the 28th Mordad [August 19, 1953] coup. They confessed that they supported the suppressive, dictatorial, and corrupt Pahlavi shah for twenty-five years. Please pay attention. We are in the year

1379 [by the Islamic calendar], more than forty years have elapsed since 1332 and the coup d'etat of the 28th Mordad. It is only now that they are admitting that they were behind the coup d'etat. They admit that they supported and backed the dictatorial, oppressive, corrupt and subservient regime of the shah for twenty-five years. And they are now saying that they supported Saddam Husayn in his war against Iran. What do you think the Iranian nation, faced with this situation and these admissions, feels? . . . In the course of those days, during the war, we repeatedly said in our speeches that the Americans are helping Saddam Husayn. They denied this and claimed they remained impartial. Now that 12 years have elapsed after the end of the war, in a center [the American-Iranian Council] this American Secretary of State is officially admitting that they helped Saddam Husayn. The question is, what good will this admission do us? . . . What good does this admission—that you acted in that way then—do us now? . . . An admission years after the crime was committed, while they might be committing similar crimes now, will not do the Iranian nation any good.

And that was the end of the Clinton administration's bid for reconciliation with Iran. Clearly, the history of Iranian-American relations is crucial to our policy now and in the future. And just as clearly, untangling it is going to be a bear.

THE
PERSIAN
PUZZLE

From Persepolis to
the Pahlavis

To understand the labyrinth of U.S.-Iranian relations, there are at least three things that you need to know about the seven millennia of Iranian history before the twentieth century. The first is that the land that is today Iran is the heir to a long line of remarkable predecessors. In its day, the Persian Empire was a superpower like nothing the world had ever seen—with a monotheistic religion, a vast army, a rich civilization, a new and remarkably efficient method of administration, and territory stretching from Egypt to Central Asia. All Iranians know that history well, and it is a source of enormous pride to them. It has given them a widely remarked sense of superiority over all of their neighbors, and, ironically, while Tehran now refers to the United States by the moniker "Global Arrogance," within the Middle East a stereotypical complaint against Iranians is their own arrogant treatment of others.[1]

The second important aspect of Iran's early history that still defines the Iranian state and has had a tremendous impact on U.S.-Iranian relations is that for the last five hundred years, Iran has been the only Shi'i Muslim state in the world. Though 90 percent of all Muslims are Sunni, there are a number of countries where Shi'ah make up either a majority (Bahrain, Iraq, Iran) or a significant minority (Lebanon, Saudi Arabia, Syria, Yemen). But only Iran adopted Shi'i Islam as its state religion. Although the Sunni-Shi'ah divide is not as caustic as other interreligious splits, it is not a trifle either. There are important aspects of Shi'ism that have helped shape Iranian political culture in ways that are quite different from that of other Muslim nations. What's more, it has heightened both Iran's sense of uniqueness and its sense of isolation. For Iranians, Shi'ism is a key element of their culture, and for many Arabs and other non-Iranians, the terms "Shi'ah" and "Persian" were long considered synonymous.

Last, for roughly a century and a half beginning in the early 1800s, a weak Iranian state became prey to powerful external actors, principally the European great powers. Iranians (Persians, as they were then still known) were accustomed to looking down on Europeans as barbarian adherents to a superseded religion and a primitive civilization. Now, suddenly, they were trouncing the shah's armies, carving up their lands, making and unmaking governments, monopolizing their markets, and treating their land as battleground, playground, and campground with no regard for the needs or desires of the Iranians themselves. It was humiliating; it was frustrating, and it was frightening for Iranians to be so vulnerable and so constantly manipulated by these foreign powers. And it reinforced a powerful sense of xenophobia coupled with an inferiority complex among Iranians to complement their superiority complex.

Elaine Sciolino has covered Iran since the revolution and is one of the most knowledgeable journalists writing on Iran, yet even she admits in her book *Persian Mirrors* that "whenever I think I understand Iran, it throws me a curve."[2] Iran is a maddeningly complicated state and society, and even a cursory understanding of its motives today requires knowing a fair bit about the forces that have shaped the nation over time.

Ancient History

When the first tribes entered Iran after the last ice age, they found an inhospitable land. The territory of Iran is fenced in by three great mountain ranges—the Alborz in the north, the Zagros in the west and south, and the Mekran in the southeast. In the center is a great plateau that is itself mostly uninhabitable. Two vast deserts, the Dasht-e Kavir and the Dasht-e Lut, in the east of the central plateau, render roughly half its territory unfit for agriculture. It has few navigable rivers.[3]

The mountains and deserts, the poor soil, and the lack of good rivers made communications difficult in ancient Iran. As a result, the population became deeply fragmented. In those parts of the land that were fit for agriculture, secluded villages and isolated towns—with only a few big cities—became the rule. Nomadic tribes who depended on herding livestock inhabited the rest. Because of the discrete separation of so much of the population, Iran became a patchwork of ethnic, religious, tribal, and other groupings, all of whom seemed to find constant reasons for conflict with their neighbors.[4]

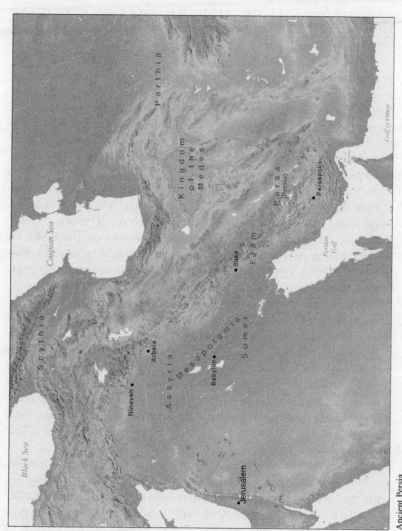

Ancient Persia

Thus, it may seem odd that so difficult a land would produce one of the world's first great multiethnic empires. Perhaps a hard land made for hard people who could then conquer their softer neighbors? Whatever the reason, for centuries of the ancient world, the empire that emerged from ancient Iran was a superpower in a league by itself.

The first people to settle and establish a civilization in what would become Iran, however, were hardly world beaters. The Elamites lived in the far southwest of the land, close by to what was then the great civilization of Sumer—mankind's first true civilization, the home of the biblical Garden of Eden, and the ancient precursor of modern Iraq. Elam suffered from the superior power of the Sumerians as much as it benefited from their more advanced culture and technology.

In the second millennium B.C., migratory waves from eastern Europe brought the Indo-European race of Aryans into Persia. Three groups of Aryans swept in and settled in different parts of the country: the Scythians, who conquered the far northwest from their strongholds around the Black Sea; the Medes (or Mada), who settled in a wide swath of land in the center of the country; and the Persians (or Parsa), who eventually made their home in the south, in what would eventually become Iran's Fars (derived from "Pars") province. Other elements of the Aryan race would spread westward from their primordial homeland into northern Europe, to constitute the Germanic and Scandinavian peoples whom the Nazis would make so much of.[5]

For many centuries, it was the Medes who dominated ancient Iran. They were forced to unite quickly and develop an effective society to stave off the fearsome Assyrian Empire to their west. At that time, Assyria ruled Mesopotamia and much of the Near East with a highly developed and highly brutal war machine. In constant warfare with the Assyrians, the Medes rarely fared well, but, aided by the Zagros Mountains, they were ultimately able to hold back the Assyrian incursions.

Although the term "Mede" would remain in European usage as a synonym for "Persian" for millennia, little has survived of their history or society. The era of the Mede ascendancy saw the birth of one of the world's first monotheistic religions—Zoroastrianism. Zoroaster ("Zarathustra" in Greek) lived from roughly 628 to 551 B.C. and preached of a single great god, Ahura Mazda, of whom all other gods were simply poorly descried parts. Zoroastrianism was deeply concerned with the eternal relationship between good and evil, and many scholars believe that, even in modern Iran, Zoroaster's focus on this permanent struggle remains an important element lurking beneath the surface of much religious and secular philosophy. Khomeini's obsession with the struggle between good (epitomized by Islam and Iran) and evil (the West, the United States) is often described as a manifestation of this deep-seated Iranian trait. Zoroastrianism was also the first religion to preach the notion that humans would face judgment after death based on their actions in life, and that each soul would then spend eternity in either Paradise or perdition. Zoroastrianism became the chief religion of the Medes (and the Persians) and would dominate Iranian spiritual life until the Islamic conquest more than a thousand years later.[6]

Ultimately, most of what we know of the Medes regards their eventual displacement by the Persians. In 636 B.C., the Elamites were crushed in battle by the great Assyrian king Ashurbanipal. This defeat opened the way for the rise of the Persians. The defeat of Elam (the Persians' neighbors to the west) created room for the Persians to expand their land and power. With their new status, the Persian kings allied themselves with the Babylonians, and together they defeated the Assyrians, sacking the Assyrian capital of Ninevah in 612 B.C. In about 559 B.C., Cyrus II (later called Cyrus the Great) took the throne of Persia. It was Cyrus who took a state that had made itself regionally important, and turned it into the vast Persian Empire. Drawing on the new power provided by the combined lands of Persia, Elam, and parts of Assyria, Cyrus turned on the Medes and conquered them. He quickly followed this victory with successful campaigns against the Parthians and Hyrcanians farther to the east, before turning west and smashing the fabulously wealthy King Croesus of Lydia (in present-day northern Turkey), and incorporating Asia Minor into his empire. After his Lydian victory, Cyrus turned south, conquering Babylon, where he freed the Jews from their captivity and permitted them to return to Palestine—thereby earning considerable praise in the Bible's Book of Isaiah. When Cyrus finally died, he was followed by his son Cambyses II, who added Egypt to Cyrus's colossal Persian demesne.[7]

In 522 B.C., when Cambyses' son Darius ascended the throne as the king of kings of Persia, his empire was the greatest in the world. It stretched from the Aegean to Afghanistan, from the Black Sea to the Blue Nile. It was estimated to have contained 50 million people, an unimaginable population for that time. So vast an empire was difficult to govern with ancient communications and organization, and Darius's greatest achievement was a thorough internal reform of the empire. He built roads—2,500 kilometers' worth of them. He created a system of provinces ruled by satraps (governors) capable of acting on his behalf. He instituted a standardized system of weights and measures and introduced uniform gold and silver coinage. His commercial reforms made Persia a trading juggernaut that dominated the markets of the ancient

Near Eastern world. And Darius built a magnificent new imperial capital at Persepolis with an eclectic architectural style that attempted to blend elements of the motifs of all of the many subject peoples of the empire.[8]

Darius also mounted the first Persian invasion of ancient Greece, which looms so large in the Western consciousness. It was Darius whose forces landed at Marathon in 490 B.C. only to be defeated by the Athenian hoplite army. Darius's defeat by so tiny and insignificant a nation as the Athenian city-state spurred his son and successor, Xerxes, to mount a much grander expedition. In 480 B.C., Xerxes led a massive force of possibly as many as 200,000 troops across the Hellespont to conquer all of Greece. At Thermopylae, he was detained by the illustrious, doomed stand of 300 Spartan warriors and their great king, Leonidas, whose sacrifice inspired their squabbling countrymen to unite against the Persian foe. Later that year, the Athenian fleet scored a stunning victory over the Persians at Salamis, forcing Xerxes to halt the invasion. The next year, at Plataea, a combined Greek army led by the Spartans smashed a Persian force, ending the Persian threat to Greece and setting a limit on Persia's westward expansion.[9]

A century and a half later, Greece would come back to bite the Persians. In 334 B.C., Alexander the Great, king of Macedon and the leader of a Greek confederation, invaded Persia. For the Greeks, Persia was the world's great superpower and had been for as long as any could remember. Attacking it was the ultimate act of defiance, and anyone who could conquer it would achieve fame unmatched for all the ages. This was precisely the sort of challenge that appealed to the young, headstrong Macedonian monarch. In 334, Alexander crossed the Hellespont with a force of about 35,000 men and proceeded to conquer the greatest empire the world had ever known. In 331, he defeated the Persian Army at the Battle of Arbela (in modern-day northern Iraq) by charging directly at the Persian king, Darius III, who fled the field and so demoralized his troops. The next year Alexander occupied Persepolis and burned it. Eventually, he would push on into Afghanistan and India, before turning back when his exhausted troops mutinied.

Having conquered Persia, Alexander was determined to rule it; he reorganized the empire and attempted to fuse his Greco-Macedonian base with his new Persian conquests. He instituted a common currency, made Greek the "official" language of the entire empire, devised a unified bureaucracy, and even went so far as to order 10,000 of his Greek soldiers to marry Persian women at a mass ceremony at Susa in 324. But Alexander contracted a fever and died the very next year, and without him, his empire could not hold together. It was divided up among a number of his generals. Mesopotamia fell to Seleucus, who made his capital at Babylon and used it as a base to conquer the Iranian heartland. For the next century, the Iranian lands were ruled by the Seleucid Greeks, who brought Hellenistic influences to Persia.[10]

The Seleucids were eventually displaced by the Parthians—a central Asian people descended from the Scythians, who were, in a sense, returning to their old stomping grounds. The Parthians were able to conquer and hold Mesopotamia as well as the Iranian lands, and for several centuries they contested control of Armenia and the Levant with the Roman Empire. The Parthians left almost no surviving records, and scholars speculate that they may not have kept any themselves. But the Parthians too would pass, defeated in 227 A.D. by Ardeshir of Sasani, who would establish in their place the Sassanid Empire. The Sassanids ruled Iran until they in turn were overthrown by a new power rising in the south, Islam.[11]

The Islamic Invasion

The Sassanids fought ten wars with Rome, many more with the migrating Huns, and developed a highly centralized state firmly grounded in Zoroastrian teachings. But by the sixth century A.D., they were losing their grip on power thanks to revolts among their military nobility, internal discontent, and a series of costly and unsuccessful wars against the Byzantines. They were certainly not ready for the storm that broke upon them in the middle of the next century.

In 622, the Prophet Muhammad made his famed *hijra* (migration) from Mecca to Medina, beginning the Islamic era. Two years later, his followers defeated the Meccans in the Battle of Badr, bringing the new religion back to his homeland and inaugurating the first of the Islamic conquests. The new faith spread like wildfire among the tribes of western Arabia, firing them with a zeal that made them nearly invincible in battle. Within a year after Muhammad's death in 632, the entire Arabian Peninsula had fallen to Islam. Five years later, victory at the Battle of Qadisiyah would bring them control of Ctesiphon, then the capital of Mesopotamia. The Islamic armies then broke the power of the Sassanids at Nahavand in 642, although not until 700 was Iran fully pacified.[12]

In some ways, the Islamic conquest changed everything for the Iranians, and in other ways it did not change that much. The Iranians were slow to convert to the new religion. Not until the ninth century were a majority of Iranians Muslims. Unlike many other lands of the Islamic empire, Arabic did not entirely supplant Persian as the language of the masses—the elites learned it, but most of the population continued to speak variations of Pahlavi, the Persian tongue of the Sassanids. Moreover, the Muslim conquerors actually adopted a great deal from their Iranian subjects. They retained the Sassanid monetary system, incorporated Sassanid court ceremonies into their own, and borrowed many Sassanid administrative mechanisms, including the office of *vizier* (minister) and the *divan* (a budgetary office). The practice of veiling and seclusion of women—wealthy, freeborn noble women—came from the Persians, too, although both customs were also practiced to some extent by the Greeks and Romans.[13]

Under the first two Islamic dynasties—the Umayyads and the Abbasids—Iran remained firmly within the orbit of the larger Islamic empire. However, the decline of the Abbasids in the tenth and eleventh centuries allowed Iran's rulers to begin to assert a degree of independence from the center. This process was reinforced by climatic change. Over the centuries, irrigation had introduced salinity into the Iranian soil, leading to desertification, which forced formerly settled agricultural communities to adopt nomadic ways of life that made them more difficult to control by centralized authority.[14]

Overall, these patterns left Iran vulnerable to invasion by warlike tribes from central Asia—greatest among them the Seljuk Turks, who conquered Iran in the early twelfth century. Nevertheless, the Seljuks recognized themselves to be culturally inferior to their Persian subjects, and they quickly adopted many local practices. Not all Iranians accepted the Seljuks, and one group of Isma'ili Shi'ah created a secret sect that sent out fanatical members to murder their political opponents. In Arabic, these zealots were called the Hashashiyyun (because it was believed they smoked hashish before departing on their missions), which became corrupted in European usage to "assassins."

Of far more devastating consequence were the Mongol invasions that began in the thirteenth century. First Genghis Khan blazed a trail of slaughter and destruction across Iran, followed by his grandson Hulagu, who extended the bloody Mongol conquests farther west, sacking Baghdad in 1258. The Mongols did terrible and, in many cases, permanent damage—destroying fragile underground water tunnels and massacring so many Iranian males as to radically alter parts of Iran's topography and demography. A second wave under Tamerlane (Timur the Lame or Timur Lang) in the fourteenth century was gentler only by comparison with its predecessors—the razing of the great cities of Isfahan and Shiraz being cases in point. The Mongols were skilled at obliterating things but poor at building anything lasting of their own. They left behind little but a legacy of misery after their passing.

Shi'ism Comes to Iran

In the wake of the chaos left by the Mongol rulers, Iran became a cockpit to be fought over by a variety of Turkic and Afghan peoples. For that reason, it is somewhat remarkable that an indigenous group, the Safavids, would finally succeed in reunifying the country—the first native dynasty to rule the land in more than a millennium. The Safavids began as a militant Sufi (mystic) sect of Shi'i Islam. After conquering the great northwest Iranian city of Tabriz in 1501, the Safavids moderated many of their more extreme beliefs—such as the notion that their leaders were divine—and launched a series of offensives that soon brought the rest of the traditional Persian realm under their control. However, this stability came with a price: they demanded that all of the inhabitants, the vast majority of whom were Sunni Muslims, convert to Shi'ism.[15]

Thus it was the Safavids who brought the Shi'i version of Islam to Iran. Although Shi'ism is often associated with Iran because Iran is the largest Shi'i country today, its origins have nothing to do with Iran. Instead they derive from the earliest days of the Islamic empire.

After the death of the Prophet Muhammad, there was disagreement among his followers over who should be named his successor (*caliph*) as leader of the Muslims. Although an important minority of the original companions of the Prophet favored 'Ali, cousin and son-in-law of Muhammad, the majority backed Muhammad's longtime companion and father-in-law, Abu Bakr. 'Ali eventually became the fourth successor to the Prophet, but his murder in the garrison town of Kufa in southern Iraq reopened the debate on succession. (He was assassinated in 661 by a dissident soldier, one of a group who opposed his lenient treatment of the rebellious governor of Damascus, Mu'awiya.) Upon the death of 'Ali, his followers, or partisans, demanded that the succession remain within the family of the Prophet and to its only survivors, the sons of 'Ali—Hasan and Husayn. Members of the dominant merchant clans of Mecca and Medina, however, backed the claims of another prominent tribe, the Umayyids, led by Mu'awiya. Hasan gave up his claim and Mu'awiya was named caliph.

But not everyone accepted Hasan's decision. Those followers of 'Ali who rejected Mu'awiya became known as the "party of 'Ali" or, in Arabic, the Shi'at 'Ali, later abbreviated to Shi'ah. 'Ali's youngest son, Husayn, became the leader of the Shi'ah, although he made no claim to the caliphate as long as Mu'awiya lived. When Mu'awiya died in 680, Husayn hoped to claim the caliphate, but he and seventy-one of his followers were waylaid at nearby Karbala by a far greater force under Yazid, the son of Mu'awiya, who (naturally) believed that the caliphate should pass to him. Husayn and his followers were slaughtered at Karbala on the tenth day of the month of Moharram. Husayn and his brother Abbas were buried in Karbala, which became—together with their father's tomb in Najaf—the holiest sites in Shi'i Islam. The tenth day of Moharram, the day of *Ashura* ("tenth" in Arabic), became the holiest day of the Shi'i religious calendar, when the faithful wail and even flog themselves bloody to excoriate themselves for, figuratively, not having come to the defense of Husayn at Karbala. Indeed, the martyrdom of Husayn and the mythology of the fatally doomed cause became important touchstones of the Shi'i faith.

The Shi'i and Sunni sects of Islam have a great deal in common—far more, arguably, than the doctrines of Protestant and Catholic Christianity, for example. And although born of a blood feud, the Sunni-Shi'i split has not been a particularly gory one; again, there is nothing in Islamic history like the appalling wars of the Reformation that devastated Europe during the sixteenth and seventeenth centuries. A key distinguishing feature of Shi'ism, however, is the concept of the Imamate. Shi'is believe that the succession from the Prophet rightly should have passed to 'Ali and then to 'Ali's blood line. Most Iranians are Twelver Shi'ah, the mainstream Shi'i denomination. As their name implies, Twelvers believe that there were twelve imams: 'Ali, then his sons Hasan and Husayn, and nine others. The twelfth imam was taken into hiding to protect him from the enemies of Shi'ism when he was just a baby, and later it was announced that he had entered into a form of occultation and would return only at a much later date in messianic fashion as the Lord of the Age, the Mahdi, who will bring an era of justice followed by ultimate judgment for all mankind.

The concept of the imamate is important because it contributes to another key difference between Sunni and Shi'ah. In its simplest form, the Sunni faith maintains that God has given mankind everything we need to live our lives properly in the form of the Quran and the sayings and histories of the Prophet, the proper interpretations of which were finalized in the ninth and tenth centuries. Shi'is believe that the imams were themselves divinely guided, and so it fell to them to lead the community in righteous fashion, which they did by definition. The loss of the twelfth imam consequently posed a problem for the Shi'ah: Who was going to lead them? This problem led eventually to a reliance upon men called *mujtahid*s—those capable of practicing *ijtihad* (the ability to interpret the holy scriptures). These were religious leaders responsible for guiding the community in the absence of the imam. At the pinnacle of the Shi'i religious hierarchy, the most respected and revered *mujtahid*s were granted the title *marja-e taqlid* (source of emulation). Effectively, the concept behind this structure held that only those most learned in Islamic jurisprudence (the *mujtahid*s) were capable of interpreting the scriptures to determine how men and women should live their lives in the absence of the twelfth imam. Everyone else had to look to a source of emulation (a *marja-e taqlid*), who were always highly respected *mujtahid*s, and follow their example to live righteous lives. In the nineteenth century, the notion of a *marja-e taqlid al-mutlaq* (the "absolute" or "supreme" *marja-e taqlid*) as the ultimate exemplar for all Shi'ah to follow also entered Shi'i theology and would become the root of Ayatollah Khomeini's concept of *velayat-e faqih,* or "rule of the jurisprudent."[16]

The emergence of the *mujtahid*s and the concept of the *marja-e taqlid* at the peak of it all gave rise to a fairly elaborate religious hierarchy within Shi'ism that is not matched by Sunni Islam. Would-be mullahs (a Persian term for a cleric that in Arabic is rendered *'alim*) begin by attending a seminary, a *madrasah,* often in one of the great centers of Shi'i learning (called *hawza*s) at Qom in Iran or Najaf in Iraq. From there, they might go on to be the local mullah in a village or teach under the guidance of a higher-ranking cleric in one of the seminaries themselves. In time, as they demonstrated their learning, their familiarity with the Quran and other Islamic scripture, and their ability to deal with questions posed by their students or congregants, they might be accepted as a *hojjat-ol Islam* ("proof of Islam"). If their wisdom and prestige were to continue to rise, they might be acclaimed as an ayatollah ("sign of God"), which requires them to write a lengthy dissertation elaborating on how people should conduct themselves in day-to-day life as a guide for their followers. Finally, at the very top, is the exalted rank of *ayatollah al-uzma* (grand ayatollah, literally "greatest sign of God"), which is a relatively recent rank that was used to distinguish the very top ayatollahs after "title inflation" raised many lesser figures to the rank of ayatollah and so diminished its cachet. All of the grand ayatollahs were *marja*s, and in the nineteenth century, a *marja-e taqlid al-mutlaq* was then named from the handful of grand ayatollahs.

The Qajar Dynasty and the Early Modern Era in Iran

Having brought Shi'ism to Iran, the Safavids held power from the sixteenth to eighteenth centuries. In 1722, Ghilzai tribesmen from Afghanistan conquered much of Iran, effectively emasculating the dynasty. Various external and internal groups contested power in Iran until 1795, when the Qajars—a Turkic tribe who had migrated to Iran from Central Asia in the fourteenth century—were able to defeat their rivals and claim the throne of a reunified Persian state.[17]

The Qajars would not rule happily for very long. The world was changing all around Iran, and not necessarily to its advantage. The rise of maritime commerce meant that many of the trade routes that had once passed from the Far East through Iran to the West now sailed around the mountainous land altogether. Without that trade, Iran's cities declined. This, coupled with further growth in nomadism, further weakened the strength and control of the central government. Meanwhile, the European states were growing powerful and creeping ever closer to Iran. In 1763, the Iranian ruler Karim Khan granted the British East India Company the right to build a base and a trading post at Bushehr on the Persian Gulf.[18] More dangerous still, to the north, the Russians were slowly digesting new conquests in the Black Sea area and setting their sights on targets even farther south.

Persia (as it was then still called) and Russia first came to blows in 1804, when their imperial ambitions collided in Georgia. In a nine-year war, the Russians prevailed decisively, forcing the Iranians to cede all of their lands in the Caucasus and to agree to give up the right to maintain any naval forces in the Caspian Sea.[19] But in the age of the Great Game between Russia and Britain, as these opponents sparred and fenced across the length of Asia, Russia's victory could only increase British interest in the country. With the shah (king) of Persia still smarting from his drubbing by the Russians, it was not difficult for British envoys to convince him to sign a protectorate agreement with His Majesty's government. The Definitive Treaty of 1814 pledged British support for Persia in return for Persian promises that no other foreign troops would be allowed into Iran and that only British officers would be allowed to train the Persian Army—a French training mission having formerly served that purpose since 1807.[20]

The signing of the Definitive Treaty officially made Iran a pawn in the Great Game. The shah had hoped to use British support to defend his realm against the Russians in the near term and use British military assistance to rebuild his army so that he could eventually avenge his losses to the Russians. The European powers had other things in mind. The Russians sought to rule Persia. The British saw Persia as yet another buffer to the "jewel in the Crown" of India. Thus they wanted an independent Persia, stable and strong enough to withstand the Russians but not strong enough to constitute a threat to India itself.[21] Inevitably, it was the Iranians who lost out in this struggle.

In 1826, the Persians launched an offensive into the Caucasus to try to regain the lands they had lost in 1813. Their timing was terrible. The British were then allied with the Russians against the Turks in the War of Greek Independence and so provided no aid to Iran against the Russians. After some initial Persian victories, the Russians regained their balance and began to systematically demolish the shah's forces. By 1828, the Persian armies had been so badly mauled that the shah was forced to sign the humiliating Treaty of Turkmanchai. It confirmed Persia's loss of all of its former possessions in the Caucasus, forced Persia to grant economic concessions and extraterritorial privileges to Russian citizens, and saddled the shah's government with enormous war reparations. It was a stunning blow to Iranian self-confidence, and it would not be the last.[22]

Many of the trends established at the beginning of the century would plague Iran right till its end. A variety of vicious circles emerged that slowly sapped the strength of the Qajar state. Desertification, changing trade patterns, the growth of European manufacturing (which could produce better goods more cheaply than traditional Iranian handicrafts workshops), and the persistent problems of communications across Iran's mountains and deserts helped impoverish the nation and weaken the central government. However, the shahs of Persia were slow to recognize this weakness and continued to embark on foreign wars that generally turned out to be not just humiliations but expensive ones to boot.[23]

Over time, various Iranian political elites did recognize the increasing gap between themselves and the Europeans in military, commercial, and bureaucratic efficiency, and attempted to institute programs of broad reform similar to those attempted by their Egyptian and Turkish coreligionists. However, Persia lacked the wealth of either Egypt or Turkey to purchase European weaponry, manufacturing plants, and expertise. Thus these efforts at reform were often costly failures that Iran could not afford.[24] Nor were they helped by the international financial markets, which saw a century-long decline in the price of silver—the basis of Persia's currency—thus making it ever harder for the Iranians to pay for imports.[25] More damaging still, the decline in the silver market caused massive inflation in Persia, prices rising by 600 percent between 1850 and 1860.[26]

The inefficient Qajar state had great difficulty extracting resources from this increasingly poor nation. Corruption was rampant among the shah's ministers, and the shahs themselves spent extravagantly, including on monstrously expensive sojourns in Europe in which they would move much of the court to Paris, London, Italy, or some other European locale for months at a time. As the century wore on, these trends in turn prompted a pattern of behavior familiar to other, less developed countries: the Qajars began to borrow—to pay for their wars, their defeats, their efforts at reform, their corruption, their luxuries, and their increasingly unbalanced trade. But because their reform efforts bore little or no fruit and they refused to curb their own spending, their debts simply mounted until they were forced to begin selling concessions and the meager manufacturing capability they had to foreigners to try to pay off their debts—which reduced future revenue and made them ever more dependent on the Europeans.[27]

Because the concessions effectively deprived them of the ability to raise revenues by imposing duties on foreign goods, the regime instead imposed *internal* tariffs, which had the effect of further undermining domestic manufacturing by making goods produced in Persia even less competitive with European industrial production. Entire Iranian industries were thus wiped out by foreign competition, impoverishing Persia's middle class and artisanry. At various points, European creditors pressed the shahs to sell off Crown lands to repay debts, increasing the power of the landlords at the expense of the central government and further diminishing royal revenues in the future. Moreover, these new duties brought the shahs increasingly into competition with Iran's rising middle class, composed largely of merchants and businessmen (called *bazaari*s because their place of business was the bazaar, meaning "market" in Persian) who were being penalized for the government's financial mistakes. In response, they began to clamor for some degree of political representation so that they could defend their hard-earned capital against the depredations of an arbitrary and incompetent regime.[28]

Throughout the century, the Persians considered Russia to be their principal external threat. Russia was the giant at their doorstep, while Britain seemed distant, and interested principally in defending India, not ruling Persia. Consequently, the Persians actively encouraged British investment in the early part of the century. Of course, the British were hardly disinterested, let alone benevolent, to the Persians. Despite their treaty obligations, they failed to aid the shah during the second Russo-Persian War and forcibly turned back two Persian invasions of Afghanistan—going so far as to seize Persia's Kharg Island in the Persian Gulf and bombard its main port of Muhammarah to force the Persians to vacate the Afghan city of Herat in 1856. The British also hampered the construction of railways in Iran for fear that this would make the country both more desirable to the Russians and easier for them to invade. And both Britain and Russia intervened frequently in Persian internal, external, and commercial affairs as it suited their needs or tastes.[29]

For these reasons, at least some Persians also came to distrust and dislike the British. Yet Britain was more in favor than out among the Persian elite during the nineteenth century, and in 1872 they demonstrated their ardor by granting Baron Paul Julius von Reuter, a naturalized British subject, a monopoly over virtually all of Iran's economic and financial resources. In the words of Lord Curzon, then Britain's foreign secretary, it was "the most complete and extraordinary surrender of the entire industrial resources of a Kingdom into foreign hands that has probably ever been dreamt of, much less accomplished, in history."[30] The shah, Nasir ed-Din, was desperately short of cash to fund his extravagant trips to Europe, and the prime minister, Mirza Hosain Khan Moshir-al-Dowleh, was a Westernizing reformist who concluded that Iran would be modernized only if it turned its whole economy over to the British. (It is worth pointing out that Moshir-al-Dowleh also stood to benefit handsomely from the concession. No one was entirely selfless in late-Qajar Iran.)[31]

The Reuter Concession proved to be so abject a surrender to British commercial interests that virtually no one could stomach it. The *bazaari*s, the few remaining industrialists, the nationalists, and the Russians all fought the Reuter Concession, forcing the regime to cancel it.

Nevertheless, the Reuter Concession set the stage for dramas to come. The episode neither alleviated the government's need for cash—and its willingness to sell anything to get it—nor did it mitigate the sense of grievance growing among a wide range of Iranian society. The middle class resented the shah's despotism and his squandering the country's wealth on his own private extravagances. The *bazaari*s resented their loss of markets to foreign imports. The Shi'i clergy had long-standing ties to the bazaar: mullahs and *bazaari*s were often from the same families (one son following the path of religion, others the path of business); *bazaari* trade guilds regularly employed mullahs for a variety of ceremonies; the mullahs would often petition the government on behalf of the *bazaari*s; and much of the income of the mullahs came from tithes and other forms of charity paid mostly by the *bazaari*s. If that were not enough to stir the mullahs against the regime, they also feared the growth of Western influence and secularism, which they blamed on the shah for allowing the foreigners into the country.[32]

The simmering dissent first came to a boil in 1891 over a dispute about tobacco. Still short of cash, the Qajar regime granted a concession to a Briton, Major Gerald Talbot, for a monopoly on all tobacco sold in Persia. Tobacco was widely used by Iranians. It was also widely grown there, so the concession promised not only higher prices for smokers but lower profits for the farmers who grew it and the merchants who sold it—all of whom would be forced to sell and buy at prices set by the monopoly. The tobacco concession touched a nerve. When agents of the new Imperial Tobacco Corporation arrived in the southern city of Shiraz, the center of the tobacco trade in Iran, there were large-scale popular disturbances led by a fiery cleric, 'Ali-Akbar Falasiri, who called for a *jihad* against the tobacco company. The Tobacco Revolt quickly became a national rebellion. The *bazaari*s, the peasantry, the Westernized intellectuals, and the clergy all came together to fight the concession. A senior Shi'i cleric issued a *fatwa* (a ruling of Islamic jurisprudence) prohibiting the use of tobacco. Increasingly violent demonstrations and the nationwide boycott forced the shah to cancel the concession—although at the cost of a £500,000 payoff to the Imperial Tobacco Corporation, which only drove the Treasury further into debt.

The Tobacco Revolt would have some far-reaching consequences for Iran. By galvanizing public opinion against the granting of concessions, it badly undermined the British position in Persia because they had pursued concessions the most avidly and were the nationality associated with the Reuter Concession. It also helped expand many of the fissures that had been growing between the Qajar regime and Persian society. At the same time, it demonstrated that intellectuals, *bazaari*s, mullahs, and even some of the peasantry all had interests in common, and could change the course of their country if they united. In this sense, the Tobacco Revolt was a harbinger of what was to come.[33]

The United States and Iran: Early Contacts

American merchant ships found their way into the Persian Gulf in the first half of the nineteenth century. It was not a particularly auspicious destination. The Arabs had little to sell (although they were eager to buy American wares, particularly manufactured goods), and neither the climate nor the culture was well suited to North American tastes. Nevertheless, by the early 1850s American trade with the Gulf states had grown so extensive that the United States opened negotiations with Persia for a commercial treaty. After several false starts in which early versions were scuttled by the British—who wished to keep American traders out of their Persian markets—the Treaty of Friendship and Commerce was signed in December 1856.[34] It extended most-favored-nation status to both parties. The language of the preamble of the treaty nicely points up the vast cultural gap between the two sides, as well as the lingering pretensions of the Qajar shahs. Here are the opening lines of the *English* version of the text:

The President of the United States of North America, and his Majesty as exalted as the Planet Saturn; the Sovereign to whom the Sun serves as a standard; whose splendor and magnificence are equal to that of the Skies; the Sublime Sovereign, the Monarch whose armies are as numerous as the Stars; whose greatness call to mind that of Jeinshid; whose magnificence equals that of Darius; the Heir of the Crown and Throne of the Kayanians, the Sublime Emperor of all Persia, being both equally and sincerely desirous of establishing relations of Friendship between the two Governments, which they wish to strengthen by a Treaty of Friendship and Commerce, reciprocally advantageous and useful to the Citizens and subjects of the two High contracting parties, have for this purpose named for their Plenipotentiaries.[35]

Even then, the Iranians were beginning to grow wary of Britain, and they started to look for yet another foreign power that could protect them from the British. Consequently, one Persian draft of the treaty with the United States contained articles calling on the United States to "protect the Persian seas from the bad conduct and evil designs of the enemies of Persia."[36] The American envoy deftly struck out those clauses.

As is invariably the case with the United States, religion followed close behind trade. In 1830, the first American Presbyterian missionaries settled in Urumiyyah in Iranian Azerbaijan. They would eventually establish schools and bring over additional missionaries who set themselves up in Tabriz, Tehran, and Hamadan. They found few converts among the Muslim Iranians, but their schools did develop a small, devoted following.

Again in typically American fashion, where trade and religion blazed the trail, the U.S. government eventually followed. In 1879, the frigate USS *Ticonderoga* entered the Persian Gulf proper, the first U.S. warship to do so. Since the signing of the 1856 trade pact, the Persians had not ceased their efforts to interest the United States in their country. Again, just as they had perceived Britain as less threatening than Russia because of its geographic distance from Iran, so they now assumed the United States would be less threatening than Britain because of its still greater distance. So the Persians remained determined to bring the Americans in to give them leverage against Britain and offered very favorable economic terms to do so.[37] In 1883, Washington finally made a concession of sorts by sending a minister to open a permanent diplomatic mission in Tehran—although the United States declined to take the Persians up on their more ambitious offers.

The Constitutional Revolution of 1906

The 1891 Tobacco Revolt should have been a warning to the Qajar shahs that their rule had become tenuous, but it does not seem to have made much of an impression. In 1900–1902, with Russia now back in their good graces, the Persians secured three large loans from Saint Petersburg to pay off their existing debt and finance the court. In return, the Iranians agreed to further lower the customs duties on Russian goods and to pay off all of their debts to Great Britain and not take out new loans from London without Russia's consent. Typically, much of the loaned money went to pay for three extravagant trips to Europe by the shah. Nevertheless, so as not to completely alienate the British—and to pocket still more cash—in 1901 Persia granted William K. D'Arcy a sixty-year concession for all oil exploitation rights throughout Iran except for the five provinces bordering Russia. The Persians agreed to protect all of D'Arcy's facilities and personnel in return for a small cash payment and 16 percent of the profits.[38]

By the turn of the new century, there was a broad consensus across Iranian public opinion that the Qajar regime had to be stopped. Virtually the entire society was furious at the willingness of the shah and his ministers to give away the country's wealth and resources in the form of monopolies, favorable tariffs, and other concessions to pay for the shah's luxurious lifestyle, his foolish foreign policy adventures, and the corruption of his government. By 1906, Persia owed £800,000 to Britain and another £3,250,000 to Russia.[39] The consensus that slowly emerged was that the only way out of Iran's situation was to limit the shah's ability to grant concessions and take out foreign loans.[40]

The events of 1905 seemed to provide both the opportunity and the need for action. The need was caused by a series of economic calamities. There was a bad harvest throughout the country, coupled with a cholera epidemic. In addition, the Russo-Japanese War of 1905 caused a tightening of trade with Russia and an unwillingness on the part of the Russians to extend additional credit to Iran. The result was a sharp increase in prices—during the first three months of 1905, sugar prices rose 33 percent and wheat 90 percent. The regime found itself strapped for cash once again, and compounded the country's problems by raising additional internal customs duties and postponing loan repayments, which touched off a financial crisis.[41]

The opportunity was created by Japan's defeat of Russia in 1905. This, coupled with the revolt that followed in Russia, convinced many Iranians that Russia was too weak and preoccupied to intervene in Persian affairs. Similarly, many Iranians were affected by the rise of constitutionalism abroad. The Russian rebellion of 1905 centered on demands for a constitutional government to limit the powers of the tsar. Japan had promulgated a constitution before the war, and a movement was already developing among Turks that would lead to the 1908 Young Turks revolt. In addition, the American influence made its first impact at this time, as many Iranian intellectuals had adopted the American passion for constitutionally limited government.[42]

The result was a popular move against the regime that quickly developed widespread support. The *bazaari*s and the peasantry demanded an end to the concessions and the internal tariffs. The mullahs seconded the demands of the *bazaari*s and added a demand to limit foreign influence in Persia. The intellectuals demanded an end to the corruption of the state and greater progress toward modernity. The middle class demanded fiscal responsibility to end inflation and graft. All of these demands coalesced around the general notion that Iran needed a constitutional democracy.[43]

The revolution itself was remarkably purposeful. Throughout 1904–1905, small secret societies of intellectuals had been organizing and agitating for a constitutional government. In late 1905, they recognized that they would need the support of the clergy if they were going to appeal to Iran's masses and found sympathetic ears with two key ayatollahs—Behbehani and Tabatabai. At this point, they simply needed a cause, and one was promptly provided in December, when the governor of Tehran ordered two prominent *bazaaris* publicly bastinadoed (beaten on the soles of the feet) for failing to comply with an order to lower the price of sugar. This provided the opportunity to rally the *bazaaris* to their cause as well, and the two ayatollahs led two thousand people to take *bast* (a traditional form of sanctuary) at a shrine in Tehran to protest the governor's action and provoke a dispute with the regime. The rebels maintained a confrontation with the government throughout the winter and spring of 1906, leading to an outbreak of violence when the regime's security forces attempted to arrest leading opposition figures. This spurred more protests, with the two ayatollahs organizing a group to take *bast* in the seminaries of Qom, while intellectuals and leading merchants led a much larger group (perhaps as many as twenty thousand people) of *bazaaris*, intellectuals, middle class, and mullahs to take *bast,* this time on the vast grounds of the British legation. Indeed, the British had probably been tacitly supporting the movement all along in response to the recent pro-Russia policies of the shah.

The shah himself was dying. This, the strong support by the merchants for the constitutionalist movement, and the constant public agitation by the intellectuals and the mullahs were too much for him. In August, he agreed to the formation of a national consultative Majles (Parliament) and an electoral law granting suffrage to all male Iranian citizens over thirty who owned property, regardless of religion. The new Majles held its first meeting on October 7 and by the end of the year had produced a Constitution modeled after that of Belgium (which was then considered the most progressive in Europe). The shah signed the Constitution on December 30, 1906, just a week before his death.[44]

The triumph of the constitutionalists was to prove short-lived, however. The new shah, Mohammad 'Ali, wanted nothing to do with a constitutional monarchy and began to set things in motion to undo what his father had done. Having achieved their immediate aims, the diverse coalition favoring the Constitution began to crumble. The mullahs and the intellectuals split over the issue of secularism—the mullahs did not care at all for the electoral law allowing any Iranian male to vote regardless of religion. Once the *bazaaris* got many of the internal tariffs and foreign concessions annulled, they lost interest, ceding the field to the large landowners, who quickly came to dominate the new Majles and who had little interest in real reform. Finally, the constitutionalists still had to deal with the foreigners, who seemed to think they owned the country. Here the greatest problem was a threat created by events having nothing to do with Persia.

On August 31, 1907, Britain and Russia unexpectedly put an end to the Great Game by signing the famous Anglo-Russian Agreement. The cause was Germany. Both London and Saint Petersburg were increasingly concerned by the ever more powerful and ever more belligerent German Empire, which had been born from the ashes of French defeat in 1870. By 1907, they had become so fearful that they decided to resolve their differences and ally against Germany. A major element of their agreement concerned their competition for markets and influence in Persia, and they worked out what was to them a very equitable settlement (although much less so to the Iranians): they carved the country into three bands, or spheres of influence, with Russia having complete sway in the northern band, Britain having exclusive rights in the southern band, and the central band generously left to the Iranians themselves. Within these zones, they granted each other complete rights not merely to sign agreements but to apportion revenues from Iranian government customs, its postal and telegraph services, and its fisheries, to pay off Persian loans to their banks.[45] Of course, once the Russians and British had settled their differences, it was not long before they began to see an independent-minded Iranian democracy (however nascent) as being problematic to their interests.

In 1908, the shah was ready to strike back. He had carefully built up his forces, he had the support of the large landowners and even some conservative clergy, he also had some degree of British and Russian backing, and the divisions among the constitutionalist coalition had seriously weakened their strength and popular appeal. Army units, including the famed Cossack Brigade, which was Russian-officered and widely considered the most effective unit in the Iranian Army, seized control of the Majles and much of Tehran, arrested leaders of the constitutionalist movement and summarily executed some of them.[46]

Then things got confusing. The shah faced strong opposition from constitutionalists in Tabriz who had joined with local Azeri nationalists, and his coup devolved into a protracted siege of the city. Other groups, including tribal leaders, then also made bids for independence or greater power elsewhere around the country. The chaos that seemed to be emerging throughout Persia alarmed the British and Russians, causing them to drop their support for Mohammad 'Ali. Meanwhile, constitutionalist propagandists appear to have made considerable headway in convincing the British public that they should support the Iranians in achieving the kind of constitutional government Britain already had. The result was that in 1909, the constitutionalists launched a counteroffensive of their own. Russian troops entered Iranian Azerbaijan and broke the shah's siege of Tabriz. British-backed Bakhtiyari tribesmen (one of Iran's largest tribes), along with constitutionalist forces from Azerbaijan and elsewhere around the country, marched on Tehran and deposed the shah, replacing him with his young son Ahmad.[47]

Back in power, the constitutionalists set out to implement the broad series of reforms that had never really gotten started before the shah's counter-revolution. Their greatest problems were restoring central government control over the country and dealing with Iran's daunting web of debts, concessions, corruption, and inefficiency. Recognizing that they lacked the ability to address these issues, but not wanting to give the Russians and British any more of a role in their country, they turned to different foreigners. They formed a Gendarmerie and brought in Swedes to train and officer it. And to deal with their financial problems, they brought in an American, William Morgan Shuster, as their economic adviser.[48]

None of this made the British or Russians happy. In particular, they strongly disliked Morgan Shuster. He was prickly and self-righteous, and seemed to harbor the strong, traditional American repugnance for European imperialism. In one telegram back to Washington, Shuster complained that the British and Russians would stop at nothing to undermine him, including "calling me [a] Jew."[49] In 1911, Shuster began establishing a tax collection service and proposed a former British officer to head it. The Russians objected that under the terms of the 1907 Anglo-Russian Agreement (never adopted or ratified by the Iranians in any way) only Russian officials would be employed in northern Iran. In addition, Shuster had the temerity to try to collect taxes from several Qajar nobles in league with the Russians, to which Saint Petersburg also objected. They eventually persuaded their British allies that Shuster and the new government in Tehran were jeopardizing their comfortable division of the country. With the British reluctantly on board, the Russians then mounted a new invasion of northern Iran, occupying the cities of Rasht and Anzali and issuing an ultimatum that demanded the dismissal of Shuster, Persian agreement not to hire any additional foreign advisers without Russian and British consent, and—to add insult to injury—reimbursement for the costs of the invasion. Not to be left out, British forces occupied key strategic points in southern Iran. In Tehran, the government and security forces pressed the Majles to comply with the Russian demand. When the Majles refused, it was forcibly disbanded in December 1911, ending Iran's first experiment with democracy.[50]

The 1906 Constitutional Revolution was a searing experience for Iranians. In the minds of many people, it had been mounted to seek redress for and bring an end to the depredations of a corrupt monarchy and rapacious foreign interests. Democracy was not the aim of the revolutionaries but their method. In this sense, democracy was simply a tool in the arsenal of nationalism. The constitutionalists were fired by the conviction that only if the people controlled the government could they stop the shah and his crooked ministers from selling their livelihoods and patrimony to the foreigners. But in the end, what most Iranians would conclude from the course of the revolution was that it was the foreigners who were the greatest problem for Iran. The relative ease with which the Russians and British raised up and then toppled the different factions led many Iranians to believe that the only way they could seize control of their destinies was to get the foreigners out. Thus, 1906 burned into many Iranian hearts the idea that nationalism—Iran for the Iranians and the foreigners out—was the essential precursor for any and all other changes they hoped to make in their government, their society, and their lives.[51]

World War I

The outbreak of the First World War in 1914, less than two years after the end of the Constitutional Revolution, left Iran in shambles. The resurrected monarchy declared itself neutral, but that was as well respected by foreign powers as Persia's sovereignty had been over the past century. An important part of the reason for this was that on May 26, 1908, William D'Arcy finally struck oil at Masjid-e Sulayman in southwestern Iran (in the "neutral" band between the British- and Russian-controlled territories). In 1911, Winston Churchill, as first lord of the Admiralty, made the fateful decision to convert the Royal Navy from coal-burning to oil-burning ships, thereby making the newly discovered Iranian oil fields vital to British naval power. To cement the relationship, on the eve of war, the British government acquired a 51 percent share of the Anglo-Persian Oil Company (APOC), which owned D'Arcy's concession in Iran. So important was Persia's oil to the Royal Navy that after the war began, in 1915, London agreed to a secret treaty with its Russian ally granting them control of Istanbul and the Turkish Strait after the war in return for giving Britain control of the formerly "neutral" band of territory in central Iran where the new oil fields were located.[52] Ultimately, Britain's ill-fated invasion of Iraq was mounted with logistical support from Iran and was intended to protect the oil fields from a Turkish incursion.[53]

By war's end, Iran had become a battleground, with Ottoman Turkish, Russian, British, and indigenous military forces crisscrossing its territory at various times. Turkish and Russian troops fought several battles in Iranian Azerbaijan, and following the Russian Revolution, British forces mounted expeditions against the Communists from—and provided sanctuary for White Russian forces in—northern Iran. The result was an economic catastrophe. Northern Iran was the country's breadbasket, and much farmland there had been ruined by the invading armies. Peasants had been taken from their fields and forced to serve in the armies. Irrigation works that required careful upkeep had been destroyed. Cultivated areas and livestock had been pillaged and left to rot. In addition, the presence of large numbers of foreign troops meant that there were more mouths to feed with less food. The result was a famine that may have killed as many as 2 million Iranians out of a total population of a little more than 10 million.[54] Moreover, the civil strife that had accompanied the Constitutional Revolution had left the central authority of the state weak and allowed the emergence of powerful local leaders, including tribal shaykhs who were then picked up as local proxies by different foreign nations. In a number of cases, some of these Iranian groups attempted to carve out their own autonomous or even independent states.[55]

To the extent that anyone was in control of Iran by the end of the war, it was the British. British troops were deployed widely throughout the country, and London used its position of preeminence and the weakness of Iran's government to try to turn the entire country into a British protectorate. They bribed and coerced their puppets in Tehran to sign the Anglo-Persian Agreement of 1919, which granted Britain the exclusive right to provide all expert advisers to Iran, officer and supply the Army, build railroads and other infrastructure, and develop a joint committee to revise the Persian tariff system (to Britain's inevitable advantage). In return, the British agreed to recognize Persian sovereignty and territorial integrity (whatever that meant) and provided a loan of £2 million over twenty years at 7 percent interest. In addition to the "stipend" paid to the shah and the commissions paid to the court, further impetus was added when Red Army forces invaded Persia in response to the British and White Russian forays from Iranian territory and attempted to establish an independent Communist republic in Gilan province. This only prompted the government in Tehran to huddle closer to the British.[56]

But once again, the Iranian people drew the line where their government was happy to tread. The population protested against it, the Majles would not ratify it, and the Azerbaijanis were so incensed by it that they declared an independent Azeri Republic in April 1920. Meanwhile, the British acted as if the treaty had been ratified, taking over the Iranian Army (including the Cossack Brigade), promulgating a tariff law that gave British imports very favorable rates—and equally unfavorable rates to Russian imports—and effectively taking over Persia's finances. Having helped create this mess, the British slowly reached the conclusion that things had gotten so chaotic in Iran that a British postwar government obsessed with bringing down costs decided to withdraw all of Britain's troops in Persia by 1921, leaving a weak government in Tehran that was patently incapable of dealing with the centrifugal forces that had been unleashed in the country.[57]

Thus by the end of the First World War, the peoples of Iran had fallen very far by any standards, but especially far by their own. Every Iranian knew something of the glory of ancient Persia, the power of Parthia and the Sassanid Empire, and the importance of the Safavids' making Iran the first Shi'i state in the world. The pride they felt in their past did not correspond at all to the frustrations they felt with their present. In particular, the nation's traditional xenophobia—bred from a climate that fostered isolation—had been aggravated by the relentless foreign intervention and the humiliation that Iranians felt in not being able to do anything about it. This long century of weakness and dominance by foreign machinations had a traumatic impact on Iranian political culture and has reverberated throughout Iranian history to this day. Since then, if there has been a "goal" of Iranian foreign policy, it has been ending the foreign interference that, to so many Iranians, has seemed to be the source of all of their problems.

CHAPTER 2

Reza the Great

The misery and strife that engulfed Iran after the First World War created a moment ripe for a man on horseback. In 1921, that man appeared. He was Reza Khan, a tall, powerful figure and the commander of what had once been known as the Cossack Brigade—the most potent military force in all of Iran—but which had been purged of its Russian officers and expanded to divisional strength in the turbulent years since the Constitutional Revolution.[1]

Reza Khan's coup was a gradual one, and at first he was only a supporting player in it. The liberal journalist Sayyid Zia-al-Din Tabatabai was the principal figure at first, although as in so many other instances in the later history of the Middle East, it was the military figure behind the political front man who eventually emerged on top. On February 21, 1921, Reza Khan brought his Cossack Division into Tehran, arrested sixty prominent politicians, assured the shah that he was there to defend the monarchy from an imminent revolution, and demanded that Sayyid Zia be made prime minister. Reza Khan himself was made commander of the Iranian Army. By May, he had forced Sayyid Zia and a number of other original supporters out of the government and had himself named minister of war. In 1923, the shah appointed him prime minister, and two years later the Majles officially deposed the Qajars and installed Reza Khan as shah—at which point he took the royal name Reza Shah Pahlavi. (The dynastic name "Pahlavi" he took from the name for the Middle Persian language, that of the pre-Islamic Sassanids.) Only four members of the Majles opposed his accession to the throne, one of them a European-educated Iranian nationalist named Mohammad Mosaddeq.[2]

Reza Shah was not unpopular when he took power; in fact, large segments of Iranian society backed him as the only obvious solution to their troubles. Many Iranians wanted a strong, dynamic government capable of dealing with Iran's crippling internal and external problems. Although he almost certainly took power with the connivance (if not the active support) of the British,[3] Reza Shah was unmistakably his own man and determined to reduce foreign influence in Iran, thus winning the adulation of Iranian nationalists—and much of the population was ardent nationalists after the hardships they had suffered at the hands of foreigners for the prior several decades. The *bazaari*s saw him as a force for law and order who would end the violence and the chaos and make it possible for Persia's economy to revive. Because Reza Shah was a determined modernizer, many of Iran's reform-minded intellectuals initially saw him as a kindred spirit, if not a new leader. In fact, even the four Majles deputies who had opposed the foundation of his dynasty strongly supported his steps to centralize and modernize the country. Reza Shah was also mindful of the mullahs at first, deferring to their principal interests, at least until he was firmly ensconced on the Peacock Throne. Indeed, the best evidence indicates that most of the Majles deputies truly believed in Reza Khan when they voted to make him shah in 1925.[4]

Reza Shah was also very much a man of his times. He fit the mold of the autocratic modernizer typical of the interwar years. The closest analogy was Kemal Atatürk, whom Reza Shah unabashedly admired. However, there was much about Reza Shah's goals and methods that accorded with those of Mussolini and Franco, and even with aspects of Stalin and Hitler. He was barely literate and mostly uneducated, but he was obsessed with modernity and industrialization; committed to secularization; devoutly nationalist; enamored of a powerful, modern military; ruthless and dictatorial in his methods (and adherent to an "ends justifies the means" philosophy of government); and determined to create a "new" Iranian man. Like so many of his contemporaries, he too espoused the quasi-Fascist mantra of exercise and physical fitness. Like them, he also believed that dress and other aspects of physical appearance were critical to the social engineering he hoped to accomplish.[5]

In these aims, Reza Shah had his work cut out for him. The Iran he took over in 1925 was about as poor, backward, fragmented, and impotent as could have been imagined. Persia had only 150 miles of railroad, about 800 miles of road, and only one relatively modern port—the city of Anzali on the Caspian Sea. Iranian agriculture was virtually unchanged since the eighteenth century. Many scholars estimate that Iran was one of the poorer nations in Asia. In a

sist that foreigners call the country "Iran," rather than Persia—which, after all, really stood for only part of the country and did not accurately reflect the fact that many of his subjects were not ethnic Persians. To make his point, he ordered the Iranian postal service to return all letters with addresses in "Persia."[14] Similarly, he withdrew his diplomatic representation to the United States (even after so much avid courting of Washington) because the *New York Daily Mirror* had published an editorial calling him a British stableboy.[15] He likewise broke diplomatic relations for a time because a French political cartoonist made a joke playing on the similarity of *shah* and *chat* ("cat," in French).[16]

The next priority for the new shah was gaining full control over his country. Reza Shah hoped both to gather up the parts of Iran lost to separatist movements and tribal uprisings, and to turn back the slow trend toward entropy that had plagued Iranian rulers for centuries. Almost immediately after he had ensured that the new regime was firmly in control in Tehran, he began reorganizing the Iranian military for war and then launched a series of campaigns to crush the various separatists. He integrated his own Cossack Division, the South Persia Rifles (formed by the British), the Swedish-trained Gendarmerie, and a grab bag of other paramilitary units into a single Persian Army. He also took many of his own Cossack Division officers and assigned them to key posts in many of the newly absorbed formations. Then he launched this force in an almost counterclockwise offensive. He started in the spring of 1921 in Khorasan, in northeast Iran, where he crushed a local revolt led by a Colonel Mohammed Taqi Pesian. In the fall, he moved on to the Caspian province of Gilan, where the withdrawal of the Red Army had left Kuchek Khan's Gilani Republic vulnerable and disorganized. In the summer of 1922, Reza Shah's forces pushed farther westward, to crush a breakaway Kurdish movement and a revolt against his rule in Azerbaijan.

While Reza Shah was busy consolidating his control in the north, he had to keep looking over his shoulder to the south, where he feared that the British might be working to undermine it. Britain already had an agreement with Shaykh Khazal, the tribal chieftain of Khuzestan province in extreme southwest Iran (where all the oil fields were located) that gave them a kind of protectorate over the province. There were rumors that the British were trying to convince Khazal to declare independence, which fed into Reza Shah's innate suspicions of the British. So he hustled south with his army and asserted his control over Khuzestan in 1924 before Khazal or the British could make a move toward independence (if they ever intended to do so). No sooner had Reza Shah established his authority over Khuzestan than he raced east to

Luristan, where Persian Army units had been defeated by some of the wilder tribesmen. In bitter fighting, he broke the power of these tribes and returned Luristan to central government control. He then turned to deal with the Bakhtiyaris and the Qashqa'is—two of the biggest and most powerful tribes in Iran—subduing them with a combination of negotiation and force. Finally, he headed back north to put down a Turkoman revolt along the Caspian before returning to Tehran. Even Reza Shah's staunchest critics had to admit that he had performed brilliantly in restoring central government control to so fractious and fragmented a society.[17]

As a military officer, it was natural for Reza Shah to favor a strong Army. However, his determination to minimize foreign intervention and his herculean efforts to unify the country after taking power convinced him that building up Iran's military strength was critical if it was going to remain a strong, centrally controlled nation-state. Consequently, he made the expansion and improvement of his armed forces one of his highest priorities. He began sending officers to study at French and German military schools and explicitly emphasized the training of the officers so that he could quickly expand the Army as the Germans under General Hans von Seeckt were secretly doing in Weimar Germany. He introduced conscription, both to build a greater sense of nationhood among the isolated communities of the country and to furnish a manpower base for the enlarged Army he desired. He founded a navy and an air force and established military factories to produce small arms and ammunition for the armed forces. He revised the recruitment system, regularized promotion, and increased pay. By 1941, Reza Shah had taken the hodgepodge force of 40,000 men in five divisions that he had welded together in 1925 and turned it into a cohesive military of 127,000 men organized into 18 divisions, with 100 tanks.[18]

Paradoxically, it was Iran's oil money that made much of this possible. Just as the oil helped bring the foreign powers (particularly the British) into Iran, so too did they allow Reza Shah a degree of independence that his predecessors had lacked. Although Iran's oil revenues remained small compared to what they would eventually grow to, they were large enough to allow him to support such a sizable standing army. It also allowed him to finance his ambitious modernization program without resort to foreign loans. What's more, his hope was that the modernization effort itself would build an Iran strong enough to be able to stand up to the foreigners. Thus Iran's independence grew along with its oil wealth, in a pattern that would continue on into the reign of his son, with important consequences for both Iran and the United States.

Modernization

The modernization and industrialization of Iran were the major projects of Reza Shah's reign. Like Atatürk, Mussolini, and his other fellow modernizing dictators, the new shah was determined to pull his people into the twentieth century whether they liked it or not. To this end, he inaugurated a mammoth range of reforms, construction projects, reorganizations, and other changes. The sheer breadth of the effort was staggering.[19] Among them:

• He greatly expanded and modernized Iran's infrastructure. He built 14,000 miles of roads, 6,000 miles of telephone lines, power plants, and railroads— including the monumental Trans-Iranian Railroad, which linked the Caspian ports and Iran's principal agricultural lands in the north to the oil fields and the Persian Gulf in the south. He started an air service. By the late 1930s, all of Iran's cities had electric power. The number of cars in Iran rose from 600 in 1925 to 25,000 in 1942. By 1933, the cost of moving goods in Iran had fallen to one third the 1920 rate, and the time had been cut to one tenth of what it would have been in 1920.[20]

• He overhauled Iran's legal system. He introduced new criminal and civil codes based on French models. He abolished the Shari'a courts, guaranteed religious minorities equal protection under the law, established a hierarchy of civil courts with magistrates employed by the state, and wiped out the bandits and highwaymen who infested the countryside.

• He mandated a major reform of Iran's finances. He instituted a uniform land tax and an income tax, promulgated a new commercial code, permitted the creation of joint stock companies, reorganized and modernized the state's fiscal system, and created Bank Melli as a central bank to regulate the country's money supply (a function previously performed by a private British bank). Not surprisingly, state revenues increased tenfold under Reza Shah.[21]

• He instituted new trade practices. He signed new commercial treaties with many Western states that imposed higher tariffs on many goods with the goal of both increasing state revenue and protecting Iran's nascent industries.

• To administer the new finances and oversee his vast modernization program, he created a modern state bureaucracy. The 1926 Civil Service Reform Act established a new bureaucracy with educational standards. Within this system, he created a modern system for collection of revenues. He took the Rube Goldberg agglomeration of offices and functions that he had inherited from the Qajars and reorganized them into a rational new bureaucracy of 90,000 full-time personnel in 10 principal ministries.[22]

• He made a major effort to expand and improve Iran's meager educational programs. He set up a comprehensive public school system to teach primary and secondary education to both sexes and relied on state revenues to cover all costs, making it free to every Iranian citizen. He required all schools to teach in Persian and to follow the public school curriculum to standardize education. He established Tehran University and a number of other, smaller institutions of higher learning, including thirty-six teachers' colleges and thirty-two vocational schools. The number of students in primary school jumped almost sixfold between 1925 and 1941; the number in secondary school doubled; and the number of those in institutions of higher education rose fivefold. For the cream of Iran's crop, Reza Shah even established programs to pay for them to study abroad—and 1,500 did so by 1938.[23]

• He "modernized" the status of women. He insisted that Tehran University admit women and made sure that the state schools provided equal education. He brought women into factory work, teaching, nursing, and other sectors of the workforce. He began encouraging women to unveil and later required it—complete with orders to the gendarmes to begin tearing off or cutting veils in public.[24]

• He fostered industrial production. He founded the Agriculture and Industrial Bank in 1933 to provide low-interest loans to small businesses, revised Iran's tariffs and quotas to product industry, built sixty-four state-owned factories, and created other incentive programs for industrialization. By 1941, there were seventeen times as many modern manufacturing plants in Iran than there had been in 1925. As a percentage of Iranian income, manufacturing grew from virtually nothing to about 5 percent between 1926 and 1947, and the industrial workforce grew to almost seven times its 1900 strength.[25]

• He expanded and enhanced the provision of health care. He established a Pasteur Institute in Tehran with a Frenchman at the head to improve public health, established Iran's first medical school, passed a law implementing a series of measures to prevent and combat infectious diseases, founded the Society of the Red Lion (Iran's version of the Red Cross), built numerous local clinics, mandated free medical treatment for the poor and compulsory vaccinations, and began the inspection and certification of brothels. Reza Shah's efforts to increase the numbers of physicians succeeded in pushing down the ratio of doctors to population from 1 to 11,000 in 1924 to 1 to 4,000 in 1935.[26]

He instituted a number of other changes to bring Iran into the "modern" world. He introduced the metric system and a modern solar calendar. He mandated the use of surnames, civil marriage and divorce requirements, and the wearing of "modern" dress. He even forbade camel caravans from entering Iran's cities.[27]

Nevertheless, there were also very real problems with the new program of reform and modernization. For one thing, it neglected Iran's agricultural sector, in which the vast majority of Iranians were still employed. As a result, agricultural production stagnated, causing a decline in living standards of Iran's vast peasantry. The result was a drop in the domestic demand for consumer goods, which, when coupled with the world financial crisis, the low productivity of Iranian workers, and the poor quality of Iranian goods (all of which made it very difficult for Iran to export) crippled the economy. To make matters worse, the regime kept prices artificially high as a way to try to stimulate revenue for industry, but the only real impact of this was to trigger painful inflation. The planning and organization of the reforms often left much to be desired, and the mistakes they engendered helped prevent the modernization program from achieving anything like its stated goals. Many of Reza Shah's reforms were both cruel and inefficient. For instance, he forced nomadic tribes to settle when the only land available for them to do so was inhospitable, resulting in thousands of deaths. Similarly, many of the laws he passed effectively legalized the "serfdom" of the Iranian peasants and their control by Iranian landowners. In many factories and even in handicrafts, women and children were horribly exploited. Still other reforms produced only mixed results. For example, while education clearly increased markedly under Reza Shah, by the end of his reign it was still the case that less than 10 percent of the country's population had any elementary education and less than 1 percent had received a secondary education.[28]

What's more, as was also true for Reza Shah's fellow autocratic modernizers, the new shah's determination to modernize Iran came with a heavy price. He quickly disappointed the constitutional reformists by proving that he was no democrat. He rigged elections; censored or shut down newspapers; banned labor unions; outlawed the Communists; and broke up political gatherings. He intimidated, arrested, tortured, and even murdered his opponents. He established a secret police network throughout the government and the country, and in 1928, he placed the Majles directly under Army supervision, thereby reducing it to nothing but a rubber stamp.[29] The regime's repression became so severe that in 1934 one U.S. Embassy official described it as "strongly reminiscent of Soviet Russia in the period of militant communism, 1917–1921."[30] He was also deeply corrupt. He extracted bribes and extorted money from tribal leaders and confiscated land and wealth or forced their owners to sell to him at absurd prices or be murdered or exiled. He went so far as to divert irrigation canals to force owners to sell their land or to better water his own.[31] Through these methods, he made himself the richest man in Iran, and by 1941 he reportedly owned 15 percent of Iran's arable land.[32]

Nor were all Iranians enthusiastic about Reza Shah's version of "modernity," especially the large percentage of religious Muslims, who disliked the shah's imposed secularization. Families that at first were delighted to send their girls to the free public schools abruptly began withdrawing them when the regime insisted that all teachers and schoolgirls should be unveiled. Many men disliked the mandated European-style Pahlavi brimmed hat, which was specifically designed to make it difficult to pray by touching one's head to the prayer mat in the traditional Islamic manner. Moreover, many of the reforms hit the clergy very hard. The disbanding of the Shari'a courts, the requirements for civil marriage and divorce ceremonies, the creation of the public schools (which competed with the religious schools), and the standardization of curricula all took important sources of revenue and influence away from the mullahs. The shah also set up a government agency to oversee religious endowments, which were another critical element of the clergy's funding. Finally, Reza Shah established a theological faculty in Tehran—separate from the religious seminaries in Qom—at which all young clerics had to present themselves and undergo an examination to obtain a license to preach. The test was very strict, and 90 percent of candidates failed. He justified this as a way of getting rid of "charlatans" from the ranks of the mullahs, but it further embittered the clergy, who were not accustomed to having to pass a government test to practice God's law.[33]

As the 1920s and '30s passed, Reza Shah's rule became increasingly unpopular thanks to Iran's deepening economic hardship, burgeoning corruption, the dislocation caused by the massive changes, and the callous manner in which the shah treated his people. The *bazaaris*, Iran's traditional middle class, were unhappy about secularization but equally unhappy about the shah's emphasis on industrialization and his mistaken economic policies, which ruined native industries and raised their costs of doing business. The new, Westernizing middle class disliked his repression and the fact that, despite all their new education and progressive ideas, they generally had little role in state policy, little political influence, and little ability even to express themselves in public. The cities teemed with illiterate, unemployed, and unemployable refugees from the countryside, who lived in squalid conditions and were exploited by Iran's troubled industries. Indeed, many Iranians simply disliked how Reza Shah's reforms were increasingly bifurcating their society between the new, increasingly Westernized and increasingly wealthy upper classes, and the traditional, increasingly impoverished lower classes. Over time, Reza Shah, who had started out so popular, was forced to rely more and more on outright repression to maintain control over his country.[34]

By the end of the 1930s, as the Second World War approached, there is little doubt that Reza Shah Pahlavi had changed the face of Iran. But many of the changes he had wrought were superficial, and they had come at the cost of alienating large segments of society. Had the war not intervened, the frustration and fear he had caused among his people might have produced a popular reaction against his rule and his modernization. The sentiments he had stirred certainly contributed to the reformist movement that coalesced around the figure of Mohammad Mosaddeq after the war. Indeed, the combination of forces that began to emerge in opposition to Reza Shah's modernizations was broadly similar not only to Mosaddeq's coalition, but also to those that mounted the earlier Constitutional Revolution in 1906 and the later Islamic Revolution of 1979. It may be that Reza Shah's premature fall prevented his son from recognizing that his path was headed toward the collapse that engulfed Iran in 1979.

The Fall of Reza Shah

It is ironic that, in the end, it was the foreigners who brought down Reza Shah Pahlavi. The ardent nationalist who had come to power determined to build an Iranian state that could withstand foreign machinations was overthrown by the brute strength of the same old foes whose constant interference in Iranian affairs had created the circumstances for Reza Shah to take power. Whatever his other achievements, and these remain widely debated, there is no question that he failed to accomplish his highest priority and insulate Iran against foreign influence.

You could argue that Reza Shah brought it on himself. He was fascinated by the rise of modern Germany. Some Iranian elites assumed that as a fellow Aryan state, their nation was a natural ally for Nazi Germany, given its obsession with race. They do not seem to have understood that Hitler's kind of Aryans had blond hair and blue eyes—they were not "Orientals." There are stories told that it was the Iranian Embassy in Berlin that first suggested to

Reza Shah that he change the name of the country from "Persia" (land of the Parsa) to "Iran" (land of the Aryans). He clearly was affected by Hitler's methods. And he saw in Germany what he and other Iranians had once seen in America—a powerful third country that could help Iran to keep Britain and Russia at bay. But he underestimated the power (and the proximity) of the Russians and British and overestimated the power (and reach) of the Germans. By 1941, there were more than a thousand German advisers, businessmen, and officials in Tehran alone, and another thousand outside the capital. And the Germans *did* want an alliance with Reza Shah in case Rommel's Afrika Korps or their Army Group South racing across the Ukraine toward the Caucasus were able to reach Iran's borders. In fact, German agents even made contact with the Nazi sympathizer General Fazlollah Zahedi, to try to convince him to lead a tribal revolt if the Wehrmacht got within striking distance of Iran.[35]

After the German invasion of Russia in June 1941 pushed Stalin into Churchill's arms, there was probably little chance that Iran would avoid foreign occupation. Especially since Reza Shah had built the Trans-Iranian Railway, linking the Persian Gulf with the Caspian, Iran was simply too good a route to get supplies to the embattled Red Army for the Allies not to occupy it. Of course, Reza Shah's flirtation with the Germans—and his former anti-British activities—only sealed the matter for London. In August 1941, the British and Soviet governments demanded that Reza Shah expel all of the Germans in Iran and place the Trans-Iranian Railway and Iranian port facilities entirely at their disposal. When Reza Shah refused, Russian and British forces invaded the country. Some units of the shah's Army stood their ground, but most collapsed quickly before the European formations. In less than two weeks it was all over. Reza Shah himself was sent into exile, and on August 25, 1941, his twenty-one-year-old son, Mohammad Reza, was installed by the Allies on the Peacock Throne as Mohammad Reza Shah Pahlavi.[36]

The new shah remained mostly in the background at first. No one thought him terribly capable, and with their troops occupying the country, the British and Russians made all of the key decisions anyway. During this period, both the Majles and the prime minister were able to usurp considerable authority and, as Habib Ladjevardi has suggested, Iran probably came closer to being a functional constitutional monarchy during the war years than at any other time before or since.[37] Mohammad Reza Shah always assumed that he would be more than a figurehead monarch—which was what the Allies had intended. He mounted a cautious but determined effort to regain the position, powers, and property his father had formerly held.[38]

Perhaps the most important notion that Mohammad Reza Shah brought to the throne with him, however, was the importance of building an Iran strong enough to stand up to the European powers. There is no doubt that his father had drilled this into him throughout his education because it was the most important guiding principle of his own reign. But it was a lesson reinforced many times over by the sudden and swift demise of his father's regime, which had seemed so awesome just weeks before its embarrassing collapse. Indeed, throughout Mohammad Reza Shah's years in power, minimizing foreign influence and increasing Iran's power and independence were probably his greatest priorities. Thus, he likely faced a bitter irony of his own when, given what he had hoped to achieve, he heard the revolutionary crowds in 1978 railing against him for having sold Iran out to the West.

The Ugly Americans

The Second World War not only marked the debut of the new shah; it was also the first large-scale contact between Americans and Iranians. When the United States entered the war after the attack on Pearl Harbor, Washington deployed troops directly to Iran to help move the mountains of supplies that the "Arsenal of Democracy" was sending to aid the Red Army. Ultimately, 30,000 Americans manned the long supply lines from the Persian Gulf through the Zagros and Alborz Mountains up into the Soviet Union.[1]

And Iran was crucial to the provision of Lend-Lease aid to the Soviets, which in turn was a critical component of Allied victory in World War II. Because the Soviet histories are untrustworthy—and the Soviets themselves may not have known the actual figures—it is impossible to know what percentage of the Russian war effort was provided by Lend-Lease, but the figures that are available make clear that it was extremely important. The United States and Britain provided nearly $18 billion worth of equipment.[2] The United States alone sent 12,500 tanks, 380,000 trucks, 35,000 jeeps, 8,000 tractors, 22,000 aircraft, 15 million pairs of boots, 62 million square yards of wool, 107 million square yards of cotton, 34 million uniforms, 4.2 million tons of food, 11,800 railroad cars, 956,000 miles of telephone cable, 35,000 radio stations, and 380,000 field telephones.[3] By the end of the war, two thirds of all of the trucks in the Red Army were American.[4] Although it took some time for the Allies to make the Iranian route serviceable, by 1943, 34 percent of all Lend-Lease aid to Russia was passing through Iran. By the end of the war, the Iranian route had accounted for 26 percent of all Lend-Lease assistance to the USSR.[5]

Many Iranians feared that, this time, the British and Russian governments intended a permanent division of Iran. A variety of Iranian officials, believing the United States to be benign and uninterested in Iranian affairs, pleaded with American administrators and diplomats to evict the Russians and British from Iran and simply run the Lend-Lease operations there themselves. This was a ridiculous idea that said more about the naïveté of the Iranians than about the nature of the Iranian-American relationship; the United States was not about to start a row with its British and Russian allies because of Iranian fears of what they might do in the future (especially since the first American troops did not arrive until December 1942, by which time the Russians and British had already been operating in Iran for a full sixteen months). However, the United States did agree to try to reassure the Iranians by seeking a joint declaration from all three Allied powers affirming that the takeover of Iran was temporary and it would regain its independence after the war. This led to the January 1942 Tripartite Pact, in which the three allies guaranteed Iran's territorial sovereignty and independence. In addition, to try to attach meaning to these guarantees, all three agreed to withdraw their troops from Iran no later than six months after the end of the war. None of this allayed the fears of most Iranians, who had been victimized by the British and Russians too many times in the past to trust their words this time.[6]

While Iranian officials were trying desperately to keep the United States in, the evidence suggests that many average Iranians would have preferred that the Americans get out. U.S. military personnel showed little cultural sensitivity and often treated the Iranians as impediments to their mission. Cables between the State Department and the U.S. Embassy in Tehran discussed a wide range of bad behavior, including distressingly frequent automobile accidents in which American personnel had killed or injured Iranians and/or destroyed their property. There were also too many "incidents of drunkenness and rowdyism," which the diplomats feared would have an adverse effect on American prestige in Iran.[7] This is not necessarily to blame the U.S. troops; it was a mass-conscript army in which few had ever been outside their hometowns, let alone to the exotic Middle East—and there was a war to be won. Nevertheless, while the Americans never came in for quite the same criticism as the hated Russians and British, the overall impression left on the Iranians by the American service personnel was not a very positive one.[8]

While Iranians tended to be disappointed with the United States (rightly or wrongly) for what they saw, they might have been much happier if they could have heard what was going on behind the scenes.[9] As early as January 1943, shortly after the first American troops set foot in Iran, a State Department policy memorandum decried the imperial ambitions of the British and Russians and stated unequivocally that it should be U.S. policy to build an independent Iran, strong enough to stand up to its old imperial nemeses.[10] That August, Secretary of State Cordell Hull wrote President Franklin Roosevelt a memorandum in which he reaffirmed this position, arguing that "it is to the advantage of the United States to exert itself to see that Iran's integrity and independence are maintained and that she becomes prosperous and stable."[11]

This rationale prompted a series of actions designed to produce a more independent, stable, and prosperous Iran after the war. At the "Big Three" Conference of Roosevelt, Churchill, and Stalin in Tehran in December 1943, FDR convinced his two colleagues to put into the conference's joint statement (called the Tehran Declaration) that they all recognized "that the war has caused special economic difficulties for Iran," and promised to preserve Iran's unity and independence, and to promote Iranian development. He also got them to reaffirm their commitment in the Tripartite Pact to withdraw all of their troops from Iran within six months of the end of hostilities.[12] In the meantime, Washington made Iran eligible for Lend-Lease assistance. Although the United States did provide moderate levels of direct aid (roughly $7.8 million in Lend-Lease), the most important American support to Iran came from a number of assistance missions.[13] The United States dispatched three different military missions: one to train the Iranian Army, one to coordinate the movement of materiel to Russia with the Iranian government, and one to assist the Iranian Gendarmerie—this last led by Colonel H. Norman Schwarzkopf, the father of the commander of Coalition forces during Operation Desert Storm in 1991. Schwarzkopf in particular developed a real affinity for the Iranians and performed extremely well in reforming the Gendarmerie.[14]

In addition, the infamous Arthur Millspaugh returned to Iran at the head of yet another financial advisory mission. Millspaugh was sent to reform Iran's public finances and was given the authority to set prices, raise taxes, and manage the budget. Unfortunately, Millspaugh contributed to the unfavorable impression of Americans left in the minds of many Iranians. He was no less difficult in 1943 than he had been in 1927. Upon returning to Tehran he laid out a program of price controls, rationing, revision of the tax codes to make them more progressive, raising income taxes, budget cuts, and an internal Treasury loan. In these efforts, Millspaugh ran head on into the interests of Iran's upper classes, who rejected his progressive income taxes and efforts to eliminate corruption, as well as Iranian nationalists (including Mohammad Mosaddeq), who simply objected to a foreigner running Iran's affairs. In addition, his desire to cut the military budget again provoked the anger of the shah. In late 1944, history repeated itself when Millspaugh tried to fire the head of the Iranian National Bank, prompting so much opposition from the Majles, the government, and the Iranian elites that he was himself forced to resign.[15]

America's good intentions but mixed implementation had even less of a positive impact on the Iranian people than they might have because the war was disastrous for the Iranians. Once again, they found themselves occupied by foreign powers, their (admittedly unpopular) government deposed, and the foreigners turning Iran's resources to their purposes with little regard for the well-being of the Iranian populace. In particular, Iran suffered from severe inflation (at times reaching 450 percent) and widespread famine. The massive influx of foreign troops meant there was a much greater demand for food and virtually everything else that Iranians had to offer, and the foreigners brought large checkbooks with them to pay for it, driving prices through the ceiling and making it very difficult for the average Iranian family to afford what it needed to survive.[16]

This situation was greatly complicated by three other problems. First, Allied transport monopolized Iran's roads and railroads, as well as the trucks and rolling stock that moved on them, meaning that too little transport was available to move food and other goods. Second, the Russians again occupied northern Iran (the country's breadbasket), and they seized Iranian manpower and equipment for their own needs, leaving too little to work the farms. Finally, there was another bad harvest in 1942, which pushed a fragile system over the edge. By the end of that year, the U.S. Embassy in Tehran was reporting that the government could keep only two days' worth of wheat (the staple of the Iranian diet) on hand. At least according to the American diplomatic correspondence, the U.S. recognized the problem and was trying to address it with Allied personnel and supplies in country, but Americans were meeting considerable resistance from the Russians and British, who cared little about the welfare of the Iranians.[17] This state of affairs led to violent bread riots in 1942, followed by famine and large-scale loss of life (albeit not on the level of that experienced during World War I). It is no wonder that the American Office of Strategic Services (the forerunner of the CIA) station in Tehran constantly reported that the Iranian people were deeply unhappy, angry at Russia and Britain in particular, and increasingly pro-Nazi, with crowds cheering Hitler's appearance in newsreels.[18]

The Soviet Withdrawal Crisis

For Iranians the end of World War II meant one thing: the end of occupation, they hoped. The Americans remained firmly committed to that goal and reminded both the British and Soviets that Japan's formal surrender on September 2, 1945, set the deadline for full evacuation of Iran at March 2, 1946.

Stalin, however, did not seem to share Washington's conviction that an independent Iran would be a positive development. Although his true intentions remain unknown, he seemed determined to see how much of Iran he might be able to annex or break up into smaller, less threatening satellite states. He started early in the war. In October 1941, fifty-three Marxists who had been jailed by Reza Shah formed the Tudeh (Masses) Party. Although originally not Stalinists, they were persuaded to join the Soviet cause and thereafter received considerable Russian assistance. The Soviets encouraged the Tudeh to get out into the countryside and raise the political consciousness of the peasantry, who still accounted for two thirds of Iran's population in the 1940s.[19] Simultaneously, Moscow worked hard to stir separatist sentiment among Iran's Kurdish and Azeri minorities, both of whose homelands conveniently bordered the Soviet Union. The Russians freed Kurdish, Azeri, and Communist prisoners from the shah's jails, and provided them with the skills, funds, and motivation to go out and stir up the population. Moreover, the Russians sent large numbers of troops, technicians, officials, propagandists, labor agitators, and others to take over as much of Iranian civil society in the north of the country as they could, going so far as to establish a new, Soviet-controlled school system.[20]

In the autumn of 1944, the shah made the situation worse by clumsily trying to rig the elections for the new Majles. The ensuing popular outrage galvanized a broad coalition of opposition groups against the shah, including pro-British Majles deputies, tribal leaders, the upper class, middle-class intellectuals, *bazaari*s, right-wing nationalists, and the Tudeh. The Soviets saw this as a propitious moment and had the Tudeh make a broader grasp at power. Moscow demanded an oil concession in the north to match the British concession in the south, and had their Majles deputies—Tudeh Party members, Kurds, Azeris, and others—support the idea. They also staged violent strikes in Isfahan and a few other smaller cities. In so doing, they overreached and ruined whatever chances they might have had of gaining some advantages in the country through internal channels. Iran's middle and upper classes saw the Tudeh's methods as lawless, while Iranian nationalists saw them as a threat to their sovereignty. This act prompted the Majles (again led by Mohammad

Mosaddeq) to forbid the government from issuing any further oil concessions to anyone.[21]

So Stalin switched to a different approach: the Soviets just decided to stay and "create facts on the ground." On August 2, 1945, the new "Big Three"—Truman, Attlee, and Stalin—met at Potsdam to decide the fate of the postwar world. This time, the conference declaration stated that all Allied troops must be withdrawn from Tehran right away and the rest in stages from the remainder of the country.[22] But Soviet actions suggested a different intention. Immediately after the conference, the Russian press launched a massive campaign against Iran, supporting the creation of separate Azerbaijani and Kurdish states. They dispatched several hundred Turkish Communists to help the Tudeh Party and brought key Kurdish leaders to a "conference" in Baku, where Soviet apparatchiks promised them financial aid, weapons, military training, and other equipment to launch a revolt.[23]

By November, the Azeris were ready. They had long-standing grievances against the central government; they provided the most taxes of any of Iran's provinces but did not receive commensurate benefits, and instead the regime forbade them to use the Azeri language in business or to teach it in schools. That November they elected a provincial assembly, and in December they declared autonomy.[24] When Iranian government troops were sent to get control of the unruly province, they were blocked by Soviet forces—still deployed in Iran and showing no sign of leaving. In January 1946, the Kurds followed suit and proclaimed a Kurdish People's Republic, which immediately signed a mutual defense pact with Azerbaijan.[25]

Iran thus had the honor of becoming the arena for the first crisis of the Cold War, and it fell to the United States to solve the problem. The Truman administration was not looking for a fight with the Russians so soon after the end of the war, but they were also determined to get Stalin out of Iran. For the moment, they urged Iranian nationalists to bring the matter before the new United Nations Security Council and await the expected withdrawal of Soviet troops in February.[26]

The withdrawal never came. The last American soldier left Iran on January 1, 1946. The British moved more slowly (they may have been waiting to see what the Russians would do), but they were in the process of leaving and announced that all of their troops would be out by March 1. Not only did the Russians not say anything about leaving, but in January, Soviet propaganda began to promote the absurd but ominous claim that the people of Tehran also demanded "liberation." That same month, the Iranians tried to have their case raised in the UNSC, but when the Russians walked out of the proceedings in protest, the new body tabled the issue. To emphasize their point, Moscow directed the Tudeh to begin widespread agitation in favor of the Soviets—including mounting labor strikes, creating street disturbances, and disseminating propaganda. In 1946, the Tudeh had roughly 150,000 members and was the largest and most effective political organization in Iran, so this was a serious threat.[27] The Soviets first restricted and then eventually halted delivery of food from the north.[28] Most dangerous of all, observers on the ground reported that the Russians actually continued to *increase* their troop strength in Iran.[29]

This series of events convinced Washington that it needed to step up the pressure on Moscow. President Truman alerted American military forces to be ready to deploy to Iran, including three combat divisions in Austria awaiting their return to the United States. These moves seem to have finally gotten the Russians' attention, and on March 24, Moscow announced that all Soviet troops would be withdrawn.[30]

Simultaneous with the American moves, the Iranians had decided it was time to take matters into their own hands. The Majles had elected Ahmad Qavam, an experienced politician of the old establishment, as prime minister. The shah had opposed him because Qavam's stature made him a potential rival for power, but he had little choice in the matter. While Washington ratcheted up the pressure on Moscow, Qavam conducted a series of negotiations with the Soviets, and got the Russians to agree to withdraw their forces in return for the promise of an oil concession in northern Iran. As many Iranians tell it, Qavam knew that this was a safe move because the Majles would never ratify the concession. Moreover, in a side letter, Qavam gave in to a key Russian demand regarding the status of Azerbaijan. And he convinced the Soviets of his good intentions by bringing the Tudeh Party into his government—to the consternation of the shah—and giving them three cabinet posts. As a result, Moscow thought it was negotiating with a sympathetic leftist, rather than a wily nationalist.[31]

In May 1946, Soviet forces finally pulled out of Iran. The Russian withdrawal set several things in motion. First, it fatally weakened the position of the Kurds and Azeris and allowed the Iranian Army to reoccupy the rebellious provinces—which benefited the shah, who had pressed for immediate military reoccupation against Qavam, who wanted to uphold his deal with the Russians. Second, it greatly weakened the Tudeh, whose great supporter was seen as abandoning the field. Third, it triggered a revolt by the powerful Qashqa'i tribe, which created a state of internal emergency that either forced Qavam or provided him with the opportunity (sources differ and the evidence is ambiguous) to evict the Tudeh from the government. Last, it set up a vote by the Majles that rejected the Soviet oil concession.[32]

Traditionally, American historians (and President Truman himself) told the story that it was an "ultimatum" from Truman that convinced the Russians to pull out of Iran in 1946. On the other hand, a different version offered by Iranians and Western scholars of Iran minimizes the importance of the American involvement and instead emphasizes Qavam's clever diplomacy. The truth appears to be more a combination of the two.

There simply was no ultimatum from Truman to Stalin, although the United States did make clear its anger to the Russians for their malfeasance.[33] Nevertheless, it seems a bit more than mere coincidence that, within weeks of Washington turning up the diplomatic heat and alerting military forces for a move to Iran, the Russians declared themselves ready to leave the country. It is also hard to buy the story that Qavam's oil concession did the trick by itself. Josef Stalin did not voluntarily give up territory anywhere if he thought he could hang on to it without a fight. Evidence from newly declassified Soviet archives does indicate that the Russians believed there was significant oil in northern Iran (although British geologists had not found any up to that point, nor have there been any major finds there over the past sixty years) and that this was an important motive during the crisis.[34]

Thus, it seems most likely that Russian withdrawal came as a combination of the U.S. threat; the prospect of gaining an oil concession in northern Iran, the price for which was withdrawal of their troops; and possibly the hope of bolstering Qavam, whom the Russians may have believed was their best chance to gain a sympathetic Iran.[35] A number of scholars have pointed out that Qavam may have been much more of a leftist than generally recognized.[36] For instance, after the Soviet withdrawal, Qavam had wanted to negotiate a settlement with the Kurds and Azerbaijanis that would respect his deal with Moscow, but the shah refused to negotiate and instead sent in the Army.[37] Qavam also made a determined effort to try to get the Majles to approve the Soviet oil concession, which does not fit well with the notion that Qavam purposely struck the deal with the Russians in order to get their troops out, knowing that the Majles would not ratify the concession.[38]

All of this suggests that Stalin may have seen a complicated picture in Iran that ultimately made withdrawal the best route for him to get what he wanted. Various sources attest that he was not interested in a war for Iran but that he was willing to see if he could bluff his way into acquiring the northern part.[39] However, northern Iran was not enough of a priority for Stalin to up the ante once Truman signaled a willingness to fight. On the other hand, he may have (rightly or wrongly) seen Qavam as a sympathetic prime minister who was trying hard to grasp all of the reins of power. For Stalin, withdrawing from Iran therefore had not only the benefit of dampening the risks created by enraged Iranian nationalism and the risk of war with America, but it probably was the best way of helping Qavam, and Stalin may have seen Qavam as the best (or merely a viable) means of ensuring a friendly government in Iran.

Picking Up the Pieces

Once again Iran had been battered by a world war. Eventually, it would recover from the famine and inflation, but the effects of the war seemed to undo even the positive developments of Reza Shah's modernization efforts. In 1946, Iran was one of the poorest countries in the world.

Indeed, the war had exacerbated a number of problems left from the days of Reza Shah. It had further reinforced the power of the landowners who had taken advantage of the hard wartime conditions to buy up much of the previously independent land from debt-ridden peasants willing to sell their plots cheap. Consequently, few Iranians owned any land anymore and those farmers who did not (the sharecroppers) found themselves starving or barely scraping by. And most Iranians were still farmers or dependent on farmers. In 1950, 55 percent of the population still lived in villages averaging 100 inhabitants, and the mean size of an Iranian village was still just 250. The tax system was further perverted to weigh even more heavily on the lower classes by the landowners who controlled the Majles during the war. The government maintained a monopoly on wheat and paid prices below market rate (to make it available at low prices to the urban poor) but in so doing not only added to the burdens of the struggling farmers, but contributed to an overall decline in wheat production such that Iran was forced to begin importing. The end of Allied requisitions and the resumption of foreign imports also crippled the *bazaaris* and Iran's struggling industries. Finally, the country's instability and its lack of a mature legal and political system frightened off the foreign investors Iran had been expecting.[40]

Iran's principal hope was the United States. As far as the Iranians were concerned, it was the United States that got the Russians out of the country in 1946. According to former Secretary of State Dean Acheson, the U.S. ambassador to Tehran cabled Washington in December 1946 "that in the Iranian view the quick collapse of the Tudeh Party was due to the conviction of everyone—the Russians, the Iranians, and the Azerbaijanis—that the United States was not bluffing but solidly supporting Iranian sovereignty."[41] Iranians watched the creation of the various postwar U.S. aid programs and hoped that they too would receive some of the largesse America was distributing.

Many Iranians, the shah first among them, also sought a closer relationship with the U.S. out of fear of communism and the USSR. All throughout his life, Mohammad Reza Shah feared Communist subversion and Soviet invasion. He frequently exaggerated both of these threats and was quick to dismiss internal problems as the result of Communist plots, but it was a driving force in his policy. He sought American aid not only for domestic economic reasons but also to shore up his defenses from this two-headed menace. He was not alone in this position. Iran's upper classes, although mostly pro-British, worked hard after the war to involve the United States in Iranian affairs. Iranians wanted the United States in their country to keep the Russians out (and, for some on the left, to keep the British out too).[42]

The United States did not ignore Iran, but it did not fulfill the Iranians' dreams either. After the war there were a great many broken and destitute nations, and Iran was not the most wanting nor the most important in American eyes. Billions of dollars were poured into Europe and East Asia—the cockpits of the world wars—and Iran had to make do with millions. Washington's thinking about Iran, developed principally by then–Undersecretary of State Acheson, focused primarily on Iran's internal stability. Acheson concluded that Iran would never be able to defend itself against a determined attack by the USSR and, therefore, that task should be left to American deterrence. Acheson was also concerned that building a large military, as the young shah planned, in the hope of taking on the Russians would be a colossal distraction and a strain on Iran's resources. Consequently, Acheson consistently urged Tehran to concentrate on political reform and economic development as the best means of achieving stability and prosperity and let Washington worry about dealing with the Russian threat.[43]

In 1946, the United States extended Iran a loan of $3.3 million, and another for $22.5 million in 1947. These were not insignificant sums, but they were less than Iranians wanted and Washington refused to waive interest payments on them. In 1948 and 1949, the United States did not provide any direct economic aid at all and Tehran was told that it should apply for assistance from the new World Bank. On the military side, the Truman administration steadfastly fended off the shah's ever more insistent requests for funds and weaponry. Washington provided only a token $10 million military grant in 1950.[44] However, it did expand the American advisory mission to the Iranian Army and continue the program with Iran's Gendarmerie. In addition, the United States provided a series of assessment missions and economic expertise.[45] Most of this simply whetted Iranian appetites for more, and when it was not forthcoming they felt betrayed. As one U.S. Embassy assessment explained in 1950, "The Iranians built a dream world in which our part was to loan them $250 million, and when we played our role only to the extent of making a $25 million loan, the Iranians thought we had let them down."[46]

A nonevent in 1946 provides a revealing glimpse into the Iranian side of the U.S.-Iranian relationship. As soon as the Soviets were out of Iran, the shah began sparring with Prime Minister Qavam. Initially, the shah offered the United States very favorable oil concessions if Washington would help him regain absolute power, but the United States demurred.[47] Then, in October, the shah sent an emissary to the U.S. Embassy in Tehran to ask the ambassador whether Washington would object if the monarch decided to oust the prime minister. The envoy did not get the answer he sought, so the shah grudgingly refrained.[48] If this story is true, it is noteworthy because the shah of Iran chose not to depose his prime minister for fear of incurring the wrath of the United States. From an American vantage point, it is just not clear what he was afraid of. The United States was giving very little aid to Iran, so Washington had minimal leverage there to use against the shah if we were displeased. Likewise, by the end of 1946, the American military that had helped defeat Nazi Germany was being rapidly demobilized, and—given our actions earlier that year in getting the Soviets out of Iran—it was highly unlikely that President Truman was going to invade Iran even if the troops were available.

This was the beginning, however, of a theme that would run through U.S.-Iranian relations for the next thirty-three years: Iranians believing that the United States had the ability (and the desire) to control their destinies even when we did not. This is not to suggest that the United States never interfered in Iranian affairs—we did, and at times in very unpopular ways—but the extent of that interference was wildly exaggerated by Iranians, even those who should have known better, like the shah. In later years, Mohammad Reza Shah would depose a number of prime ministers without breathing a word to the United States—and in some cases would oust prime ministers Washington really liked. But even he would never lose the sense that the United States was pulling all the strings in his country.

The one potential bright spot in the postwar Iranian firmament was oil. Over the years, Iranian oil exports had grown dramatically and Iran had become the key producer of the British empire. In 1914, Iran exported less than 300,000 tons of oil. This had grown to 1.5 million tons in 1920, then to 6.5 million tons in 1941, and to 16.5 million tons in 1945.[49] The problem was that the Iranians themselves were seeing very little of the profit. If Iran had controlled all its own oil revenues, it would have made £275 million in 1950, as an example; however, under the terms of the 1933 concession—and after the Anglo-Iranian Oil Company (AIOC, the former APOC) got done cooking the books—it made only £37 million.[50] To add insult to injury, the company paid its Iranian employees a pittance and treated them like slave laborers.

The sense that AIOC was fleecing their country created a growing anger among Iranians, while the treatment of AIOC's Iranian employees inevitably produced a general strike in July 1946. His Majesty's government (the majority shareholder in AIOC) responded in all too typically imperial fashion: London deployed a naval force to threaten the main refinery at Abadan and recruited tribesmen and ethnic Arabs from Khuzestan province and sent them to brawl with the striking workers. Dozens were killed and more than a hundred injured in the street fights that ensued. In the end, the British reached a compromise, agreeing to observe Iranian labor laws in return for an end to the strike. By then, the workers were tired of the violence and desperate for a paycheck, and they returned to work. But AIOC quickly reneged on its end, and there was effectively no change in its treatment of its Iranian employees.[51]

Iran's political scene was no better after the war. Politics remained largely the purview of a small elite, most of them plutocratic landowners whose chief interest was maintaining their status and wealth. Their principal source of competition was the young shah, who was determined to regain the autocratic position his father had once held. Prime Minister Qavam proved a disappointment. He rigged the 1946 Majles elections to remain in office. However, in another pattern that would recur throughout Iranian history, the broad party that he had built in opposition to the shah and the British could not remain cohesive. There were simply too many groups with too many competing interests; once they were in power, their other differences emerged and pulled them apart.[52]

Meanwhile, the shah's power continued to grow as Iran's military power revived. Like his father, Mohammad Reza Shah retained a tight grip on the armed forces, lavishing them with resources and making sure to closely associate his own fortunes with those of the military. By 1949, he had rebuilt the Army to a strength of 120,000 men.[53] Moreover, the huge boost in their morale after crushing the Azeri and Kurdish separatist movements in 1946 redounded to the benefit of the shah, who had favored the military solution as opposed to Qavam's preferred political approach. The shah's political fortunes were also buoyed by Qavam's problems, which allowed royalist Majles deputies to take a centrist position, playing the crucial swing vote in debates between the rightwing pro-British bloc and Qavam's left-of-center Democrats. In late 1947, the shah felt strong enough to oust Qavam and install his own prime minister.

Background to the Oil Nationalization Crisis

In February 1949, the shah narrowly survived an assassination attempt. The assassin's identity was never fully established. His papers showed that he worked for a religious newspaper (and therefore might have been a religious extremist), but he also paid dues to the journalists' union affiliated with the Tudeh Party. Whatever his true motives, the shah saw in the failed assassination attempt both a boon and an opportunity. The boon came from a huge boost to his popularity for having survived the attack (although he failed to recognize that this had nothing to do with him personally). The opportunity was to crack down hard on two major independent power centers in Iran, the Communists and the clergy. He declared martial law, introduced changes to the Constitution to allow him to dissolve the Majles, banned the Tudeh, arrested many of its leaders, and arrested or deported a number of leading clergy who had been taking an active role in politics. In July, he went too far, attempting to fix the Majles elections, and when this became known, it triggered widespread opposition to his bid for autocracy.[54]

The shah's repressive policies combined with another cause to produce a remarkable political coalition. This other cause was the British oil concession. The AIOC was a rapacious and careless company. They were determined to maximize immediate profits without regard for Iran or even for the ill will they were creating for themselves. The company lied and manipulated its books to underpay the Iranian government to the tune of billions of dollars.[55] AIOC also indulged in bribery of Iranian officials, attempted to manipulate Iranian internal politics, armed local tribesmen in return for their support, and consistently violated the terms of the 1933 compromise on the concession in terms of improving working conditions, training Iranian personnel, and promoting more Iranians to positions of greater authority. The British went so far as to import labor from India for jobs Iranians believed should rightly have gone to them.[56]

The working conditions of AIOC's Iranian employees were unconscionable: they were paid 50 cents per day and lived in a shantytown called Kaghazabad ("paper city," for the principal means of construction) without running water or electricity. They had no vacation, no sick leave, and no disability compensation. An Israeli who worked for several years at Abadan wrote that the Iranians there were "the poorest creatures on earth. . . . They lived during the seven hot months of the year under the trees. . . . In winter times these masses moved into big halls, built by the company, housing up to 3,000–4,000 people without wall or partition between them. Each family occupied the space of one blanket. There were no lavatories. . . . In debates with

British colleagues we often tried to show them the mistake they were making in treating the Persians the way they did. The answer was usually, 'We English have had hundreds of years of experience on how to treat the Natives. Socialism is all right back home, but out here you have to be the master.' "[57] Averell Harriman, visiting Abadan in 1951, cabled Truman that the slums he saw there were "shocking for housing of employees of a large Western oil company." And later that the British held "a completely nineteenth century colonial attitude toward Iran."[58]

The result was the formation of the National Front in October 1949. This was a broad coalition embracing much of Iranian political society, all of whom were now united in their desire to limit the designs of the shah and seek redress from the British. The National Front managed to gather together reformist liberals of the new middle class, socialists, nationalists and ultranationalists, *bazaari*s (the "traditional" middle class), and various religious groups, including some right-wing extremists.[59] Among the Muslim groups, the most important figure by far was Ayatollah Abolqasem Kashani, whose father had been killed fighting the British in Mesopotamia in World War I. This fractious bunch coalesced around the eccentric figure of Mohammad Mosaddeq, an elder statesmen of Iranian politics with a long record of opposing both the Pahlavis and the foreign oil companies. In 1949, Mohammad Mosaddeq seemed to be the very embodiment of the two causes that mattered most to the majority of the Iranian body politic.[60]

Once the shah's tampering was exposed, the elections were canceled and rescheduled, and when they were finally held in the late fall, they were among the most free and untainted in Iran's history. Only eight actual members of the National Front were elected to the Majles, but many of the other deputies were sympathetic to its aims and demonstrated a willingness to follow Mosaddeq's lead.[61] What's more, the chaos that followed the cancellation of the July elections allowed the Tudeh Party to resurrect itself almost immediately. Mosaddeq never cared for the Tudeh, but as fellow enemies of the shah and the oil companies, he could count on their support in achieving his two principal goals.[62]

Escalation to Deadlock

Thus, the drama began in 1949, when the Iranian government demanded a renegotiation of the British oil concession. Encouraged by their parliamentary victory over the shah and driven by Iran's dire economic circumstances, Iran's nationalists expected a dramatic reversal in the terms of the concession. However, the British were not in the giving vein. Many of the AIOC's executives were both numbingly greedy and terrifyingly insensitive to the Iranian perspective. Indeed, many were astonished and even disappointed by the "ingratitude" of the Iranians for not being thankful to the AIOC for pumping, refining, and selling their oil for them.[63] For the British government, the majority shareholder of AIOC, the question of Iranian oil was more than a matter of greed. AIOC was heavily dependent on Iranian oil production, which accounted for 76 percent of the company's total production in 1949–1950, and AIOC was very important to the British economy.[64] Postwar Britain was in economic straits, running a trade deficit of $1 billion per year and struggling to recover from the war. Consequently, the $142 million in annual taxes paid by the company, plus the government's share (at that point about 60 percent) of AIOC's $93 million in annual profits was of great importance to the well-being of the national economy.[65]

As should have been expected, the initial negotiations did not solve the problem. At that time, most Iranians wanted a fifty-fifty split of all profits coupled with revised and transparent bookkeeping procedures to put an end to AIOC's creative accounting procedures, as well as improved working conditions. American oil companies had agreed to a fifty-fifty deal with Venezuela earlier and it was rumored that a similar deal was in the works with Saudi Arabia; if the Americans could grant such deals, the Iranians expected the same from the British. But AIOC had no interest in a fifty-fifty deal, and the British government feared that agreeing to an even split would set a precedent for British oil interests elsewhere around the world. All they were willing to offer was an increase in the minimum annual royalty to £4 million, a further reduction in the area in which AIOC could drill, and a promise to train more Iranians for administrative positions.[66] The offer was not just absurd, it was insulting: Iran had made £16 million that year, so the increase in the minimum royalty was irrelevant; the reduced AIOC concession area would still contain all of Iran's proven oil fields; and the company had repeatedly and flagrantly disregarded its previous promises to train and promote more Iranians.

Nevertheless, the shah demanded that the cabinet accept the British offer and present it to the Majles for ratification. Mohammad Reza Shah granted the British the same exaggerated respect he applied to American influence and feared that they would overthrow the government if Iran did not accept.[67] When the government attempted to sell the new agreement to the Majles, the Parliament virtually revolted. It refused to ratify the agreement and began a move to nationalize the oil fields outright.

———

Across the Atlantic, the Truman administration was deeply unhappy with this turn of events, and particularly with AIOC and the British. Acheson, now the secretary of state, and Assistant Secretary of State for Near Eastern Affairs George McGhee sympathized with Iranian nationalists against British imperialism. They also were extremely concerned that British greed would drive Iran into the arms of the Communists. And they were unhappy with the shah, who had dropped an American-inspired anticorruption campaign almost as soon as it had begun. In addition, Acheson and company did not believe that Mosaddeq and other Iranian nationalists were Communists, and considered them the best men to reform the political system and ensure that Iran did not drift into the Soviet orbit. Consequently, they were very disturbed that London would be setting itself up as the enemy of Mosaddeq's National Front. From the start, Acheson and American diplomats urged the British to be flexible and generous with the Iranians, and even suggested they would be comfortable with outright nationalization as long as Tehran compensated AIOC at a reasonable rate for its losses. At least one of Acheson's subordinates launched into a tirade at visiting British officials for risking the "loss" of Iran to communism by their continued unwillingness to strike a fair deal with Mosaddeq.[68]

As far as Washington was concerned, things turned from bad to worse. In 1949–1950, there was another bad harvest in Iran, which triggered a depression and accompanying starvation, unemployment, and civil unrest.[69] The year 1950 also saw the outbreak of the Korean War and the launch of a more assertive American approach to containment of the Soviet Union. Suddenly, defending a vulnerable Iran against Russian encroachment or Communist takeover loomed large in American minds. The United States signed a mutual defense agreement with Tehran in May, approved a $25 million Export-Import Bank loan (although it was never actually imparted because of problems on the Iranian side), began a program of military assistance that would provide an average of $23 million per year in military aid through 1956, inaugurated an Agency for International Development (AID) program for Iran, and supported an Iranian application for a $10 million loan from the World Bank. Washington also began to press the British harder to compromise with Iran on the oil concession, suggesting that a fifty-fifty split would be fair and appropriate.[70]

Unfortunately, the British struck first. In secret, they demanded that the shah replace the current prime minister with General 'Ali Razmara, whom they considered both a stronger personality than the shah and more compliant with their will. Upon taking office, Razmara pledged to curb the powers of the shah and to revive the anticorruption campaign, which led many Iranians to believe that he had been installed at Washington's behest, not AIOC's.[71] But

Razmara was probably doomed to fail. The shah spent his time working to undermine the new prime minister, while the Majles remained just as adamantly opposed to the British proposal. Razmara suggested to the British that they sweeten the deal by agreeing to allow the Iranian government to inspect AIOC's books periodically, begin to train some Iranians for managerial jobs, and make some royalty payments in advance in the name of supporting Iranian national development. But the Brits remained intransigent.[72]

The Iranians formally voted down the AIOC offer in November 1950. The very next month, ARAMCO (the conglomeration of American oil firms operating in Saudi Arabia) agreed to a fifty-fifty profit split with the Saudi government. Recognizing that this could further embolden the Iranians, the British ambassador to Tehran proposed that AIOC immediately do the same. This proposal might have averted the crisis and passed the Majles: in the debate within the Majles oil commission in November, Mosaddeq had proposed outright nationalization of the oil fields but had been voted down by the rest of the committee, who were still interested in achieving better terms with the British. The fifty-fifty deal might very well have been the better terms they were looking for. But AIOC and the British Foreign Office rejected the idea out of hand.

The announcement of the Saudi deal and the absence of any hint of a change on the part of AIOC effectively eliminated the moderate position within the Majles. Mosaddeq and the extreme nationalists were now in control, and in mid-February 1951, the Majles oil commission adopted Mosaddeq's earlier proposal and recommended full nationalization of the oil fields. Despite public demonstrations in favor of nationalization, Prime Minister Razmara rejected the recommendation and within three weeks he was assassinated by a Muslim extremist tangentially affiliated with one of the parties of the National Front. Razmara was succeeded as prime minister by Mosaddeq himself, and so on April 30, 1951, the Majles voted to nationalize all of Iran's oil production, with the shah obediently signing the bill two days later.[73]

In London, the response of the British was equally extreme. The most innocuous step they took was to put Iran's "illegal" nationalization on the agenda at the U.N. Security Council. At the other end of the spectrum, London began drawing up plans for an invasion of Iran code-named "Buccaneer" with 70,000 troops to be landed by sea, and the maximum possible brought in by air to seize the oil fields in a *coup de main*.[74] They also began a military buildup in the area by deploying additional naval forces to the Persian Gulf and a paratroop brigade to Cyprus to get the process moving. This was not the first time the British had considered this possibility—the British ambassador to Washington had first floated the idea with U.S. officials in the fall of 1950—

but now the planning was in earnest.[75] In the meantime, AIOC shut down the oil fields, fired 20,000 Iranian employees, and convinced all of the other international oil firms not to lift Iranian oil. They were greatly aided by the fact that there was a worldwide oil glut. Thus, Iranian production was not missed and the other firms all agreed to collaborate with AIOC to discourage other governments from adopting full nationalization.[76] To ratchet up the pressure further, the British government froze all Iranian assets in British banks, it prohibited the export of key British commodities (such as sugar and steel) to Iran, and eventually began using the Royal Navy to enforce a blockade of Iran's oil exports to take care of the occasional tanker attempting to smuggle Iranian oil.[77]

The Truman Administration Steps In

As far as Washington was concerned, things were getting out of hand. The Truman administration feared that the Anglo-Iranian row would lead either to a rift in the Western alliance or to the fall of Iran to the Soviet Union. The Americans remained convinced that Mosaddeq was a genuinely popular nationalist with strong anti-Communist credentials whose views accurately reflected those of a large segment of Iranian society. They were deeply concerned that the British continued to somehow believe that Mosaddeq was unpopular, and they feared that continued intransigence on the part of the AIOC would only further inflame Iranian nationalist sentiment. Moreover, the United States was terrified that a British invasion of Iran would trigger a Soviet counterinvasion.[78]

Meanwhile, both sides demanded that the United States take a position in the dispute. This produced a lukewarm statement from the State Department that was mostly sympathetic to the Iranians but called for a negotiated settlement. Privately, the administration decided that the United States needed to take a more active role in mediating the dispute lest the situation spiral into open warfare. When Acheson learned that the British were, in fact, planning an invasion, he delivered a strong warning to the British ambassador to Washington that the United States would not support military intervention in Iran—a point he was forced to reiterate to His Majesty's government at various points during the crisis.[79] Truman cabled British Prime Minister Attlee to encourage him to reopen negotiations with Iran immediately and not allow the two sides' positions to become entrenched. In public, however, the U.S. ambassador to Iran made Washington's stance even more transparent by telling *The Wall Street Journal,* "Since nationalization is an accomplished fact, it would be wise for Britain to adopt a conciliatory attitude. Mossadegh's National Front party is the closest thing to a moderate and stable political element in the national parliament."[80]

The British were incensed by the American tilt toward Tehran. The staunch American opposition convinced Attlee to take the invasion plan off the table in July, but it did not end British interest in creating regime change in Tehran. London instead began planning for a covert action campaign to try to oust Mosaddeq's government.[81] Remarkably at the time—but as would become the norm in later years—Mosaddeq's government responded to what was seen in most capitals—including London—as a very pro-Iranian American statement with a bizarre demarche protesting Washington's interference in Iran's internal affairs.[82]

After considerable debate, the Truman administration decided to try to mediate the dispute by dispatching Averell Harriman, the former wartime ambassador to Moscow and a close confidant of the president, to Tehran in July 1951. After many weeks of painful and peculiar talks, Harriman and his team convinced Mosaddeq to receive another team of British negotiators. All of Harriman's efforts came to naught because the British negotiations still would not agree to nationalization, and the Iranians would not accept anything less.[83]

In October 1951, the U.N. Security Council took up the Iran-AIOC dispute, and Mosaddeq himself made the journey to New York to defend his country before the world. It was only then that the American people finally got a good, long look at the Iranian prime minister, and they were not quite sure what to make of him.

Dr. Mohammad Mosaddeq was like nothing Americans had ever seen before. He was a scion of the Qajar royal family, the ultimate establishment figure whose relatives had held the prime ministership twenty times in the last century but who had adopted the cause of Iranian nationalism and constitutionalism as his passions.[84] He was a true eccentric: he famously held cabinet meetings and received foreign dignitaries while in bed, dressed in his pajamas. He was a hypochondriac and frequently begged off public events or played for sympathy by claiming to be at death's door, but he was not very particular about his appearance and grooming. He had a flair for melodrama and employed rather hackneyed theatrics that outsiders considered foolishness—crying during his speeches, hobbling on a cane one minute and then breaking into a trot the next—but that hit all of the right chords with his countrymen. Indeed, many foreigners underestimated Mosaddeq because they assumed his outward idiosyncrasies indicated a weak man underneath.[85]

Moreover, Mosaddeq was a mass of contradictions. In particular, he studiously cultivated the impression that he was totally devoted to the letter of the law and unbendable in his uprightness. In actuality, he treated the law as entirely malleable and placed reason and pragmatism well ahead of dogmatic adherence to it. Roy Mottahedeh, a well-known specialist on Iran and Shi'ite Islamic law, notes that much of Mosaddeq's academic work, including his doctoral dissertation, was an overdrawn (if not outright fanciful) argument that Shi'i jurisprudence enshrined above all the notion that the law was determined by commonsense reasoning and that a lawmaking body "could pick and choose whatever it considered appropriate among the sources of Islamic Law."[86] Although this would have appalled any well-versed *madrasah* student, it said a great deal about Mosaddeq's view of the law.

Mosaddeq was also the incarnation of an extreme form of Iranian nationalism; indeed, xenophobia would probably be a more accurate term. Iran was a politically immature nation at the time, and the Iranian people were obsessed with humiliating the British—to the detriment of everything else. Mosaddeq embodied that reckless (even suicidal) sentiment. During their negotiations in Tehran, Mosaddeq once famously reproached Averell Harriman regarding the British: "You do not know how crafty they are," he told Harriman, the former American ambassador to London, "You do not know how evil they are. You do not know how they sully everything they touch."[87] Shi'i Iran was reared on the story of Husayn's martyrdom and taught to glorify the suicidal sacrifice in pursuit of the noble but hopeless cause—and that was precisely what Mosaddeq offered his countrymen. Unfortunately, this made him exactly the kind of impractical and quixotic figure that pragmatic Americans found inexplicable. For instance, Mosaddeq told the Majles oil commission in 1951 that to defeat communism, Iran needed money, and to get that money it had to nationalize its oil industry. But when questioned as to how nationalization would bring in revenue if it simply triggered a boycott, he responded: "I have no intention of coming to terms with the British. Rather than come to terms with the British, I will seal the oil wells with mud."[88]

Yet playing to the world in New York in September 1951, Mosaddeq was dazzling. He twice addressed the Security Council, but, claiming illness, he spoke at times through his son. At points he seemed meek and helpless, at others he roared. He electrified his audience. He also converted a number of formerly skeptical Americans of the correctness of his cause. And he embarrassed the British by producing a number of documents found in the AIOC offices after they were nationalized that demonstrated widespread (and largely illegal, as well as unethical) interference in Iran's political affairs. In the end, he not only triumphed, he prevailed. The Security Council agreed with Iran that the nationalization was an internal matter and therefore did not fall under its jurisdiction.[89]

After his victory in New York, Mosaddeq spent several weeks in Washington at the invitation of President Truman, who hoped to use Mosaddeq's stay to try again to work out a compromise between the Iranians and British. Assistant Secretary of State George C. McGhee spent many long hours with Mosaddeq, struggling to craft an agreement. Although he could not get the prime minister to budge on the issue of nationalization, he did work out a compromise position that would have allowed the AIOC back in to market Iranian oil with a financial arrangement that would establish something close to a fifty-fifty profit split. But the British would not accept it; although they would not admit it openly, they remained categorically unwilling to accept nationalization and were really willing to consider only the terms of a reformulated concession. There was effectively no overlap in their positions, and Mosaddeq returned to Iran in mid-November without a settlement.[90]

For his part, Mosaddeq had also failed to achieve his primary goal. He had come to Washington hoping that the United States would agree to provide Iran with economic assistance and to press its oil companies to buy Iranian oil to break the British embargo. Truman and Acheson were sympathetic, but felt constrained by their ties to Great Britain. The American position was further complicated by the international context. In October, Winston Churchill—another leader famous for conducting business in his pajamas—had returned to 10 Downing Street, and the old Tory quickly indicated that he had no sympathy for the Iranians and believed the whole matter should be cleared up with a bit of gunboat diplomacy. In addition, 1951 was the height of the Korean War, and Churchill bluntly told Truman that British support in Korea (where it was desperately needed) would come at the price of American support in Iran. Nevertheless, Truman and Acheson still promised Mosaddeq additional technical assistance and continued military aid. But Mosaddeq had naively assumed that the anticolonialist Americans would leap to Iran's defense, and now he was deeply disappointed.[91]

Mosaddeq Shah

The spring 1952 Majles elections loomed large. Cracks had already begun to develop in the broad façade of the National Front. Part of this was due to the efforts of the British, whose covert action network in Iran was busy funneling money to opposition parliamentarians and newspapers. Mark Gasiorowski, the leading non-Iranian scholar of the 1953 crisis, has also suggested that CIA operatives in Iran,[92] who were supposed to have been focused on the Soviets, may have decided to act entirely on their own initiative and aid the British in making trouble both for the Tudeh Party and for Mosaddeq.[93] However, of equal or greater importance were two other factors. First, the economic impact of the British embargo was beginning to hurt. Iranian oil production had fallen from 660,000 barrels per day (bpd) in 1950, to 340,000 bpd in 1951, to just 20,000 in 1952.[94] Tens of thousands of oil industry workers had lost their jobs, and numerous other Iranians who depended on the oil workers as customers and the industry for business were feeling the effects as well.[95] Finally, differences were beginning to reemerge in the loose coalition that Mosaddeq had brought together under the National Front banner. With the shah remaining largely in the background and the oil industry nationalized, the coalition had lost its binding forces. Middle-class Iranians became frustrated with the ongoing crisis with Britain. Members of the clergy began to remember their distaste for Mosaddeq's secularism, and, in particular, Ayatollah Kashani began to flex his own political muscles independent of Mosaddeq. Indeed, Mosaddeq would accuse Kashani of attempting to rig the Majles elections.[96]

It was Mosaddeq himself, however, who ended up manipulating the elections in rather blatant fashion, albeit mostly out of a desire to combat the American and British efforts to subvert the Majles. He knew that his greatest support would come from Tehran, and he had gerrymandered and sequenced the elections to give the greatest emphasis to the capital. When the results for the first 79 seats (out of 136) came in, it became clear that the National Front was not going to carry the house; the National Front had won only 30 of them, and the remainder were all from areas where the National Front had little support. So Mosaddeq did something completely unexpected: he called for an emergency session of the cabinet and convinced it to vote to halt the elections on the grounds that they were being corrupted by foreign agents—which they were, although the extent was unclear and there was no actual evidence to substantiate the charge. By stretching certain ambiguous clauses of the Iranian Constitution, Mosaddeq argued that this was possible as long as the 79 Majles deputies already elected did not veto the cabinet's decision, which they did not.[97] Mosaddeq held on to power but had resorted to undemocratic methods to do so.[98]

It is surprising that immediately after the fiasco of the 1952 election Mosaddeq would take an enormous political gamble, but that is exactly what he did. When he submitted the names of his cabinet to the shah, he included his choice for minister of war. Although it was the prime minister's right to appoint the minister of war, no one ever had, instead leaving that post to be filled entirely at the discretion of the shah as part of his prerogatives over the military. When the shah refused to accept Mosaddeq's choice for war minister,

Mosaddeq resigned. The rejoicing in London could probably have been heard in Tehran. The British saw this as their moment to regain control of Iran and *their* oil industry. They convinced (it is unclear how) a very reluctant shah to reappoint the (by then) pro-British Ahmad Qavam, of Soviet-withdrawal-crisis fame, as prime minister. However, when Qavam announced that he planned to reverse many of Mosaddeq's policies and that all who objected would be arrested, the Iranian people revolted. The next day there were massive popular demonstrations in Tehran and other cities. Inevitably, things spiraled out of hand with greater and greater demonstrations, resulting in bloodshed and troops mutinying over the bloodshed. In all, 69 people were killed and about 750 wounded. Four days later, the shah asked Qavam to resign and recalled Mosaddeq as prime minister.[99]

At that moment, Mosaddeq had effectively overthrown the shah. When they met, the shah acceded to Mosaddeq's control of the War Ministry. He went so far as to ask Mosaddeq whether he would retain the monarchy, acknowledging that Mosaddeq's popularity and control over the institutions of government were such that the shah was powerless to oppose him. Mosaddeq replied that he would allow the shah to remain as shah, but only if he reigned but did not rule.[100]

By subverting Iran's election process and rallying popular support to depose the shah's prime minister, Mohammad Mosaddeq, the lifelong constitutional democrat, had effectively made himself dictator of Iran. It is unclear whether this was his intention all along, and it was a "popular" dictatorship in that the demonstrations in July had given him a kind of mandate from the masses, but it was hardly democracy.

Mosaddeq himself did seem to recognize what had transpired and moved quickly to consolidate his power. He cut the military's budget by 15 percent, announced that in the future Iran would buy only "defensive" weapons, transferred 15,000 men from the Army to the Gendarmerie (which was not as closely associated with the shah), purged 136 senior officers, rearranged the high command to put officers he trusted into the top slots, and announced the formation of two commissions—one to investigate corruption in arms procurement and the other to examine the system of military promotions. With the armed forces effectively neutered, he then declared martial law.[101] Next, he extracted from the rump Majles a law granting him emergency powers for six months to "decree any law he felt necessary for obtaining not only financial solvency, but also electoral, judicial, and educational reforms."[102]

Countercoup

In retrospect, the last half of 1952 merely set the stage for the climactic events of 1953. Mosaddeq quarreled more and more frequently with Ayatollah Kashani and other National Front leaders over cabinet appointments and Mosaddeq's emergency powers. That fall, the ambitious Kashani broke with Mosaddeq—possibly at the urging of several other ayatollahs who objected to Mosaddeq's secularism—and so gravely weakened the National Front.[103] At the end of the year, when his emergency powers were up, Mosaddeq had the Majles renew them for another twelve months.

The most important event was a final bid by the lame-duck Truman administration to find a negotiated solution to the Anglo-Iranian impasse. This time, the Americans were willing to press hard and make real sacrifices to get American oil companies to cooperate with the U.S. government against the British embargo. What's more, the British had finally come around to accepting nationalization and were ready to agree to a fifty-fifty profit split. But now Mosaddeq scuttled the deal himself. He demanded that the British pay $50 million in damages and lost revenues. This was probably the most important of the many opportunities Mosaddeq missed by his single-minded hatred of the British. Had he been willing to accept this deal, it almost certainly would have precluded the coup. Moreover, by remaining obstinate, Mosaddeq convinced the Eisenhower administration that he could not be reasoned with when they took office in 1953.[104]

In response, the British stepped up their covert activities, making contact with the retired General Fazlollah Zahedi (the same man the Nazis had hoped would lead a tribal revolt on their behalf during World War II) to convince him to mount a military coup against Mosaddeq. When the prime minister got wind of this, he broke diplomatic relations with Great Britain and closed down the British Embassy, thereby denying MI6 a base from which to operate in Tehran.[105] This prompted the British to make their first overture to the CIA, which could still operate from an embassy in Iran and had a lot more money than the British. Deputy Director of Central Intelligence Allen Dulles, Deputy Director for Plans (Operations) Frank Wisner, and the chief of Near East operations, Kermit "Kim" Roosevelt (grandson of Teddy), were all enthusiastic about the idea. However, they purposely withheld the plan from the Democrats, who "were considered too sympathetic to Mosaddeq."[106] Eisenhower had already won the U.S. presidential election, and Dulles's brother, John Foster, was slated to be the new secretary of state. Dulles himself would move up to become the director of central intelligence. The CIA officers thought that the Eisenhower administration would gladly rush in where the Truman administration had feared to tread, and they were content to sit on things until after the inauguration.[107]

Once again, Mosaddeq misjudged the Americans, assuming that the Eisenhower administration would do for him what the Truman administration would not. With Iran's economy feeling the pinch of the embargo, Mosaddeq needed economic assistance and American political pressure on the British, and he needed them fast. In fact, some analysts believe that Mosaddeq may have dismissed the final effort of the Truman administration to broker a compromise deal with the British because he expected that the Eisenhower administration would take Iran's side completely in the dispute.[108]

In a theme that has recurred throughout modern Iranian history, Mosaddeq assumed that the United States considered Iran a vital nation, and that Washington would never risk losing Iran to the Communists (who might take control if Iran were reduced to chaos or were spurned by the West). Believing that he was reinforcing this fear, Mosaddeq warned the new administration that if he did not get what he wanted from them, he would turn to the Soviet Union. Of course, this was the worst thing he could possibly have done. Unlike Acheson, John Foster Dulles, and many of those around him, had a great deal of difficulty distinguishing between nationalists and Communists, and Mosaddeq's foolish threats simply confirmed to them that Mosaddeq was at best unstable and at worst possibly a Soviet agent. To add fuel to the fire, Mosaddeq began to flirt with the Tudeh Party as his coalition frayed. Although the Tudeh would eventually reject Mosaddeq's overtures, there was enough common ground (in opposing both the royalists and now the mullahs) for them to work in tandem at times.[109]

The Eisenhower administration brought with it a very different *weltanschauung* from that of the Truman people. Barry Rubin has pithily described the difference as "While Truman and Acheson felt social change was inevitable—and thus should be encouraged in a manner consistent with American interests—Eisenhower and Dulles tended to see reform movements as disruptive and as likely to be captured by local Communists. The Iran experience marked the transition from a U.S. policy based on the first perception to one based on the second."[110] The one member of the new administration who was not convinced that Mosaddeq had to go from the start was the president, who was somewhat sympathetic to the eccentric Iranian.[111] Over time, however, Ike too was brought around. The unwillingness of Mosaddeq to go along with the final compromise deal of the Truman administration despite Iran's economic needs weighed heavily on him. Moreover, the Dulles brothers had the CIA's covert action personnel in Tehran foment disturbances in the guise of the

Tudeh, which allowed them to convince Eisenhower that Mosaddeq's government was unstable and therefore vulnerable to a Communist takeover.[112]

By June 1953, the CIA's covert action program, code-named Operation Ajax, to destabilize Iran and topple the Mosaddeq government was ready.[113] The Agency's propaganda instruments in Iran (which previously had been battling with their Soviet counterparts for Iranian hearts and minds) would be turned against Mosaddeq. The United States and Great Britain would support the efforts of General Zahedi to foment a military coup, and the Agency would help him try to reach out to other royalists in the Army. They would also attempt to stir up tribal and popular unrest to make it difficult for Mosaddeq to rule and convince other groups that his continued rule was a threat to Iranian stability. The CIA would secure the cooperation of the shah and the support of Ayatollah Kashani and other important political leaders who had already broken with Mosaddeq or seemed to be in the process of doing so. Finally, the U.S. government would deny Iran any financial or other assistance.[114] They swung into action immediately.

The British had not waited for the Americans. They and General Zahedi had already started provoking fights with the government and trying to convince various Army factions to join with Zahedi during February and April 1953. They also worked to convince key Iranian politicians and tribes to turn against Mosaddeq.[115] But when the Americans arrived with huge amounts of cash to spend (by the standards of 1953 Iran), they welcomed the reinforcements. Six new newspapers suddenly appeared on the streets of Tehran in the summer of 1953, all of them spewing venom against Mosaddeq.[116] Richard Cottam, a leading scholar of Iran and, at the time, one of the CIA's leading Iran propagandists, estimated that by the end of the summer, four fifths of the newspapers in Tehran were under CIA influence.[117] Likewise, as soon as the covert action program was approved, President Eisenhower notified Prime Minister Mosaddeq that the United States would not be able to provide Iran with any economic assistance.[118]

Eisenhower's letter came at a particularly dark time for Mosaddeq. Among the Iranian people, he remained the most popular figure in the country by a wide margin, but he was losing his grip on the country's political elites. His coalition was deeply fractured, thanks to his own increasingly dictatorial rule, the economic problems facing the country (Iran had lost $200 million in revenue from the oil blockade by then),[119] and the inevitable entropic forces working on a coalition that came together to oppose things that no longer existed rather than to pursue a common agenda. And the CIA and MI6 covert action campaigns that were aimed at these fissures were undoubtedly exacerbating the problems; wherever there were cracks, Western agents were working to pry them open into great, wide rifts. Kashani was by now completely estranged from Mosaddeq, as were a variety of leftist and center-nationalist leaders and the important Bakhtiyari tribe.[120] With few allies remaining, Mosaddeq gave the Tudeh a freer rein, simply as an expedient to find some support against his multiplying enemies. Mosaddeq's desperation to deal with Iran's economic matters and his growing internal problems caused him to pilfer treasuries throughout the government and to press for ever greater control. In July, fearing that he was about to lose a vote of no confidence in the increasingly obstreperous and Western-controlled Majles, Mosaddeq took a further, and dramatically unconstitutional, step by calling for a popular referendum to dissolve the Parliament.[121]

Mosaddeq's gambit was to try to make it possible for him to rely solely on the support of the one group that still backed him with some degree of vigor: the Iranian people. Many of his closest advisers warned him against the referendum, and a number deserted him when he ignored their advice.[122] But even in calling for the popular referendum, Mosaddeq seems to have lost some of his faith in his support among the people. There were separate ballot boxes for "yes" and "no" votes, and they were generally set up on opposite sides of a room so that a person's vote was hardly secret. There were other charges of even more deliberate tampering. Not surprisingly, on August 3, Mosaddeq "won" the referendum with more than 99 percent of the vote.[123] "Mosaddeq, the constitutional lawyer who had meticulously quoted the fundamental laws against the shah, was by now bypassing the same laws and resorting to the theory of the general will," in the words of Ervand Abrahamian.[124] To rub his enemies' noses in his "victory," Mosaddeq disbanded the Majles and lifted the prosecutorial immunity of Majles deputies.[125] At that moment, Mohammad Mosaddeq was the undisputed, unconstitutional ruler of Iran.

Despite all of this, the CIA coup d'état against Mosaddeq was a very nearrun thing. It started the night of August 15. The United States, working through a variety of intermediaries (including Norman Schwarzkopf, Sr.) but mostly through Kim Roosevelt, had persuaded a reluctant and fearful shah to sign a pair of royal decrees—*firmans*—that deposed Mosaddeq as prime minister and named General Zahedi in his place. Technically, this did not quite conform to the 1906 Constitution (in which the shah confirmed the decisions of the Majles), but it was close enough to be able to make the average Iranian assume it did. Besides, given the liberties that Mosaddeq had recently taken with the Constitution, the *firmans* were downright punctilious. The plan was for a loyal military officer to take the *firmans* to Mosaddeq and arrest him that night. The next day, the *firmans* would be published, agitators and rabble-rousers paid by the CIA would organize street demonstrations in favor of Zahedi, loyal Army units would be brought in, and Ayatollah Kashani (who may have indirectly received $10,000 for his help) would send his minions into the streets in support of Zahedi as well. The shah himself, terrified that things would unravel, chose to wait at his villa on the Caspian with a plane at the ready to whisk him out of the country at the first sign of trouble.[126]

Mosaddeq had been tipped off and was ready. When Zahedi's men arrived in the middle of the night, he claimed that the *firman*s were illegal and forged, and he had Zahedi's lieutenant arrested. The next morning he reported to the nation that there had been an attempted coup and those responsible were being rounded up. The shah jumped into his plane and fled, Zahedi and his comrades went into hiding, and the CIA believed that the coup had failed. But Kim Roosevelt refused to give up, and over the next few days he began to turn things around with some important help from a number of middle-rank Army officers still loyal to the shah. He convinced the shah—now in Baghdad on his way to Rome—to publicly announce that he had signed the two *firman*s. He then convinced several newspapers to print the *firman*s on the front page. Next, Roosevelt used his paid agitators to get the Tudeh out onto the streets of Tehran (by posing as Tudeh leaders themselves) and begin demonstrating violently in favor of Mosaddeq, which he expected to arouse the emotions of the royalists and frighten the centrists. He encouraged others, and Kashani's people, to turn out their own followers to oppose the Tudeh. Although it is unclear whether it was the CIA-British contacts that prompted him to do so, Kashani did turn out large numbers of his loyalists, and others joined in. These riots (and overtures by Zahedi) in turn attracted military units loyal to the shah (including the Imperial Guard) to Tehran, who then turned against the pro-Mosaddeq crowds and the prime minister himself. The climactic day, August 19, ended with a bloody battle at Mosaddeq's house where Army units loyal to the different sides slugged it out with tanks and infantry and as many as 300 were killed before the royalists prevailed. Mosaddeq escaped over the roof but was later caught and put under arrest. The shah then returned home in triumph to the seeming adulation of at least a portion of the Iranian people.[127]

The Legacy of the Coup

For most foreigners, the collective memory of Iranians for Mohammad Mosaddeq might seem contrary and ironic. He is remembered as the man who stood up to the West, even though his whole strategy for nationalization hinged on receiving vast economic aid from the United States. He is remembered as the man who challenged despotism, even though he established an autocracy that might have been as complete (although probably not as repressive) as either Pahlavi had he remained in power. He is remembered as the man who was betrayed by the United States, even though the Truman administration tried repeatedly to save him from himself and he ultimately rejected a deal that Washington worked out that most Iranians probably could have lived with—and that probably would have staved off the coup. He is remembered as a paragon of virtue and a scrupulous champion of the law, even though his own time in office was marked by a series of unconstitutional actions. There are elements of truth in each one of these aspects of the Mosaddeq myth. However, just as Americans know virtually nothing about the man, so Iranians know only part of the truth, and what they do know is often as problematic as what Americans do not.

Like John F. Kennedy's among Americans, the myth of Mohammad Mosaddeq—and of the utopia that he would have created had he survived in power—has become a fixture in Iran's political imagination. Even astute observers of Iranian history are capable of rather fanciful claims regarding "what might have been" if Mosaddeq had not been removed from power, as well as the purely evil consequences that followed from his overthrow. Witness the leaps of causal faith in this claim by one Iranian writing about 1953: "It is a reasonable argument that but for the coup Iran would now be a mature democracy. So traumatic was the coup's legacy that when the shah finally departed in 1979, many Iranians feared a repetition of 1953, which was one of the motives for the student seizure of the U.S. embassy. The hostage crisis, in turn, precipitated the Iraqi invasion of Iran, while the revolution itself played a part in the Soviet decision to invade Afghanistan."[128]

What is most knotty for the United States is that the popular Iranian version of history portrays Mosaddeq as a wildly popular prime minister forging a new, democratic Iran fully in command of its own destiny, who was overthrown by American agents to prevent Iran from achieving political and economic freedom. The event itself was a source of tremendous anger against the United States for Iranians, who assumed that the United States had been responsible for the coup long before actual evidence to that effect began to surface. It completed Iranian disillusionment with the image of the United States as a grand, munificent benefactor of Iran. After the coup, and more and more as the tragic-mythic version of the coup spread, Iranians increasingly believed that the United States was a malevolent power that had replaced the British as the insidious force controlling Iran's destiny and preventing it from achieving its rightful stature and prosperity.[129] As usual, that myth is not right, but it is also not entirely wrong either. There is a kernel of truth in it, and therein lies the rub; the United States *did* help to overthrow Mosaddeq, and it *was* culpable in the establishment of the despotism of Mohammad Reza Shah that suc-ceeded him.

How much was Mosaddeq's fall the result of the United States?[130] That question has never been fully answered and probably never will be. Richard Cottam, who is generally sympathetic to Iranian nationalists, summed up the prevailing view that "Regardless of foreign participation, Mossadegh could not have been overthrown if significant elements of the population had not lost faith in his leadership."[131] Mosaddeq had alienated important segments of the Iranian elite through his own actions—principally his refusal to deal with the British and so end the embargo, and his concentration of power in his own hands to dictatorial levels. The British and Americans did help exacerbate these splits, but the evidence is compelling that they intensified trends already under way. It is difficult to find evidence to suggest that any of the major op-ponents to Mosaddeq who brought about his downfall (particularly his former allies in the National Front, whose abandonment of him in 1952–1953 drasti-cally undermined his support in the Majles) did so in response to Western overtures.[132]

Even during the August coup itself, key developments were the work of actors who appear to have wanted nothing to do with America or Britain but did oppose Mosaddeq and seized the opportunity created by the foreign pow-ers to further their own goals. For instance, many of those who joined the anti-Mosaddeq crowds on the decisive nineteenth of August appear to have reflected genuine popular discontent and been motivated by leaders (like Kashani) just as distrustful of the United States and Britain as they were op-posed to Mosaddeq.[133]

Nevertheless, the American (and lesser British) role was critical in Mosad-deq's overthrow. It seems unlikely that his domestic foes would have been able to put aside their own differences to move against him. An Iranian scholar has written that "The coup was a product of the close collaboration of Mosaddeq's domestic and foreign opponents, even though the role of the two foreign pow-ers, especially the United States, in organizing and financing it was all but in-dispensable. Mosaddeq's Iranian opponents were too divided and too unsure of themselves as well as each other to organize and act in unison. Some of them, notably the shah himself, even suspected that the British were secretly behind Mosaddeq and so they were hesitant to commit themselves. On the other hand, the foreign powers could not possibly have brought down Mosad-deq by a coup without the cooperation of his domestic opponents."[134] In other words, by the time that Kermit Roosevelt showed up in Tehran there was a great deal of kindling laid at Mosaddeq's feet; all the CIA had to do was strike the match. But it is just unclear that had Kim Roosevelt not shown up with a book of matches when he did, other Iranians would have done it them-selves.

Of course, in the Iranian version of the story, the CIA and British MI6 take on supernatural powers. The coup demonstrated that they (and the CIA partic-ularly) could work miracles. Consequently, it was assumed that the Western intelligence services *could* be behind almost anything and, when coupled with the tendency of Iranians to see themselves as "the center of the universe," this quickly turned into the ingrained conviction that they *were* behind everything. Given how important Iranians perceived their own country to be, they could not imagine that the CIA was not spending great time and effort manipulating every segment of their society. This inflated sense of the CIA's power and determination to rule Iran would play an important role in generating anti-Americanism among Iranians angry at the shah's policies but convinced he was little more than the all-powerful CIA's cat's-paw.

A last important legacy of Mohammad Mosaddeq was his martyr complex. Martyrdom and the story of Husayn dominate Shi'i theology, and this is one reason why Mosaddeq himself doubtless found it easy to assume that role. Throughout his brief time in power, Mosaddeq pushed his convictions to an absurd extreme that courted disaster in what seemed to be a purposeful man-ner. Mosaddeq's example encouraged the belief among Iranians that staking out an extreme position, even if it would inevitably result in great hardships for oneself or for Iran as a whole, was the right course of action. The fact that Mosaddeq was even more popular after his overthrow than when he was prime minister has only reinforced that notion. This tendency would be resurrected to an even greater extent during Ayatollah Khomeini's reign, when Iran almost seemed to be actively seeking its own destruction by taking on the whole world and hewing to causes that had long been lost.[135]

Because he made himself a martyr, Mosaddeq's own political agenda took on an almost sacred importance in later years. Fulfilling his dream became not just an unimpeachably correct approach in many Iranian minds but a holy obligation for some. Unfortunately, the legacy of Mosaddeq's ideas has not al-ways been a positive one for Iranians. Mosaddeq was obsessed with foreign interference in Iranian affairs, believing it to be the root cause of all of Iran's problems, and therefore did his countrymen a great disservice by allowing his fixation on foreign conspiracies to be a distraction and even an obstacle to policy courses that could have addressed tangible problems. In particular, throughout the oil nationalization crisis, Mosaddeq made it clear that all he cared about was removing all traces of foreign influence from Iran, not trying to achieve what was best for the Iranian economy.[136] (Of course, in Mosad-deq's mind, these were one and the same.) Although at times he claimed that he was not an extremist, but merely forced to the extreme by others, the evidence suggests the opposite.[137] Even before he was prime minister, when he led the Majles special commission on the oil concession, Mosaddeq was the only member of the commission who would settle for nothing less than full nationalization right from the start. He argued to the commission in 1951 that "the British-dominated oil industry, not the landowning system, was the principal cause of all Iran's misfortunes."[138] After acquiring his dictatorial powers in 1952, Mosaddeq might have tried to implement wide-reaching political and social reforms, but he did not. The reforms he made were rather modest, and instead he remained focused on the nationalization issue and his own political power.[139]

Consequently, his obsession with foreign interference in Iran—extreme even by the standards of his day—and his guiding assumption that the elimination of all foreign influence was a necessary precondition to Iranian political freedom and economic prosperity, became even more firmly ingrained in the Iranian political mythos. Just as George Washington's famous warning against "foreign entanglements" grew to be an article of faith for many Americans and became deeply problematic for American foreign policy in the twentieth century, so too has Mosaddeq's obsession with eliminating suspected foreign influences over all other policy considerations become an Iranian bête noire to this day.

What's more, Mosaddeq became his own self-fulfilling prophecy and, in so doing, his lesson became burned into Iran's collective psyche. Mosaddeq was consumed with foreign conspiracies to interfere in Iran, influence Iranian behavior, keep the country servile to Western interests, and remove independent-minded governments. That fixation on foreign plots provoked a foreign plot that did overthrow him. Ever since, Iranians—already predisposed to conspiracy theories and inevitably blaming everything but the weather on foreign subversion—have had one firm, incontrovertible fact with which to back all of their assertions and conjecture: the United States *did* overthrow Mosaddeq. Neither we nor they can ever escape that truth. We *should* not forget it; they *will* not.

CHAPTER 4

The Last Shah

In a cable to the Foreign Office in London in the autumn of 1953, one British official described the return of Mohammad Reza Shah Pahlavi after the fall of Mosaddeq as follows: "After leaving Tehran last August with what must have been little hope of returning he suddenly found himself swept back on a wave of popular enthusiasm. Almost all experienced observers here, both Persian and foreign, are agreed that this enthusiasm was generated more by the Persians' deep rooted feelings for the institution of the monarchy than by any strong sentiments in favour of the person of the Shah. Unfortunately, His Majesty has, I understand, interpreted it largely as a demonstration of personal affection. This and the doubtful quality of much of the advice he receives from his court have not made it easy for him to make an accurate appraisal of the present state of the country."[1]

Another story has it that news of Mosaddeq's fall reached the shah while he and the empress were dining in Rome, to which they had fled when the coup plot had initially gone wrong. Upon hearing the news, he is reported to have shouted, "I knew it! I knew it! They love me!"[2]

Indeed, the young and still relatively inexperienced shah did believe that his people loved him.[3] This desire to be loved—and his inability to recognize that he mostly was not—would plague Reza Shah Pahlavi's reign from start to finish. His father does not seem to have cared whether he was loved as long as he was feared, and he ruled accordingly; but it was all-important to Mohammad Reza, and he found himself perennially caught between the desire to be loved and the need to be feared. Unfortunately for the United States, over the course of the twenty-five years from 1953 to 1978, Iran's strategic position and its oil wealth would serve as binding forces, tying America tightly to Mohammad Reza Shah's fortunes, our own popularity rising and declining with his until his fall took us down with him.

Restoration

Immediately after the coup, the shah and his new prime minister, General Zahedi, rounded up most of Mosaddeq's chief supporters, but there was little bloodshed. Mosaddeq himself was imprisoned and in January 1954 was put on trial in public in what proved to be a mistake for the regime. Mosaddeq summoned all of his old eloquence and histrionics and mesmerized the Iranian people one last time. Although he was convicted and sentenced to three years in prison followed by permanent house arrest, in the court of public opinion he swept the field. Indeed, much of his persistent legacy in Iran comes from the vindication he won through his performance at his trial.[4]

Ultimately, it was the Tudeh who paid the heaviest price. Although it was not the principal mover on either side, the CIA/MI6 covert action program had successfully tied it to Mosaddeq—in both word and deed. Many Tudeh members did take to the streets to support Mosaddeq, even though the party leadership had decided to stay out, because they were convinced by Western covert propaganda and agents provocateurs that the party leadership had decided to support the prime minister against the shah. What's more, the shah, Zahedi, and many of those around them also believed that the Tudeh was a threat—that it had supported Mosaddeq and was planning to push the country into the arms of the Russians (which, on the last point, it essentially was). The restored regime launched a massive crackdown in which 1,400 were arrested by the end of September 1953 and another 700 by the end of the year.[5]

A key unintended consequence of the coup was that it destroyed the rough balance of power among the Majles, the shah, and the prime minister that had existed since Reza Shah's fall in 1941.[6] The coup and the political pogroms that followed it destroyed the power of both the Majles and the prime minister and silenced the independent political voices that once had existed on both the left and the right. What's more, the shah learned his lesson from the coup. He saw in Mosaddeq's fall the opportunity to permanently cripple the Majles and build the kind of police apparatus that his father had and that he now understood was critical to his hold on power.

In the summer of 1954, the shah dealt with the Majles. He thoroughly rigged the elections, doing so in blatant fashion. He went so far as to have many of the thugs who had led the CIA's demonstrations and street brawls in

August 1953 patrolling the polling places to ensure that Iranians voted the "right" way. Unsurprisingly, 60 percent of the new Majles deputies came from the traditional landowning classes, who were the shah's strongest supporters.[7] The very next year, he dispensed with General Zahedi (who had come to power thanks to American and British intervention) and instead began appointing prime ministers entirely subservient to himself. After that, the Majles became little more than a rubber stamp for the shah, and, in Barry Rubin's memorable phrase, the prime minister became nothing more than the shah's "executive assistant."[8]

Then Mohammad Reza Shah turned to constructing an effective internal security apparatus. He requested help from the United States, who sent Army Colonel Stephen J. Meade, on loan to the CIA, to help Iran organize a modern intelligence service. At least initially, the CIA tried to keep the shah's new intelligence unit focused on the Soviets, providing only basic training in tradecraft, Russian language skills, and mostly innocuous information on the Tudeh. Meade urged the shah to keep domestic and foreign intelligence separate and tried hard to entice the Iranians to work on the Soviet target. But the shah had other ideas. The new intelligence unit handled both internal and external security, and initially focused principally on the internal threat. In fact, during its first year of operation, it uncovered a Tudeh network within the Iranian armed forces that justified to the shah both his paranoia about communism and the need to create the kind of pervasive security presence that could eliminate just these sorts of threats. Thus, the new intelligence service quickly became a favorite of the shah, and in 1957 it was reorganized, expanded, given greater power, and renamed the National Intelligence and Security Organization (Sazman-i Ittili'at va Amniyat-i Kishvar, or SAVAK).[9]

Initially, the shah had chosen to rule through the military, declaring martial law and forming a cabinet led by General Zahedi and consisting of one third generals.[10] However, with the military's loyalty assured, Zahedi gone, and the Majles cowed, the shah's political power was effectively complete. He could now confront Iran's great lingering problem, its economy. Many of the problems Iran had faced at the end of World War II persisted, albeit not in quite as virulent a form. Agriculture remained locked in the grip of a tiny landed minority, who kept most of the peasantry in a state of enforced serfdom. Because the landlords now thoroughly dominated the government (90 percent of all bureaucrats in 1956 came from this class), there was no desire to enforce efforts to deal with this problem even when the shah tried to do so.[11] The clergy, which itself owned significant land, mostly colluded with the landlords in this one area.[12] More and more rural Iranians emigrated to the cities in hope of opportunities that did not exist in the countryside anymore. But there they found only different kinds of problems. Industry remained meager, and Iranian products generally could not compete with foreign imports. Shantytowns grew apace, ringing all of Iran's cities, as the rural poor transformed themselves into urban poor.[13]

But slowly, Iran did begin to emerge from its economic stagnation in the 1950s, helped along by two powerful forces: oil and American aid. In 1954, the restored Iranian regime put its oil industry in order. Ironically, although the British succeeded in ousting Mosaddeq, they ended up with a worse deal than if they had accepted the fifty-fifty split when it had first been proposed in 1949. The new arrangement granted Iran control of its oil resources, plus a fifty-fifty profit split. Production, however, was now divided up among a consortium of foreign firms in which AIOC (renamed British Petroleum, or BP) still retained the lion's share with 40 percent, but Royal Dutch Shell and nearly a dozen American companies controlled the rest. Still, no one had to feel sorry for BP. They demanded compensation for their losses and got it—both from the shah, who agreed to pay £25 million over ten years, and from the other oil companies, which paid BP nearly $600 million over time.[14] Nationalization of Iranian oil also meant that Iran could now sell the rights to explore and pump oil in other areas of Iran, including offshore, where they secured more profitable deals from American and Italian firms. As a result, Iranian oil revenues grew slowly but smartly from $90 million in 1955 to $285 million in 1960 to $482 million in 1964.[15]

The other desperately needed injection of funds that Iran received during the 1950s came from the United States. Now that the Iranian government was "made in the USA," even if most Iranians only suspected it, Washington felt it vital to provide the restored regime with the economic aid it needed to consolidate its hold and stabilize the country. It started right away with Kim Roosevelt literally handing General Zahedi nearly $1 million in unspent CIA funds from the coup. Washington followed this up within three weeks with another $68 million in emergency aid. More funds continued to flow, and between 1953 and 1956 the United States ended up providing roughly $200 million in economic assistance (and another $200 million in military aid). By the end of the decade, American economic aid to Iran since Mosaddeq's fall would reach $611 million.[16]

Of course, where the Pahlavis were concerned, the moment that Iran's economy began to recover was the moment that their focus shifted to the military. As always, Mohammad Reza Shah saw his own fortunes bound up with those of the Iranian armed forces. His use of the military against the Azeris and Kurds in 1946 had allowed him to triumph over Qavam, and the loyalty of key military units in 1953 had been vital to toppling Mosaddeq. What's more, the shah despised the powerlessness he felt before the foreign powers—the United States, the USSR, even the British—and believed that a powerful Iranian military was the single most important element in achieving geopolitical independence for Iran. But paradoxically, the shah concluded that building up a powerful military machine to make Iran more independent first required getting even closer to the United States, because only America could provide the finances and the weaponry to build that great Iranian military. This became one of the primary drivers, and possibly the most important, in the close ties the shah forged with the United States.

The shah decided that the only way to convince Washington to give him what he wanted was to make himself a key ally of the United States in the Cold War with Russia. Of course, this came easily to a man so suspicious of communism and the ruler of a country that had been repeatedly invaded by Russia, but there was more than just a convergence of perceived threats at work. Thus Iran's alliance with the United States was seen by the shah as mostly a temporary, tactical expedient. Even within the Eisenhower administration, there were considerable numbers of people (starting with the president) who questioned the utility of selling massive amounts of weaponry to Iran given both its competing economic needs and its dubious ability to use the equipment. In response, the shah stressed Iran's importance as a frontline state against the USSR and the ease with which the Red Army could reach the Persian Gulf and its oil fields if Iran were not better armed. To prove his anti-Communist credentials, he signed Iran on to the Baghdad Pact of 1955, an alliance of Turkey, Iraq, Iran, Pakistan, and Great Britain, which was intended to be the right flank of NATO (and which later morphed into CENTO, the Central Treaty Organization, in mimicry of its European antecedent). The shah joined the Baghdad Pact against the advice of the British, who thought the Iranian economy too fragile to support the kind of military expenditures the creators of the pact envisioned. Indeed, he still signed on even though the United States chose not to explicitly join the pact, which Washington engineered, preferring simply to "associate" itself with the treaty.[17]

In the end, the shah's efforts paid off. It was an uphill fight. The United States was far more concerned about the internal threat to Iran created by a vulnerable economy and would have preferred the shah to invest his money in political and economic reforms projects. Nevertheless, with no one else for the Americans to turn to, the shah's persistent demands eventually carried the day. Between 1953 and 1961, the United States provided Iran with approximately $500 million in military assistance that allowed the shah to expand his armed forces from 120,000 to 200,000 men.[18] By 1956, Iran hosted the largest U.S. military aid mission in the world.[19] The Eisenhower administration also provided Mohammad Reza Shah with a host of other assistance; various American assets helped the shah quell the Qashqa'i tribal revolt in September and rig the 1954 elections, in addition to helping start the intelligence service that eventually became SAVAK.[20]

In spite of all of its anti-Communist mania, the Eisenhower administration had considerable ambivalence about Iran. It started with their view of the shah himself, whom they considered weak, vacillating, vainglorious, and callow. In addition, the shah did not share Washington's conviction that the greatest threat to Iran came from Communist subversion capitalizing on Iran's weak economy. Instead, he complained constantly that he was not getting the military aid to which he believed Iran was entitled. The shah whined that in the 1950s (while Iran had been receiving $500 million for its military and had the largest U.S. military aid mission) the United States had given twice as much aid to Yugoslavia (this was virtually all economic assistance), three times as much to Turkey, and four times as much to Taiwan.[21] At various points during the 1950s, Americans dropped hints that they would not be averse to a strongman from the military displacing Mohammad Reza Shah, but the shah's control over the levers of power proved too strong.[22]

Although the money flowing from Washington might have suggested otherwise (and certainly did to many Iranians), the Eisenhower administration tried hard to keep Iran at arm's length. In particular, the CIA shut down its covert action programs in Iran in the mid-1950s and instead turned its attention fully to gathering intelligence on the Tudeh and the Russian presence in Iran and developing a liaison relationship with SAVAK also designed to provide information on Russia and communism.[23]

Paradoxically, while the United States was trying to keep its distance from Iran, many Iranians resented the growing American presence in their country. Muslim political activists in particular were angered by what they viewed as the lax morals of American culture seeping into Iran.[24] Iran's middle class, especially the traditional *bazaari*s, feared that American aid was allowing Washington to gain control over their country, and they assumed that the price for U.S. aid was doing America's will—which they believed was confirmed in the overthrow of Mosaddeq, the signing of the Oil Consortium Agreement, and Iran's adherence to the Baghdad Pact. They also did not like the way that U.S. aid contributed to corruption in their government as Iranian officials became ever more skilled at skimming money off American aid programs. Finally, and most ironic of all, they blamed Washington for Tehran's heavy emphasis on spending on the military rather than on education, social progress, and economic reform.[25]

By the late 1950s, Mohammad Reza Shah seemed completely in control in Iran. He had again fixed the 1956 Majles elections, packing the Parliament with apolitical figures dependent on the regime for their authority. He created two political parties—the National Party as the party of the government and the People's Party as the loyal opposition—that were both so entirely beholden to the regime that they were known by Iranians as the "yes and yes, sir" parties.[26] By 1957, with the new SAVAK up and running, the shah felt comfortable enough to lift martial law in Tehran (which had been in place since the August 1953 coup). The next year SAVAK proved its worth (and its ability to protect the regime) by snuffing out a coup plot by General Valiollah Qarani, the commander of the Army's intelligence branch.[27]

Then events elsewhere in the region rocked the seeming complacency of the Pahlavi regime. In 1958, the Lebanese and Jordanian governments invited in foreign troops to save them. American Marines landed in Lebanon, ostensibly to protect the Lebanese government from Communist subversion but in truth to help the Maronite Christians hold power in the face of challenges from Lebanese Muslims. The young King Hussein of Jordan was threatened by Nasserist elements in his military and elsewhere in Jordan, and the British Paras came to his rescue. But it was in Iraq that the ax fell. In July 1958, Nasserist military officers overthrew the Iraqi monarchy in bloody fashion. So hated had the British-supported king become that the Iraqi people treated this coup d'état as a popular revolution. Immediately, Baghdad withdrew from the Baghdad Pact, forcing the State Department to scramble to convince the remaining members to reform as CENTO.[28]

In Tehran, the Iraqi Revolution was a thunderbolt—the Pahlavis had been close to the Iraqi Hashemites and the Iraqi king had seemed no less secure in his throne than Mohammad Reza on his. Moreover, the victory of the Nasserists in Iraq conveyed a sense that pan-Arabism was on the march throughout the region. Nasser himself had overthrown Egypt's King Farouk in 1952; in 1955 he had allied himself with the Soviet Union and signed the "Czech" Arms Deal for massive Soviet military aid. Syria had followed, and then had actually merged with Egypt under the umbrella of the pan-Arabist United Arab Republic, in 1958. Arabs began to whisper that the large Arab population of Khuzestan province in far southwestern Iran (which had once been known as "Arabistan" and now contained most of the country's oil wealth) should rise up and throw off the Persian yoke. On top of all this, the Soviets themselves began to press the shah, promising him weapons and money if he came around, and threatening that if he did not, then Moscow might have to invoke the 1921 Soviet-Iranian Treaty (which permitted the USSR to intervene in Iran if it was being attacked by a third power from Iran) against the "foreign bases" in Iran.[29] In response, the shah decided he needed to strengthen the country's ties to the United States and to Israel—the two "natural enemies" of the Soviet Union and the Arab radicals.[30]

The shah's new overture found a receptive audience in both Tel Aviv and Washington. The embattled Jewish state was desperate for allies of any kind, and a fellow Middle Eastern country that shared its problems with Arab nationalism was a perfect fit. It was also a propitious moment for the United States. The years 1957 and 1958 had seen Sputnik and the start of the missile gap, another Berlin crisis with Moscow, the crisis with Communist China over Quemoy and Matsu, and now the problems in the Middle East. Few in Washington were blind to the problems in Iran: a 1958 CIA study argued that the shah would be overthrown if he did not soon begin a process of domestic reform, and a congressional committee investigating American aid to Iran found widespread irregularities and misuse of funds.[31] Indeed, a National Security Council Directive stated that the United States would press the shah to reform domestically, and that if he refused, Washington would identify and support a successor.[32]

However, concern about the Soviet Union once again trumped these other considerations. The shah came up with a perfunctory anticorruption campaign and a seven-year development plan, and Washington contented itself that that would be enough. Eisenhower met the shah in December 1959 and did not even raise the issue of reform. The U.S. government had apparently been aware of the Qarani coup well before SAVAK and had kept quiet about it, perhaps suggesting that the administration was then not averse to a change in the regime. (The shah later learned that the United States had known about the Qarani coup and had said nothing, increasing his own distrust of America.)[33] But after the fall of the Iraqi monarchy, Washington reversed course. Later that year, General Teymour Bakhtiyar, the head of SAVAK, was on a visit to the United States, and when he met CIA Director Allen Dulles and Kim Roosevelt, he told them he wanted to overthrow the shah and wanted their help. Dulles and Roosevelt were noncommittal in reply but then immediately informed the shah of Bakhtiyar's disloyalty.[34]

Thus, far from looking to identify a successor, the United States was now helping the shah to stay in power. To make that point public, in March 1959, the United States and Iran signed a bilateral defense agreement that proclaimed that "In the case of aggression against Iran, the Government of the United States of America, in accordance with the Constitution of the United States of America, will take such appropriate action, including the use of armed forces, as may be mutually agreed upon and as is envisaged in the Joint Resolution to Promote Peace and Stability in the Middle East, in order to assist the Government of Iran at its request."[35]

The decade did not end particularly well for the shah despite the treaty with the United States, the increase in American aid, and his growing oil revenues. His regime overspent on its seven-year development plan and on the armed forces, exacerbated by pervasive corruption that drained much-needed capital from the treasury. In response, the regime began to run a deficit and to take loans from abroad, and eventually to just print money. The situation suddenly exploded into a crisis when the 1959 harvest turned out to be a bust. Inflation jumped and the regime turned to Washington and the IMF for assistance. The IMF offered $35 million and the United States another $8 million to get Iran's finances under control, but both insisted on immediate curbs on government spending and other reform measures.

The result was an immediate increase in unemployment and corresponding public demonstrations. To make matters worse, there were considerable "irregularities" by both of the shah's tame political parties. It made a mockery out of even the façade of democracy, and inflamed popular sentiment against the monarch. In March there was rioting in Tehran, and by August the shah was forced to cancel the Majles elections altogether. When they were eventually restaged later in the year, the electoral fraud was even worse—the shah got the deputies he wanted, but at the cost of making his people very unhappy. Thus, with a brand-new American administration taking power in Washington, the shah had a full-blown economic and political crisis on his hands.[36]

The Stillborn Reforms

In 1960, John F. Kennedy and the Democrats recaptured the White House, and his election had a profound impact not only on the United States, but on Iran. Mohammad Reza Shah Pahlavi never cared for JFK. First, there were personal difficulties. Kennedy was everything that Mohammad Reza aspired to be—dashing, charismatic, worldly, intellectual, a war hero, and genuinely popular—and it all seemed to come so effortlessly to Kennedy, while the shah struggled. Second, Kennedy's administration brought with it a fundamentally different approach to American foreign relations than that of the Eisenhower administration, one that did not mesh with the shah's preferred course. In particular, the Kennedy administration stressed economic development, social change, and political reform over conventional military assistance.

What's more, Kennedy and his advisers suggested that they expected these changes would likely require "revolutions" around the world, by which they simply meant dramatic changes from past practices of government, but which the shah seems to have taken literally. For instance, in a 1962 speech at the White House, Kennedy warned that "Those who make peaceful revolution impossible will make violent revolution inevitable."[37] Mohammad Reza Shah apparently saw such hyperbole as being a warning directed at him personally, that if he did not agree to political and economic reforms along the lines of what Kennedy wanted, the United States would start a popular revolution in Iran.[38] As always, it was never clear why the shah believed that Washington could or would take such action—let alone that Kennedy's broad exhortations were actually veiled threats intended specifically for Iran—nonetheless he did, and he acted accordingly. Especially at that moment, in 1961, the shah needed American help to deal with his domestic mess.

In reality, the Kennedy administration's perspectives on Iran were much more complicated than the Iranians ever fathomed. On the one hand, they were concerned about Iran's stability. In early 1961, the journalist Walter Lippmann had a conversation with Soviet Premier Nikita Khrushchev in which the Russian famously singled out Iran as a country headed for revolution because of the misery of its people and the corruption of its government. Lippmann reported Khrushchev's boast to Kennedy, who heard something similar from Khrushchev himself at their 1961 summit, during which the latter boasted that Iran was a "rotten plum" about to fall. Kennedy reportedly saw this as a challenge, prompting him to make Iran a priority for his program of American-assisted reform.[39] Kennedy directed the State Department to form a special task force on Iran, which was headed by Assistant Secretary of State for Near Eastern Affairs Phillips Talbot. In May, this task force presented its recommendations, which included increasing American economic aid, providing full political and diplomatic support to the new reformist Amini government, and exerting gentle but firm long-term pressure on the shah to broaden his base of support by bringing the moderate opposition into the government. The task force also suggested that the United States should increase its contact with opposition groups and encourage moderate oppositionists as a way of undermining extremists.[40]

Nevertheless, American leverage with the shah was limited, and Washington feared that if it pressed him too hard, he would take up with Moscow.[41] And in fact, the shah did begin to flirt with the Russians, going so far as to pledge not to allow the deployment of foreign (i.e., American) nuclear missiles on Iranian soil in September 1962, just before the Cuban Missile Crisis. But this was all tactical for Tehran. The shah remained as anti-Communist as ever, and his overtures to Moscow were intended almost entirely as a means of gaining leverage over Washington.[42]

As usual, events intervened to force the hand of both the shah and the Americans. In May 1961, 50,000 teachers took to the streets in Tehran to protest their wages and working conditions. The police had to call in several companies of infantry and even a battalion of paratroopers to help them control the protesters. One of the striking teachers was killed and many more injured in the violence that inevitably ensued. With considerable encouragement from Washington and the memory of what had befallen his Iraqi counterpart fresh in his mind, the shah dissolved the Majles he had worked so hard to pack, and appointed Dr. Ali Amini as prime minister. This was a bitter pill for the shah to swallow. He deeply distrusted Amini, a moderate reformer who had been the minister of finance in Mosaddeq's government. Amini was the American candidate; he had been ambassador to Washington, he had developed a friendship with then-Senator John Kennedy, and he had strong ideas about the rule of law, representative government, and progressive economic policies. The shah admitted to one journalist that the Kennedy administration had forced him to appoint Amini.[43] Once in power, Amini ousted many of the worst of the shah's flunkies from the government. In their place he brought in technocrats and reformists, including the radicals Hassan Arsanjani as minister of agriculture and Mohammad Derakshesh as minister of education.[44]

It was Amini and his lieutenants, Arsanjani in particular, who really inaugurated the broad program of social and economic reforms that the shah later repackaged as his "White Revolution." Amini had the advantages of having American support and not having a Majles to deal with (although this also opened him to charges of being illegitimate). On the other hand, Amini had a colossal task in front of him. Corruption in the Iranian regime was rampant—skimming of funds, soliciting of bribes, charging of commissions, nepotism, and the padding of payrolls with hundreds of "consultants" and those "awaiting assignment" who never showed up for work but still received half pay. Iran's taxation system was horribly regressive; the rich simply did not pay, and so, to find revenues where it could, the regime taxed sugar and other staples of the lower classes. The rise of education and mass communication meant that a more politically aware populace, and particularly a more politically active middle class, was becoming disgruntled that they did not have political influence commensurate with their economic contributions and education. Iranian agriculture remained nearly feudal: most of the land was owned by wealthy absentee landlords (56 percent of the land was in the hands of 1 percent of the population),[45] who contracted with peasants at disadvantageous rates to serve as sharecroppers. And inflation continued to climb; even the government was admitting that it was in double digits by 1962, while private estimates placed the actual numbers even higher.[46]

Amini was a serious reformer. He started with economic austerity and imposed real anticorruption measures. He pressed Arsanjani to devise a meaningful land reform program, and Arsanjani needed little encouragement. Arsanjani was a true radical whose principal goal was to break the power of the large landlords. His efforts eventually coalesced into the 1962 Land Reform Act, which forced landowners to sell the state all agricultural property in excess of one entire village (!) or parts of up to six different villages, although it did allow for exemptions for orchards, tea plantations, and mechanized fields, all of which were recognized to be more efficient in larger parcels. Landlords were to be compensated based on their previous tax assessments and paid out over ten years, while land bought by the state was to be promptly sold back to the sharecroppers working those plots at modest rates.[47] The extent of the land problem in Iran becomes obvious when you consider that allowing an absentee landlord to continue to own just one entire village constituted radical progress. And it *was* radical progress, the kind that invariably stirs opposition.

Amini and his reformist cabinet also received important help from the United States, both via economic aid ($80 million in economic grants and $77 million in loans in 1961–1962)[48] and a vast range of assistance programs. The United States provided food under the Food for Peace program (which buys surplus American agricultural products and sells them to designated countries via grants or low-cost loans payable in local currency). It provided Ex-Im Bank loans to build highways, ports, airports, railroads, power plants, and water treatment facilities. Washington granted loans to Iran's Industrial Mining and Development Bank, which in turn lent to agricultural and industrial projects like textile and cement plants, pest and water control projects, and the creation of agricultural cooperatives. Americans helped establish health programs in Iranian universities, created a network of rural health care centers, and set up programs to bring qualified Iranians to the United States to train as doctors and public health care officials. The United States encouraged providing greater authority to local government, including village councils, and established programs to provide aid directly to these municipal administrations for construction projects and agricultural loans. Americans set up apprenticeship programs for every occupation from blacksmiths and carpenters to automobile and locomotive repairmen, to plumbers and foundry workers. Iran soon boasted one of the largest AID missions in the world.[49]

In addition, the United States doggedly pressed the shah to concentrate on supporting Amini's reforms, rather than nurturing his long-standing obsession with foreign and domestic threats. The Kennedy administration convinced a reluctant shah to agree to scale back the Iranian military from 240,000 men to only 150,000 men and to employ Iranian military personnel in civic action programs.[50] Washington cut its military aid to Iran, from $85 billion in 1960, at the end of the Eisenhower administration, to $58.6 billion in 1961 and then to $44.7 billion in 1962.[51] Even the CIA distanced itself a bit further from SAVAK. The Agency's training mission was removed, ostensibly because its job was done. However, the fact that Iran immediately brought in Israeli Mossad personnel to take the place of the Americans suggests that politics played a larger role.[52]

Although the Kennedy administration was pleased, Amini's reforms were going too far for some influential Iranians. In October 1962, the cabinet approved the Local Councils Law of 1962, which created local governments throughout Iran to try to decentralize some power away from the regime in Tehran. Many of Iran's mullahs rose up to protest it, including a then-little-known cleric named Ruhollah Khomeini. Khomeini and his cohorts had three objections to the law: it gave women the vote, it allowed elected officials to take the oath on the holy book of their choice (thereby allowing religious minorities to hold office), and it did not limit religious minorities to vote only for specially designated representatives.[53] Many of his fellow mullahs also railed against Amini and Arsanjani's land reform program, calling it un-Islamic and unconstitutional. (Of course, the law would have stripped much of the land owned by the clergy too.) Khomeini doubtless shared their sentiments but was clever enough not to say so publicly, recognizing that the peasantry liked the land reforms. Many landlords and mullahs (including Khomeini) began to claim that Amini's reforms were all an American plot to further reduce Iran to servitude. The only "evidence" they had for these plots was that Amini and his reforms were popular with the Kennedy administration, but that was all they needed.[54]

In the end, however, it was the shah and the middle class who were Amini's undoing. Amini repeatedly clashed with the shah over cutting the military budget as part of his austerity measures. Moreover, the initial round of land redistribution was extremely popular among the peasantry, which did little to improve the shah's feelings about Amini and Arsanjani.[55] As for the middle class, Amini's anticorruption campaign and efforts to battle inflation seemed to matter little to them. Instead, led by Mosaddeq's old National Front, they excoriated him for ruling without a Majles and refusing to call for elections—points on which they had been much less adamant ten years earlier, when it had been Mosaddeq himself ruling without a Majles.

Between January 1960 and January 1963, there were a dozen protests that turned into riots in the streets of the capital. Beginning in October 1961, Tehran University became the scene of a number of violent demonstrations. These culminated in a bloody clash in January 1962. Students bizarrely chanting "Long live Dr. Mosaddeq! Down with Amini!" and the inevitable "Down with the shah!" provoked the shah to dispatch police and paratroopers to break up the demonstrations. They did so with great brutality, beating people up and trashing university buildings. Again the National Front blamed Amini. In non-sensical and politically foolish fashion, the National Front launched a relentless full-scale media war against him. The shah could not have asked for anything more. He had tolerated Amini because it was necessary, but when the middle class and the intellectuals (who should have been Amini's staunchest supporters) turned on him, it allowed the shah to oust him and again install a docile creature of the court, Asadollah Alam, as prime minister in July 1962.[56]

The White Revolution

With Amini out of the way, the shah gathered power back into his own hands. He and Alam rigged the 1963 Majles elections, producing a safe majority of monarchists and technocrats happy with the shah and the status quo. Alam also watered down Arsanjani's Land Reform Act.[57] But what the shah had begun under duress, he came to embrace as his own. For some time, he had seemed to understand that there were problems with Iran's distribution of land and had made some modest efforts to deal with it. Soon after his 1953 restoration, he began redistributing some of his own personal fiefdoms and by 1958 had sold off 500,000 acres to 25,000 peasants at low prices.[58] Moreover, he did not try to stop the land reform program; he merely sought to make it redound to his own credit and to weaken some of its most radical (i.e., progressive) measures. At some point in the early 1960s, he also realized that land reform was genuinely popular and that this was a way to finally reach his people and achieve the adulation he craved.

Indeed, it is important to understand the shah's own aspirations to understand the White Revolution. Mohammad Reza Shah Pahlavi was not a man of strong character.[59] Psychologists could no doubt have a field day discussing his relationship with his father and the various qualities it produced in the son. He was clearly insecure on his throne; he saw plots everywhere and feared (or resented) anyone with any independent standing as a rival. But he also saw himself as a modern, young monarch. Like Kennedy, and very much in the mold of his father, he wanted to be thought of as "modern" and as leading his people to a brighter future. Consequently, he increasingly attempted to associate himself with Iran's liberal intellectuals. Rather than a despot propped up by a powerful army and a traditional, landed autocracy, he wanted to be seen as a leader of the vanguard of Iranian society, forging a path toward enlightenment and greatness for his people. Land reform seems to have played into that image of himself. In fact, he conceived that land reform could become part of a much broader program of modernization that, he hoped, would make him the darling of the intelligentsia and the savior of his people. Although he never would have suggested as much, it was an effort to legitimize his regime by making himself the ruler who brought Iran to modernity and prosperity.[60]

So in January 1963, Iran held a referendum on what was formally known as "The Revolution of the Shah and the People" but was colloquially called the "White Revolution." Not surprisingly, it passed with 99.9 percent of the vote, but the obvious tampering should not suggest that the program was unpopular, at least at first.[61] The initial version consisted of six principles:

1. Land reform
2. Nationalization of the forests and pasturelands
3. Profit sharing for workers
4. Privatization of state factories
5. Revised electoral laws intended to give greater representation to workers and farmers (but which Arsanjani would employ to grant women suffrage)
6. Foundation of a Literacy Corps to send recent college graduates out into the countryside to teach reading and writing to the peasantry

Later, six more would be added:

7. Creation of a Health Corps to improve rural health services and educate more health care professionals
8. A reconstruction and jobs corps
9. Rural courts of justice
10. Nationalization of the waterways
11. National reconstruction
12. An educational and administrative reconstruction[62]

The shah also began a major campaign to industrialize the Iranian economy. Like his father, the shah was obsessed with building a modern industrial base for the prestige, to diversify Iran's economy, and to reduce its dependence on imported manufactured goods. He did attempt to attract foreign investors to Iran, but initially most of the investment in Iranian industries came from the government itself. In addition, the regime levied tariffs of as much as 200 or even 300 percent on certain goods to try to shelter nascent Iranian industries from competition with overseas manufacturers.[63]

The peasantry were enthusiastic supporters of the White Revolution when it was first unveiled. They wanted land reform to continue and also saw advantage in the Literacy Corps, the rural judiciary system, and the Health Corps.[64] Many women were pleased to finally have a political voice (they were granted suffrage in February 1963), and the idea of profit sharing did appeal to the small but growing cadre of industrial workers. At its core, however, the White Revolution was about land reform, and although it ultimately fell short of its goals, it was not without impact. In particular, during the initial stage of land reform in 1962–1964, the White Revolution effectively broke the power of the landowning "Thousand Families" who had monopolized Iran's rural economy and society. The landowners, including the tribal chiefs, lost their ability to hold the peasantry in a quasi-feudal status. Although virtually all retained large landholdings, and thus some degree of economic influence, their status as rural power brokers was gone.[65]

But praise for the White Revolution was not unanimous across Iran's socioeconomic hierarchy. The wealthy landowning class hated it, for obvious reasons. But so too did the middle classes, including the liberal intelligentsia, who saw it as a sop to foreigners and an effort to buy off the backward peasantry. Because the White Revolution did not deal with basic issues of political and social justice, it did little to address their primary grievances. Even many women lost enthusiasm for the White Revolution once they realized that while they could now vote, in a nation without real political parties or fair elections, their votes were just as meaningless as those of their husbands and brothers.[66]

This was a major miscalculation on the part of the shah. In the past, one of the few segments of Iranian society he could count on for support had been the landed aristocracy, which in turn wielded enormous power over the peasantry. By breaking the power of the landowners over the peasantry, he deprived himself of that power base and alienated the one class most committed to the monarchy. He did it in the hope of shifting his base of support from the reactionary aristocracy to the progressive elements of the middle class, but because they saw nothing in the White Revolution that addressed their concerns, this bid failed. The one class genuinely pleased with the shah after the first phase of the White Revolution was the lower class—the peasantry and industrial workers—but they too soured on it when the "revolution" failed to live up to their expectations.

The result was a significant narrowing of the shah's base of support to the professional bureaucracy (who were wholly dependent on the monarch for their sinecures and graft) and the security services. So, for example, the Majles elected in 1963 was the first to have fewer than 50 percent of its members come from the landlord class.[67] As a result, the shah was increasingly forced to rely on repression to maintain control over Iranian society. SAVAK began to spread deeper and deeper throughout Iranian society, and its methods became more and more brutal.

The group that opposed the White Revolution most vigorously, however, was members of the clergy. Land reform cut into the wealth of the religious establishments and hurt the village landlords, who were often the mullahs' most important patrons. Some may have simply disliked a shah interfering in their affairs, and it may have conjured memories of the humiliations they had suffered at the hands of his father. For others, there were matters of principle involved—such as women's suffrage—that were unconscionable. Still others were xenophobes who saw land reform as an American scheme and so opposed it on the grounds that anything the United States wanted to see in Iran could, by definition, only be bad for Iran. Very few of them ever seem to have asked whether land reform might actually benefit the people of Iran.[68] Indeed, by making clear their animosity to the White Revolution and insinuating that it was somehow "against" Islam, the mullahs reversed the sentiments of many peasants who had initially seen land reform as beneficial.

Once again, the mullah who led the charge was the Ayatollah Khomeini, who rose out of the obscurity of Iran's religious center of Qom on the back of this issue to take a position on the national stage. Beginning in March 1963 with a written statement, Khomeini blasted the White Revolution. He called it "a serious threat to Islam."[69] He claimed that it was the product of a Jewish, Baha'i, and American conspiracy to humiliate and subvert Islam.[70] (The Baha'i are an offshoot of Shi'ah Islam whom many Shi'ah, especially the clergy, consider apostates.) He railed against the shah and his ties to America and Israel. His words were so powerful that they inflamed a number of his most zealous followers to create street disturbances.[71]

At the beginning of June, on the occasion of Ashura, Khomeini again ripped into the shah and his White Revolution. He told the Iranian people, "We have come to the conclusion that this regime also has a more basic aim: they are fundamentally opposed to Islam itself and the existence of a religious class."[72] This provoked the regime to arrest Khomeini on June 5. The very next day, shopkeepers, mullahs, office workers, teachers, students, unemployed workers, guild leaders, members of the National Front, factory workers, and tens of thousands of others took to the streets in Tehran, Qom, Shiraz, Isfahan, Mashhad, and Tabriz in protest. For three days they protested while the regime tried to get control over the situation. In the end, the shah called out the troops, who savagely attacked the demonstrators. As many as three hundred people were slaughtered before the Army cleared the streets, although the rumor mill quickly inflated that figure tenfold. Khomeini was put under house arrest for six months, but it was a great victory for him. He was now a national figure, and his act of protest and his unbending determination vaulted him over many other senior religious figures within Iran's Shi'i religious hierarchy.[73]

America's reaction to the new White Revolution was rather tepid, at least within the U.S. government. The American press loved it and saw it as the fulfillment of all of the Kennedy administration's dreams for Iran, as did many of the American aid workers, at least initially.[74] However, in Washington and the U.S. Embassy in Tehran there was considerable skepticism. The CIA prophetically warned that the planning for the White Revolution had left much to be desired and long-term economic development was a rather low priority for the shah. They believed that Iran was spending too much on its military and feared that the final version of land reform was carving up the parcels too small for efficient planting and harvesting. The embassy in Tehran chimed in, noting real concerns about the dearth of managerial skills as well as economic and technical knowledge among the shah's bureaucrats. They observed that right from the start many projects faced endless delays while Iranian agencies bickered and that there was no plan for an investment program that would allow for sustainable development. The Bureau of the Budget wrote an even more pessimistic report that concluded that Iran lacked the economic and administrative structure to manage the changes it had set in motion. Moreover, those in the field lost their enthusiasm for the White Revolution quickly as they saw the inefficiencies in the Iranian system manifest themselves and as more and more Western-trained experts were fired or ignored for counseling against some of the more ambitious aspects of the agenda.[75]

Many Iranians saw the United States as the prime mover in the White Revolution and as a malevolent force throughout Iran. Indeed, many Iranians simultaneously blamed the United States for the White Revolution *and* for the lack of change in the country. A 1963 poll of young Iranians by a West German public opinion group found that 85 percent thought that American aid to Iran "worked to make the rich richer" and only 8 percent thought it "improves the standard of living of the many." Half of those polled said that the United States "is too much on the side of having things remain as they are." Finally, 33 percent saw America as "aggressive," compared to 19 percent who thought the same of the USSR.[76]

Kennedy's assassination in November 1963 proved important for American-Iranian affairs. JFK and the people around him had a real interest in pursuing development abroad. One of Kennedy's legacies, of course, was the Peace Corps, an organization of idealistic young Americans trying to provide hands-on assistance to the people of the poorest nations of the world. Consequently, they had wanted to see real reform in Iran and had been willing to press the shah hard to get it. They had made some real progress until Amini's ouster.

Lyndon Johnson also had his idealistic side, but his primary interest was in making America a better place, not necessarily the world. For Johnson, the Great Society was his principal agenda, and the deepening conflict in Vietnam tended to monopolize the time and resources that he had left for foreign affairs. In terms of American policy toward Iran, Johnson allowed the various aid programs begun under Kennedy to continue, but they lost their political momentum. The shah no longer felt any real pressure from Washington to reform his political system, eliminate corruption, widen participation, curb military spending, and improve the lives of his citizens. It is not that Johnson opposed any of those objectives or cut programs (indeed, aid levels remained fairly constant),[77] just that they were no longer a priority. Moreover, because of the troubles in Vietnam, the Johnson administration was not looking for additional confrontations with foreign countries.[78] All of this meant that the shah increasingly was able to run his country the way he wanted to, without foreigners telling him what to do—or warning him that what he was doing would result in disaster. It was the beginning of the long descent for both the shah and the United States.

The White Revolution Loses Steam

As for the White Revolution, it soon began to disappoint. It was not an abject failure. It brought benefits to the Iranian people, principally in terms of extending literacy and health care into the countryside, enfranchising women, and providing a few other modest benefits.[79] The literacy rate rose from 14.6 percent of the population in 1956 to 29.4 percent in 1966 and then to 47.5 percent in 1976.[80] The creation of the Health Corps also had an impact; the number of doctors in the population had increased by one third since the end of Reza Shah's reign.[81] Similarly, there were some increases in Iranian industrial production as a result of the corresponding drive to increase Iran's manufacturing sector. For instance, the number of workers in manufacturing rose from 815,000 in 1956 to 1.9 million in 1972, and the manufacturing sector went from contributing 45.4 billion rials to Iran's GDP in 1963 to 138.1 billion rials in 1972.[82]

Overall, however, the White Revolution failed to deliver on its promises. Many of its failures would not manifest themselves until well into the 1970s, but some were apparent within just a few years of the start. This was particularly true of land reform, the heart of the whole program. After the initial wave of popularity passed, problems began to crop up. Many landlords with close ties to the shah were able to use their influence to have their lands exempted. The exemptions for mechanized farms, orchards, and tea plantations also took considerable land off the table. Moreover, because the old landlords were allowed to retain sizable holdings, they generally kept the most productive tracts and gave up the least desirable. As a result, little of Iran's most desirable land (and in a country of deserts and mountains there was too little of this to begin with) was made available to the peasantry.[83]

Second, the redistributed plots were generally too small to be productive. The average parcel of land sold under the terms of land reform was 10 acres. Because of Iran's topography, rainfall, and other climactic conditions, only 50 percent of land can be cultivated during a given year while the other half needs to lie fallow, leaving the average peasant family with 5 acres to farm every year on average. The problem is that in Iran it requires 8.5 acres of land per year to sustain a family of five (the average rural family size in 1966) at subsistence level.[84] (And of course this would be even worse for families with more than five members.) Consequently, by 1971, 78 percent of the peasants who owned land had less than the minimum needed for subsistence farming and 32 percent of peasants still did not own any land at all.[85] And this does not take into consideration the hundreds of thousands of Iranian peasants who simply gave up on rural life because they could not survive on the redistributed lands and so sold their tiny parcels back to the old landlords (for a pittance) and headed to the cities.[86]

The inadequacy of the land distribution was a consequence of the amateurish and inadequate planning that went into the White Revolution and that would haunt Iranian modernization throughout the 1960s and '70s. Another manifestation of this problem was the failure to put in place government programs or low-cost loans for farming equipment, fertilizer, and other agricultural supplies. The tiny size of the plots being distributed meant that farmers could not accumulate a surplus to allow them to purchase what they required themselves, so they needed help from the government. Unfortunately, there was none forthcoming. Consequently, as late as 1978, there were more than 2 million peasant farms in Iran but only 50,000 tractors. In some cases, agricultural collectives filled the gap, but these were far too few to make a meaningful difference.[87] The absence of these vital inputs further reduced the productivity of peasant farming. Iran's agricultural production actually slowed as a result of land reform and increasingly fell behind population growth. Agricultural production grew by only 2 to 2.5 percent per year during 1963–1977, while consumption of agricultural products grew by an average of 12 percent per year, forcing Iran to begin importing ever greater quantities of foodstuffs.[88]

Similar problems arose with industrialization. Just as Iranian planners failed to anticipate the needs of all of the new, small landholders for low-cost loans to help them get started, so too did they fail to anticipate the need of would-be entrepreneurs for low-cost business loans.[89] As a result, there was little capital available for any but the very wealthy. Ironically, many of the wealthiest landowning families took the money they made when they were forced to divest much of their land and put it into industry. Thus, by 1975, forty-five Iranian families controlled 85 percent of the country's manufacturing firms.[90] Moreover, because the shah's bureaucrats did not recognize the need for improved technical education to train industrial workers, Iran's educational system remained mired in traditional rote memorization and emphasized Islamic studies and the humanities rather than engineering, math, and the sciences. Not surprisingly, Iranian worker productivity remained extremely low. As one example, in 1976, General Motors found that it took forty-five hours for Iranian workers to assemble a Chevrolet while German workers could assemble the same car in twenty-five hours.[91]

The failure of the White Revolution caused problems for Iran in a wide range of areas. For instance, the problems with land reform created a massive migration to the cities. Iran's urban population soared from less than 30 percent to nearly 50 percent in just the twenty years from 1956 to 1976.[92] Housing could not keep pace with this deluge, causing rents to soar and shantytowns to sprout in thick rings around Iranian cities. This in turn bred anger—even desperation—among Iran's lower classes. Similarly, the formation of the Health Corps and its programs for free medical care raised the hopes of many Iranians, but by 1970 two thirds of the population still had no access to medical facilities.[93] One of the worst legacies of the White Revolution was that it sparked new expectations of a better life in the minds of many Iranians, especially among the lower classes, but then failed to deliver.[94]

The Texan and the Shah

Lyndon Johnson considered himself a great friend of Mohammad Reza Shah. Johnson had made two trips to Iran while vice president (the Kennedy folks considered him a major liability and tried to keep him out of town as much as possible) and had been treated royally in Tehran. This was another element in the sudden evaporation of American pressure on Iran to make serious economic and political changes. Johnson had little desire to tell his friend the shah how to run his country. Besides, Johnson saw the shah as a bulwark of the West against communism and actually encouraged him to rule with a firm hand to keep domestic problems under control.[95]

Unfortunately, their new relationship did not begin on a good note. In October 1964, less than a year into Johnson's administration and just a month before the American presidential elections, the Majles approved a new law providing all American military personnel and their dependents with full diplomatic immunity. It was a close vote, especially for a hand-picked Majles— 70 voted in favor, 62 against, and a number abstained.[96] There was nothing particularly extraordinary about the treaty. The United States had similar agreements with Germany, Japan, and South Korea. Indeed, it is standard procedure to this day for the United States to insist that American military personnel and their dependents in other countries be tried only by American courts.[97] Mosaddeq himself had approved an identical Status of Forces Agreement (SOFA) while he had been prime minister.[98] But to the Iranian people, the SOFA looked like the kind of extraterritoriality demanded by the British and Russians during the bad old days of the nineteenth century. There was public grumbling across the country.

Then it got worse. Twelve days later, the Majles voted to accept a $200 million loan from a consortium of private U.S. banks that was intended to allow the shah to purchase more American weapons. To most Iranians—with Mosaddeq's exhortations to prevent the shah from selling the country to the foreigners still ringing in their ears—this was an outrage. To all and sundry, the shah had seemingly sold the country's sovereignty to the United States for $200 million worth of weapons. It was the Qajars all over again.[99]

Once more, the Ayatollah Khomeini gave voice to the sentiments of all Iranians. On October 26 he told a packed audience in Qom, "They have sold us, they have sold our independence. . . . If some American's servant, some American's cook, assassinates your *marja* [religious source of emulation, invariably a high-ranking ayatollah] in the middle of the bazaar or runs over him, the Iranian police do not have the right to apprehend him! Iranian courts do not have the right to judge him! The dossier must be sent to America, so that our masters there can decide what is to be done! . . . They have reduced the Iranian people to a level lower than that of an American dog. If someone runs over a dog belonging to an American, he will be prosecuted. But if an American cook runs over the Shah, the head of state, no one will have the right to interfere with him. Why? Because they wanted a loan, and America demanded this in return."[100]

Khomeini's broadside expressed what many Iranians believed. However, after the terrible bloodshed in June 1963, few were willing to challenge the shah openly by taking to the streets again. They admired Khomeini, but they were not going to risk their lives for him—at least not yet. Khomeini was again arrested and this time was exiled, first to Turkey. But he then found his way to the great Shi'i shrine city and center of learning of Najaf, Iraq. There he was himself hailed as a *marja,* the highest rung of the Shi'i religious hierarchy. And there, among the great Iraqi ayatollahs, Khomeini lowered his voice for a time while he found his way and established his credentials, and he ceased to trouble the shah for several years.[101]

In case there was any doubt, it was the United States that took most of the blame. The Iranian people were furious that the United States would so blatantly attempt to humiliate Iranians and trample their sovereignty under foot. Even the shah and his court found a way to pin the country's problems on the Johnson administration. Originally, Iranian officials had assured Washington that the SOFA would pass through the Majles quickly and easily and without protest. After the firestorm it sparked, however, the shah's regime blamed the omniscient United States for not knowing that it would create so much popular animosity and blamed Washington for having damaged the shah's position (on purpose, some insinuated) by pushing it through the Majles when it was obviously going to provoke the people's anger.[102]

The "omniscient" United States was increasingly blind and ignorant when it came to Iran. The shah had never stopped suspecting the United States. Washington's role in the Qarani coup plot (when the Eisenhower administration had said nothing to him about a plot it knew about) and in Mosaddeq's overthrow (if the United States could overthrow Mosaddeq, why not him?) convinced Mohammad Reza Shah that America had both the will and the capability to play kingmaker in Iran if it wanted to do so. The shah ordered SAVAK to keep an eye on the Americans, and it dutifully complied, attempting to bug the U.S. Embassy, monitor American intelligence operations against the Tudeh and the Soviets in Iran, and even mounting operations inside the United States itself. The CIA hoped to maintain close ties to SAVAK as a way of keeping an eye on the Iranians, and it did have occasional success recruiting SAVAK officers. However, SAVAK kept the Agency at arm's length, demanding information and training but giving little in return.[103] Moreover, Tehran forbade American personnel from meeting with Iranian oppositionists and did everything it could to keep the United States from trying to gather any information on Iran. CIA officers were strictly directed to maintain their focus on the Soviets and the Communists and to gratefully accept whatever tidbits of information SAVAK deigned to provide about Iranian internal affairs. American foreign affairs officers were similarly forced to restrict themselves to conducting business with the shah's regime and not to try to find out what was going on in the country itself.[104] Shaul Bakhash relates that by the late 1960s, when he was still a journalist in Iran, he saw no point in talking to diplomats at the U.S. Embassy on Iran's domestic politics anymore because "they knew nothing."[105]

In response, Washington did nothing. The Johnson administration was increasingly preoccupied with Vietnam and the Great Society, and the president saw no point in picking a fight with his friend the shah. What's more, during the 1960s, the power relationship between the two countries gradually changed to Iran's advantage. American aid to Iran began to dwindle as Iran's oil wealth began to grow. Increasingly, America needed the shah—his oil, and his oil dollars to be spent on American products—more than the shah needed the United States.[106] In the mid-1960s, oil prices began to rise and Iran's oil fields were able to pump more, plus Tehran was able to negotiate a number of favorable deals (75/25 profit splits) for its offshore oil fields, all resulting in growing revenues.[107] Iran made $372 million off oil in 1963, but by the end of the decade the figure had risen to $791 million. In contrast, U.S. aid to Iran dropped during that same period from $103.5 million to just $4 million.[108] At a time when the United States was running deficits to pay for the war in Vietnam, it seemed hard to justify $100 million or more for a country that was making close to $800 million in oil revenues.

In fact, in 1966, the Johnson administration declared Iran a developed nation that no longer required an American AID mission. What had once been the largest AID mission in the world closed the next year. Once again, this rankled Iranians, most of whom felt they still needed development assistance. They saw this as a sop to the shah, who now wanted Iran to be seen as a First World industrialized nation ready to join the ranks of the European and North American nations. They also resented the fact that the American aid workers who actually tried to help average Iranians were being withdrawn and replaced by American businessmen coming to Iran to sell the country weapons and industrial equipment that did nothing for the vast majority of the populace.[109]

This last argument should not be overstated, at least not for most of the

1960s. As long as the Kennedy and Johnson administrations were in charge, there were strict limits on the numbers and types of weapons sold to the shah. There was a recurrent bureaucratic battle between the Pentagon and the State Department regarding arms sales to Iran. State wanted to make the shah happy and encourage him to continue the White Revolution (which looked more and more successful as the United States became more and more dependent on the shah's regime for its information). The Pentagon opposed this approach, arguing that the Iranians neither needed the weapons they wanted nor could use them terribly well once they got them. Moreover, the military pointed out that after the 1967 Six-Day War—in which Israel smashed the Arab armies of Egypt, Syria, and Jordan—the shah did not have much to fear from the radical Arabs; the Iraqis were bogged down in a guerrilla war with their Kurdish insurgents (whom the shah was supplying); and the Russians were on such good terms with Tehran that they were even selling it some weaponry. In short, Iran did not face a strategic threat that justified its military expenditures. To its credit, the White House mostly sided with the Pentagon in these disputes.[110] As a result, the American side of Iranian military expenditures rose only from $61 million in grants and sales in 1963 (virtually all in grants) to $130 million in 1970 (virtually all in sales).[111]

Nevertheless, this was mostly a rearguard action. Particularly when oil prices began to pick up steam after the Six-Day War, Iran's oil clout was hard to ignore, especially since it allowed the shah to pay in cash for goods that translated into American jobs. As Iranian oil production grew, it made Iran an ever more important part of the oil market, with the ability to cause price disruptions by varying its production if it wanted to, giving the shah additional leverage. Moreover, the shah consistently hewed to a very conservative foreign policy that made him even more appealing to those in Washington looking for allies at a time when the United States was so bogged down in Vietnam that it had little ability to focus elsewhere. The shah assisted royalist guerrillas in Yemen against the Nasserist military government in Sanaa. He armed the Iraqi Kurds against the military governments in Baghdad. And he became very close to the Israelis, who even had a "virtual" embassy in Tehran.[112]

As the decade progressed, it also became harder for Americans to justify not selling to Iran ever greater quantities of arms, heavy machinery, and whatever else the shah wanted. First, there was considerable growth in the Iranian economy during this period, which looked like progress to most Americans. For instance, real GDP per capita more than doubled between 1963 and 1970, from $518 to $1,045.[113] Economic growth between 1963 and 1973 averaged 10 percent per year, one of the highest rates in the world during that period.[114] As far as opposition was concerned, Americans, particularly American officials, had little access to the Iranian people and so knew little about their grievances. The public opposition that the United States saw came largely from reactionaries—aristocratic landlords and medieval clerics—whom many Americans assumed would be drowned out as modernization and "progress" enriched the lives of the rest of Iranian society.[115] Indeed, the Department of State's semiannual report on Iran in September 1969 referred to Iran's "almost monotonous domestic political stability."[116] Even American academics, who often had better exposure to the Iranian populace, were very circumspect about criticizing the shah's economic policies because the Iranian economy was growing so quickly that it seemed possible that, in the end, all of the petulance might be submerged beneath the rising tide of Iranian wealth.[117]

And the shah was never happy with what he got. He complained incessantly that there were weapons he was not being sold, or not being sold in appropriate quantities. He also believed that American aid should continue because of the various threats Iran faced. He was obsessed with new "toys," military hardware to parade rather than training and infrastructure to build actual capability.[118]

As far as the shah was concerned, these purchases were absolutely essential to achieve his geopolitical aspirations. He wanted to be the strongman of the Gulf region and to hold sway over the region as his predecessors had in the era before the Europeans had arrived. Events in the 1960s and early 1970s also heightened his determination to make Iran independent of the United States. Kennedy's pressure on him to engage in unpleasant reforms had left a bad taste in his mouth. Moreover, America's withdrawal from Vietnam and its failure to support its Pakistani allies against India in either 1965 or 1971 apparently led him to conclude that the United States could not be counted on to come to Iran's defense in a pinch. He increasingly sought to diversify Iranian arms purchases—buying up big-ticket items from Britain, France, and even Russia—as a way of diminishing his dependence on the United States.[119]

The Beginnings of an Armed Opposition

Given these circumstances, it should not be surprising that the shah's policy generated opposition, including, at both fringes, guerrilla movements to try to topple his regime. The regime had founded a large number of universities in the 1960s and '70s, and these became hotbeds of protest against the shah. Students all across Iran tended to be unhappy about their poor living conditions and often inadequate education and anxious about their future job prospects as unemployment and underemployment persisted through the 1960s despite the rapid expansion of the economy.[120] Moreover, during this period, the regime slowly ratcheted up its pressure on the mullahs—harassing and arresting those it thought subversive, depriving others of land or livelihoods, and closely monitoring their activities. SAVAK tended to be more covert when dealing with the clergy than Reza Shah's security services had been, but they could be just as tenacious and brutal when given free rein. This encouraged some mullahs to incite religious zealots to attack the regime, and others to simply look the other way.[121]

The results were not long in coming. In January 1965, Prime Minister Hassan Ali Mansur was killed by the son of an ironworker distressed by the economic problems afflicting the lower classes. The investigation revealed that he was affiliated with a right-wing religious group. In April, the shah survived another assassination attempt, this time by a member of his own elite imperial guard. The assassin was found to have been a member of a left-wing group of middle-class intellectuals opposed to the regime.[122]

These grievances coalesced into larger guerrilla movements in Iran determined to wage an insurgency against the regime. In 1965, the Mujahideen-e Khalq was founded by religious militants formerly associated with the National Front. Their goal was to wage a terrorist campaign against the government that would shake the power of the state and demonstrate to the Iranian people that it was possible to rise up against the government in the hope of triggering a popular uprising. Eventually, some members of the group would conclude that Marxism was the ideal path to achieving Islamic salvation for Iran, causing the group to split into an Islamist MEK and a Marxist MEK. Both would continue to fight the regime.[123] Several years later, three small opposition groups merged to form the Feda'iyan-e Khalq. They were refugees from the Tudeh and Marxist groups within the National Front who later became critical of the Stalinist Tudeh and Iran's Maoists and instead adopted Che Guevara's model of armed struggle.[124]

Sucked into the Vortex

The assassinations. The unhappiness of the mullahs. The popular disgruntlement. The carping of the middle-class intellectuals. All of these developments should have been warning signs to the United States. But they weren't. Distracted by our domestic campaigns and the misery of Vietnam, unable to monitor Iranian society in any sort of objective fashion, and perhaps desirous of believing the rosy picture painted by the Iranian court, America proceeded blindly down the path laid out by the shah.

This is another one of the ironies of the Iranian-American relationship. The common Iranian sentiment is that the United States stood firmly behind the shah, encouraged him to buy arms, pressed him toward industrialization, aided SAVAK in oppressing the Iranian people, and cared not a jot about the welfare of the Iranian people. In this version, it is the United States that is the mover and the shah who is the tool. This story is not entirely false. Johnson in particular saw the shah as a solid ally; a stable pro-American government in an increasingly troublesome world; and a ready source of income in a time of mounting budget deficits. But the argument is more wrong than right. First, it omits the efforts of the Kennedy administration, which not only believed in progress from the ground up as the best way of ensuring prosperous, contented American allies but actually pressed the shah's government to conform to its prescriptions. Second, it fails to recognize that beginning in the mid-1960s, it was the shah who had the upper hand in the relationship.

Mohammad Reza Shah needed America, but by the end of the 1960s, America needed him more. As Mark Gasiorowski has cogently argued, Iran's increasing oil wealth allowed the shah to pursue the ever greater independence from the United States that he had always desired. American firms may have been more than willing to sell Iran whatever the shah wanted and Washington may have been a bit too willing to give him his way, but it was the shah who constantly badgered, hectored, and threatened the United States to get what he wanted—not the other way around. Likewise, Washington probably had too cozy a relationship with SAVAK and may have purposely ignored the stories of its terror and its tortures, but at most, the United States was an accomplice, not the inspiration. Certainly the United States never participated in the repression of domestic dissent, as Iranians believed. Moreover, throughout the 1960s there were voices of caution within the U.S. government that were always heeded to a greater or lesser extent. The shah had to fight to get F-4 Phantoms, and he never got the M-60 tanks he wanted from the Johnson administration. The shah himself complained bitterly of America's niggardliness with its armories. And in the end, the Johnson administration could content itself with the incontrovertible statistics of rapid Iranian economic growth, which at the time seemed like an unadulterated good.

The shah increasingly felt himself unencumbered by the American relationship. For the first time in centuries, an Iranian monarch had real leverage against the foreign powers, and he was not bashful about using his new advantages. As long as America's policies coincided with his own goals he was glad to help execute them, but when there was a difference, he did not hesitate to advocate his interests over those of the United States. Although Washington made it clear that Americans wanted low oil prices, the shah pushed the world price as hard as he could. He took from the CIA what SAVAK needed and gave back only what he was willing to part with. He built Iran's armed forces and industries, diversified his suppliers, and cultivated friends and allies with a deliberate eye toward increasing his independence from the United States and perhaps someday even setting Iran up as a rival. Especially after the colossal increase in Iran's oil revenues in the 1970s, the shah talked constantly about making Iran one of the five great powers of the world with the third most powerful military.

While American policy was not selfless or mistake-free toward Iran during the 1960s, the common Iranian notion that the United States paid *too much* attention to Iran and bullied the shah into taking paths deleterious for the Iranian people because they served American interests does not bear up. To a great extent, the problem was the opposite. When American officials did pay close attention to Iran (under Kennedy), they tended to push for what they believed best for the Iranian people—and what most average Iranians probably would have wanted too, at least in the abstract. The problems arose because the United States lost interest in Iran and lost its ability to steer the shah as it once had. It is this pattern that set the stage for the disaster of the 1970s, when obscenely high oil revenues and the utter neglect of the Nixon administration combined to create a catastrophe for both the shah and his American allies.

Come the Revolution

In the Persian Gulf region, it is hard to get away from the oil, and in many ways the Iranian Revolution also begins with oil. A case can be made that it was the oil that caused the revolution. In the early 1970s, the shah began a campaign to boost Iranian oil revenues that succeeded beyond his wildest dreams. Money poured into Iran, and that money changed everything. Iran's economy overheated, corruption went haywire, officials in Tehran lost all touch with reality. It ended up twisting the Iranian economy, threatening its social structure, and stressing the autocratic political system past the breaking point. Iran was not a happy country before the oil boom, but afterward, it was a powder keg.

The oil also lashed the United States more tightly to Iran than had ever been the case before. After the oil boom, America needed Iran in ways it never had in the past. Suddenly, what happened in Iran was critical to the American economy, and to the entire global economy. When the shah's regime went down, the United States went down with it—and was blamed for its fall.

Pillars, Proxies, and Realpolitik

Richard Nixon and his national security advisor/secretary of state, Henry Kissinger, brought to Washington a hard, dispassionate view of the world. They saw the world through the prism of the global confrontation between the United States and the Soviet Union, and they treated international politics as a grand chess match between the two superpowers. They were extraordinarily sophisticated in their playing of that game, demonstrating a willingness to employ every tool in America's foreign policy kit from military force to arms control and from covert action to humanitarian assistance. They also deserve credit for a number of important successes for U.S. foreign policy. The opening to China, the start of the Middle East peace process that would culminate at Camp David under the Carter administration, and the various arms control treaties with Russia were all salient events that began with Nixon and Kissinger and had long-lasting benefit for the United States.

But theirs was a fairly one-dimensional view of the world, and its focus on great power politics often came at the cost of creating major problems for the United States in the Third World. In places like Angola, Cambodia, Chile, and Iran, it produced troubles that would beleaguer the United States for many years. For Nixon and Kissinger, Third World states were little more than pawns in their battle with Moscow. They were not terribly concerned with what went on inside those countries, as long as their governments responded properly to the moves dictated by Washington. In that sense, they tended to see the shah as a "good" pawn—they both liked him personally and believed that the two countries shared an essential convergence of interests. They tended to overlook those instances when the shah did not follow Washington's script and instead emphasized the occasions when Iran did exactly as America hoped. If keeping the shah in the game meant looking the other way to some excesses at home, they appear to have been willing to do so.[1]

In a certain sense, the problems started in 1968, when Great Britain announced that it would no longer be able to support its former imperial obligations, and so would be withdrawing its forces from "east of Suez." Oil from the Persian Gulf region had long ago become a vital global commodity, and the region itself was considered highly unstable. Consequently, some other nation was going to have to watch over the Gulf region to make sure that internal or external problems did not jeopardize the world's oil supplies, and that other nation could only be the United States.

For the incoming Nixon administration, the solution to the problems of the Persian Gulf region grew out of a new approach to Vietnam that itself evolved into a more generalized policy toward the Third World designed to allow the United States to devote more of its resources and attention to the new Great Game with the Soviet Union. In 1969, the president announced what would come to be called the Nixon Doctrine. The initial conception focused on Asia and when applied to the Vietnam War was known as "Vietnamization." The idea was that while the United States should provide support, the Vietnamese should fight the war themselves. Eventually, this evolved into the overarching Nixon Doctrine, which stipulated that the United States would lean on regional proxies to defend themselves and their neighbors, maintain stability, and ensure that American interests were looked after while the United States concentrated on the Soviets.

In the Persian Gulf, the Nixon Doctrine was applied with a vengeance in a strategy that came to be known as the "Twin Pillars." When the British withdrew in 1971, it meant that all of the Gulf emirates formerly under their protection became independent states—South Yemen (formerly Aden), Oman, Bahrain, Qatar, and the UAE. None was considered stable, and all were feared to be vulnerable to Nasserist takeover. Kuwait had been independent only since 1961, at which point the Iraqis had immediately claimed it as rightfully belonging to them, and many Iranians had long considered Bahrain to be Iran's "lost" fourteenth province.[2] To further pique American concerns, Soviet warships first began regular patrols of the Gulf in 1968. On the other hand, the Nixon administration recognized that the Soviet Union was not particularly threatening to the Arabian Peninsula (it was ultimately too far from Russia, and at the time there was no Soviet presence in the Horn of Africa) and that inserting American troops into a region already rife with Pan-Arabist nationalism would not help matters. They concluded that the region was better policed by a regional sheriff in accord with the Nixon Doctrine, and the shah of Iran seemed perfect for that role. Of course, State Department Arabists pointed out that Iran was not an Arab country and that the Arabs probably would resent the United States relying on Persians as Washington's regional proxy. To avoid this perception, the Nixon administration paired Saudi Arabia with Iran as the second, albeit weaker, "pillar" of American policy.[3]

The decision to rely on the shah as America's regional proxy reflected something of a misreading of the shah on the part of Nixon and Kissinger. They saw him, in Kissinger's memorable phrase, as "that rarest of leaders, an unconditional ally," someone whose views and policies matched those of the United States precisely and in all respects.[4] The shah did share many of America's general goals in the region—he sought stability, he opposed Nasser and other Arab radicals, he supported the state of Israel, he opposed communism and the Soviet Union, and he sought to prop up many of the other conservative monarchies of the region. But there were also important differences between Iran and the United States, and the combination of America's unconditional support and Iran's new oil wealth caused the shah to set off in directions that the Nixon administration probably would not have favored if Tehran had ever made its intentions explicit. Moreover, the shah had never forgotten his distrust of the United States and his desire to make Iran strong enough to be fully independent and impervious to foreign influence.

The shah was thrilled to take on this new role on behalf of his friends

Richard Nixon and Henry Kissinger.[5] For him it meant an opportunity to do things his way. Most Iranians saw the new relationship as having further subordinated Iran to the United States. Indeed, as Ali Ansari points out, the appellation "policeman of the Gulf," which the shah was often called, was translated into Farsi as "Gendarme," which had servile connotations. It reinforced the view of many Iranians that the shah was the lackey of the United States.[6] But the shah knew better. He understood that playing this role for an America deeply distracted by Vietnam and great-power politics gave him leverage. At the very least, it meant that America would stop telling him how to run his country if it expected him to look after its interests in the Persian Gulf. And, in fact, the Nixon administration did just that, virtually eliminating all criticism of Iranian human rights abuses, resisting any effort to convince the shah to reform his political and economic systems, refraining from passing judgment on the White Revolution and other Iranian internal policies, and essentially leaving it up to the shah to run Iran's affairs.

Mohammad Reza Shah's role as one of America's Twin Pillars in the Gulf and his ability to pay cash for arms also meant that the doors to America's armories were finally thrown open to him. At the end of May 1972, Nixon and Kissinger stopped off in Tehran on their way back from Moscow. In lengthy meetings with the shah, the president outlined the Twin Pillars policy and the role he hoped Iran would play. The Iranian monarch graciously accepted, and in return the president agreed to allow Tehran to purchase any nonnuclear weapon it wanted from the United States. At the end of their meeting, President Nixon looked across the table to the shah and said, "Protect me."[7] Upon their return from Tehran, Kissinger spelled out the new approach to the foreign policy bureaucracy, prompting immediate protests from the military, which did not believe that the Iranians should be given carte blanche to buy American arms. But Kissinger laid down the law: "Henceforth, decisions on purchases of U.S. military equipment would be left primarily to the government of Iran."[8]

The shah also seems to have recognized that his new status as America's regional proxy opened up other vistas. Iran's growing oil wealth, and the weaponry he was buying with it, allowed him to think about playing a bigger role in the Middle East. In the past, his goals had largely been defensive—seeking to deter a Soviet invasion and ultimately become strong enough to withstand any foreign pressure. By the beginning of the 1970s, they had become considerably more grandiose. The shah increasingly saw himself as the regional hegemon. He might not have aspired to conquer any of the Arab lands, but he did seem to want to be the arbiter of their fates—the ruler from whom all had to seek permission and indulgence.[9]

Consequently, Iran became more active in regional politics. Many of its actions did fall closely into line with what Washington wanted in terms of preserving the stability of the region and minimizing Soviet/Communist influence. In 1973, Tehran sent troops to Oman to help the new government battle Dhofari insurgents supplied by the militantly Marxist government of South Yemen. That same year Iran helped the pro-American Pakistani dictatorship crush Baluchi rebels whose territory spanned their mutual border. The shah also provided arms to Somalia against the Soviet-backed Ethiopians during the Ogaden War of 1976–1978 and even took a hand in supporting American efforts in places that had little to do with Iran—such as Vietnam and sub-Saharan Africa.[10]

However, far from being America's "unconditional ally," much that the shah did served his interests without necessarily serving our own and at times ran counter to what Washington might have wanted. For instance, in 1971 the shah took over the small islands of Abu Musa and the Tunbs, which were claimed by the new government of the UAE. This certainly was not helpful to the United States, which wanted the shah to play the role of protector, and not bully, of the small Gulf states.[11] The shah opposed both publicly and privately the small American military presence in the region; he wanted no restraints on his ambition to dominate the Gulf, and he saw the U.S. Navy base in Bahrain as a rival to his own suzerainty.[12] Finally, the shah breached U.S. law by transferring American weaponry to Pakistan during its war with India in 1971 and to Turkey during its war with Greece over Cyprus in 1974 without Washington's permission. The Pentagon tried to point out these violations, but no one in Tehran or the White House was listening.[13]

In a textbook case of the tail wagging the proverbial dog, in 1972 the shah convinced the Nixon administration to join his own efforts (and those of the Israelis) in supporting the Kurds of northern Iraq, who were again battling the central government in Baghdad. The CIA and State Department, including the U.S. ambassador to Iran, urged the White House to stay out of this fight because, they warned, the Kurds would inevitably be betrayed by the Iranians, and that would redound to everyone's detriment. The Kurds had appealed directly to the United States for support in 1971 and again in early 1972 but had been rebuffed because providing such assistance was not seen as consistent with American interests in the region. But when the shah broached the idea with the Nixon administration, suddenly everything changed, and tens of millions of dollars of covert American assistance started flowing, making it possible (along with the deployment of Iranian combat troops) for the Kurdish peshmerga to stymie Baghdad's forces. Kurdish leaders have stated that they never would have opted for a military showdown with Baghdad without

American assistance—and a guarantee that the United States would not allow the Iranians to abandon them. But in March 1975, the shah did just that. He sat down with Iraq's strongman, the young Saddam Hussein, in Algiers and quickly sold out the Kurds in return for Iraqi acquiescence on a range of border issues. Both the Nixon administration and the Kurds were blindsided by the Algiers Accord. Neither was happy about it, but many Kurds paid for it with their lives, because without American and Iranian support, they were swiftly crushed by Saddam's army.[14]

Finally, the new policy toward Iran also led to a further reduction in American intelligence-gathering operations in Iran. The shah complained frequently and forcefully about U.S. efforts to discern what was going on inside his country, and over time, so as not to offend America's regional proxy, U.S. officials increasingly complied. The volume of CIA political reporting on Iran in the early 1970s actually dropped below that of the late 1940s, and the U.S. Embassy in Tehran had few officers who could speak Farsi or who had previously served in Iran.[15] After all, the Iranian Ministry of Foreign Affairs and SAVAK personnel all spoke English, and since they were the only Iranians the Americans were allowed to speak to, what point was there in learning Farsi?

OPEC and the Oil Boom

The policy issue on which the shah most differed with the United States—and that ultimately had the greatest impact on both countries—was the price of oil.[16] As the world's largest consumer of oil, the United States wanted the price low. As the second greatest exporter of oil and a man with a long shopping list, the shah wanted it high, and in the end, he got his way. The Organization of the Petroleum Exporting Countries (OPEC) had been formed back in 1960 with Iran as a charter member. However, it had not made much of a mark during its first decade of existence.[17] That began to change in the early 1970s as demand for petroleum products finally began to overtake supply, creating a seller's market. The free world's demand for oil rose from 19 million bpd in 1960 to more than 44 million bpd in 1972.[18] Suddenly the producing countries had real leverage with the oil companies. In 1970, the shah wrung a revised deal out of the consortium that had been exporting Iranian oil since 1954, boosting Iran's share of the profits to 55 percent. Then, in February 1971, Iran led the OPEC countries in a battle with the oil companies over oil prices that OPEC won. Daniel Yergin describes this as the "watershed" for OPEC, marking the moment when "initiative had passed from the companies to the exporting countries."[19] As a result, Iran's oil revenues nearly doubled in the space of a year, from $885 million in 1971 to $1.6 billion in 1972.[20]

Yet the 1971 Tehran Agreement did nothing but whet Mohammad Reza Shah's appetite for more. In January 1973, the shah announced that he was taking over the oil consortium altogether, completing the nationalization begun by Mosaddeq twenty-two years earlier. The United States was furious (American firms held a sizable stake in the consortium), but the shah would not budge—and, of course, this time there was no possibility that the United States might overthrow the shah.[21] Then, in October 1973, Egypt and Syria launched their surprise attack on Israel that started the Yom Kippur/Ramadan War. Again, Iran saw an opportunity to boost its oil revenues and, at an October 16 meeting, urged the other Gulf oil states to raise prices, resulting in a hike from $3.01 per barrel to $5.12. The next day, the Arab states announced an embargo on oil sales to the United States and a cut in production starting at 5 or 10 percent (different countries adopted different levels) and increasing by 5 percent every month until the United States agreed to cease its support for Israel and the Israelis agreed to withdraw to the 1967 borders. Iran was not part of the war effort and was on good terms with Israel, so it did not participate in the embargo. Instead, it continued to sell oil, actually ramping up production by another 600,000 bpd, thus capturing a larger share of the market and taking advantage of the sudden increase in prices to reap a tidy profit.[22]

That was still not enough for Mohammad Reza Shah. In December 1973, the OPEC oil ministers met in Tehran again and the shah convinced them to boost prices still further, to a (then-astronomical) price of $11.65 per barrel. The initial price increases and the embargo had already caused a massive oil crisis throughout the West, and this new boost threatened to greatly exacerbate it.[23] Nixon wrote a personal note to the shah outlining the "catastrophic problems" the price increase was causing and urging him to reconsider. The shah's response completely dismissed Nixon's request.[24] He went so far as to tell one journalist that America and the other industrialized nations "will have to realize that the era of their terrific progress and even more terrific income and wealth based on cheap oil is finished. . . . Eventually, they will have to tighten their belts; eventually all those children of well-to-do families who have plenty to eat at every meal, who have their cars, and who act almost as terrorists and throw bombs here and there, they will have to rethink all these aspects of the advanced industrial world. And they will have to work harder. . . . Your young boys and young girls who receive so much money from their fathers will also have to think that they must earn their living somehow."[25]

So much for America's "puppet" and "proxy" in the Gulf. Former NSC staffer Robert Hormats summed up the American perception of these events succinctly: "The Shah turned around and screwed us."[26] Ultimately, the oil crisis would run until March 1974 and, thanks in large part to the shah's efforts, would result in a 276 percent increase in oil prices—the single greatest increase in oil prices from a supply disruption in history.[27] The New York Stock Exchange lost $97 billion in value in six weeks (the equivalent of more than $400 billion in 2004 prices).[28] The oil embargo was a terrible price shock for the Western economies and threw them into recession ("stagflation" is the term used to describe the unusual—and extremely painful—combination of economic stagnation and high inflation that ensued). In turn, this prolonged recession, coupled with the stain of the Watergate scandal, helped bring down the Republican Party in the 1976 presidential election.

For Iran, the ultimate impact of the oil price increases was no less catastrophic, although few recognized it at the time. Oil revenues, which had stood at $885 million in 1971 and had climbed to $1.6 billion in 1972, reached $4.6 billion in 1974 and then skyrocketed to $17.8 billion in 1975.[29] Tehran seemed suddenly to be awash in money, and the shah could afford anything he wanted. Iranian planners, who had never been particularly effective, lost all grounding in reality. They seemed to have more than enough money to solve all of their problems and indulge all of their fantasies. Literally overnight, the $36 billion originally allocated to the shah's Fifth Development Plan nearly doubled to $63 billion without anyone having thought through the consequences or anticipating any of the requirements.[30] As Shaul Bakhash put it, "You would not have imagined how badly one could distort an economy in just two years. I would not have believed it had I not seen it myself."[31]

Iranian arms purchases increased in the same astronomical fashion as its oil wealth. In 1972, the shah took advantage of Nixon's open-ended commitment to buy the brand-new F-14 fighter—the most advanced and most expensive fighter in the world, which no other country had been allowed to purchase. But once the oil revenues started to roll in, the sky became the limit; the shah began reading magazines such as *Jane's Defence Weekly* as if they were shopping catalogues, seeing articles about new weaponry and picking up the phone to order them. Iran bought tanks, armored personnel carriers, artillery pieces, radars, surveillance equipment, fighters, antiaircraft guns, antitank missiles, surface-to-air missiles, frigates, corvettes, and amphibious assault ships; and always the top of the line, no matter how expensive. The shah increased the size of his armed forces from 255,000 men in 1971 to 385,000 in 1975.[32] Iran's defense budget grew from $1.4 billion in 1972 to $9.4 billion in 1977.[33]

Moreover, several negative relationships between Iranian oil revenues and arms purchases developed. The more money the shah had, the more he spent on weaponry, the more additional weapons he wanted, the more he tried to boost Iranian oil production and jack up oil prices still further. Indeed, a major motive in his maneuvering on oil prices in 1973 was the spur of the Nixon administration's 1972 offer to allow him to buy whatever arms he wanted from the United States. Now that the whole American arsenal was for sale to him, he needed even more money to buy all of the items that had been denied him in the past.[34]

Meanwhile, U.S. officials were deeply concerned about the hemorrhage of American dollars pouring out to pay for Middle Eastern oil. Thus, few in Washington were unhappy that the shah was turning around and sending billions of those dollars back to the United States to pay for arms (and a whole range of other purchases). To some extent, American officials encouraged the shah's spending spree to minimize the damage to the U.S. trade deficit. They pressed hard for the shah to buy American to make sure that the United States—not one of its European allies—got those petrodollars back.[35] Iranian arms purchases from the United States alone grew from $524 million in 1973 to $3.9 billion in 1974.[36] In August 1975, the shah signed another deal for $10 billion more in American arms, including 300 F-16 and 200 F-18 fighters (which were still under development at the time). Such acquisitions were ridiculous; it would have taken a decade just to train the pilots and ground crew to handle so many ultramodern aircraft, especially on top of the 150 F-14s Iran had ordered. Between 1972 and 1977, Iran would spend over $16 billion on American weaponry alone and accounted for one third of all American arms sales. In 1977, Iran actually represented half of all American arms sales. And of course, the shah was simultaneously buying from Europe and Russia too.[37]

Nor did Iran's billions pour back out for weaponry alone. The shah spent wastefully on civilian goods too. The August 1975 arms agreement with the United States also included a $40 billion commercial sales agreement. Later Iran would sign another economic agreement for a further $15 billion in sales, including eight large nuclear power plants. Despite being the second largest exporter of oil, Iran was desperately short of power. All of the equipment, appliances, weapons, and other systems Tehran was purchasing required electricity, and the sudden surge in demand overstrained Iran's modest power grid, causing rolling blackouts even in Tehran, while much of the countryside was still without electricity altogether.[38]

A great deal of Iran's new oil wealth simply went to line the pockets of the shah's courtiers. The Iranian system had been corrupt for centuries, but when the oil billions began to pour in, graft too exploded to unimaginable proportions. Congressional investigations uncovered some evidence of that graft, but there was a consensus that this was only the tip of a vast iceberg. For instance, Grumman officials admitted to paying the Iranian defense minister a $28 million commission on the $2.2 billion F-14 deal.[39] A June 1972 cable from the U.S. Embassy in Tehran on "Corruption in Iran—A Problem for American Companies" named General Electric, Northrop, Boeing, Cities Service, McDonnell-Douglas, RCA, and Neill Price as companies it knew to be buying the influence of Iranian officials and members of the royal family via bribes, commissions, and payoffs. They also suspected a great many others. The mere fact that they felt it necessary to write a fifteen-page cable is another example of the extent of the problem.[40]

An Economy out of Control

While the shah and his courtiers were wallowing in Iran's new wealth, the Iranian people were increasingly unhappy, and one important cause was Iran's misfiring economy.[41] Although not all of the news on the economic front was bad, the regime pursued a complicated web of economic policies, many strands of which caused considerable hardship. Overall, this skein afflicted Iran's middle and lower classes in a range of ways that reinforced most of the worst features of the existing system.

The regime's approach to agriculture continued to do more harm than good. When Tehran finally recognized that agriculture was suffering from too many small farms with no ability to pay for farm machinery or supplies, its solution was to demand that farmers sell their farms and collectivize. To enforce this fiat, the central government razed entire villages or transferred their populations in a page out of Stalin's own collectivization handbook. In the early 1970s, Tehran reduced its assistance and investment funding to Iran's 50,000 rural villages.[42] There had been far too little of this in the past, and diminishing such programs further just when the oil boom was starting and the government seemed awash in cash caused widespread resentment. The inadequacy of government financing for peasant farmers forced many into serious debt, which was compounded by the regime's enforcement of low prices for foodstuffs, particularly wheat. This made food cheaper for the urban poor but further destroyed the ability of Iran's farmers to make a living. By the middle of the decade, the cost to produce a bushel of wheat exceeded the government's floor price.[43]

These foolish and callous policies accelerated the process of the peasantry reselling their newly distributed land back to their former landlords (at a loss). However, the peasants generally did not go back to being sharecroppers. Instead they fled to the cities, and the large landholders generally did not reinvest their profits in either agriculture or industry but sent them overseas. As a consequence, agricultural production could not keep pace with the demand from a growing populace, and by 1977 the government was importing 25 percent of Iran's annual food needs for the price of 10 to 20 percent of its annual oil revenues, even though the cost of imported wheat still exceeded the production cost of domestic wheat.[44]

Those living in the cities were in turn buffeted by the combination of rapid urbanization and poor planning. The population of the cities continued to grow faster than new housing, especially since the government made little effort to subsidize low-cost housing. This led to soaring rents and ballooning shantytowns. Rents in Tehran rose by roughly 300 percent in 1971–1976, and by 1975 the average middle-class family in Tehran was spending 50 percent of its income on housing.[45] The percentage of urban families living in only one room increased from 36 to 43 percent between 1967 and 1976 despite Iran's superficially high growth rates.[46]

Once again, the government showed little regard for its citizenry. Broad new boulevards were plowed through ancient neighborhoods, and superhighways were driven through the shantytowns themselves.[47] In 1973, the French journalist Eric Rouleau warned that the terrible economic circumstances in Iran's cities were prompting a rise in alcohol and narcotics use, while the absence of "safety valves" such as independent trade unions or opposition parties that would allow people to air their grievances and seek peaceful redress were creating volatile undercurrents among the populace.[48]

The sudden influx of oil wealth also brought with it tremendous inflation, adding to the miseries of the lower classes and threatening the status and the savings of the middle class. In 1970, according to its own figures, the government had gotten inflation down to just 1.6 percent, but it then rose to 4.2 percent in 1971, to 9.8 percent in 1973, to 14.2 percent in 1974, and to 27.1 percent in 1977.[49] The International Monetary Fund concluded that the Iranians were actually underreporting inflation by almost half, and a leading scholar on the economic aspects of the revolution estimates that inflation actually averaged 50 percent annually from 1975 to 1977.[50] The government responded with a plan to raise taxes, which infuriated the *bazaaris*, who were already being crippled by the combination of inflation and price controls and did not need new taxes added to their problems. The regime backed off on the tax scheme but instead adopted practices equally offensive to the *bazaaris*: an "antiprofiteering" campaign by which members of the government's political party (most of whom knew nothing about business practices) inspected the bazaars and brought charges against nearly half a million shopkeepers and small businessmen leading to 250,000 fines, 23,000 banned from selling in their hometowns, 8,000 jailed, and an unknown number sentenced to forty lashes.[51]

Because of the inappropriate growth strategy adopted by the shah's government, the massive expansion of Iran's economy did little to deal with employment problems. Between 1962 and 1971, Iran's GNP effectively doubled, but this was driven almost entirely by the oil sector, which required comparatively few jobs. On the other hand, Iran had had a tremendously high birthrate over the past twenty years (roughly 3 percent annually), and the net effect was a serious shortage of jobs by the early 1970s. Employment increased by 23 percent in 1962–1971, but the economically active population grew by 75 percent.[52] In other words, the number of new workers coming onto the market was greatly exceeding the ability of the Iranian economy to create jobs for them.[53] To make matters worse, rather than training Iranians to take jobs in the new industrial, service, and transport sectors, Iranian firms had hired 300,000 Indians, Pakistanis, Filipinos, Koreans, Americans, Europeans, and Afghans. Since many of the Americans and Europeans were brought in to handle skilled positions, it reinforced the popular perception that foreigners were taking the most desirable jobs from Iranians and running Iranian society.[54]

Nor did industrialization fill the gap created by the demise of Iran's agricultural economy. The regime's lending and investment policies gave preference to Western-style industries that produced heavy goods such as cars and technologically sophisticated ones such as televisions. Although this emphasis on industry did produce some modest growth (the percentage of GDP produced by the manufacturing sector grew from 11 percent in 1960 to almost 14 percent in 1970), it did not play to Iran's strengths.[55] It also did little to address unemployment since few Iranian workers had the requisite skills for these jobs. This in turn meant that: (1) the plants that were not dominated by foreign workers tended to be highly cost-ineffective; (2) a number of Iranian industries produced high-end goods that the average Iranian could not afford and that foreigners did not want; (3) in favoring heavy industry, the government undermined small crafts and consumer goods that Iranians both needed and were good at making, which in turn required imports to make up for the shortfalls; and (4) the policies contributed to a wide gap in wages between the comparatively few skilled Iranian workers and the vast majority of unskilled laborers. A 1972 study found that Iranian industrial goods were 25 to 35 percent more expensive than the global average and often of inferior quality.[56] Overall, Iran's heavy manufacturing sector tended to be something of a white elephant that provided little employment or revenue for Iran's economy and was sustained mostly by constant infusions of government funds.[57]

The malfunctioning economy created a number of other problems. For instance, inflation and unemployment, the destruction of Iran's agriculture, and the horrendous living conditions in Iran's cities created health problems, including malnourishment. A study in 1972–1973 found that 44 percent of the population was undernourished and 23 percent was receiving less than 90 percent of the World Health Organization's standard for minimum daily caloric intake.[58] On the other hand, the massive increase in the Iranian bureaucracy in response to the flood of petrodollars—and the absence of any other work for so many Iranians—meant that those who did have jobs increasingly found them with the government. By 1978, one fifth of all civilian households depended on the state for their livelihoods, which meant that they were highly vulnerable to government cutbacks and their salaries inevitably lagged far behind inflation.[59]

Ironically, the country's sudden, massive flood of oil revenues only served to exacerbate the resentment of the Iranian people. Many Iranians thought that the expenditures on weaponry were unnecessary at best, especially since Iran did not face a real threat and the military had so frequently been used as an arm of state repression.[60] Likewise, the mind-boggling new wealth of the shah and his court only highlighted the growing gap between Iran's superrich and the rest of the population.[61] According to the Central Bank of Iran, in 1960, the 60 percent of Iran's population in the "middle-income range" saw their percentage of consumption drop from 46.7 percent in 1960 to just 26.5 percent in 1970, while that of the top 20 percent of the population grew from 44 to 64 percent.[62] Nevertheless, the regime did little to alter its badly regressive tax structure to take some pressure off the lower classes.[63] The animosity that many middle- and lower-class Iranians felt at the growing economic division was sharpened by the widespread (and mostly correct) sense that the superrich had made a great deal of their money from corruption, from the favors of the shah, and from exploiting Iran's warped politicoeconomic system. Ali Ansari observed that corruption, "normally tolerated as an accepted part of social and economic life, now grew to such proportions that even the tolerant considered it obscene."[64]

Many Iranians also expected a bit more of a "trickle down" of the oil wealth than the mere trickle they actually experienced. For example, they saw the influx of consumer goods but were unable to take advantage of it themselves. The government and its retainers bought goods and equipment by the boatload, but because they had not considered the limited capacity of Iranian ports, ships were forced to wait an average of 100 days before being able to off-load their goods. Similarly, because the regime's provisions to expand the country's transportation infrastructure proved hopelessly inadequate to its booming demands, even when those goods were finally off-loaded, they often sat quayside for as long as six months before they could be picked up, and since the regime had made no provision for additional warehouses, many of those goods sat out in the burning Persian Gulf sun, where they were ruined long before they could be sold or used. Billions were flushed away through such mistakes—"bottlenecks," they were regularly called.[65]

For the average Iranian, the reports of these bottlenecks created a sense that the incompetence and avarice of the shah and his regime were depriving them of what little benefit they might have expected from Iran's sudden windfall. Here as well, the atrocious planning—or lack thereof—by the regime was a major contributing factor. One famous example told by economist Robert Looney concerns the government's plan to modernize all of Tehran's bakeries with Western equipment. Because Western firms did not produce baking equipment to handle traditional Iranian bread, modernizing the bakeries also meant forcing them to switch to English processed bread and French baguettes. The entire enterprise turned out to be an absurd waste of money because Iranians generally refused to eat the new European breads.[66]

The Winter of Their Discontent

The economy was not the only thing that Iranians had to complain about. For most people, nothing really seemed to be living up to the regime's promises, and they grew frustrated that Iran's oil wealth was doing comparatively little to improve their lives. Iran's lower classes were most unhappy with the impact of Iran's distorted economy on their already difficult lives. However, the primary grievances of Iran's middle classes were as much social and political as they were economic.

Of all of the different groups hurt by Iran's economic dislocation, its traditional *bazaari* middle class may have been the hardest hit. The *bazaari*s were battered by almost every aspect of the regime's economic policies, from its regressive taxes to its antiprofiteering campaigns to its lending policies to its price controls to its emphasis on heavy industry and imports.[67] The incredible new wealth of Iran's upper classes meant that they could now import whatever they wanted, while unemployment, inflation, and the low wages of Iran's lower classes meant they had little to spend. The regime did not help matters by encouraging the establishment of huge Western-style department stores that threatened to demolish the bazaar's place in Iranian commerce. To give some scale to the problem, Iranian imports grew from $400 million in 1958–1959 to $3.5 billion in 1974–1975 to $18.4 billion in 1975–1976.[68] Even those *bazaari*s who did well by selling consumer goods during Iran's boom still increasingly felt that their gains were not keeping pace with Iran's fast-growing economy.

Iran's "new" middle class, composed mostly of doctors, lawyers, professors, bureaucrats, and other white-collar professions, was also affected by the economic problems. Inflation destroyed these people's savings and reduced their salaries to a pittance.[69] Nor did education offer the path out that middle-class families and their children had hoped. There were not enough schools to honor the shah's promises of free education. In 1975, illiteracy still topped 60 percent, and while this was a considerable improvement over the 80 percent mark it had approached in 1966, it hardly reflected the shah's pretensions to a modern, industrial society.[70] Worse still, the schools continued to teach mostly by traditional methods of rote memorization and to emphasize traditional topics of Islamic studies and the humanities.[71] Consequently, many high school graduates lacked the skills to get decent jobs. The real growth in primary and secondary schooling also created a rush for places in colleges and other institutions of higher learning, and the regime's efforts simply could not keep pace with the demand. In 1961, of those students who passed the final high school exam, 36.3 percent found places in universities. By 1978, only 12.1 percent could.[72]

For those few who did get in, Iran's universities suffered from poor academic, housing, and educational conditions. Teachers were frequently dismissed or arrested by the regime for suspicion of being subversives and attempting to corrupt the youths.[73] Finally, whereas in earlier years a university graduate was virtually assured a job in the government if he could not find one with a corporation, there were simply too many university graduates (and with too few useful skills) to find them jobs in the bureaucracy, contributing to the unemployment problem.

Yet the middle classes also remained deeply unhappy about Iranian political life and the paltry opportunities for them to exercise any influence over the country's policies—especially those that affected their own well-being. The shah continued to manipulate elections to produce safe majorities while muzzling the press. He extended government control over unions and trade guilds. He suppressed the National Front and all other independent vehicles of political expression.[74] Worst of all, in March 1975, he arbitrarily disbanded his pet two-party system and instead formed a single political party called Hizb-i Rastakhiz (the Resurgence Party). Every Iranian was expected to join the Rastakhiz Party, which was an effort to unite and mobilize the Iranian people along the lines of other twentieth-century totalitarian parties such as the Nazis and the Communists (albeit without quite their ideology). The shah famously announced that it was now time for every Iranian to choose sides and that "those who don't want to be part of the political order can take their passports and leave the country."[75] Every bureaucrat was forced to join or lose his or her job. The rest of the country was also expected to join, and functionaries were sent around to places of business to register members, although the state was too inefficient to punish those who did not. Iran's middle class in particular resented this intrusion into their political lives: it was bad enough not to be allowed to participate in politics as you wanted, but it was even worse to be told that you had to participate in a certain way, and that if you did not, you ought to just leave the country.[76]

This threat seemed real enough to many Iranians because of the growing terror inspired by the shah's SAVAK. All Iranians disliked the shah's police state, but the middle classes most of all, if only because they were more politically aware and therefore more carefully monitored than the lower classes. Although SAVAK may not have been as pervasive and arbitrary as Saddam Hussein's Mukhabarat or Josef Stalin's KGB, it nonetheless succeeded in spreading terror throughout the state. By the 1970s, Iran may have resembled the police state of George Orwell's *1984* more than either the Russian or Iraqi models: like Orwell's Oceania, Iran was a state where nothing was efficient except the secret police (as opposed to Russia and Iraq, where even the secret police were inefficient, but they compensated with massive, indiscriminate violence and murder). SAVAK actually appears to have been quite good at discovering who was a "subversive" (accepting that its standard for subversive behavior at times encompassed even the mildest forms of political disagreement with the regime) and mostly leaving the rest of the country alone. In that sense, the Iranian "terror" was much less pervasive than that of Stalinist Russia or Saddam's Iraq. Yet, as in Iraq and Russia, people disappeared from their homes, there were no trials and no respect for human rights, executions were commonplace, and the methods of torture practiced in Tehran's Evin Prison were every bit as sadistic and horrific as those developed at the Lubljanka or Abu Ghraib. Because it was efficient and the punishments it meted out were so extreme, SAVAK seems to have been highly effective at instilling terror throughout the society with fewer personnel and fewer extrajudicial killings than either the Russians or Iraqis. International human rights groups found evidence of "only" thousands of such deaths, compared to the hundreds of thousands and millions slaughtered in Iraq and Russia, respectively.[77]

There was also a strong sense among Iranians from all walks of life that their government had proven itself to be callous and incompetent and that the shah was living in something of a fantasy world—cut off from the reality of his country, surrounded by sycophants who dared not tell him that his visions were leading Iran to the brink of disaster, and indulging a cult of personality that both bewildered and alienated most of his subjects. As an example, the new Rastakhiz Party published a handbook entitled *Philosophy of Iran's Revolution,* in which it proclaimed that "the Shah-in-Shah [king of kings] of Iran is not just the political leader of Iran. He is also in the first instance the teacher and spiritual leader, an individual who not only builds his nation roads, bridges, dams, and qanats, but also guides the spirit and thought and hearts of his people."[78] His regime also began to call him "Farmandar" (Commander) in addition to another title he had earlier given himself, "Aryamehr" (Light of the Aryans). In 1971, the shah staged a five-day spectacle for hundreds of foreign dignitaries and royalty to celebrate the 2,500th anniversary of the Iranian monarchy. Setting aside the questionable accuracy of the claim, many Iranians were incensed that the shah would spend $100 million to $200 million (reports varied) on such extravagances as flying in food daily from Maxim's of Paris for such a crowd while there was famine in Sistan and Baluchistan provinces.[79]

The regime's isolation and surreal perspective manifested itself in a variety of ways. The government blamed inflation on "price gouging" by the *bazaari*s, the stagnation of Iranian agriculture on the ignorance of the peasants, and the inability of its fabulous oil revenues to cover all of its frivolous spending on corruption by foreigners and the treachery of the Arabs who were preventing Iran from maximizing its oil revenues.[80] Iran scholar Nikki Keddie suggests that "Without anyone to contradict him, he [the shah] may have really believed the picture he presented in his words and books of himself as an enlightened ruler leading his people to a better life in a strong, independent Iran, opposed only by 'black and red reactionaries' (religious fanatics and Communists). It is not credible that he did not know of the tortures he often denied, and he cannot have believed all he said, but did believe his beneficent picture of himself, underestimated Iran's problems, and overestimated his ability to solve them."[81]

The Rise of the Mullahs

Iran was always a religious country. Perhaps because it was the only Shi'ah-led nation for so long, Iranians clung to Islam and saw in it a source of strength and guidance well beyond what became the norm in many other nations. It was not by accident that Ayatollah Kashani and other mullahs were Mosaddeq's most important allies—and his greatest bane when they turned against him. The 1960s and 1970s, however, witnessed a deepening of religious belief throughout the country. This phenomenon seemed to be tied to a variety of different factors. One important element was urbanization. As peasants left their rural life and headed to the unfamiliar world of the cities, they looked for something they could cling to that would provide them with a sense of balance in what seemed to them a topsy-turvy world. Consequently, mosques and *hay'ats* (prayer and religious discussion groups) sprouted all through Iran's new slums.[82]

A second cause was that Iran's new oil wealth rapidly integrated Iran into the global economy, bringing Iranians into contact with Westerners to an extent many had never before experienced. Typically, whenever a traditional non-Western society has been confronted by the combination of Western culture and modernity (which often seem indistinguishable), it has produced some kind of backlash in which religion has played a prominent part. In Iran, the economic and physical dislocation that many Iranians experienced, coupled with their sudden exposure to the strange and uncomfortable world of the West, caused many to seek refuge in something traditional and comfortable: Islam.

In addition, the regime's own actions further enhanced the status of the clergy. Because the regime was fiercely secular and disparaged the traditional religious aspects of Iranian society, the mere act of embracing religion was also an act of defiance against the regime. Many young women began wearing the veil more as a political gesture rather than as a sign of new devotion. By the same token, the regime was somewhat wary of taking on religion too directly. The shah tried hard to portray himself as a deeply religious man and cultivated ties to important ayatollahs. While the regime certainly did mistreat and even kill mullahs, it did not do so indiscriminately for fear of provoking the religious establishment. It was similarly cautious about violating the traditional sanctuary of mosques. As a result, the mosque was one of the few places in Iran where people felt they could speak their minds and "breathe freely" without fear of SAVAK. And since the shah had prohibited political parties and otherwise emasculated the secular political opposition, all that remained were the mosques and the mullahs.[83]

As for the clerics, it is hard to imagine what more the shah could have done to antagonize them. He stripped them of much of their land. He cut government subsidies. He took over the Awqaf organization, the central body that oversaw the vast range of religious endowments that spanned the country. He closed down publishing houses that produced religious books and disbanded religious organizations on campuses across Iran. He placed government restrictions on religious pilgrimages to Iraq and Saudi Arabia. He created a "Religion Corps," which, like the Literacy Corps and the Health Corps, was sent out into Iran's villages to educate Iranians in the state-sanctioned version of Islam. His security forces arrested, imprisoned, tortured, and even executed many clerics, including future revolutionary leaders such as Ayatollah Husayn 'Ali Montazeri, 'Ali Akbar Hashemi Rafsanjani, and 'Ali Husayn Khamene'i. In 1974, the regime tortured to death the fifty-four-year-old Ayatollah Husayn Ghaffari.[84] By one count, the regime killed, arrested, tortured, or exiled at least six hundred clerics during the 1970s alone. The shah even attempted to supplant Iran's Islamic calendar (which dated the year 1 from Muhammad's flight to Medina in A.D. 622, according to the Christian calendar) with a new calendar, based on the founding of the Persian Empire by Cyrus the Great. This was a terrible affront to devout Iranians and suggested that the shah was putting the monarchy ahead of Islam.

There was also a range of more indirect threats that the mullahs responded to with equal or greater concern. The reactionary clergy opposed the shah's efforts to improve the lot of women by giving them equal rights with men in family law and encouraging their greater integration into the workforce. They opposed the shah's secularization, his affection for so many attributes of the West, his tolerance of religious minorities such as the Jews and the Baha'i, and his relations with Israel. His reforms of law and education threatened their livelihoods in the religious law courts, as document writers, and as teachers. His very emphasis on modernization seemed to call into question the relevance of the mullahs in Iranian society.[85] The anthropologist Michael Fischer has argued that the shah's focus on economic modernization was seen as a threat to many of the younger religious students and freshly minted mullahs, whose sense was that Iranians no longer considered religion vital to their lives.[86]

No one benefited from these different trends more than the Ayatollah Khomeini. From Iraq, he continued to educate new students, who returned to Iran bearing the wisdom of the "Imam," as Khomeini came to be called. In particular, as the mosques and *hay'at*s spread, they began to adopt the practice of playing cassette recordings of sermons by famous ayatollahs, either because no mullah was available or as an additional benediction at their gatherings. Khomeini's students smuggled tapes of his sermons into Iran, and his no-holds-barred attacks on the shah, his court, his thugs, and every other aspect of his corrupt police state became wildly popular.[87] Influential thinkers and rising religious leaders all came to pay homage to him in Najaf and to join his circle of followers. In part because Khomeini encouraged it and in part because the threat from the government made it necessary, the seminary students and the clergy themselves established a nationwide network to try to communicate their message to the Iranian people, which in time became a network to mobilize the Iranian people.

Sparks

By 1977, Iran was something of a tinderbox thanks to all of these different sources of unhappiness. By their actions as well as their inactions, the shah and his retainers had managed to alienate just about every segment of Iranian society. The Army remained loyal to its king, as did the seniormost bureaucrats. However, even the great landlords were deeply ambivalent; they certainly did not want a revolution, but they thought little enough of Mohammad Reza Shah and his regime (after all that he had put them through) that they were not going to fight for him. Everyone else seethed at the various injustices perpetrated by the shah against them, their family, their friends, and their interests. So great was popular animosity toward the shah that anything he promoted or that his regime demanded immediately became an object of ridicule. Hence young, well-educated women began to demand segregated education even though coeducation had been a major victory for their grandmothers.[88]

Inevitably, the bull market in oil that the shah had been riding ran out. The recession in the West, caused to a considerable extent by OPEC's price hike, forced a slowdown in activity and spurred conservation efforts that resulted in reduced oil consumption (and therefore, reduced oil prices) just a few years later. Because Iran's production continued to grow, the result was not a decline in oil revenues but a plateauing. The problem was that the projects that the regime had started assumed rapidly *increasing* oil revenues to be able to pay for them. Unexpectedly short of cash, the government stopped or slowed many huge projects for roads, airports, docks, communications centers, and other major facilities. This in turn threw 400,000 construction workers (a prime occupation for the unskilled laborers who had migrated from the countryside) out of work by July 1978.[89] In addition, the regime ended all state credits and financing for small businesses (which was inadequate to begin with), undermining many of the bazaar merchants. They stopped hiring civil servants, which meant that even greater numbers of university graduates had no jobs. And they expanded price controls, placed limits on income, curtailed investment, and added a variety of other measures that crippled the activities of small businesses. After the sudden acceleration of 1973–1974, in 1976–1977 the regime was slamming on the brakes. Its drastic measures threw the country into recession, drove up unemployment, and brought popular animosities to a fever pitch.[90]

Then along came the Carter administration. Jimmy Carter began his presidency in January 1977 with two strikes against him as far as Mohammad Reza

Shah was concerned. Carter believed that human rights considerations should weigh heavily in decisions regarding arms sales and that the United States should show greater restraint regarding weapons sales. This was the last thing that the shah needed. He feared that Carter was another Democrat like Truman or Kennedy, who would try to pressure him to reform.[91] And Carter did reverse the Nixon-Kissinger decision to allow Iran to purchase whatever non-nuclear weapons from the United States it wanted.[92] However, before Carter could start pressing Iran to make reforms, the shah decided to preempt the new president by loosening up a bit on political discourse, freeing some political prisoners, and easing a number of other aspects of his police state.

The shah had actually taken the first tentative steps in this direction in mid-1976, even before Carter's victory in the November election. By then, Mohammad Reza Shah was aware that he had cancer, and apparently it was threatening enough to make him start thinking about his own mortality. He wanted his son to succeed him, and it is possible that he started to relieve some of the pressure on Iranian society in hope that this would create a better atmosphere for his son to take power in. Of greater importance, however, he saw Carter as a presidential candidate and feared him as another Kennedy even then. So did other Iranians: one newspaper serialized Carter's book *Why Not the Best?* during 1976, which was taken as an oblique warning to the shah that the Americans were going to demand change.[93] And Carter fed this expectation by specifically attacking the shah's human rights record during the election campaign. For his part, the shah wanted to make sure that he did not become an election problem for his friends in the Ford administration, so he took steps to take the punch out of Carter's attacks.[94] He ousted a number of his old advisers, including Prime Minister Amir Abbas Hoveyda, who had been strong proponents of hard-line positions, and replaced them with a number of liberals and technocrats, including Jamshid Amuzegar, a highly regarded economist, as prime minister.[95]

Much to the shah's chagrin, Carter defeated Ford in the election, at which point Tehran accelerated its liberalization efforts to try to undermine the pressure from Washington that the shah thought inevitable.[96] For instance, in 1977, Iran invited in delegations from the International Committee of the Red Cross, Amnesty International, and the International Commission of Jurists to examine the country's social and political conditions. The shah attempted to clean up his regime's practices to a certain extent before these various groups conducted their surveys, and he agreed to reform Iran's Military Justice and Penal Code regarding detention and due process in response to the ICJ recommendations. He also eased restrictions on the press and promised an end to the use of torture by SAVAK.[97]

But the pressure that the shah feared never came. The Carter administration did not make human rights an issue with the shah after it took office. It was not that Carter administration officials ignored the issue—they did raise it with him on a regular basis—but they certainly did not press him as he had feared, and they were, perhaps, a bit too willing to accept his assurances that he was making dramatic gestures in this area. Instead, the Democrats decided to stick with the Twin Pillars strategy out of a combination of the mistaken impression that the shah was still very much in control of Iran, the post-Vietnam desire to keep the United States from engaging too deeply in regional issues, and the fact that Carter too had higher priorities than dealing with the shah.[98] The United States had built two highly sophisticated electronic intelligence collection sites in northern Iran that allowed American intelligence personnel to collect information on the USSR's ballistic missile tests at its ranges in Central Asia. The Carter administration, like all of its predecessors, considered those sites so valuable that it did not want to do anything that might cause the shah to close them down.[99] Finally, the Carter administration was nearly desperate to get OPEC to lower oil prices—which continued to cripple Western economies—and they needed the shah's help to do so.[100]

The administration's policy toward Iran should have been evident to anyone watching its actions with anything approaching an objective eye. In May 1977, Secretary of State Cyrus Vance visited Tehran and barely mentioned human rights. A senior member of Vance's party told reporters that the United States was very pleased with the reforms on human rights that Iran was already making and therefore sanctions were out of the question. In fact, Vance promised American approval for the sale of another 160 F-16s to Iran (at a cost of $1.8 billion) as well as 7 AWACS aircraft (for $1.23 billion)—which at that time were brand-new and had not been sold outside of NATO. The shah was reassured enough to later increase his order to 300 F-16s.[101] The administration then fought a hard battle with the Congress to get approval for the sale—which should have been a clear sign of Washington's commitment to the shah.[102]

Typically, however, what mattered in Iran was not what was actually happening but what the Iranians *believed* was happening. The rumor spread that Vance had told the shah to reform, or else he would be removed from his throne just as Mosaddeq had been. They saw the shah's initial moves toward liberalization—both those before Carter and those prompted by his election—and assumed that the administration was forcing the shah to be more respectful of human rights. They further assumed that Carter would protect Iranians if they chose to take actions to express their grievances against the shah.

Newspapers decided to try to press the limits of their new freedoms, with the leading *Kayhan* asking "What Is Wrong with Iran?" and receiving 40,000 letters from Iranians complaining about different aspects of government policy. Intellectuals and professionals began to form new groups and even political parties. Liberals such as Karim Sanjabi revived the National Front, while Mehdi Bazargan brought back the Liberation Movement of Iran. Various groups and individuals started circulating "letters of grievance"—open letters to the prime minister and the shah written by prominent moderates such as Shapour Bakhtiar and Daryush Foruhar. A large group of Iranian lawyers demanded strict adherence to the rule of law and an end to the regime's special courts. Beginning in October 1977, students began to protest regularly on campuses.[103] In fact, these protest movements by liberal secularists spread so quickly and seemed to encounter so little resistance from the regime that even Ayatollah Khomeini off in Iraq noticed and ordered his minions to begin to mobilize their network of religious supporters to join the movement.[104]

There were other signs of the building unrest. In August 1977, the mayor of Tehran had sent bulldozers to plow through one of the slums of the city to make way for a new highway—without so much as warning the poor living there. This time, the denizens rose up against the authorities and a number of people were killed in fierce fighting.[105] On October 23, 1977, Khomeini's eldest son, Mustafa, died under mysterious circumstances in Iraq. There were memorial services all across Iran, and many turned into protests and demonstrations against the government.[106]

In November 1977, the shah and the Empress Farah visited the White House. Thanks to Iran's oil wealth and policies going back to Reza Shah, there were many Iranians studying in the United States. These decided to use the shah's appearance to deliver a protest message six thousand miles from home. Thousands of anti-shah students began pouring into Washington. The Iranian Embassy caught wind of the storm gathering and started busing in Iranian military cadets and pro-shah students of their own to try to counteract the oppositionists. On November 15, when the Carters received the shah and the empress on the White House lawn, they did so amid a scene of bedlam, with thousands of Iranian students screaming and fighting and swarming around the gates of the White House. The police used tear gas on the students (all of them; they did not discriminate), which blew back into the faces of the Carters and the Pahlavis. With tears running down their faces, they cut short the ceremony and retreated into the White House proper.

Although once again the visit was a great diplomatic success and the two couples got along extremely well, back in Iran it was read completely differently. There the oppositionists assumed that the tear gas incident could have happened only if Carter had ordered it. Thus it was widely touted as a sign that the United States had abandoned the shah, therefore making him (somehow) vulnerable.[107] In a wonderful bit of understatement, President Carter's director for Persian Gulf affairs, Gary Sick, has observed that "This misunderstanding, though minor, was symptomatic of the perceptual gulf that separated the two societies and that bedeviled relations throughout the entire crisis."[108]

Obviously, a reckoning was in the offing. It came in early 1978. First, after his successful trip to Washington, the shah was now certain that Carter would not interfere with his governance of Iran, and he again began to crack down on the various protest movements he had unleashed the previous year.[109] In December, government thugs attacked and beat up a number of leading oppositionists (including Daryush Foruhar) while bombs exploded at the homes of others, including Mehdi Bazargan.[110] In December, religious oppositionists organized demonstrations against the government on the holy days of Tasu'a and Ashura and were attacked by regime security personnel.[111] Then, in January 1978, the Carters reciprocated with a visit to Tehran. The president's various public statements were effusive in their praise of the shah, including a famous toast at the state dinner in which Carter called Iran "an island of stability in a turbulent corner of the world."[112]

The Iranian people now felt betrayed. It was finally clear to them that Carter was not going to enforce his own rhetoric about human rights—at least not in Iran. Indeed, again demonstrating the vastly exaggerated sense of American power over (and attention to) Iran, many Iranians believed that the White House had ordered the shah to reimpose draconian repression.[113] What was seen as Carter's treachery brought forth a flood of anti-Americanism that had been lurking inside many Iranians for a long time. Without ever realizing it, Americans had become deeply hated by a wide swath of Iranian society.

To some extent, this hatred was a result of Americans just being Americans—and not being Iranians—and being in Iran. The mammoth military and civilian contracts the shah was signing with American corporations required ever-larger numbers of Americans in Iran to train Iranian personnel, set up facilities and equipment, and often run them as well. By July 1976, there were 24,000 Americans in Iran. By late 1978, there were 45,000.[114] Most of the Americans were in lucrative, high-profile positions in which they were superior to most of the Iranians they were in contact with. "Almost all of them," one Iranian wrote, "seemed to have more money than they were judged to deserve."[115] This often confirmed the unshakable conviction of many Iranians that the Americans were actually running their country. The fact that President Nixon appointed former DCI Richard Helms as ambassador to Tehran in 1974 only reinforced the sense that the CIA was pulling all of the strings in Iran and that now the United States had become so confident, arrogant, and brazen that it was not even going to try to hide it anymore. To give a sense of just how willing Iranians were to believe the worst about the United States, Khomeini claimed in 1977 that Washington had a secret plan to build American colonies outside of major Iranian cities, and this inane fantasy was widely taken as fact.[116]

There were also problems at an interpersonal level. Certainly some Americans behaved badly; others were simply unfamiliar with the culture and thus made mistakes without even knowing it. Although they were not generally housed in separate residential facilities, the Americans generally kept to themselves, which to the hypersensitive Iranians was often taken as snubbing them.[117] In addition, some (perhaps many) of the American salesmen who came to Iran during the 1970s brought a single-minded determination to part the shah from Iran's money with little regard for the country. Many Iranians focused on these unscrupulous businessmen and perceived it as a reversal from the selfless Americans who had come to Iran between 1942 and 1968 and who had built a reputation of incorruptibility among Iranians. This new breed was more than willing to engage in bribery or whatever else was needed to secure contracts. While the Americans no doubt considered it merely "the price of doing business in Tehran," xenophobic Iranians could turn the relationship around and blame the United States for bringing corruption to Iran.[118] One Iranian poet called Americans "a tribe that worships gold."[119]

This raises another factor in this ferocious anti-Americanism, namely the displacement of anger at the shah onto the United States as his ally or colonial "master." Many Iranians were deeply unhappy that the shah was squandering money on military equipment and foreign policy adventures that they assumed were being dictated by Washington. They accepted without question the notion that the shah could not be making such decisions for himself and that the United States wanted him to buy vast quantities of its weapons (which, on this last point, was not entirely incorrect, of course). It never occurred to them that some of the things the shah was doing ran directly counter to what the United States actually would have wanted. An obscure, flaky intellectual named Abol Hasan Bani Sadr, who attached himself to Ayatollah Khomeini's circle, complained that "The economic health, social welfare and cultural integrity of the nation are being sacrificed so that the Shah can continue to rule within the framework of American strategic objectives."[120] In fact, many oppositionists called Mohammad Reza Shah "the American king."[121] The fact that he seemed so envious of the West and so solicitous of its opinions, while remaining so tone-deaf to the complaints of his people, made many Iranians further resent the West and particularly its leader, the United States.

Still another aspect of Iran's anti-Americanism stemmed from its confrontation with Western culture, Western economies, and Western technology. All of these bred insecurities and animosities among Iranians—just as they have in countless other societies around the globe.[122] Azar Nafisi was a professor of English literature in Iran during the revolution, and in her magnificent memoir of that period, *Reading Lolita in Tehran,* she relates the anger of one of her students at the United States: " 'All through this revolution we have talked about the fact that the West is our enemy, it is the Great Satan, not because of its military might, not because of its economic power, but because of, because of'—another pause—'because of its sinister assault on the very roots of our culture. What our Imam calls cultural aggression. This I would call a rape of our culture.' "[123]

In the 1960s, a secular intellectual named Jalal Al-e Ahmad popularized the term *gharbzadegi,* which is usually translated as "Westoxication" (being intoxicated or "drunk" on the West) but could also be translated as "Westernitis," "Westamination," or "Euromania." Al-e Ahmad's work was little more than an expression of rage, an attack on the West and everything it stood for, often in completely incoherent and inaccurate fashion. For instance, Al-e Ahmad blamed the rural migration to the cities on the mechanization of Iranian agriculture, which he claimed was the result of America's desire to recycle petrodollars by selling tractors and other farm equipment to Iran—which was precisely the opposite of the problem that had actually driven so many peasants to leave farming and move to the cities. But the work touched a nerve, and the concept became wildly popular throughout Iran.[124]

By the early 1970s, just about everyone in Iran was blaming the United States for just about everything. The religious Right, the Marxist Left, the liberals in between; the upper classes, the middle class, and the lower classes all had their particular conspiracy theories, all of which had only one common characteristic: the central role of the United States. In fact, even the regime joined the chorus. When the shah became concerned by the increasing number of guerrilla and terrorist attacks on the regime, he began to encourage Iran's press to claim that the United States was responsible for the various maladies plaguing the country.[125] Of course, the problem that he did not recognize was that in the minds of his own people, he was indistinguishable from the Americans. As a result, acts of violence against Americans increased along with attacks on the regime throughout the period before the revolution. In November 1971, there was an attempt to kidnap U.S. Ambassador Douglas

MacArthur II, followed by the assassination of Lieutenant Colonel Lewis Hawkins, a military adviser, on June 2, 1973. Other murders followed, and between 1971 and 1975 there were thirty-one bombings and threatened bombings directed against American organizations and facilities—including two bombings of the embassy itself.[126]

The Revolution Unfolds

It was Carter's unintentionally offensive remarks in Tehran that set into motion the chain of events that became the Iranian Revolution. Immediately afterward, Khomeini blasted Carter for being a hypocrite, promoting human rights only where it was convenient for the United States because it had no military or commercial interests. On January 7, the regime responded with a misstep of its own, placing an anonymous editorial in the newspaper *Ettela'at* that blamed all of the recent protests on "Red and Black" reactionaries (meaning Communists and Islamic extremists). For good measure, the piece insinuated that Khomeini was a foreigner, an agent of the British, a drunkard, and a closet homosexual. The next day, there were massive demonstrations in Qom, Iran's religious center, to which the shah's police responded with violence, killing several people (including mullahs) and wounding many more.[127]

These events did three important things. First, they outraged the public; even those who did not agree with Khomeini considered him an upright and devout man who should not have been slandered, while killing religious students and mullahs who were protesting such an insult to one of the *marjas* (sources of emulation) was equally unconscionable. Second, it made the religious opposition coequal with the various secular groups that had kicked off the protests and had carried virtually all of the burden of opposition throughout 1977. In fact, in the minds of many Iranians, it knitted together all of the different protests into one grand opposition alliance. Third, it elevated Khomeini as a symbol of the revolution. He was not yet its undisputed leader, but he achieved a position of prominence not equaled by any other oppositionist, and this allowed him eventually to drive the revolution in the direction he wanted.

Khomeini's rise as the focal point of the revolution was critical to its course and arguably to its success. In Khomeini, the opposition suddenly had a leader capable of mobilizing great masses of Iranians; without him, it would have been much harder for the middle-class oppositionists—left, right, or center—to do so. In addition, there were two key aspects of Khomeini that proved to be the defining elements of the revolution. First, Khomeini was insistent, right from the start, that the shah had to go. No compromise was possible. Had the various middle-class parties remained the leading elements of the opposition movement, there is every reason to believe they would have compromised. In fact, their leaders—such as Shapour Bakhtiar and Mehdi Bazargan—were willing to reach deals with the shah's regime. But not Khomeini. For him, the revolution could not succeed, nor could it be considered a success, if the shah remained even as a figurehead.

The second key principle that Khomeini brought to the revolution was implacable anti-Americanism. As he so frequently pointed out, he believed the United States was satanic. Khomeini truly seems to have conceived, in his Manichean worldview, that the United States, along with Israel and occasionally the Soviet Union, was the source of all evil in the world. No one knows why he believed this—perhaps the fact that he was arrested in 1963 for leading opposition to American-inspired reforms and again in 1964 for opposing the American Status of Forces Agreement. Whatever the reason, by 1978 it was a defining element of his political agenda. In this sense, Khomeini embodied the extreme form of xenophobia directed at the United States that Mosaddeq had embodied during his own era, albeit directed at the British. Obviously, the styles of the two men were very different, as was their specific target, but the intensity of their conviction that everything wrong with Iran stemmed from foreign machinations and that solving any of Iran's problems therefore required wholly exorcising the British/American presence from Iran was the same. With Khomeini playing a leading role (and ultimately *the* leading role) in the revolution, it became—in one respect—a collective manifestation of anti-Americanism. Because anti-Americanism was already prevalent throughout Iranian society by the 1970s, and because the shah was widely considered an American puppet, it seems likely that the protest movement that began in 1977 would inevitably have had some anti-American aspects to it. But it was Khomeini who made the revolution *about* anti-Americanism, just as he made it *about* the overthrow of the shah.

An important tradition of Shi'i Islam is that memorial services are held for the dead not only immediately after the passing but at prescribed intervals afterward. Most important is the forty-day anniversary, the *arba'een*. In January 1978, Grand Ayatollah Shariatmadari—one of the four most eminent religious figures in Iran—called for all Iranians to observe the *arba'een* of those killed at Qom on January 8 by spending the day praying at home or in the mosques. Shariatmadari (who did not particularly care for Khomeini or his radical ideas) was from Azerbaijan, so people in the Azeri capital of Tabriz took his request most to heart. While there were observances of the *arba'een* on February 17 all across the country, in Tabriz they turned into antigovernment protests, which brought out the police, which led to violence and scores of people killed and wounded. The next day, religious leaders all across the country asked Iranians to observe the *arba'een* of those killed in Tabriz.[128]

And off it went, with each *arba'een* creating the deaths to generate another *arba'een*. On March 29, there were demonstrations in fifty-five cities; five of them turned violent and several hundred people were killed. The uprisings persisted for another three days in about a half-dozen cities, including Tehran. On May 10, there were violent protests in twenty-four different cities, the Army had to deploy tanks in some of them, and, in Tehran, riot police dumped tear gas into the central bazaar to try to control the crowds. Riots continued across the country for several days in early May.

At this point, the shah and his regime seem to have recognized the pattern that was emerging and moved to break it. He tried to employ a classic "carrot-and-stick approach," or what is typically called the "iron fist in the velvet glove" in these kinds of situations. He unleashed SAVAK to go after the leaders of the protests with threatening letters, leaflets accusing them of being American puppets (!), kidnapping some, beating up others, bombing their offices, and a host of other nasty tricks. Members of the Rastakhiz Party were formed up into a vigilante force called the Resistance Corps, which was steeled by police officers out of uniform and used to attack meetings of student groups, political parties, and other opposition events. At the same time, the shah made a number of concessions to public grievance. He eased up on "profiteers," amnestied some *bazaaris*, banned films that the mullahs considered "pornographic," sacked the head of SAVAK, issued an ethics code for the members of the royal family to try to control graft, and promised free Majles elections in the fall.[129]

The regime also reached out to the three seniormost clerics in Iran—Grand Ayatollahs Shariatmadari, Golpaygani, and Najafi-Mar'ashi—all of whom seem to have been a bit nervous that the radicals (that is, Khomeini) were trying to hijack this protest movement. They called for "peaceful demonstrations" and the return of constitutionalism, and explicitly said that the shah's removal was not necessary for Iran to have a better future. Khomeini responded by continuing to call for the overthrow of the "pagan regime." During the latter part of June, July, and on into early August, there was a noticeable diminution in the unrest. There were still outbursts—a funeral that led to violence in the Iranian holy city of Mashhad in late July and a massive demonstration that turned ugly in Isfahan in early August—but there simply weren't the size, scale, provocativeness, and prevalence of the protests that had accompanied the *arba'een*s. This was seen as a triumph for the "quietist" ayatollahs and the regime's new tactics over Khomeini. But it did not last.[130]

On August 19, a fire set at the crowded Cinema Rex movie theater in Abadan killed 377 people. Although it was the sixth fire set in twelve days and all of the others had been set by Islamists who opposed the showing of "sinful" movies, the rumor nevertheless spread that SAVAK had set the fire and had locked the doors to trap the people inside. Outlandish as this was, the rumor itself caught fire and ignited the Iranian population. The next day, there were mammoth demonstrations in Tehran.[131] Two weeks later, on the occasion of another Muslim holiday, the 'Id al-Fitr, 400,000 people gathered for a protest in Tehran. In the past, the mullahs had usually been able to call out some tens of thousands for rallies; hundreds of thousands was literally a new order of magnitude. Every day after the 'Id (September 4), people poured out into the streets in ever-greater numbers, even though many liberal oppositionists and moderate clerics began calling for restraint. By September 7, the number in Tehran reached 500,000, all chanting "Death to the Pahlavis," "America out of Iran," "Khomeini is our leader," and "We want an Islamic republic."[132] Similar riots broke out in fifteen other cities across Iran.

That night, the shah took the velvet glove off the iron fist. He declared martial law and ordered the Army out onto the streets of the capital and many other Iranian cities. He put Major General Gholam 'Ali Oveisi, the man who had led the successful crackdown in 1963—for which he had earned the sobriquet "the butcher of Tehran"—back into his old post as governor of Tehran. The problem was that not everyone got the word about martial law in time, and on the very next day, September 8, various lower-class groups set up barricades and began throwing Molotov cocktails at Army vehicles throughout south Tehran. A crowd of 5,000 people, many of them students, gathered together at Jaleh Square, and the Army decided to make its point: around two hundred people were killed in Jaleh Square and several hundred more in military crackdowns across the city. That day forever after became known as Black Friday to Iranians.[133]

The next day, several important things happened. First, fearing a repetition of 1963, Khomeini shifted tactics. He called on people across Iran to go on strike, rather than continuing to demonstrate en masse where they would be vulnerable to attacks by the Army. Over time these strikes grew, and they became one of the key instruments of the revolution during its latter phase. Meanwhile, the shah decided that he had overstepped, and to try to appease the population for the Jaleh Square massacre, he sacked his highly unpopular minister of court, Amir Abbas Hoveyda. However, far from appearing to his people like a balanced "carrot-and-stick" approach, the shah's actions made him appear vacillating (which he was) and uncertain. He reportedly wept at the cabinet meeting that day.[134] This behavior emboldened the opposition and undermined the steadfastness of his supporters.

Another party that was beginning to worry about the shah's mixed message to his people was the United States, and to try to counteract that trend, President Carter called the shah to express his support. The shah was so pleased with their conversation that he released the transcript to the press, which to the Iranian people now looked as if Carter had called the shah to congratulate him on the Jaleh Square massacre. It only enraged the population—against the shah and against his American "masters."[135]

The Americans were not blind to the events in Tehran. But the Carter administration did not have a great deal of experience with Iran. The administration was at a delicate stage in the negotiations of the Camp David peace talks and the SALT II treaty with Russia, and its principals were inclined to allow their subordinates to keep an eye on what seemed to be minor disturbances in Iran.[136] What's more, virtually all of the Iran experts in Washington—as well as throughout the Middle East and even in Iran, for that matter—believed that the shah would be able to weather this storm. He had handled many domestic disturbances in his thirty-seven years in power and had overcome even significant unrest, as in 1963 and '64.[137] The Jaleh Square massacre was the first time that Washington had an inkling that there was something very different going on.[138]

In October the situation became worse. On October 6, the shah made a terrible mistake: he demanded that Saddam Hussein expel Khomeini from Najaf, where the shah felt he was able to make too much trouble inside Iran.[139] Still wary of provoking his powerful neighbor, Saddam complied. It wasn't much of a sacrifice, as Khomeini was managing to stir up Iraq's Shi'ah too. Khomeini eventually made his way to Paris, where telecommunications and press exposure gave him more prominence in Iran, a better ability to communicate with his disciples, and therefore *greater* influence over events, not less. On the eighth and ninth, there were antigovernment riots in a dozen cities, and starting on October 16 (the *arba'een* for Black Friday) there were massive demonstrations in Tehran, Mashhad, Qom, and Hamadan coupled with wave after wave of strikes that lasted the rest of the year. These strikes crippled Iran's already fragile economy, and on October 27, for the first time, opposition groups took control of an entire city, Babul in northern Iran. The end of the month was marked by huge protest gatherings and bloodshed in thirty-six different cities. Worst of all, the oil field workers collectively walked out on strike.

The Crisis of the Ancien Régime

By the beginning of November, the entire country seemed to have stopped in its tracks. Iran's economy was dead, and its societal life focused entirely on the battle of wills between the people and the shah. On November 5, Tehran exploded into violence again in response to clashes between students and regime security forces at Tehran University the day before, when soldiers had fired on students pulling down a statue of the shah. That same day, mobs burned banks, liquor stores, Western business establishments, movie theaters, and hotels. They chased the American advisers out of the Ministry of Labor and temporarily overran the British Embassy.

Two days earlier, President Carter's national security advisor, Dr. Zbigniew Brzezinski, had called the shah directly to try to stiffen his spine. Brzezinski had told the shah that while the United States preferred a peaceful, political resolution to the crisis, Washington was prepared to stand by him no matter what course of action became necessary. Washington's concern had deepened throughout October and into early November. Brzezinski's call was part of a coordinated campaign by the administration to demonstrate its support to the shah and convince him to deal more decisively with the crisis. In addition to the phone call, Secretary of State Cyrus Vance made a public statement so supportive of the shah that journalists wanted to know if his statement meant that the Carter administration was backing away from its earlier commitment to liberalization in Iran. The next day, the U.S. ambassador to Iran met with the shah to reiterate Washington's support.[140]

Nevertheless, within the palace, debate raged, all of it swirling around the peripatetic figure of the shah. Some urged greater conciliation, but the leading voice was from a group of military officers led by Major Generals Oveisi, Manuchehr Khosrowdad (the commander of Iran's airborne forces), and Abbas 'Ali Badrei (the commander of the Imperial Guard), who had been urging a comprehensive and ruthless crackdown on the opposition for months. They pleaded with the shah to put them in charge of the government and allow them to use force as they saw fit. But the shah would not make up his mind. Perhaps because of his cancer, he did not want to use all-out force against his people. In his memoir, the shah would bitterly claim that he had asked for confirmation from Washington for the message conveyed by Dr. Brzezinski's phone call.[141] To a certain extent, this was just false: Ambassador Sullivan never heard the shah request such clarification.[142] Moreover, a phone call from the president's national security advisor *is* confirmation; that is what foreign governments want when they request such confirmation, and, in truth, it is unheard of for a foreign government to ask for "greater" confirmation than the national security advisor's spoken assurance. Brzezinski too believes that at the end of their phone call, the shah was not in any doubt as to where the United States stood.[143] In fact, on November 14, the shah told an American businessman whom the White House had sent as a private emissary (another element in its effort to assure the shah of Washington's support) that the only other help the United States could provide would be to "tell the leaders of the political opposition what you are telling me, that at the highest levels you support me fully in my efforts to restore order and stability and that you look towards me as the key to continued strength, stability and prosperity for Iran."[144]

Instead, the shah appears to have been looking for someone else (the United States) to make his decision for him. By all accounts, the shah genuinely did not want to be the author of a vast new bloodbath, one that probably would have made 1963 pale by comparison. But neither did he want to give up his throne, and he seemed to recognize that that was the choice he had left. At the very least, he wanted to be able to pin the blame for his actions and their consequences squarely on the United States. If he could have done that, it would have made his decision much easier, possibly even self-evident in his own mind.[145] Thus, what he wanted was not confirmation that the Carter administration supported him but a statement that would appear to be a command from the Americans to use massive, indiscriminate force. He wanted to be able to tell the Iranian people that he had been *ordered* to use violence by Iran's masters in Washington. But because the White House was not in a position to order the shah to do anything—the United States was hardly Iran's "master," and just months before the Americans had been the supplicant, begging Tehran to lower oil prices—and because it was unimaginable that the Carter administration, even its biggest hard-liners, such as Brzezinski, would have made the kind of statement that the shah wanted, he never got it.[146] Indeed, at a later meeting with Ambassador Sullivan, the shah would finally make this desire more transparent. Brzezinski writes that in Sullivan's readout from their meeting, "The Shah asked then whether he was being advised to use the iron fist even if it meant widespread bloodshed and even if it might fail to restore law and order. Sullivan reported that he responded by saying that if the Shah was trying to get the United States to take the responsibility for his actions, he doubted that he would ever get such instructions from Washington. He was the Shah and he had to take the decision as well as the responsibility."[147]

Without the clear command from Washington that would have allowed him to shift the blame for large-scale bloodshed on to the United States, the shah waffled. Finally, on November 6, he announced a half step: he appointed a military government, but rather than putting the hard-liners in charge, he turned to General Gholam Reza Azhari, a mild and retiring general who was least likely to antagonize the opposition but, for the same reason, also unlikely to deal forcefully with the protests. What's more, in announcing the new government on November 6, the shah issued a stunningly apologetic statement to try to mitigate the inevitable popular anger at him that he knew would follow. But the apology was taken as a further sign of weakness and only convinced the opposition leadership (especially Khomeini) that it had him on the ropes.[148]

This was probably the last moment the shah had to avert his fall. After this early-November decision, the situation came apart completely. On November 26, more than a million people marched in protest of the regime in Mashhad, with lesser (but still huge) numbers in Qom, Tehran, Isfahan, and other major cities. With revolutionary propaganda working on their sympathies and their officers frustrated and divided, the Army rank and file began to crack. Troops began to desert, while others became so reluctant to fire on demonstrators that their officers had to do much of the shooting themselves. In December, a whole division based at Mashhad fell apart in a mass of mutinies and desertions. Overall, the military was suffering an average of 1,000 defections per day.[149] Meanwhile, the protests just got bigger and bigger until, on December 10 and 11—the holy days of Tasu'a and 'Ashura again—as many as 9 million people joined demonstrations across the country, a million in Tehran alone.[150] Nine million people marched and chanted, demanding the shah's death, Khomeini's return, and America's eviction. Charles Kurzman, author of an excellent book on the revolution, believes that these two days may represent the largest protest event in history.[151]

Of course, turning points are generally obvious only in retrospect, and the United States did not realize that the game in Tehran was over. On December 28, the president sent a cable to Mohammad Reza Shah that tried one last time to get him to act decisively. The cable recommended strongly that (1) the shah should end his vacillation and act; (2) a civilian government that could restore stability was preferable; but (3) if that was impossible, the shah should appoint a "firm military government" that would end the disorder and violence; and (4) if none of these options was feasible, the shah should consider establishing a Regency Council (i.e., step down from the throne in favor of his son) to supervise the current military government. In his own instructions, Sullivan was told to make clear that it was Washington's judgment that it would likely be impossible to restore the shah's former absolute power. The United States was effectively telling the shah that it wanted him to get control of the situation however he could, even if that meant sacrificing his own position to a greater or lesser degree.[152]

Sullivan delivered his message the next day, only to have the shah tell him that he simply did not have the heart to order a serious crackdown.[153] Instead, he ended martial law, deposed the military government, and asked the aged liberal democrat Shapour Bakhtiar to form a government of reform. On January 16, 1979, the shah and his family packed their belongings and fled the country. Unlike in 1953, they never returned.

America and the Iranian Revolution

True revolutions are extraordinarily complicated events. They are rare occurrences in human history. No one really knows why they happen. No one has been able to diagnose the precise combination of factors that produces one. Academics have been pondering that issue for decades, and no one has been able to come up with a general cause or even combination of causes. Like so many human events, revolutions appear to be intensely idiosyncratic. Hardship, misery, and repression are constants of human existence, unfortunately. But revolution is not. For every example of an impoverished, oppressed nation that has risen up and overthrown its oppressors at some point in time, there are a hundred or a thousand examples of others that haven't.[154]

For that reason, I find it difficult to blame American policy makers for not anticipating the Iranian Revolution. In retrospect, the revolution appears obvious, but beforehand, there was no reason to believe that Iran would actually descend into violent upheaval. There had been similar moments of rebellion, and the shah had dealt with them swiftly and effectively. Moreover, because revolutions are such rare and idiosyncratic events, it is always difficult to predict them anywhere at any time, and the smart bet is to assume that a revolution will not occur rather than that it will. Very few people actually predicted the Iranian Revolution. Most Iranians would not have predicted it in early 1978, nor would they have predicted its outcome even at the end of that year. Moreover, Khomeini alone among the various opposition leaders seemed to have a clear idea of the end state he envisioned for Iran, and that that end state would comprise a novel form of government without the shah and with every last vestige of America extirpated from the country.

Nevertheless, American policy makers must bear some blame. It is one thing to say that revolutions are hard to predict; it is something entirely different to suggest that because they are hard to predict, policy makers should act as if predicting them is impossible. Certainly, we do know a fair bit about the circumstances that are more likely to produce revolutions, and Iran in the late 1960s and especially the 1970s was slipping ever deeper into the kind of state that is most conducive to germinating a full-blown revolution. American policy makers often claimed after the fact that because they were largely blinded to developments inside Iran by the shah's deliberate policies toward the United States, they were unable to see those warning signs. Again, there is truth to this point, but again, it is not the whole truth. Ultimately, there were actions that the shah was taking and developments inside Iran that were obvious to everyone inside or outside Iran, and many were monstrously misguided. If nothing else, the obvious economic and social problems should have made American policy makers think harder about the possibility that there were other problems that they weren't seeing. At the very least, the obvious problems alone should have made American policy makers question their conduct toward Iran.

In the aftermath of the Iranian Revolution, the familiar charge of "intelligence failure" was heard all across Washington. Was there an intelligence failure in Iran? Yes, there was. American intelligence collectors (including embassy officials) gathered too little information on the mood of the Iranian people, the problems in the economy, and the rise of the network of mullahs (and Khomeini in particular).[155] American intelligence analysts failed to challenge their assumptions that the 1977–1978 disturbances were just another in a long line of such events in modern Iranian history and that the shah was a strong, decisive leader who had survived such challenges before and would be willing to do whatever was necessary to maintain control.[156]

However, the charges of an intelligence failure have been greatly exaggerated. Part of the problem lies in bureaucratic politics having nothing to do with Iran. In 1977, Admiral Stansfield Turner—an outsider—took over the CIA. Turner became DCI immediately after the CIA had gone through the worst period of its thirty-year existence, when in 1974–1975 Congress had conducted devastating hearings that had revealed CIA involvement in several assassination and coup plots during the 1950s and '60s, as well as a number of other less-than-savory activities. At the time, the Agency, and particularly its dominant Directorate of Operations (the spies), were a caricaturish old boys' network that refused to admit that it had done anything wrong and refused to change its ways. Turner's charge was to remake the CIA and he started out by trying to clean house in the DO. He fired and retired a number of Agency "legends." But the DO did not go down without a fight, and it started a vicious war of rumors against Turner that eventually included the idea that he had been responsible for the intelligence failure in Iran by "gutting" the clandestine service and putting too much emphasis on satellites and technical surveillance. It is a fable that has stuck to this day.[157]

The other element of mistaken blame is that the key failure in Iran was not one of intelligence at all (collection or analysis) but of policy. I mean this in two ways. First, in the narrow sense that it was a mistake for the United States to allow the shah to dictate America's intelligence collection in Iran. The reason that the collectors provided so little on the Iranian people, the opposition, and the mullahs was almost entirely because the United States had stopped trying to collect on those groups out of deference to the shah's wishes. A major reason that the analysts were wrong—and clung to what proved to be misguided assumptions—was that most of the intelligence they were provided was the recycled misinformation doled out by the SAVAK to its American liaison officers. Indeed, since the Iranian Revolution and entirely because of it, the United States has often gone out of its way to demonstrate that it will not allow a host government to dictate its intelligence operations or whom its diplomats can meet.[158]

The larger policy failure in Iran was to tie ourselves so tightly to the shah's regime. In Iran, we hitched our wagon to a falling star. That was our great mistake. As Gary Sick, among others, has pointed out, by 1978 no one in Washington wanted to make "the call," meaning that no one wanted to actually be the one to give voice to what everyone could see with his own eyes, that our entire position with the world's second-largest oil exporter in the critical Persian Gulf region was about to collapse.[159] There are times when it may be impossible for the United States to adopt such a course of action, and there are those who argue that this was the case with Iran in the 1960s and '70s. I do not believe that this was the case. If the Johnson, Nixon (especially), Ford, and early Carter administrations had been a bit less focused on the superpower competition and a bit more willing to treat the Third World on its own terms, we might have avoided not just the fiasco in Iran but others as well, including possibly the Vietnam War. Had we not invested virtually our entire Persian Gulf position in the shah's Iran, we might have been more willing and able to press him to reform (and thereby possibly even head off the revolution) and to distance ourselves from him when the people began to move against him.

The shah brought the Iranian Revolution on himself. At the strategic level, his many mistaken policies created tremendous animosity against his regime across the breadth of Iranian society. At a tactical level, he mishandled the manifestations of that unhappiness from start to finish in 1977–1978. While the Carter administration did not cover itself in glory during the revolution, ultimately there was nothing they could have done. Only the shah could save himself, and he simply was not up to the task. The United States could not run his country for him, nor could it invade and take it over to prevent his regime from collapsing.[160] Ultimately, the United States' greatest mistake was not in failing to prevent his fall but in following policies that made his fall so injurious to our interests.

All this said, the Iranian version of events is flat-out wrong. Especially by the early 1970s, the United States was not the arbiter of Iran's fate. Indeed, the United States had allowed itself to be reduced to a subordinate position in the U.S.-Iranian relationship. To the extent that anyone was manipulating anyone, it was the shah who was manipulating the United States through his ability to influence oil prices, his ability to determine where billions of petrodollars would be spent, his monopoly over strategic freedom of action in the Gulf region, his lobbying and propaganda network in the United States, and his control over virtually all of the information the United States received from his country.

The vast range of problems Iran experienced in the early 1970s had little to do with the United States. In walking through the list of things working at cross-purposes in Iran, especially in the realm of the economy and the country's social development, it is hard to find the United States involved at all— or even to imagine what the United States might have done to try to alleviate some of these problems. Iran's dislocations were almost entirely the product of the rapid growth of Iran's oil revenues, the poor planning of the shah's regime, and a wide range of extremely deleterious decisions made wholly by the shah and his ministers (and at times against foreign advice). Nevertheless, a case can be made that the United States was not entirely blameless. It would have been better for Iran if we had said "no" a bit more on arms and other sales. Although here, those who argue that the shah invariably would have just bought what he wanted elsewhere are almost certainly right.[161] That would have cost the United States billions of dollars, but it also might have hindered the Iranian people from developing the notion that Washington was *forcing* the shah to purchase American weapons. Then again, the Iranians have consistently shown themselves to be so wedded to their foreign conspiracies, and so impervious to real evidence to the contrary, that even that is hardly certain.

Moreover, contrary to the common Iranian theory, Iran's problems were not derived from close attention paid by Washington to Iran and the careful manipulation of Iranian affairs; indeed, quite the opposite. To the extent that the United States contributed to Iran's problems, they were generally caused by neglect on the part of Washington and an unwillingness (or inability) to get involved in Iranian affairs. On those few occasions after World War II when the United States really took an interest in Iranian affairs, it did so to push political, economic, and social reform. Although it has gotten very little credit from the Iranian people at the time or since, the Kennedy administration tried hard to persuade the shah to embark on real political and economic reforms intended to improve the lot of the Iranian people across the board and so stave off a revolution. So too did the Truman administration. The Johnson administration made much less of an effort, but it deserves credit both for sustaining most of Kennedy's ground-up developmental aid programs and for giving ground only grudgingly on the shah's demands for weaponry, heavy machinery, assistance to SAVAK, and other pernicious policies. The levee burst with the Nixon administration, which simply abdicated any responsibility for Iranian internal affairs, a policy continued by the Ford and Carter administrations.

The one area in which the United States' neglect of Iran was most damaging—and most difficult to forgive—was in the sphere of human rights. The shah's police state terrorized the Iranian populace. Tens of thousands may have been tortured by SAVAK, and at least thousands were murdered. Despite the efforts of Iranians and others to prove it, no evidence has ever been produced that the United States directly aided SAVAK in this grisly record or even provided general advice and assistance.[162] The United States never even sold Iran tear gas or riot-control equipment until late in the revolution.[163] But we did turn a deaf ear to those pleading for our help to stop these practices.

Ultimately, the United States was not culpable in the crimes committed by the shah's regime against the Iranian people; we were simply indifferent to them. A lot of other countries were equally indifferent, and our own ability to influence the shah's behavior was much less than it had once been. But we were not powerless. The mere hint that the Carter administration might make an issue out of human rights prompted the shah to take actions that he otherwise would not have. At the very least, we could have put more distance between ourselves and a regime whose misdeeds were impossible to disguise.

For this reason, the Iranian Revolution is an important lesson for American foreign policy more broadly. On many occasions the United States has ignored repression and human rights abuses by autocratic regimes in the name of expediency. The shah's regime lasted for another twenty-five years after Washington reinstalled him on his throne in 1953. At times, the shah's friendship paid off. He did help us in a number of ways in the Persian Gulf in the 1960s and '70s.[164] There have been other examples in history when our friendship with autocratic regimes paid off for even longer. But in the case of Iran, in 1978–1979, the autocracy was undone by its own inefficiencies and repression, and at that point, our friendship—our willingness to look the other way at the shah's terroristic reign—cost us dearly. Matched against the twenty-five years of benefit we derived from our alliance with the shah, we now have suffered through twenty-five years of harm produced by that very same friendship. And the harm has had real consequences, as the families of the 240

Marines killed in Beirut in 1983 and the 19 soldiers killed in the Khobar Towers attack in 1996 would all attest.

There may be times when the best interests of the United States demand a temporary alliance with repressive, autocratic regimes, but we should recognize that history has often demonstrated that there is a very real long-term cost for such policies. What's more, we should not see it as an either/or proposition—that either we support the dictator or we don't. The Kennedy administration's approach of maintaining strong ties to Iran while also pressing the shah (and aiding him) to reform suggests that it is possible to do both. Even under the Kennedy administration, the United States was unfairly blamed by the Iranian people, so it may have been that even had the policy been maintained, America still would have been a target for Khomeini and Iran's other revolutionaries, but successful reforms might have sufficiently defused the pressure that created the revolution. Even if it did not, it is hard to imagine that there would have been the same level of venom displayed by Iranians for the United States.

We must also recognize that, fairly or not, the United States is held responsible for actions that no other country is. The Europeans, the Japanese, and a host of other nations were equally cozy with the shah. An argument can be made that they were even worse offenders because they made virtually no effort to moderate the shah's behavior while the United States at least made some, however weak and sporadic by the end. Yet they came in for much less of the blame. As long as the United States is the world's only superpower, that pattern is likely to remain the norm. Because of our power, our wealth, and our role as the global leader, we will be held responsible for things that no one else is, and not just for what we have done but for what we have not done as well.

The United States has the capacity to act in ways and in situations that no other nation on earth does. While the common form of the Iranian complaint—that the United States was an active cause of Iran's misery—is unfair and unsubstantiated by the evidence, we can recognize that a more realistic version of their complaint has substance to it. The United States could have acted to curb the shah's behavior in a way that no other nation on Earth could have, and by failing to act, we did contribute to their suffering. I absolutely do not condone the murderous and misguided atrocities perpetrated by Iranians against Americans during the revolution and ever since, which they claim to be revenge for what they believe we did with the shah while he was in power, but I cannot say that we are entirely faultless in the anger that has produced their unpardonable behavior ever since. We do bear a portion of the blame for the misery that preceded the revolution, and so we also bear a portion of the blame for the misery that has followed.

CHAPTER 6

America Held Hostage

On the morning of January 17, 1979, the newspaper headlines in Tehran blared, "SHAH RAFT!" The shah has gone. Two weeks later, on the morning of February 2, they would likewise trumpet, "IMAM AMAD!" The Imam has come.[1]

The revolution had prevailed, and the old regime, which had become the focus of so much hatred, was finished. But revolutions are inherently destructive events. They are about tearing down the status quo, and the principal motivating force of the masses who make the revolution is a conviction that the status quo must go. Rare is the revolution in which the people know clearly beforehand what they want *instead of* the existing regime. This is why virtually every revolution is followed by a period of disorder. When the revolution succeeds, the institutions that preserved order in the past are gone, but new ones can be built only by people recognized as having the authority to act on behalf of the revolution and a clear sense of what it is that the revolution sought to create, not just what it sought to break. Typically, there is no shortage of people claiming they satisfy those criterion but, at least for a while, none who truly can.

So it was with the Iranian Revolution. A great many people had taken part in the revolution. In fact, one assessment contends that it was probably the most popularly engaged revolution in history, with 10 percent or more of the Iranian population participating in demonstrations and general strikes while only 2 percent of the French population and less than 1 percent of the Russian population had participated in their respective revolutions.[2] With so many people taking part and no long-standing organized opposition as an alternative to the shah's regime, it's not surprising that there seemed to be as many ideas about the postrevolutionary government as there were people taking part in it. Iranians had supported the revolution for religious reasons, economic reasons, political reasons, tribal reasons, ethnic reasons, and purely personal reasons, and the overlap among these different causes was often nonexistent.[3] In addition, the revolution had been quite bloody. Despite the shah's reluctance to employ maximal force to crush the revolt, roughly 3,000 people still died and many more were wounded during the fourteen-month revolution.[4] A last element adding to the chaos was that the shah had built a highly centralized state designed to be wholly responsive and loyal to him, and when he fell, that system collapsed. The revolutionaries had to embark upon a painful process of putting Iranian government and society back together again, and to do so in a manner consistent with the goals of the revolution.[5]

Moreover, Iranian society has a powerful tendency toward anarchy. Perhaps it is the independence inherent in a country where mountains and deserts carve up the land into tiny communities almost completely isolated from one another. Perhaps it was Iranians' experiences with centuries of weak and corrupt regimes that made ignoring or rebelling against government edicts relatively easy. Whatever the reason, a dominant pattern of their history is that the Iranian people have resented and resisted every government they have had over the last two millennia. And so for many Iranians, the revolution was welcomed simply because it got the central government off their backs. One American official tells the story that he traveled to Iran shortly after the revolution to survey several American government facilities throughout the country. During the course of that trip he headed out into the Qashqa'i tribal regions around Shiraz, where he found that the people were ecstatic about the revolution. In talking to them, he found that their enthusiasm for the revolution focused on two wonderful benefits: they no longer had to pay taxes, and they could now hunt in the shah's game preserves. They knew little about Khomeini and less about what should or could follow the shah—just as long as they did not have to pay taxes and could hunt in the shah's game preserves.[6]

The result of all this was chaos. Different groups all across the country took control of their school, their factory, their business, their town, their neighborhood, and so on. A great many people saw in the breakdown of order the opportunity to rectify personal grievances. Peasants attacked landlords, sometimes killing them on the spot; soldiers shot their commanding officers; groups arrogated to themselves various police and judiciary powers and arrested and executed people in the name of the revolution. The Kurds, Azeris,

Arabs, Turkomen, and Baluchis all tried to take control over their ethnic homelands. The whole country seemed ready to disintegrate.[7]

One group ultimately did prevail—the radical mullahs. They did so because they had three great advantages. They had the network of mosques and *hay'at*s that had performed so well in organizing people to demonstrate against the shah during the revolution. They had the powerful Iranian affinity for Islam and the widespread notion among the lower classes that if something was said to be "Islamic" it had to be good and if it was said to be "un-Islamic" it had to be bad. And they had Khomeini.

No one knew what role Khomeini would play in the future government, nor was there universal agreement that he was the undisputed leader of the revolution. But he was unquestionably the most popular figure among Iranians, by far. When he arrived back in Tehran on February 1, 3 million people lined the streets to greet him. When he retired to Qom after two weeks in the capital, the general expectation was that he would perform a purely supervisory role as "Imam," providing legitimacy to the new regime and little more. At that time, he gave no impression that he wanted to play a direct role in the management of the nation.[8] But very quickly it became clear that he would. Whether he had always intended to and merely feigned ambivalence or he really had no interest in governing but was not going to allow anyone else to take Iran in a direction he did not prescribe—thereby necessitating his assumption of power—may never be known. Whatever his intentions, Khomeini quickly became the arbiter of postrevolutionary Iran.

Since the revolution, Iran has never been the kind of monolithic state it was in the past. There has been a constant cacophony of voices all claiming to speak for the Islamic Republic and endless political infighting among individuals and groups. But right from the start, Khomeini emerged as the guiding light and defining spirit of Iran. He was the one person who could transcend the rancorous Iranian political battles and define the nation's course in a way that silenced most—and often all—opposition. While lesser figures bickered and squabbled over every conceivable issue, it was Khomeini who made the ultimate decisions, and it was Khomeini who molded the Islamic Republic in his own image. And it was Khomeini who ultimately drove the U.S.-Iranian confrontation that emerged.

The Ayatollah

Ruhollah Musavi Khomeini was already seventy-seven years old by the time he was thrust into the world's spotlight in 1979. He was born in the town of

Khomein outside Tehran (Shi'i clerics traditionally take the name of their place of origin; thus Iraq's Ayatollah Sistani, for example, took his name from his home province of Sistan in far eastern Iran). By the time he came to prominence, he was virtually a caricature of an anachronistic Middle Eastern zealot. "Khomeini was the archetype of the medieval prophet emerging from the desert with a fiery vision of absolute truth," Gary Sick has written. "His God was a harsh and vengeful deity—full of fury, demanding the eye and the tooth of retribution for human transgressions of divine law. Khomeini, in more than a decade of angry exile, had elaborated the doctrine of a utopian Islamic state and then endowed it with sacred inevitability. This philosophical system was as stark as it was comprehensive. It held the answers to all questions, and the answers were absolute and final."[9]

The core of Khomeini's political philosophy was a concept known as *velayat-e faqih,* which means "rule of the jurisprudent." Khomeini was a devotee of Plato (a rarity among mullahs), and in his utopian Islamic society, the state would be ruled over by a theocratic philosopher-king—a man so learned in Islamic law that all of his peers and all of his countrymen would recognize that only he could provide "right-minded" guidance. Michael Fischer notes that Khomeini was never able to cite textual bases for the concept of *velayat-e faqih,* largely because it was derived essentially from *The Republic* rather than the Quran.[10] Unlike Mohammad Mosaddeq, who deviated from traditional Shi'i thought by emphasizing individual and collective reason to the point where it became mere expediency, Khomeini broke with the same traditions but in the opposite direction, emphasizing that because Islam provides a complete system of law and morality, only the most learned in Islam could govern properly. Although most foreigners tend to see Khomeini as the very embodiment of dogmatic Shi'i Islamic theology, in actuality, this notion ran directly contrary to the mainstream tradition in Shi'i Islam, which held that all governments were illegitimate as long as the twelfth imam remained in hiding, and therefore it was unseemly for mullahs to involve themselves in politics. Khomeini insisted on precisely the opposite.[11]

Not every Iranian idolized Khomeini or believed him worthy of the title "Imam." Many of the clergy, including Iran's seniormost ayatollahs—the *marjas* Shariatmadari, Golpaygani, and Najafi-Mar'ashi—thought his ideas virtually sacrilegious and his methods extraordinarily dangerous. They also feared that by mixing Islam with politics, Khomeini would ultimately turn many people off to religion (a fear that took two decades to realize but did ultimately prove prophetic).[12] Other Iranians did not care for Khomeini, his methods, or his ideas but had supported him simply because he gave voice to their feelings about the shah's regime. Charles Kurzman quotes an Iranian intellectual as telling him, "I hate Khomeini, but if anyone says anything bad about him I get angry. Why, you ask? Because I hate the shah even more."[13]

Nevertheless, Khomeini held a magnetic appeal for a great many segments of Iranian society. The Iranian body politic has traditionally revered piety, austerity, and consistency to a specific set of values among its leaders, and Khomeini practiced each to an extreme. This alone made him seem virtually messianic in his devotion to his ideals and to his religion. Khomeini also had the gift of being able to speak to the people of Iran in their own language and in the idiom of Islam, which they found comforting. He stressed that Islam offered a complete guide to life; in a modern world where many Iranians felt that they had lost their bearings, this too was reassuring. He also managed to be all things to all people: the *bazaaris* saw him as the quintessential mullah-champion of their interests. Ignorant of most of his specific beliefs, the modern middle class misconstrued him to be a reformer who would complete the work Mosaddeq had left unfinished. The lower classes saw him as a revolutionary who would undo all of the injustice of the old system and raise them up to be equals with the rest of society in every way. Even many among the traditional land-owning classes saw him as a reactionary (a good thing, as far as they were concerned) clergyman who would re-create the old system the way it had been before the Pahlavis had ruined things. And, of course, all Iranians appreciated his single-minded determination to oust the shah and extirpate the American influence from Iran.

Over time, Khomeini would demonstrate that virtually every aspiration attributed to him (with the exception of his personal austerity and his blind hatred for the shah and the United States) was untrue—but it never seemed to matter. His reputation for piety and devotion, coupled with his fiery charisma, left Iranians blinded to the reality. Although he had made no secret of his intention to create a theocratic system based on the radical concept of *velayat-e faqih,* few during or even immediately after the revolution were aware of it and most simply assumed that the "Islamic Republic" he kept talking about was whatever they hoped it would be. It was the best of all possible worlds, and each individual inevitably defined that differently. Even fifteen years after his death, Khomeini has the same hold over many Iranians.[14] In his book *Persian Pilgrimages,* Afshin Molavi tells of a cab driver and part-time tour guide in Mashhad who explained to him that "I supported Khomeini because he promised us a better economic life."[15] Of course, nothing could have been further from the truth: in response to an aide pressing him to concentrate more on alleviating Iran's economic problems, Khomeini had famously retorted, "We did not make the revolution to lower the price of watermelons." But Khomeini remains the embodiment of all good things to many Iranians—whatever those good things may be.

Khomeini was obsessively—even mindlessly—opposed to the United States. At times he got so carried away by his own hatred that he said things that on their face were farcical, such as proclaiming shortly after his return from exile that "The Great U.S. Satan has dominated our country for the past 2,500 years."[16] Throughout the course of the revolution and thereafter, Iranian moderates among the leftists, the liberals, and even the clergy were willing to accept a new relationship with the United States. Khomeini simply refused and blocked every effort at reconciliation. Khomeini redefined the goal of the revolution as the total cleansing of American influence from Iran, including America's puppet, the shah. Consequently, the success of the revolution was predicated upon the hardest possible line toward the United States, and anyone suggesting moderation was by definition betraying the revolution. Although at times Khomeini referred to the shah as "Yazid," the caliph who had had Husayn martyred at Karbala back in the seventh century, more often it was Jimmy Carter he called Yazid, while the shah was merely "Shimr"—the general who had actually struck the blows against Husayn and his companions.[17] The Imam's constant theme about the United States was that (echoing Mosaddeq about the British), "All our problems come from America."[18]

Grasping at Straws

In the chaos that followed the fall of the shah, all sides made bids to gain control over the country. For his part, Khomeini remained determined to tear down the last vestiges of the shah's regime but seemed tentative about how much to involve himself in creating a new one—or precisely what that new government should look like. Iran's leftists and liberals saw this as the moment to assert themselves and take what they saw as their natural place in defining the new political structure. After all, they had started the revolution, their guerrilla groups had played a key role during the protests, and they—not the benighted mullahs—were the ones with the political acumen to organize and run a new government. Of course, the radical clergy had other ideas and, with or without direction from Khomeini, set out trying to build a theocratic state. Meanwhile, Shapour Bakhtiar's government, the last appointed by the shah before his departure on January 16, struggled to hold on to power. But Bakhtiar's fate depended on the Iranian military, and the Iranian military was looking to America.

As noted in the previous chapter, Washington woke up late to the fact that the shah's regime was truly collapsing. The Carter administration's efforts to try to stiffen Mohammad Reza Shah's spine were too tardy to have any impact (and almost certainly would not have been decisive even if they had come much earlier in the crisis, unless the shah had been of a very different mind regarding the use of indiscriminate force). Not until the end of December did Washington begin to talk seriously about the need for a military crackdown—and about trying to get the shah to step aside and let the generals take charge if he remained unwilling to order such a crackdown. Only at this point did the divisions within the Carter administration manifest themselves openly. Brzezinski and others on the NSC staff essentially argued for a military takeover, while the State Department—led by both Secretary Vance and Ambassador Sullivan—argued for supporting the moderate liberals.[19]

As the shah's regime disintegrated in early January, their debates became rancorous, but in retrospect, both groups were operating under completely false assumptions and neither approach was likely to have had any chance of success. The NSC position assumed that the shah's armed forces were somehow capable of taking over the country. To encourage and help plan a military takeover, the White House ordered General Robert "Dutch" Huyser to Tehran on January 4. Huyser was to be the new Kim Roosevelt. Huyser had extensive contacts with the Iranian armed forces, and he took his mission very seriously. However, within just a few weeks, he was forced to concede that the Iranian armed forces could not do the job: the military continued to lose roughly 1,000 soldiers to desertion or defection every day, leaving the officers unsure of the loyalty of their troops; the generals were deeply divided and some were already cutting deals with different opposition factions; and there were no plans for gaining control over the key nodes of the country and no real ability or willingness to conduct such planning. Naturally, some Iranian generals looked to Washington to do it for them, but the United States lacked the capacity (let alone the desire) to take over the boiling cauldron of Iran. If the Iranian military could not do so, no one could.[20]

On the other hand, the State Department's position was equally misguided. At the same time that Huyser was dispatched to try to mount a military takeover, State reached the conclusion that Khomeini was not a threat to the United States because he could not govern; he would have to install the middle-class liberals in power because (echoing their own assumptions) only they had the skills to build a new government and run the country.[21] Some State Department Iran experts went so far as to argue that the result might actually be even better for Iran and the United States than the shah's regime had been.[22] Thus, while Huyser was working with Iran's generals to try to push the military into a coup d'état, Ambassador Sullivan was working just as feverishly to help the various secular oppositionists, and particularly the liberals, pull together a coalition government of their own. Very quickly, this too was proven to be a pipe dream—Khomeini demonstrated that he could make or break any government, and only he would determine who would rule.

President Carter took the obvious middle position: he hoped that the State Department was right that Iran's liberals would be able to take and hold power—and he wanted to give that approach a chance—but he was willing to have the Iranian military mount a coup if the liberals were not up to the task. Ultimately, Brzezinski and Vance would no doubt have said the same thing (and had done so in early November); where they all disagreed was on timing. Brzezinski felt that the government was already collapsing and the moment was at hand for the military to act. Vance still thought that it was further away and the U.S. should concentrate on assisting the liberals. The president fell somewhere in between, believing that there was still a chance for the liberals to succeed but that the time was short enough that they needed to start hedging their bets by sending Huyser to stiffen the Iranian military's spine and start preparing for the coup they all feared would be necessary. Huyser himself noted this in his memoirs, recalling about the written orders he was sent that "there was disagreement about its meaning within the Cabinet. Brzezinski wanted it to convey to the Iranian military a green light to stage a military coup, and considered that it did so. President Carter intended it to convey such a meaning as a last resort."[23] Huyser himself tended to act in accord with the president's vision, trying to convince the military to stand by the Bakhtiar government while simultaneously encouraging them to start planning and preparing for a military takeover if that became necessary—only to quickly realize that the Iranian armed forces were capable of neither by early January.[24]

It is worth noting here that, just as many Iranians feared, the United States did try to intervene to stop the Iranian Revolution. At the time, the revolutionaries were convinced that the United States intended to replay the events of 1953 by overthrowing the new, popular government and reinstalling the monarchy. Many of their actions at the time were intended to deter or prevent just such an eventuality. It seems paranoid to read about their fears and undertakings now—and they were paranoid. But as the old saw goes, "Just because you're paranoid doesn't mean that someone's not out to get you." And we were out to get them. President Carter did so reluctantly, and only as a last resort, but not only was he prepared to support a military coup, he sent General Huyser to Iran to make it happen. The central purpose of the Huyser mission was to try to convince the Iranian military to take over the country and snuff out the revolution, and to assist them in doing so. The fact that Cyrus Vance was not as gung ho as John Foster Dulles, or that it failed to live up to the success of Operation Ajax, does not make it any less real. Here was more fodder to feed the conspiracy theories that already consumed Iran's collective psyche.

The Scramble for Iran

On February 9, the fate of both Bakhtiar and the Army were sealed. The *homafar*s (warrant officers) at Doshan Tappeh Air Force Base, who were staunch supporters of the revolution (the *homafar*s had the best technical skills but were treated as second-class citizens in the shah's military), tried to take control of the base. Elements of the Imperial Guard intervened to stop them, prompting the *homafar*s to call for help from other revolutionary elements. Leftist guerrillas, particularly the MEK and the Feda'iyan, answered their call, and in a two-day pitched battle, the Imperial Guard was forced to retreat. At that point, the shah's armed forces were broken. If the vaunted Imperial Guard could not stand up to the hordes of ragtag revolutionaries, who could?[25] Defections throughout the ranks increased dramatically, and many officers put their entire units at the disposal of the new revolutionary authorities. If the Army could not support and protect him, Shapour Bakhtiar was also finished. With Khomeini railing against him ever since he had returned from France on February 1, Bakhtiar recognized that his days were numbered and fled. The new Revolutionary Council declared his government dissolved and authorized Mehdi Bazargan, another liberal oppositionist, but one with strong ties to the Islamists, to put together a new, revolutionary government.

At the U.S. Embassy and at the State Department, Bazargan's appointment was met with relief and applause. He seemed to be just what the United States wanted and precisely what State and the embassy had claimed was inevitable: Khomeini would recognize that a theocracy was impossible and would turn to friendly liberals to rule instead.[26] The embassy redoubled its efforts to develop a new relationship with the Bazargan government and to help him consolidate power—limited though America's ability to do anything in revolutionary Iran was. However, their vindication was to prove short-lived.

Bazargan's key problem was that he was not in charge of very much. There were a great many people and organizations doing things in Iran, but few of them looked to him for orders or even guidance. Most simply did what they believed best, at times based on their own interpretations of statements made by Khomeini or other leaders. Many had guns, money, and followers and listened to no one but their own chiefs. Certainly the leftist groups, led by the MEK and the Feda'iyan, fell into this category. The Tudeh Party also came back from the dead and set about rebuilding its strength on the ground. Then there were the tribes, which generally reasserted control over their traditional lands and often wanted nothing to do with a new central government. The Kurds, Azeris, Baluchis, and some Arabs in Khuzestan also began to agitate for autonomy, if not outright independence.

However, the greatest challenges to Bazargan's authority were from the various Islamic organizations that seemed to spontaneously emerge across the country. Of these, the most important were:

- **The Revolutionary Council.** Originally composed of seven mullahs chosen by Khomeini, seven secular oppositionists (including Bazargan), and two generals considered loyal to the revolution, this body was intended to unify the various opposition movements and bring coherence to the process of constructing a new government. They were granted supreme administrative and legislative authority, and it was this group that named and approved Bazargan as the new prime minister—once Khomeini had publicly approved him for the post. When Bazargan and his colleagues left the Council to run the new provisional government, however, Khomeini filled the vacant slots with more people loyal to himself. As a result, very quickly the Council became little more than an instrument for the radical clergy to exercise control.[27]

- **The *komitehs*** (literally revolutionary "committees"). *Komitehs* were groups of Islamists that sprouted throughout the country in bands of anywhere from a few dozen to several hundred and put themselves in control of something—a piece of land, a city block, an institution, anything at all. Many of the members of the *komitehs* were **Hizballahis** (Hizballah means "Party of God" and comes from a reference in the Quran; they were also known at times as **"Ansar-e Hizballah,"** or "Partisans of the Party of God"), the most extreme adherents to Khomeini's brand of militant Islamism, and handled security and "enforcement" for the *komitehs*. (This is *not* the familiar Hizballah terrorist group from Lebanon, which is discussed in chapter 7.) Most *komitehs* were based around a local mosque or mullah. In Tehran alone there were at least 1,000. They arrogated to themselves the powers of justice, administration, security, and enforcement. They took the law into their own hands by setting up roadblocks and checkpoints and "arresting" or executing anyone doing anything they construed as un-Islamic or antirevolutionary—and they had terrifyingly broad definitions of these activities. For instance, chess was deemed antirevolutionary because of its abstract association with monarchy; thus possession of a chess set could be a capital offense. They were somewhat similar to the Soviets who emerged after the Russian Revolution, but they were often more bloodthirsty, more arbitrary, and less responsive to central control.[28]

- **The Pasdaran** (Sepah-e Pasdaran-e Enqelab-e Islami, or "Islamic Revolutionary Guards Corps" [IRGC]). The Revolutionary Guards were created by Khomeini in May 1979, after attacks on several key Khomeinist leaders, and were charged with restoring order and defending the revolution. Although one of their first responsibilities was to fight the MEK, a number of the original groups that were formed into the IRGC had been part of the Islamist branch of the MEK. From an initial muster of 6,000, they grew to more than 100,000 within a year and were used to quash autonomy movements by Kurds, Turkomen, and Baluchis. They also served as a counterpart to the regular armed forces, which was repeatedly purged but never trusted because of its original ties to the Pahlavis and long American tutelage.[29] Later, Khomeini would create the **Basij** (Haid-e Basij-e Mostazafan, or "mobilization forces"), as a vehicle for men to make themselves available as needed to the revolution without becoming full-time Pasdars—something like a reserve component for the Revolutionary Guards.

- **The *bonyad*s** (Islamic charitable foundations). With the shah's state gone, there was a great deal of official and royal family property and wealth left still in the country. The radical mullahs established the *bonyad*s to administer these assets, ostensibly for the direct benefit of the Iranian people. In practice, the *bonyad*s came into the possession of immense wealth and economic resources and put them at the disposal of Khomeini and his followers—or used them to line their own pockets. The most famous and powerful of all was the Bonyad-e Mostazafan (the Foundation for the Dispossessed), which took control of the former Pahlavi Foundation as well as hundreds of companies, factories, housing units, agricultural lands, and substantial holdings in the West, amounting to tens of billions of dollars.[30]

- **The revolutionary tribunals.** These sprang up spontaneously all across Iran, usually led by a mullah who took upon himself the role of judge, jury, and prosecutor. They charged people with offenses such as "un-Islamic behavior" and "offending the revolution" and meted out biblical sentences: two middle-aged women accused of prostitution were buried up to their chests and then stoned to death. Khomeini himself set the tone for the tribunals in pronouncing that "Criminals should not be tried. The trial of a criminal is against human rights. Human rights demand that we should have killed them in the first place when it became known that they were criminals."[31] Hojjat-ol Islam Sadeq Khalkhali, Tehran's notorious "hanging judge" (who had absolutely no legal training), was famous for such wisdom as "There is no room in the Revolutionary Courts for defense lawyers because they keep quoting laws to play for time, and this tries the patience of the people" and "Human rights mean that unsuitable individuals should be liquidated so that others can live free."[32] In many cases, a trial in one of these tribunals consisted of nothing more than the "judge" reading the accusation and then sentencing the defendant—often to immediate death. In the first eighteen months of the revolution, they were responsible for the summary execution of at least 1,500 people.[33]

- **The Islamic Republic Party.** Created in 1979 with Khomeini's blessing by his disciple Ayatollah Mohammad Beheshti, the IRP became the principal vehicle by which the radical mullahs exerted their will and ultimately gained control over the revolution and then the state. By bringing together virtually all of Khomeini's top lieutenants, they also made themselves the titular authority over all of the other revolutionary institutions. Over time, the *komiteh*s, Pasdaran, revolutionary tribunals, *bonyad*s, and even the Revolutionary Council came under the control of the IRP members. When that happened, despite the fractiousness of the IRP, their opposition made it impossible for Bazargan (or anyone else) to set an independent course because the residual governmental structure simply could not compete with the resources and sway of this lineup.[34]

Nevertheless, Khomeini's campaign to gain full control over Iran's levers of power continued to proceed slowly. Again, we do not understand why: it may have been because he had not yet decided to turn Iran into a full-blown theocracy (although even if that was the case, his minions were making it well nigh inevitable by creating these various institutions); or, as seems more likely, he remained unsure that the Iranian people would accept his vision and so decided to implement it slowly and methodically. There were considerable numbers of Iranians who admired the leftists and the liberals, and the MEK and the other leftist militias had won considerable praise for their role in defeating the Imperial Guard in February. Thus, Khomeini did not feel he could simply sweep them aside; they had to be marginalized incrementally. In March, the new regime held a referendum with a single question: "Do you want the monarchy to be replaced by an Islamic Republic?" Khomeini refused to allow any other system of government to be put on the referendum, and at that time, few Iranians had any idea what the Imam meant by an "Islamic Republic." In protest, many of the secular groups boycotted the referendum, including the MEK, the Feda'iyan, the Tudeh, the Kurds, the National Front, Bazargan's Iran Freedom Movement, and Ayatollah Shariatmadari's followers. Nevertheless, 20 million people voted, and 98 percent voted "yes."[35]

This allowed Khomeini and his supporters to call for the creation of a constitutional committee to give substance to the people's will. There were enough secularists on this committee so that the original Constitution looked fairly similar to the 1906 Constitution, but the liberals and leftists complained bitterly all the same. This turned out to be a huge mistake. It allowed Khomeini to create an Assembly of Experts to revise the Constitution, and the IRP used its various levers of power (including violence and intimidation) to ensure that it had a strong majority in this body. The result was a new Constitution, modeled very much along the lines of Khomeini's vision of an Islamic Republic and centered on the concept of *velayat-e faqih*.[36]

The Embassy Is Taken

It is against this background of Iranian domestic political struggles and fears of American intervention that the infamous hostage crisis played out. An indication of the importance of the political context was provided by a prior incident. On Valentine's Day 1979, just two weeks after Khomeini's return from exile, 150 members of the Marxist Feda'iyan-e Khalq attacked and overran the U.S. Embassy in Tehran. Khomeini and the radical clergy immediately denounced the attack. One of Khomeini's closest followers, Ibrahim Yazdi, rounded up several hundred students at Tehran University and led a counterattack that freed the embassy. They restored all of the American personnel and criticized the behavior of the leftists.[37]

On November 4 of the same year, a group of three hundred or more Islamist students again attacked and overran the embassy. They took sixty-six American diplomats and Marines hostage (one would be released in July 1980 for medical reasons, while thirteen women and African Americans were released just two weeks after the takeover in protest of America's discriminatory racial and gender policies; so the students announced).[38] They physically and psychologically abused many of the hostages.[39] They did it with the connivance of another of Khomeini's close followers, and within thirty-six hours of the takeover, Khomeini had given this identical act his seal of approval.[40]

The ostensible difference between the two takeovers was that on October 22, the United States had admitted the shah, who was dying of cancer, for medical treatment. But in February it had been widely expected that the shah would eventually make his way to the United States, and at that time, none of the revolutionary leaders had said a word about it. Moreover, during the hostage crisis, both the students and Iran's Islamist leadership often mentioned America's admitting of the shah as almost an afterthought in their thinking. Nor did they release the hostages when the shah was forced to leave the United States after his medical procedures were completed on December 15 or when he died in Egypt on July 27.

In understanding the hostage crisis, it is worth starting with the motives of the students themselves.[41] They were a ragtag lot, assembled just two days before the attack by a half-dozen ringleaders. They were generally very religious, ardent followers of Khomeini—although not members of any particular party—idealistic, and deeply naive. The inspiration for the attack apparently was a pair of sentences in a statement by the Imam that "It is incumbent upon students in the secondary schools and universities and the theology schools to expand their attacks against America and Israel. Thus America will be forced to return the criminal, deposed Shah."[42] But what drove all of their thinking was the memory of the 1953 coup. Their conversations were laced with references to Mosaddeq and his fall at the hands of the CIA. It is unclear why, but they believed that admitting the shah was the start of a new American covert operation to thwart the revolution.[43] They decided to take the embassy both as a means of forestalling a new coup and to avenge the earlier overthrow.

In that latter sense, admitting the shah was principally viewed by the students as a further—and deliberate—humiliation of Iran by the United States that demanded a response. For instance, one of the leaders of the student group convinced another to take part by asserting simply, "The U.S. has decided to admit the shah. Look, do we need any more proof about what they think of the Iranian nation [*sic*]. There may even be another plot under way against us."[44] Likewise, Massoumeh Ebtekar, who eventually emerged as the spokesperson for the students, has since written that "The young men and women who participated in the embassy takeover did so based on their conviction that their action was in line with the Imam's policy. We believed then that action was essential; we were determined to take a stand against past and possible future humiliation by the United States."[45] Another student leader, challenged by one of the hostages as to why the students were taking over the embassy blurted out, "To teach the American government and the CIA a lesson, so it will keep its hands off other countries, and particularly Iran!"[46] One of the hostages, Colonel Charles Scott of the defense attaché's office, found the same in talking to his captors:

It was a situation where truth didn't matter. Perceptions were much more important. A large portion of the Iranian people believed that the United States had the ability to pull strings and return the Shah to power. Iranians believed that we were about 1,000 times more powerful in directing their internal affairs than we ever were. The truth is that at this time we had practically no influence in Iran. Our only purpose for being there was to try and establish a relationship with the new regime. But when the Shah was admitted to the United States, we opened Pandora's box for the hardline revolutionaries. They could say, "Look what America did in 1953! They're getting ready to do it again! Another coup is in the wind! They're going to return the Shah to power!" That accusation held a lot of water with a lot of people. Most Iranians believed it. It's hard for many Americans to understand that the entire Iranian population felt wronged by the Shah, and by America's support of the Shah. After he was admitted to the United States, they wanted to strike out at something American. You could search the entire country over, and there was only one target that they could attack. That was the American embassy in Tehran.[47]

Even today, Iranians seeking to justify the taking of the embassy voice this theme as the central issue of the embassy takeover. In August 2000, Hojjat-ol Islam Mohammad Mousavi Khoeiniha, who was Khomeini's liaison to the students in the embassy but later went on to become the publisher of a leading reformist newspaper supportive of Mohammad Khatami, would write, "The historical memory of the Iranian nation, and in particular the revolutionaries, of the United States–inspired coup of August 1953, that resulted in the overthrow of Dr. Mohammad Mossadegh, needs an honest appraisal. That event resulted in the return of Shah Mohammad Reza Pahlavi to Iran and the continuation of his dictatorial regime. When all the implications of this tragic episode in our history are taken into consideration, an unbiased arbiter would surely judge the students' action (in 1979) has [*sic*] having been the only real avenue for seeking justice from the American government."[48]

In short, for the students who took the embassy, for the Iranian revolutionary officials who supported them, and for much of Iran, the taking of the embassy was a response to the 1953 coup against Mosaddeq. To some extent, it was about preventing a repeat performance. However, what stands out from all of the various statements made both at the time and since is that a far more compelling cause for the Iranians was revenge. It was an act of vengeance for the 1953 coup, designed to humiliate the United States, to cause pain to the American people, and to assuage the angry psychological scars that the Iranian people still bore from that event.

Although Ebtekar and most of the students adamantly believe that Khomeini did not know about the plan to take the embassy until after it had happened, there is some reason to believe that he did.[49] The students deliberately brought Khoeiniha into the plot and asked him to seek the Imam's blessing for it. He later told them that he was certain the Imam would approve but that it would be best for Khomeini if he could honestly say that he had not known about it beforehand. Of course, that is precisely what a good subordinate says when he has informed his superior and the superior wants the action to proceed but wants to be able to disavow any knowledge of it afterward if it turns out to be a fiasco. Thus, Khomeini could allow it to move forward and judge after the fact whether it was serving his purpose. Despite all of his leadership of the revolution and his willingness to hew fixedly to a course when it was important to him, at other times—particularly on tactical issues of how to achieve a goal—Khomeini "led from the rear," waiting to see which course was most popular and then embracing it.

Moreover, there is evidence that he did know: prior to the student attack, the police who normally ringed the embassy were nowhere to be found, suggesting that Khomeini or someone else very senior was aware of the preparations and wanted to see it succeed.[50] Likewise, one group of Americans was able to escape the embassy during the takeover but was later accosted in the street by either Pasdars or Hizballahis (they were dressed in camouflage uniforms and were carrying Iranian Army G-3 assault rifles) and marched at gunpoint back to the embassy.[51] Clearly, the students had some help from people in high places. Ultimately, however, this is not a terribly germane point: what matters most is that in less than two days, Khomeini had enthusiastically blessed the takeover, even after having condemned the same act just nine months earlier.[52]

Khomeini's motives were doubtless far more complicated than those of the students. First, these were *his* loyalists, not godless Marxists like those who had taken it in February, and they were important to his ongoing struggle with the various secular groups. Approving of the takeover in February would have been another important victory for the leftists, and Khomeini was trying to weaken them, not strengthen them. Although disavowing the students who took the embassy the second time might have hurt Khomeini in a very mild way, the more important issue is that once it became clear that it was very popular, embracing it allowed Khomeini to ride the coattails of his student followers.[53]

Khomeini's obsessive hatred for the United States was a central motivating force in his decision making. He was as devoutly anti-American as he was devoutly Muslim. Anti-Americanism was not a tool he used to achieve power; rather, it was one of his primary goals—and to some extent, the achievement of power was an instrument toward achieving that goal. Khomeini repeatedly stated that Iran was ready to accept collective martyrdom rather than "submit" to America—and he said exactly what he meant. (His behavior throughout the Iran-Iraq War confirmed his willingness to force Iran to endure terrible damage in pursuit of his cosmic struggle with the infidels.)[54] Moreover, "Imam Khomeini believed that the shah was a puppet installed and supported by America to secure its regional interests," Ebtekar explains. "Once he had been ousted, the revolution would naturally have to confront imperialism face to face if it hoped to hold to its original path. In this context we could understand what the Imam meant when he described the embassy takeover as a 'second revolution, greater than the first.' The first confronted the despotic dynasty and brought it down. The second took dead aim at the root of all our sufferings, the imperialist system itself." Given that Khomeini was certain he would have to confront the United States itself at some point, he may have reasoned that the embassy takeover—with genuinely self-motivated students leading the way—was the best tactic to rally the entire nation to the cause.[55]

Khomeini may have had other interests as well. A year after the revolution, Iran was not in terrific shape. Certainly it was not the Islamic Paradise that many Iranians thought they had been promised. Inflation and unemployment were both soaring, while skilled Iranians—and their money—were fleeing the country as quickly as they could. Industry and key services were crippled by this loss of personnel and capital. Three counterrevolutionary plots were discovered during the summer. The revolution's key supporters remained fanatically devoted, but there was considerable grumbling among the masses, and the middle class watched unhappily as the secular oppositionists were systematically forced out of positions of authority.[56]

Iran's economy had not recovered much at all and in many ways was worse off than it had been under the shah. Iran's oil production had dropped disastrously as a result of the massive disruption and neglect from the strikes, the revolution, and the loss of foreign oil workers. In addition, Khomeini and many of those around him were deeply ambivalent about Iranian oil exports, reasoning that it was the oil that had brought on so many of Iran's problems with the West, and so they did not make restoring Iranian oil production a high priority—not only was the revolution not about the price of melons, it was also not about the price of gas either. Consequently, Iranian oil production dropped from 5.9 million bpd in 1978 to just 1.3 million bpd just before the start of the Iran-Iraq War in September 1980.[57] Likewise, Iran's new ideologically driven government created other problems for the economy. For instance, when a dispute arose with Moscow (another government the Imam did not care for) over a plan to more than double Iranian natural gas sales, the Iranian response was to simply stop selling natural gas altogether—depriving the country of roughly

$100 million per year at 1979 prices.[58] It may have been the case that Khomeini was deliberately seeking a confrontation with the United States as a way of diverting people's attention from these mundane problems—problems for which his ideology had few answers and that were creating divisions within the revolutionary leadership—and instead shift the focus back to their collective hatred of the United States.[59]

Finally, there were the interests of the various political groups jostling for power within the Iranian hierarchy. The hostage taking was a disaster for the moderates, both secular and clerical, and a godsend for the radical mullahs, Khomeini included. Just days before, Bazargan and Ibrahim Yazdi had met with Zbigniew Brzezinski in Algiers, where they had both gone for Algeria's independence day celebration. Attacking the United States was a perfect way for the radicals to undermine Bazargan and the moderates, who were now publicly associated with the United States. Indeed, the day after Khomeini gave his ringing endorsement of the takeover, Mehdi Bazargan finally tendered his resignation, noting that he simply could not accept responsibility for the consequences of this action.[60] The seizure itself and the 444-day standoff also allowed the radicals to smoke out the moderates and then disgrace them. Anyone who could not hold to the Imam's line for the entire crisis immediately was branded an accomplice of the United States. And eventually, all of the moderates recognized the damage being done to Iran by the ongoing crisis and argued for ending it. In the highly charged atmosphere of the standoff with the United States over the hostages, extreme anti-Americanism became the only litmus test for loyalty to the revolution, and this allowed the radicals to push out many of their more moderate rivals.[61]

In addition, by taking over the embassy so quickly, the students prevented the staff from destroying all of the classified documents stored there. Many of the most sensitive were obliterated, but others were merely shredded. In an act of remarkable cleverness and determination, teams of students painstakingly reassembled these documents and eventually published eighty-one volumes' worth, along with their Farsi translations. Although the students, and the Iranian leaders, would insist that the documents betrayed widespread and ongoing American interference in Iranian affairs, in truth they were rather unremarkable. Indeed, they demonstrated the very limited range of contacts the embassy had with Iranian society. As an example, Ebtekar claims that "One of the non-classified documents we found described American cultural policy in our country. We interpreted the document as a plan for long-term cultural disintegration." The document in question is actually just three paragraphs long. The third and key paragraph reads, "In brief, the revolution was against privilege and rapid Westernization. I believe it is essential that we keep this firmly in view as we go about trying to promote U.S. interests by entering into ongoing communication processes with influential Iranians. There are, of course, specific communication tensions, but the deep-seated tensions stemming from revolt against privilege and Westernization underlie most of the other limited tensions we may address."[62] This was the master plan to subvert Iran's culture.

If the documents provided less than compelling evidence of American plots, they did furnish plenty of undeniable evidence of secret contacts between embassy personnel and various moderate Iranian leaders. In none of the documents was there even a hint that these figures ever offered to sell out their country to the United States. Instead, they simply indicated a desire to have good relations with the United States and often sought assistance from America in convincing the shah to compromise; making peace with the armed forces; securing spare parts for Iran's American-built weaponry; and balancing against the Russians, whom they feared were again aiding the Kurds.[63] However, what the students and other Iranians objected to was the tone taken by these Iranian leaders in the conversations. The documents described that, in most of their conversations with members of the American Embassy, they would make remarks about how other Iranians were going too far in their anti-American zeal and that this was hurting Iran. Here's how the students saw it: "The Iranian side would display a sense of inferiority in the face of the West and express its eagerness—or the eagerness of its government—to enjoy the blessings of the United States."[64] Again, what mattered was not what actually was said but how; they chose to interpret the tone of the remarks as being somehow submissive to the United States, and this is what was beyond the pale. Consequently, the takeover of the embassy, and the revelation of these contacts, proved to be a tremendous boon to the radicals in their campaign to oust the moderates and take complete control over the Iranian government.

America's Dilemmas

The seizure of the embassy was hardly a surprise to the U.S. government. In fact, it had been long expected. After the Valentine's Day attack, American officials from top to bottom recognized that the embassy and its personnel were a target for retaliation by various factions of Iranians, all of whom seemed to have very different agendas, goals, and philosophies but were in complete agreement on one thing: that America was responsible for all of Iran's problems. They also recognized that admitting the shah to the United States (as they had promised when he departed Iran in January) could trigger such an attack. The shah's influential friends David Rockefeller and Henry Kissinger called President Carter to urge him to admit the shah, and Carter reportedly responded, "What will you do when they seize our embassy?"[65] On another occasion, Carter famously remarked that he did not want the shah in the United States playing tennis while Americans in Tehran were being kidnapped or killed.[66] After the February attack, the embassy had sent home its dependents and the overwhelming majority of its personnel (going from a staff of roughly 1,400 down to about 50) and greatly reduced the amount of classified documentation on hand, because of the risk.[67] In fact, Washington-area Iran experts and the embassy repeatedly warned that if the United States were to admit the shah, the Iranians would likely attack the embassy.[68] Consequently, many of the hostages later said that they had felt betrayed when they heard that the Carter administration had allowed the shah in for medical treatment on October 22.

In the administration's defense, the shah was desperately ill and his doctors stated that the surgery could be performed only in the United States; what's more, many felt (and were being encouraged in this view by David Rockefeller and Kissinger) that the United States owed this small gesture to a man who had been America's ally for many decades.[69] President Carter's own humanitarian impulses also weighed in his decision; as he would later say, the United States had always been a haven for those in distress and the thought of rescinding his earlier invitation to the shah now that he was so gravely ill pained him deeply.[70] The United States informed the Iranian government and made it clear that the shah would stay only as long as was necessary for the operation and immediate recovery.[71] Nevertheless, the administration could have taken additional precautions with the embassy, such as further reducing its manning and documents (both had been allowed to creep back up after the February events) and devising contingency plans in the event of an attack during the weeks between September 28, when the administration first learned of the shah's medical predicament, and October 22, when the shah was admitted.[72]

The taking of the hostages finally got the attention of the American people. In truth, this was a key motive of the students. It was part of their desire for revenge for the 1953 coup. All through 1979, militant Iranians had been frustrated by the fact that the American media and the American people simply were not paying attention to them and to their revolution. The sudden drop in Iranian oil production as a result of the revolution caused another spike in oil prices, a recession in the United States, and painfully long lines for gasoline. While many Americans were angry and frustrated about the gas lines and the economy, few seem to have blamed—or even acknowledged that the source of the problem was—the Iranian Revolution.

The Iranian extremists wanted Americans to know that they had struck a great blow against the United States in deposing Washington's "puppet," but America mostly ignored them. Revenge is about psychological satisfaction, and how could the Iranians feel that sense of satisfaction if the United States did not even seem to acknowledge their acts of vengeance? Once the embassy takeover had America's attention, they never ceased to harangue American audiences with chants of "Death to America" and long litanies of claimed American plots and abuses—against Iran and many other countries. This was more than just background noise for the Carter administration. These constant images of Iranians blaming America for everything wrong in the world, the sense of anger that a country would commit such an offense against us, and the demand to do something about it became driving emotions for the American public—and their elected officials knew that they had to do something to address these passions.[73]

The problem was, what to do? Before the seizure of the embassy, Washington had resolved to try to build a new relationship with the moderates in the Iranian government, exactly as State had urged. This seemed to be enjoying some initial success—Bazargan had even made it possible to close down the two listening posts on the Soviet border and extract the Americans working there quietly and without any disturbances.[74] However, once Bazargan resigned it was unclear whether there was anyone whom the United States could work with in Tehran.

The other problem that popular frustration raised was that it made it difficult for the Carter administration to defuse the crisis. The hostages served two interrelated purposes for the Iranians. First, as long as the holding of the hostages was seen to be causing pain to Americans, it provided psychological gratification to Iranians. Second, as long as the crisis provided that psychological gratification, supporting additional confrontation (and humiliation) of the Americans was a winning political position in Tehran. In other words, the more attention Americans paid to the hostage crisis, the more valuable it was to the Iranian radicals in their domestic fight to drive all other political groups out of the new regime. The situation was made even more difficult by the personality of the president. Jimmy Carter was a deeply religious man who cared passionately about others—hence the importance of human rights to his foreign policy—and who took the plight of the hostages to heart.[75] Consequently, Carter became personally committed to the hostage crisis, which also increased its value to the Iranians. Thus, the hostage crisis became something of a vicious cycle: the longer it went on, the more frustrating it became for the American people, the more President Carter agonized over what to do, and therefore the more valuable it became for the Iranians.[76]

Washington had still another problem to contend with: the Iranians were completely ignorant about the United States. Even the Western-educated courtiers of the shah's regime routinely operated under bizarre misimpressions of the United States, its capabilities, and its interests in Iran. Those now in charge of Iran's affairs were generally not even that knowledgeable. In many cases, they lacked any experience of America or Americans. One of the Algerian diplomats who eventually brokered the deal to free the hostages commented, "These weren't negotiations. They were more like a seminar. In Tehran, we explained to the Iranians the American legal, banking, and political systems. In Washington, we explained the politics of revolutionary Iran."[77] So the U.S. government was forced to try to persuade a group of people whose ideas about America and the world were immature, ignorant, and fantastic to gain the release of fifty-two American hostages who the Iranians truly believed were spies sent to enslave their country.

Ultimately, the United States did not have many options. The administration considered a range of military operations: coercive strikes against Iranian military and economic targets (air bases and oil facilities), a blockade, mining Iran's major harbors, seizing a piece of Iranian territory (Kharg Island, which has a major oil export terminal), and a rescue mission similar to what the Israelis had pulled off at Entebbe just three years earlier.[78] However, they just as quickly concluded that none of them was an attractive option. President Carter made it clear that his overriding goal was to get the hostages released alive, and the National Security Council agreed that the coercive strikes were more likely to provoke the Iranians to kill some of the hostages than to let them go free.[79] Seizing Kharg Island (exactly the course the British had taken in 1856, when they had successfully coerced Persia to give up the conquered city of Herat) seemed likely to result in considerable American and Iranian casualties, and again offered little guarantee that it would convince the Iranian government to free the hostages rather than just stiffen the Iranians' spines.[80] Planning for a rescue mission did begin. However, it had a low priority at first because the location of the embassy in downtown Tehran, the difficulty of getting real-time intelligence indicating the location of the hostages, and the distance from either friendly bases in the region or the North Arabian Sea (which is the closest that the navy was willing to sail a carrier in those days) was more than 1,000 miles over hard terrain, making such an operation very risky. The two military options that seemed most reasonable were mining or a blockade, but it was unclear that either would actually exert enough pressure on Tehran to convince it to give up the hostages (and it might just cause the people to rally around the government and therefore harden them in their determination not to free the hostages). There were also concerns that the Iranians would retaliate by going after oil tankers in the Persian Gulf, which would drive up gasoline prices so that the average American would suffer the consequences.[81] Moreover, there was an initial consensus that the crisis would not last long enough for the kind of slow pressure exerted by either of those forms of coercion to be effective, and therefore it was not worth the risk.[82]

Nor was there a covert action option. At different points, members of the NSC raised the possibility of repeating the 1953 coup or simply covertly strengthening the opposition to Khomeini, but this was not to be. The CIA's Directorate of Operations (DO) had been devastated by the congressional hearings during the Ford administration and by DCI Turner's subsequent purge of the DO.[83] Moreover, the United States did not have the assets available in Iran. Before the revolution, the CIA had been severely circumscribed in its ability to deal with any Iranians except for members of the shah's regime itself. Because of the revolution, even those contacts were gone; most had either fled the country or been executed or imprisoned by the revolutionary tribunals. The Iranian exile community had grandiose claims both for its abilities and for the degree of popular willingness to act against Khomeini (which Saddam Hussein would take to heart in 1980, to his grief) but no evidence that there was any fire beneath their smoke. Typically, the rule of thumb for covert actions is that where no such capability exists, it takes at least five years to build one—this being the approximate amount of time needed to find and hire operatives, establish cover for them in the country, allow them to make contacts among the locals, identify and recruit agents, and finally plan and prepare for the operation. Given that the United States would be starting from scratch in Iran, there was little enthusiasm for embarking on a five-year project that was still likely to fail. As Admiral Turner observed, "Covert actions to overthrow governments work best when the situation is unstable and only a small push is needed to change it, as was true with Mossadegh."[84] For all of the unhappiness in Iran, Khomeini remained extraordinarily popular, and an effort to unseat the revolution was a nonstarter.[85]

The debate over the hostage crisis fell prey to a vast philosophical chasm between the dovish secretary of state, Cyrus Vance, and the hawkish national security advisor, Zbigniew Brzezinski, that would dominate foreign policy making during much of the Carter administration. From the start of the crisis, Vance wanted to try to find a negotiated solution and was willing to make considerable concessions to the Iranians to do so. Brzezinski was inclined toward a military option. However, because none of the military options seemed palatable and because Carter made clear his preference for exhausting diplomatic options before trying the military approach, the State Department position prevailed. In some ways, this approach did play to one of the few advantages that the United States had: international support. Iran's blatantly illegal actions in seizing, incarcerating, and mistreating the hostages—coupled with the summary executions, assassinations, torture, and other widespread violence in Tehran—had left a bad taste in the mouths of much of the world. Consequently, as part of Vance's diplomatic campaign, the Iranians were deluged by pleas from world leaders to release the hostages. Beyond this, Washington did what it could to find an emissary who could negotiate between Iran and the United States but met with little success.[86]

Throughout November the tension between the two sides escalated despite Vance's resistance to any effort on the U.S. side that might turn up the pressure on Iran. The problem was that the Iranians simply were not playing along. Early on, many members of the National Security Council wanted to slap sanctions on Iran as a way of putting some pressure on Tehran (and showing the American people they were doing something), but State managed to whittle it down to merely prohibiting the delivery of military spare parts bought by the shah.[87] On November 12, the Foreign Ministry in Tehran announced four conditions for freeing the hostages: return of the shah to Iran for a fair trial, return of the shah's assets, an end to interference in Iran's affairs, and an apology for past American crimes against Iran.[88] The same day, Washington learned that Iran planned to announce that it would no longer sell oil to the United States (a largely symbolic gesture since oil is fungible and we could simply buy it from another country without upsetting the oil markets). To preempt the Iranians, the Carter administration announced that it was prohibiting the purchase of Iranian oil by Americans.[89] Two days later, the administration learned that the Iranians were about to start withdrawing all of their assets from U.S. banks, mostly to deny the United States a source of leverage, but again Washington reacted faster and froze all of their assets, to the tune of $12 billion. For good measure, Carter cut off all trade with Iran except exports of humanitarian goods such as food and medicine.[90] These actions did appease the hawks, as they seemed to exert some additional pressure on Tehran.

Some of the administration's efforts to engage the broader international community to pressure Iran also began to bear fruit: on December 4, the U.N. Security Council passed a resolution calling for the immediate release of the hostages without any reference to Iran's claimed grievances—exactly as the United States had wanted. On December 15, the International Court of Justice likewise found for the United States, directing Iran to free the hostages and restore America's diplomatic property immediately.[91] But none of it had any impact. Indeed, the administration became somewhat desperate to find interlocutors who might be able to reach Khomeini and persuade him to start negotiations with the United States (let alone cut a deal!). In their desperation they reached out to Christian Bourguet, a French lawyer, and Hector Villalon, an Argentine businessman, whom the Iranians had recruited to try to have the shah extradited to Iran but who were genuinely willing to try to help. Once again, it was unclear that these two really could deliver on anything they promised, and the affair ended badly. Astonishingly, Villalon forged a letter from Carter to Khomeini that accepted American guilt for numerous injustices done to Iran in the desperate hope that this would convince Khomeini to open negotiations. Of course, the Iranian government did no such thing and instead released it to the public, requiring Washington to prove that the letter was forged and explain what it had been doing working with such bizarre intermediaries.[92] It was a lesson that the United States would have done well to learn right then: when dealing with the Iranian government, there are many unofficial go-betweens who claim to know the right people and be able to deliver an agreement, but invariably the affair will end badly if you take them up on it.

As the winter wore on, things got progressively worse for the United States. At the end of December, the Soviet Union invaded Afghanistan. This stunning development radically altered the geopolitical context of the hostage crisis, particularly for Brzezinski, but also for many others. The administration became determined to forge an Islamic coalition to oppose the Soviets in Afghanistan—an effort that would turn into the large-scale Arab support for the Mujahideen guerrilla campaign that did ultimately drive the Russians out but also created a proving ground for Usama bin Ladin and other Islamist terrorists. Under those circumstances, many in the administration, including Brzezinski, became very skittish about resorting to a military option against Iran for fear that it would both drive Iran into the arms of the Soviets and destroy the Islamic coalition against Russia they were building.[93]

Moreover, the administration ran into the limits of its diplomatic leverage. In early January, Washington attempted to follow up on its success at the United Nations by having the Security Council adopt multilateral sanctions against Iran. Immediately, our European and Japanese allies began to balk. In another lesson that has held true to this day, they proved glad to talk at the Iranians but unwilling to do anything. By mid-January, the United States had pressured, wheedled, cajoled, and begged nine other countries to vote for the resolution (which would have allowed it to pass by a 10–2 vote with three abstentions, not very good by UNSC standards) only to have the Russians veto it to spite the Carter administration for its angry reaction to their Afghan invasion. Washington then tried to get the European and Japanese allies to adopt the same sanctions anyway, even without the United Nations' blessing, but all of them refused.[94] This strongly suggests that none of them wanted to go along with the sanctions to begin with, and it seems highly likely that those who voted in favor of the resolution did so knowing full well that the Russians were going to veto it. In the Security Council, it is a rare vote that is a surprise. Countries make their decisions based on bilateral negotiations conducted outside the formal sessions, and when the vote is finally taken, everyone knows exactly what to expect. Especially given the public animosity between the Russians and Americans at that time, it would have been quite obvious that the Russians were going to veto, thereby making it easy for any country so inclined to make an empty gesture of solidarity with the United States by voting in favor—except that the Carter administration then called their bluff by asking them to make good on their prosanctions vote. At this point, they were forced to hide behind rather paltry excuses for inaction. It was not the last time our European and Japanese allies would disappoint us when it came to taking action against Iran for its various misdeeds.

At the end of January, Iran held its first presidential elections, and Khomeini's candidate naturally won with 75 percent of the vote.[95] Iran's new president was Abol Hasan Bani Sadr, a secular intellectual who had fallen in with Khomeini while he was in Najaf. Bani Sadr was a well-known moderate too—in fact, during the early days of the revolution, when the United States had been trying to connect with Iranian moderates, a CIA officer working undercover as a businessman had offered Bani Sadr a $1,000-per-month "consulting fee."[96] He had apparently refused the money, but it would come back to haunt him later anyway. As Iran's finance minister at the time of the embassy takeover, Bani Sadr had declared it unwise and illegal.[97] Thus, the administration again became hopeful that this would provide an opportunity to open negotiations, but it didn't. The Iranians continued to refuse direct contacts, and the indirect contacts remained maddeningly useless.

Still another problem that arose for the Carter administration and that would become a theme in Iranian-American relations in the future was Iran's bargaining style. All of the intermediaries on the Iranian side insisted that the United States make concessions up front to which the Iranians could then respond, but with no guarantee that they would.[98] The Americans pointed out that that was not a negotiation: in a negotiation, both sides agree to trade off concessions to try to reach a compromise in which *both* simultaneously achieved their goals. What the Iranians were proposing was that the United States start propitiating Tehran, and if at some point the American offerings were acceptable, the Iranians would do something for us—but then again they might not, although they would certainly keep whatever concessions we had already made. At one point during the crisis, when one senior American official was told that this was the Iranian demand and then asked why this should be a problem, he responded, "Our problem is in giving everything away up front with no assurance that the hostages will actually be released."[99] This too is a pattern that has held true to this day.

Operation Eagle Claw

By April, President Carter was growing impatient. The limited economic sanctions he had imposed so far were clearly having no impact in Tehran. The international community had taken some mild actions but was unwilling to take the kind of steps that might have put real pressure on Iran. What's more, Vance's efforts to negotiate a settlement were going nowhere simply because there was no one in Tehran who seemed both able and willing to negotiate. On April 7, Washington finally broke diplomatic relations with Iran (over Vance's objections). The administration also cut off the remaining trade with Iran and began denying visas to all Iranians. Washington also asked the Europeans and Japanese to do the same, but they again begged off. Only by threatening to start mining Iran's harbors was the administration able to get the allies to adopt even the most modest sanctions against Iran.[100]

Meanwhile, the Iranians remained completely wrapped up in their own internal political wrangling. In March, Iran held its first elections for a new, 270-seat Majles. The IRP went all out to fix the vote, including beating up rival candidates and threatening people who did not vote for IRP nominees. Again, many of the secular groups boycotted the elections, which did nothing but add to the IRP's final tally of seats. Khomeini's brother Morteza Pasandideh protested that the IRP had even rigged the vote in the Imam's hometown itself. It was a two-stage election, and at the end of the first round the MEK, the National Front, and other secular parties all charged that the elections should be invalidated by the widespread fraud perpetrated by the Islamists. Of course, it was all to no avail. In the end, the IRP and its allies ended up with 130 seats, by far the largest bloc but a disappointment, especially given their labors to rig the election. What helped them was that most of the other deputies were independents or members of small, unaffiliated parties. Moreover, the IRP used its control of the Council of Guardians—a committee of twelve members charged with certifying the Islamic credentials of any candidate for elective or appointive office, as well as any law passed by the Majles—to reject a number of important political figures from other parties who had been elected despite the IRP's efforts. Thus, Abdul Rahman Qasemlu, the main Kurdish leader; Karim Sanjabi, the head of the National Front; Admiral Ahmad Madani, who had run against Bani Sadr for president; the leader of the Qashqa'i tribe; and Abolfazl Qasemi, leader of the Iran Party, were all summarily disqualified.[101]

In April, the disgraceful Majles elections sparked unrest on many Iranian university campuses, prompting Khomeini to complain about "Western influences" there. Within days, Hizballahis, Komitehs, Pasdars, and other revolutionary thugs had stormed Tehran University and other colleges, beating up and arresting students and faculty members. Eventually, Khomeini opted to simply shut down all of the universities for three years, until the faculty and student bodies could be purged and the curricula and textbooks completely rewritten to comply with his unique vision of the world.[102] Simultaneously, there was a battle within the Iranian political establishment. The Majles repeatedly refused to accept Bani Sadr's choices for prime minister and instead forced him to appoint Mohammad 'Ali Raja'i, an IRP party hack whom Bani Sadr detested. Bani Sadr famously told Raja'i to his face in one meeting, "You have been talking for an hour and have lied twelve times."[103] But it did not end there, as Raja'i demanded that members of the cabinet be chosen based on their Islamic and revolutionary credentials, while Bani Sadr insisted just as firmly that they be determined by skills and experience. The difference led to a drawn-out fight over the cabinet, and even the compromise solution brokered by Khomeini left many key ministerial slots unfilled since they could not agree on a candidate.[104]

As a result, Carter decided to try a unilateral military solution to the problem. All throughout the fall and winter, the military and intelligence communities had been preparing for a hostage rescue mission. On April 25, they put it into action. Everyone, even its staunchest supporters, recognized that it was hardly a sure thing. Brzezinski originally considered it such a long shot that he preferred seizing Kharg Island or the blockade instead until the Russian invasion of Afghanistan caused him to decide that those options were even riskier. Even then, he pushed to conduct punitive air strikes in conjunction with the rescue attempt so that "If the rescue succeeded, that would be all to the good; if it failed, the U.S. government could announce that it had executed a punitive mission against Iran, because of its unwillingness to release our people, and that unfortunately in the course of that mission an attempt to rescue the hostages had not succeeded."[105] Nevertheless, by the time the mission was launched, many in the administration had come around to believing (or simply convinced themselves) that it had a reasonably good chance of success.

In truth, the mission was exceptionally difficult and probably should have been considered a long shot at all times. The plan was for the brand-new U.S. Army Delta Force to be airlifted into Iran at night on heavy Navy helicopters.[106] Because the helicopters did not have the range to make it all the way from a carrier in the North Arabian Sea to Tehran, they would stop at a remote location 200 miles south of Tehran (code-named "Desert One"), where they would be met by C-130 Hercules transports carrying fuel bladders. The helicopters would refuel there and then fly on to a remote location outside of Tehran ("Desert Two"), where they were to arrive before dawn and hide during the day. From there, the Delta Force soldiers would be trucked into Tehran in vehicles provided and driven by CIA operatives. They would assault the embassy, free the hostages, and move them to a soccer stadium next door to which the helicopters would have flown to meet them.[107] The helicopters would then fly the entire group to another nearby airfield, where they would transfer to C-141 cargo planes for the final escape under cover of U.S. Navy fighters.

The plan did not survive contact with the enemy's weather. One of the most difficult parts of a very difficult mission was simply flying the eight helicopters (six were considered the minimum necessary, and two others were brought as spares) the 600 miles to Tehran at night, without lights, at low altitude, and in complete radio silence. Although the teams had practiced the mission repeatedly under desert conditions, they were unaware that in Iran at that time of year, the climactic conditions often produce vast clouds of suspended dust particles that cut visibility and can cause mechanical failures. During the flight in to Desert One three of the helicopters experienced mechanical problems or warning of mechanical problems. That left only five, and the commander on the spot reluctantly decided that he could not go ahead with the mission without the six that the exercises had indicated were the minimum needed for success. To make matters worse, a helicopter collided with a C-130 during the departure from Desert One, killing eight Americans. The military option had failed.

Reaction across the United States was mixed. On the one hand, many people were angry and disappointed that the mission had failed and blamed the administration for doing a half-assed job—for instance, critics were quick to ask why so few helicopters had been employed. On the other hand, many other people believed that the rescue mission had been a noble failure: worth a shot but, because of the complexities, foreordained never to succeed. The most interesting reaction was inside the Carter administration. There, a combination of sentiments seemed to prevail: a sense that Vance had been right to eschew the military option all along; a sense of relief that the military option had been tried, it had been found wanting, and therefore would not have to be tried again; and resignation to the fact that there now was little way to press the Iranians to move faster on the hostages than they wanted to. And indeed, after the failure of the rescue mission—and a brief period of consideration of a bigger follow-up that did not last for very long—there simply was no more consideration of the military option. It was off the table.[108]

Not with a Bang but a Whimper

It took another nine months after the failure of the rescue mission before the hostage crisis was finally resolved. After the rescue mission, the Europeans finally announced their long-awaited sanctions against Iran, and they were so meaningless as to be insulting to the United States. They merely embargoed trade with Iran that fell under contracts signed after the hostages had been taken on November 4. Contracts signed before November 4 were not only not affected but could be retroactively "expanded," thus eliminating the need for any company to sign a new contract with the Iranians.[109] Clearly, there would be no increase in the level of economic or political pressure on Iran.

At that point, and even without the presence of Secretary of State Vance, who had resigned in opposition to the hostage rescue mission, the Carter administration concluded that all it could do was to wait for the political situation in Tehran to clarify to the point where the Iranians would decide that they were ready. And so the most powerful nation on Earth sat and waited. In September, the Iranians finally decided that they were ready. A relative and close associate of Khomeini, Sadeq Tabatabai, made it clear that Iran wanted the hostages released quickly and would do so on terms more favorable to the United States than Washington had even offered.[110] We still do not know why Khomeini decided that it was time for the hostages to be freed. It undoubtedly had something to do with Iran's internal politics. By September, Khomeini's control over Iran's government had greatly improved (although it was not yet complete): his disciple, Bani Sadr, was president; the IRP dominated the Majles, and while they were obstreperous, they were his followers too; a new cabinet was about to be confirmed that would be dominated by the IRP; and the secularists seemed to be in retreat.

Nevertheless, if it all seemed too good to be true, it was. Almost immediately, IRP hard-liners in the Majles began demanding far more humiliating terms from the United States and brought the process to a halt. That was just enough of a delay for two other major problems to crop up. The first was that on September 22, Iraq invaded Iran, kicking off the eight-year Iran-Iraq War (which is discussed in chapters 7 and 8). This wrenched Tehran's decision making back into chaos and again precluded any kind of movement toward a resolution.

The second issue was that at some point in the September–October time frame, Khomeini seems to have changed his mind on timing. While Khomeini's practical political needs from the hostages seem to have been satisfied by the fall of 1980, his hunger for revenge was not yet sated. Apparently Khomeini decided that he would hold on to the hostages for a while longer to try to unseat Jimmy Carter as president to extract further—and specifically parallel—revenge for the 1953 coup. Ibrahim Yazdi, in an interview in the 1990s, stated that Khomeini believed that releasing the hostages prior to the November election could swing the vote Carter's way and that holding on to them would probably ensure Carter's defeat. Yazdi said that Khomeini chose to hold them until the day Carter was out of office as a way of demonstrating that he could topple an American leader just as America had toppled Mosaddeq.[111] Two other of my predecessors as director for Persian Gulf Affairs at the NSC, Howard Teicher, who served in the Reagan administration, and Bruce Riedel, who served in the Bush 41 and Clinton administrations, support this contention by stating that in early 1980 there was considerable classified intelligence indicating that Khomeini was determined to "humiliate, weaken and otherwise undermine President Carter's chances for re-election," and so he purposely strung out the hostage crisis because he knew that Carter's personal association with this ongoing source of frustration was hurting his standings with the American public.[112] It is worth noting that if this is true—and there is no particular reason to doubt Yazdi, Teicher, or Riedel on this point, especially since Khomeini did not hide his hatred of Carter—it would constitute the same kind of blatant Iranian interference in American internal affairs that Iranians have constantly (and at times correctly) complained about by the United States.

Ironically, both of these issues also seem to have ultimately turned around on the Iranians and become important incentives to finally end the crisis. As the war with Iraq worsened, Tehran recognized that its political isolation was inflicting real costs in terms of its inability to purchase arms and ammunition for its American-made arsenal. Likewise, it does seem to be the case that once they had contributed to the defeat of Jimmy Carter, the Iranians became concerned about what the new Reagan administration might do, given their tough talk during the campaign. This too appears to have prompted the Iranians to get things wrapped up before the new president took over the White House.[113] In addition, there was a sense in Tehran that the hostage taking was hurting Khomeini's dream of "exporting the revolution" to the rest of the Muslim world. Far from being encouraged to emulate Iran in throwing off a despotic regime and building in its place an Islamic theocracy, other Muslims were shocked and embarrassed by the violence and irresponsibility of the new regime.[114] Thus for all of these reasons, the hostages went from simply not having much more value for Iran, as was the case in the early fall when Behzad Nabavi, Iran's chief negotiator, said that "the hostages are like fruit from which all of the juice has been squeezed out," to becoming positive liabilities for the regime.[115]

In a series of negotiations worked out by Deputy Secretary of State Warren Christopher and Sadeq Tabatabai in Algeria, the United States and Iran finally reached an agreement. The administration took some satisfaction in the fact that the Iranians got virtually nothing in the deal. The United States pledged not to interfere in Iran's internal affairs and agreed to release the assets frozen on November 12. Even then, $7.95 billion was put in an escrow account to cover American claims against Iran. Altogether, the Iranians got only about $2.3 billion of their money back.[116] Of course, what the Iranians really "got" from the hostage crisis had been 444 days' worth of the psychological gratification they craved and, for the radical Islamists, a useful weapon to consolidate their control over the new government. As a last, petty act of vengeance, Tehran would not allow the hostages to be freed until the very moment Jimmy Carter was succeeded by Ronald Reagan as president. The Iranians watched the inauguration on television and only at the precise moment that Ronald Reagan finished taking the oath of office was their plane allowed to take off, but on January 21, 1981, the hostages were free at last.

America and the Hostage Crisis

If the 1953 coup was the defining moment of the U.S.-Iranian relationship for Iranians, the 1979–1981 hostage crisis was the defining moment of the relationship for Americans. In American minds (and, in fact, those of the rest of the world too) there was no justification for so blatant an act of international criminality. As Americans saw it, the Iranians had simply attacked us. As far as the American public was concerned, the United States had not done anything to warrant such treatment. Of course, the reality is a bit more complicated. In actuality, we had dispatched General Huyser to Iran for the express purpose of instigating a coup d'état against the revolution, even if only as a last resort. The Iranian revolutionaries did not know this at the time and so had no proof of America's hostile actions toward their revolution, but this central element of their paranoid fantasies ultimately turned out to be very real.

The hostage crisis has left a terrible scar on the American psyche. It is an episode so frustrating that most Americans have simply preferred to forget about it, ignore it, and minimize it as much as they can. However, few Americans have ever forgiven the Iranians for it. It is America's great underlying grievance against Iran, and as such it has been the "elephant in the living room" of U.S. policy toward Iran ever since. We never discuss it openly, but the residual anger that so many Americans feel toward Iran for those 444 days has colored every decision made about Iran ever since. Whenever Iran has done something malicious since then (and they have done plenty), this anger magnifies the outrage Americans feel. Whenever Iranians have attempted to reach out to the United States (rare and problematic though these efforts have been), this same anger has created a very high threshold for reciprocating. Indeed, one reason subsequent American administrations have been reticent to pursue a rapprochement with Tehran is that this latent anger is so volatile and can be so easily brought back to the surface by a political opponent that few have been willing to take the risk. Ever since November 4, 1979, no American political leader has wanted to open himself or herself up to the charge of "coddling" the Iranians. It is not a winning strategy in post–hostage crisis America.

The United States has very real policy differences with Iran that are likely to make any rapprochement very difficult, especially in the short term. There is also no question that emotional obstacles also play a very significant role in our differences, and if at some point we can resolve the policy differences, we are going to have to confront these emotional obstacles as well. That means that the Iranians are going to have to come to grips with their anger at America for our role in the 1953 coup and our friendship with the shah. It also means that Americans are going to have to learn to deal with their anger over the hostage crisis.

The two greatest sources of anger and frustration for most Americans caused by the hostage crisis derive from the sense of injustice and powerlessness that it caused us. For so many Americans, a key point is that the taking of the embassy was wrong. By that we mean that it was wrong not only from an international legal standpoint, but also in the sense that we were innocent of the charges that the Iranians leveled against us and that they claim motivated them to launch the attack. The other half of our emotional baggage relating to the hostage crisis is the blinding frustration provoked by the fact that the United States of America, with all its wealth and all its power, allowed a small, weak nation like Iran to hold fifty-two of its citizens hostage in one of the more outrageous acts of state terrorism of the twentieth century.

The first issue gets to the question of the level of American complicity in Iran's unhappiness with the shah and our interference in Iran's internal affairs. As I have tried to describe in the previous three chapters, Iranians have tended to greatly exaggerate both of these matters. For the most part, the shah did what he wanted, not what America wanted, and when America's "interference" was greatest (during the Truman and Kennedy administrations) it was directed at getting the shah to reform his methods and improve the lot of the Iranian people. Much of our "interference" in Iranian affairs on those occasions was economic aid, and most people—including the Iranians at the time—are eager to have it and resentful when they *don't* get it. The shah was neither our creature nor our puppet, and consequently a very great deal of Iran's animosity toward the United States is undeserved. Moreover, in the specific circumstances of November 1979, it is absolutely untrue that the United States was preparing to overthrow the revolution: the Carter administration's decision to admit the shah was a wholly humanitarian gesture. For all of these reasons, I remain convinced that the United States has been chastised and attacked unfairly by Iranians. If, at some point in the future, the United States and Iran do begin a new rapprochement and, in the course of those conversations, the Iranians demand another apology from the United States for its past misdeeds, I believe that the American administration should agree to do so only if Iran makes a similar apology for the taking of the embassy and its other misdeeds.

All that said, we are still not blameless. We may not have been planning a counterrevolution in November 1980, but we did try to do so ten months earlier. The Iranians' fears were not baseless. In my own thinking about the hostage crisis, the Huyser mission looms very large. Along with the 1953 coup, it is the worst instance of negative American interference in Iranian affairs—and it is understandable why Iranians would be just as angry about it as we are about the hostage crisis. This should not be taken as a statement that the United States should never engage in covert action to overthrow foreign governments, nor should it be seen as absolution for the seizure of the embassy. It is simply to say that we should not feel quite as aggrieved about the seizure of the embassy because, in truth, we were not as innocent as we believed.

The sense of frustrated powerlessness that so many Americans felt at the time, and that contributes to our ongoing anger at Iran, gets to the question of whether the Carter administration might have handled the crisis differently. There are three realities that bear on this question. First, Vance's strategy of patience coupled with limited pressure and limited concessions ultimately "worked" in the sense that all of the hostages came home alive. It is impossible to get around that fact. As frustrating as it was to endure, it got the job done. Thus the relevant question is whether there was another approach that would have brought the hostages home sooner or that would have been less damaging to our interests abroad.

Second, the Carter administration's Republican opponents did not offer much of a critique of the actual strategy employed. Reagan himself only ever talked cryptically about a "secret plan" to handle the hostage crisis. If such a plan ever existed, Reagan never revealed what it was.[117] Even after he took office, Reagan declined to explain what his secret plans had been, claiming that they were "still classified"—begging the question of when the campaign documents of a political party were ever classified.[118] All of this strongly suggests that the Reagan team did not have a strikingly different notion of how to handle the hostage crisis. It seems more than a little likely that this approach was intended to be a mirror of Eisenhower's famous 1952 campaign remark "I will go to Korea," which was designed to suggest that he had a plan to resolve that interminable standoff when he actually did not.

Other high-ranking Republicans who criticized the Carter administration's handling of the crisis were more specific in their charges, and they focused on the argument that the Democrats had paid too much attention to the whole affair, thereby keeping it useful to Khomeini and the Iranian radicals. Their principal criticism was that Carter should have lowered the visibility of the crisis (a difficult feat given the degree of public outrage), not that he should have taken decisive actions to try to force the Iranians to give in.[119] This isn't much of a critique. It suggests that there was no other obvious, markedly different course of action that the United States might have pursued. Most of the senior Carter administration officials have actually agreed with it since the end of the crisis. However, while downplaying the crisis might have helped, there is no certainty that it would have, nor is there anything to suggest that it would have dramatically improved the outcome.[120] Ultimately, the clock was driven by Iran's internal politics, and those internal politics had not played out until the fall of 1980. There is little to suggest that lowering the visibility on the American side would have affected those internal politics sufficiently to have gotten the hostages home significantly sooner. It probably would have helped diminish both our own frustration with the situation by keeping it lower on the American agenda and might also have ameliorated the international sense of American weakness and indecision that the crisis created, but probably not by much.

Third, as long as one starts with the goal that the Carter administration did, that America's overriding priority was getting the hostages out alive, the actual strategy employed was probably the only one that *could have* worked. Covert action was simply not an option because the capabilities did not exist and revolutionary Iran was an awful candidate for an externally instigated coup d'état. And any of the military options could have gotten one or more of the hostages killed, thereby failing that primary goal. (At least one scholar has noted that since the rescue mission entailed the same risk—and since the planners estimated that even a successful raid would result in the death of two to four hostages—Carter should not have opted for the rescue based on his own criteria.)[121] Consequently, the strategy adopted probably was the only one that could have met Carter's goal. Tweaking it to try to downplay the whole affair, as both Republicans and Democrats have suggested, might have made it a bit less painful, but that was about it.

However, a different question can be asked: Would there have been other courses of action available if the United States had adopted a different, but still plausible, goal during the crisis—and could those other courses of action have produced a markedly better outcome? Specifically, a colder-hearted administration might have decided that the principal goal of the United States once the embassy was taken was to preserve the credibility of American deterrence and that the lives of the hostages were secondary to that goal. Callous as that may sound in retrospect, such a policy would not have been particularly anomalous: diplomats and Marines all know that their lives cannot come before vital national interests, a point expressed by a number of the hostages after their release. Such a course also could have been justified strategically. The hostage crisis made the United States look weak in the eyes of the world, and weakness invites challenge. It seems fairly certain that this impression of weakness contributed to Iran's decision to challenge the United States in Lebanon in the 1980s and throughout the Persian Gulf in the 1980s and early 1990s; Iraq's decision to invade Kuwait in 1990 and then to remain there even after the United States committed 500,000 troops in 1991; Syria's willingness to challenge us in Lebanon in the 1980s; and possibly to other international confrontations that followed (although it is hard to be certain that it did or, if it did, of how much it was a factor compared to other causes). Nonetheless, throughout the 1980s and '90s, the legacies of the Iranian hostage crisis, Vietnam, and the withdrawal from Lebanon all contributed to a common international perception that the United States was weak and cowardly, and this did influence the thinking of various leaders who chose to confront us at different times.

Thus, a different administration could have plausibly adopted this different set of goals. In such a hypothetical alternative scenario, the question then becomes whether it would have made sense to employ another military option in addition to or instead of the hostage rescue attempt. Because Iraq attacked Iran in September 1980, considerable information is available about how Iran under Khomeini was likely to have reacted under various forms of military attack, and none of it suggests that the outcomes of such an alternative scenario would have been much better for the United States.

In this alternative scenario, the United States could have had one of two specific objectives. We could have demanded that the Iranians return the hostages and then tried to coerce them into doing so, accepting that any prompt release of the hostages would be a victory (because we had forced them to do something that they did not want to do) even if some of the hostages were killed in the process. Such a successful act of coercion would probably have eliminated the damage to our deterrent posture that our policy during the real hostage crisis actually caused. On the other hand, we could have implemented a purely punitive response in which we opted to cause tremendous damage to Iran to demonstrate that it would pay an unacceptable price for having taken the hostages. The key word in that last sentence is "unacceptable." For a punitive approach to have succeeded in restoring America's deterrent posture, it would have to have been able to inflict so much damage on Iran that both the Iranians and other rogue regimes would have concluded that the retaliation greatly outweighed the pain that the United States suffered by the taking of the embassy and the killing of however many hostages ended up dead. If it did not, those states still would have had the incentive to challenge the United States in the future in the expectation that they too could inflict more pain on us than we could bear but that we could not inflict more pain on them than they could bear. The problem was that revolutionary Iran had so little of value and such an abnormal set of values, and was so willing to accept pain, that it would have been extremely difficult to meet those standards short of a full-scale invasion of Iran or the use of nuclear weapons—neither of which was an option that any American policy maker would have ever entertained as a solution to the hostage crisis.

The obvious target for any military campaign was Iran's oil. Four of the military options that the Carter administration considered—seizing Kharg Island, air strikes, mining, and blockade—were really directed at Iran's oil exports. The most important air strike being considered was that against the Abadan refinery, and both the blockade and mining were really designed to block tankers from lifting Iranian oil. The problem was that, at least at first, revolutionary Iran cared little about its oil. As noted above, Khomeini was deeply ambivalent about Iran's oil because of its historical impact on Iranian society and had allowed Iranian oil production to fall from 5.9 million bpd to 1.3 million bpd. At the start of the Iran-Iraq War it would fall still further, to just 700,000 bpd.[122] During that war, Iran did feel pressure to ramp up production and exports because it needed the money to buy tanks and artillery pieces to keep Iraq's armies out of its territory (and then to fulfill the Imam's dream of liberating the Shi'i holy sites in Iraq). However, in a war against the United States in which there was no threat of actual invasion, the Iranians would probably not have felt the same need. Khomeini himself would not have bemoaned the loss of Iranian oil exports, and he doubtless could have convinced the Iranian people to support him for a very long time. Given the kind of sacrifices the Iranian people actually made during 1980–1988, there is little reason to believe that they would have been unwilling to make similar sacrifices in the event of a war with the United States.

Hitting the F-14 bases would have done almost nothing. No more than ten to fifteen of Iran's seventy-five were even operational by September 1980, and it seems unlikely that U.S. air strikes could have done more damage than that. Certainly there would have been some psychological impact from having American jets blow up these aircraft rather than simply losing them to maintenance problems, but it is hard to imagine that it would have been a painful enough blow to cause the Iranians to give up the hostages. Nor does it seem likely that the threat of additional such strikes against the rest of Iran's air force would have done the trick. Again, Iran lost roughly two thirds to three quarters of its air force to sabotage, poor maintenance, lack of spare parts, and other problems related to the revolution during 1979–1980, but this effective loss of any meaningful air power had no impact on its decision making in the war against Iraq. Given the tremendous anti-Americanism that Khomeini had injected into the Iranian Revolution, there is little reason to believe that the loss of the country's air force would have been enough to shock the Iranian people into agreeing to Washington's demands or even convincing them that taking the embassy had not been worth the costs.

Other than the oil exports, it is unlikely that the blockade or mining (two different tactics to accomplish the same goal, halting maritime trade) would have had much impact either. Iran did still grow considerable amounts of food, and—of far greater importance—Iran has long land borders that would not have been affected by the naval blockade. It seems highly likely that after an initial period of adjustment (which might have been painful) the Iranians would have modified their trade patterns accordingly and been able to meet most of their needs. It was not viable for the United States to shut down all of Iran's land borders either militarily or diplomatically (as we mostly did with Iraq during the 1990s). The Carter administration tried repeatedly to get multilateral sanctions passed against Iran and failed flat out because few countries had any interest in cutting their trade with Iran. The loss of oil revenues might have made it harder to pay for food imports, but Iran would doubtless have found ways to export some oil overland; again, the willingness of the Iranian people to make sacrifices in the heady days after the revolution was so great that they likely would have been able to shake off easily whatever pain such a blockade would have created.

Overall, it is critical to keep in mind the more generalized experience of the Iran-Iraq War. Iran suffered horrific damage during that war and its people made astonishing sacrifices, yet it took eight years of beating their heads against a wall and losing hundreds of thousands of young men in senseless human-wave attacks, with nearly the whole world lined up against it, before Iran gave up. In hindsight, most outside observers (and even some Iranians) recognize that the war was not worth the hardships they endured, but that recognition has not convinced anyone that therefore the Iraqi invasion was worthwhile, nor would a similar experience have redounded to America's benefit.

Although the United States could have inflicted different kinds of damage on Iran than Iraq did, unless we were willing to employ nuclear weapons or mount a full-scale invasion (both of which were simply inconceivable in the circumstances), it is unlikely that the amount of pain we could have inflicted on Iran would have been significantly greater than that caused by the war with Iraq—which was very great. What's more, being attacked by the Great Satan would have played into Shi'i martyrdom complexes probably even better than did Saddam Hussein's invasion. Khomeini had already painted the United States as Yazid, the caliph who ordered the death of the revered Husayn—so what could have fit better into the ayatollah's worldview than for Yazid/America to attack Husayn/Iran, which would be helpless under the blows of the attacker but would ultimately triumph? Iran's masses would have flocked to Khomeini's banner probably even more enthusiastically than when the Iraqi Shimr attacked.

Moreover, because it seems unlikely that any of these strategies would have forced the Iranians to change their behavior significantly, at some point the United States would have tired of the game, and at that point the Iranians would have claimed victory. They would have outlasted us, and that would have eroded our deterrent just as our withdrawals from Vietnam and Lebanon did and just as our inaction during the actual crisis did, just in a different way. Consequently, it is hard not to conclude that any such American military campaign would have led to a much louder and bloodier outcome than the actual course adopted by the Carter administration, but not necessarily a quicker or better outcome.

Perhaps it will help to assuage our lingering anger from the hostage crisis to understand that the sense of powerlessness we felt was probably inherent in the confrontation. Because of the nature of the Iranian body politic at the time, there was very little that the United States could have done that would have been justified by the circumstances that could have significantly changed the outcome. I still find it maddening to write this, even as I do so. But I believe that it is the truth. Of course, for those same reasons, Iran did not benefit from its actions. Khomeini benefited from them, as did other radical mullahs, but the Iranian nation did not. The hostage taking and Iran's conduct throughout the crisis made it an international pariah, a position it continues to occupy, more or less, to this day. In the end, the Iranians got nothing for it. To the extent that it helped solidify the radicals' control over their government, their current unhappiness can also be traced back to the hostage crisis. In truth, the Iranians did not even get very much of the psychic gratification they so craved because what they failed to understand at the time (and since) was that the United States never cared a jot for Iran, just for the hostages. The hostage crisis did not make Americans any more sympathetic to Iranians or any more mindful of our own complicity in their history, as they had hoped. As Ted Koppel put it to me, "What the Iranians still have not figured out is that Iran is just as irrelevant to the American people today as it was twenty-five years ago."[123] In the end, the hostage crisis was not good for anyone.

At War with the World

The 1980s was the defining decade of Iran's modern history. After the shah's regime collapsed the nation was virtually tabula rasa: a clean slate upon which the Iranians might have drawn anything, at least in theory. The trials they endured during the 1980s helped determine the shape of the new nation they created. The 1980s were also an important counterpoint to the experience of the revolution itself. What had once seemed so hard about the revolution—overthrowing the shah—appeared in hindsight to have been the easy part, and the difficult part was building a new state afterward. Moreover, because the 1980s was the only period of time in which Ayatollah Khomeini, the "founding father" of the modern Iranian state, was alive and in power, it took on added significance. As is often the case, the decisions that Khomeini made in response to the exigencies of those years became guideposts for what was acceptable in terms of both ends and means after he passed from the scene. The Iran that the United States must deal with today is, in many ways, the Iran created by its experiences in the 1980s.

An important element of this process of redefinition was the clash of revolutionary ideology with reality. As Khomeini and the radical clerics consolidated their power, they remained determined to pursue the more grandiose aspirations that their dogma implied. As a result, Iranian decision making often had a surreal quality to it—whether it was insisting that women wear the *chador* (the head-to-toe veil); banning music (all music), dancing, the intermingling of genders, and much foreign literature; or demanding that Iranian armies liberate Baghdad and then Jerusalem long after it was clear that they could do neither. At other times, however, more pragmatic elements in Tehran were able to gain temporary ascendancy, at least on specific diplomatic and military matters, because reality had so intruded on the radicals' fantasy world that Khomeini recognized (for a little while) that he risked jeopardizing the revolution by continuing to pursue its most extreme objectives. This tension produced significant swings in Iranian behavior that made it even more difficult for outside observers to predict Iran's course, and that became the crucial element in the Reagan administration's misguided bid to end its own agonizing hostage ordeal with Iran.

When the Reagan administration took office in the wake of the 1979–1981 hostage crisis, its initial reaction was to steer clear of Iran. Most Americans remained angry and frustrated at Tehran, and the experience of the hostage crisis had convinced most American policy makers that the Iranians were either irrational or emotionally unbalanced because of the revolution and that therefore no good would come from a relationship of any kind. Mired in the renewed Cold War with Russia, the Reagan administration's greatest fear—unjustified in retrospect—was that Iran would join the Soviet camp, and since American efforts of any kind seemed more likely to drive them in that direction than to have any positive impact, they initially adopted a "Hippocratic" posture with Iran of focusing foremost on doing no harm. As the decade progressed, however, the United States would grow increasingly troubled by Iran's behavior, as a result of its victories on the battlefield, its aggressive efforts to subvert the Gulf oil monarchies, its violent confrontation with Israel, its widespread support for terrorism, and its endless rhetorical and diplomatic (not to mention terrorist) attacks on the United States. These concerns would prod a reluctant Reagan administration to gradually increase American involvement in the Iran-Iraq War to the point where, in the end, Washington's role became an important factor in Iran's defeat.

Saddam Rolls the Dice

Throughout the revolution and the early days of the hostage crisis, there was one other character waiting in the wings, intensely interested in the drama being played out in Tehran. Saddam Hussein felt he had a stake in all these affairs. The events of 1979 and 1980 seem to have filled him alternately with great hope and great fear. His mighty rival, the shah, who had humiliated him in 1975 by forcing him to sign the Algiers Accord, was gone. Iran was thrown into chaos and seemed weak and at war with itself. But in the midst of it all was rising the specter of the visionary ayatollah, calling out to Muslims everywhere to repeat the feats of the Iranian people against their own "shahs."

By the fall of 1980, the Iranians, and particularly the mullahs, were a bit high on their own success. They had overthrown the shah of Iran and utterly humiliated the United States of America, holding fifty-two Americans hostage for 444 days and revealing (at least in their own eyes) the superpower to be nothing but a paper tiger. Moreover, the Iranians were building an Islamic Republic, which many of Iran's devout Shi'ah were certain was a realization of the ideal system of government—at least until the return of the *mahdi*. Although it had not been a part of the rhetoric of the revolution, now that they had enjoyed such unexpected success in the face of such daunting obstacles, some among them began to think in terms of spreading their revolution. Khomeini himself led this cry, announcing, "We shall export our revolution to the whole world. Until the cry 'There is no God but God' resounds over the whole world, there will be struggle."[1]

One of the states that Iran singled out for particular attention was Iraq. Khomeini believed that he could appeal to Iraq's oppressed Shi'i majority to throw off Saddam Hussein's (Sunni) totalitarian regime. Khomeini held a grudge against Saddam from his fourteen years in exile in Najaf and sudden eviction at the shah's behest in 1978. Khomeini still had considerable contacts in Iraq, and Iran backed the terror campaign unleashed by the Shi'i ad-Dawa group (now popular members of the new, post-Saddam Iraqi government). After the revolution, Khomeini repeatedly called on Iraq's Shi'ah to launch a jihad against Saddam's regime, while Tehran's propaganda organs regularly referred to Saddam as a "puppet of Satan" and "mentally ill."[2] Iran set up camps to train Iraqi Shi'ah in guerrilla warfare techniques. The new Iranian regime also let it be known that it no longer felt bound by any of the shah's agreements—including the 1975 Algiers Accord—and they ominously noted that in traditional Islam there were no borders dividing the faithful.[3]

There is no question that Saddam saw all of this as a threat. Throughout his reign, Saddam was sensitive to unrest among Iraq's Shi'ah, and he genuinely feared that Khomeini would rouse them against him, given what the ayatollah had already achieved against the shah. The Dawa were also a serious problem for Saddam, having come close to killing both Foreign Minister Tariq Aziz and Information Minister Latif Nusayyif Jasim in early 1980, and enjoying considerable support among the Shi'ah of southern Iraq. Initially, Saddam did try quietly to reach a modus vivendi with the new revolutionary regime in Tehran, but Khomeini would have no part of it and instead turned up the rhetorical heat on Baghdad.[4]

However, Saddam also saw opportunities in postrevolution Iran. Saddam, and other Iraqi leaders before him, had long cast a covetous eye toward Khuzestan province in Iran with its considerable Arab population and oil fields that were almost as extensive as Iraq's own. Iraq had harbored the Khuzestan Liberation Movement since the 1960s, although it had done little other than to issue the occasional call for its brethren to rise up against the Persians.[5] On April 30, 1980, they were revived in dramatic fashion, seizing the Iranian Embassy in London and holding twenty-one hostages for six days until the British SAS stormed the building and overpowered the attackers. In so doing, they suddenly reminded the world of their existence and the cause of the Arabs of Khuzestan. What's more, Khuzestan lay on the Iraqi side of the Zagros Mountains, meaning that if an Iraqi army could dash across its plains and seal the mountain passes before the bulk of Tehran's ground forces could get through them, it could effectively preclude resistance by Iran. Saddam saw the chaos in Iran and the efforts (which he exaggerated) of its ethnic minorities—including the Arabs of Khuzestan—to secure greater autonomy from Tehran. While Khomeini's propagandists called on the Shi'ah of Iraq to throw off the Sunni yoke, so Saddam's mouthpieces called on the Arabs of Khuzestan to throw off the Persian yoke. Moreover, Baghdad began to infiltrate its own operatives into Khuzestan to make contact with the separatist forces there and conduct sabotage operations against Iran's oil industry.[6]

Saddam thought that invading Iran would be easy. Former Iranian officials and high-ranking officers from the shah's military fled in droves to Iraq, where they set to work trying to convince Baghdad to help them regain their country. Even Shapour Bakhtiar and General Oveisi made their way to Baghdad, where they persuaded Saddam that the Iranian Army had been so debilitated by desertions and purges after the revolution that Iraq's armed forces would be able to sweep it aside with ease. They also claimed that the Iranian people despised Khomeini and the mullahs and would overthrow them if given half a chance. Arab tribal chiefs from Khuzestan added to this fog by pledging to bring their tribes over to Saddam's side if Iraq would invade Khuzestan. Based on this misinformation, Saddam conceived the idea that by seizing the province he would ignite a new revolution in Iran, one that would oust Khomeini and replace him with a government more amenable to Iraqi interests—and that would allow Iraq to hang on to Khuzestan and its oil riches. If he succeeded, he would possess 11 million bpd of oil production, roughly 20 percent of global consumption in 1980, and would achieve his dream of making himself the leader of the Arab world.[7]

A Most Pathetic Blitzkrieg

On September 22, 1980, Saddam crossed his own Rubicon, hurling nine divisions at Iran. Three armored and two mechanized infantry divisions drove into

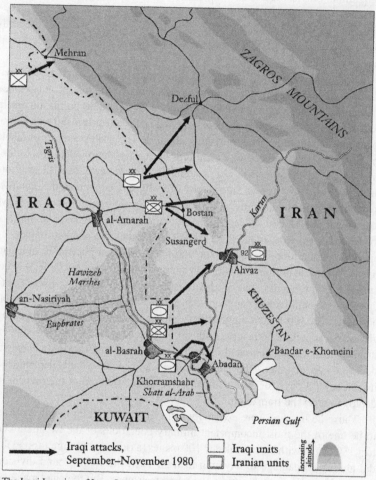

The Iraqi Invasion of Iran, September 1980

Khuzestan itself with the aim of securing the major cities, major roads, and, most important, the Zagros Mountain passes, through which Iranian forces would have to move to reinforce or retake Khuzestan. Farther north, three Iraqi infantry divisions and another armored division were ordered to seize the northern passes through the Zagros that the Iranians would have to use if they wanted to try to launch a counteroffensive directly against Baghdad. According to several former Iraqi generals, the whole operation was to be wrapped up in two weeks.[8]

The attack caught the Iranians totally unprepared. Although there had been months of constant skirmishing along the borders and Iranian reconnaissance operations had detected the buildup of Iraqi forces at various points, no one in Tehran either took the threat seriously or was able to tear himself away from the political infighting to do anything about it. The shah's once formidable military had been reduced to a shambles by the revolution. The revolutionaries purged 7,500 officers in just two months after the revolution. In addition, three coup attempts during the summer of 1980 only convinced the *komiteh*s to cut deeper, and by the time of the Iraqi invasion, the armed forces may have lost as many as 12,000 officers to the revolution. Other officers, and many of the troops, simply deserted; since the fall of the shah, no one had trained, no one was maintaining his equipment, and few were even present at their garrisons. What few military units the revolutionaries possessed were largely occupied trying to regain control of Kurdistan and other fractious ethnic areas. Overall, Iran could muster no more than about 500 operational tanks, probably no more than 300 functioning artillery pieces, and fewer than 100 operable aircraft to resist the 2,500 tanks, 1,400 artillery pieces, and 340 fighter-bombers that Baghdad had concentrated for the invasion. Only one Iranian division was deployed in Khuzestan—the 92nd Armored—and it was so badly depleted that it took several days for even company-sized formations from the division to deploy to meet the Iraqi assault.[9]

Thus, the Iranians were extremely fortunate that the Iraqi invasion proved to be one of the most incompetent military operations of the twentieth century.[10] It began with an air strike by 100 planes (a ridiculously small force) that did almost no damage to anything in Iran. Then the Iraqi ground divisions stumbled into Khuzestan against almost no resistance. But they had made virtually no preparations: they did not have any logistical support plans, no schemes of maneuver, no communications plans, no way of contacting the Arab tribes that were supposed to support the invasion, and nothing more than the most vague objectives ("conquer this city," "secure that mountain pass") to go on. One former Iraqi general remembered angrily that "Our troops were just lined up on the border and told to drive into Iran. They had an objective, but no idea how to get there or what they were doing, or how their mission fit the plan, or who would be supporting them."[11] Moreover, Iraq's tactical formations demonstrated an inability to move more than a few kilometers per day or to quickly overcome even the most meager Iranian resistance, even with their overwhelming advantages in numbers and firepower.[12]

The revolutionaries may not have been ready for the Iraqi invasion, but they reacted to it quickly. Khomeini called for the creation of an "army of twenty million." Across the country, mullahs began rounding up volunteers, organizing them into Basij formations and dispatching them to the front under Pasdaran control. Garrisons were raided and arms and ammunition assembled and sent to the front by train, truck, car, or whatever other transport was available. Tehran launched a propaganda campaign to rally the nation against the foreign threat. Former junior officers of the shah's Army were recalled to service and sent to the front to take charge of the scattered Iranian units resisting the Iraqi advance. In Khuzestan itself, mullahs and other revolutionaries rounded up bands of fighters from Pasdaran units, Basij formations, *komitehs*, and whatever else was at hand, gathered what arms they could, and went off to fight the Iraqis.[13] Because of the incompetence of the Iraqi armored formations, tiny bands armed with small arms were often able to tie down much larger Iraqi units simply by their presence.[14]

As a result, the Iraqi invasion failed to live up to the plan for a two-week blitz across Khuzestan that Saddam had ordered. Ultimately, the deepest any Iraqi unit penetrated into Iran was just 65 kilometers, and in most sectors the Iraqis got no farther than 20 or 30 kilometers. The only city the Iraqis were able to take was Khorramshahr, which sat just across the Shatt al-Arab waterway from Iraq, but they did so only after four weeks of horrific combat that cost Baghdad 8,000 casualties and the loss of more than 100 tanks and APCs to Iranian infantry equipped with small arms, light antitank weapons, and Molotov cocktails.[15] Iraqi armored columns fell short of reaching the main cities in Khuzestan, and they never even got close to the mountain passes. Worse still, Iraqi forces actually overran the city of Susangerd but then failed to garrison it, allowing it to be retaken without a fight by Pasdaran units. All in all, it was a miserable performance. In September and October, Saddam and his flunkies had boasted that Iraq's troops had no definitive stopping point and that they intended to see Khuzestan independent—"independent" under Iraqi control, of course. But by the end of November, with the Iranian resistance hardening, the balance of forces rapidly shifting against the Iraqis as Iran continued to pour troops and materiel into the border regions, and the seasonal rains turning Khuzestan into a sea of mud that made any further advances impossible, Saddam was forced to concede that the invasion had not lived up to his expectations.[16]

Counterattacks, Foreign and Domestic

By late November 1980, Iran's military crisis had passed. The Iraqi units had effectively stopped themselves by their bumbling, glacial advance. They had been slowed by tiny pockets of Iranian resistance and had failed to take anything of real value. In particular, because the Iraqis had failed to seal the passes through the Zagros, Tehran had succeeded in rushing hordes of soldiers to the front lines—poorly trained, armed, and organized soldiers, but men willing to fight and die for the Islamic Republic all the same. Iranian forces had been outnumbered by the Iraqis 6 to 1 in the theater of operations at the start of the campaign, but by early December, they had cut Iraq's numerical advantage to just 2 to 1—more than adequate to halt the shambling Iraqi offensive.[17]

At that moment, Iran's ferocious internal politics came back to the fore. In truth, at no time during the war did the various factions stop fighting one another. The Iranian people may have set aside their differences and rallied to the flag, but the mullahs never did. In particular, the IRP never ceased hounding Bani Sadr. In response, the president had chosen to concentrate on the war. It seemed to be the one area where his power was unchallenged, the one issue on which he did not find himself constantly undercut by radical clerics and their henchmen. In keeping with his emphasis on secular professionalism, Bani Sadr had concentrated his efforts on rebuilding Iran's shattered regular armed forces, and he shared the professional military's disdain for the amateur zealots of the Revolutionary Guard and the Basij. Beginning in December 1980, even the sanctuary of his command of the war effort was denied him. The IRP railed that under his cowardly leadership the armed forces were insufficiently aggressive. They claimed that regular Army units were hanging back and letting the Pasdars and Basijis do all of the fighting. The fact that the Iraqi advance was stopped seemed to suggest that it was now time for the new Islamic armies to go over to the offensive.[18] The IRP's attacks had more to do with politics than military tactics, as numerous IRP members attested in publicly proclaiming that they would rather lose much of the country to Iraq than allow a secular government under Bani Sadr to restore the prestige of the regular armed forces.[19] In January 1981, Bani Sadr caved in to the pressure to go on the offensive.

The result was a fiasco. Iran's armed forces had come a long way in just a few months, but they were not yet ready for a major attack. In addition, Khuzestan's terrain remained very muddy, channeling movement into narrow assault corridors. To make matters worse, the mullahs and Pasdars at the front frequently communicated in the clear, which allowed the Iraqis to intercept enough information to have a fairly good idea of what was afoot. Consequently, Baghdad had concentrated several of its best armored formations to await the Iranian assault.[20] On the night of January 4–5, Tehran launched its 16th and 92nd Armored Divisions in an effort to envelop three or four Iraqi brigades around Susangerd and push them back from the outskirts of Ahvaz (Susangerd sits just northwest of Ahvaz). Initially, all of Iraq's advantages were outweighed by the sheer incompetence of its forces, and the Iranians made good progress. But on January 7, the 16th Armored Division was forced by the mud to attack along a single road hemmed in on three sides by Iraqi armor. When the Iraqis opened fire, the Iranians tried to get off the road and maneuver but many got stuck in the mud, making them sitting ducks. The Iranian division lost two thirds of its tanks, forcing Tehran to call off the entire operation.[21]

The disastrous Battle of Susangerd effectively finished Bani Sadr. If he could not lead Iran's armies to victory, what good was he as a president? Never mind that the mullahs had goaded him into launching the offensive prematurely. From that moment on, Bani Sadr was systematically and humiliatingly stripped of his powers by the IRP-controlled Majles. He was attacked relentlessly by the IRP-controlled media. He was denied access to the vast economic resources of the IRP-controlled *bonyad*s. He had no real counterpart to the Pasdars, Hizballahis, and *komiteh*s, who could rally popular support and engage in street violence. His allies were persecuted by IRP-controlled courts, while their own thugs went free. As the Majles illegally deprived him of powers specifically granted the president by the Constitution, Bani Sadr publicly protested, only to have Khomeini, of all people, scold him for "disobeying" the Majles and accuse him of trying to establish a cult of personality. In desperation, Bani Sadr turned to the MEK, whose members tried to stage rallies on his behalf but were physically stopped and beaten by Hizballahis and Pasdars. In June, Bani Sadr and Masud Rajavi both fled to Paris, at which point the Majles declared Bani Sadr incompetent to govern and issued a warrant for his arrest.[22] Far from bringing a more reasonable government to power, Saddam's invasion had helped ensure that the IRP—the most radical of all of the Iranian factions—was left with uncontested control of Iran.

Iran's internal problems did not stop with Bani Sadr's fall, and for months the Iranian leadership was consumed with the battles in Tehran rather than those against Iraq. The basic issue was that the MEK recognized that unless it could somehow turn things around, its days were numbered. Having openly declared for Bani Sadr and seen the Imam declare for the IRP—and force its leader into exile—the MEK had made itself a primary target of the IRP's wrath. It decided that the best defense was a good offensive and tried to decapitate the IRP leadership in the hope of either toppling the regime or forcing a compromise. On June 28, 1981, a massive explosion inside the IRP headquarters succeeded in killing much of the party's top leadership. Ayatollah Behesti (the leader of the party and the organizational genius behind much of Khomeini's success), twenty-seven Majles deputies, four cabinet ministers, and dozens of others were all killed in the blast. Two days later, a bomb narrowly missed killing Hojjat-ol Islam 'Ali Khamene'i as he delivered the Friday sermon in Tehran. Sensing that this was their last chance to survive (let alone take power), the Feda'iyan-e Khalq, the Communists, and other leftist groups also joined in the bloody campaign. Thereafter, the MEK and its leftist allies launched a sustained terror campaign that assassinated roughly two hundred government officials by the end of August. Then, on August 30, the MEK pulled off another dramatic coup, smuggling a bomb into the prime minister's offices and killing President Raja'i (who had succeeded Bani Sadr in blatantly rigged elections), Prime Minister Mohammad Javad Bahonar (who had in turn taken Raja'i's old office), and three other senior officials.[23]

Naturally, the regime reacted with concomitant ferocity. They cracked down on the MEK and the other leftist groups as hard as they could, arresting, torturing, and killing almost indiscriminately. On one day in September 1981, 149 people were hanged or shot by firing squad. The next week, another 110 were executed on a single day.[24] The MEK would later claim that altogether, 7,746 people had been killed in executions, street battles, and assassinations.[25] In the end, only the IRP—with Khomeini's full backing—remained standing. What's more, this internal battle somehow changed Khomeini's thinking, because as a result, he lifted his previous ban on clerics occupying senior government positions and had the faithful 'Ali Khamene'i named president to succeed Raja'i. At this point, Iran was a full-fledged theocracy.[26]

This change in leadership in Tehran also accelerated a change in Iran's conduct of the war. In April, Iran launched an attack in the northern sector, near Qasr-e Shirin, and with the IRP increasingly ascendant in Tehran, their commanders were able to prevail in the debates over tactics. So for the first time, the Iranians used large numbers of Pasdaran formations filled out with Basijis in human-wave attacks. Contrary to the dire warnings of Iran's professional military officers, the Iranians overran the Iraqi front lines and won the battle. This victory convinced them to try the same tactic on several other occasions on the southern front, and their successes in these battles convinced the mullahs and the Pasdaran that large-scale infantry assaults relying on the Islamic fervor of the Revolutionary Guards and the Basiji were both the key to defeating Iraq and a new way of "Islamic" warfare.

Eventually, the Iranian military forces hammered out a new military and a new approach to offensive operations. The purging of the officer corps, the deliberate sabotaging of equipment, the shortage of spare parts due to the U.S. arms embargo, and the lack of maintenance on most Iranian vehicles drastically reduced both the firepower and the mobility of Iranian forces. Nevertheless, the Iranians worked around these problems by conducting offensive operations using massed Revolutionary Guards and Basijis to assault Iraqi positions with fire support from Iranian Army armor and artillery formations. These massed human-wave assaults were horribly wasteful of manpower but frequently swamped the defenses or panicked the Iraqi soldiers into abandoning their positions. Once the Pasdars and Basijis had punched through the Iraqi lines, mobile Army detachments would exploit the breakthrough. These units moved quickly (as quickly as they could given their very limited mobility) and conducted deep maneuvers that resulted in large-scale envelopments of Iraqi formations. This combination allowed the Iranians to conserve their limited numbers of operational tanks, APCs, artillery, and other heavy weapons and employ them only when they could be decisive.[27]

Using these new tactics, the Iranians launched a series of limited offensives against the Iraqi forces dug in across Khuzestan. They proved stunningly successful. In September 1981, the Iranians relieved the Iraqi siege of Abadan and retook the east bank of the Karun River. In November and December, they rolled up the Iraqi front lines in central Khuzestan, near the town of Bostan, and drove a deep wedge into the Iraqi lines. In March 1982, they turned their attention to the major Iraqi formations left in a salient in northern Khuzestan, threatening the city of Dezful. In a weeklong battle, the Iranians conducted an impressive (if slow-moving) double envelopment that obliterated some of the best formations in the Iraqi Army. Iran crushed the remaining Iraqi forces in Khuzestan at the end of April and retook the city of Khorramshahr at the end of May, at which point it had effectively liberated all of its territory.[28] In June, with the dregs of his army fleeing pell-mell back to Iraq, Saddam magnanimously announced that he was "withdrawing" his units to Iraq so that Iran and Iraq could join forces and send their armies to fight together against the Israelis, who had by then launched their invasion of Lebanon.[29] Here as well, Saddam was to be disappointed by the Iranians.

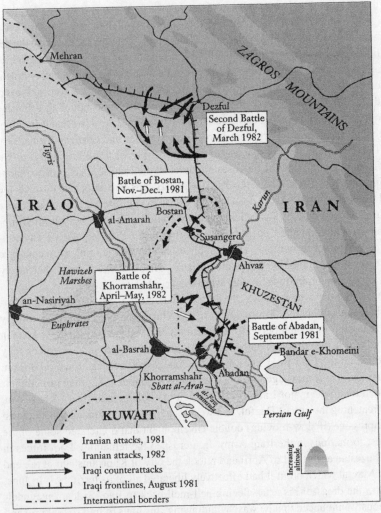

Iran's Counteroffensives, 1981–1982

The Road to Karbala

In Tehran there was euphoria. The armies of Iran—the armies of Islam, the armies of the Imam—had driven back the forces of the infidel Saddam Hussein and the despised Arabs. But immediately, the government in Tehran fell into factional debates once again. A pragmatic group of mullahs favored making peace with Iraq so that Iran could concentrate on setting its domestic house in order. There was still a great deal to be done. Iran's political structure remained immature, and its economy had never recovered from the revolution. Some also recognized that while regaining Iranian territory was one thing, toppling Saddam Hussein's police state was something very different.[30]

Inevitably, these pragmatists were staunchly opposed by the most radical wing of the IRP as well as the commanders of the increasingly powerful Pasdaran, who saw the war as a jihad. They demanded the export of the revolution and the liberation of Iraq (and all of the Gulf states, and, on some days, all of the Islamic world) from secularism, Westernization, and autocracy. As was most often the case, Khomeini sided with the radicals. He seems to have concluded that the war was a sign that it was his God-given mission to spread the Islamic Revolution beyond Iran.[31] In his words, "It is not a question of a fight between one government and another. This is a rebellion by blasphemy against Islam." He pledged to fight until "the government of heathens in Iraq topples."[32] On June 21, 1982, against the advice of many of Iran's generals, he ordered the invasion of Iraq and publicly demanded the overthrow of Saddam's regime. For the next five years it would be "war until victory" for Iran.

In mid-July the armies of the Islamic Republic were ready. Iran decided to launch its first offensive into Iraq against the city of al-Basrah, Iraq's second largest. Southern Iraq is heavily Shi'ah, which the Iranians saw as a natural constituency. Tehran knew that the Shi'ah chafed under Sunni rule and hated Saddam in particular. The Iranians assumed that if they could take al-Basrah it would spark a Shi'ah revolt that would at least secure all of Mesopotamia in a new Iranian-dominated Iraqi state, if not sweep Saddam Hussein and his Sunni supporters from power altogether. In addition, al-Basrah was conveniently located within striking distance of Khuzestan, where Iran now had a well-developed military infrastructure that could support large-scale operations into Iraq.[33]

Meanwhile, the Iraqis had not been idle. First, and of greatest importance, Saddam began sacking and killing the flunkies he had put in charge of the Iraqi military, replacing them with competent professional officers and giving them greater leeway to run the war the way they thought best. He bought tons of military hardware and and conscripted nearly every able-bodied male to the colors, so that even though Iran's population was twice as large, Iraq consistently had more men under arms. The Iraqis recognized that al-Basrah was the logical place for an Iranian attack, and Baghdad's combat engineers proved themselves to be first-rate: building trenches and earthworks, laying minefields and concertina wire, constructing tank firing ramps and artillery pits, and massively expanding "Fish Lake" and other water obstacles. The Iraqis dug in deep and awaited the Iranian assault.[34]

Iran's Ramadan al-Mubarak ("Blessed Ramadan") offensive in mid-July 1982 was conducted using the same forces and tactics that had worked so well in driving the Iraqis out of Iran. But now, against well-entrenched Iraqi forces fighting for their own homeland, the Iranians stumbled. The fighting was ferocious, with wave after wave of Basijis marching into the automatic weapons fire of the fortified Iraqi lines, often bringing nothing into battle but a Quran and a headband proclaiming their willingness to be martyred for the Imam. Mullahs were everywhere, urging on the faithful, encouraging them to march through minefields to clear the way for the better-armed Pasdars and Army units following. But so too were Iraqi tanks, artillery, and air strikes everywhere, and, in the end, firepower bested manpower. After two weeks of vicious combat, the Iranians called off their attack.[35]

But the Iranians refused to give up. The Imam had given them an order—to liberate the holy city of Karbala and depose Saddam's heathen regime on their way to Jerusalem—and they were not daunted. So they tried again in August, and when that failed, they shifted their forces farther north along the direct approaches to Baghdad and tried again in October. When that too failed, they shifted back to the south and in November tried again. In September 1982, the Saudis—who were terrified that the Iranians would overrun Iraq and then turn on them—proposed a peace deal that would have included a payment of $70 billion in reparations to Iran. Saddam immediately accepted it. And many of the pragmatists in Iran desperately wanted to accept the Saudi offer and use so phenomenal a sum to repair the damage from the Iraqi invasion and the revolution, and begin to build a new Islamic society. But the ayatollah wanted no part of Saudi Arabia's blood money; he was determined to liberate Karbala, then Baghdad, and then Jerusalem.[36] And so the Iranian attacks continued. The Iranians made common cause with the Iraqi Kurds and attacked in the north. They found ways into the swamps between al-Basrah and Baghdad and attacked there. They tried in every place and in every way they could, and each time the results were the same: through surprise and sheer weight of numbers, their forces could usually achieve a local breakthrough. However, the Iraqis had learned to build their defenses in depth, so invariably the cumbersome Iranian infantry formations would run into a second and then a third line of defense, and the horrible casualties inflicted by each successive Iraqi line, coupled with the inevitable (if not terribly well executed) counterattack by Iraqi armor would stop the Iranian attack cold after only rather modest gains.[37]

Stalemate

Despite their losses, the Iranians would not give up, nor would they change their tactics. Among themselves, they began to justify their losses by arguing that they were now pursuing an attrition strategy—bleeding Iraq's smaller population—that would lead to eventual victory if only because Iraq could not sustain the same casualties that Iran could.[38] Moreover, the combination of their victories in 1981–1982, the ideological appeal of relying on hordes of infantrymen often armed with only their faith in God, and the fact that they always seemed to be coming so close to breaking through the Iraqi lines each time kept Iran's leaders wedded to the same approach. They kept convincing themselves that next time, they would certainly break through.[39]

The Iranians were not entirely foolish to believe this. Saddam Hussein was equally nervous about the ability of his fragile regime, kept in power largely by terror, to withstand this constant onslaught. Although the Shi'ah had disappointed the Imam and had not risen up to welcome the Iranian armies—and had, in fact, fought courageously against the hated Persians—Saddam was not sure how long that would last. In particular, the Shi'ah made up more than 80 percent of the lower ranks of his combat formations, who bore the brunt of the fighting and the bulk of the casualties. Saddam noted too that the Iranians kept coming close to breaking through Iraq's lines, and he could not be certain that they never would. Thus, though it seemed that Saddam had finally stabilized the military contest, he actually became increasingly determined to find some way to bring the war to an end by ratcheting up the pressure on Tehran in other areas.

Saddam tried a range of gambits, but Iran was able to withstand them all. The first was a strategic air campaign that Iraq mounted against Iran's cities. By about 1983, the Iraqi Air Force had won air superiority by default. The Iranians were so short of spare parts, munitions, and other consumables for their American-built aircraft that they mostly ceded the sky to the Iraqis and instead husbanded their resources to protect critical assets and support major offensives. Although Iraq had launched sporadic attacks on Iranian cities from the earliest days of the war, in 1982, in response to Iran's assault on al-Basrah, the Iraqis launched sustained air, rocket, and missile strikes on Iranian cities, but these were poorly planned and conducted in desultory fashion—a few dozen here, a few dozen there. It was painful for Iran but not a serious threat. Moreover, there was a real imbalance in Iran's favor during these exchanges: Iraq's most important cities—Baghdad, al-Basrah, Mosul, Irbil, Kirkuk—were all within about 200 kilometers of the border, whereas Iran's most important cities—Tehran, Isfahan, Shiraz, Tabriz, Mashhad, and others—were generally much farther away. Tehran itself was 600 kilometers from the Iraqi border. Thus it was difficult for Iraq to sustain air operations against Iranian cities, while Iran could always cobble together a quick strike against Iraqi cities. Moreover, Scud missiles—which both Iraq and Iran eventually possessed— have a range of only 300 kilometers, so that whenever Iraq started bombing an Iranian border town with aircraft and/or Scuds, Iran could retaliate with Scuds against Baghdad itself but Iraq could not retaliate against Tehran. Finally, there was an imbalance in pain thresholds: Saddam was nervous that his oppressed citizenry would not tolerate being bombarded, while the Iranians were certain that their fanatically committed population would. At various points during the war, Saddam would get frightened or frustrated enough to start another "war of the cities," only to be reminded that the Iranians could actually inflict more pain on him than he could on them, at which point he would again call off the attacks for a while.[40]

Khomeini and the clerics also found Saddam's second major effort, attacks on the Iranian oil industry, equally unpersuasive in getting them to call off Iran's relentless invasion attempts. As with the strikes on each other's cities, right from the start, both sides conducted halfhearted (or half-witted) attacks on each other's oil facilities. Initially, both concentrated on the other's oil installations: refineries, terminals, and storage facilities. Neither side was able to do much damage. The Iranians had few planes available and great difficulty contending with Iraqi air defenses, while the Iraqis could not effectively execute strike missions against targets even as "small" as a major oil refinery. Initially, the Iraqi air strikes were also very inaccurate, in part because the Iraqis insisted on attacking only from high altitude and in part because their pilots were atrocious. In 1984, Iraq began to receive the strike version of the Mirage F-1 with advanced AS-30L laser-guided bombs. Baghdad sent its best pilots to France to train on the Mirage, and the combination of its best pilots, good training, a capable plane, and an excellent weapons system made a small but noticeable difference. However, even with the Mirage F-1s, the Iraqi air strikes never did enough damage to prevent Iran from repairing the facility in a matter of weeks or even days.[41]

Because of the Iraqis' early difficulties targeting Iranian oil facilities, in 1983 they shifted gears and launched a campaign against Iranian oil tankers in the Gulf. Initially, this too was not terribly successful because the only platform Baghdad had for attacking ships at sea was Super Frelon helicopters with Exocet missiles. The Super Frelons had a limited range and the Exocet had a small warhead that did little damage to most supertankers. In this area as well, the purchase of the French Mirages helped Baghdad. Not only did the Mirages have a longer range, but they were capable of refueling each other in flight, thus allowing for considerably longer strike missions. The training the Mirage pilots had received from the French also paid off. Nevertheless, the Iraqis still suffered from their insistence on using the Exocet missile (rather than more powerful ordnance) as well as their incapacity to properly identify targets ahead of time. On most missions, a Mirage would fly at medium altitude along the Saudi coastline, turn in to the center of the Gulf, flip on its fire-control radar, and fire at the largest ship it detected. This was no way to run an antishipping campaign, and it produced very middling results.[42]

Geography conferred important advantages on Iran in the oil war, too, that made it possible for Tehran to weather the Iraqi campaign. Iran's oil fields were generally located farther away from the border than Iraq's were, and, with the exception of the massive refinery and storage tanks at Abadan, most of Iran's other oil-related facilities were located well down the Persian Gulf coast. In addition, Iran had a pipeline network that allowed it to divert substantial amounts of oil to the export terminals at the southern end of the Gulf, where it was difficult for the Iraqis to get at them. On the other hand, the majority of Iraq's oil flowed out of terminals at its southernmost tip, just across the Shatt al-Arab from Iran. Iranian artillery fire across the Shatt shut down most of this traffic, while the Iranian Navy destroyed the offshore Iraqi oil terminal at Mina al-Bakr just two days into the war. Iraq was able to partially compensate for these losses via pipelines through Turkey and Syria, but in April 1982—after months of trying to get a better deal from the Iraqis—Hafiz al-Asad cut off the Syrian pipeline altogether and declared his support for Iran. At that moment, Iraq's oil export capacity was reduced to just 600,000 bpd, down from 2.5 million bpd at the start of the war. Eventually, Iraq was able to increase the throughput of the Turkish pipeline to nearly 1 million bpd, but not until 1985, when it opened a new pipeline through Saudi Arabia, was it able to get back to prewar export levels. Consequently, the Gulf states themselves had to start providing massive loans to Iraq to keep "the eastern flank of the Arab world" from succumbing to Khomeini's Shi'i Persian hordes.[43]

The last sign of Iraq's fear and desperation was its resort to chemical warfare. By late 1983, Baghdad had stockpiled enough mustard gas to begin using it against Iranian combat formations, and the mustard was soon followed by choking agents such as phosgene and then nerve agents such as tabun, soman, and sarin. The chemical warfare attacks inflicted horrifying damage on the mostly unprotected Basijis and Pasdars. Iranians scrambled to purchase gas masks, but these could do little against the blister and advanced nerve agents, which could kill by contact with exposed skin. Moreover, many of the Iranian soldiers had grown beards to demonstrate their Islamic fervor, which made it impossible to get a proper seal with their gas masks. All told, Iraq probably inflicted about 50,000 casualties on Iran with chemical warfare agents during the course of the war.[44]

Adventures in Lebanon

Throughout the period of Khomeini's ascendancy, Iran remained committed to the export of the Islamic Revolution.[45] Iran's collective perception was initially messianic: in deposing the shah and building the Islamic Republic, it was doing God's work on Earth, and it was to spread that blessing to the rest of the Muslim world, if not every nation on Earth. Later on, during the war, these same methods would serve as a defensive weapon that Tehran used to try to pressure the other Gulf states to stop supporting Iraq. At other times, export of the revolution came to be a more basic element of Iranian foreign policy, a way for Tehran to gain influence in parts of the world or parts of the region in which it otherwise would not. Finally, the export of the revolution also served Iran's (and particularly Khomeini's) obsessive hatred of the United States and Israel. It was a way in which Iran could lash out at the Great Satan and the Little Satan, and it could be done in ways that played to Iran's strengths and our weakness.

Thus, shortly after the revolution, Iran began to provide money, advice, and other support to radical Shi'ah groups in Bahrain, Kuwait, Saudi Arabia, and Iraq, in the hope of helping them to throw off the yoke of tyranny and realize a true Islamic society as well.[46] The Iranians set up a camp at Manzariyeh Park, near Khomeini's residence, to train terrorists in small-arms and explosives use and, in particular, how to conduct suicide attacks.[47] In 1979 and again in 1980, the Iranians supported uprisings among the Shi'ah majority of Saudi Arabia's eastern province of al-Hasa—which just happens to be where most of the Saudi oil fields are located.[48] In 1981, Iran established the Supreme Council of the Islamic Revolution in the World, and the Pasdaran created an Office of Liberation Movements, headed by Mehdi Hashemi—the son-in-law of Ayatollah Khomeini's heir apparent, Ayatollah Husayn 'Ali Montazeri.[49] In December of that year, Bahrain broke up a coup plot involving 150 Shi'ah who called themselves the Islamic Front for the Liberation of Bahrain, based in Tehran.[50] In 1983, a coup plot discovered in Qatar also turned up suspicions of Iranian involvement.[51] That fall, Khomeini called for an "Islamic uprising" during the Hajj (the annual pilgrimage to Mecca, which is one of the responsibilities of every Muslim to perform at least once). Montazeri himself called the Saudis a "bunch of pleasure-seekers and mercenaries" and asked, "How long must Satan rule in the house of God?"[52] For the next five years, the Iranian contingent at the Hajj started riots against the Saudis and the United States. In 1987, the anti-American demonstrations of the Iranian contingent turned into an assault on the Grand Mosque, provoking a firefight with Saudi security services that resulted in the deaths of 402 people.[53]

Of course, not everyone in Iran's power structure favored the export of the revolution over all other goals. Many of the same pragmatists who had urged Khomeini to end the war after the eviction of Iraqi forces from Iranian territory in 1982 also sought to moderate Iran's external behavior for fear of the impact it was having on Iran's war effort by isolating Iran and generating international support for Saddam. The pragmatists were able on occasion to convince the ayatollah to turn down the rhetoric, rein in the Revolutionary Guards (who were the prime vehicle for exporting the revolution in all its different forms), and extend an olive branch to various countries. However, it generally took them weeks if not months to convince Khomeini to do so, and typically the radicals could convince Khomeini to reverse himself in days.

Saddam Hussein grasped the importance of this commitment to exporting the revolution among Iran's leadership in the spring of 1982 as he scrambled to find ways to deflect the imminent Iranian invasion of Iraq. So in May 1982, he ordered the assassination of the Israeli ambassador to London, Shlomo Argov. His rationale for doing so had little to do with Israel and everything to do with the war against Iran. It was clear to all in the Middle East that the right-wing Begin government in Israel was eager to launch a major invasion of Lebanon to try to clear out the PLO enclave there, which was serving as a base for attacks on Israel. Saddam calculated that killing Argov would be enough to trigger the Israeli invasion, and he was proven right in that expectation. However, he was wrong about the connection that mattered most to him—which was that Khomeini's own hatred of Israel would prompt him to call off his invasion of Iraq and instead redirect the Iranian armies against Israel. Khomeini did intervene against the Israelis in Lebanon, but he did not halt the invasion of Iraq to do so. Instead, he found another way to fight Israel in Lebanon and declared that his armies would march on Jerusalem, but by way of Karbala (in Iraq), not Beirut.[54]

On June 6, 1982, in response to the Iraqi-organized assassination in London, Israel launched its long-anticipated invasion of Lebanon. The Israelis had two goals: to rid the country of the PLO and to create a new government dominated by their allies in the Maronite Christian community.[55] They succeeded quickly and easily in their first goal, but the second proved considerably harder. Moreover, as a result of Israel's effort to achieve its first goal, a Multi-National Force (MNF) of American, British, French, and Italian troops was deployed to Beirut to supervise the peaceful departure of PLO troops and prevent a final battle in and among Beirut's civilian population. When the PLO departed, so too did the foreign forces, leaving Lebanon to the Israelis, the Syrians, and the myriad ethnic and religious militias that had sprouted there after the outbreak of civil war in 1975.[56]

The Israeli invasion caught Khomeini's attention, as well as that of the leadership of the IRP and the Pasdaran. As they saw it, here was the "Little Satan," the instrument of the United States, attempting to expand the borders of the new crusader state by taking over more Muslim lands. The guardians of the Islamic Revolution were not going to stand idly by. So in the summer of 1982, Iran dispatched 1,000 Revolutionary Guards under the command of Mohsen Rafiq-Dust to set up shop at Baalbek in the Bekaa Valley and help drive the Israelis out of the country.[57] Many of the Iranians already had extensive connections to the more extreme elements of Lebanon's Shi'i community and were able to ingratiate themselves quickly into Lebanese society and attract numerous adherents.[58]

The Iranians found fertile soil in the Bekaa, which made recruiting easy. Lebanon's obsolete Constitution divided power among its various ethnic and religious communities based on a census more than fifty years old at that point. As a result, by the early 1980s, Lebanon's Shi'i population—which had grown to become the largest bloc within Lebanon's patchwork demography—was furious that it still was accorded status and authority behind the Christian and Sunni Muslim communities. A Shi'i militia called AMAL (for Afwaj al-Muqawama al-Lubnaniya, or "Battalions of the Lebanese Resistance") was formed to protect Shi'i territory and advance Shi'i interests. However, AMAL was secular and led by moderates who were principally interested in rearranging the power-sharing structure of the old, corrupt Lebanese government. This left a sizable number of Islamic extremists who hoped to create a wholly new society deeply dissatisfied, and throughout the late 1970s, groups would break away from AMAL to form their own, more radical organizations. In addition, after the Ba'th regained power in Iraq in 1968, it began to expel foreign-born Islamic fundamentalists as a threat to its hold on power. A sizable number of Lebanese Shi'ah had studied at the great seminaries in Najaf as students of Shaykh Muhammad Husayn Fadlallah and Ayatollah Khomeini while he was in exile in the city. These young mullahs were expelled from Iraq in 1977 and returned to Lebanon. The Islamic Revolution in Iran, led by Khomeini himself, ignited the emotions of these groups, so that when Rafiq-Dust and his company of Pasdars arrived in the Bekaa, people flocked to their banners.[59]

Given their initial successes, the IRGC contingent in Lebanon quickly doubled in size.[60] They set up an intelligence network; began providing training; furnished money, weapons, and other supplies; reached out to the various radical splinters from AMAL; and began to establish a variety of social services that would provide Lebanon's impoverished Shi'ah with the basic support that no one else could or would. They created a Lebanese "Hizballah" to supervise all of these activities and to serve as an umbrella organization that would coordinate the activities and resources of the many radical Shi'ah groups already involved in the fighting—against the Israelis, the Maronites, the Sunnis, and on occasion AMAL. Over time, the Iranians knitted many of these groups together such that by early 1984, Hizballah had become a cohesive entity rather than a coalition. Nevertheless, some of the groups continued to exist and operate independently in parallel with Hizballah itself.[61]

Through it all, Iran was the principal moving force behind Hizballah, providing it with an organizational structure, training, material support, moral guidance, and often operational direction. Hizballahis themselves readily acknowledge that "it would have taken an additional 50 years for the movement to score the same achievements in the absence of Iranian backing."[62] Indeed, the Hizballahis and Iranians have always been on the same ideological page. Hizballah not only accepts the concept of *velayat-e faqih* but acknowledged Khomeini (and later Khamene'i) as the *faqih* and Iran as their model of emulation. Indeed, an important element of Hizballah philosophy from the very beginning was Khomeini's brand of pan-Islamism, which held that Lebanon and Iran were two indissoluble parts of the same nation.[63] In addition, as radical Islamists whose spiritual leaders had studied with Khomeini, the Hizballahis also shared Iran's extreme anti-Americanism, magnified by their own country's painful history with Israel.[64]

When Israel invaded Lebanon, it did so with the connivance of one of the Maronite Christian militias, led by Bashir Gemayel, who was elected president of Lebanon after the invasion. On September 14, 1982, Gemayel was killed by a Syrian terrorist, enraging his followers and terrifying the Israelis that their carefully laid plans were about to disintegrate. The result was the massacre of thousands of innocent Palestinians in the Sabra and Shatilla refugee camps in

West Beirut by Maronite militiamen, an act so appalling that the United States, France, Italy, and eventually Great Britain pledged to return their troops to Lebanon as peacekeepers to prevent additional tragedies.[65]

Unfortunately, the Reagan administration did not understand what it was getting itself into. Bashir Gemayel was succeeded as president by his older brother, Amin, and Washington treated him as the legitimate chief executive of all of Lebanon. The problem was that none of the other ethnic groups (and few even of the other Maronite militias) saw him that way. To them, he was simply the leader of one Maronite militia, and often that is how he acted. Thus, in November 1982, Gemayel ordered the American-trained Lebanese Armed Forces (LAF) to retake positions in the Shuf Mountains south of Beirut in conjunction with his own militia, the Lebanese Forces. At that point, the other ethnic and religious leaders called on their followers in the Army to desert—which they did en masse, leaving generally only the other Christians in the LAF. Nevertheless, the United States believed that it was aiding the legitimate government of Lebanon and its national armed forces to restore stability over its sovereign territory. What the rest of Lebanon saw, however, was the Christian United States (along with Italy, France, and Britain) assisting its pro-Israeli coreligionists to expand the territory under Christian control. Without realizing it, the Reagan administration had taken sides.[66]

Then it got worse. As part of his agreement with Israel, Bashir Gemayel had promised to sign a peace treaty once Jerusalem had helped him to achieve power. Now that Bashir was dead, Israel and the United States pressured Amin Gemayel to make good on his brother's promise. Amin was more cautious than his brother, but he was now so dependent on Israeli and American support that he could not refuse. As their negotiations drew to a close, various groups in Lebanon disrupted the negotiations and attacked the United States for its new role as the Maronite protector. On April 18, 1983, one of the world's first truck bombs was detonated outside the U.S. Embassy in West Beirut, blowing off the front half of the building and killing sixty-three people, seventeen of them Americans. Undaunted, the United States, Israel, and the Gemayel government pressed ahead, signing a peace treaty on May 17. It was a historic occasion for Israel—its second peace treaty with an Arab state—but it did not last.[67]

The Syrians, the Iranians, and virtually all of Lebanon's various Muslim sects opposed the agreement, as did several of the Maronite militias. Lebanon's Druze population (the Druze are a highly secretive sect of Shi'i Islam who live in the Levant) began shelling the Maronite and LAF positions in Beirut with Syrian backing, prompting the Israelis to increase their own support to the LAF and the Maronites.[68] However, as the fighting escalated and Israeli casualties continued to mount, Jerusalem decided to withdraw from central Lebanon, retiring back to the Awali River, just north of the Israeli border. This effectively left the Maronites and the LAF to their own devices, and they were no match for the Druze, the Syrians, and the other Muslim militias. The retreat also uncovered the MNF positions in West Beirut, which were overlooked by the Shuf Mountains; the Marines immediately began taking sporadic fire, first from snipers and then from Syrian and Druze artillery batteries. By late September, LAF units had been surrounded at Suq al-Gharb in the Shuf Mountains, and in desperation, Amin Gemayel turned to the United States for help. Once again, Washington misunderstood what it was getting itself into. This time, President Reagan declared that Suq al-Gharb was of "strategic significance" to the United States, deployed American military officers with the LAF units, and authorized the Sixth Fleet to start shelling Druze positions in the Shuf. The fact that the French (the old Lebanese crusader power) joined in did little to ameliorate the anger of the Lebanese Muslim factions and their Syrian and Iranian supporters.[69]

Inevitably, there was a response. On the morning of Sunday, October 23, a suicide bomber drove his truck bomb into the middle of the U.S. Marines complex near Beirut International Airport, killing 241 Marines. Moments later, a similar truck bomb detonated at the French compound, killing 57. Two weeks later, another truck bomb was driven into the Israeli military headquarters at Tyre, killing 60. In every case, Islamic Jihad claimed responsibility for the attack. Here is where things get confusing. No one can prove even today whether Islamic Jihad was something separate from Hizballah. In the West, there is absolute conviction that Islamic Jihad was part of Hizballah or even just a name that Hizballah invented to cover its role.[70] Hizballah itself denies having mounted the attacks. However, what everyone seems to agree upon, including senior Hizballah leaders, is that a man named Imad Mughniyah and the Iranians were ultimately behind it. In particular, Iran's ambassador to Syria, Hojjat-ol Islam 'Ali Akbar Mohtashemi, "supervised" the planning of the attacks.[71] Imad Mughniyah was himself a close compatriot of Shaykh Fadlallah of Hizballah, reports directly to Tehran (often bypassing the Hizballah command structure), and would go on to lead many other terrorist attacks for Iran.[72] Regardless of who pulled the trigger, there was little debate that it was Iran that was behind the attack.[73]

Now it was time for internal political problems in the United States to make themselves felt. By early November, American intelligence had collected considerable information regarding the roles of Hizballah and Iran and, to a lesser extent Syria, in the Marine Barracks attack. What's more, they had also identified the Shaykh Abdallah Barracks as the Pasdaran headquarters in the Bekaa, and the training camp where a range of Shi'i terrorists were being trained by the Iranians—and where it was believed the attack on the Marine Barracks had originated. A pointed debate erupted within the U.S. government over whether to mount a retaliatory strike (in conjunction with the French) against the Shaykh Abdullah Barracks. The Reagan administration was deeply divided and often just as deeply undisciplined. The hawks, led by Secretary of State Shultz and the NSC staff, pressed hard for the strike, believing it was important for the United States to back up its tough rhetoric about holding terrorists responsible for their actions. The doves, led by Secretary of Defense Caspar Weinberger, had opposed American involvement in Lebanon from the start and fought to hamstring the operation and thereby speed its termination. They did this less out of an analysis of Lebanon or American interests there and more from a philosophical conception that categorically opposed limited uses of force. On November 14, President Reagan approved the strike and the French were notified that the operation was on for November 16. But on his own initiative, Weinberger superseded the president's orders and canceled the strike hours before it was scheduled. In Washington, there was a monumental row. As far as Hizballah and the Iranians were concerned, they had once again stuck the United States in the eye and gotten away with it. France—whose planes had been in the air when it had been told that the raid was off—felt betrayed.[74]

In early December, various Muslim militias stepped up their attacks on the Marines at the airport, likely emboldened by the failure of the United States to retaliate for the October 23 terrorist attack. The United States responded by shelling Druze targets in the Shuf again. Indeed, Washington had moved the giant battleship USS *New Jersey* to the Levant, and it joined in the bombardment. Anchored barely a quarter mile from the Lebanese coast, the first salvo from the battleship's sixteen-inch guns shattered windows and blew doors off their hinges all along the waterfront.[75] The Syrians too joined in, firing at American reconnaissance aircraft overflying Lebanon. On December 4, to try to send a signal to Damascus, the United States mounted an air strike against Syrian surface-to-air missile batteries, but it turned into a disaster arguably as ugly as Desert One; the strike did little damage, two American planes were shot down, and the public outrage that followed convinced Damascus that "the United States could not stand the heat of even a small-scale confrontation with Syrian forces," as Secretary of State George Shultz grimly put it.[76] Even the guns of the Sixth Fleet could not save the Maronite forces, who were systematically driven back by the Druze, supported by AMAL, the Syrians, and Hizballah. By early February, the Muslim forces had pushed the Maronites out of West Beirut, leaving the MNF isolated in unfriendly Muslim territory and increasingly victim to harassing fire from the hills overlooking the airport. In Washington, the Congress debated how fast the Marines should be withdrawn, and the press heaped scorn on the Reagan administration. On February 7, 1984, the United States pulled its troops out of Lebanon altogether, and one month later Amin Gemayel abrogated the peace treaty with Israel.[77]

America's policy in Lebanon was a disaster. It was a disaster for U.S. policy toward the region, and it was a disaster for U.S. policy toward Iran. It was a mistake to have intervened in Lebanon at all. Even with the benefit of 20/20 hindsight it is difficult to see how anyone could have solved the Lebanese conundrum in 1982. It took Syria another nine years (for a total of sixteen since its initial intervention) and a willingness to employ terrifying amounts of violence to pacify Lebanon under its control. Thus the Reagan administration cannot be faulted for not devising a realistic political plan to end the violence there, but without such a plan, as Secretary of Defense Weinberger argued, sending American troops in was at best futile. We compounded that error by intervening in the way we did—with limited forces, with heavy restrictions (from the Pentagon) on the capabilities and actions of those forces, tied to Ariel Sharon's fantasies about remaking the Lebanese state and ignorant or innocent of the powerful factors at work in that unhappy country. It was virtually foreordained that our Lebanese intervention would come to grief of some kind.

The presence of Iran's radical Revolutionary Guards should only have added to our caution. The Revolutionary Guards collectively shared Khomeini's blind hatred of the United States, and they were charged with conducting military and terrorist operations in pursuit of Iranian interests in Lebanon. Once American troops entered the country, it was only a matter of time before the Revolutionary Guard found a way to strike at them. Worst of all, America's hasty retreat after suffering 260 killed in all—at a time when the Syrians and Lebanese were counting their dead by the thousands and Iraqis and Iranians by the tens of thousands—conveyed the impression that the United States could not stomach a fight. In actuality, Washington had finally figured out that it had been a mistake to intervene in the first place, that American troops were not serving a useful purpose, and therefore any casualties were not worth it. But that is not how it was seen in the region. There, the withdrawal from Lebanon was seen in the context of both Vietnam and the earlier hostage crisis, and the lesson learned in many parts was that if you can inflict a little pain on the Americans, they will run. It would be an important aspect of Iranian policy toward the United States for many years thereafter.[78]

America's Tilt Toward Iraq

For the first few years of the war, the United States remained largely aloof. Neither combatant was a particular favorite of Washington.[79] As Shultz recalled, "Resentment of Iran still ran deep in the United States after the seizure of our embassy and people in November 1979 and the long agony of the hostage crisis that was so debilitating to the Carter administration."[80] In fact, although the United States had absolutely no contact with Iraq regarding Saddam's decision to invade—and never even discussed an invasion with Saddam's government, let alone gave it a green light—many in Washington took great private satisfaction that the mad mullahs and their followers were finally getting what many Americans saw as their just rewards.[81]

Nevertheless, at first there was no love lost for Saddam Hussein's regime either. It was not because he was an odious tyrant. The Reagan administration came to office without the same fetish for human rights that the Carter administration had nurtured. Consequently, during those years, the United States kept company with a number of odious tyrants. The problem was that he was not one of *our* odious tyrants, and we believed that he was actually one of *their* odious tyrants. In the early 1980s, Washington still divided the world between the Communist bloc and the free world, and we assumed that Saddam was a member of the former. Iraq had been receiving weaponry from the Soviets since 1958 (although it had also started buying from the Europeans, particularly the French, in the 1970s, after Saddam and the Ba'th took power in Baghdad). It had signed a Treaty of Friendship with the Soviets in 1972. And it was one of the leading Arab radical states, along with Syria and Libya, that was most opposed to Israel and that looked to the Soviet Union as their superpower patron. Thus, early on, America's policy toward the Iran-Iraq War was essentially "A pox on both your houses." As many American officials used to joke, the only bad thing about the war was that someday it would have to end. Nevertheless, recognizing that open warfare in so fragile and important a part of the world risked real instability, the United States eventually supported some halfhearted peace measures in the U.N. Security Council and declared an arms embargo and a program to try to curb foreign arms sales called Operation Staunch.[82]

Over time, however, that view began to change.[83] The most important element in Washington's change of heart was its abiding antipathy for Iran. American officials considered Iran one of the greatest threats to American interests on the planet: it was maniacally anti-American and highly aggressive, which made preventing Iran from growing any stronger—let alone overturning any of the other Gulf oil kingdoms—a vital national interest. This context was critical because all of Iran's actions were interpreted in light of it.

The sense that Iran was an aggressive threat to America's vital interests was reinforced by Iran's efforts to export its revolution. Trying to undermine the governments of Kuwait, Bahrain, and Saudi Arabia was not passive behavior. Likewise, Iran's interference in the Lebanese civil war could hardly be justified as defensive in nature. And when its Hizballah proxies began to launch terrorist attacks on American peacekeepers there, this pushed Iran into yet a new level of threat to American interests. However, the developments that actually triggered the American shift were Iran's sudden run of victories on the battlefield. By mid-1982, the Iraqis were not the only ones who were afraid that Iran was about to conquer Iraq, overthrow Saddam's regime, and then mount subsequent invasions of Jordan and Israel and/or the Gulf states. After the systematic way in which the new Iranian armies had shredded Iraq's better-equipped ground forces and driven them out of Iranian territory, there were widespread fears that Iran would be able to export the revolution on the shoulders of Pasdaran infantry.[84]

This fear prompted a reorientation of American policy to help Iraq enough that it would not be defeated by Iran. It did not represent an actual effort to promote Iraq's own aims—few in Washington were interested in that. The U.S. "tilt" toward Iraq came in February 1982, when the Reagan administration removed Iraq from its list of terrorism-supporting states. Washington claimed that this was in recognition of diminished Iraqi support for terrorism, but at the time, the evidence of such a diminution was scanty at best.[85] Nevertheless, taking Iraq off the terrorism list—no matter how cynical the reasoning— removed a number of hurdles that would have hindered U.S. support for Iraq. Soon thereafter, Washington began passing high-value military intelligence to Iraq to help it fight the war, including information from U.S. satellites that helped Iraq fix key flaws in the fortifications protecting al-Basrah that proved important in Iran's defeat the next month.[86]

U.S. support for Iraq increased throughout the war, especially as Iran's battlefield fortunes looked increasingly dangerous. Starting in 1983, the United States provided economic aid to Iraq in the form of Commodities Credit Corporation guarantees to purchase U.S. agricultural products—$400 million in 1983, $513 million in 1984, and climbing to $652 million in 1987. This allowed Iraq to use money it otherwise would have spent on food to buy weapons and other military supplies. In March 1985, the United States began issuing Baghdad high-tech export licenses that previously had been denied. The sophisticated equipment Iraq bought with these licenses proved crucial to its weapons of mass destruction (WMD) programs. In addition, Washington kept ratcheting up its level of intelligence cooperation with Baghdad, eventually authorizing a liaison relationship between U.S. intelligence agencies and their Iraqi counterparts. Perhaps more than anything else, the high-quality intelligence the United States regularly furnished Baghdad regarding Iranian forces and operations proved vital to Iraq's conduct of the war.[87] U.S. allies followed suit and started selling Iraq virtually anything it wanted in terms of arms and WMD.

As part of the "tilt," the United States turned a blind eye to Iraq's various misdeeds. The Iranians couldn't have cared less that America ignored Saddam's domestic abuses, even his near-genocidal Anfal campaign against Iraq's Kurds. However, they were outraged by Saddam's use of chemical warfare (CW) against their troops. They knew that Saddam was acquiring vast amounts of equipment, know-how, and supplies for weapons of mass destruction from America's allies (particularly Germany) and even some from America itself. For most Iranians, this was proof that the United States was encouraging or ordering its Iraqi puppet to use CW. Of course, Saddam was no more America's puppet than the shah had been, and Washington was hardly ordering him to do anything. The Reagan administration mostly just did not care. In March 1984, a U.N. report documented Iraq's usage of CW, at which point the United States issued a rather pro forma denunciation of Iraq's misdeeds. Washington did press the Europeans—especially Germany—to tighten their export controls, but these were little more than slaps on the wrist and did not have any discernible impact. The administration refused to further censure Iraq or even reduce its own support, and it blocked a congressional resolution that would have imposed sanctions on Iraq.[88]

In its terror that Iran was going to win the war, the United States was willing to ignore whatever the Iraqis believed was necessary to hold on, including using chemical warfare—which did seem to be fairly useful in stopping Iran's human-wave attacks. Thus, it was not so much a conscious decision to condone Iraq's use of chemical warfare against Iran, although some officials did do precisely that, as much as it was a general lack of interest in whatever horrible things were befalling the Iranians.

The Iran-*Contra* Mess

Consequently, it was a shock for the country to learn that the Reagan administration—those champions of the hard line who had excoriated the Carter administration for not being tougher with the Iranians—had been trying to trade arms for hostages with the very same people. The story goes back to Lebanon during the days of the Israeli occupation and the multinational intervention. On July 4, 1982, four Iranians—three diplomats on the staff of the embassy in Beirut and one journalist—were stopped by a Maronite Christian checkpoint and were never heard from again. The Iranians publicly protested, but given that this was the nation that had taken over the American Embassy and was trying to overthrow the governments of a half-dozen regional states, there was little international sympathy. The Iranians decided to take matters into their own hands: on July 19, David Dodge, the acting president of the American University of Beirut (AUB), was kidnapped. Dodge would later spend part of his captivity in Tehran. His kidnapping was almost certainly a response to the disappearance of the four Iranians, but Iran's thinking was unclear. No one ever delivered a "ransom note" to the U.S. government, which would have been expected if the Iranians had grabbed Dodge under the assumption that the United States controlled the Maronites and therefore they needed leverage against Washington to get us to force the Maronites to give up the Iranian hostages. Alternatively, it may be that they simply believed that kidnapping Americans would jeopardize the American presence in Lebanon, which was crucial to the Maronite hold on power. However, if the Iranians or anyone else ever proposed swapping Dodge for their diplomats to one of the Maronite groups, it has not come to the attention of the U.S. government.[89] Whatever the answer, the United States suddenly had another hostage crisis with the Iranians.

Then others got into the act. On December 12, 1983, six bombs were detonated in a ninety-minute period across Kuwait. The U.S. and French Embassies, a power station, the control tower at Kuwait International Airport, an oil depot, and the compound of an American defense contractor were all bombed. None of the attacks did much damage. Islamic Jihad again took credit, and the method by which it communicated its claim made it credible. However, the Kuwaitis quickly caught seventeen members of the Iranian-backed Iraqi Shi'ah group ad-Dawa who had actually conducted the attacks. This supported the supposition that Islamic Jihad is largely a cover name used by Hizballah and/or the Iranian Revolutionary Guard. (Indeed, now that ad-Dawa has become a respectable part of the Iraqi political scene, its leaders admit that the seventeen who blew up these targets were directed by the Pasdaran, although they claim that it was a "rogue" operation that was disdained by the rest of ad-Dawa.) Nevertheless, Iran's fingerprints were once again all over the attacks. The next month, when the trial for the "Dawa 17" was supposed to begin, Americans started disappearing in Lebanon. One of the Dawa members apprehended by the Kuwaitis was the brother of Imad Mughniyah. So Mughniyah murdered Malcolm Kerr, the president of AUB, and then began grabbing hostages—three in January–March 1984, including the CIA's Lebanon station chief, William Buckley, and CNN's Lebanon bureau chief, Jeremy Levin—to try to use them to get his brother and the other Dawa prisoners freed. Several of these hostages also ended up in Tehran, and Buckley was eventually tortured to death.[90]

More followed. In December 1984, Peter Kilburn, a librarian at AUB, was taken hostage. In January 1985, Reverend Lawrence Martin Jenco was abducted, although February brought some good news as Jeremy Levin was able to escape with some aid from the Syrians, of all people. (Which underscored that Syrian and Iranian interests in Lebanon were not always identical.) Nevertheless, on March 16, Terry Anderson, the Associated Press bureau chief, was taken, followed in June by David Jacobsen and Thomas Sutherland of AUB.[91]

By 1985, the United States was long gone from Beirut, and it is hard to imagine that after our undignified retreat anyone, even the Iranians, still believed we pulled all the strings in Lebanon. Hence that is not a likely explanation for why hostages continued to be taken. Mughniyah had his justification, but he was not responsible for all of the kidnappings. It may be that the Iranians thought they could use them to force Washington to scale back its support for Baghdad. Alternatively, it may be that other groups in Lebanon took American hostages on their own in the hope of making themselves important to Tehran and Damascus by doing so.

Nevertheless, Mughniyah was getting impatient. So on June 14, 1985, he led a team of Hizballahis who hijacked TWA flight 847, flying from Athens to Rome to New York. For three days, the plane shuttled back and forth between Algiers and Beirut, and the hijackers killed U.S. Navy diver Robert Dean Stetham and dumped his body on the tarmac in Beirut. They demanded the freeing of the Dawa 17 as well as 766 Lebanese (mostly Shi'ah) held by the Israelis. The Israelis made it clear that they had been intending to release the 766 prisoners anyway and were willing to do so if that was what the United States wanted. However, Secretary Shultz and other hard-liners in the Reagan administration refused to negotiate with terrorists, and the crisis began to drag on. At that point, Iran's influential Majles Speaker, 'Ali Akbar Hashemi Rafsanjani, convinced Khomeini that Iran did not need another hostage crisis with America, especially in the midst of the war with Iraq. With Khomeini's blessing, Rafsanjani began to pressure the hijackers to bring the matter to a close. Ultimately, however, the administration did ask Israel to release the 766 prisoners—albeit to do so in a way that tried to save face for Washington—and this concession plus the Iranian pressure convinced the hijackers to give up their hostages on June 30.[92]

The TWA flight 847 crisis was problematic in two ways. First, the Reagan administration had gone back on the president's pledge not to negotiate with hostages and so convinced other Iranians and their terrorist protégés that the United States could be compelled to make deals—including putting pressure on Israel to make deals—when faced with a terrorist act. As Shultz predicted, that legacy has haunted America's policy in the Middle East to this day. Second, it convinced many in Washington that (1) Iran was the right address to deal with the problem of terrorism in the region and (2) that there were Iranian "moderates" or "pragmatists" whom the United States could work with to end the hostage problem and perhaps even address other bilateral problems. The first point was eventually proven correct, but the second was only half right.

By late 1985, Iran had real problems. Its economy was straining under the pressure of the war. Shortages of food produced hunger and malnutrition, and housing shortages caused Iran's shantytowns to flourish again. The American arms embargo (and a worldwide oil glut) added to its problems because it meant that the regime had to spend its hard-currency earnings on black-market sources of American-made weapons and ammunition, rather than using them to help alleviate the economic problems at home—and even then, the Iranian armed forces were starved for ammunition and spare parts for their American weapons.[93] Meanwhile, the war had bogged down and the casualty count continued to rise.

These problems inevitably fostered disaffection among the Iranian people themselves. In April, there had been a series of antiwar and antigovernment demonstrations in Tehran, spurred in part by the March 1985 iteration of the "war of the cities." The regime was forced to turn the Hizballahis and Pasdars loose on the streets to suppress the protests. Mehdi Bazargan, the former prime minister, remained in Iran as the head of the Iran Freedom Movement (IFM). While he was increasingly excluded from politics, he still had considerable popular respect, and in early 1985 he warned that Iran must return to the rule of law or the country would explode. Ironically, that only prompted the Hizballahis to trash the IFM's offices and the regime to ban Bazargan from running for the Majles elections that year.[94]

The Islamic Republic was always a deeply fractious place, and the problems that Iran faced in late 1985 brought out widely differing notions of how to deal with them. The pragmatists stressed that Iran needed to ensure the survival of the revolution and believed that the best way to spread the revolution was by becoming a source of admiration that the rest of the Islamic world would seek to emulate—and all of this meant fixing Iran's problems at home. It also meant ending the war and repairing relations with other countries (including the United States) so that Iran would have access to the international trade and capital it needed to correct its internal problems. The pragmatists were strongly supported by the *bazaari*s, who wanted rational—not revolutionary—economic policies. They were opposed by the hard-line revolutionaries, who stressed that Iran needed to export the revolution to the rest of the Islamic world in literal form and create a new Islamic power bloc capable of defying both East and West. This debate became personalized in the form of Majles Speaker Rafsanjani, who led the pragmatist group, and Prime Minister Musavi and Ayatollah Montazeri, who led the radicals. For his part, Khomeini seemed emotionally sympathetic to the hard-liners, but he was realistic enough to recognize the merit of the arguments of the pragmatists, and so he could be persuaded by either side at different points.[95]

In Washington, the hijacking of TWA flight 847 had brought the issue of the hostages back to the forefront of President Reagan's concerns. During the TWA crisis, the family of the hostage Reverend Lawrence Martin Jenco pointed out to the president that he was making a swap of 766 prisoners from Israeli jails for the 39 Americans on the TWA flight but had declined a similar deal of the Dawa 17 held in Kuwaiti jails for the seven Americans being held in Lebanon. It was a powerful argument.[96]

Thus, the driving force for Iran-*contra* was the same as it had been for the last hostage crisis with Iran: a president who cared deeply about the fate of those who had been kidnapped. By 1985, Reagan wanted the hostages in Lebanon freed, and his staff was determined to find a way to do it. Robert M. Gates was then the deputy director of Central Intelligence, a disinterested observer with a keen eye for all that happened. His explanation best captures the motives of those on the American side: "There seems to me little question that, personally, Reagan was motivated to go forward with the Iranian affair almost entirely because of his obsession with getting the American hostages freed. And that obsession affected [DCI William] Casey strongly. Reagan was preoccupied with the fate of the hostages and could not understand why CIA could not locate and rescue them. He put more and more pressure on Casey to find them. Reagan's brand of pressure was hard to resist. No loud words or harsh indictments—none of the style of Johnson or Nixon. Just a quizzical look, a suggestion of pain, and then the request—'We just have to get those people out'—repeated nearly daily, week after week, month after month. Implicit was the accusation: what the hell kind of intelligence agency are you running if you can't find and rescue these Americans?"[97] This was also the view of all those around him who were involved in the Iran-*contra* fiasco.[98] George

Shultz remembered in his own memoirs that after TWA flight 847, "Pressure mounted on the White House and from the White House to 'do something.' Ronald Reagan felt a deep sense of personal responsibility for the fate of those seven unfortunate Americans."[99]

Just as there were Iranians who were considering the possibility of reaching out to the United States, so too were there a small number of Americans who believed that the United States should try to improve relations with Iran. One of those Americans was Robert C. "Bud" McFarlane, President Reagan's national security advisor at the time. Although he was staunchly opposed by both Secretary of State Shultz and Secretary of Defense Weinberger, McFarlane believed that it was possible and desirable. Then the Israelis entered the picture, in the form of Foreign Ministry official David Kimche. Although by this time Baghdad had begun to moderate its stance toward Israel and the Middle East peace process as part of the price for Washington's "tilt" toward Iraq, the Israelis still considered Iraq their enemy—and since nowhere is the notion that "the enemy of my enemy is my friend" more often applied than in the Middle East, the Israelis were attempting to help Iran. They had opened a channel to sell arms and ammunition to Iran through an Iranian middleman named Manuchehr Ghorbanifar. Ghorbanifar's contacts within the Iranian government had led the Israelis to believe that a group of "moderates" existed who were attempting to overthrow Khomeini. However, the Iranians wanted American-made Tube-Launched Optical-Tracking Wire-Guided (TOW) anti-tank missiles, and by law Israel needed American approval to transfer them to another country. In addition, Ghorbanifar claimed that, to prove their bona fides, the Iranians would be willing to free the seven American hostages kidnapped in Lebanon. Kimche wanted to know if McFarlane was interested. Of course he was: here was an opportunity not only to make contact with Iranian moderates but maybe even to help overthrow Khomeini, and the prospect of freeing the hostages would justify the entire operation for President Reagan.

And so it began. Between May 1985 and October 1986, Robert McFarlane, Oliver North, and a handful of other American officials mostly at the NSC and CIA authorized—with President Reagan's explicit consent but over the objections of Secretaries Shultz and Weinberger—repeated shipments to Iran of TOW antitank missiles (2,000 in all), 18 Homing-All-the-Way-Killer (HAWK) surface-to-air missiles, and several planeloads of parts for other HAWKs that the shah had bought but that had become inoperative over the years because of poor maintenance. In addition, they provided the Iranians with intelligence regarding the Iraqi military, which the Iranians demanded as a quid pro quo for the intelligence the United States was providing Iraq about Iranian forces. These negotiations were conducted with the help of a bizarre collection of middlemen, who were often found to have greatly exaggerated or even lied to one or both sides about what the other had promised. In every case, as far as the Americans were concerned, the deal was supposed to have been that the Iranians would have the seven Americans held hostage in Lebanon released in return for the latest shipment of arms. In every case, the Iranians failed to do so, although that never stopped the Americans from agreeing to yet another arms shipment in return for yet another promise of the hostages. On three occasions, the Iranians did see to the release of a single hostage—just enough to keep the Americans coming back for more. However, in September and October 1986, just before the clandestine effort was exposed and shut down, three more Americans were kidnapped in Lebanon, suggesting that the Iranians and their terrorist proxies planned to keep the unequal process of trading the occasional hostage for regular shipments of weapons and intelligence going for a long time.[100]

Fortunately, fate intervened to turn this misguided effort off. On November 3, the Lebanese weekly newsmagazine *ash-Shira'a* revealed the story of McFarlane's trip to Tehran. At that point, all of the details started coming out, including the even less well known fact that the profits from the weapons sales to Iran were being illegally diverted to fund the Nicaraguan *contra* guerrillas then battling the Sandinista government. The Congress had denied the administration funding for the CIA program to support the *contras,* but the NSC and CIA had found a way to tie one harebrained scheme to the other.

A great question mark has always been what the Iranians were up to. At this point, we do not have anything like a definitive account from the Iranian side. The most likely explanation stems from the combination of Iran's real problems in 1985 and the divisions within the Iranian government over how to address them. Rafsanjani was extremely close to Khomeini and also strongly in favor of creating an opening to the United States as a way to end Iran's isolation. As early as 1983, he had made the shocking statement in a Friday sermon that Iran would recognize any country that "honored" the revolution—widely seen as a trial balloon that relations with the United States should be normalized.[101] Rafsanjani undoubtedly convinced Khomeini that he ought to be allowed to explore such an opening in secret.[102] This made possible the various contacts between the Americans and the string of Iranian personalities all linked to Rafsanjani. However, the hard-liners continued to fight the effort. This seems to be why the Iranians ended up taking us to the cleaners: because of his larger policy interests, Rafsanjani and his allies probably would have been willing to obtain the release of the hostages, as he had with TWA flight

847, but the hard-liners' resistance consistently limited the ability of the pragmatists to make good on their promises. The hard-liners also, no doubt, saw this as an opportunity to obtain the missiles and spares that the Iranian military so desperately needed on the cheap and likely encouraged their cohorts in Lebanon to grab more Americans to keep this one-sided deal going.

Once the initiative leaked, however, Khomeini—as he had done to Rafsanjani and the pragmatists before—quickly distanced himself from the whole affair, leaving the pragmatists to take the blame.[103] The Associated Press reported that in a speech nearly a week after President Reagan's public disclosure of the affair, "Khomeini accused the unidentified officials of falling prey to 'foreign propaganda' from the White House, which he called the 'Black House.' 'I never expected such things from these people,' he said. 'At this time they should be screaming at America.' " While Khomeini could be convinced, after much effort, to adopt a pragmatic course, it rarely lasted for long, and especially not when it was seen as tying him to the United States. So once it was revealed, he immediately sold out Rafsanjani by denouncing it as a rogue operation by people who had meant well, even though they had acted wrongly (which, as a good subordinate, Rafsanjani did not dispute). Nevertheless, Khomeini moved to protect Rafsanjani and the other pragmatists by silencing pleas from the radicals for a full investigation of the matter.[104] The ayatollah had no interest in having his able and faithful servant come to grief, nor did he want his own role in the events exposed.

The Reagan administration's handling of its own Iranian hostage crisis was hardly better than the Carter administration's. Ultimately, Carter did not cut a deal with the Iranians (although it is clear that the administration was willing to do so in terms of issuing apologies and resuming arms sales once the hostages were released). Reagan, however, tried to. Based on numerous accounts by his chief lieutenants, Reagan appears to have been just as anguished about the fate of the seven Americans held in Lebanon and Iran as Carter was about the fifty-two being held at the embassy. The Reagan administration wisely kept the president's feelings quiet, learning that lesson from Carter's mistakes. However, the effort to trade arms for hostages was horribly damaging from a domestic political standpoint: two senior members of the administration were convicted of a number of crimes, six others were pardoned by President Bush before they could come to trial, former National Security Advisor McFarlane attempted to commit suicide, and the president's political advisers were at times concerned that the Congress would begin impeachment proceedings. Foreign policy initiatives don't end up much worse than that.

The affair was no less disastrous for U.S. foreign policy. The Reagan administration had convinced the terrorists in Lebanon and their backers in

Tehran that, contrary to its rhetoric, it would bargain for hostages. Consequently, not until December 1991 were all of the American hostages in Lebanon freed. Moreover, coupled with the retreat from Lebanon, Iran-*contra* seems to have confirmed some Iranians in their conviction that the United States was a paper tiger. This interpretation contributed to a pattern of aggressive Iranian behavior toward the United States for the next ten years. Because the United States had sold several thousand missiles plus parts for several thousand more in defiance of Operation Staunch—the arms embargo on Iran—American efforts to prevent other countries from selling to Iran were badly undermined. Washington remained fortunate that by then, Iran's hard-currency earnings were too meager to allow Tehran to buy sizable amounts of weaponry. Moreover, Washington had betrayed the faith of the moderate Arab states—let alone Iraq—in its solid support for their cause. Iran-*contra* made the Gulf states wary of the United States as a potential defender, a distrust that influenced their behavior in the run-up to Saddam's invasion of Kuwait in 1990 and that the first Bush administration had to overcome when it sought to deploy troops to Saudi Arabia to defend the Kingdom in August 1990.[105] America had a lot to do to make up the ground lost by Iran-*contra*.

The Imam's Legacy

As the Iran-Iraq War entered its sixth year, the Iranian people had lost most of their passion for the revolution. The adrenaline from the fears of the early days of the Iraqi invasion was gone, as was the euphoria of their victories of 1981 and '82. Now the Iranians were increasingly confronted with the hardships of life under an interminable war and an oppressive theocratic regime. A victor had not yet been declared in the struggle between reality and ideology in Tehran, but the people of Iran were already the clear losers.

For many Iranians, the 1980s were thus the long period of disillusionment that all revolutions eventually experience. All of the hopes and dreams set free by the revolution were slowly and painfully dashed. The Islamic Republic proved to be something less than the paradise they had imagined. Internal politics became far more rancorous than they had been under the shah and were often resolved through violence. Repression changed its form and its targets but, if anything, became worse than it had been when SAVAK seemed to rule the country. The economy did not improve; it got worse. Like other revolutionary regimes before, the Iranians had also been surprised and dismayed when other nations did not follow their lead in overthrowing their own governments and adopting the blessings of the Islamic Republic—let alone that their efforts to spread the revolution were provoking animosity rather than gratitude. By 1986, the energy and enthusiasm of the revolution had largely drained away. It increasingly required the whip of the Hizballahis and other revolutionary organs to maintain public "support" for the more extreme courses of the regime.

These realizations were shared by some members of Iran's new political elite, who attempted to steer Tehran's policy in directions that would not be quite so damaging. However, in so doing, they ran into many of the most fundamental tenets of the revolution—and their fanatical and entirely unscrupulous advocates within the power structure. The constant tug-of-war between these groups was responsible for the inconsistency of Iranian behavior during those periods. However, in the end, it all came down to Khomeini, whose semidivine status made him the final arbiter on all such matters. In the minds of most Iranians, Khomeini alone continued to tower above all of the disappointments of the revolution he had promised would solve all of their problems.

Khomeini's words and deeds had a profound impact upon the Iranian state. To this day, Iranians struggle with his legacy. Indeed, for Iran, the history of the 1990s and the beginning of the twenty-first century has been the story of how the nation has labored under Khomeini's legacy in both domestic and foreign affairs. Unfortunately, much of that legacy has been complicated or even downright pernicious.

To a great extent, the history of U.S. foreign policy toward Iran during this same period of time has been the story of how Washington struggled with Iran as it struggled with Khomeini's legacy. After the embarrassing debacle of Iran-*contra,* American policy toward Iran became defensive and reactive, and arguably has remained so ever since. The Reagan administration worked to repair the damage done by Iran-*contra* to America's position in the Middle East and had to deal with an Iran increasingly emboldened against the United States by the weakness displayed during the hostage crisis, the Lebanon intervention, and the Lebanese hostage saga. For the most part, Washington reacted to what emanated from Tehran. That is not to say that the United States did not initiate policy actions of its own, but those initiatives were driven principally by the tone and actions set by Iran.

This pattern would continue beyond the Iran-Iraq War. In part because of our long and troubled relationship with Iran, in part because Iran itself remained a deeply troubled nation, and in part because Iran just was never that important to the United States, Washington allowed the Iranians to take the lead in determining the course of the relationship. Thus Khomeini's handling of Iran, and of U.S.-Iranian relations, in the last days of his life—at the end of the Iran-Iraq War and in the first days after its conclusion—became the touchstone for the confrontation between Tehran and Washington that would follow.

Al-Faw and al-Basrah, Again

By 1986, the Iran-Iraq War itself had settled into an uncomfortable routine. The Iranians would launch a major offensive into Iraq about once per year, coupled with smaller attacks every one to three months, using their usual mix of Pasdaran, Basiji, and regular Army formations. Especially in their major assaults, they would typically break through the first, and maybe the second, Iraqi lines of defense before being halted by deeper fortifications and concentrated armor, and artillery, air strikes, and often chemical warfare too. The battles were bloody but inconclusive. Indeed, by 1985 the Iranians were actually scaling back their offensives to try to keep down casualties. For the first time, Tehran could not be quite so profligate with its manpower.

However, the Iran-*contra* affair offered the mullahs a glimmer of hope. The intelligence that the Americans had provided had helped the Iranians gain a more accurate sense of Iraq's defenses. In turn, this suggested an important weakness in the Iraqi line along the al-Faw peninsula at the far southeastern tip of Iraq—just across the Shatt al-Arab waterway from Iran. In addition, the TOW and HAWK missiles the Iranians had received gave them added firepower to resist the inevitable (but inevitably clumsy) Iraqi counterattack that they knew to expect and that generally had helped stop every previous Iranian assault into Iraq. Now Iran's masses of light infantry had the weapons to beat back Iraq's hordes of tanks and aircraft.[1]

So Iran devised a new offensive, carefully prepared its forces opposite al-Faw, and launched its best units across the river during the night of February 10–11 in one of the most daring operations of the war. The Iranians attacked in driving rain that helped cover their movements, allowing them to catch the Iraqi defenders by surprise. Baghdad had assumed that Iran lacked the equipment to cross the Shatt, especially at al-Faw, where the river is at its widest. Consequently, the peninsula was held by poorly trained and motivated Iraqi Popular Army forces that collapsed when they were suddenly attacked by battle-hardened Pasdaran assault teams. The Iranians poured troops into al-Faw and began pushing northwest toward al-Basrah and the port of Umm Qasr.

By the morning of February 11, the Iranians were across the river and behind Iraqi lines. They had finally achieved the great breakthrough they had been hoping for since 1982, and their commanders recognized the opportunity and goaded their troops to move as fast as possible before the Iraqis could regroup. For their part, the Iraqis panicked. Baghdad sent units hurrying south toward al-Faw without organizing a coherent defensive scheme. As a result, the Iranians easily defeated several hasty Iraqi counterattacks and kept moving toward al-Basrah. The Iranians had also been able to repair a number of their American-made Cobra attack helicopters, and these began ranging across the peninsula, picking off Iraqi tanks. In its desperation, Iraq even threw its air force into the fray, flying several hundred attack sorties during the first couple of days of the battle. But thanks to the HAWKs, and because the Iranian troops were largely light infantry, and therefore presented few high-value targets (and the Iraqi pilots were mostly awful), the Iraqi Air Force did little damage as well.

In the end, however, the Iranian forces were not up to the task. They were still hamstrung by shortages of trucks, jeeps, cars, armored personnel carriers, and all other manner of transport. As a result, Iran's unwieldy masses of light infantry could not pursue as quickly as Iraq's better mechanized forces could retreat. These shortages also crippled Iran's logistical support, which fell farther and farther behind its slow-moving infantry. Although they regularly performed better than the hapless Iraqis, Iran's own forces were still quite mediocre. Their commanders often showed more determination than tactical skill, and while zeal can take you a long way in combat, there are times when it is just not enough. Meanwhile, the Iraqis crammed armored and mechanized formations onto their front lines and eventually brought in their Republican Guard and special forces brigades, which together were eventually able to stop the Iranian advance. Just over two weeks after the start of the offensive, Iran had shot its bolt, al-Basrah was saved, and the Iranian troops began to dig in at the northern end of the al-Faw peninsula.[2]

Iran was, however, strong enough to hang on to its hard-won foothold. Baghdad had built up enough strength in the area that on February 22, it was able to launch a major counterattack to try to expel the Iranians from al-Faw, mustering three division-strength columns. The Iraqis threw everything they had at the Iranians. They committed the air force in full, flying as many as two hundred ground-attack sorties per day, in addition to enormous quantities of artillery and heavy doses of chemical warfare. They kept up these attacks for three weeks, but now that the Iranians were dug in and armed with TOWs and HAWKs courtesy of the United States, they made little progress. After several weeks of fruitless combat, the Iraqis were forced to call off the attack because they were suffering heavy losses.[3]

The Iranians were ecstatic and somewhat unrealistic about what they had achieved. They believed that they had won a tremendous victory and could now threaten al-Basrah from the east, northeast, and south—the city seemed all but theirs. However, that great victory set into motion forces that would lead to their defeat in less than two years.

Baghdad is where the shock of the Iranian victory at al-Faw was felt most intensely and most quickly. It prompted Saddam Hussein to allow his professional military officers to run Iraq's war operations completely and to allow them to restructure the Iraqi armed forces as they saw fit. So the Iraqi general staff took the Republican Guard—at that time, about three brigades of highly loyal, well-equipped troops—and turned them into the core of a new Iraqi Army. The Guard was expanded to twenty-eight brigades by plucking all of the best soldiers and officers from the rest of the Army. These brigades were then grouped under six divisional commands, provided with Iraq's best weaponry, and given intensive training and additional pay and privileges to keep them motivated. The result was a force with markedly greater combat skills than the rest of the Iraqi armed forces, one that was more than a match for the best Iranian units.

Meanwhile, success had bred dissension among the Iranians. The obvious next target was al-Basrah. But a major debate arose among the commanders—and among their political masters—over how to go after Iraq's second city. The problem was that over the years the Iraqis had never stopped fortifying al-Basrah, and now, after the fall of al-Faw, they redoubled their efforts. Eventually, the Iraqis constructed six concentric rings of fortified lines around al-Basrah, each of which the Iranians knew would be difficult and costly to overcome. Iran's most experienced and professional commanders in the Army and even some in the Revolutionary Guard were wary of attempting a direct assault and proposed a strategy of making numerous small attacks on the perimeter of the city's defenses, using surprise to catch the defenders off guard, cause casualties, and take some terrain, and then quickly shifting their effort to a different sector to keep the Iraqis off balance. The idea was that such a strategy would allow them to whittle down the outer Iraqi defensive lines before launching a major thrust. The firebrands among Iran's generals, mostly in the Revolutionary Guard, however, argued for a direct thrust with massive force, capitalizing on the psychological advantage they had gained from the victory at al-Faw and again relying on the superior devotion of their troops to overcome Iraq's advantages in firepower and fortifications. The debate became so vitriolic that the Army's ground forces commander, Brigadier General 'Ali Sayyid Shirazi, actually came to blows with the Pasdaran commander, Mohsen Reza'i, prompting Khomeini to relieve Shirazi, who had been one of the key architects of the al-Faw operation.[4]

The politicians also became involved in the debate. Khamene'i and most of the more conservative clerics sided with the Army, while the radicals naturally abetted the Guard. Interestingly, as a result of the Iran-*contra* affair, Raf-

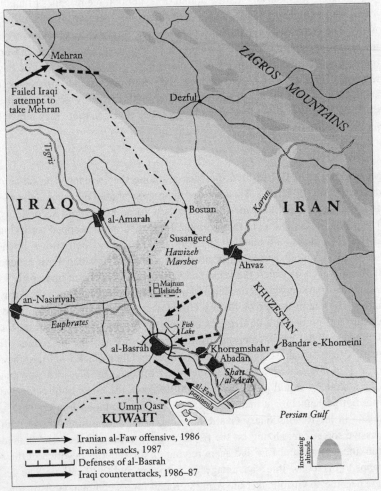

Iranian Offensives, 1986–1987

sanjani and a number of his allies also supported the Pasdaran position, principally to demonstrate their commitment to the revolutionary cause. As a result, it was the Revolutionary Guard that prevailed.[5]

By January 1987, the Iranians were ready to launch what they expected to be their final assault to capture al-Basrah. They concentrated a very large force of as many as 200,000 men and brought their most experienced Revolutionary Guard and Army divisions in for the attack. They knew that the Iraqis were fixated on their positions on al-Faw, because those positions were already across the Shatt al-Arab and therefore an attack from the south would not require Iranian troops to make a water crossing. Tehran cleverly played on this fear by launching a diversionary assault in late December that crossed the Shatt just north of the al-Faw position—as if to turn the flank of the Iraqi defensive lines facing south toward al-Faw as part of a major thrust out of al-Faw—and the Iraqis bought the Iranian ruse. When the real assault came from the east and northeast of al-Basrah on January 5, the Iraqis were caught by surprise. With that advantage, plus the number and quality of forces they had mustered, the Iranians quickly punched through the first two Iraqi defensive lines ringing al-Basrah.[6]

Both sides then pushed reinforcements into the area as fast as they could. Baghdad in particular began committing its best units, including Republican Guard formations, to the defense of al-Basrah. The Iraqis poured chemical warfare onto the waves of Basij and Pasdaran units leading the assaults. Iraq even unleashed its air force against the Iranians, conducting as many as five hundred sorties on some days, in an all-out effort to halt the Iranians. For the next month, the Iranians kept up the pressure on al-Basrah, feeding in more and more units to launch one attack after another. Through sheer determination, they continued to inch forward. By late February, however, Iraq had redeployed sufficient numbers of Republican Guard and special forces units to its fortified lines to put up a stout defense along the entire front. For their part, the Iranians had lost so many men breaching the Iraqi defenses (probably on the order of 70,000 to 80,000 casualties) that they could not keep the offensive going and were forced to bring it to a halt—although not before they pierced five of the six Iraqi fortified rings and penetrated to within a few kilometers of al-Basrah.[7]

Earnest Will

Another ripple effect of Iran's conquest of al-Faw was that it knocked over a line of dominoes that eventually brought the United States into the war, much to Iran's ultimate regret. This too began with Saddam Hussein, who once again started casting about for other ways to inflict pain on Tehran in the hope that this would convince the mullahs to call off their offensive or even make peace. Once again, he opted to try to strike at Iran's oil exports. This time, the Iraqi attacks were modestly successful, causing a drop in Iranian exports from 1.6 million bpd to 1.1 million bpd.[8]

The Iranians responded by ramping up their own attacks against the oil tanker traffic in the Persian Gulf. These tankers were generally not carrying Iraqi oil, which by then was largely being piped directly to Turkish ports on the Mediterranean and Saudi ports on the Red Sea. Instead, they went after the tankers carrying oil for the Gulf states themselves. This was fair game as far as the Iranians were concerned because the Gulf states were feeding Iraq tens of billions of dollars. In particular, the Iranians went after the Kuwaitis, who were allowing the Iraqis to use their ports to receive arms shipments.[9] During the height of Iran's offensive against al-Basrah, Iran struck twenty oil tankers in the Gulf, fifteen of which were Kuwaiti.[10]

The Iranians were quite resourceful in these attacks. Their air force had been worn down to about fifty to seventy operational aircraft, and so its utility was very limited. So too had the Iranian navy suffered losses and, as a result, Tehran held back its remaining large surface ships for major operations. Instead, Iran turned to a variety of other tactics. The Iranians began to use small boats equipped with antiship or even antitank missiles. They also fitted out other small boats as suicide craft that could ram another ship, detonating an explosive charge. They turned to shore-based antiship missiles, particularly the Chinese Silkworm (a clunky naval cruise missile but one with a big enough warhead to be quite deadly if it hit something). Iran deployed Silkworms on the al-Faw peninsula itself, where they could be fired across the Persian Gulf and over Kuwait's completely flat Bubiyan Island and hit ships in Kuwait Bay. They started work on sites for Silkworm launchers along the Persian Gulf coast at the strategic Strait of Hormuz, where they could virtually shut down tanker traffic to the Gulf. In addition, to press Kuwait on one more front, the Iranians again encouraged Kuwait's Shi'ah population to demonstrate against the government and conduct sabotage operations.[11]

Now it was Kuwait's turn to do something unexpected. Since they did not have a capable navy of their own, the Kuwaitis decided to rent one. They asked the United States if Washington would reflag eleven Kuwaiti tankers (that is, reregister them as "American" ships flying the U.S. flag) and so bring them under the protection of the U.S. Navy. American warships had been escorting U.S.-flagged merchant ships through the Gulf since the beginning of the war, and the Kuwaitis wanted us to do the same for them. Washington hemmed and hawed. The Persian Gulf was becoming a chaotic and dangerous place, and

America's admirals had little desire to get involved in the fracas between Iran, Iraq, and the other Gulf states. But the Kuwaitis were not about to take "no" for an answer. So they turned to the Russians. Alone among the GCC states, Kuwait had a long-standing relationship with Moscow, much to Washington's annoyance, and the Russians leapt at the opportunity; here was an opportunity to legitimize a Soviet military presence in the strategically vital Persian Gulf. The Kuwaitis and Soviets quickly agreed to a deal whereby three Kuwaiti tankers would fly the Russian flag. This instantly changed the minds of the cold warriors in the Reagan administration, who notified the Kuwaitis that the United States would fulfill their original request and reflag the eleven Kuwaiti tankers.[12]

None of this actually deterred the Iranians, but with both superpowers getting involved, they realized that they had to be more careful. This seems to have been the product of a debate between pragmatists—led, as usual once more, by Majles speaker Rafsanjani—and radicals centered principally in the Pasdaran.[13] The result was a compromise. Rather than come out and confront the U.S. Navy in particular, they opted to conduct what Tony Cordesman and Abraham Wagner have called "the naval equivalent of a guerrilla war." Operating from Iranian offshore oil rigs, Iranian small boats manned by Revolutionary Guardsmen boarded, seized, harassed, and attacked ships all throughout the Gulf, including a Soviet freighter in a rather obvious warning. In addition, they began to lay mines in the shipping channels. One of the Soviet-flagged Kuwaiti tankers struck a mine in the northern Gulf on May 16, 1987. Before this could lead to an escalation between Iran and the USSR, however, fate intervened. The very next day, an Iraqi Mirage inadvertently put two Exocet missiles into the side of the American frigate USS *Stark,* killing thirty-seven sailors.[14]

Although this may not have made sense in the world of Iranian conspiracy theories, where Iraq was America's puppet, the fact that Washington immediately shifted blame for the incident from the Iraqis who had conducted the attack to the Iranians—for creating a hostile environment in the Gulf—did. As far as the Iranians were concerned, this was just more proof that America would stoop to any level to destroy the Islamic Republic. On the other hand, there was considerable fear among the Gulf Arabs that the United States would now pull out of the Persian Gulf, just as it had pulled out of Lebanon in 1984. Although there is no evidence of this, it would be reasonable for the Iranians to have believed the same—as far as they were concerned, they had proven that the United States was weak and cowardly both during the hostage crisis and in Lebanon. And in fact, Iran did ratchet up its confrontation with the United States, launching more attacks on ships and laying more mines, including off the Kuwaiti oil port of al-Ahmadi.[15] To clarify their position still further, the Revolutionary Guards put up a banner in their Tehran headquarters that announced, "The Persian Gulf will be the graveyard of the United States."[16]

Washington was not going to back down either, however. The Reagan administration was smarting from the painful retreat from Lebanon and the fiasco of the Iran-*contra* affair, and some of its most senior officials welcomed the opportunity to demonstrate that the United States would stand up for its vital national interests.[17] As Weinberger put it, "I was sure that if we did turn down the Kuwaiti request, we would be demonstrating once again to our friends, and to potential adversaries in the Middle East and elsewhere, that we were not a reliable, strong, or useful friend in any crisis."[18] In addition, American decision makers unanimously agreed that Gulf oil exports *were* a vital interest of the United States and had to be defended.[19]

However, the Reagan administration once again went out of its way to limit its confrontation with Iran. The administration clung to the notion that it wanted to remain neutral in the war and not provoke Iran to retaliate. Iran was aggressive, anti-American, and unpredictable, and U.S. policy makers were leery of getting into a fight with it. In particular, they feared that Iran would escalate by mounting terrorist attacks against the United States elsewhere around the region or the world. Given that Iran did not believe the United States was neutral and did try to escalate as best it could, this restraint ultimately served little purpose. Nevertheless, the U.S. Navy was prevented from being too aggressive.[20]

In July 1987, American warships began to escort the reflagged Kuwaiti vessels under Operation Earnest Will, with a full carrier battle group steaming in the North Arabian Sea just outside the Strait of Hormuz. Ironically, as part of the very first convoy, the reflagged supertanker *Bridgeton* struck an Iranian mine. This victory only encouraged the Iranians to be even more aggressive in their mining operations, which provoked a number of European countries to send naval forces to the Gulf to help keep them in check. Iran responded in early September by launching Silkworms against targets in Kuwait from the site on the al-Faw peninsula.[21]

Meanwhile, the United States had devised its own solution to the Iranian mining problem. Washington dispatched special forces units to the Gulf, which, with highly advanced sensors, helicopters, and optical equipment, identified the various Iranian vessels laying the mines. During the night of September 21–22, American special forces helicopters cloaked to operate with relatively little noise and employing a variety of night vision equipment followed the *Iran Ajr* as it left port, sailed out into the middle of the Gulf, and began laying mines. After confirming that the *Iran Ajr* had laid six mines and was in the process of leaving more, the Americans attacked. The Iranians had no idea they had been watched the entire time and were quickly overcome. The next day, the United States showed off the ship, its mines, Iranian charts showing where the mines were to be laid, orders from higher authorities ordering the minelaying, twenty-six crew members, and videotape of the crew members discussing their minelaying operations. The Iranians had been caught red-handed.[22]

The net effect of this was merely to provoke the Iranians. The more pragmatic clerics in Tehran, again led by Khamene'i and Rafsanjani, were arguing to scale back the naval operations in the Gulf for fear of further compromising Iran's already fragile international standing. Far from providing the pragmatists with a stronger argument to make this case, the humiliating exposure of the *Iran Ajr* actually allowed the radicals to prevail again by arguing that Iran needed to show the Americans that it would not be so easily deterred.

In particular, the impact of Iran-*contra,* coupled with Lebanon and the hostage crisis, again seems to have played a role. The Iranians apparently saw American restraint—in merely capturing an Iranian minelayer rather than mounting a larger retaliation—as another sign of American timidity. So they turned up the heat, and at the end of September an Iranian frigate boldly attacked a Greek tanker with missiles and gunfire, even though two American warships were within six miles.[23] In mid-October they fired Silkworms three times at targets in Kuwait Bay. On October 15, they hit the supertanker *Sungari* and, the next day, the U.S.-flagged *Sea Island City.* Again, Washington showed restraint, retaliating only by destroying an Iranian offshore oil platform being used by the Revolutionary Guards as a base. Three days later, they fired another Silkworm at the Sea Island oil-loading facility in Kuwait Bay.[24] Earlier in October, the Iranians had tried to mount a large-scale attack by Pasdaran naval units on Saudi offshore oil facilities but were prevented from doing so by powerful Saudi and American naval forces that had been readied to meet them. Then, in November, Iranian-backed dissidents attempted to bomb the Kuwaiti Interior Ministry, and in March 1988, Iranian proxies began a campaign of terrorist attacks against Saudi facilities outside the Kingdom.[25] The Iranians were not going to back down.

Iran Vanquished

All of the various strands of the war finally came together in 1988 to produce a cascade of defeats for Iran. The tremendous enthusiasm and willingness to sacrifice inspired in the Iranian people by the revolution had carried them a great distance. They had driven Iraq's Army out of their territory and banged on the gates of al-Basrah for six years. They had held their own against Iraq's larger, better-equipped armed forces, which had been supported by the technology of the West, American intelligence assets, weapons of mass destruction, and tens of billions of dollars not just from Iraq's own treasury but from all of the Gulf states. Iran had even found innovative ways to prevail against the greater firepower, mobility, and technology of Iraq's (admittedly mediocre) military. It had been an impressive performance. But for Iran, it all came apart in 1988.

The first ominous sign was that popular support for the war, which had been weakening over the last two years, began to slide quickly. Pasdaran units began to conduct demonstrations in favor of "forgiving" Saddam Hussein. The pool of volunteers for the Basij virtually dried up, forcing the regime to begin drafting young men for the first time. Many Iranians grumbled against the war and even dodged the draft. As a result, the units at the front no longer had the pools of manpower they had once had, and they were forced to husband their resources by conducting smaller attacks than in the past. Leading politicians in Tehran began to talk about attrition strategies and triumphing by stirring revolution in Iraq.[26] Indeed, in private, a number of Iranian senior officials had begun to urge Khomeini to end the war after the al-Faw operation ran out of steam short of al-Basrah, but the Imam would not hear of it.[27]

Meanwhile, Iraq had been working hard to address the geographic imbalance that had hurt it through the various "wars of the cities." With European assistance, Iraq had devised a way to modify its Scuds to fly more than twice their normal range—finally putting Tehran within reach of the Iraqi missile force. On February 29, 1988, Iraq launched the first five of what it called its new "al-Husayn" missiles against Tehran. During February, March, and April, the Iraqis launched more than two hundred al-Husayns against Iran, almost all targeted at Tehran and Qom. The impact was devastating. The citizens of Tehran and other eastern Iranian cities had never been exposed to a sustained missile bombardment campaign, having suffered only sporadic Iraqi air strikes during the previous seven years. Moreover, rumors began to circulate that the Iraqis had developed CW warheads for the al-Husayn. The regime exacerbated the situation by foolishly trying to prepare the population for such an eventuality, which turned widespread anxiety into mass panic. In the final months of the war, Iranian civilians fled the cities in droves: more than a million people deserted Tehran in the first month of the Iraqi missile strikes alone, and more fled in succeeding months.[28]

At the battlefront, things got even worse. In addition to expanding and remaking the Republican Guard, Iraq's top leadership—now freed of Saddam's political shackles—set about teaching the Guard and a few other capable Iraqi units a new way to conduct offensive operations. The most important element of this new approach was detailed scripting of military operations. Exhaustive plans were given to the Republican Guards and the handful of competent regular Army divisions to learn backward and forward. For months beforehand, the Guard and Army units would practice executing these operations. The Iraqis built vast full-size mockups of the relevant terrain and practiced executing their scripted operations on them. Eventually, they reached the point where the entire operation could be performed from memory.[29]

In April 1988, the Iraqis felt ready to try out their new Army and their new method of offensive operations. They mounted an offensive to clear the Iranians out of al-Faw, and whereas in 1986 they had stumbled, in 1988 they rolled. To some extent, they were punching at air, because after the failure of the Karbala V offensive to take al-Basrah, the Iranians recognized that they did not have the manpower to hold al-Faw and had greatly reduced both the size and capability of their forces there. Baghdad concentrated 100,000 men of the Republican Guard and the Iraqi VII Corps against the 15,000 second-rate Iranian troops manning the positions on al-Faw. On April 17, they kicked off a tremendous bombardment with conventional artillery and chemical warfare. Then the Guard and the VII Corps launched their scripted and memorized offensive. In thirty-five hours, the Iraqis secured the peninsula and captured much of Iran's equipment intact. All things considered, it was a stunning turnabout for Iran, which had not fallen victim to a successful Iraqi ground offensive since October 1980.[30]

On the same day that the Iranian Army was reeling from its loss to the Iraqi Army on al-Faw, the Iranian navy suffered an equally crushing defeat at the hands of the U.S. Navy in the Persian Gulf. Days earlier, the Iranians had planted a new minefield in the Gulf in anticipation of an American convoy due to pass through that stretch of water in just a few days. When the convoy sailed through, the frigate *Samuel B. Roberts* struck a mine, wounding ten sailors. On the eighteenth, the U.S. Navy responded to the mine attack by executing Operation Praying Mantis. The American ships began by destroying three more offshore oil platforms that the Pasdaran had been using as bases to attack shipping in the Gulf. This time, however, the Iranian navy came out to fight. Light attack craft, F-4 Phantoms, and even Iran's largest warships sortied from Bandar Abbas and other harbors to take on the American forces. The Iranian missile boat *Joshan* started the battle by firing a U.S.-made Harpoon antiship missile at an American cruiser (it missed) and was immediately sunk in a hail of missiles and gunfire. Iranian small boats and a pair of F-4s also tried to strike various American ships in the Gulf, and several of the boats were sunk

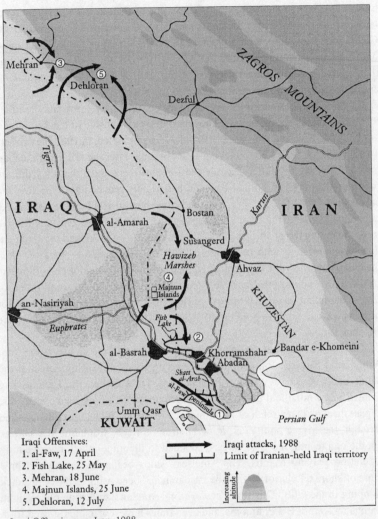

Iraqi Offensives:
1. al-Faw, 17 April
2. Fish Lake, 25 May
3. Mehran, 18 June
4. Majnun Islands, 25 June
5. Dehloran, 12 July

Iraqi attacks, 1988
Limit of Iranian-held Iraqi territory

Increasing altitude

Iraqi Offensives vs. Iran, 1988

or damaged, as was one of the F-4s. Later, the Iranian frigate *Sahand* fired on planes from the USS *Enterprise,* which was providing air support for the operation. The *Enterprise* aircraft immediately put two Harpoon missiles and four laser-guided bombs into the *Sahand,* sinking her. Finally, in a remarkable act of stupidity, the Iranians also sent out the frigate *Sabalan,* sister ship to the *Sahand,* late in the day, and it too fired three missiles at a passing American A-6 Intruder. The Intruder promptly put a 500-pound laser-guided bomb neatly down the *Sabalan*'s smokestack, crippling the ship, although the Joint Chiefs of Staff refused permission to the *Enterprise* to finish off the Iranian frigate.[31]

Over the next three months, the Iraqis mounted four more major ground operations against Iran, each one larger, more ambitious, and more successful than the last.[32] In May, they struck the Iranians near Fish Lake, just east of al-Basrah, knocking back the Iranian armies that had been poised on the outskirts of the city for so long. In June, they attacked at Mehran, and again in the Hawizeh Marshes, conducting a massive double envelopment there that destroyed six to eight of Iran's best divisions. Baghdad launched its last operation at Dehloran in July, driving forty kilometers into Iran and performing another devastating double envelopment. In all of these attacks, Iraq employed tremendous artillery and CW barrages, used the Republican Guard and its other capable units, operated according to the rigid method of set-piece offensives they had devised in 1986–1987, and enjoyed overwhelming advantages in firepower and numbers. For example, in June, at the Battle of the Hawizeh Marshes, the Iranian forces could muster no more than 50 or 60 operational tanks, while the Iraqis deployed nearly 1,500. By the end of July, Iran's ground forces had been decimated and were incapable of preventing the Iraqi military from driving into Iran and occupying whatever they wanted.

July also saw the final act played out between Iran and the United States in the Gulf. Praying Mantis had finally convinced Iran's admirals that they should not take on the U.S. Navy, but it had not completely dissuaded the Pasdaran naval forces from acting provocatively in the vicinity of American warships. On July 3, soon after Iran's crushing defeat in the Hawizeh Marshes, Iranian fast attack craft came out to attack Gulf shipping not far from a U.S. Navy surface action group. Two tankers sent out distress calls, and one of the Iranian boats fired at a U.S. helicopter. The American ships then moved to engage the Iranians, and in the midst of their skirmishing, a regular flight—Iran Air 655—left Bandar Abbas airfield (which was both a civilian airport and a military base) on its twice-weekly flight to Dubayy in the UAE. The plane's trajectory took it straight at the American ships, and the state-of-the-art air defense cruiser USS *Vincennes* somehow mistook it for an Iranian F-14 coming out to join the fray. In the heat of battle, the *Vincennes* fired two surface-to-air missiles that brought down the plane and its 290 passengers and crew. It was the sixth worst disaster in aviation history.[33]

The shoot-down of Iran Air flight 655 was an accident, but that is not how it was seen in Tehran.[34] The Iranian government assumed that the attack had been purposeful. Even its most sophisticated students of world affairs, such as U.N. Ambassador Mohammad Mahallati, called it a deliberate attack.[35] What's more, they assumed that the shoot-down had been the second part of a message from the United States, the first half having been Operation Praying Mantis. Tehran convinced itself that Washington was trying to signal that the United States had decided to openly enter the war on Iraq's side and was now willing to do anything—including killing Iranian civilians—to bring down the Islamic Republic. Thus, as far as Tehran was concerned, America could be expected to use its full military might against Iran if the fighting continued.[36] Meanwhile, the international community was virtually silent regarding the entire incident, which drove home to many Iranians the realization that they had so isolated themselves internationally that no other country would support them now that the United States was determined to destroy them.[37]

This set off another round of furious debate within the Iranian leadership, although by then it was really just a monologue by the pragmatic mullahs, who were trying desperately to convince Khomeini to end the war. The situation had gotten so bad that even the radical clerics had dropped their support for continuing the war. Thanks to the missile attacks, the awful casualties from the front, and now the Iran Air flight 655 shoot-down, the Iranian public had reached its breaking point. In June, an open letter from former prime minister Mehdi Bazargan to Khomeini demanding that he end the war circulated widely throughout the country.[38] That month, Khomeini had made Majles Speaker 'Ali Akbar Hashemi Rafsanjani commander in chief of all of Iran's armed forces, to deal with the military crisis and the ongoing feuds between the Army and the Pasdaran. After Iraq's sweeping victory at Dehloran in mid-July, Rafsanjani called a council of commanders from both the Army and the Pasdaran to assess Iran's strategic situation. The conclusions of that conference were unanimous and unmistakable: Iran no longer had the resources to defend the country against Iraq and the United States. A majority seconded Rafsanjani's conclusion that Iran had to bring the war to an end.[39] Khamene'i, the Assembly of Experts, the leaders of the Majles, the cabinet, and the government's senior military and economic advisers all concurred, and they appointed Rafsanjani their spokesman to convince the imam. After considerable discussion, Rafsanjani convinced the ayatollah that pursuing the war any longer would lead to the destruction of the Islamic Republic, and very grudgingly, Khomeini finally agreed.[40] On July 20, the Imam informed the nation through a written statement that "I had promised to fight to the last drop of my blood and to my last breath. Taking this decision was more deadly than drinking hemlock. I submitted myself to God's will and drank this drink for His satisfaction. To me, it would have been more bearable to accept death and martyrdom. Today's decision is based only on the interest of the Islamic Republic."[41]

Khomeini's willingness to bow to reality rather than accept martyrdom was important for the future of Iranian decision making. It demonstrated that the Islamic Republic was capable of allowing pragmatism to govern even its most important foreign policy causes. However, of equal or greater importance was the fact that the ayatollah was willing to accept defeat only after six years of utterly fruitless efforts to achieve his grandiose aspirations and a series of catastrophic developments on the ground, at sea, and on the home front. Had it not been for that string of defeats, he might well have persevered even longer, and in so doing would only have prolonged his country's misery. Iran got nothing from its decision to invade Iraq—something predicted by many other Iranians when the decision was taken in 1982. In fact, the country paid a horrific price for Khomeini's stubbornness. It would not be the last time that the Iranians persisted in a policy that caused them tremendous harm for the sake of a principle that only they understood. Moreover, when Khomeini did finally accept reality, it was too late for him to gain anything from it. Had he quit the war in 1982, Iran could have reaped enormous advantages—including $70 billion from the Gulf Arabs. By the time he finally did, all that Iran got was an end to its misery. And it was not only Iran that suffered for Khomeini's mindless adherence to misguided belief; every other nation that involved itself in this conflict suffered in direct proportion to its involvement—the United States, the Gulf states, Lebanon, Israel, and Iraq (although it is hard to feel any sympathy for Saddam since it was his own foolishness and avarice that had gotten everyone into the mess of the Iran-Iraq War to begin with). In the end, Iran was willing to accept reality, but only after it had beaten both itself and Iraq bloody trying to deny it and, in persisting, had deprived itself of considerable gains that could have been achieved if only it had been less convinced of its own infallibility.

America and Iran in the 1980s

The Reagan administration came to office wanting to have little or nothing to do with the angry, difficult nation of Iran. By the time they left, the United States was in an undeclared war with the Iranians. Washington was dragged, kicking and screaming, every step of the way into this fight, and once again the Iranian version of the history—which claims that the United States encouraged (or ordered) Iraq to invade Iran and then sought out opportunities to assist Iraq—is 180 degrees from reality. But naturally, so too is our own vision of a strong, consistent American foreign policy in the 1980s that sought to confront rogue nations like Iran that supported terrorist groups.

The United States studiously ignored Tehran until its battlefield victories conjured the nightmare of an Iranian victory over Iraq that would allow the ayatollah's armies to push either westward into Jordan and Israel or southward into Saudi Arabia and the Gulf states. Indeed, our eventual involvement in the tanker war (through the reflagging effort) was driven entirely by the threat to the Gulf states, not Iraq (or Israel, for that matter). Even then, the United States tried to limit the support it provided Iraq. Certainly the agricultural credits, civilian goods, and intelligence the United States supplied to Saddam Hussein's regime were useful to the Iraqi war effort, as was the willingness of the United States to encourage its European allies to provide Baghdad with the things the United States would not. However, the United States did observe its own arms embargo of both states—although it actively tried to prevent Iran from acquiring weapons while merely not providing them to Iraq. What's more, the Reagan administration tied itself into knots to avoid a direct military confrontation with Iran, much to the dismay of its own hawks, who feared that such signs of reticence would only embolden Iran's anti-American radicals.

Certainly, the United States did not seek out confrontation with Iran. If Washington had wanted to, there were much more aggressive and potent approaches it could have taken. Washington could have provided American weaponry—the best in the world—to Iraq. The administration could have sent an expeditionary force to aid the Iraqis. It could have sunk the rest of Iran's navy, obliterated its coastal facilities, and completely shut down its oil trade. It could have mounted punishing air strikes against Iranian military and intelligence targets in retaliation for each hostage taken and each terrorist attack conducted by Hizballah or other Iranian proxies. In the post-9/11 world, my guess is that if this history were repeated, the American people would demand that their government do so. But at the time, the United States did not.

Critics often complain that the U.S. government "doesn't have a policy" toward such-and-such a country or about such-and-such an issue. Generally, this isn't true. Most of the time the U.S. government does have a policy toward every country and every issue; it's mostly just that the particular critic doesn't like the policy or, sometimes, doesn't understand it. However, in the case of Iran in the 1980s, it is probably true that the United States did not have a "policy" toward Iran in the sense of a clearly defined goal for what Washington wanted to do with Iran and a strategy that explained how the United States would seek to achieve that goal. This was largely a result of the revolution and the hostage crisis. To American policy makers, Iran appeared to be such a bizarre and troubled country, so intensely anti-American, and so unpredictable that no one in Washington thought anything could be done with them or to them that could possibly benefit the United States in any way. There was a strong sense that Iran was a tar baby—any involvement with it would only bring the country to grief. And of course, the Lebanese intervention and the Iran-*contra* affair seemed to be proof of that conviction. The lesson Washington learned from those experiences was that whether America came into contact with Iran willingly or unwillingly, in the end we would regret it. Thus, the best Washington could do was to avoid Iran and hope that it avoided us too. It was only the threat to the vital oil exports of the Persian Gulf that brought a reluctant United States into contact with Iran once again. Then the Reagan administration did everything it possibly could to prevent the confrontation from escalating and to convince the Iranians that if they just kept to themselves, so too would we. It would be left to the George H. W. Bush administration to begin to formulate an actual policy toward Iran.

Parting Shots

The awful war with Iraq was finally over for Iran, and reconstruction could commence. As always, the Iranian people looked to their imam to guide them in this new phase of their country's life. At that point, the ayatollah seemed to understand that there was a great deal that needed to be done in Iran and that he likely would not be around to oversee it all. So he took a number of actions on foreign and domestic policy that seemed designed to guide Iran's behavior long into the future. These would become the seals on his legacy and consequently would be critical to his successors in defining the limits of their policies long after he was gone.

Even before the end of the war, Khomeini recognized that the governmental structure he had created was running into problems. There were too many independent centers of power competing with one another: the president, the prime minister, the Majles, the Army, the Pasdaran, the *bonyad*s, the revolutionary tribunals, the *komiteh*s, the Council of Guardians, and so on. All of these different institutions were capable of blocking a policy initiated by one of the others and all were capable of some degree of independent action.[42] The result was a bizarre combination of paralysis on broad issues of general policy and "freelancing" on tactical matters. Setting broad policy directions required achieving consensus among these different institutions, and because the Iranian political scene had devolved into its usual fragmented cacophony, that rarely ever happened. Within the Iranian polity, there were dozens and dozens of tiny bands, each of which had its own unique set of ideas. Because these groups could generally agree on lots of things that they did not want, it was easy for them to band together to block policies pushed by other groups. But because they could not agree on what they *did* want, they could not put together broad enough coalitions to actually enact coherent policies.

Nevertheless, because each institution also had a considerable degree of autonomy—and because Khomeini often failed to punish those who exceeded their briefs—on specific issues they could often press the edge of the policy envelope and take actions that were not necessarily sanctioned by anyone. By and large, it required Khomeini's personal intervention to unite Iran's fractious political shards around a particular policy and to bring wayward institutions into line.[43]

Khomeini's first instinct was to try to disband and curb some of the institutions. Thus he brought the *komiteh*s under the control of the IRP, and eventually they were submerged within a new umbrella organization for the internal security formations called the Law Enforcement Forces (LEF). Then the IRP itself was dissolved. The revolutionary tribunals were replaced with a central judiciary system, ostensibly controlled by the government. The position of prime minister was abolished and many of its powers transferred to the president. Yet these fixes did not solve the underlying problems. The *komiteh* members simply became Revolutionary Guards or Hizballahis, with the same roles and activities. The judiciary retained many of the features of the old revolutionary tribunals, and because there were few precedents of Khomeini ever having disciplined them, they continued to do as they saw fit in their sphere of governance.[44]

Later Khomeini tried creating new organizations to try to mediate disputes among the existing ones. The most important of these was the Expediency Council, which was intended to resolve differences between the Council of Guardians and the Majles.[45] But this too failed because all it did was to create yet another institution with some degree of independence and a certain amount of power. It was just one more player in a game that already had too many.

By the beginning of 1988, Khomeini seems to have realized that without a very strong *faqih,* like himself, the system would devolve into anarchic paralysis. Indeed, the only reason Iran had had any semblance of a unified policy and forward motion on that policy during the war years was that he had been there to set the policy by fiat and enforce its execution, largely by his own personal prestige. But by 1988 he was eighty-six years old and had been having health problems for several years. His successor was unlikely to have the same stature that he did, which meant that he would have to strengthen the institutional position of *faqih* to allow his successor to drive the Iranian system forward without his own charisma and unique status as "the Imam."

Thus, in January 1988, in the midst of yet another crippling political deadlock within the regime, Khomeini authored a letter, ostensibly written to Khamene'i and the Council of Guardians, in which he proclaimed that the authority of the *faqih* was absolute and his duty to preserve the Islamic Republic took precedence over all others. The Imam explained that the state, ultimately embodied in the *faqih,* was empowered (by God) to take whatever action necessary to preserve the Islamic Republic, even if this meant going against well-established religious law or the objections of senior clerics and jurists. Indeed, Khomeini indicated that the state/*faqih* could even supersede the five pillars of Islam (daily prayer, charity, the pilgrimage to Mecca, the statement of faith, and daytime fasting during the holy month of Ramadan) laid down in the Quran itself, if it were necessary for the preservation of the Islamic Republic. But this did not help, either—in part, because critics pointed out that this flirted with the cardinal sin of *shirk,* or usurping the unique sovereignty of God, by suggesting that the orders of the *faqih* (who was merely a man, no matter how learned) could take precedence over God's word as revealed to the Prophet Muhammad.[46]

And so, at the end of his life, Khomeini was leaving behind a governmental system that barely managed to curb excessive independence and break constant logjams when he was alive and provided no real evidence that it could be made to work without him. It was a very unfortunate inheritance for his heirs.

The Reconstruction Debate and the Rushdie Affair

Another of Khomeini's legacies was badly confused policy guidelines. This too was reinforced by the actions he took during his final days. At that time, the principal policy issue facing Tehran was the conduct of postwar reconstruction. There was no debate that Iran had a great deal of work to do to repair the damage from both the war and the revolution that had preceded it. The country was a mess. Two million people had been displaced or fled their homes, and as many as eighty different cities and towns had suffered significant damage. The port of Khorramshahr (once Iran's main oil export terminal) and the vast Abadan refinery had been destroyed. The oil-loading facilities on Kharg and Sirri Islands had been badly damaged. Inflation rose to 40 to 50 percent in 1988 and unemployment topped 28 percent in 1986 (despite the mass mobilization for the war), while agricultural production was worse than ever.[47] Iran's annual population growth rate stood at a staggering 4 percent, and in part for that reason, per capita income had dropped 40 percent since the revolution. Food imports now stood at $3 billion per year, while oil revenues had fallen to $9 billion. The CIA calculated that the war had cost Iran $160 billion over its eight years.[48] The total cost of repairing all of the damage from the war and the revolution was usually estimated at around $450 billion.[49] On top of all that, Iran had suffered more than one million casualties, with as many as 400,000 of those killed—and this from a population of 47 million in 1986.[50] It was a terrible war that left deep physical and emotional scars.

Naturally, a sharp debate broke out over how to go about reconstruction. As usual, the pragmatists, led by Khamene'i and Rafsanjani, argued that Iran should reconcile with foreign nations to attract aid and capital from both international financial institutions and foreign investors. They stressed that Iran simply did not have the resources to rebuild the country in any sort of rapid fashion without such foreign assistance. They were opposed by many of the same wartime radicals, who favored a "self-help" approach whereby Iran would rely only on its own resources and the abilities of its people to rebuild their country. They argued that the people were ready to make more sacrifices for reconstruction and therefore it was unnecessary for Iran to allow foreigners to participate in reconstruction. Since one of the purposes of the revolution had been to get the foreign influences out of Iran, reconstruction should not become a vehicle by which those same influences could slink back in.[51]

Khomeini's heart was with the radicals, but he recognized the validity of the pragmatists' arguments. He seems to have understood that the Iranian people were tired of war, tired of deprivation, even tired of his imposed social controls. The Imam repealed the ban on chess and allowed some Western forms of music in. The regime even loosened up a bit on free speech. Khomeini likewise decided for the pragmatists in a major debate over whether foreign trade should be controlled entirely by the government, as the radicals wanted, or partially determined by the private sector, as the pragmatists argued. He also allowed the pragmatists to start mending fences with many foreign nations, including France, Britain, and Kuwait. European hostages held by various pro-Iranian groups in Lebanon were suddenly released.[52]

In fact, things were going so well for the pragmatists that they decided to press on the most sensitive issue of all: relations with the United States. In October 1988, Mithileshwar Singh, an Indian-born U.S. resident who had been held hostage in Lebanon by Islamic Jihad for twenty months, was unexpectedly freed. The next month, on the anniversary of the taking of the embassy, the usual demonstrations at the scene of the crime were unusually small and subdued. Rumors began to circulate in Tehran. The conservative newspaper *Jomhuri Islami* published an editorial stating, "We have nothing to lose by establishing proper relations with the superpowers of the West based on justified rights of the Islamic Republic."[53] This was followed by a statement by Iran's deputy foreign minister that if the Americans "change their policies and treat us with mutual respect and nonintervention in our affairs, the relations with the United States will be like that with other countries."[54] This was hardly an unqualified overture, but for Iran, it was a dramatic shift.

January 1989 saw a new administration take power in the United States, that of the first President Bush. Even before they had taken office, the members of the new foreign policy team recognized the change in tone emanating from Tehran. They decided to extend a hand to the Iranians, to let them know that if they were ready for a better relationship, so too was the United States. At the very least, they wanted to see what might be accomplished with a careful act of reciprocity. So in his inaugural address, President Bush asked for Iran's help in freeing the remaining American hostages in Lebanon and famously assured the Iranians that "Goodwill begets goodwill." It was a small gesture, but it caused a huge stir in Tehran. Meanwhile, in an even more dramatic departure from past practices, Rafsanjani began to give interviews to Iranian media in which he went so far as to say that attempting to win a military victory over Iraq had been "too big a bite" and that Iran's Constitution had been written too quickly and was "incomplete."[55] Then Supreme Court Justice Musavi Ardabili remarked that the hostage crisis had gone on for too long and that the war with Iraq "should have been stopped after the liberation of Khorramshahr."[56]

As far as Khomeini was concerned, things were getting out of hand. A modest rapprochement with a few Western nations was one thing, but making up with the Great Satan was beyond the pale. Similarly, calling into question what were ultimately his own decisions about the conduct of the war against Iraq and suggesting that the structure of the Islamic Republic was less than ideal was going too far. Something had to be done to stop all of this and demonstrate the limits of tolerable dissent. Conveniently, an Indian-born Muslim writer named Salman Rushdie wrote a book called *The Satanic Verses* that offended some Muslims.[57] The ayatollah had the instrument he needed.

For five months, Iran had ignored the book and the protests among Muslims that it inspired. Then, on Valentine's Day 1989, Khomeini issued a *fatwa*—a ruling of Islamic jurisprudence—that announced that "The author of *The Satanic Verses* book, which is against Islam, the Prophet and the Quran, and all those involved in its publication who were aware of its content, are sentenced to death. I call on zealous Muslims to promptly execute them on the spot they find them so that no one else will dare to blasphemize Muslim sanctities." One of the *bonyad*s then offered a $2.6 million reward for Rushdie's death.[58] Khomeini's decree set off a worldwide firestorm, with his devotees bombing bookstores that sold *The Satanic Verses* in London, Italy, and California, as well as a New York newspaper that supported people's right to read the book. Many who publicly opposed the *fatwa* were threatened, attacked, and even killed, including an *alim* (a Muslim cleric) in Belgium, and the book's Japanese translator, who was assassinated by the IRGC.[59]

Rushdie was a prizewinning author living in Britain, and death threats against him were not the kind of thing the West could ignore. Many of the European governments that had just restored diplomatic relations with Iran recalled their ambassadors in protest. But Khomeini continued to rail that the book was proof that the West was implacably hostile to Islam. Eight days after his initial *fatwa*, Khomeini issued a "very important" address in which he warned that "It is not necessary for us to pursue the establishment of extensive ties (with the West)."[60]

Khomeini's *fatwa* may have seemed bizarre and trivial to many Westerners, but to Khomeini it was critical. As he pointed out in his same "very important" address, the book had been a "godsend" that helped Iran out of a "naive foreign policy."[61] Khomeini's response to *The Satanic Verses* was thus principally about Iran's own policy debate. The Imam was determined to overturn the liberalizing trends in both foreign and domestic affairs—which he probably had acceded to without recognizing fully what a Pandora's box (from his perspective) he was opening. Rushdie's book became the vehicle to try to shut it.

Imam Raft

Having recognized the need to set Iran's house in order before he died, Khomeini moved to address other issues of importance. At the end of March, he stunned the country by announcing that Ayatollah Montazeri was no longer his successor. Although Montazeri had remained a radical on foreign affairs, he had increasingly fallen in with the pragmatists on domestic policy.[62] By the end of the war he had begun to speak out publicly on the need for freedom of the press and to argue for better treatment of political prisoners. At one point, he went so far as to write Khomeini a private letter warning him that "the crimes of your Intelligence (and security Affairs Ministry) and your prisons are far worse than those of the Shah and his SAVAK."[63] After the war, he brought these complaints out into the open, saying that Iran had become known in the world only for its executions.[64] Along with Montazeri, a number of important members of the pragmatist camp were also dismissed, in particular several senior members of the Foreign Ministry who had been most supportive of a new dialogue with the West and the United States.[65]

Montazeri's sudden dismissal created something of a crisis within the regime, because none of Khomeini's other close associates had the religious credentials to succeed him as *faqih*. On the other hand, Iran's other grand ayatollahs (*ayatollah 'ozma,* the rank a Shi'i cleric must attain to be considered a "source of emulation" or *marja-e taqlid*) who did have the necessary credentials opposed the entire concept of the *velayat-e faqih*.[66] The Imam's solution was rather direct: he ordered that a constituent assembly convene to begin a revision of the Constitution. The new version deemphasized the religious credentials of the *faqih*—or *rahbar,* "Supreme Leader"—and instead argued that his public support and knowledge of social and political issues were equally important. The new Constitution also defined the powers of the Supreme Leader more clearly and greatly expanded them. It abolished the prime ministership and shifted most of those powers to the president.[67]

Finally, the Imam moved to tie up all of Iran's loose ends in terms of political dissent. He launched a wave of arrests aimed at anyone left with any sort of affiliation to the MEK and other opposition groups. Few in Iran shed any tears for the MEK at this point because it had sided with Saddam during the war and had even furnished a small army that Iraq had launched into Iran late in the war. Several thousand were executed by hanging or by firing squad in what Amnesty International called "the biggest wave of secret political executions since the early 1980s."

On June 3, 1989, Khomeini finally died. There was an outpouring of grief from millions of Iranians. But then it was time for the important business of succession. On June 5, the Assembly of Experts announced that Khomeini's faithful, if uninspiring, servant Hojatt-ol Islam 'Ali Khamene'i would be the new *faqih*/Supreme Leader.[68] In the days that followed, members of the regime also let it be known that Khamene'i was now to be considered an ayatollah, even though this title typically is won by acclamation from peers and followers, not promotion. In fact, the Shi'i religious establishment of Qom refused to acknowledge Khamene'i with this title and has not to this day.[69] In theory, the *faqih*/Supreme Leader ought actually to be a grand ayatollah, and therefore worthy of being a *marja-e taqlid*—someone whom the entire nation could look to as a source of guidance. But Khamene'i's supporters apparently recognized that the rank of ayatollah was enough of a stretch for him, and they would not push it further by claiming that he was a grand ayatollah.

Once Khamene'i moved up to the role of Supreme Leader, his compatriot

'Ali Akbar Hashemi Rafsanjani took his former slot as president of Iran in brazenly rigged elections at the end of July.[70] To most outsiders and many Iranians, this seemed to be a remarkable turnabout in Iranian domestic politics and an overwhelming victory for the pragmatists. However, they were all to be badly disappointed. Azar Nafisi remarked about Khamene'i that "From a tepid liberal he turned overnight into an irredeemable hard-liner." Whereas once Khamene'i and Rafsanjani had been seen as an almost inseparable partnership at the head of the pragmatist camp, over time they began to part ways.

Although it is possible that Khamene'i was always a hard-liner at heart and simply played the pragmatist during the 1980s, it seems far more likely that he was sympathetic to both arguments (hence his "tepid" liberalism) but found himself pushed into the camp of the hard-liners by the circumstances of his accession. Khamene'i's poor credentials—and the need to rewrite the Constitution for him to become *faqih*—left him without a great deal of legitimacy to rule. The most important source of his legitimacy as far as the vast majority of Iranians were concerned lay in his adherence to Khomeini's precepts, and thus his most important task was faithfully executing the Imam's will. Ultimately, Khomeini was the source of all legitimacy in postrevolutionary Iran, and that meant Khamene'i had to be careful to remain firmly within the parameters outlined by the Imam. In the final year of his life, among the Rushdie *fatwa,* the dismissal of Montazeri, the final crackdown on dissidents, and his condemnation of relations with the West (and particularly the United States), Khomeini had made it very clear that his vision of the Islamic Revolution was the most radical, dogmatic, ideological, uncompromising, and anti-American version of it. If Khamene'i were to be seen as legitimate by the Iranian people, he would have to adhere to that legacy.[71]

In addition, Khamene'i needed the radicals to defend his legitimacy. By their nature, the pragmatists were not overly concerned with Islamic or revolutionary credentials: their whole point was to pursue policies that they thought best for Iran on technocratic grounds regardless of religious or other ideological purity. They were unlikely to question Khamene'i's fitness to be *faqih.* However, the same could not be said for the radicals, who saw themselves as the spiritual guardians of the Islamic Revolution. If they did not like Khamene'i's policies, and particularly if they believed he was deviating significantly from the radical policies Khomeini had endorsed at the end of his life, the radicals would have moved to undermine or topple him on those grounds. That was a threat Khamene'i certainly could not abide. Moreover, Khamene'i needed to run the government, and its key institutions—particularly its most powerful and independent, such as the Pasdaran, the judiciary, the *bonyads,* the Council of Guardians, and the Assembly of Experts—were all dominated by the radicals. For all of these reasons, the new Supreme Leader ultimately turned out to be much more of a hard-liner than anyone had expected.

Nevertheless, Khomeini had been fully cognizant that the decisions he made in the last days of his life would have a profound impact in shaping Iran long after he was gone. Because he had so dominated the Iranian Revolution, and because the country he left behind was something of a political shambles, those final decisions became the defining features of Iranian politics ever since. Khomeini's legacy became the banner of large segments of Iranian society. It has defined Khamene'i's tenure as Supreme Leader, and it later defined the reformist opposition that eventually emerged in the mid-1990s, both in terms of what was considered permissible dissent and what their central grievances became. To this day, many of Iran's domestic and foreign policy debates are born of the ongoing intellectual, religious, and political struggle with the legacy of Khomeini. So too, then, America's ongoing confrontation with Iran is a struggle with a nation grappling with the Imam's legacy.

CHAPTER 9

Collision Course

The conclusion of the Iran-Iraq War in 1988 had allowed Tehran's leadership to begin to think about something other than the all-consuming war with Iraq. The costs of the war also forced them to ask some basic questions about the nature of revolutionary Iran. The revolution was over, the war was over, now what kind of a country did they want to build? However, Khomeini's death, so soon after the war and before so many basic issues had been sorted out, locked his successors into a number of patterns, values, and goals that would prove debilitating and dangerous over time. Some of Iran's leaders would show real creativity in skirting the boundaries the Imam had laid down on a variety of issues. However, they were not able to overturn them altogether, try though they sometimes might, and they were least successful in charting new courses on some of the most important aspects of Iran's foreign policy—its relationship with the United States, opposition to the Middle East peace process, and export of the revolution.

Understandably, Iran had also learned some very unhealthy lessons from its experiences in the 1980s. Based on the hostage crisis, Lebanon, and the Lebanese hostage crisis, many Iranian leaders concluded that the United States was so sensitive to casualties that even small numbers could cause Washington to cut and run. They did learn from their own experience during the tanker war that if challenged overtly, the United States was capable of inflicting severe damage on Iran, but those same events also seemed to suggest that the United States was loath to take such action and would not do so unless provoked in a clear and unmistakable way.

The crucial ingredient that was then added in the early 1990s was the determination of the United States (during both the Bush and Clinton administrations) to forge a new peace between Israel and its Arab neighbors. This was anathema to both Iran's ideology and its strategic position, at least as the Islamist theocracy conceived of it. Although it was not the only source of trouble, America's determination to make peace and Iran's determination to wreck it put the two countries on a collision course, leading to a series of escalations by each side—although Iran seemed to be conscious of the game it was playing while the United States often did not. As a result, the two sides almost came to blows once again in 1996.

Thus, the end of the 1980s and the start of the 1990s saw all of the various elements of U.S.-Iranian relations that had been forming over the decades come together. The result was a direct confrontation that rapidly intensified to the brink of war. With the "distraction" of the Iran-Iraq War removed from the scene, America and Iran confronted each other directly: Iran in a deliberate way, the United States because it was dragged into the confrontation by Iran's aggressive attacks.

The Bush Administration and the Overshadowing of Iran by Iraq

Iran was never wholly absent from the first Bush administration's agenda, but it tended not to be a primary consideration either. The Bush team had a few other things on their plate. In 1989, the Berlin Wall fell and the Cold War evaporated with it. That same year, democracy nearly broke out in China, until it was extinguished at Tiananmen Square. In 1990, Saddam Hussein invaded Kuwait in a misguided effort to solve his economic problems through military conquest and achieve his dream of becoming the dominant power in the Arab world—a dream that had been frustrated by his failed invasion of Iran ten years before. The Bush administration worked hard to build an unprecedented international consensus and multilateral coalition to eject Iraq from Kuwait and then unleashed the forty-three-day Persian Gulf War, which freed Kuwait and smashed Iraq's military power. The Gulf War was followed in quick succession by the reunification of Germany, the collapse of the Soviet Union, the creation of its successor states, humanitarian catastrophes in northern Iraq and Somalia, and finally the administration's own Madrid Conference, which inaugurated a new Middle East peace process. In the course of four years, it was an administration that accomplished an astonishing amount.

Early on, some senior Bush administration officials were interested in testing whether Iran had changed its views toward the United States—and whether it would be possible to establish enough of a relationship to convince Tehran to lean on its Lebanese terrorist allies to release the remaining hostages. President Bush himself had been vice president during the Iran-*contra* debacle and had been privy to at least some of those events. His national security advisor, Lieutenant General Brent Scowcroft, had been one of the members of the Tower Commission, which had investigated the Iran-*contra* events. Both came to office hoping to improve relations with Iran because of these experiences, although that history also made them cautious.

The administration eased some of the sanctions that had been applied to Iran during the Iran-Iraq War. In addition to the president's inaugural message, Washington proposed covert meetings in Europe between American and Iranian officials. Although there were indications that the Iranian pragmatists wanted to accept the deal, in the end they were unable to. In particular, having been so badly burned by the revelation of the Iran-*contra* connection, Rafsanjani apparently did not trust the United States to keep such meetings secret. Instead, a channel was opened between Washington and Tehran using the courageous and talented U.N. envoy Giandomenico Picco, who began a lengthy series of negotiations to get the hostages released. Picco was able to work out a deal in which Iran would get the hostages released in return for American support for a U.N. Security Council resolution that squarely blamed Iraq for starting the Iran-Iraq War—which had the benefit of being true and which Iran wanted both for emotional reasons and to establish a basis for war claims against Iraq.[1] The willingness of the administration to try to reach out to Iran during its first years in office even extended to an embarrassing incident in which an unknown Iranian called the White House and managed to convince senior administration officials that he was a representative of Rafsanjani—prompting President Bush to return the call, believing that he would be speaking to the president of Iran, only to realize that the person on the other end was *not* Hashemi Rafsanjani.[2]

Indeed, all of the administration's early efforts came to naught. While Rafsanjani and others around him might have been interested in an official dialogue with the United States, they were in no position to act on it. When the pragmatists were finally able to convince the rest of the Iranian regime that the hostages were doing more damage to Iran's international relations than they were worth, it was too late. By the time the last hostages were freed in 1991, Iran and its proxies had done so many other belligerent things in the meantime—such as the brutal murder of Lieutenant Colonel William Higgins (who had been held hostage by Islamic Jihad since February 1988) on July 31, 1989—that no one in Washington was interested in improved relations any longer. The administration recognized that there was a faction within the Iranian regime that wanted better relations, but they concluded that the United States could not start a rapprochement with a *faction* inside the Iranian government; until Iran as a whole was ready, it would be a waste of America's time—and a potentially embarrassing one, as their own experiences with Iran-*contra* reminded them.[3]

When Iraq invaded Kuwait on August 2, 1990, the attention of the world focused on the Persian Gulf once again and American forces returned to the region in strength. Tehran was wary of the deployment of American and other Western forces in the Gulf, suspecting that it was all just a ruse to cover a buildup for an American invasion of Iran. However, with nearly 700,000 American, European, and Arab troops on hand, the Iranians were in no position to try anything provocative. So they watched and waited to see what the Americans would do. Breaking Saddam's military power could only benefit them, and the Iranians hoped (like many others in the region) that the United States would finish him off, although at the same time, they were afraid that Washington would replace Saddam with a pro-American regime that might be almost as bad for Tehran.

Ultimately, of course, the United States did not ensure Saddam's fall from power after the sweeping victory of Operation Desert Storm, and, ironically, Iran had a good deal to do with it. Within twenty-four hours of the end of the Gulf War on February 28, 1991, revolts broke out among demoralized Iraqi soldiers sick of Saddam's repressive rule and catastrophic foreign policy adventures. The revolt spread quickly among the Shi'ah of southern Iraq and the Kurds of the north, and Saddam faced the most serious internal challenge of his entire twenty-five-year rule. At that moment, the Shi'ah and Kurds looked to the United States—which throughout the war had encouraged them to rebel against Saddam—to aid them now that they had done so.[4]

The United States chose not to, however, and Iran was arguably the most important reason why. The administration drew back out of concern that the success of the Iraqi "intifadah" would cause the country to fall into chaos or shatter along ethnic and religious lines, leaving a power vacuum in the region and no state to balance Iran. In Secretary of State James Baker's words, the United States did not assist the rebels "primarily out of fear of hastening the fragmentation of Iraq and plunging the region into a new cycle of instability. The Shia were quite naturally perceived as being aligned with Iran, and the Kurds, who had demanded an independent state of Kurdistan for decades, were very fragmented in their leadership and were a constant source of concern to Turkey."[5] To some extent, the Iranians had even contributed to the problem by allowing members of the Badr Corps (Iraqi Shi'ah dissidents who had fled to Iran, where they had been armed and trained to fight Saddam's regime) into southern Iraq to aid the intifadah.[6] This reinforced the fears of the Bush administration that Iran was angling to take over part or all of Iraq and was using the intifadah as the vehicle for its conquest. So, much to the later regret of both Iran and the United States, Washington did nothing and Saddam crushed the rebels and held on to power.

After the Gulf War, senior Bush administration officials again entertained the possibility of improved relations with Iran and renewed Picco's efforts to get the hostages freed. However, there was division within the administration. Some looked at Iran's behavior during most of the war, when it had stayed on the sidelines and had not made any trouble for the United States, and saw this as a sign of progress in Iran. Others focused on the fact that Tehran had allowed members of the Badr Corps into Iraq during the intifadah and saw it as a sign of renewed malevolent intent. What tipped the balance against Iran was the brutal murder of former prime minister Shapour Bakhtiar in August 1991 by three Iranians connected to the Revolutionary Guards (two were later convicted by a French court). At that point, no one in Washington could make the case that Iran was not still involved in terrorism, and so the idea of rapprochement with Iran was dropped. With characteristic bad timing, the pragmatists (through Picco's good offices) then succeeded in convincing Tehran to release the remaining hostages. But when they did so, the United States said little more than "It's about time." This snub undercut Rafsanjani and the pragmatists. By that time, Iran's expectations had grown to the point where it had expected that the United States would lift its economic sanctions on Iran and unfreeze its remaining assets, in return for the freeing of the hostages. This was wildly overoptimistic, reflecting Iran's naiveté about American politics, but it was apparently widely believed in Tehran. When their action was met with no response from the United States at all, the Iranian pragmatists felt betrayed. Likewise, the radicals felt their own position confirmed, since Iran had gotten nothing for freeing the hostages. American officials said that they saw no reason to reward Iran and its Lebanese proxies for having taken the hostages in the first place.[7] "A criminal does not get rewarded for stopping the crime spree and turning himself in. At most, he gets leniency," as one former administration official put it to me.[8]

In some ways, the action taken by the Bush administration that had the most far-reaching impact on U.S.-Iranian relations was one of its last, and one that ostensibly had nothing to do with Iran. In 1991, it recognized that Saddam Hussein's defeat and the fall of the Berlin Wall created the possibility for achieving real peace in the Middle East, and it showed enormous foresight and bravery in deciding to try to pull it off. At the end of October, the United States (and the Soviets, although their political collapse just weeks later quickly rendered them irrelevant) convened the Madrid Peace Conference, which kicked off a new Middle East peace process between Israel and all of the remaining Arab confrontation states. For Tehran's radicals, this new peace process was a dire threat. Khomeini and the religious radicals he represented harbored a fierce anti-Semitism and anti-Zionism. Although the Iranian people did not have quite the same level of hatred for the Jewish state as the Arabs, or their own radical mullahs, it was still the case that Israel was disliked (or even hated) by many, and Israel's association with an issue usually cast it in a negative light. Moreover, many Iranians had absorbed the constant refrain of the mullahs that the Middle East peace process consisted of the United States' bullying weaker Arab states into making concessions to Israel. Thus, the Bush administration's effort to revive the Middle East peace process struck the wrong chord in Tehran. The struggle between Iran and the United States over the peace process would become the central battle of the undeclared war waged during the early 1990s.

Wrestling with the Great Satan

The reason that the Bush administration's early overtures to Iran were never accepted in Tehran stemmed largely from the continuing evolution of domestic politics after Khomeini's death—and America's continuing role as Iran's biggest political football. During his 1989 presidential election campaign, Rafsanjani had remained true to his past positions. He had stressed the importance of allowing the private sector to regulate trade while the government tried to stimulate growth, investment, and employment. On foreign affairs, he observed that the ayatollah's famous comment that Iran should favor "neither East nor West" did not mean that Iran should not have relationships with either.[9] Upon taking office, Rafsanjani appointed a cabinet that excluded key radicals (although he was not able to snub them entirely), included many new faces who promised change in Iranian policies, and stressed technocratic competence over loyalty to the revolution.[10] Initially, he and Khamene'i worked well together and were largely able to steer the course of Tehran's policy. They stressed the importance of tending to Iran's failing economy and used that to justify doing little to export the revolution.[11]

Hojjat-ol Islam 'Ali Akbar Hashemi Rafsanjani may be a true moderate, but his policies have consistently been subordinated to what is best for his career. Rafsanjani is wildly ambitious—Iranians believe that he wants to succeed Khamene'i as Supreme Leader. He is also a thoroughly unprincipled political animal, notorious for abusing Iran's electoral laws to make elections turn out his way. Throughout his time in the spotlight, Rafsanjani has famously compromised his principles whenever it was convenient for either the survival or the advancement of his political career. Thus, it would be a mistake to attribute altruistic motives to his positions. Since the earliest days of the revolution, he has repeatedly advocated a rapprochement with the United States. It seems to be based on his reading of the practicalities of the situation: Iran needs good relations with the rest of the world, and the United States is the most powerful and important country in the world, so it is useful to have good relations with the United States. This is not to say that he has not sold that position out whenever it was expedient to do so. In 1989, right after the Rushdie *fatwa,* when Iranians were scrambling to demonstrate their anti-Americanism and thus adherence to the imam's line, Rafsanjani pronounced, "If for every one Palestinian today, they execute five Americans, or English, or French—outside Palestine, not inside—such wrongdoings will not be repeated. It is not difficult to kill the French or Americans, although it is somewhat difficult to kill the Israelis, as they are a bit scarce."[12] He was the ultimate barometer of Iran's political leanings and would say whatever was necessary not to seem out of step. But inevitably he would resurrect the idea of reaching out to the United States when he felt the political traffic would bear it.[13]

In the early 1990s, Rafsanjani faced three problems in trying to get relations with the United States on track. First, the radicals were down but not out. They continued to draw strength from Khomeini's legacy and his final acts, and they still controlled a great many Iranian institutions, which they were able to use to slow and hamstring the new policy course. Their own position espoused a sort of "Islamic socialism" in which the government controlled all foreign trade, limited landholdings, imposed higher taxes on the rich, and provided extensive social services for the poor. They opposed the pragmatists' efforts to woo Iranian expatriates to bring their expertise and capital back to Iran and railed against private enterprise, debt rescheduling, and the pragmatists' efforts to reach out to international financial institutions for help. The newspaper *Salam,* a leading radical mouthpiece, claimed that the IMF and World Bank had "evil imperialist" objectives and that "We will not be able to satisfy our hunger with the loaf of bread that the West will loan us."[14] Moreover, the radical position was supported in many cases by the population itself, which continued to advocate key elements of the revolutionary mantra. For instance, there was widespread popular opposition to the idea of accepting foreign loans because of Iran's unfortunate earlier history with Qajar shahs having accepted European loans that had then become vehicles for the Europeans to gain control over the country.[15]

If Rafsanjani's first problem was that Iran's leadership was roughly divided among pragmatists and radicals—and the radicals were still strong enough to thwart many of his initiatives—his second problem was the reverse. Despite the two broadly discernible movements of "pragmatists" and "radicals" in Iran, the country was anything but homogeneous—or even split—politically. Instead, Iran's polity was (and still is) severely fragmented. Analysts consistently and correctly use the term "kaleidoscopic" to describe Iranian politics.[16] Every person has his or her own unique perspective; it is rarely the case that individuals, let alone groups, share identical perspectives, and every time you change the circumstances of an issue—or switch to a different issue—it is like twisting the kaleidoscope: all of the pieces immediately realign in a different fashion. This was part of the fragmentation that Khomeini faced toward the end of his life, and it got much worse after his death, especially as the issues Iran had to confront became both more perplexing and more intractable. This fragmentation made it extremely difficult for Rafsanjani to build a wide enough coalition to be able to break what was still the ultimate foreign policy taboo for Iranians.[17]

Rafsanjani's last problem was that, increasingly on foreign policy issues, and particularly with regard to relations with the United States, Middle East peace, and exporting the revolution, he was opposed by the Supreme Leader himself. Khamene'i's determination to adhere to Khomeini's legacy to preserve his own legitimacy seems to have led him to make the conscious decision to support Rafsanjani on domestic political issues but to side with the radicals on foreign policy. After all, anti-Americanism and export of the revolution were fundamental elements of Khomeini's vision and closely identified with his years in power, while the Imam had never paid much attention to issues such as whether the economy should be privatized or nationalized. Indeed, Khomeini's various statements and writings on domestic affairs were often so confused, ambiguous, and contradictory that Khamene'i, Rafsanjani, and the pragmatists were able to cite the Imam's words for virtually everything they did—leaving the radicals protesting lamely that they were abusing the spirit, if not the letter, of the Imam's legacy.[18] Thus, by following the radicals on foreign policy, Khamene'i was supportive of them in an area most closely and clearly associated with Khomeini's legacy, while he followed the pragmatists on an issue the Imam had not cared much about and where his views had been less clear.

During his first few years in office, Rafsanjani had again tried to explore the possibility of better relations with the United States. He had taken President Bush in his inaugural address at his word and tried to demonstrate some "goodwill." In 1990–1991, when all of the remaining American hostages in

Lebanon were freed, Rafsanjani commented in public that it was Iran that had freed them.[19] He had also tried to expand back-channel communications with the United States. The two countries had been using the Swiss (the "protecting power" that looked after American diplomatic interests in Tehran) to exchange messages, and Rafsanjani's people suggested developing this channel into a fuller set of negotiations. In 1990, Rafsanjani had his vice president, 'Ata'ol-lah Mohajerani, publish a piece in *Ettela'at* that advocated negotiations with the United States. There is little doubt that Rafsanjani used Mohajerani as his stalking horse, to see how others would respond to such a suggestion. It did not go over well.[20]

In the wake of the Rushdie *fatwa* and the Imam's last acts, anti-Americanism remained a tremendously powerful force in Iran. In response to the Bush administration's early overtures, Khamene'i led a chorus denouncing the possibility of better relations. For example, in March 1990, he gave a speech in which he blamed all "arrogant powers," with "the satanic and demonic American power" at their head, for "leading humanity toward decadence ... [and] mocking and ridiculing all spiritual values." In another speech that month he described the United States as "the embodiment of the Devil and corruption."[21] Radio Tehran commented in 1990 that if Iran were to abandon "the only vital element of the revolution in the arena of its global struggle ... that is, the struggle against America," the country's revolutionary identity and strategic aspirations would be lost.[22] Thus, the radicals were able to snuff out Rafsanjani's overtures to the United States almost immediately. The discussions about expanding the Swiss channel were publicly exposed, forcing Rafsanjani to give up the whole initiative. Similarly, articles appeared throughout the Iranian press blasting the Mohajerani trial balloon. The response was so negative and so furious that Rafsanjani's office was forced to claim that the piece had not reflected the president's views—although it was widely known that it had.[23]

Even then, Rafsanjani did not entirely give up. When he was most strongly resisted by the radicals—and increasingly by Khamene'i—he would pull back, but whenever he thought he could he would trot the idea out again. Moreover, Rafsanjani had greater success selling the idea of reaching out to the Europeans (including Great Britain, the old enemy) as a way of attracting the trade and capital he sought for reconstruction, and to a considerable extent as a way of conditioning Iranians to the idea of normal relations with Western powers to prepare the groundwork for his desired rapprochement with the United States. To a great extent, the radicals accepted Rafsanjani's European overtures for precisely the opposite reason: if Iran could get trade and capital from Europe, they believed it would make it unnecessary to make up with the

United States.[24] Not surprisingly, Iranian policy often seemed (and, in fact, was) highly contradictory. A National Intelligence Estimate from October 1991 (written while I was at the CIA) contained the remarkable judgment that "Rafsanjani's goals vis-à-vis the United States are to reduce bilateral tensions and US economic and political pressures on Iran and to limit US military presence and political influence in the Persian Gulf." We recognized that these goals were in practice mutually exclusive but were not entirely sure that the Iranians did.[25]

Iran's New Foreign Policy

Although Rafsanjani never gave up on his efforts to improve relations with the United States and did have some success in repairing relations with Europe and some of Iran's Arab neighbors, the Iranian grand strategy that emerged in the early 1990s reflected a very different orientation. Ultimately, the same powerful, underlying aspects of Iranian domestic politics that killed the early efforts by the Bush administration and Iran's pragmatists to reach an accommodation would lead Tehran to adopt a new, aggressive, and aggressively anti-American foreign policy at the start of the new decade.

There were a number of strategic factors that also influenced a policy already being driven by the continuing ideological fixation of Iran's elites. The destruction of Iraq and the fall of the Soviet Union created both defensive fears and offensive opportunities for Iran. Both suggested that the United States would be unrestrained in throwing its weight around in the Persian Gulf or the Middle East more broadly, and this was a threat to Iran. In particular, the Iranians feared that at some point America would seek to mount a Desert Storm–type operation against them. The buildup of America's peacetime military presence in the region after the Gulf War, the bellicose rhetoric directed at Iran from some quarters of Washington, the establishment of new American military bases in Qatar and new military agreements with the UAE (which was closer to Iran than to Iraq), and the major American initiative to strengthen ties to the GCC militaries and help them enhance their capabilities all seemed very threatening to Iran. Although the American military moves were mostly intended to contain Iraq, not Iran, in Tehran they looked like the logical precursors to a repeat of Desert Storm, this time against Iran.

At the same time, the fall of the USSR removed a threat from the north and created new Muslim states in Central Asia potentially friendly to Iran, while the destruction of Saddam's armed forces removed a major threat to Iran from the west. The Soviet Union's collapse also unleashed its arms industry, which suddenly was willing to sell Iran systems—such as *Kilo*-class attack submarines and advanced naval mines—at bargain prices that the USSR never had. This meant that Iran could again indulge its own regional hegemonic aspirations. Indeed, there was a remarkable continuity of Iranian thinking in this area from the shahs to the mullahs.[26]

A second factor for Tehran was the rise of various Islamist movements elsewhere throughout the region. The late 1980s and early 1990s saw the electoral triumph of Islamists in Algeria (who were promptly prevented from taking office by the Algerian military), the rise of an Islamist government in Sudan, Hizballah's growing popularity in Lebanon, the emergence of the Palestinian fundamentalist group HAMAS as a rival to the secular PLO for the principal opposition to Israel, the growth of the Muslim Brotherhood in Jordan, a flourishing of Islamist groups such as the Gama'a Islami and Egyptian Islamic Jihad in Egypt, and the growth of Sunni and Shi'i fundamentalist movements in many of the Gulf countries. There was a sense among Iranians that these new groups and governments were natural allies of Tehran. Indeed, many of them—even the Sunnis—looked to the Iranian Revolution as a model for what they hoped to someday achieve. Some Iranians explicitly argued that the Islamist wave was an overpowering historical force that would transform the Middle East the way that the Renaissance had transformed Europe. Thus, Iran had an incentive to pursue a radical foreign policy to ride this wave and tap into this tremendous political force that shared many of Iran's goals, particularly the destruction of Israel and the eviction of the United States from the region.[27]

Finally, there was the threat created by the Middle East peace process that the Bush administration kicked off in Madrid in 1991. At the most basic level, many (probably most) Iranian officials continued to regard the state of Israel as an unwanted "crusader state" implanted by the Christian West on Islamic lands. Thus, the idea of a peace process that would further legitimize that nation, even if only on its earlier borders, was anathema to the power brokers in Tehran. The ideology of the revolution and Khomeini's legacy demanded that they block it. However, there were other considerations of a strategic variety at stake. Iran had few allies in the world, the most important of which was Syria. If Syria made peace with Israel, a major source of their shared strategic goals would disappear, and so too might their strategic partnership. Moreover, Syria's ongoing confrontation with Israel made Damascus condone Iran's presence in Lebanon. Again, if Syria signed a peace accord with Israel, this likely would include the disarming of Hizballah in Lebanon. But for Iran, its support of Hizballah and its role in Lebanon were crucial because they were the only way that Iran had any influence in the Levant. For a nation that aspired to play a major role in the Middle East, Iran could not afford to lose its one foothold in the Levantine cockpit.[28]

All of these different factors, both ideological and strategic, crystallized into a new Iranian foreign policy at the start of the 1990s, and that characterized Iranian international actions through the first half of the decade. This policy saw the United States as Iran's principal foe and believed that Washington was attempting actively to weaken Iran, to prevent Iran from playing its "natural" role as the hegemon of the Persian Gulf region, and even to create the pretext for military or other action against Iran to overthrow the government. Thus, Iran would forge an alliance of like-minded states and groups that opposed the United States and rejected its Middle East peace process. This Iranian-led alliance would act as a counterweight in the region to the American alliance, which effectively included Egypt, Jordan, Morocco, the GCC, Turkey, and Israel. Moreover, Iran would work actively to try to undermine the governments of the U.S. allies in the region and encourage local resistance to the American presence (including mounting terrorist operations)[29] in an effort to drive the United States out of the Persian Gulf and, hopefully, the entire region.[30]

However, the Gulf War had injected another important new element into Iran's thinking: caution. In just forty-three days, the United States, with rather marginal assistance from its European and Arab allies, had pulverized the same Iraqi Army that had destroyed Iran's own ground forces just two years before. This seems to have cleared up any lingering Iranian misimpressions about U.S. military capabilities. This (and the memories of Praying Mantis) seems to have convinced even the radicals in Tehran that what had kept the United States from inflicting much greater damage on Iran in the 1980s was a lack of will, not a lack of power. As best we can tell, the Iranians seemed to look at American behavior during the hostage crisis, the Lebanon withdrawal, the tanker war, and now the Gulf War together, concluding that there were real limits on Washington's willingness to employ force and that therefore the key to fighting America was to do so in ways that did not cross our "trip wires" for the use of force. This is what the U.S. military refers to as "asymmetric warfare"—another country attacking the United States in ways that play to its strengths and prevent us from employing our own. Iran seems to have been the first country after the Gulf War to craft an asymmetric strategy against the United States. Consequently, one of the main goals of its own new, aggressive foreign policy was that it wanted to try to drive the United States out of the Persian Gulf region without taking the kind of action that would prompt America to replay Desert Storm against it.

As a result, beginning in 1991–1992, the Iranians adopted a more aggressive and assertive foreign policy, but one designed never to cross a threshold that would justify a massive American military assault. They organized a conference in Tehran in opposition to the Madrid Conference, which included delegations from many rejectionist groups and countries. They embarked on major diplomatic campaigns to woo the new governments of Central Asia and to provide support to Muslim groups waging battles for self-determination everywhere from Bosnia to Nagorno-Kharabakh to Kashmir. They quickly deepened their ties with the new Sudanese government. Tehran and Khartoum exchanged high-level visits, signed trade deals, and crafted an agreement on military cooperation, while Iran sent military and intelligence advisers from the Revolutionary Guard to Sudan.[31] The Iranians began to support Egypt's Gama'a Islami to try to pressure, if not undermine, Hosni Mubarak's regime—one of America's most important allies in the Middle East and a key player in the peace process.[32] Because the Arab-Israeli peace process was such a threat to Tehran's interests (both ideological and strategic), the Iranians also made a major effort against Israel. They encouraged Hizballah and Palestinian Islamic Jihad (an extremely pro-Iranian terrorist group, but different from the Islamic Jihad that operated in Lebanon) to cooperate with HAMAS and provided military and financial support to do so. Indeed, Iran may have been providing HAMAS with as much as $30 million annually in the early 1990s.[33]

In addition, in 1992, Iran evicted the UAE from Abu Musa Island in the Strait of Hormuz—which they had jointly administered since the shah had landed troops on the island in 1971. Tehran probably meant to show the Gulf Cooperation Council (GCC) states that Iran intended to play a dominant role in the Gulf and that the United States (which did nothing in response to this action) could not help them. Later that year, the Iranians staged large-scale naval and air maneuvers in the Gulf to demonstrate their prowess and their ability to project power into the Persian Gulf. This marked the beginning of a new Iranian policy of confrontation with the Arab Gulf states. Moreover, it caused an uproar in the Arab world, which the Iranians blamed on American propaganda. In a good indication of how obtuse they could be with their Arab neighbors, the Iranians repeatedly stressed in a number of venues that they were willing to "forgive" the Arabs for their anger over Iran's seizure of Abu Musa—an act of Persian condescension that only further enraged many Arabs.[34]

As part of its strategy of driving the United States from the region, Iran also greatly increased its intelligence, covert action, and terrorism activities. The Iranians augmented their funding to numerous opposition groups (mainly but not entirely Shi'i) throughout the Gulf states and began to plan direct terrorist operations against Israeli targets worldwide, which would bear fruit later in the 1990s. They mounted a campaign of comprehensive and aggressive surveillance of Americans in the region with the very deliberate intention of developing attack profiles for assassinations, suicide attacks, bombings, and other forms of terrorism. Iranian intelligence personnel began to regularly and aggressively scout American facilities throughout the region. They tailed American personnel, learning their routes to and from work, their places of residence, their security precautions, and their routine behavior, all with an eye toward conducting terrorist attacks at some point in the future.[35]

Washington could never determine the purpose of these widespread, relentless, and extremely disturbing Iranian reconnaissance operations. It was entirely possible that they were part of an aggressive offensive intended to find targets of opportunity for immediate attack, suggesting that Tehran wanted to strike at the United States but simply lacked the opportunity. Alternatively, Iran's strategy may have been a more circumspect offensive, in which the intelligence agencies were ordered to conduct contingency planning in the event that the leadership in Tehran decided that it wanted to launch an attack to advance a particular goal or react to an American move. Finally, it was possible that Iran was simply looking to develop contingency plans for attacks on Americans as a deterrent. Because American officials discussed these Iranian activities with the press, the Iranians knew that Washington was aware of them and may have intended them merely as a message to the United States that an attack on Iran would be met with a widespread campaign of terror against American personnel and assets overseas. Although the last explanation appears to have predominated toward the end of the decade, in the early 1990s, when Iran was on the offensive against America, it seems that one of the two offensive explanations was the more likely.

It may have been that the two different offensive strategies were a topic of debate within Tehran. Iran's radicals doubtless wanted to conduct such attacks as often and as soon as possible, but others in Tehran were unsure that they would be able to keep their involvement secret and knew that if they could not, it could prove damaging to Iran in terms of international condemnation, massive American retaliation, or both. There seems to be little doubt that the Iranians believed that such attacks would be a useful element in their effort to drive the United States out of the Gulf region. They believed that if they could cause enough casualties to American military forces in the region—as they had in Lebanon—we would leave. But the question they had to ask themselves was whether the Bush (and later the Clinton) administration would be as reluctant to retaliate for Iranian-inspired terrorist attacks in the Gulf as the Reagan administration had been in Lebanon. Given the Bush administration's handling of Iraq both during and after the war, the Iranians decided not to test it, but the new Democratic administration would be another story.

The final element of Iran's new foreign policy was the military dimension. Although this was an asymmetric campaign against the United States relying principally on diplomacy, propaganda, subversion, and terrorism, there was also a military component to it. However, that military component was wholly defensive. Tehran's goal was to build up its military forces as best it could to defeat an American military operation launched from the Persian Gulf and/or to shut down Persian Gulf oil shipments. The Iranians wanted to make themselves strong enough that an American assault on Iran (which would have to come from the Gulf) would be so costly that the United States would be deterred from doing so or would quickly give up the operation when American casualties began to mount. They also wanted to be able to threaten to shut down oil exports through the Gulf as another asymmetric approach to the United States—effectively saying to Washington, "If you use force against us, we can use it against you too, and in ways that you will find very painful."[36]

Consequently, the Iranians began a sustained buildup of their air and naval forces to be able to project power into the Persian Gulf. They took advantage of the falling prices on Soviet-style military hardware caused by the end of the Cold War and the collapse of the Soviet Union to stock up on weapons from Russia, China, and North Korea in particular. Between 1991 and 1997, Iran bought roughly $1.4 billion worth of equipment from Russia and other former Soviet republics, including *Kilo*-class submarines, SU-24 strike aircraft, MiG-29 fighters, advanced naval mines, and some ground force equipment. During that same period, it spent about $1.3 billion on antiship missiles, missile patrol boats, air-to-surface missiles, and technology for its own ballistic missile development program from China. The North Koreans, however, dominated Iran's ballistic missile needs, providing Iran with the old Scud-B and the longer-range Scud-Cs, as well as technology that was instrumental in the development of Iran's series of Shahab short- and medium-range ballistic missiles.[37]

Another aspect of this military strategy was the acquisition of nuclear weapons. The shah had had an interest in nuclear weapons, but it was actually rather restrained given his approach to other aspects of military power. He did have a nuclear weapons program, but it had not progressed beyond basic research and was not lavishly funded. Given how he threw money at things that mattered to him, the fact that he did not drown his nuclear weapons program in cash suggests that it was not a high priority.[38] However, he did want nuclear *energy* very badly. Iran had energy problems that produced rolling blackouts across the country, including in Tehran. In addition, in the 1970s there were fears that Iran's oil reserves would be exhausted in about thirty years' time, and the shah deliberately planned to use Iran's oil money to build a nuclear power grid that would be up and running before that occurred.[39] At the start of the Iran-Iraq War, Iran discontinued the nuclear program because Khomeini apparently believed that nuclear weapons were against Islam.[40] However, as information began to surface that Iraq was pursuing nuclear weapons, the Iranians decided that they needed to match Saddam, and in the mid-1980s they resurrected the program. The end of the war did not diminish Iran's desire for nuclear weapons. Instead, Iran actually began to pump additional resources into its program and—as the world only learned in 2003–2004—was able to take advantage of the expertise of Dr. A. Q. Khan, the "father" of the Pakistani nuclear program, and other members of the Pakistani government who were anxious to earn a little cash on the side.[41]

Iran's logic for accelerating its nuclear weapons program was very straightforward: if you want to pursue a policy that runs contrary to the vital interests of the United States, you must be able to deter an American invasion, and the only sure way to do that is to have a nuclear arsenal. It was a conclusion shared by many other countries around the world—including Iraq and North Korea. Deterring the United States was not the only motive Iran had for acquiring nuclear weapons (deterring Israel, building prestige, and dealing with a revived threat from Iraq were also considerations), but it was its most important incentive.[42]

Dual Containment

When the Clinton administration took office in January 1993, Iran had already adopted its new, hard-line foreign policy. Although not all of its aspects had manifested themselves, the broad contours were clear. Moreover, the new American foreign policy team interpreted the history of the Bush administration's overtures to Iran just as their predecessors had: the United States had tried to reach out to Iran, which had not only refused but had stepped up its animosity toward the United States. National Security Advisor Anthony Lake warned the new foreign policy team that Americans had a bad habit of being seduced by the siren song from Tehran and then badly betrayed by it—and he was not going to allow the new administration to be humiliated as its predecessors had. As for the eventual release of the hostages, that was viewed principally as something the Iranians had done purely out of self-interest. The Clinton team believed the Iranians had finally realized that the hostages had become a serious liability for them and that releasing them served their interest in wooing Europe—with its potential trade and aid—as a substitute for jettisoning their anti-American ideology and mending relations with the United States. Thus, as far as the Clinton administration was initially concerned, the Iranians had proved themselves to be implacable foes, impervious to gestures of kindness. Much of the professional bureaucracy suspected that Rafsanjani had been behind the release of the hostages and that it had probably been intended as a reciprocal gesture, but they too conceded that it just was not enough to build a new relationship. Given all of Iran's actions designed to drive the United States from the Gulf, undermine its allies, and destroy the state of Israel—and to do so via terrorism and subversion—it was clear that the pragmatists were not in control in Tehran, which made a policy of trying to foster engagement fruitless.[43]

The second critical element of the Clinton team's thinking about Iran derived from its interest in the Middle East peace process. The new administration quickly took up the challenge of trying to forge a comprehensive peace among Israel and its Arab neighbors. A number of the new senior Clinton administration officials believed ardently that the Arab-Israeli dispute was the single greatest source of instability in the region, and their predecessors in the Bush administration had created an opportunity they were determined to take advantage of. The peace process would include the Palestinians, Syria (and its Lebanese vassal), and Jordan. But this meant that Israel's other security concerns—those beyond the immediate confrontation states—had to be addressed. In other words, the administration had to do something about Iraq and Iran. Both were vehemently opposed to the status quo and determined to prevent the peace process from succeeding. They were also very willing to abet the various Palestinian (and Lebanese) rejectionist groups however they could and, if unconstrained, could also build formidable conventional and non-conventional (weapons of mass destruction) military capabilities that could threaten Israel more directly.[44]

The U.S. government was already well attuned to the threat from Iraq. But Iran was a different story. Frequently during the 1990s, Iranian actions were noted in Washington but did not necessarily spur senior administration officials to action. To some extent, Iran's nefarious activities were considered par for the course—Iran was an aggressive, anti–status quo, and anti-Semitic power, and it was no surprise that they were doing aggressive, anti–status quo, anti-Semitic things. At times, only when the Israelis made it clear to Washington that they were alarmed enough by the latest round of the Iranians' misbehavior to call into question their ability to take further steps on the peace process would this galvanize Washington to take steps against Iran in an effort to reassure Jerusalem and keep the process moving forward.

Throughout the Clinton administration, but especially early on, it was often Israel's security concerns and the interrelated needs of the peace process that were the main prods to U.S. action on Iran. (Israel was not alone in this: Egypt, Saudi Arabia, and other Arab states also felt threatened by Iran during the early 1990s, and they too pressed Washington for a tougher line toward Tehran—Israel's was often just the loudest among many voices.) As was obvious even at the time but has since been demonstrated repeatedly, Israel was willing to move ahead in the peace process only if it felt reasonably secure. I stress "reasonably" secure because there were terrorist attacks on Israelis throughout the 1990s, and it often took all of Israeli Prime Minister Yitzhak Rabin's will and reputation to keep Jerusalem on the negotiating track. Iran's support for these terrorist attacks, and its slow but unwavering pursuit of nuclear weapons, frightened Israelis, and those fears were a major issue for the peace process. Consequently, the Israelis—from Rabin to Peres to Netanyahu to Barak—stressed to the Clinton administration that if they were going to "take risks for peace," as President Clinton famously phrased it, the United States was going to have to limit Iran's ability to attack them.[45]

The Clinton administration's initial answer to this need was a policy known as "Dual Containment," which was devised by Clinton's first senior director for Near East and South Asian affairs at the National Security Council, Martin Indyk.[46] In a speech to the organization he founded, the Washington Institute for Near East Policy, Indyk laid out the policy of Dual Containment:

> The Clinton administration's policy of "dual containment" of Iraq and Iran derives in the first instance from an assessment that the current Iraqi and Iranian regimes are both hostile to American interests in the region. Accordingly, we do not accept the argument that we should continue the old balance of power game, building up one to balance the other. We reject that approach not only because its bankruptcy was demonstrated in Iraq's invasion of Kuwait. We reject it because of a clear-headed assessment of the antagonism that both regimes harbor towards the United States and its allies in the region. And we reject it because we don't need to rely on one to balance the other.[47]

In other words, there would be no more "Twin Pillars" or "Tilt Toward Iraq." Both had proven disastrous. The Persian Gulf region was too important to have its stability left to fragile and outdated balance-of-power politics. Moreover, because American military might was so great and unrivaled, it was possible for the United States to prevent both countries from again trying to overturn the status quo in the region by force without having to turn to another unreliable regional proxy.

Indyk went on to say that although they were calling the policy "Dual Containment," that was not to be construed as implying that the policy would be applied uniformly to both. Quite the contrary: while both nations were to be contained, the approaches and even the goals would be quite different. In the case of Iraq, the Clinton administration would pursue a very aggressive form of containment—far more so than what had ever been employed against Russia. Although the Bush team had failed to remove Saddam, it had left a fairly robust multilateral regime intended to keep Iraq in check through a combination of draconian sanctions, inspections to root out Iraq's weapons of mass destruction programs, no-fly zones over the north and south of the country, and an increased American military presence on Iraq's borders.[48] The new administration would use this to keep Iraq weak, force it to comply with all of its obligations to the United Nations, and make a modest effort to encourage regime change via support to Iraqi opposition groups and pursuit of war crimes charges against Saddam and his chief henchmen.

Their approach to Iran would be very different. Indyk went out of his way to stress that the U.S. government had no problem with the nature or makeup of the Islamic Republic, only with its behavior in terms of human rights abuses, widespread support of terrorist groups, pursuit of weapons of mass destruction, opposition to the peace process, and efforts to subvert neighboring governments. Moreover, the strategy to be employed hardly rivaled the bellicose tone of the Iraq strategy:

. . . in the absence of dramatic changes in Iran's behavior, we will work energetically to persuade our European and Japanese allies, as well as Russia and China, that it is not in their interests to assist Iran to acquire nuclear weapons or the conventional means to pose a regional threat. Nor do we believe it is in their interests to ease Iran's economic situation so that it can pursue normal commercial relations on one level while threatening our common interests on another level. We will pursue this effort of active containment unilaterally, maintaining the counterterrorism sanctions and other measures enacted by previous administrations to encourage a change in Iranian behavior. However, we recognize that success will require multilateral efforts since much of what Iran seeks in order to build up its military power is obtainable elsewhere. In this regard, we will seek to impress upon our allies the necessity for responding to the Iranian threat and the opportunity now presented by Iran's current circumstances.[49]

Nevertheless, it is important to note that, at least initially, there was very little to the Iranian side of Dual Containment. The United States committed itself to maintaining its arms embargo on Iran and a variety of other sanctions, mostly related to Iran's inclusion on the annual State Department "terrorism list." The United States also stated that it would work to convince other countries likewise not to sell weapons and nuclear materials to Iran and to limit their economic contacts as well. The United States did not indicate that it would make any efforts to overthrow the Iranian regime. There was no stated willingness to use military force to make Iran comply with America's will. Indeed, there was not even a comprehensive set of economic sanctions in place and U.S. trade with Iran was actually quite substantial at this time. As a result of the measures by the Bush administration to scale back the sanctions on Iran, the United States actually became the largest single buyer of Iranian oil, via the overseas subsidiaries of American companies.[50]

The central aim of the Iranian segment of Dual Containment was merely to constrain Iran's ability to make trouble in the Middle East through a rather modest series of measures—most of which were already in place—until Iran's behavior changed. In describing the policy, administration officials often did stress their hope that the "pressure" exerted on Iran by the sanctions and American diplomatic efforts would cause Iran to change its behavior, but in private, they generally understood that this was highly unlikely; regarding Iran, Dual Containment was principally a defensive strategy, not an offensive one.

Early on, the part of Dual Containment that focused on Iran was more declaratory than operational. This point should not be seen as a criticism. Containment can legitimately be a purely declaratory policy, meaning that it can be nothing more than deterrence. A key element of most containment regimes is the defining of "red lines" that would trigger the use of force. This is nothing but words, but by establishing a deterrent threat it can be the most important element of containment. This was the case with American containment of the Soviet Union during the Cold War: the most important element of that policy was our rhetorical assertion that we would go to war if Russia or its proxies invaded Europe, Japan, South Korea, and later the Persian Gulf under the Carter Doctrine. Ultimately, containment of the Soviet Union succeeded because the Soviets never chose to test that rhetorical assertion. The Iran part of Dual Containment was a policy designed to reassure Israel that the United States would keep Iran in check while Jerusalem embarked on the risky process of peacemaking and placed some limited constraints on Iran's freedom of action. But it was not the start of an aggressive new American action to cripple the Iranian economy or to weaken its political structure.

The one area where the new administration suggested that it would take new action to try to impose additional constraints on Iran was in terms of pressing its allies in Europe and Japan to diminish their trade with Iran. However, this ran smack into Europe's own new policy toward Iran, which the Europeans called "Critical Dialogue." At a European Union summit in Edinburgh in December 1992—just weeks before the Clinton administration took office—the European Union had announced that, "Given Iran's importance in the region, the European Council reaffirms its belief that a dialogue should be maintained with the Iranian Government. This should be a critical dialogue which reflects concern about Iranian behaviour and calls for improvement in a number of areas, particularly human rights, the death sentence pronounced by a Fatwa of Ayatollah Khomaini against the author Salman Rushdie, which is contrary to international law, and terrorism. Improvement in these areas will be important in determining the extent to which closer relations and confidence can be developed. The European Council accepts the right of countries to acquire the means to defend themselves, but is concerned that Iran's arms procurement should not pose a threat to regional stability. In view of the fundamental importance of the Middle East Peace Process, the European Council also expresses the wish that Iran will take a constructive approach here."[51]

The Critical Dialogue reflected a fundamentally different philosophy from the American approach. Washington's philosophy was to make it clear to Iran that it would be met with force if it attempted to attack any of the Persian Gulf monarchies and that it would pay a price (a modest one, initially) for its continued anti-American, anti–peace process, and anti–status quo behavior via sanctions. Europe's approach, or so its diplomats claimed, was to show Iran that there were rewards for acting as a good citizen of the world. Whether anyone actually believed this is just unclear. In practice, the Critical Dialogue was little more than a façade for European trade with Iran despite Iran's persistence in taking actions that Europe too found distasteful if not abhorrent.[52] In 1994, the three Iranians indicted for the 1991 assassination of Shapour Bakhtiar came to trial. One of them was Zeynalabedine Sarhadi, a great-nephew of Rafsanjani and an "archivist" at the Iranian Embassy who had been accused of helping organize the killers' escape to Switzerland. The court convicted the other two but freed Sarhadi on the grounds that the prosecution had not proven that he had participated in the actual murder. As Reuters news agency noted, "Had [Sarhadi] been convicted, Paris would probably have been forced to impose diplomatic sanctions on Iran." Bakhtiar's widow, among others, accused the French court of bowing to politics in finding Sarhadi innocent.[53] Often it took the popular outrage of European publics at Iranian actions to force their governments to take even mild action to reproach Iran, such as in 1995, when a wave of popular protests against Iran's continuing active promulgation of the death sentence on Salman Rushdie moved the Danish Parliament's Foreign Affairs Commission to boycott a meeting with the visiting Iranian deputy foreign minister Mahmud Vaezi.[54]

On other occasions, even public outrage was not enough. For instance, in October 1993, Germany invited Iranian Intelligence Minister 'Ali Fallahian—the man behind much of Iran's terrorist activities—for a visit to Germany and extensive meetings with his German counterpart, Bernd Schmidbauer. "The Fallahian visit caused a furor in Germany," according to Charles Lane. "Opposition politicians, human rights groups, and the German press raised sharp questions about the Kohl government's dealings with the man believed responsible for so much terrorism—and, presumably, for the ongoing efforts to carry out the death sentence *fatwa* Iran's religious authorities have pronounced on British author Salman Rushdie." Fallahian had already been implicated in the brutal murder by Iranian agents of four Kurdish dissidents at the Mykonos Restaurant in Berlin in September 1992. In fact, the German Federal Crime Office wanted to arrest Fallahian upon his arrival in Germany but was prevented from doing so by Chancellor Kohl's office.[55] Indeed, by 1996, German Foreign Minister Klaus Kinkel would admit that Germany was "fully aware of the evil things that Iran has been doing and is still doing. . . . The Americans and the Germans agree as to the general assessment of what Iran means by way of terrorism . . . support of Hezbollah, Hamas, and Jihad." But this would have no impact on the Critical Dialogue.[56]

Dual Containment failed to change Iranian behavior because it was a policy that relied only on sticks and, especially early on, rather small sticks at that. Critical Dialogue similarly failed (if it ever was truly meant to try to change Iranian behavior) because it was a policy of nothing but enormous carrots that were provided regardless of what Iran did. Thus it simply rewarded Iran's bad behavior. However, since it did make quite a bit of money for European (and Japanese) companies, and since there were no constituencies within their electorates who took on Iran's aggressive and dangerous behavior as a major cause—and because European governments rarely evinced Washington's level of commitment either to the peace process or to the stability of the Persian Gulf—the European governments had little incentive to change.

Inadvertent Escalation, 1992–1995

Not surprisingly, the Iranians (especially the radicals) loved the Critical Dialogue but did not care for Dual Containment. The fact that the announcement of the American policy was not accompanied by meaningful new actions was lost on them. Nor did they like it any better when a year later Clinton's national security advisor, Anthony Lake, called Iran a "backlash state" and a "rogue" regime in a *Foreign Affairs* article that took Indyk's Dual Containment policy and applied it on a global scale to a series of anti–status quo countries, including North Korea, Syria, Libya, and Cuba as well.[57] Nor did they like the sound of Secretary of State Warren Christopher's remarks at Georgetown University later that year, when he stated flat out, "Iran is the world's most significant state sponsor of terrorism and the most ardent opponent of the Middle East peace process. The international community has been far too tolerant of Iran's outlaw behavior. Arms sales and preferential economic treatment, which make it easier for Iran to divert resources to terrorism, should be terminated. The evidence is overwhelming: Iran is intent on projecting terror and extremism across the Middle East and beyond. Only a concerted international effort can stop it."[58] Tehran might not have disagreed with the assertions, but it would have characterized them differently, and most important of all, the tone seemed belligerent and ominous.

Some Iranians no doubt assumed that all of this meant the United States would try to do to Iran what it was already doing to Iraq—indeed, many American and European critics failed to grasp the differences in the two separate strategies grouped under the Dual Containment rubric, so it is hard to imagine that at least some Iranians did not make the same mistake. For others, especially for Tehran's radicals, simply because the policy explicitly stated that the United States would try to prevent Iran from accomplishing some of its goals (such as blocking the peace process and toppling the governments of the Gulf oil monarchies), it was something like a declaration of war. Indeed, rather than recognizing that containment was a *defensive* American policy adopted in reaction to their own *offensive* foreign policy, the radicals—and much of the Iranian populace—saw it as further proof of the malevolent designs and single-minded focus of the United States on Iran.

These developments set the stage for the U.S.-Iranian confrontation of the early 1990s. Between 1992 and 1996, this confrontation became increasingly rabid. The Iranians worked actively to implement their strategy to drive the United States out of the Gulf, expand their influence throughout the region, and derail the peace process. Although their policy predated the Clinton administration, the announcement of Dual Containment spurred them to apply it more aggressively to try to thwart the American effort to box them in. The Iranians supported opposition groups around the Gulf. They continued to provide funding, weaponry, advice, and operational guidance to Hizballah in Lebanon, as well as considerable funding and possibly other support to Palestinian Islamic Jihad and HAMAS. In turn, PIJ and HAMAS ramped up their terrorist attacks on Israel to try to throttle the peace process, which had picked up speed with the 1993 Oslo Accords between Israel and the Palestinians. Two American allies, Israel and Turkey, developed an informal alliance during the 1990s, prompting Iran to step up its support for the Kurdish Workers' Party (PKK), which had engaged in a murderous terrorist campaign against Ankara for more than a decade. In October 1994, Jordan signed a peace treaty with Israel that had been long in the making and was therefore quick in execution. Iran loudly condemned the treaty and urged its Syrian ally to end its negotiations with Israel. Meanwhile, in March 1992, Hizballah, working in conjunction with the Iranian Embassy, detonated a bomb at the Israeli Embassy in Buenos Aires, killing twenty-nine. To make sure that no one mistook its handiwork, Hizballah later released a surveillance tape of the embassy. In 1994, this time working through both Hizballah and local neo-Nazis, the Iranians bombed a Jewish community center in Buenos Aires, killing eighty-five and wounding two hundred others. There were several other terrorist attacks directed at Jewish or Israeli targets in Buenos Aires in 1992–1996 that likely were also conducted by Hizballah, but in these cases there is too little evidence to do more than speculate.[59] Beginning in 1993, the State Department's annual *Patterns of Global Terrorism* began referring to Iran as the world's "most dangerous state sponsor of terrorism."[60]

Of course, Rafsanjani and other pragmatists never gave up on their ultimate objective of repairing relations with the United States, even if it was clear that they would have to take baby steps at first. In 1993, they set their sites on Saudi Arabia, whose fixation on the threat from Iraq in the wake of Saddam's invasion of Kuwait had diminished its fear of Iran somewhat, suggesting that Riyadh might be amenable to a rapprochement. King Fahd showed some receptivity to the idea, hosting a visit by Iranian Foreign Minister 'Ali Akbar Velayati that secured the Saudis' agreement to increase the number of Iranians who would be allowed to take part in the Hajj that spring to 115,000. But the radicals put an end to this too. At the Hajj, the Iranian authorities who led the Iranian contingent defied the Saudi police and held a "Disavowal of the Infidels" ceremony (a rally in which they blamed America and Israel for all of the ills of the world and demanded the destruction of both). That was the end of that.[61]

Dual Containment also opened up a new diplomatic course more in keeping with Iran's current foreign policy. Since Iran was working to forge a new anti-U.S., anti-Israel (and anti–moderate Arab states) alliance among the various Middle Eastern states and terrorist/opposition groups that shared its objectives, some in Tehran recognized that Iraq might be a good candidate for inclusion. Thus, in October 1993, Iran's deputy minister of foreign affairs, Mohammad Javad Zarif (an extremely capable diplomat closely associated with the pragmatist position), journeyed to Baghdad to see if the Iraqis were interested. This was a stunning reversal. Just a year before, Iranian warplanes had bombed Iraq, striking a camp occupied by the MEK (which had been evicted from France in the 1980s and so had moved to Iraq—where it had been armed by Saddam, fought alongside Iraqi forces during the Iran-Iraq War, and, after the Gulf War, even participated in the suppression of the Shi'ah and Kurds on Baghdad's behalf). Ultimately, Zarif's talks in 1993 broke down, but on several other occasions during the 1990s, Iran would try again. Especially toward the end of the decade, it was the Iraqis who consistently balked—even though most outside observers felt that the relationship would be much more beneficial to Iraq than to Iran, whose standing among the Europeans and Japanese could only suffer by association with Saddam Hussein.[62]

By 1995, Iran's aggressive foreign policy was in high gear. In January, Tehran concluded a deal with Moscow for the Russians to build a nuclear research reactor at Bushehr (where part of the shah's nuclear program had been based). Although the reactor was ostensibly for research purposes only—and would have been difficult to use to build weapons—many feared that Iran would use it as a cover to allow it to develop expertise and import items ostensibly for peaceful purposes that could then be diverted to a weapons program.[63] In June 1995, President Hosni Mubarak of Egypt (a key American ally and an important part of the Middle East peace process) was nearly assassinated in Addis Ababa, Ethiopia. The Egyptians quickly concluded that Sudan had mounted the hit using the Gama'a Islami, but they believed that Iran had also been involved. Iran was providing the Sudanese with considerable aid and advice, including in intelligence matters, and through Sudan was supporting the Gama'a, so the connection was plausible.[64] In Bahrain, a variety of Shi'i organizations—many of them with ties of one kind or another to Iran—began mounting public protests for greater political representation and economic reforms. By the late spring, these disturbances had grown to such levels that the government was forced to make a number of concessions in the hope of defusing the popular unrest. In truth, Iran seems to have played only an ancillary role in pushing the Shi'i protests, but this was not entirely apparent at the time.[65]

Needless to say, none of this looked as if Iran was backing down or even that Dual Containment was constraining Iran's ability to destabilize the region. Meanwhile, America's early efforts to shut down Russian and Chinese military (including missile and nuclear) sales to Iran were going nowhere. The Chinese and Russians mostly denied that Iran was a threat, that it was trying to build nuclear weapons, that they had control over the companies striking the deals, or that the deals even existed. Washington's frustration prompted the administration to turn up the heat. The U.S. intelligence community made a major effort to identify Russian and Chinese deals with Iran, which high-level U.S. officials—including Secretaries of State Christopher and Albright, Secretary of Defense Perry, and even Vice President Gore—then used to prove their points in Moscow and Beijing and demand that this trade end. Gore in particular fought an endless series of battles in his regular meetings with Russian Prime Minister Viktor Chernomyrdin in which he painfully extracted any number of Russian commitments to end either particular sales or entire categories of weapons trade, only to find the Russians violating them soon after. Eventually, during the latter half of the 1990s, these violations became so egregious and inexcusable that the administration imposed sanctions on a dozen Russian firms and successfully convinced the Chinese to end their missile sales to Iran—at least for a while—for fear that Washington would do the same to them. Nevertheless, even these measures did not shut down all arms trade to Iran.[66]

Iran's increasing aggressiveness also affected the United States because of the fear it conjured in Israel. In particular, the Israelis were increasingly concerned by Iran's support for the various radical Palestinian rejectionist groups and Hizballah. Yitzhak Rabin was under tremendous pressure from Israel's right wing to take direct action against the terrorists and even to halt the peace negotiations until the Palestinians themselves reined in their own extremists. In turn, Rabin pressed the United States to do more to help him with these attacks. One of the many courses of action that the Israelis pressed for was tougher action against Iran. Jerusalem was one of the few places on Earth where Dual Containment was not regularly misunderstood. The Israelis knew full well that the policy was not intended to put the same kind of pressure on Iran that it put on Iraq—and that was what upset them; Israel felt that Dual Containment was not putting much pressure on Iran at all. Although the policy had had a demonstrable effect on Iran's rearmament—forcing Tehran to consistently halve its planned arms purchases—it had not convinced Iran to desist from its aggressive foreign policy. The Israelis wanted the United States to turn up the heat on Iran in the hope that this would prompt it to rein in Hizballah, HAMAS, and PIJ. (Of course, Iran was not the only country supporting these groups, nor was it the only country the Israelis wanted the United States to pressure to try to cut support to these groups.)[67]

Israel's pleas for assistance found their most fertile ground in the U.S. Congress. For electoral, strategic, and moral reasons, there have long been a great many staunch supporters of Israel on Capitol Hill. What's more, in 1995, the Republicans had just swept into power in Congress thanks to new House Speaker Newt Gingrich's "Contract with America." Just as America was inevitably a political football in Tehran, so beginning in 1995, Iran became a political football in America. The new Republican-controlled Congress knew a good issue when they saw one. Thanks to America's long, unpleasant history with Iran, from the hostage crisis to its new aggressiveness, there was zero political support for Iran in the United States. Indeed, Iran's behavior was so self-evidently offensive to the average American (and even the average European) that it became easy to ask why the United States was not doing more to try to press (or even get rid of) the regime in Tehran.

The problem for the Clinton administration was that the Republican argument was compelling from a strategic perspective. The Iranians were not moderating their behavior and were endangering the peace process by sponsoring attacks on Israel, and they were also engaged in an aggressive foreign policy designed to undermine American interests in the Gulf. Dual Containment had, so far, done little to persuade Iran to change its behavior. Moreover, American trade had actually grown to embarrassing levels: by 1995, the United States was Iran's third largest trading partner, its sixth largest purchaser of exports, and the largest purchaser of its oil.[68] This point alone was crippling America's efforts to implement those aspects of Dual Containment that called for multilateral sanctions and restraint in economic ties to Iran. The Europeans, Japanese, and Russians could all shrug off American pleas not to sell this or that to Iran (including Russian nuclear reactors) because U.S. companies were doing so much business with Iran themselves. In fact, many foreigners justifiably saw Dual Containment as an economically driven policy just as cynical as the Critical Dialogue: the Americans were ignoring their own trade with Iran but standing on moral principles and strategic logic to persuade the Europeans, Japanese, and Russians to prevent their own companies from doing the same.[69] Dual Containment was caught in its own loopholes.

In January 1995, with some help from the Israelis, Senator Alfonse D'Amato (R–N.Y.) decided to close those loopholes.[70] He introduced legislation that would ban all U.S. trade with Iran, including all trade conducted through overseas subsidiaries of American firms. Initially, the administration was tepid about the idea. Given how difficult maintaining the international sanctions on Iraq was already proving, it was leery of putting another country into that category. In addition, the administration did not like the idea of Congress mandating such a dramatic foreign policy shift. No administration, Democrat or Republican, likes to see Congress meddling in what it considers the sole purview of the executive branch—a battle that has been going on since the *Federalist Papers*. Some among the Clinton team proposed that the administration beat Congress to the punch by banning all trade with Iran itself through an executive order. But there were also others who were reluctant to take so dramatic a step.[71]

Hashemi Rafsanjani seemed to understand that this was a critical moment for U.S.–Iranian relations. If Washington banned all trade with Iran, it would be seen in Tehran as a major escalation in the ongoing confrontation. It would also eliminate one of his own most important arguments for moderation in Iranian policy toward the United States—the importance of American trade to Iran. Thus, in 1995, amid so much anti-American and anti–status quo activity by his own government, he tried once more to make a gesture to the United States to turn around the pattern of mutual hatred that was starting to spiral out of control. Again, it would be dangerous to ascribe altruistic motives to a man so famous for his corruption, his political expediency, and his own willingness to condone violence and repression. Far more likely, Rafsanjani believed that better relations with the United States were necessary for Iran to be able to fully restore its economic and political ties with the rest of the world.[72] Yet the fact remains that he tried once more to patch up relations with the United States.

His vehicle this time was the American oil company Conoco. Iran was considering a new production agreement for two of its offshore oil fields, the first time it had done so since the revolution. It was a good contract, probably worth about $1 billion to the winner, but the real importance lay in being the first foreign firm to be able to get back into Iran and so gain the inside track on even bigger deals expected in the future. Initially, it looked as if the contract would go to the French company Total, but on March 6, 1995, most of the world was taken by surprise when Iran announced that the U.S. firm Conoco had won the deal.[73] We do not know how Rafsanjani convinced Khamene'i (who would have had to approve the deal) to go along with awarding it to an American firm. Most speculation focuses on the importance to Iran's trade with Europe, Russia, and Asia of having a clear deal with an American company that would make it difficult, if not impossible, for the United States to press other countries not to trade with Iran. On the American side, there was nothing actually illegal about the deal, and for months beforehand Conoco had been consulting with the State Department to ensure that the deal was politically feasible. As Conoco executives would point out, they had had twenty-six separate meetings with State Department officials, and in every one of those meetings, the State Department had assured them that the deal would be approved if the Iranians granted Conoco the contract.[74]

In effect, the Conoco announcement brought all of the contradictions of American policy toward Iran out into the open and forced Washington to decide whether it wanted to have its cake or eat it. In particular, it focused attention on the D'Amato bill. At that moment, an unlikely hawk appeared: Secretary of State Warren Christopher, who had been the deputy secretary of state throughout the Carter hostage crisis and had conducted the final negotiations with the Iranians that had led to their release (and so, unquestionably, the senior administration official with the most firsthand experience of the Iranian regime). Just days after the awarding of the contract, Christopher denounced it as "inconsistent with the containment policy that we have carried forward," adding that "wherever you look you will find the evil hand of Iran in the region."[75] The Israelis and a number of Arab governments also weighed in, urging the United States to scuttle the deal. And much to the dismay of Conoco and the chagrin of all the American officials who had been telling them that the deal would not be a problem, the administration did just that.

On March 14, 1995, President Clinton announced that the Conoco deal was inconsistent with U.S. policy, and the next day, he signed an executive order prohibiting all oil development deals with Iran so that the issue would not arise again.[76] A number of factors prevailed. First, it was U.S. policy to deny Iran hard currency (which it needed to buy weapons, nuclear materials, and support terrorist operations), and the contract would have meant a considerable influx of hard currency to Iran. Second, the Israeli (and Arab) imprecations weighed heavily on the minds of the administration officials working feverishly on the Middle East peace process, which was still making progress despite mounting terrorist attacks against Israel. With the memory of the horrific attacks in Argentina in particular on many minds, few in Washington were charitably inclined toward Tehran. Third, few in Washington saw the contract as an overture from Tehran. The deal was clearly in Iran's interest, and many in the administration believed that it was nothing but a cover to allow the Europeans and Russians to sell Iran anything they wanted to. In this sense, Washington saw the Conoco deal exactly as the hard-liners in Tehran did: not as the start of a new relationship with the United States but as the ultimate display of American hypocrisy, which would prompt Europe, Japan, and Russia to abandon their few self-imposed constraints on trade with Iran—i.e., on weapons and sales of dual-use technology. At that point, Washington feared and Tehran's radicals hoped, it would be open season in Tehran.[77]

The Conoco deal helped resolve the administration's impasse over a total ban on commerce with Iran. Many of the specific motives that had led to its prohibition could also be expanded into general principles about U.S. relations with Iran. The extent of trade between the two countries was unseemly and impossible to reconcile with the moral and strategic rationale of Dual Containment. For that reason, it was a perfect excuse for the Europeans, Japanese, Russians, and others to ignore (mostly) the American requests not to sell to Iran.[78] It was like demanding that these other countries go on a diet while we were busy stuffing ourselves. We recognized that we would have greater moral authority to do so if we went on the diplomatic equivalent of a hunger strike. Finally, it would be a major demonstration of our support for Israel and America's willingness to take far-reaching action to try to help it with its security problems—and thus, hopefully, to give Rabin some domestic cover to keep plodding along the difficult road to peace.

With all this in mind, on May 6, 1995, Clinton signed a new executive order that banned all trade and all other financial and commercial transactions with Iran, including by the foreign subsidiaries of American corporations.[79] Overnight, American trade with Iran dropped to essentially nothing. No one could accuse the Clinton administration of hypocrisy anymore.

The imposition of the executive orders did cause some pain to Iran, but not a great deal. The Iranians were able to find new buyers for their oil at effectively the same prices. Of greater importance, the new moral clarity of the administration's approach did not have a noticeable impact on Europe, Japan, or Russia. Russia did modestly curb its arms sales to Iran and delayed its nuclear sales to Iran, but in this case, American bilateral pressure tied to Russian President Boris Yeltsin's need for American economic and diplomatic support was of far greater consequence than any strategic (let alone moral) argument that the United States made regarding the threat from Iran. "We do not believe that a trade embargo is the appropriate instrument for influencing opinion in Iran and bringing about changes there that are in our interests," explained German Economic Minister Günter Rexrodt.[80]

Given this weak international response to the strengthening of the American position on Iran, the Republicans in Congress went looking for other means of exerting pressure on Iran. House Speaker Newt Gingrich in particular recognized the key weakness of Dual Containment, that it was a policy predicated on "sticks" and that, even with the new total embargo, the sticks were too small. Of course, Gingrich was an astute politician, and he recognized that, given the popular antipathies to Iran, the Democrats were vulnerable to charges that they were not being active enough in trying to change Iran's roguish behavior. In particular, Gingrich asked why the United States was not mounting a greater covert action program to try to topple the Iranian regime.

So Gingrich did what any legislator with the power of the purse would: he began pushing to have $18 million added to the CIA's covert action program on Iran, to be used specifically to try to overthrow the government.[81] The Agency did have a modest covert action program against Iran that had been in existence since the Bush administration. However, the effort was making little progress: "It was a joke, and everyone knew it was a joke," one former senior administration official remembered.[82] Another former senior U.S. government official who had been involved with the program commented that when he had first taken a new job where he had some involvement with the Iran CA program, his predecessor had handed him the file and explained that although there was nothing to it and no one believed that it could accomplish anything, "it would be an embarrassment *not* to have a covert action program against Iran," so they had kept it going. In other words, it had been nothing but a bureaucratic cover-your-ass exercise: no one wanted to have to go before Congress and say that there was no CA program against a country as troublesome as Iran, so the Agency maintained one simply for the sake of it. The effort consisted mostly of anodyne efforts to introduce factually accurate information into Iranian news media and to expose Iranians to Western culture. One particular effort got the nickname of the "Great Books" campaign, because it sought to smuggle classics of Western literature into the country.[83]

The basic problem with mounting a covert action program against Iran was that there was no real point to it and enormous potential risks from exposure that outweighed any possible benefits. Although the intelligence community had noted the growing disenchantment of the Iranian people with their government over the years, there was no sign of any determination on the part of sizable segments of the population to take action against the government. Consequently, there was no expectation that the government was on shaky ground, and covert action from abroad has historically worked to overthrow a government only if it is already in dire straits and just needs a last push. What's more, every U.S. government expert on Iran was intimately familiar with the Mosaddeq coup and the ferocious anti-Americanism it had furthered—and the hypersensitivity of Iranians to any American involvement in their affairs as a result of it. Consequently, the Iran experts at the CIA were far more concerned about not getting caught—and thereby feeding Iranian paranoia that the Americans were again trying to subvert their country—than about trying to accomplish what little they might. In light of its historical experiences, it was a reasonable position, and many Republicans in the Senate joined the Democratic administration in opposing Gingrich's move.[84] There was one other problem: thanks to sheer managerial incompetence and abysmal tradecraft on the CIA's part, the Iranians had managed to uncover effectively the Agency's entire Iran operation, which had been operating out of a facility in Frankfurt, Germany. As a result, Tehran had systematically rolled up American assets in Iran, and the Agency was left with effectively nothing in Iran that might have done anything if there were something for it to do.[85]

None of this stopped Gingrich, who fought relentlessly to have the money appropriated for the Iran covert action campaign. Eventually, through sheer determination, Gingrich won and the White House agreed to set aside the money for the Iran campaign, in return for his agreement that the money would not be specifically appropriated for overthrowing the Iranian government (which was not U.S. government policy) but merely changing Iranian behavior, which was.[86] But now there were two problems. First, there was still no good use for the money. The appropriation of the money had not changed the fact that the Agency had virtually no assets in Iran and no good ways of influencing Iranian behavior without having it backfire on the United States. Second, Gingrich had done it all in the open, so headlines all around the world blared that the United States was ramping up its covert action campaign against Iran. Not only did this contribute to the first problem by putting the Iranians on notice that we were going to try to step up our covert action campaign against them, but it also played perfectly into the hands of Iran's radicals—the public debate over the covert action campaign by itself created the backlash that U.S. government officials had been working so hard to avoid.[87]

Iran's reaction was exactly as predicted. One Majles deputy condemned the United States as "a renegade government whose logic was no different from Genghis Khan or Hitler."[88] The radicals in Iranian Hizballah threatened that they had "access to U.S. interests all over the world, even in the United States. We will strike them in Europe and other parts of the world if the United States takes action against the Islamic Republic of Iran. The (Iranian) government and the leader (Ayatollah Khamene'i) are now preventing us from taking action, but as soon as they give us the green light no place will be safe for the Americans. . . . Each of us is a powder-keg and the United States is very vulnerable."[89] Iranian Foreign Minister Velayati sent a written note to the U.N. Security Council demanding that it prohibit the U.S. covert action program, which "violates international law." Velayati argued that "The United States' current policy is nothing but a flagrant support of state terrorism in a clear and official form. . . . The UN should rapidly react to the decision."[90] The Majles itself announced that it would allocate $20 million "to counter the Great Satan" and combat the American plan. Broadcast live on Tehran radio, the Parliament approved spending the money "to uncover and neutralize U.S. Government conspiracies and interference in Iranian affairs, to sue the United States in international legal bodies and to inform world public opinion about U.S. violations of the U.N. charter."[91] Even Assad Homayoun, Iran's last chief of mission in Washington under the shah and an important opposition leader to the Iranian government, lamented that "The United States is sending the wrong signal. I don't think covert operations are necessary. Eighteen or 20 million dollars will not change the government."[92]

In Gingrich's defense, there was a case to be made for what he was doing. He was creating what Russell Baker once called an "overt covert action" operation.[93] Gingrich wanted to put pressure on Iran and almost certainly recognized that the CIA was correct when it said that there simply was no realistic possible way to do so through covert action. By making the issue public and by very publicly raising the money allocated to the program, the debate itself became the form of pressure on the Iranians. The $18 million had no impact on the government of Iran in terms of what it enabled CIA's covert action personnel to do—that was determined by the circumstances, which were beyond their control. But it did have an impact on the government of Iran because it made clear to them, to their people, to potential oppositionists, and to the Europeans, Japanese, and Russians that the United States was truly determined to force Tehran to change its behavior (if not overturn the government altogether).

This kind of campaign is not necessarily a foolish strategy, especially when you have no other real covert action options. No country, and certainly not a small, relatively weak country like Iran, wants to be the target of a U.S. covert action campaign and will at times react more to the existence of the program than to its actual impact. The problem was that Iran was not the average Third World country—it was a country whose identity was bound up with anti-Americanism and whose leadership believed that the best defense was a good offense. The public debate over America's covert action program did not cause Iran to moderate its behavior. Instead, it provoked it to escalate.

Amid all of the ruckus over the covert action money, on November 4, 1995, Israeli Prime Minister Yitzhak Rabin was assassinated by a right-wing Israeli extremist. Although no one realized just how devastating Rabin's loss would ultimately prove to be to the cause of peace in the Middle East, everyone knew that it was a major blow to the hopes of millions of Israelis and Arabs. There was an outpouring of grief, not just in Israel and the West but even in Arab capitals across the Middle East. Virtually alone among the mourners, the Iranians rejoiced. Rafsanjani himself welcomed Rabin's death, adding that "The peace issue planned by America and the Zionist regime is far worse than the war which has been imposed on innocent Palestinians, and in fact the peace issue is a new way to further enslave the Palestinian nation and to trample on its rights."[94] Likewise, the pragmatist Speaker of the Majles, 'Ali Akbar Nateq Nuri, scolded President Clinton, saying, "When it comes to someone like Salman Rushdie, an apostate who has insulted the religious sanctities of over one billion Muslims—you defend him, or a criminal like Yitzhak Rabin. Shame and revulsion upon you, truly."[95] Because Rabin had been so universally respected for his courage in trying to make peace, Iran's crowing over his death was as devastating to its international reputation as any terrorist attack it might have sponsored. In the United States, it was another sign that Iran was a rogue nation, wholly opposed to the values of the rest of the world.

CHAPTER 10

To the Brink

In 1996, all of the trends that had been brewing for the past four years threatened to come to a violent head. As far as the Iranian leadership was concerned, with Khamene'i and the radicals firmly in charge, the United States had declared war on Iran. Washington had imposed comprehensive trade sanctions, it was pushing for other nations to do the same, and it had unveiled a new $18 million covert action program against them. In their minds, the ghost of Kim Roosevelt was no doubt resurrected once more. It is also unclear whether they recognized that these American actions were largely a response—and a reluctant one at that—to Iran's own aggressive effort to drive the United States out of the Gulf and derail the Middle East peace process. Nor is it clear that this was relevant to them even if they did. As far as Tehran's hard-liners were concerned, including Khamene'i, they had been locked in a life-or-death struggle with the United States for decades, and this was simply another round. Consequently, in response to what they perceived as American escalation, the Iranians stepped up their attacks on America and its allies in the Middle East.

Their first target was Israel and the new government of Shimon Peres, who had succeeded Rabin as prime minister. If anything, Peres was more devoted to the cause of peace than Rabin had been, and this did not suit Iran at all. Besides, the Iranians were certain that Israel had been behind both the imposition of the comprehensive sanctions in the spring of 1995 and Gingrich's drive to ramp up the U.S. covert action program in the fall. In late February, HAMAS and PIJ launched four suicide attacks on Israel in nine days, killing fifty-nine

Israelis. The blow to Israel, so soon after Rabin's death and at a time when the peace process was moving unsteadily, was devastating. Although HAMAS was determined to halt the peace process and had few constraints on when and how it would act to do so, PIJ's participation in this coordinated series of blasts points to Iran as the ultimate moving force. In the words of Israeli terrorism expert Meir Litvak, "Whereas Hamas was always an independent Palestinian movement [albeit one with considerable Iranian support], Islamic Jihad became an instrument of Iranian policy in the Arab-Israeli conflict."[1]

Then it was Hizballah's turn. Back in 1993, Israel and Hizballah (under heavy Syrian pressure) had reached an agreement defining the limits of their guerrilla war in southern Lebanon; Israel agreed to avoid attacking Lebanese civilian targets if Hizballah agreed to confine its own attacks to the Israeli soldiers still occupying a narrow security zone in southern Lebanon. In March 1996, Hizballah suddenly stepped up its attacks on Israelis in Lebanon, doing so with a twist: it began to launch the attacks from civilian locations. There was no reason to suspect that Hizballah was responding to orders from Damascus, and in general, Hizballah is less closely tied and less responsive to Syria than to Iran. Tehran was clearly at work again, tightening the screws on Israel at a particularly delicate moment, as Shimon Peres was facing a tight re-election battle with right-wing challenger Benjamin Netanyahu, and the elections were set for May.

Whenever Israeli troops tried to retaliate against these Hizballah attacks, they ended up hitting civilians, as the Hizballahis doubtless expected—and probably intended. Hizballah then "retaliated" by launching Katyusha rockets into northern Israel in clear violation of the 1993 agreement but claiming that they were doing so only in response to Israel's having struck Lebanese civilian targets. Some of the causes that Hizballah cited to justify additional Katyusha attacks were even more transparent—such as claiming that a Lebanese civilian had been killed by a mine that they insisted Israel must have planted.[2] Syrian Foreign Minister Faruq ash-Shara assured Washington that Damascus would bring the campaign to an end, but after a short pause Hizballah resumed its attacks into northern Israel, further indicating that the Syrians were not driving the Hizballah attacks, Iran was.[3] As the two sides continued to trade volleys in late March and early April, pressure mounted on the dovish Peres to take dramatic action to put an end to the exchanges.

On April 11, Peres bowed to the pressure and launched Operation Grapes of Wrath, a campaign of air, naval, and artillery strikes against targets throughout Lebanon including not only Hizballah but Lebanese infrastructure and economic targets as well. Israel's ill-considered strategy was to create massive refugee flows and threaten Lebanon's nascent reconstruction as a way of putting pressure on the Lebanese and Syrian governments to get control over Hizballah. The sixteen-day operation turned out to be a minor fiasco for Israel. More than 150 Lebanese civilians were killed (including more than 80 in a shelling incident at a U.N. compound at Qana), and 200,000 were forced out of their homes. The Lebanese were so incensed by Israel's callousness that Hizballah's popularity shot up, while Jerusalem earned considerable international opprobrium for its tactics, even though most governments sympathized with the pressures and frustrations that had driven the Peres government to that point.[4]

Overall, it was another victory for Hizballah and Iran. To demonstrate its gratitude to its Lebanese proxies, Iran boosted its financial assistance to Hizballah to $100 million per year after Grapes of Wrath ended.[5] And thanks in part to the Iranian-motivated terrorist attacks by PIJ, HAMAS, and Hizballah, Peres lost the Israeli election on May 29 to Netanyahu, who was unwilling to pursue the Middle East peace process with the same determination as Rabin and Peres, just as Tehran had hoped.[6] Martin Indyk, the American ambassador to Israel at the time, has since commented that in 1996 the Iranians proved that terrorism could topple a government.[7] In truth, as Jimmy Carter would no doubt have added, it was at least the *second* democratically elected government the Iranians had helped topple.[8]

Terrorism in the Gulf

The action then shifted back to the Persian Gulf region, and specifically back to Bahrain. The country's Shi'i majority had not been mollified by the modest measures of the government in 1995. The ruling Khalifa family continued to drag its heels on vesting a Parliament with real authority so that the Shi'ah could have a greater say in their own governance. Thus, in the spring the rioting broke out anew and with much greater fury than the year before.

The Bahrainis blamed the Iranians. They claimed that the Revolutionary Guards were funding, supplying, organizing, and even directing the opposition groups. This was probably an exaggeration. The United States looked hard at the Bahrain riots and could find little evidence of significant Iranian involvement. For the most part, it was a genuine popular protest—something the Khalifas did eventually recognize and actually moved to correct. As a result, today Bahrain is (at least for the moment) on the cutting edge of political reform in the Arab world, such as it is. However, at the time, the Bahrainis were certain that this was yet another Iranian attempt to overthrow their government, as Tehran had tried to do in 1981. The Iranians were not entirely blameless; they had funded and helped organize many of the groups that did mount the protests, but it seems that having gotten them started, the groups took on a life of their own and eventually became self-sustaining entities that did truly reflect the political aspirations of Bahrain's Shi'ah. Of course, no one in the Gulf believed it. Since virtually every one of the GCC states had been attacked by Iran in some way at some point during the 1980s and '90s—and since all of them were wary of their own Shi'ah populations—they were all ready, even eager, to blame Iran. It was much better to blame Iran than to admit that the local Shi'i populations were unhappy with their lot and willing to rise up to try to change it. In January, the Bahrainis even expelled an Iranian diplomat connected with the Revolutionary Guard for assisting the oppositionists.[9]

The extent of Iranian involvement in the riots soon became secondary in the minds of the Gulf Arabs and the U.S. government. In early June, Bahrain announced that it had discovered a plot including at least forty-four people (twenty-nine of whom had already been arrested) for conspiring with Iranian support to overthrow the government of Bahrain. In Washington, the Bahrainis provided documentary evidence of the connections between the group, which called itself Bahraini Hizballah, and the Pasdaran's "Export of the Revolution" branch, the al-Quds Forces (Arabic and Farsi for "Jerusalem" Forces). To make their point to the rest of the world, the Bahrainis then televised confessions made by six of those arrested in which they stated that they had been trained in Iran and by Hizballah in Lebanon and had received guidance from an Iranian intelligence officer who claimed to report directly to Khamene'i.[10] The fact that the United States had just announced in July 1995 that its naval forces headquartered in Bahrain were to be upgraded to a full fleet (the Fifth Fleet), implying a sustained high level of American naval forces in the Gulf, was almost certainly an element in Iran's motivation. Indeed, one of those arrested noted in his televised confession that he had been ordered by Iranian officials to gather information on American forces in Bahrain.[11]

Meanwhile, the riots continued to get worse, creating an ominous situation in the Gulf region and convincing the Gulf states that the Iranians were determined to use any method they could to bring down their governments. The Saudis privately warned the Iranians to cease their activities in Bahrain, and they told the Bahrainis that either Manama got control over the situation or Riyadh would. To back up these points, Riyadh began to move Saudi Arabian National Guard units to a position where they could intervene in Bahrain. Later in June, a summit of GCC ministers issued a joint statement demanding that Iran stop interfering in Bahrain's internal affairs and Manama pulled its ambassador out of Tehran.[12]

On June 25, 1996, just days after the GCC ministerial statement condemning Iranian interference in Bahrain, an enormous truck bomb obliterated half of a building at the Khobar Towers housing complex in eastern Saudi Arabia. Khobar Towers was one of many facilities that housed American military personnel deployed to defend Saudi Arabia and contain Iraq after the Gulf War. Nineteen Americans were killed and another 372 were wounded.

A previously unknown group called Saudi Hizballah (actually, Hizballah al-Hijaz, or "The Party of God of the Hijaz," the name for the holy territory of western Saudi Arabia used by those opposed to the Saudi royal family rather than "Saudi Arabia") was quickly proven to be behind the operation. Eventually the Saudi and American governments were able to establish that this group had been created by the Iranian Revolutionary Guard; many of its personnel had been trained in IRGC camps in Iran and the Bekaa Valley, and in 1994 the Pasdaran's al-Quds Forces had directed them to begin planning for attacks on Americans in the country. At that time, this was probably part of the broader Iranian effort to surveil and develop attack plans against a wide variety of American targets throughout the region. Only in late fall 1995—amid the public furor over Gingrich's proposal to add $18 million to the CIA's covert action program to try to overthrow the government of Iran—were they directed to attack the Khobar Towers complex, which they had first begun to reconnoiter in June 1995. The IRGC then provided them with additional funding, advice, and other forms of support—such as furnishing the explosives and an expert in bomb design from Lebanese Hizballah.[13]

Khobar Towers was Iran's first blow against the United States itself (rather than one of our Middle Eastern allies) since Hizballah and Islamic Jihad had released the last hostages in Lebanon in 1991. Within weeks, the U.S. government had a strong case that Iran was likely behind the attacks, but, as is so often the case, did not have the kind of evidence that would stand up in a court of law.[14] (That evidence was not released to the United States until 1999.) In particular, the U.S. intelligence community was very leery of saying definitively that Iran was behind the attacks even though there was a consensus among the analysts that it likely was. By this point, Bill Clinton was fed up with the Iranians, according to several of his aides. The president had gone out on a limb to support Shimon Peres in the Israeli election, knowing that the peace process would continue to make the kind of progress it had under Rabin only if Peres were reelected, and it had basically been the Iranians who had cost Peres the election.[15] They had attacked the peace process ceaselessly, they were responsible for terrorist attacks around the world, they constantly surveilled and harassed American personnel overseas, and they were working hard to undermine America's allies in the region. He asked that options be developed for a military response, and he made it clear that he wanted to hit hard. As Richard Clarke remembers it, the president told his top national security advisers, "I don't want any pissant half-measures."[16] For that reason, he also did not want to go to war half cocked. Clinton and his senior advisers wanted to be sure that if they did mount a major military operation against Iran, they had the full support of both the American people and the international community, and that meant having a strong case that Iran was behind the bombing.[17]

Very quickly, it became clear that it *would* be possible to build just such a case. When the Saudis want to, they can handle internal security with considerable efficiency and alacrity, especially since their security services are not bound by the same law enforcement constraints as those of the United States and other Western nations. After Khobar Towers, the Saudis were determined to find the people responsible, and their methods quickly bore fruit in the form of witnesses, evidence, and then members of the cell themselves. Washington learned that the Saudis had built an ironclad case against Iran, but the Saudis were being highly secretive about it. The Clinton administration wanted full access to everything that the Saudis found, including the culprits themselves. In particular, Washington stressed to the Saudis that it would severely damage U.S.-Saudi relations if the Kingdom summarily tried and beheaded the suspects, as the Saudis had done on a number of occasions in the past.[18]

This was where the administration ran into its first problem. The Saudi royal family split over whether to provide the United States with the information and access to the suspects. One part of the Al Sa'ud wanted to provide everything, expecting that this would prompt the United States to launch military operations against the Iranians whom they feared and hated. But others did not. These princes had a variety of different motives. Some simply did not like having the United States in the Gulf (or the Kingdom) and felt that providing the evidence that would trigger an American military response would only involve the United States more deeply in the region. Their feeling was "Better to allow the Gulf states to work out their differences among themselves without the interference of the infidel Americans." Other princes strongly disliked publicizing the fact that Saudi Arabian Shi'ah had taken up arms against the regime. The Saudis are intensely private by nature, and the Al Sa'ud have long tried to maintain the fiction that Saudi Shi'ah are not discriminated against and are fully supportive of the regime. The evidence Riyadh had collected in the Khobar Towers case made clear that at least a segment of the Shi'ah had been dissatisfied enough to turn to Iran for assistance in striking out at the government.[19]

Finally, the Saudis were nervous that the United States would just make relations with Iran worse by launching a military strike. Riyadh has never ceased to be disappointed by American military operations in the region, and that was particularly true in the mid-1990s. In 1979, when the Iranian Revolution shook the Saudi monarchy, President Carter dispatched a squadron of F-15s to the Kingdom as a demonstration of America's military commitment; the planes were sent *unarmed* in the wrongheaded belief that this would convince the Iranians that the United States did not have any hostile intent toward the revolution. All it did was convince the Saudis that Washington could not be counted on.[20] The massive American military campaign of the Gulf War was something of a tonic, but even then, the Saudis had wanted the United States to continue the war and finish off Saddam (contrary to the erroneous portrayal of them as having wanted us to stop the war for fear that the Shi'ah would take over).[21] They were again very disappointed when we left him in power, even if unintentionally. All through the first half of the 1990s, they had seen the Bush and (particularly) Clinton administrations launch cruise missile "pinpricks" against Saddam for egregious acts of aggression—including trying to kill former President Bush and the emir of Kuwait. Many key Saudis believed that providing the United States with the access we wanted would provoke us to launch a small, useless retaliation that would both enrage the Iranians and convince them that the United States was not willing to hit them hard enough to actually get them to back down. In those circumstances, the Saudis felt it was much better to preclude an American military move altogether, given that it would only provoke the Iranians to lash out at them again.[22] However, the Saudi royal family operates by consensus, and in cases like this one where there is no consensus, they do nothing. So weeks and then months passed with the United States pressing for the evidence and Riyadh unable to come to a decision.

A similar debate was taking place in Washington. At the same time that the administration was pressing the Saudis hard to share their evidence, senior officials were trying to figure out what to do if Riyadh complied. The Pentagon's various war plans for Iran were dated; what's more—as was often the case during the 1990s—the uniformed services were reluctant warriors. They were chary of a war with Iran, and in their exposition of the options they tended to stress the extremes of either all-out invasion or minor cruise missile strikes. Nevertheless, there were several options: a full-scale invasion involving a half-million or more American troops drawn up in the immediate wake of the revolution; air and naval strikes against Iranian coastal emplacements, which had been considered during the tanker war of the late 1980s; and a simple air and/or cruise missile strike at one or more Iranian military or WMD sites. The last option seemed to be ruled out by the president's rather categoric statement that he didn't want any "pissant half-measures." At the other end of the spectrum, no one thought the American people were ready for a full-scale invasion of Iran and the costs that would likely entail. As a result, most discussion focused on middle-range scenarios that envisioned large-scale air and naval strikes against Iranian coastal facilities (naval ports, air bases, Silkworm launch sites, air defense batteries) or military, intelligence/terrorism, and WMD sites elsewhere around the country. Even with these options, there was considerable discomfort among many in the administration, who assumed that the Iranians would retaliate with more terrorist attacks for our military retaliation. Although this was not necessarily an assessment shared by the government's Iran analysts, it weighed on the minds of many Clinton administration officials as they pondered whether to strike if it came to that. The military in particular seemed to regard such a scenario as beyond dispute, and this drove them to their extreme options of invasion or a cruise missile pinprick. Nevertheless, the Joint Staff dutifully began work on refining all of the options, predicated on Washington's being able to get access to the Saudi information so that it could make its case properly to the country and the world, and that was still not forthcoming.[23]

As the weeks passed, it became clear that the debate within the royal family was being won by those opposed to providing the information. Prince Bandar bin Sultan, Saudi Arabia's longtime ambassador to the United States, told Clinton's national security advisor, Sandy Berger, that if the United States could guarantee a massive military campaign against Iran (and just what that meant was unclear), Saudi Arabia would provide the information. Berger, a lawyer by training, replied realistically that the U.S. government "could not promise what it would do on the basis of information it had not seen."[24] Although that was the only intelligent thing Berger could have said on the spur of the moment, Riyadh likely took it as a sign that the Clinton administration would never be willing to mount a major operation. Matters were probably not helped when, at the end of August 1996, Saddam decided to attack the Kurdish-held city of Irbil—which most of the region considered to be under the protection of the United States. Washington wanted to mount a sizable military response against Iraqi targets in southern Iraq, which would require the use of Saudi air bases. But the Saudis had little interest in the Kurds and disliked the public blowback they got each time infidel American warplanes struck fellow Muslim Iraqis. So Riydah turned the request down, forcing Washington to opt for yet another round of cruise missile strikes and the expansion of the southern no-fly zones. To American officials, if Riyadh would not condone a military response against Saddam for yet another blatant act of aggression, it seemed unlikely they would do so against Iran. For their part,

the Saudis probably saw the meager American response to Iraq's latest bel-
ligerence as still more proof that the Clinton administration would be willing
to hit the Iranians hard enough to provoke them, but not hard enough to deter
them. The fact that Washington had intended to mount a much larger response
and that their own rejection had precluded that effort was no doubt lost on
Riyadh.[25]

ILSA

If President Clinton was fed up with Iran, the U.S. Congress was fed up with
America's allies. Iran's behavior over the past twelve months had been unpardonable. The Europeans had acknowledged as much on numerous occasions,
but it did not seem to matter. In June 1995, Iran's deputy minister for foreign
affairs, Mahmud Vaezi, had met with an E.U. delegation in Paris and announced that Iran would soon repeal the *fatwa* on Salman Rushdie, a key point
for the Europeans. He then publicly retracted the statement. Norway called its
ambassador home in protest. No other E.U. member took any action.[26] In November, after the Iranians so publicly praised the assassination of Yitzhak
Rabin, the German Parliament voted to disinvite Iranian Foreign Minister Velayati, who had been scheduled to attend a conference on Islam and Europe.
Other European leaders "regretted" and otherwise disdained the Iranian remarks, but took no action.[27] February 1996 saw the series of suicide attacks
in Israel that killed fifty-nine Israelis and ultimately scuttled Shimon Peres's
reelection chances. In March, the European Union announced that it was seriously considering revising its Critical Dialogue with Iran in light of the suicide attacks and Iran's hailing of those attacks as "divine retribution." The
French in particular announced that they were considering new diplomatic options in light of Iran's actions. Nothing came of any of it.[28] That same month,
a German court handed down an arrest warrant for Iran's intelligence minister, 'Ali Fallahian, for having ordered the 1992 assassination of the Iranian
Kurdish leaders in the Mykonos Restaurant. It had no impact on German
policy vis-à-vis Iran.[29] In May, the Belgians intercepted a strange shipment
headed for Hamburg, Germany. Although the cargo was listed as "pickles," inside they found a massive mortar, designed to throw a 275-pound explosive
charge about 650 meters—militarily useless but perfect to be mounted on the
back of a flatbed truck and used for a terrorist attack against a civilian facility.
The shipment had originated in Iran and was being carried on an Iranian
freighter. Neither the Belgians nor the Germans took any action as a result
of it.[30]

So the Congress decided to act. Specifically, Iran's old nemesis Senator Alfonse D'Amato did, introducing a bill that called for "extraterritorial" or secondary sanctions on any foreign corporation that invested in Iran's oil industry in excess of $40 million, which was later lowered to $20 million. (Senator Kennedy would eventually add Libya to the bill in response to the pleas of the families of the victims of the Pan Am flight 103 bombing). The bill was clever. It provided the president with two sets of waivers—on the usual grounds of "national interest" or if the parent country of the company was itself applying sanctions against Iran—and it required him to impose two different kinds of sanctions from a list of six possible against any company found violating the investment ceiling.[31] On July 23, 1996, with Khobar Towers still fresh in their minds, members of Congress voted to pass the D'Amato bill: 409–6 in the House and 96–2 in the Senate.

Much of the executive branch hated the D'Amato bill. In fact, for many, "hated" was too mild a word. Few had any sympathy for the Iranians, or for the feckless Europeans for that matter. That, however, was not the issue. The foreign policy bureaucracy's concerns lay in America's larger policy interests. Secondary sanctions were directly contrary to the principles of free trade, which the United States had fought tirelessly to promote for the past fifty years. Indeed, Washington diplomats and economic policy officials were still engaged in constant battles with the Europeans and Japanese in particular to liberalize their trade policies. Worse still, secondary sanctions were forbidden by the World Trade Organization, and the United States was the greatest champion of the WTO. In fact, American diplomats increasingly recognized that the WTO could be an extraordinarily effective tool in fostering economic and political reform across the Third World because countries were desperate to join but had to conform to the WTO's political and economic guidelines to do so. Many in the executive branch feared that the D'Amato bill would completely undercut the United States' vital interests in advancing free trade and promoting reform in the Third World.

On the other hand, there were those who favored the bill. Many of President Clinton's domestic policy advisers thought it would be sheer stupidity for the White House not to endorse the bill: the president himself had imposed comprehensive economic sanctions on Iran, Iran had just killed nineteen American servicemen, painfully few Americans thought anything good about Iran, and the bill had passed with so overwhelming a margin that a veto could easily be overridden—in which case, the secondary sanctions would still have come into existence and Clinton's opponents would still have been able to claim that he was soft on Iran.[32] Others in the executive branch, including many of Clinton's senior Middle East and counterterrorism advisers, were fairly sympathetic to ILSA. In particular, they saw it as a useful tool to try to convince the Europeans, Japanese, and Russians that they needed to start taking serious actions to punish Iran for its continuing aggressive and destabilizing activities. Although I was never privy to his personal thoughts on this matter, I always suspected that for President Clinton himself, who famously weighed every aspect of an issue before making a decision, the decisive factor was probably also the most obvious: Iran was run by a nasty, aggressive, anti-American regime that had just killed nineteen Americans and wounded almost four hundred more; it deserved everything it got in return.[33] On August 5, President Clinton signed the D'Amato bill into law as the Iran-Libya Sanctions Act of 1996, or ILSA.

Of course, the Europeans, Russians, and others were furious. They fulminated against ILSA, complaining that it was not just illegal but an outrageous act of economic warfare against America's oldest allies. They complained of American hypocrisy, pointing out that the United States had worked tirelessly against the Arab secondary boycott of Israel but had now imposed one of its own—not against Iran but against countries that traded with Iran, which up until only the year before had included the United States. The European Union issued an edict forbidding European companies from complying with ILSA and threatened to begin formal proceedings in the WTO against the United States. The Europeans also insisted that ILSA would have no impact on their actions, out of principle if not economic self-interest.[34]

Yet ILSA did have an impact. For nearly a year afterward, no one would touch an Iranian oil field. Indeed, after the passage of ILSA, the Iranians put out tenders for eleven different oil field development deals, many of them potentially highly lucrative. Not one of the tenders was picked up even though many foreign firms showed considerable interest. The sanctions contained within ILSA allowed the president to bar any company making investments in Iran that exceeded the $20 million threshold from any commercial transactions with the United States. Given how important the American market was to most foreign corporations, few were willing to risk their ability to do business with the United States in return for being able to invest in Iran. The numbers did not add up. In truth, there were other issues involved as well. In particular, Iran was a terrible investment risk. Its oil industry was a shambles; the country was overseen by a theocratic, totalitarian system capable of changing course overnight and making decisions against its own economic interests in the name of ideology; it was still highly anti-Western; and there was no real rule of law or the other kinds of legal, economic, and political assurances that most businesses seek before sinking $20 million or more into a deal. But it is also impossible to escape the fact that until May 1998, when the United States and European Union struck a deal in which Washington agreed to provide

ILSA waivers to European corporations in return for the European Union's commitments to increase its cooperation with the United States on nonproliferation and counterterrorism, only one such contract had been signed with Iran—by a consortium led by the French firm Total.[35] After the May 1998 agreement, the floodgates opened, and in 2003, the Congressional Research Service could point to a dozen different deals struck between Iran and foreign firms that would have exceeded the ILSA threshold despite the fact that Iran's investment climate had not improved much in the interim.[36]

The Mykonos Verdict

In late 1996 and early 1997, Iran continued to feel the backlash from its own aggressive foreign policy. The United States remained frustrated by the Saudis' unwillingness to provide the evidence they held against Iran, but American opinion leaders continued to demand that the United States retaliate with overwhelming military force against Iran if it could tie Tehran to the Khobar bombing.[37] There was also a great deal of discussion in the American media over what the options for retaliation might be, which aroused fears in Tehran that a decision to retaliate was close to being made.[38] Although the Iranians disparaged ILSA and the unilateral American sanctions, both had had an impact. Neither was enough to force Iran to desist from its pursuit of weapons of mass destruction, support for terrorist groups, or violent opposition to the peace process (the three stated goals of U.S. policy), but they did hinder Iranian plans and actions. The Iranians were not happy to see their tender offers go wanting, and they chafed at their inability to raise more hard currency. They continued to have trouble finding the cash to pay for their military spending plans and were forced to postpone plans to buy various forms of weaponry, including missile technology, because they simply lacked the hard currency to do so. Some terrorist groups actually complained that Tehran had cut its funding to them. The United States prevented Iran from obtaining loans from either the World Bank or the IMF and also convinced some of its allies not to extend important loans to Tehran.[39] As Jahangir Amuzegar noted in 1998, "In short, the overwhelming majority of bilateral oil and gas deals involving capital investment or transfer of technology have been effectively blocked by Washington. A senior Iranian official is reported to have said: 'Everywhere we try to go, we see the Americans there first, trying to convince people not to deal with us.' "[40] This pressure paid off too, as countries as diverse as China, South Africa, Japan, and Australia all backed out of deals with or loans to Tehran.[41]

Consequently, Iran's economic ties to Europe (and Japan and Russia) took on even greater significance because of the problems it was experiencing with other countries thanks to the American efforts. April 1997 thus produced another setback for Iran when a German court handed down the verdict in the trial of the five men (four Lebanese and one Iranian) accused of killing the Iranian Kurdish leaders at the Mykonos Restaurant in Berlin in 1992. Not only did the court find four of the five (including the Iranian) guilty of the murders, but it boldly stated that the assassinations had been ordered by Iran's "Committee for Special Operations" of Supreme Leader Khamene'i, President Rafsanjani, Minister of Information and Security (i.e., Intelligence) Fallahian, and other top officials.

The Iranians had been afraid this might happen. Even in late 1996, Iranian officials had issued various not-so-veiled threats to the Germans. In August, Fallahian told Iran's official news agency, IRNA, that a guilty verdict "will affect our relations with Germany and our interests. The Germans are smarter than to think we ignore these."[42] An important religious figure, Grand Ayatollah Musavi Ardabili, publicly assured the Germans that he would not call for the death of the prosecutors in the case: "There will be no fatwa like the one laid on Rushdie," he told the *Frankfurter Allgemeine Zeitung*. "As long as the federal prosecutor Bruno Jost does not insult Allah or Mohammed, a fatwa will not be ordered."[43]

They were no more apologetic when the verdict was actually issued. Moreover, because Iran did not have an independent judiciary of its own, Tehran assumed that the verdict was a political move by one insidious conspiracy or another. Iran's interior minister, 'Ali Mohammad Besharati, "denounced the baseless decision of the Berlin court in the so-called Mykonos trial as a plot of international Zionism against the religious and revolutionary values of the Iranian people."[44] Likewise, Iran's deputy minister of culture and Islamic guidance, 'Ali Akbar Asha'ri, "described the plot of the Berlin court against the Islamic Republic of Iran as a 'deceitful move' in a coordination with the White House and the Zionist Entity [Israel]."[45] There were many others, all of the same quality and tenor. Tehran retaliated by announcing that one thousand Iranian families would file a class action lawsuit against the various German firms that had helped Iraq develop chemical weapons during the Iran-Iraq War.[46]

The initial European response was quick and toothless, but still Iran took exception. Germany withdrew its ambassador from Tehran and expelled four Iranian diplomats who were actually intelligence officers. The Iranians retaliated by expelling four German diplomats from Tehran. On April 10, a European conclave called at Germany's request agreed to withdraw all European ambassadors from Tehran and to suspend the Critical Dialogue with Iran. A slightly more meaningful gesture came several weeks later, when the E.U. foreign ministers jointly agreed to halt all meetings with Iran at the ministerial level and to cooperate in blocking intelligence activities in Europe. Nevertheless, several months later the European Union decided to allow its ambassadors to head back to Tehran and to allow these other measures to subside. Still angry, the Iranians refused to allow the German ambassador to return for some time.[47]

In Washington, the European reaction to the Mykonos verdict was met with everything from bemusement to outrage. For years, Europeans (particularly the Germans) had refused to accept Iran's involvement in terrorist affairs, while at the same time saying that if there ever were "solid" evidence of such involvement, that would be a different story. Now their own judiciary not only had found Iran guilty of an act of terrorism in Germany but had taken the unexpected step of stating that senior Iranian officials had been complicit in it. The German government recognized that this was a categorically different level of evidence—one it could not dismiss. Yet its response was to suspend the Critical Dialogue *and do nothing to limit Germany's trade with Iran.* The Critical Dialogue was supposedly the stick—it was how the Europeans raised their concerns about Iranian behavior, although it was an open secret in both Washington and Tehran that many European diplomats flat-out told their Iranian counterparts that their "critical" comments were purely perfunctory, uttered so that they could tell Washington they had done so. (Indeed, the Iranians used to brag about this.) The Critical Dialogue was supposed to be the *punishment* Iran received for its bad behavior. Trade and finance were supposed to be the reward that Iran got for its good behavior. So in response to the Mykonos verdict, the European Union had decided to "punish" Iran by suspending the punishment of the Critical Dialogue while still giving Iran the reward of trade, financing, and other commercial relations. American officials were incredulous.

In part because the Europeans would not take any action, and in part because the Clinton administration felt it important to do something, even while it continued to allow its hands to be tied by the Saudis' intransigence, Washington opted for a form of covert retaliation against Iran. Previously, the CIA and other American intelligence services had not reciprocated or retaliated against Iran's extremely aggressive surveillance and targeting of American personnel because neither the Bush nor the Clinton administration was looking to start a covert war with intelligence services as capable, extensive, and unconstrained as Iran's. However, in 1997, the United States mounted a large-scale covert action that "outed" Iranian agents across the globe as a way of demonstrating that if Washington wanted to, it could wage a devastating campaign against Iran's intelligence services. A number of Iranian operatives were expelled by their host nations, and the Iranians do appear to have been greatly surprised by the operation as they reined in their intelligence assets afterward.[48]

Heeding the Warning Signs

At some point, even the hard-liners in Tehran seemed to have gotten the message that they had gone too far. The events of 1996 and early 1997 confronted them with the realization that their constant escalation of attacks on the United States, Israel, and the moderate states of the region—coupled with their overly cavalier attitude toward the Europeans' support—had left them teetering on the edge of several possible disasters. In America, there was serious talk of massive military operations against Iran in retaliation for Khobar Towers. The Iranians could not know that the Clinton administration had ruled out a full-scale invasion, and thus the specter of an Iranian version of Desert Storm loomed in their thinking. Iran's wary response to an operation ultimately as small as Praying Mantis in 1988 suggests that even those who may have discounted the possibility of an actual invasion likely did not want to provoke even a more limited American response, such as those actually being contemplated. We do not know exactly what the impact of the CIA's covert action in 1997 was inside Tehran, but the fact that Iran did quickly tone down its operations suggests that it too had been something of a shock. Tehran appears to have decided that it had pushed the United States to a point where war—overt or covert—was suddenly a real possibility, and that was a line they had not intended to cross.

Likewise, Iran's relations with Europe were suffering. Although European governments continued to bend over backwards not to take any action against Iran, that does not seem to be how it was viewed in Tehran. Europe's parliaments, judiciaries, and popular groups were increasingly adopting anti-Iranian positions (to varying degrees). Regardless of how they got there, Iranian decision makers all seemed to accept that they were running an increasing risk of having the Europeans impose sanctions on them, reduce their trade, or otherwise cooperate more with the Americans. The pro-Iranian governments in Europe were having greater and greater difficulty holding the line, and the fact that ILSA could be so roundly condemned in Europe and yet have an impact was a similarly ominous sign. It was a subtle but unmistakable sign that, if forced to choose, Europe would side with America over Iran. The Iranians seem to have realized that their policies were pushing Europe to make that choice—a choice the European governments did not want to make.

The result was a sudden turnabout in the Iranians' behavior. They stopped aggressively surveilling and targeting American personnel—although they doubtless continued to do so in more circumspect fashion. Iranian warships in the Gulf began to keep a more respectful distance from U.S. Navy vessels. Iranian support to Gulf dissidents, particularly in Bahrain, diminished. In March, Iran began a process of rapprochement with Saudi Arabia after Rafsanjani met Saudi Crown Prince 'Abdallah at an Islamic summit and the Iranians expressed a willingness to tone down their behavior. At the Hajj that year, the Saudis allowed the Iranians to hold their "Disavowal of the Infidels" ceremony, and the Iranians did so in very low-key fashion. Later in the spring, Iran and the Saudis agreed to resume direct flights—another sign of serious progress.[49] Saudi Arabia was a key state for the Iranians' new effort to demonstrate that they could be good citizens of the world. The Kingdom was the key to the GCC states (which would have to be the launching pad for any major American military operation against Iran) and was also a crucial ally of the United States, capable of acting as a moderating force on Washington.

It seems likely that the United States and its allies would have seen other signs of moderation from Iran, at least in the short term, had things continued on as they had in the past. But it is the nature of the Middle East, and especially of Iran, that things do not simply continue on in a steady progression. In May 1997, something else unexpected happened that seemed to completely shuffle the deck: much to everyone's surprise, including his own, a previously rather minor figure in Iranian politics, Hojjat-ol Islam Mohammad Khatami, won a landslide victory in Iran's presidential election, and he did so on a platform of radical, liberal change.

America and Iran in the Early 1990s:
Assessing Containment and Confrontation

America's Iran policy turned out all right in the end, and that makes it hard to criticize. However, it ultimately turned out well in 1997 because of the deus ex machina of Mohammad Khatami's election. American policy did contribute to Khatami's election. By 1997, one of the things that the Iranian people had tired of was their isolation in the world and, in particular, the relentless enmity of the United States (itself a product of Iran's relentless enmity toward America). They saw other nations reaping the economic benefits of globalization and they wanted it too, and since the United States was the very embodiment of globalization—both in a general sense and in the specific sense that the United States ultimately determined which states would be made full members of the global economy—they wanted a government that would bring an end to that enmity. Yet no one in the United States could have predicted that the outcome of our policies would be to help bring about that change, nor did Khatami's election end all of our problems with Iran, as the next two chapters discuss. Thus, it would be inappropriate to suggest that since Khatami's election was ultimately a good (temporary) outcome for the United States and a different policy might not have contributed to his election—or even might have precluded it—it is not worth asking whether America's policy toward Iran was the right one during the late 1980s and early 1990s.

Although I am willing to ask the question, I have a difficult time coming up with a different answer other than the defensive form of containment that the United States actually adopted. Although an American coined the term and we have been its most skilled practitioners, Americans have an inherent dislike of containment. It is a mostly passive policy, and Americans are inherently drawn to policies that seem to "do" more. "Don't just stand there, do something" is as quintessentially an American approach to foreign relations as it is to every other aspect of our culture. Containment is also a somewhat ambiguous approach that is neither war nor peace and so crosses our famous desire to have clear distinctions between "good guys" and "bad guys." Finally, it is a strategy of patience, something else famously lacking in the American political collectivity. Consequently, it is constantly the case that people proclaim containment to be a failure not because a containment regime is weakening, but simply because it has not yet achieved its stated goals. Such was the case with containment of Iran in the 1990s, where critics regularly pointed out at various points that since Iran had not changed its behavior, the policy had failed. Of course, this was ridiculous. By that criterion one could have claimed that containment of the USSR had failed at every point up until the country's final dissolution in 1991. Containment can be measured as a success or failure only in retrospect; there are often no tangible signs of progress until the very end, and that is something else that we as an impatient and practical-minded people dislike.

Since World War II, containment has been an important strategic option of American foreign policy. However, because of its inherent frustrations, it has rarely been adopted as the best possible approach and instead has generally been the course the United States has chosen because it was the least bad option available. Frequently it has been our default policy against foreign regimes we dislike but are unwilling (or, occasionally, unable) to bear the costs of overthrowing via direct military operations, covert action, or some other stratagem. On other occasions, all of the alternative policies appeared less likely to achieve America's objectives, either because there were competing objectives or because we feared unintended consequences. Thus, containment has served the country well, but in every case the policy was savagely attacked and only weakly defended, largely for the reasons enumerated above. This too was the case with containment of Iran.

Containment of Iran sort of succeeded by 1997. The Iranians did begin to change their behavior, fearing that they were close to provoking an American military operation and/or European trade sanctions. Whether either was justified or which was more important will probably never be known. Nevertheless, it was only a partial success because, had it not been for Khatami's election, it is unclear whether that change would have been permanent. There is reason to believe that Rafsanjani and the pragmatists had won a tactical victory but had not changed the strategic direction of Iran's policies. In a year or two, Iran might have reverted back to a more refined version of its aggressive foreign policy of the early 1990s, and unless some other development made a new policy possible, the United States probably would have found itself forced to apply containment once again. Containment had also achieved some important secondary objectives during its application against Iran in the 1990s. It had hindered Iranian rearmament and considerably impeded Iran's progress toward a nuclear weapon (although that may have been as much a result of incompetent direction on Iran's part as of our efforts). It had helped Yitzhak Rabin with his domestic politics and so was an important element of the progress Arab-Israeli peace made during that stretch of time. Indeed, the fact that Iran was a critical factor in the stalling of the peace process at different points indicates how important containment was and suggests that if it could have been strengthened by greater multilateral participation, more might have been accomplished. Had there been no PIJ and HAMAS attacks in 1996, Peres might have won the Israeli election, and he undoubtedly would have made progress on the peace process a higher priority than Netanyahu did. Ultimately, there were other, more direct obstacles to peace that likely would have brought the process up short in any event, but the "what ifs" are tantalizing and depressing.

Containment tends to shine most by comparison, and when compared to the other policy options the United States might have adopted in the late 1980s, its merits do stand out more boldly. If containment achieved, at most, a limited and possibly temporary victory in 1997, Europe's Critical Dialogue was an utter failure. Here it is important to remember what Critical Dialogue consisted of: it was a policy of allowing (even encouraging) trade and other commercial dealings with Iran while lecturing Tehran about its bad behavior. At no point in its history did Critical Dialogue achieve a change in Iranian behavior. What ultimately did contribute to the (again, limited and possibly temporary) change in Iranian behavior in 1997 was the threat of possible sanctions, which was *not* part of the Critical Dialogue. The governments adhering to the Critical Dialogue continued to insist that they would not sanction Iran in any way, even after the conclusion of the Mykonos trial. It was only the threat of action by parliaments, judiciaries, and European publics themselves that made the Iranians fearful. The threat of sanctions was never a part of the Critical Dialogue; in point of fact, threatening sanctions was precisely what the U.S. government had repeatedly urged on Europe and been rebuffed on every occasion. To the extent that the Critical Dialogue really was designed to try to change Iran's behavior, it was actually counterproductive. It allowed the Iranian radicals, who opposed moderating Iran's behavior and taking a more constructive approach toward the United States, to insist that Iran did not need good relations with the United States because it could get what it needed from the Europeans, who would continue to trade and aid them regardless of their actions toward Israel, the United States, or anyone else.

Supporters of the Critical Dialogue have at times defended it by comparing it to American policy toward China. Their claim is that their policy of constant rewards and trade with Iran was no different from American efforts to deal with China by locking it into interdependent trade relations and convincing Beijing to focus on economic, rather than geographic, growth. This is a false analogy. First, China understands that its relations with the United States are predicated on its behavior on a number of issues, including domestic human rights and its actions toward Taiwan. The pace and depth of American relations have always been determined by China's behavior, and Beijing knows that were it to embark on truly egregious behavior, the U.S. Congress would find ways to punish it regardless of what the executive branch might want. This has not fully eliminated Chinese misbehavior (from an American perspective), but it has greatly mitigated it. China does test missiles near Taiwan in moments of great strain, for example, but it does so knowing that this will hurt its relationship with the United States, even if only temporarily. Consequently, the Chinese limit those occasions to when they feel it absolutely necessary to do so. Of greater importance, China today is a very different country with very different goals and policies than Iran was in the 1989–1997 time frame. China may want the United States out of East Asia, but it is not aggressively trying to force us out, nor is it waging a terrorist campaign against American forces and allies in Asia. Indeed, even those Americans most concerned about China's rise point to a long-term threat, not ongoing asymmetric warfare. If the Chinese were to adopt such a strategy, they seem to understand that it would cause an immediate and dramatic shift in American behavior toward them. Critical Dialogue never created the same incentive structure for Iran, which actually was engaged in an ongoing asymmetric war with the United States and its allies in the region.

If Critical Dialogue was a clear failure, it is also difficult to imagine a strategy of applying greater pressure to Iran that might have worked. This is not to say that containment was perfect or that it could not have been bolstered. It is self-evident, based on Iran's behavior, that the original containment regime inaugurated in 1993 was far too weak. It would have been better to incorporate at least some of the changes that were later adopted right from the start. Nevertheless, it would have been difficult to sustain a policy that was considerably more aggressive than what the United States ended up with in 1996 as a result of the (at times collaborative) efforts of Congress and the administration. First of all, there simply was no covert action option. As noted, the United States lacked the assets in Iran, the country was not so unstable that it could have benefited from the kind of small nudge covert action can give, and mounting a covert action campaign against Iran was only likely to play right into Iran's long-standing, emotional, and often uncontrollable psychoses regarding American interference in Iran's internal affairs. It would have been the best way to provoke Iran to do the exact opposite of what we wanted it to do. It almost certainly would have made Tehran even more aggressive and more energetic in its efforts to attack our personnel, our allies, and our interests.

Nor would a more aggressive containment regime against Iran have been sustainable in the early 1990s. During that same period of time, the United States was imposing a far more draconian and offensive version of containment on Iraq. That containment regime was supported by U.N. Security Council resolutions enacted under Article VII of the U.N. Charter and a global consensus that Saddam Hussein was one of the worst dictators of the twentieth century and therefore had to be deprived of weapons that no other country was banned from possessing. He had just invaded another sovereign state, he engaged in acts of terrorism (such as trying to assassinate former President Bush) that his minions were not clever enough to conceal their involvement in, and he routinely violated the UNSC resolutions and prevented U.N. inspectors from doing their job, even to the point of threatening them with violence. Even with all of that going for it, the containment of Iraq was already eroding by 1996 and was in quite bad shape at the beginning of the twenty-first century.[50]

Given all of the problems the United States experienced in trying to maintain a more aggressive containment regime against Iraq even with everything that it had going for it, it is hard to imagine that a simultaneous program against Iran could ever have been implemented. The fundamental problem of the containment regime against Iran was that it lacked the multilateral commitment that the Iraq containment regime had early on but that disintegrated over time, causing containment to erode with it. No European or Asian country wanted to join in sanctions on Iran, let alone mount limited military strikes against it, and those were the most important elements of the tighter containment of Iraq. It simply was not in the cards for the United States to have tried to contain Iran as it did Iraq for much of the 1990s.

A last question that is important to consider is whether the United States could have and should have retaliated against Iran for the Khobar Towers attack. For my part, I believe it would have been much better for America's deterrent posture in general, and specifically with regard to Iran, if the U.S. government could have found a way to have mounted a major military retaliation against Iran for the Khobar Towers bombing. However, I do not believe that it would have been realistic to have done so under the circumstances. The reasons for this have some important lessons regarding American policy toward the Islamic Republic of Iran.

Part of the matter revolves around the question of timing. As noted above, Khatami's election seemed to obviate the need for such a retaliation because it appeared that the Iranian government was changing dramatically and for the better. Thus, there is little reason to question the logic that once he was elected, the case for retaliation evaporated. But this still leaves open the question of whether the United States could have and should have retaliated prior to Khatami's election. After all, the United States did not know that he would be elected, so this cannot justify inaction before May 1997. In fact, Khatami did not announce his candidacy until a few months before the election, and right up until the polls closed, the universal expectation (even of Khatami himself) was that he was not going to be allowed to win.

At Khobar Towers, Iran crossed a momentous line. Through a thinly veiled proxy, it had mounted a direct attack on Americans. It is not that it had never done so before—it had on at least three occasions in Lebanon in the 1980s, including the Marine Barracks bombing—and the Reagan administration's failure to retaliate for those attacks was unquestionably mistaken. After the terrorist attacks of September 11, 2001, such unwillingness to retaliate forcefully seems equally misguided, and the lessons of 9/11 deserve to be applied retroactively in assessing previous policy decisions. We learned a terrible lesson that day that we should have learned much earlier: that an unwillingness to confront terrorist groups and their state sponsors only breeds more terrorism. No nation should be allowed to think that it can attack the United States, using its own nationals or foreign proxies, and believe that it will not suffer for doing so.

To our knowledge, Iran has not attacked us again, directly or indirectly, since. But that too should not be taken as a sign of the success of our non-response. The Iranians changed their policy in 1997 for fear that the United States would respond militarily. That assumption was built on reputation: they had seen the United States act during the tanker war, the Persian Gulf War, and, on a much lesser scale, against Iraq at various points during the 1990s, and these events had injected caution into the minds of key Iranian decision makers. Had Khatami not been elected and had the United States still failed to retaliate for Khobar, it is highly likely that the radicals in Tehran would have been able to argue that our unwillingness to retaliate, linked (as they inevitably would have) with our failures to do so during the hostage crisis, the three Hizballah attacks in Lebanon, and the holding of the various American hostages, was proof that Iran could be far more aggressive toward the United States and its allies without fear of an American military response. In other words, had Khatami not been elected and the United States not retaliated, Iran's positive shift in behavior would likely have been short-lived and the Iranian decision makers likely would have learned the wrong lesson. The threat of prompt and devastating military responses was crucial to the containment of Iran, to make it clear that there were thresholds it could not cross. Having crossed a key threshold at Khobar Towers, if Iran had not suffered such a military response, containment would have been greatly, perhaps fatally, compromised.

Nevertheless, there were many major hurdles involved in such a retaliation. Some that were raised, including finding the right targets and dealing with the possibility of an Iranian retaliation, should not have been decisive (and there is no reason to believe that they were). Plenty of targets were available: Iran's navy, its new submarine fleet, its terrorist training bases, the headquarters of the MOIS and Pasdaran, its WMD facilities, and other military targets. Any of them would have sent the appropriate message to the Iranian regime that there was a price to be paid for killing Americans. Just as the United States destroyed the headquarters of the Iraqi intelligence service in 1993 for the attempted assassination of George Bush, so too could we have taken at least that degree of action for Iran's actual killing of nineteen Americans at Khobar Towers.[51]

Nor should the potential for Iranian retaliation have been a determining factor. First, the Iranians' actual behavior after the Khobar attack, and the public calls for retaliation in the United States, indicate that they understood that they had overstepped themselves and so were unlikely to retaliate further if we did. Second, Iran had not retaliated for Praying Mantis, and most people do not believe that it retaliated for the destruction of Iran Air flight 655.[52] This too suggests that given a clear demonstration of America's willingness to employ overwhelming conventional power, Iran would back down. Third, although American officials often discussed how an escalating "tit-for-tat" of retaliations between the United States and Iran did not look good to them, it was also the case that the same hypothetical series of attacks and reactions looked even worse from Tehran's perspective. The Iranians could have blown up some buildings and doubtless killed several hundred people if they were determined and willing to sustain a protracted terror campaign, but the losses they would have suffered if the United States showed similar resolve would have been much worse from their perspective. This too would likely have given them pause before retaliating for our own retaliation.

Last, allowing for the possibility that Iran might have retaliated for our own retaliation to stop us should not have been a consideration because it would have nullified the core principles of containment and deterrence. It would have been effectively rewarding Iran for its willingness to kill civilians and its pathological hatred of the United States. It would have been a declaration that any country ruthless enough to mount terrorist attacks against the United States and possessed of enough fervor to withstand massive damage from American military strikes got a free pass and would never have to endure massive damage from American military strikes.

This logic is truly perverse: by being willing to conduct the Khobar Towers attack—and thereby demonstrate that it would and could conduct additional such attacks—Iran would be immunized from an American military response. Ultimately, this was precisely the argument of Iranian radicals, who claimed that the United States was too cowardly to respond to their challenges and so they could do as they liked without fear of U.S. retaliation. It is simply not responsible, logical, or prudent to argue that the United States should not be willing to use force to retaliate for terrorist acts committed against its nationals for fear that the same country would commit subsequent terrorist attacks. If a group or nation is determined to mount terrorist attacks, refraining from retaliation for fear of additional attacks will only encourage them.

Yet there is one last issue to consider in assessing whether the United States should have retaliated against Iran for the Khobar Towers attack before Khatami's election, and that is whether we had the intelligence to do so. It is on this point that the case for retaliating against Iran falls apart. Here as well, the light of subsequent experience is helpful. The importance of intelligence when retaliating for a terrorist operation is crucial in establishing popular and international support for the military operation both at the time and afterward. As we have learned from hard experience, invading Iraq in 2003 without strong international support and based on a case for war that turned out to be considerably weaker than was believed at the time has had very painful consequences. Without a strong case for retaliation, it is impossible to garner the necessary domestic and international support.

Moreover, in war, there are always casualties, and the United States must be able to justify those casualties to its people and its allies. Many have called into question the intelligence regarding the legitimacy of striking the ash-Shifa pharmaceutical factory in Sudan in retaliation for the al-Qa'eda attacks on the U.S. Embassies in Kenya and Tanzania in 1998—and that strike was conducted with unmanned cruise missiles against a largely unoccupied facility with little likelihood of civilian casualties.[53] As damaging to America's national security as it may be not to retaliate for a terrorist attack, it is far worse for the United States to retaliate against the wrong target. Because retaliating against Iran likely would have required the United States to conduct a large enough military operation both to make it clear to Iran that it would gain nothing from terrorist attacks and to convince it not to try to retaliate in turn, it was absolutely critical for the United States to have been right that Iran was behind Khobar. Imagine if Washington had conducted massive air and cruise missile strikes against Iran, likely killing hundreds, only to find out that Tehran had not been behind Khobar?

As it so often does in the post–Cold War world, the question of retaliating for the Khobar Towers attack comes down to the question "How good was the intelligence?" And the problem was that before Khatami's election, it was not great. Most of the CIA and other intelligence community analysts believed that Iran was behind Khobar, but they believed that to be the case based on intuition and circumstantial evidence. Ultimately, they were proven right, but there have certainly been cases (Iraqi WMD in 2003 comes to mind) when the intuition of the intelligence analysts coupled with even great masses of circumstantial evidence has turned out to be wrong. Prior to 1999, when the Saudis finally turned over their evidence regarding the Khobar attack to the FBI, the intelligence community refused to say with any degree of confidence that Iran had been behind the attack. They indicated that Iran was the most likely culprit but that there were other possibilities and they just did not have the evidence to come to a firm conclusion. This had nothing to do with whether the evidence was strong enough to stand up in the proverbial court of law; the U.S. intelligence community is perfectly capable of drawing that distinction and saying to the president, "We are convinced that Iran did this, but we believe it will be difficult to prove in public." In 1996–1997, the collective leadership of the intelligence community did not feel that they could say even that regarding Iran's involvement in Khobar. Especially in light of the debate swirling around the Bush administration's decision to go to war with Iraq in 2003, when the U.S. intelligence community did solidly (but mistakenly) believe that Iraq retained large, aggressive WMD programs, it is hard to fault the Clinton administration for refraining from taking large-scale military action when the U.S. intelligence community would not offer a solid verdict.

Certainly there is more that could have been done. In particular, the United States could have pressed the Saudis harder. We might have done more to assure them that if the evidence they provided us was as good as we believed it to be (and as it turned out to be), the United States was prepared to mount major operations. This might have done enough to strengthen the wing of the Al Sa'ud that wanted to see the United States strike Iran to allow it to carry the day. There were other diplomatic tactics we might also have employed.

However, the more general lesson from the Khobar experience is one also demonstrated by other aspects of Iranian history since the revolution. Iran is an inherently problematic country. When dealing with Iran, the United States, and every other country that does so, often finds itself torn in conflicting directions. In particular, because the Iranian regime is willing to do things that are ultimately counterproductive to its own interests (although it rarely recognizes this) and can convince the Iranian people to endure heavy sacrifices in the pursuit of abstract notions such as "resisting foreign influence," dealing with it—even from the opposite end of a cruise missile—is very difficult. The Iranians have a knack for putting other countries in frustrating situations in which no good solution is possible. The European experience with "Critical Dialogue" was not a particularly happy one either. And it is not that these no-win situations benefit Iran; it is just that the Iranians are either oblivious to the damage or willing to bear it, and able to convince themselves that their actions are achieving a psychological victory that is somehow useful to them.

I still believe that American interests would have been best served by finding a way to retaliate against Iran for the Khobar Towers attack, but I concede that the Clinton administration was right not to do so under the circumstances. On Khobar Towers, the evidence was not there before Khatami's election. And to a great extent, his election may have been the best revenge the United States could have gotten against the hard-liners who had ordered the Khobar Towers attack.

The Ecstasy and
the Agony

It has been one of the defining features of U.S.-Iranian relations over the past fifty years that Iran's domestic politics have been the most important among a range of forces determining their course. Especially since the fall of the shah, it has largely (but certainly not entirely) been Iran that has set the tone and direction of the relationship. In keeping with that pattern, the unexpected election of Mohammad Khatami in 1997, and the dramatic political battles that this event sparked in Tehran, had a profound impact on America's relationship with Iran. The latter half of the 1990s and the beginning of the twenty-first century took the United States on a roller coaster of hope and dashed expectations propelled by the remarkable changes in Iran's internal politics.

Both before and after his election, Khatami suggested that he wanted Iran to have a better relationship with the United States, although that would have to be a cautious process because of the Pavlovian opposition of so much of Iran's ruling elite and key elements of the society at large. The United States was, perhaps, a bit slow off the mark thanks to a variety of strategic rationales and its own domestic political problems with Iran. However, as Khatami demonstrated his determination to try to change Iran, the Clinton administration became increasingly convinced of his sincerity and determined to try to work with him to create a new, less antagonistic relationship. Unfortunately, Khatami was just not up to the task, and his various efforts at reform—including his willingness to reach out to the United States—prompted a backlash by Iran's hard-line conservative elements that overwhelmed him. By the start of his second term in 2001 and the accession of the George W. Bush administration in the United States, the promise of the reformists had been snuffed out, at least for the foreseeable future. With Iran's hard-liners back in charge, albeit of a fundamentally changed Iran, new versions of the same old problems between Iran and America began to creep back to the surface.

Greatness Thrust upon Him

By 1997, the people of Iran had become disenchanted with the postrevolutionary regime. The Islamic Republic had failed to deliver on its promises of a better life, a less repressive society, and a more equitable distribution of wealth. So when Hashemi Rafsanjani's second term as president ended, requiring him to step down (even though he and his supporters unsuccessfully fought for a constitutional amendment to allow him to stand for a third term), the Iranian people were looking for a change.

The most obvious problems were economic.[1] The regime had frequently put its ideas about Islamic orthodoxy ahead of economic efficiency. Iranian worker productivity remained low and Iranian bureaucratic procedures had grown hopelessly tangled, all of which hobbled the country's exports. As a result, oil remained Iran's primary export, and the low oil prices of the early 1990s caused a debilitating drop in Iranian revenues. Meanwhile, Iran's imports increased, and the American sanctions helped drive up trade costs.[2] This, coupled with a heavy debt burden left over from the Rafsanjani administration's mismanagement, resulted in continuing high levels of inflation, averaging 42 percent per year in 1995 and '96.[3] Tehran claimed that inflation fell to 17 percent in 1997, but unofficial estimates still put it at closer to 35 percent and some even as high as 50 percent.[4] Before the revolution, a dollar was worth 70 rials. By early 1997, a dollar was worth 1,750 to 3,000 rials at the various official exchange rates and close to 5,000 on the black market.[5] The regime's insistence on maintaining so arbitrarily low an exchange rate (and having multiple exchange rates for different goods and services) further crippled trade, encouraged corruption, and pushed people to put their time and money into nonproductive activities such as making money by manipulating currency exchange, rather than investing that same capital in industry or agriculture.[6] Unemployment stood at more than 30 percent.[7] Corruption grew apace throughout Iran, enriching a new class (many of whom were clerics) in the same fashion as the shah's courtiers, who had helped themselves to the public treasury before the revolution. The vast *bonyad*s, which controlled hundreds of billions of dollars in assets and whose total annual income often exceeded Iran's oil revenues, continued to distort and corrupt the economy to suit their own narrow needs.[8] Iran's economic problems contributed to a troubling rise in drug use and crime.[9]

At this point, it was much harder for Rafsanjani and the pragmatists to blame their domestic rivals for all of these problems. The radicals—and a conservative opposition that also formed in opposition to Rafsanjani's domestic policies but from a different vantage point than the radicals—were still able to hinder many of his initiatives. However, since the Majles elections of 1992, which he and Khamene'i had thoroughly rigged, his government had had greater freedom to deal with the economy, and its continuing problems were as much a result of its mismanagement as the conservatives' obduracy. Rafsanjani's technocrats had generally diagnosed the problems correctly but in some cases had prescribed the wrong answers and in other cases implemented the right answers poorly.[10] Iran's former finance minister and a keen observer of the Iranian economy, Jahangir Amuzegar, wrote, "Rafsanjani's own highly-praised economic team also badly miscalculated both its own professional prowess and the response of ordinary people. The exchange-rate unification and foreign currency management were badly botched. Bank credits to debt-ridden public enterprises were imprudently increased. Widening the tax base never came to pass. . . . Public investments were stepped up in projects of questionable value. External debt, which had been skillfully kept low during the eight-year war, suddenly skyrocketed."[11]

However, the unhappiness of the Iranian people stemmed from more than merely poor economic prospects. The dogmatic imposition of archaic codes of behavior enforced by bands of armed zealots was getting old for many Iranians. Thanks to Khomeini's misguided demand that Iranians bear more children, the country's population had grown quickly and become very young over the years. In 1995, the median age was just 17.6, and in 1997 half of the population was under the age of 24.[12] (The median age in the United States in 1997 was 34.9.)[13] Iran's vast youth population chafed under the rigid social codes imposed by the mullahs and enforced by the Hizballahis.[14] Women wanted to be able to wear fashionable clothes in public. They also wanted to be able to ride bicycles in public—something Supreme Leader Khamene'i had forbidden in 1996 because riding a bicycle (even in full chador) "attracted" men.[15] Both sexes wanted to be able to meet in public without chaperons. They wanted to be able to dance and to hold parties outside. They wanted to be able to listen to pop music and to hold hands and engage in other public displays of affection without going to prison or worse. Many Iranians of all ages wanted to be able to speak their minds and hear the voices of others. They wanted to be able to debate their country's policy and to have their voices count for something. They wanted an end to television programs that proclaimed specific intellectuals, writers, and professors by name as Israeli spies or antisocial deviants. And they wanted to be able to own satellite dishes, which would enable them to receive programs from the outside world but which the regime had declared illegal in 1995 because people were using them to do just that.[16]

Hojjat-ol Islam Sayyid Mohammad Khatami Ardakani was the beneficiary of all this frustration. To a considerable extent, Iranians voted for Khatami without knowing a great deal about him. He had been minister of culture and Islamic guidance twice, in 1982–1986 and again in 1989–1992. He had not been very much in the public eye during those terms, although he had made a splash by being forced to resign in 1992 by the theocratic establishment for having been too permissive with Iran's media and entertainment. This tantalizing fact alone made him attractive as a candidate in 1997. Other than that, he had held rather minor posts, having spent 1992–1997 as the head of Iran's National Library—about as politically important as the head of the Library of Congress is in Washington.[17] Iranians voted for Khatami not so much for who he was but for who they hoped he would be.

More than 230 candidates applied to run for the presidency in 1997, and the Council of Guardians naturally disqualified all but four of them. Majles Speaker 'Ali Akbar Nateq Nuri was the anointed candidate of the establishment; Supreme Leader Khamene'i virtually endorsed him during the campaign, and Pasdaran Commander Mohsen Reza'i issued written orders to all of his troops to vote for him. The Council of Guardians no doubt believed that Khatami was just as much of a nonentity as the other two candidates, and so by leaving a field of only their well-known candidate and three minor figures, Nateq Nuri's election was guaranteed. "Never had Iranian officials been so blatant in their backing of a single candidate," Robin Wright commented.[18] However, during the short campaign period allowed by the regime (which further disadvantages candidates outside the political mainstream, who have little time for the electorate to get to know them), Khatami caught the imagination of the Iranian voters.[19] As one of Khatami's close aides put it, "They allowed him to run because they thought he had no chance of winning. It was a gross miscalculation. By the time they realized, it was too late to stop him."[20]

Initially, Khatami simply talked about the need for change. He said that he would promote the rule of law; that he would curb corruption; that he wanted to eliminate "superstition and fanaticism" from government—which every Iranian recognized as code words for getting the government out of their social affairs. He stressed the importance of empowering civil society, which meant diminishing the totalitarianism of the central government. He talked about Iran's Constitution and of the importance of the government remaining within its guidelines. He won the overwhelming support of women and the young (fifteen was the voting age) simply because people believed that he favored social and cultural freedom and would allow the press, the arts, and the people to express themselves more freely than in the past.[21]

Of course, Khatami was a cleric with good revolutionary credentials. He was also a Sayyid—a descendant of the Prophet Muhammad. As all candidates must, he swore allegiance to the Iranian political system and to the central concept of *velayat-e faqih*. Throughout his election campaign he tried to present his ideas as being in keeping with Khomeini's philosophy. What's more, because he and all of his colleagues feared that if he went too far in criticizing the regime or promoting radical change he would be disqualified, he kept most of his comments veiled and allowed people to read into them more than he could say.

And they read everything into them that they could. Like Mosaddeq and Khomeini before him, Khatami became emblematic of change in the minds of Iranians. Hence they projected onto him all of their personal grievances and hopes for change. Like the taxi driver in Mashhad who had supported Khomeini because of his supposed interest in economic reform (which Khomeini entirely lacked), so Iranians supported Khatami because they thought he stood for changing whatever it was that they did not like. " 'I want to vote for Khatami because although he is a cleric he is very open-minded and is not scared of freedom,' said Parvin Alizadeh, a 21-year-old university student."[22] " 'I hope he wins. I hope he lives a long life,' said a middle-aged woman who was voting for the first time because 'Khatami is more intellectual and less dogmatic.' "[23] " 'Khatami will create jobs and build sport facilities for the young,' said a 20-year-old Abolfazl, hanging around a street corner in Azad-Shahr with several other youth."[24] "Several watermelon peddlers in nearby Islam-Shahr said they voted for the former minister because he was a 'Seyyed,' a descendant of the prophet Mohammed. The title was used as a campaign ploy by Khatami's supporters, and it appears to have had much appeal among the more religious voters in the provinces."[25] " 'Iran needs more freedom, it is very strict,' said one 17 year-old girl after casting her first ballot."[26] "A young man in Eslam-Shahr, which was the scene of a riot two years ago over the high cost of living, said he voted for Khatami 'because he wants to make life more fun for the youth.' " " 'The disinherited all vote for Khatami; it's the rich who want Nategh-Nuri,' said Ali, a 21-year-old machinist." Still another man said he would vote for Khatami, "although I don't know him and his program well. But people say he is good." [27]

Change was the defining issue of the 1997 presidential race, and this was reflected in tectonic shifts among Iran's political elite as well. Over time, it is the nature for political disputes to evolve. Nowhere is this more often and more quickly the case than in Iran. It is important to keep in mind the kaleidoscopic nature of the fragmented Iranian polity, which remained just as true in 1997 as it was in 1992 and 1979 and 1953 and 1906. It would not be much of an exaggeration to say that every Iranian was virtually his or her own political party. Nevertheless, as always, there were broader movements that reflected the opposing views on the most important policy issues of the day. By 1997, the domestic political factions had rearranged and reoriented themselves considerably. Many of the pragmatists of the early 1990s had become "reformists." They recognized that the state bequeathed them by Khomeini was failing to cope with Iran's various problems, foreign and domestic, and so they increasingly agitated for fundamental changes in the system. In this, they were able to dovetail their own interests with those of the broader population seeking change on the issues that affected them. Rafsanjani was part of this group, as he continued to blame his opponents in the Majles and elsewhere for having hamstrung his presidency and believed that only sweeping reform would eliminate their ability to do so. Given that this half of the Iranian political spectrum had defined itself as favoring change, those who opposed them became known as the "conservatives" (or the hard-liners, in the West) because they opposed far-reaching change. Just as there were all kinds of reformists—with every imaginable notion of what reform should consist of and why—so too those who opposed change did so for many different reasons. For instance, a number of the old radicals became conservatives because they saw the existing system as being most consistent with their revolutionary ideals.[28]

In the 1997 presidential election, Khatami was embraced by all of the different reformist groups. Thus Rafsanjani's old-style pragmatists endorsed him, as did those advocating far more extreme versions of change—in some cases even the abolition of *velayat-e faqih*. Nateq Nuri was likewise championed by all the different factions in Iran that opposed change, regardless of where they might have stood in the past. Indeed, old enemies of Nateq Nuri's from when he had been seen as an ally of Rafsanjani now became his staunchest defenders. The zealots among the Revolutionary Guard who were still as eager as ever to spread the revolution and fight the Great Satan became staunch supporters of the conservative line, as did Supreme Leader Khamene'i himself, who probably believed that any change to Iran's system could only weaken his position.[29]

There was one other issue on which Khatami became a symbol of the change that the people wanted and that the conservative establishment vehemently opposed: relations with the United States. Foreign policy was not a central issue of the 1997 election, but it was not entirely absent either.[30] For the most part, foreign policy—and particularly relations with the United States—were important largely because of their place within the Iranian domestic political struggle. The popular protest movements that had congealed in Iran in 1906, 1953, and 1979 had had many things in common, but probably the most important was that they had reflected a profound unhappiness of virtually every segment of Iranian society with particular aspects of the status quo. What was critical was that while they all had different specific complaints, they all ascribed the source of their problems to a common threat (the shah, the British, the Americans), and they all took as their savior whatever other person or entity was considered the greatest opposition to The Threat. Thus, in 1953, Mosaddeq was Iran's savior because he was the most vehement opponent of the British. Likewise, in 1979, Khomeini became Iran's savior to a great extent because he was the most vehement opponent of the shah and his American "masters."

In 1997, this same phenomenon was at work again. Because so many Iranians from so many different segments of society had soured on the status quo as enforced by the regime's establishment, whatever it was that was opposed to that establishment became desirable in their eyes. There was nothing that seemed more opposed to the Iranian establishment than the United States. Thus, as people turned against the regime, they began to look more favorably on the United States simply because it was viewed as being opposed to what Iranians opposed. Another aspect of this phenomenon was that by the mid-1990s, many Iranians had become so unhappy with their current state of affairs that considerable nostalgia for the days of the shah had crept back in. There were more frequent wistful remarks about how things had been better before the revolution. Since in Iranian minds the shah was still wholly identified with the United States, nostalgia for the shah translated into nostalgia for the United States. Last, the United States represented what Iranians wanted most. Especially for women and the young, America seemed to be the physical and spiritual embodiment of what they were deprived of: freedom, material goods, sensualism, movies, glamour, rock music, you name it. Everything that Iranians were denied had a close association with the United States in the minds of most Iranians—including the minority who opposed change. For all of these reasons, by 1997, Iran had become one of the most pro-American countries (at a popular level) in the world. Of course, what Iranians yearned for was really their idealized vision of America; just as they had projected onto Mosaddeq, Khomeini, and now Khatami whatever it was that they considered "good" at that moment, they did the same with the United States.

Therefore, one of the things that Iranians tended to see in Khatami was a leader who wanted to repair relations with the United States. They were right about this, but he was more cautious than many of his constituents seemed to recognize. Khatami had spent several years in West Germany, and, like Khomeini, had studied Western philosophy, which gave him a better sense of the West and made him more comfortable with Western ideas than many of his colleagues. In his first major campaign speech, Khatami began his remarks on foreign policy as follows: "In the field of foreign policy, we would also like to announce that we are in favour of relations with all countries and nations which respect our independence, dignity and interests. We are in favour of having relations and expanding our relations throughout the world on the basis of the three firm principles of wisdom, dignity and [national] interests. . . . If we do not have relations with an aggressive and bullying country such as America, it is due to the fact that America does not respect those principles. In addition to its long-standing animosity towards our country, after the revolution that country has also been at the head of the aggressors and conspirators against us, and still continues to be so."[31]

Iranians were intrigued. In the country's poisonous and rigid political environment, this was a remarkably pro-U.S. statement. In the convoluted language necessary for an Iranian candidate to take a controversial position, Khatami had suggested that if America changed its bad behavior (which Iranians took to mean things like the sanctions, ILSA, and the covert action program), Iran could have normal relations with it. This was a categorically different notion from Khomeini's typical view that the United States was the embodiment of evil with which Iran would never have normal relations. (Indeed, all but a few of Khomeini's statements made in extremis during dire moments of the Iran-Iraq War indicated that there would be a permanent state of war between America and the Islamic Republic.) Within Iran's kabuki-like political discourse, this was a major broadside. In fact, Supreme Leader Khamene'i felt it necessary to respond immediately, warning against any candidate showing "the least sign of flexibility toward America, Western interference and cultural aggression."[32]

That was also the last major speech Khatami was allowed to make during the campaign. After that, virtually all of his rallies and televised speeches were abruptly and arbitrarily canceled by the regime. His campaign headquarters in Tehran was suddenly closed down on the claim that it had been set up illegally, and a huge rally was banned on the grounds that the sports stadium where it was to have been held was deemed "inappropriate for a political event."[33] Indeed, because Nateq Nuri continued to denounce the United States as Iran's greatest enemy, while Khatami said very little after his initial speech had suggested the possibility of normalized relations, the contrast alone kept the idea alive in the minds of many Iranians. At other points, Nateq Nuri blasted Khatami by claiming that he secretly wanted a rapprochement with America. Far from turning voters off, it seemed to make Khatami even more attractive.[34]

As the day of the election drew nearer, Iranians increasingly sensed that this would be a much closer election than they expected. There was a frenzy of activity to get out the vote on Khatami's part—wealthy and middle-class Iranians called their relatives overseas and had them fly home to vote for Khatami. Both inside Iran and among more astute observers, there was a sense that Khatami would likely win in the hearts of Iranian voters. However, everyone inside and outside the country was also certain that Nateq Nuri would "win" because the establishment would cheat, as they always did. Their arbitrary efforts to muzzle Khatami seemed proof of that, as did the fact that effectively every other major election in Iran had seen widespread fraud. Many Iranians fervently supported Khatami and voted for him not because they expected him to be allowed to win but as a symbolic act of protest against the current policies of the regime. For many, a vote for Khatami was the only way they could express their frustration and their desire for change to a regime that never seemed to listen.[35]

To no one's surprise, on election day on May 23, there was evidence of vote rigging, intimidation, and other irregularities, but to everyone's surprise—seemingly including his own—Khatami was declared the winner.[36] Officially, the government announced that he had received 69 percent of the vote to Nateq Nuri's 23 percent, but given the charges of electoral fraud, the true numbers may have been even higher. What's more, there was a phenomenally high voter turnout of 91 percent—compared to 53 percent in the 1993 presidential election—demonstrating the popular enthusiasm for Khatami's candidacy.[37] It may be that the real numbers for Khatami were so high that the regime did not dare try to manipulate them too much for fear of sparking massive public protests. Moreover, Khatami's support spanned the Iranian political spectrum: *Iran Times* crowed, "He won in Tehran and in the provinces; he won in the villages as well as the cities; he won the votes of the poor as well as the rich."[38] The regime leadership also no doubt consoled itself that, ultimately, Khatami was one of its own—a cleric with solid revolutionary credentials—and so was unlikely to get too far out of line. The people understood that too, to a certain extent, but it did not matter. They had voted for the candidate who offered the vision most at variance with that of the regime's establishment, and he had won.[39]

The Dialogue Among Civilizations

The U.S. government was as surprised as everyone else by Khatami's victory. The U.S. intelligence community had done a good job predicting that Khatami would fare much better than originally expected, but it too had assumed that the conservatives would tamper with things just enough to be able to declare Nateq Nuri the winner. The unexpected victory immediately touched off a debate in Washington over what Khatami wanted to do and would be able to do, and how the United States should react. There were those who argued that Khatami's election was the start of a counterrevolution in Iran, while others argued that he was nothing but "old wine in new bottles"—just another revolutionary mullah, but one with a nicer smile. It was a debate that would rage in Washington until long after Khatami had proven that he actually had wanted to make fundamental change but had been unable to do so. In the meantime, the Clinton administration steered a cautious middle course. The White House welcomed Khatami's election and congratulated the Iranian people on a remarkable exercise of democracy. Beyond that, American officials stressed the existing position that the United States would be more than willing to engage in an authoritative dialogue with Iran—but one that had to be openly acknowledged, so as to avoid Iran-*contra*-like shenanigans—and hoped that the new administration of President Khatami would avail itself of that opportunity. Washington reiterated that, in those conversations, the United States intended to raise its problems with Iran's support for terrorism, pursuit of nuclear weapons, and opposition to the Middle East peace process, and that any changes in American policy could come only in response to changes in Iran's behavior on those issues.[40]

It was widely expected that Khatami would focus initially on consolidating his domestic political position, and he did make this a priority—but he did not make it the all-consuming venture that both Iranians and foreign experts expected. Khatami was an experienced enough politician that he knew he had to have control over key government institutions if he was going to have any chance of seeing his policy executed. In Iran, officials did not take actions just because the president said so. As Bani Sadr's experience demonstrated, many of them had their own loyalties and agendas that did not necessarily extend to the office of the president, especially when it was occupied by a peripheral figure such as Khatami. In addition, he had to compete for the loyalty of the Iranian bureaucracy with Supreme Leader Khamene'i, who made it clear right from the start that he was not pleased with the course Khatami seemed to be charting.[41]

Khatami had two tremendous advantages early on: surprise and fear. In fact, the conservative establishment was not just surprised by the election, it was shocked by it. The conservatives had not really understood how unhappy the populace was, and the election's unmistakable rejection of them was stunning. That sudden realization created in their minds the very real fear that the people might actually rise up against them and overthrow them under Khatami's leadership, just as they had led the Iranian people against the last Pahlavi shah. Thus, the election had left them reeling and unsure of themselves. Their new understanding of the depth of public animosity toward them also made them cautious in reacting to Khatami's initial moves. Khatami seemed to have redefined the rules of the game, and until they could get a better sense of exactly how different this new game was (and how to play it), they would step gingerly.[42]

As a result, Khatami was able to score some important successes early on. His cabinet was unanimously approved by the Majles, even though he picked many well-known liberals, including several who had previously advocated rapprochement with the United States. He also ousted many of the older hardliners in the cabinet, including 'Ali Akbar Velayati, who had served as foreign minister for the past sixteen years and was closely associated with Iran's aggressive anti-American foreign policy of the early 1990s. Velayati was replaced by former Iranian ambassador to the United Nations Kamal Kharrazi, who was criticized for having spent too long in the United States and so being too immersed in American culture. For his minister of culture and Islamic guidance (the position from which he had been fired in 1992 for being too liberal) Khatami chose 'Ata'ollah Mohajerani—whose trial balloon piece in *Ettela'at* proposing negotiations with Washington had gotten him and Rafsanjani into so much trouble back in 1989. The ironies and implications were lost on no one.[43] The conservative newspaper *Jomhuri Islami* blasted Mohajerani and other members of Khatami's cabinet as unfit to hold their posts because they lacked "hatred toward America."[44] Of course, Khatami did not get his way on everything, and he made some important concessions to the conservatives, such as reappointing Vice President Hassan Habibi under strong pressure from the Supreme Leader's office. 'Ali Akbar Mohtashemi, the former interior minister and a leading radical who had become a supporter of Khatami, complained that "Over the past few days, those who lost the last elections are putting pressure on Mr. Khatami on his choice of ministers. Our concern is that he cannot choose colleagues capable of achieving programs desired by a billion Moslems in the world."[45]

Then Khatami moved against the security services. Iran's Ministry of Information and Security (MOIS, the intelligence ministry) was considered a bastion of the reactionary hard-liners, but Khatami was determined to lay down a marker that he would have at least some say in their doings. Although the hard-liners, reportedly including Khamene'i, wanted the notorious 'Ali Fallahian to remain in charge, Khatami forced them to drop Fallahian. He was unable to get his pick, Mohammad Mousavi Khoeiniha (famous for his role in the taking of the U.S. Embassy in 1979), but he did succeed in getting the hard-liners to settle for a compromise candidate. The other armed and dangerous pillar of the hard-liners was the Revolutionary Guard and its firebrand commander, Mohsen Reza'i, who had led the Pasdaran for sixteen years. Although the commanders of the armed forces are appointed by the Supreme Leader, Khatami forced Khamene'i to drop Reza'i. According to an analysis by the Ministry of Culture, fully 73 percent of the rank and file of the Revolutionary Guard had voted for Khatami (despite Reza'i's orders to the contrary), and this almost certainly played a role as well.[46] It called into question both Reza'i's leadership of the Pasdaran and the ability of the regime to count on the Pasdars in a confrontation with Khatami if it ever came to that. In their state of shock, the hard-liners simply did not know who would support them and who would not, so they made many concessions to Khatami early on. He also secured, as his new defense minister, Admiral 'Ali Shamkhani, a respected apolitical officer.[47]

Iranians and outside observers had assumed that Khatami would have the greatest difficulty gaining control over the security services and so would leave them till last. The fact that he took them on so soon—and won—was another positive sign that he had courage, strength, political savvy, and a determination to make far-reaching changes in Iranian policy. Khatami would not have embarked on a risky confrontation with Iran's security services if he had intended only to make minor adjustments in policy.

The surprises just kept coming. Another "certainty" that Khatami disproved was that because relations with the United States were such a politically sensitive issue, he would also leave that aside and concentrate on relations with Europe, domestic politics, and building his own power base first. But Khatami thought differently. In his first press conference after the election he announced that his foreign policy would be based on "détente" and a "dialogue among civilizations." Iranians had never heard their leaders say such things. Two days later, in another press conference, he greeted the "great American people" and then spelled out his positions on the United States in more detail: "America is the source of the strains in and the severing of its ties with Iran. We are sorry that US policies have always been hostile towards the revolution, the people and our interests. . . . We will not accept bullying and domination-seeking policies, and any change in our policies towards the USA depends on changes in the attitude and positions of the USA concerning Iran's

Islamic revolution."[48] In his inaugural address before the Majles upon taking office on August 4, Khatami announced, "The government underlines that in our world, dialogue among civilizations is an absolute imperative, and shall avoid any course of action that may foster tension. We shall have relations with any state which respects our independence—that is our right to make decisions within the framework of national interest." He went on to say, "We will shake the hands of all countries and nations who believe in the principles of mutual respect" and explicitly mentioned only Israel as a country with which Iran would never have good relations.[49]

On January 7, 1998, Khatami made an even bolder gesture. He sat down in an interview with acclaimed CNN correspondent Christiane Amanpour (who is of Iranian descent) to talk about his notion of dialogue among civilizations. Khatami began the interview with a lengthy paean to America, American history, and American values. It was tremendously positive, noting the similarities between America's own philosophical foundation as a deeply religious state, and he went out of his way to paint American history in rosy hues that many Americans would not even use. He went on to discuss Iranian history and the revolution and to compare what Iran was doing then with the process of nation building the United States had undergone in the eighteenth and nineteenth centuries. He criticized American interference in Iranian affairs since World War II but did so in a tone of sorrow rather than anger and stressed how antithetical to America's wonderful values and history this was. Asked about the hostage taking in November 1979, he replied, "I do know that the feelings of the great American people have been hurt, and of course I regret it." Of course, he reiterated Iran's long list of grievances against the United States— the 1953 coup against Mosaddeq, the 1964 status of forces agreement, the sanctions, ILSA, and Congressman Gingrich's effort to add $18 million to the covert action budget to topple the Iranian government. He also denied that Iran was involved in terrorism and pursuing nuclear weapons and said that Israel was run by a "racist terrorist" regime, but even here he was careful to distinguish between the Israeli people and their government and never ruled out the possibility of an Israeli state on part of the Holy Land. Finally, on the key issue of relations with the United States, Khatami said that the time was not yet right for direct discussions but argued that the two countries should begin to build contact through exchanges of academics, authors, artists, athletes, and others.[50]

Iranians were again amazed. Their leaders did not speak like that, and certainly not in public and not to an American audience. The interview was seminal both for what it said and what it did not say. Iranians had not heard one of their leaders go out of his way to praise any aspect of the United States since

1979. It just was not done in revolutionary Iran. Khatami had discussed many items that Iranians were used to hearing from the standard litany of Iranian grievances against the United States, but they had never heard one of their leaders do so in so sensitive and constructive a manner. Moreover, Khatami never employed any of the vituperative rhetoric about the United States that was the boilerplate of Iranian political discourse. Even his remarks about Israel, in which he had taken the hardest line, were a far cry from what Iranians normally expected from their leaders. For instance, the previous September, Khamene'i had told a Pasdaran rally that Israel was trying to obliterate Palestine from the face of the earth but that Iran would see to it that Israel was wiped off the pages of history itself.[51] In fact, the whole idea that an Iranian president would want to send a message to the American people, as Khatami explicitly stated—a message that suggested that better relations were possible, if not necessarily imminent—was itself dramatic. The contrast between Khatami's statements and the vitriol still being heaped on the United States by Iranian hard-liners, particularly Khamene'i, could not have been greater. Every Iranian understood that Khatami wanted to begin a slow process that he hoped would lead to reconciliation with the United States.[52]

There were other signs of a subtle but orchestrated campaign to raise the possibility of rapprochement with the United States. When Khatami's new foreign minister, Kamal Kharrazi, was asked about the possibility of improved relations with the United States, he responded, "We are ready to work with all nations, provided they are ready to establish their relations with us based on mutual respect."[53] The newspaper *Salam,* formerly one of the most vitriolic anti-American mouthpieces, moderated its own tone and began to publish numerous letters from its readers in favor of dialogue with Washington. One such letter asked why relations with Britain (the former imperialist oppressor) were acceptable but dialogue with the United States was not.[54] However, even those Iranians who followed Khatami's more positive line toward the United States echoed Washington's own demands of "proof" of good intentions. Just as American officials wanted to see Iran take actions in keeping with its new kind words, so too the Iranians demanded that the United States change its behavior rather than just sounding hopeful in its press statements.[55]

Another step Khatami took to demonstrate his interest in improved relations with the United States was to send to America dozens of people outside his administration, but connected to it, to probe the U.S. position. Soon after his election and for years after, Iranian academics, former officials, and even businessmen made their way to Washington and got into contact with Americans inside and outside the government. They spoke to American academics, former government officials, and businesspeople—anyone who had some relationship to U.S. policy on Iran. However, because they were not current members of the Iranian government, they were also eventually able to meet with U.S. officials, and a number did so. I personally met with more than a dozen of Khatami's unofficial diplomats in various informal settings. My colleagues and my superiors did as well. They all came armed with a message and a mission. The message was that real change was taking place in Iran and Khatami and those around him wanted to explore the possibility of beginning a process of rapprochement (and they often expressed it in exactly those tentative terms). Their mission was to find out whether the Clinton administration was interested, and whether the United States would be willing and able to help Khatami to move down this path.

What they told Washington about Iranian domestic politics was simple, straightforward, and squared with what the U.S. intelligence community was saying. Khatami was fighting a fierce internal battle for greater control over Iranian policy. His greatest asset was the solid and overwhelming support of the Iranian people, but the deck was mostly stacked against him. The hard-liners were fighting him on every issue across the board, and a new relationship with the United States might be the hardest change of all for Khatami to make. They explained that this was why it was so critical for the United States to start taking tangible steps to demonstrate its goodwill toward Iran. They told us that the most obvious impediment to Khatami's efforts was the fact that all of America's recent actions toward Iran (regardless of their justification) had been hostile and the hard-liners could simply ask, "Why should we try to repair relations with Washington when they continue to lash out at us with sanctions and other forms of pressure?" This was why Khatami's associates had repeatedly called on the United States to demonstrate its good intentions with actions. If Khatami was going to make any progress, he needed the United States to demonstrate its goodwill in ways that the hard-liners would find it impossible to dismiss.

What convinced the Clinton administration that it was worth taking such steps was a series of statements, followed by actions, that demonstrated that Khatami's administration understood America's concerns and was willing to work with us to address them. In his CNN interview, Khatami had stated unequivocally that "I personally believe that only those who lack logic resort to violence. Terrorism should be condemned in all its forms and manifestations; assassins must be condemned. . . . Any form of killing of innocent men and women who are not involved in confrontations is terrorism; it must be condemned, and we, in our [turn], condemn every form of it in the world." On the Middle East peace process, he said, "We have declared our opposition to the Middle East peace process because we believe it will not succeed. At the same time, we have clearly said that we don't intend to impose our views on others or to stand in their way. In our view all Palestinians have the right to express their views about their land, including the millions of Palestinians in Diaspora. They too have a right to self determination. Only then can there be a lasting peace. We seek a peace through which Jews, Muslims and Christians, and indeed each and every Palestinian, could freely determine their own destiny. And we are prepared to contribute towards the realization of that peace."[56] This was a far cry from the admonitions to destroy Israel coming from Khamene'i and other Iranian leaders.

Perhaps most stunning of all, one of Khatami's vice presidents, Massoumeh Ebtekar (of hostage crisis fame), actually gave an interview to the Israeli newspaper *Yediot Aharanot* in February 1998, just weeks after Khatami's CNN interview. No Iranian leader had ever given an interview to an Israeli journalist since the revolution. It was unheard of. In this interview, Ebtekar told *Yediot*'s Sever Plotker, "I support a dialogue between Iranians and Israelis, but it is too early to speak of a political dialogue between Iran and Israel."[57] This by itself was a shocking gesture.

Those Iranians who served as Khatami's informal interlocutors with the United States—including those who were best connected and most accurately predicted Iranian behavior—told us that Khatami wanted to shut down Iran's terrorism operations and was working to get control of the MOIS and the Pasdaran to do so. They also told us that Khatami "understood our concerns" about Iran's WMD programs and was "ready to accommodate" our needs. If nothing else, it was a lot better than any American official had heard from an Iranian in decades and convinced the administration that it was worth exploring.

But actions spoke even louder than words. In the Persian Gulf, U.S. Navy commanders reported that Iranian warships had started behaving professionally and even *courteously* to their American counterparts. Iran went on an international charm offensive, deepening its renewal of ties with Saudi Arabia, Europe, and other U.S. allies around the world in an effort to show that it had given up its previous animosities and suspicions. Washington saw this as a good sign, but recognized that Khatami had probably been able to sell this outreach to the hard-liners because they no doubt saw it as a substitute for relations with the United States, not a precursor to them. In early 1998, the hemorrhage of Iraqi oil being smuggled through Iranian waters suddenly stopped and stayed off throughout the year. This was a dramatic change—the Iraqis had been smuggling roughly 500,000 bpd through Iranian waters, generating huge illegal profits for Saddam and very nice payoffs for the Revolutionary Guards and their hard-line masters in Tehran. It was an issue that the

United States had raised constantly with a variety of interlocutors as something the Iranians could do that would be helpful and that would demonstrate their desire to be responsible citizens of the world.[58] We learned from several different sources that Khatami had prevailed upon Khamene'i to shut down the smuggling by arguing that it was not in Iran's interest to have the sanctions on Iraq continue to crumble. The fact that it was his doing was reinforced when the smuggling resumed at the same time that the hard-liners counterattacked politically and began to take back control of the government in early 1999. Shutting off the flow of Iraqi oil smuggling in 1998 was a major gesture on the part of the Iranians and convinced the U.S. government to step up the level of its own initiative to Iran.

America's Twelve-Step Iran Program

The Clinton administration responded immediately but was somewhat constrained at first. This was a legacy of almost twenty years of animosity and five of outright (if covert) hostilities. Tony Lake had left the administration by then, but his caution against the seductiveness of Iran for American policy makers remained as a sage warning in the minds of those still in office. What's more, the administration was wary of how Congress—which had pursued Iran so rabidly for the past five years—would react. The administration spent considerable time feeling out key congressmen and allies, including the Israelis, as to how they would react to an American overture to Iran. President Clinton harbored a special affection for peacemaking, having made the processes in the Middle East and Ireland personal priorities, and he saw an opportunity in Iran that he was determined not to pass up.

As a result, Washington's initial steps toward Iran were small, but they were rapid and took many different forms. A message was sent via the Swiss. It was positive but restrained. It assured the Iranian government that the United States was ready for a direct dialogue between authorized officials of the two governments. As a way of demonstrating the seriousness on Washington's part, the message actually listed the high-ranking American officials from the White House and State Department who would participate—and they were of sufficient rank as to demonstrate a real priority on Washington's part. There was no response from Tehran.

In Washington, the U.S. government concluded that because the Swiss had delivered their messages through the Iranian Foreign Ministry, they had gone not only to Khatami, but to Khamene'i and a number of other officials of varying political persuasions. This meant that any such message became a political football once it was delivered in Tehran. So the administration started to look for a channel directly to Khatami, and Khatami alone. The first route tried was the Saudis. In early 1998, Vice President Gore traveled to the Kingdom for discussions, and he brought with him a message that he asked Crown Prince 'Abdallah to pass to Khatami. Again, the message indicated a desire for improved relations and a willingness to start formal discussions on all issues of relevance to either side. The Saudis, who had been pursuing their own rapprochement with Iran for more than a year, were delighted both in the change in Washington's approach to Iran and in its willingness to have them serve as go-betweens. Again, there was no response from Tehran.[59]

By late 1997, Clinton, his top advisers, and his Persian Gulf team at the White House and State Department had become so convinced of Khatami's sincere desire to improve relations that we began a series of gestures intended to provide the Iranian president with the ammunition that his unofficial envoys to the United States were saying he needed. In every case, the administration listened closely to what those envoys said and tried hard to make the gestures that they suggested would be best received in Tehran. The Israelis, for the most part, supported this initiative. They too saw Khatami as a force for change in Iran, and they were the ultimate realists. They argued that he certainly could not be *worse* than the hard-liners, so why not see if he could deliver on his softer rhetoric? However, there was still opposition by some in Congress, who refused to accept that Khatami was in any way different from his predecessors. Clinton decided to go forward anyway.[60]

The first gestures were, in many ways, the easiest. Since Khatami had specifically asked for more "people-to-people" contacts, Washington relaxed the visa restrictions on Iranians to make it somewhat easier to visit the United States.[61] Then, in October 1997, the State Department added the Mujahideen-e Khalq to its list of outlawed terrorist groups, making it illegal to provide them with financial assistance and allowing the U.S. government to block their assets and deny visas to their members. In truth this was a long time coming.[62] In the 1970s, the MEK had engaged in assassinations and other terrorist attacks against Americans. In the 1980s, it had waged a vicious campaign against the revolutionary regime. When they had finally been expelled from Iran in 1981, they had moved first to France but were then evicted, at which point they moved to Iraq. In Iraq, they became a wholly owned subsidiary of Saddam Hussein's regime. He armed them, paid them, and sent them on missions into Iran during the latter stages of the Iran-Iraq War. Worst of all, they had become such creatures of the Iraqi regime that they helped Saddam crush the Shi'i and Kurdish revolts after the 1991 Gulf War—for which the Iraqi people will not soon forgive them. As if to make the point, in 1998–1999, the MEK launched another series of assassinations against high-ranking (mostly conservative) Iranian officials, including the former deputy chief of the armed forces.[63] Previously, the United States had refrained from putting the MEK on the terrorism list mostly because they were ardent enemies of Iran and thus they were the enemy of our enemy. Putting them on the terrorism list did solicit some angry complaints from congressmen who had bought into the MEK's claims that they represented popular opposition to the Iranian regime—and who had actually pressed to have the State Department or CIA fund the MEK over the years.[64] It was something we had heard throughout the 1990s, when cutting a check to the MEK would have effectively meant making it payable to "Saddam Hussein."

Because adding the MEK to the terrorism list was perfectly defensible from a factual point of view, it too was an easy step to take. However, senior administration officials told the press that it was intended as a goodwill gesture to Iran and its newly elected president. In Tehran, the gesture was widely reported and had an immediate, positive splash.[65]

A month after Khatami's momentous CNN interview, Washington took him up on his offer to begin nonofficial contacts. An American wrestling team was allowed (encouraged is more like it) to compete in a tournament in Tehran. American officials stated explicitly that Washington intended it as a 1990s version of the "Ping-Pong diplomacy" that paved the way for normalized relations with China. When the wrestlers returned, having been applauded in Tehran, they were invited to the White House to meet the president in the Oval Office. The wrestlers truly deserved the honor (no one had known how the Iranians would react to them, so their trip had been an act of considerable bravery), but the point was as much to show enthusiastic presidential approval for contacts with Iran.[66] In addition, the White House let it be known to the entire bureaucracy that it wanted to encourage and facilitate people-to-people exchanges with Iran. So Iranian academics, religious figures, athletes, and the like were expeditiously granted visas, while their American counterparts were encouraged to travel to Iran for the same purposes.[67]

In May 1998, the United States struck the deal with the Europeans that granted ILSA waivers in return for greater European cooperation on counterterrorism and nonproliferation. A key element of Washington's willingness to strike that bargain was the sense that doing so would be helpful to Khatami and would be another way of demonstrating America's good intentions. That June, Secretary of State Madeleine Albright gave a speech to the Asia Society in which she called on Iran to join the United States in drawing up "a road map leading to normal relations" and noted that the United States was "ready to explore further ways to build mutual confidence and avoid misunderstanding."[68] In September, Albright attended a meeting of the United Nations' "six-plus-two" group on Afghanistan, which included Iran. The administration had hoped that Iranian Foreign Minister Kharrazi would attend and that their mutual presence would demonstrate that the two countries could work together effectively on common interests. Kharrazi declined but did send Deputy Foreign Minister Mohammad Javad Zarif, which sent a more mixed message.[69]

In December 1998, the Clinton administration removed Iran from the State Department's list of major states engaged in the production or transit of narcotics (the "Majors List" of the International Narcotics Control Strategy Report). In this case as well, the action was taken on firm factual grounds, making it easily defensible to the Congress and the public. The Iranian government was waging both a major campaign to crack down on drug use at home and fighting a shooting war against Baluchi rebels in southeastern Iran who were smuggling drugs (mostly heroin) out of Afghanistan, just across the border. There was no question that Tehran was making a major effort to fight the narcotics trade. However, Iran had been on the list because it refused to cooperate with the U.S. government, which technically did put them in violation of the relevant U.S. regulations. In December 1998, the administration decided to honor the spirit of the counternarcotics guidelines and took Iran off the Majors List. Again, administration officials noted to the press that this represented merely a factual assessment but added that they would not be unhappy if Iran interpreted it as a friendly gesture.[70]

In the meantime, President Clinton was growing impatient with the slow pace at which the United States was able to trot out these gestures, especially since pressure was growing on Khatami at home. The president wanted to ratchet up the level of U.S. support for Khatami in hope that this would allow him to make a breakthrough on relations with America. One thing that the informal Iranian interlocutors had regularly suggested—and that Khatami himself had mentioned in his CNN interview—was that the United States should apologize for its past interference in Iranian affairs, and particularly for the Mosaddeq coup of 1953, which still infuriated Iranians after all these years. Many in the executive branch, myself included, felt that if apologizing for something that the United States had done forty-five years before and that was still a source of hurt to Iranians would help achieve tangible progress in a matter of great importance today, we should do it. Others, however, felt just as strongly that such matters of national pride should not be undertaken lightly, and they fought doing so. On April 12, 1999, at a formal dinner at the White House, President Clinton took matters into his own hands. Unprompted, he decided to make a bolder gesture to President Khatami. He told those assembled (including numerous reporters who disseminated his words almost immediately):

I would like to make one more point which I think is very important in the dealings between the West and the Islamic countries, generally—and I will use Iran as an example. It may be that the Iranian people have been taught to hate or distrust the United States or the West on the grounds that we are infidels and outside the faith. And, therefore, it is easy for us to be angry and to respond in kind. I think it is important to recognize, however, that Iran, because of its enormous geopolitical importance over time, has been the subject of quite a lot of abuse from various Western nations. And I think sometimes it's quite important to tell people, look, you have a right to be angry at something my country or my culture or others that are generally allied with us today did to you 50 or 60 or 100 or 150 years ago. But that is different from saying that I am outside the faith, and you are God's chosen. So sometimes people will listen to you if you tell them, you're right, but your underlying reason is wrong. So we have to find some way to get dialogue—and going into total denial when you're in a conversation with somebody who's been your adversary, in a country like Iran that is often worried about its independence and its integrity, is not exactly the way to begin. So I think while we speak out against religious intolerance, we have to listen for possible ways we can give people the legitimacy of some of their fears, or some of their angers, or some of their historic grievances, and then say they rest on other grounds; now, can we build a common future? I think that's very important. Sometimes I think we in the United States, and Western culture generally, we hate to do that. But we're going to have to if we want to have an ultimate accommodation.[71]

It was not quite an apology, but it was closer than any American president had ever come, and the effect in Tehran was electrifying. Reformists and hard-liners alike recognized that it was a tentative, diplomatic version of an apology—just what the hard-liners had been demanding since 1979.

Washington continued to roll out additional gestures to Iran as best possible. Later in April 1999, the administration repealed part of the comprehensive sanctions on Iran to allow the sale of food, medicine, and other humanitarian goods to the country. Once again, this was wholly defensible on its own merits: it simply brought the Iran sanctions into line with the Iraq sanctions, which had been modified to provide for the sale of food and medicine in 1996 as part of the U.S.-sponsored oil-for-food resolution. But it too was meant as yet another demonstration of America's goodwill and an especially important one since the Iranians had repeatedly demanded that the United States lift the sanctions before they would resume a dialogue.[72] This hardly constituted lifting the sanctions, but by demonstrating a willingness to modify them, even if slightly, Washington hoped to signal to Iran that lifting the sanctions was a real prospect if Iran satisfied American needs on terrorism, WMD, and the peace process.

Then in December, Washington approved the sale of safety-related spare parts by Boeing to Iran to allow it to rectify a structural flaw that had been found in some of Boeing's aircraft, a number of which were still being used by Tehran. Part of the problem here was that Iran used these planes both for commercial transport and to fly arms to Hizballah via Damascus. "There's always a risk that any Iran Air plane, civilian or cargo, can be used for nefarious purposes, but the greater risk in our view would have been the possibility of a catastrophic accident killing civilians," *The Washington Post* quoted one senior administration official as saying.[73]

In the midst of all the American efforts to demonstrate goodwill to Iran and the new government, the Khobar Towers bombing reared its ugly head again. Toward the end of the spring of 1999, with Saudi-Iranian rapprochement in high gear and a clear American commitment to try to engineer the same, Riyadh finally gave American investigators access to the evidence in the Khobar Towers bombing. At that point, the United States finally had the definitive information it needed that Iran had masterminded the attack. The problem was that while the Clinton administration believed that proof of a deliberate terrorist attack demanded military retaliation, the government in Iran that had mounted that attack was partially gone—replaced by a new administration that seemed to be trying hard to get Iran out of the terrorism business and that Washington was bending over backward to help. In the partisan atmosphere after the failed impeachment effort against President Clinton, White House political advisers were concerned that the president's opponents would seize on this evidence to go after him again.[74]

The administration decided to take the heat from its domestic critics and forgo military retaliation. The whole point of a retaliation would have been to convince Iran not to attack the United States again; however, the best route to that goal was for Khatami to succeed in reforming the Iranian government. The United States could not somehow turn back the clock and bomb the old Iranian regime that had attacked Khobar Towers. All Washington could have done was to strike the Khatami government, and doing so would have destroyed any chance at rapprochement, undermined Khatami's administration because it had taken such political risks to reach out to the United States, and strengthened the position of the hard-liners—which would have *increased* the terrorist threat from Iran. Since America's goal was to *decrease* the terrorist threat from Iran, by 1999 military retaliation had become the wrong policy. If the goal was to ensure that there was never another Khobar Towers, the best way to do that once Khatami was elected was to show restraint and try to help him succeed.

So, in June 1999, two senior administration officials from the White House and State Department took a detour while on an official trip to France. They met with Sultan Qaboos of Oman at his magnificent château outside Paris. Of all the Gulf states, Oman had worked hardest over the years to maintain good relations with Iran, its neighbor across the Strait of Hormuz. The sultan was also a good friend of the United States. Washington hoped that he might be able to find a way to deliver a message to Khatami and Khatami alone. It was clear that the previous messages—through the Swiss and the Saudis—had gotten caught in the abattoir of Iranian politics and been cut to pieces. The Omanis seemed like a good last bet. The message, which Oman's foreign minister, Yusef bin Allawi, would carry, stated that the United States now had "credible" evidence that the Iranian Revolutionary Guard and Lebanese Hizballah had been involved in both the planning and execution of the Khobar Towers bombing. It acknowledged that Khatami had not been in office then but stated that it was of the highest importance to the U.S. government that those in the Pasdaran who had been responsible be brought to justice. It assured Khatami that the United States wanted good relations and had no hostile intentions toward Iran, but that it was imperative for those responsible to be held responsible by being either put on trial in Iran or extradited to Saudi Arabia (since Iran and the United States did not have a treaty of extradition, a direct transfer to the United States would have been legally impossible). The message was reportedly delivered directly to Khatami, but it does not seem to have stayed with him alone. The response that the Iranians eventually provided was that the allegations were entirely false and that it was the United States that was guilty of terrorism for its shoot-down of Iran Air flight 655 in 1988 and the money appropriated by Congress for the covert action program in 1996.[75] So much for the Omani channel.

Brawling in Tehran

While the Clinton administration made gesture after gesture in hope of providing Khatami with the ammunition he needed to convince Iran's hard-liners to accept the start of a gradual rapprochement, the Iranian president and his cohorts were engaged in, quite literally, mortal combat in Tehran. The hardliners had not been vanquished by Khatami's election, just set back. With time, they regained their balance and launched a brutal campaign against the reformist movement that employed everything from bureaucratic politics to murder and street violence.

Khatami's greatest asset was, in some ways, also his greatest liability. The surprise of his victory at the polls shocked the conservative establishment, and at least initially they did not know how to respond. As a result, they gave Khatami fairly wide latitude early on, which allowed the reformists to score some early victories. However, Khatami and his followers were themselves shocked to have won, and they do not seem to have had a defined agenda when they came to office. Like the Robert Redford candidate in the famous film *The Candidate,* having worked so hard to get elected, once they had pulled it off they turned to one another and said, "What do we do now?" As a result, they squandered many opportunities to consolidate their power in those early days, when the conservatives were running scared. For instance, Khamene'i decided to keep control over Iran's internal security forces (known as the Law Enforcement Forces, or LEF, which had been formed by combining the revolutionary *komiteh*s, the police, and the Gendarmerie) rather than allow them to come under the control of Khatami's liberal interior minister, 'Abdallah Nuri, and Khatami acquiesced. Although Iran's failing economy was a major source of popular discontent, his administration was not able to formulate an economic plan for the nation until nearly a year after his election. He never made any move to assert control over the massive quasi-governmental *bonyad*s, whose vast resources bankrolled the conservatives and dominated the Iranian economy. He also did not try to exert any control over Iran's judiciary through his control of the justice ministry.

Instead, Khatami tended to concentrate initially on easing social and political restrictions. These were important to the people and thus gladly received, but they also proved superficial in the battle to determine the course of the reform program, compared to control over key bureaucratic levers and reforming the economy. Khatami's ministers stopped strictly enforcing censorship, as well as regulations regarding dress, music, and other social affairs. They approved licenses for new, more outspoken newspapers and magazines. They encouraged Iran's writers, artists, playwrights, and filmmakers to be more bold and creative—and even critical of the government. The repressed emotions of the Iranian population came pouring out like a Prague Spring in Tehran. The president's stock only rose higher among the people as a result.

Khatami's initial moves on liberalizing social controls and pressing for even a modest opening to the United States, however, only convinced the hardliners that he was their enemy. These were the two issues closest to Khomeini's heart, preeminent in both the radical and conservative agendas, and the clearest goals of the revolution. By attacking them, and doing so right from the start, Khatami made clear that while he may have been a cleric and a former disciple of Khomeini, he was definitely not one of them. Thus the hard-liners became increasingly convinced of the need to undermine, contain, and eventually destroy Khatami (politically if possible, physically if not), even if they recognized that because of his enormous popularity, it would have to be a slow, careful process.

Their first efforts to resist the reformist tidal wave were purely defensive, principally efforts to declare certain areas off limits to reform and to rally their own supporters to demonstrate (both to themselves and to the reformists) that they were not entirely without their own mass following. Many of the hard-liners made statements warning Khatami away from certain areas, topics, and issues—most notably relations with the United States. However, in the face of this early hard-line resistance, Khatami showed real courage. Initially, he would not back down. He simply disregarded many of the warnings from his opponents—although in truth on many key issues, such as relations with the United States, he moved slowly and cautiously because he was wary of provoking a major counterattack by the conservatives. Nonetheless, he did keep moving forward on these issues, albeit gingerly. When a particularly rabid hard-liner would attack him or his policies, he would come right back and insist that it was necessary for Iran to follow the path he had charted out. When the hard-liners held a rally in favor of the status quo and revolutionary values, Khatami would come back and hold an even bigger rally in favor of change. He played tit for tat and would not give up.

Khatami's courage only provoked the hard-liners to violence and other extrajudicial attacks. It is not as if this came hard to the people who backed Ansar-e Hizballah and other vigilante groups and who had been resorting to arbitrary punishments, summary execution, and street violence for years. It started in late 1997, when the hard-liners' thugs attacked a concert and ransacked the offices of the newspaper *Salam,* which had gone from a mouthpiece of the radicals to a major reformist journal. Then, the conservative-controlled judiciary leveled corruption charges against Gholam Hussein Karabaschi, the mayor of Tehran, who was regularly referred to as the "architect" of Khatami's election victory. Even if the charges were true—and there was reason to believe they were mostly trumped up—in postrevolutionary Iran, charging a public official with corruption was like arresting someone for public drunkenness at Mardi Gras. Karabaschi's arrest sparked several days of rioting by students and other reformist partisans in Tehran.[76]

Two weeks after Karabaschi's arrest, the moderate newspaper *Jame'ah* published remarks by the new IRGC commander, Yahya Rahim Safavi, in a letter to Khamene'i in which he threatened greater violence if the reformists kept up their liberalizing activities. Safavi did not mince words, urging the Supreme Leader to deal with the "hypocrite" clergy pressing for liberalization: "We seek to tear out the roots of counter-revolution wherever they may be. We should cut the neck of some of them. We will cut the tongues of others."[77] He also claimed that many of the reformist newspapers were being funded by the United States and the MEK. Although the letter seems purposely intended to have been leaked as a warning, Mohsen Rafiq-Dust—the former IRGC leader who had led the first Pasdaran contingent to Lebanon in 1983, and was now head of the largest and most powerful *bonyad*—complained to the judiciary that by publishing the letter, *Jame'ah* had engaged in slander and "divulging military secrets." Farcical though it may have been, it prompted the judiciary to close down *Jame'ah,* and when it quickly resurfaced under another name, the judiciary ordered much wider closures of newspapers and the arrest of many prominent journalists across the country.[78]

As spring turned into summer, the hard-liners became ever more creative and bold in their attacks on the reformist camp. In June, the hard-line-dominated Majles (with Nateq Nuri still its speaker) impeached Khatami's interior minister, 'Abdallah Nuri, for having criticized the vigilante groups and defended Karabaschi.[79] That same month, Karabaschi went on trial. Not surprisingly, the judge—who was also the prosecutor—sentenced him to five years in prison, sixty lashes from a cane (generously suspended), a twenty-year ban on participating in any political activities, and nearly $1 million in assorted fines.[80] In late July, another reformist journal published photos of unveiled women, prompting the Hizballahis to firebomb its offices and the judiciary to arrest its editor.[81] The Hizballahis who did the firebombing were not arrested. Khamene'i himself encouraged such activities by declaring that "today the enemy is striking Islam from home" and urging the vigilantes to confront "the new plot hatched to destroy Islam."[82]

Things only got worse for the reformists in the fall of 1998. By then, the hard-liners had completely regained their footing and were now determined to crush the reform movement. They became more sweeping in their attacks. Starting in September, the judiciary began to close down more and more reformist newspapers, often arresting key members of the staff for such crimes as "fighting against God," which carried a death sentence. The reformists countered by quickly reopening the newspapers under different names. Within just a few weeks, the hard-liners tired of these games and the Majles passed a bill that authorized the judiciary to set up a special court for journalists and called on them to charge journalists who criticized Islamic principles (which could mean no more than discussing them "disrespectfully") with threatening national security.[83] This opened the way for an attack on Khatami's minister of culture, 'Ata'ollah Mohajerani, who was called before the Majles and threatened with impeachment if he did not enforce the law—to which he reluctantly agreed, demoralizing many of the reformists' supporters.[84] In a clear sign that the tide had shifted back to Khamene'i and the conservatives, that arch-opportunist Hashemi Rafsanjani (now the head of the Expediency Council, which mediates disputes between the Majles and the Council of Guardians) increasingly backed the hard-liners.[85]

Yet Khatami kept fighting back. After Abdallah Nuri was deposed as interior minister, Khatami immediately appointed him vice president in charge of social and developmental issues, which did not require confirmation by the Majles. He then appointed another reformer, 'Abdolvahed Musavi-Lari, as interior minister and requested that Khamene'i transfer command of the LEF to him. Khamene'i complied, although it later became clear that it was a transfer in name only, as Khamene'i had made sure of the LEF's loyalty to himself before doing so.[86] Khatami also fought back verbally, challenging the rhetorical attacks of the hard-liners with his own, constantly reiterating that Islam was a religion of tolerance, not fear and aggression.[87]

Khatami's unwillingness to simply bow to the hard-liners caused them to ratchet up the pressure still further. Here they got a bit of help from foreign affairs. In September 1998, the Taliban finally took Afghanistan's main northern city of Mazar-i Sharif. The Iranians hated the Sunni-chauvinist Taliban (and their al-Qa'eda allies), who had badly oppressed the Shi'ah of the Hazarat region of the country, and Tehran had steadfastly supported various Afghan groups opposing them. Thus, when the Taliban overran Mazar-i Sharif, they found eleven Iranian diplomats working with the Afghan opposition there, who were promptly killed by Taliban soldiers. Tehran reacted by deploying 200,000 troops to the border with Iran while the leadership debated whether to mount a full-scale invasion. The Revolutionary Guard leadership in particular reportedly wanted to attack, and the entire country was gripped with war fever. Eventually, Tehran concluded that an invasion of mountainous Afghanistan—especially given that its ground forces had not improved much since 1988 because it had focused its rearmament principally on the needs of an air-sea engagement with the United States in the Persian Gulf—would likely land Iran in another protracted attrition war. The Iranians' memories of the trauma of the Iran-Iraq War convinced them that this was not something they should seek out, so the troops were withdrawn and they turned to a diplomatic solution instead. However, the threat of war with Afghanistan allowed the hard-liners to mount an even more savage attack on the reformists in the name of national unity and remaining true to patriotic, revolutionary, Iranian values.[88]

Behind the curtain of the war scare with Afghanistan, the hard-liners escalated to new levels of violence. In September, Vice President Nuri and Minister of Culture Mohajerani—still two of the leading culprits as far as the vigilantes were concerned—were attacked and beaten up by unknown assailants after Friday prayers.[89] Then, in November, former Interior Minister Hojjat-ol Islam 'Ali Akbar Mohtashemi was attacked by a crowd while giving a public speech in Mashhad. These were the first of a long series of acts of violence by hard-line thugs, who attacked, beat up, crippled, and even killed numerous reformist supporters and leaders.[90] Later that month, however, a new form of violence took center stage: assassinations. On the twenty-second, the longtime opposition figure Daryush Foruhar and his wife were killed in their home. Foruhar by then was more a symbol than anything else, having been part of Mosaddeq's National Front and the secular opposition that had kicked off the 1979 revolution. Two days later another liberal writer was found dead under mysterious circumstances, then two more, and then, in mid-January 1999, three more.[91]

These "serial killings," as they became known, touched off a firestorm in Iran. A mysterious group espousing conservative principals claimed responsibility. Most of the hard-line leadership, including Khamene'i, blamed "foreign plots" (meaning Israel and the United States), while also noting that since those murdered were "apostates" anyway, no one should mourn them too much. However, Khatami appointed an investigative commission, and over time this investigation was able to determine that the killings had actually been committed by members of the Iranian security services. Good investigative work by the commission and by several reformist newspapers even prompted official confessions that pointed at Deputy Intelligence Minister Sa'id Imami as the operational director. What's more, they uncovered a vast conspiracy within the intelligence services that had been responsible for at least fifty assassinations of Iranian dissidents in the past ten years—both inside and outside of Iran—and that had been coordinating a campaign against the reformists inside the country. It included three separate committees composed of officials from the IRGC, MOIS, and the Supreme Leader's office and justified its killings by obtaining *fatwa*s from hard-line ayatollahs—including Ahmad Jannati, the head of the Council of Guardians—declaring different leading reformists to be apostates. The investigation turned up eighteen such *fatwa*s that had already been issued.[92]

At that point, Khatami reportedly threatened to resign if Khamene'i did not allow him to replace the intelligence minister and make other changes to the MOIS, arrest those uncovered as part of this shadow organization, and publicize some of the findings. The Iranian people were enraged over the murders, and Khamene'i apparently feared that if Khatami were to resign (and doubtless betray everything he knew to the newspapers) it could touch off a popular revolt. So Khamene'i gave in. Partially. Qursan-'Ali Durri-Najafabadi was ousted as intelligence minister and replaced with a new compromise candidate, Hojjat-ol Islam 'Ali Yunesi, with a staunch reformist, 'Ali Rabi'i, as his deputy. Rabi'i in particular then set out to cleanse the MOIS of all the hard-line elements and all those involved in terrorism. It was a remarkable bureaucratic purge, and he plowed through office after office in the ministry, firing and retiring anyone loyal to the hard-liners or anyone tied to Iranian terrorist activities. Once he had cleaned out roughly 80 percent of the ministry— and forced the hard-liners to transfer most of its nefarious activities to the Revolutionary Guards to prevent Rabi'i from eliminating them altogether— Khamene'i ordered him to stop. When the U.S. government finally learned about Rabi'i's purge, Washington took it as another good sign that Khatami was serious about getting Iran out of the terrorism business.[93]

Part of the findings of the Iranian investigative committee were released to the public, but not all. What was released all pointed to the former deputy minister of intelligence, Sa'id Imami, as having been the operational director of the conspiracy, and Imami was duly imprisoned. But the hard-line-dominated judiciary effectively stopped the process there. It announced that more than thirty others had been arrested but would not give out names or details on who or why. Worst of all, in 1999 the judiciary announced that Sa'id Imami had somehow committed suicide in prison, while under heavy guard, by somehow drinking enough of a mildly toxic "hair removal cream" to kill him. Imami's death conveniently shut down the investigation: everyone subordinate to him could only point to him, and he was now no longer around to implicate anyone above him.[94]

The Turning Point

Khatami followed up what seemed to have been a great victory in the crisis over the serial killings by again demonstrating his overwhelming popularity. In February 1999, he held municipal elections. The Iranian Constitution called for municipal councils to govern local economic, social, and cultural affairs. However, no one had ever bothered to actually establish the local councils, let alone hold elections for them. Khatami and his allies saw this as a way of diffusing authority away from the central government, which the hard-liners continued to dominate, and out to the local levels, where support for the reformists was enormous. Moreover, because there would be so many candidates (334,000 of them vying for 190,000 slots), it would be impossible for the

Council of Guardians or any other hard-line institution to vet them fully. As expected, the reformists won another lopsided victory throughout the country, even picking up twelve of the fifteen seats in Tehran. What's more, 'Abdallah Nuri, the deposed interior minister, ran in Tehran and was the top overall vote getter in the election. He became the chairman of the new Tehran city council and positioned himself to run for the Majles the next year—where it was widely assumed he would wrest the speakership from Nateq Nuri.[95]

Of course, the hard-liners counterattacked immediately. They again banned more newspapers, attacked reformist leaders, and arrested a liberal-minded cleric—Mohsen Kadivar—on the charge of "confusing public opinion." They tried to impeach Culture Minister Mohajerani but failed, so they tried to kill him instead—and failed at that too. They arrested thirteen Iranian Jews in Isfahan on a variety of odd charges, which was widely seen—including in Washington—as an effort by the hard-liners to embarrass Khatami in front of the world: if he did anything to help the Jews, the hard-liners would paint him as a friend of Israel; if he did not, the Western world would hold it against him.[96] However, the hard-liners' main attack came in the Majles, which they still dominated.

At the beginning of July, the Majles provisionally passed a bill that would have sharply curbed press freedoms, and the judiciary shut down the newspaper *Salam,* then the leading voice of the reformist movement. On July 8, a small group of students at Tehran University organized a protest against both the press law and the closing of *Salam.* That night, Hizballahis broke into their dormitory rooms, ransacked those rooms, beat many of the students up, and either threw or caused some of them to fall from their dorm windows, killing several. The next day, Khatami denounced these attacks, which sparked spontaneous protests by thousands at Tehran University and other colleges in the capital, chanting "Freedom or Death!" The Hizballahis and other vigilante squads came out to oppose them, and there was considerable carnage. The riots got progressively worse as supporters of the reformists came out to aid the students and crowds in Tehran attacked banks, the offices of conservative newspapers, and even the Ministry of Intelligence itself. The riots quickly spread to eighteen other cities across the country.[97]

A revolution was brewing. The riots "posed the most serious threat to the clerics' monopoly on power in two decades of unchallenged totalitarian rule," according to Jahangir Amuzegar. "The placards carried and the slogans chanted by the street demonstrators also crossed all forbidden lines, breaking a twenty-year record in audacity and provocation: 'Death to despots!' 'Khamenei, shame on you!' 'Rahbar, resign!' 'Khatami, where are you when your sons are killed?' 'Down with the puppet Majles!' 'Either Islam and the law or another revolution!' Some of the rioters tore up and burned pictures of Ayatollah 'Ali Khamenei—a criminal offense. None of this had been heard of since the 1979 revolution."[98]

More than ten thousand students and thousands of other supporters of the reformists were now engaged in daily combat with the Hizballahis and members of the LEF. It was a showdown that had been two years in the making. As in 1979, the students were tired and frustrated—of second-rate teachers who were ideologically acceptable, of courses crammed full of dogma but devoid of interesting or useful material, of a stultifying social life and miserable living conditions, and of degrees that were economically useless because they did not stand for any learning that was desirable to an employer. So too were many others in Iranian society, who had tasted a bit of social and cultural freedom and were now petrified that it was about to be taken away from them. Everyone also remained unhappy about the economy, which remained moribund (as much from Khatami's own inaction as from the hard-liners' obstinacy). A great many people were ready to take up arms against the establishment, as their six days of brawling with the Hizballahis demonstrated. The only real question was whether someone would lead them in a new revolution, and the someone they looked to, of course, was President Khatami.[99]

But Mohammad Khatami was not ready to lead a revolution. As brave as he had been, his courage seems to have failed him at this hour. It was disappointing for a great many Iranians, but it was also understandable. First, as is so often the case, Khatami almost certainly did not realize how fateful that moment would prove to be. He no doubt believed that there would be other chances and other ways to advance the reformist cause. Second, the consequences of such courage would likely have been very great given how willing the hard-liners were to use force, both indiscriminately against masses of protesters and discretely against specific individuals. To reinforce this point, the regime had alerted and concentrated several divisions of Revolutionary Guards around Tehran and other cities. Moreover, during the riots, twenty-four of the senior commanders of the Pasdaran sent Khatami a threatening letter, almost certainly with Khamene'i's connivance (it was eventually published by a conservative newspaper after the riots subsided). In it, the Guard commanders warned, "Our patience is exhausted and in case of nonobservance we can no longer distinguish ourselves through serenity." They warned him not to take any "revolutionary decisions" but to "act in accordance with your Islamic and national mission."[100] In other words, if Khatami did not call off the protests, they would take matters into their own hands, and their actions threatened to be very far-reaching.[101]

We know that Khatami had a series of conversations with Khamene'i (and others) about how to handle the situation. We do not know what they said to each other. Based on the actions that followed, it seems that Khamene'i probably told Khatami that if he did not order the students and other reformists to desist, Khamene'i would let the Revolutionary Guards settle the matter, and they would do so with great violence. The letter from the Guards commanders and the alerting of their units made crystal clear that this was not an idle threat. So Khatami acceded, likely believing that doing otherwise would have meant both mass killings of his followers and a wave of beatings, arrests, and assassinations against his closest adherents and possibly their families as well.[102]

On the sixth day of the riots, Khatami publicly denounced the protesters and stated that those who were spurring them were undermining both the nation and the reformist agenda. He called them "rabble rousers."[103] That allowed Khamene'i to take a cynically sympathetic stand, bemoaning the violence being perpetrated by the hard-line thugs against "my children," the protesters. The next day, the Law Enforcement Forces (not the Pasdaran) moved in and with considerable violence—but also great skill—crushed the students and other protesters. Dozens were injured, 1,400 were arrested, but few (possibly none) were killed.[104] This does not seem to have been part of the deal struck by Khatami and Khamene'i, however. Interior Minister Musavi-Lari actually ordered the LEF to halt the operation, but it simply ignored him. It seems highly unlikely that Khatami's interior minister would have tried to prevent an action to which the president had given his consent, no matter how grudgingly, nor does it seem likely that Khatami would have acquiesced in the brutal suppression of his followers.[105] Then, to demonstrate that they too could call on support from the masses, the conservatives held a huge counterdemonstration, for which they bused in hundreds of thousands of seminary students, government employees, disabled war veterans, families of those killed during the Iran-Iraq War, and other staunch supporters of the regime.[106]

No one knew it at the time, but in retrospect, the riots of the summer of 1999 were a watershed in the course of the reform movement. During the presidential elections of 1997, a split had opened up in the Iranian body politic. Because the hard-liners were unwilling to countenance any meaningful change, a middle-ground policy of gradual reform like the one Khatami attempted to pursue was going to become impossible at some point. The maximum amount of change that the conservatives were prepared to accept was too far from what most of the reformists considered the minimum acceptable. In hindsight, it is clear that neither Khatami nor anyone else was going to be able to bridge that gap. The willingness of the hard-liners to resort to extreme forms of violence to prevent going beyond their maximum threshold, and the torrent of emotion that Khatami's early changes had unleashed, meant that at some point there would likely be a major clash. Given this constellation of forces, only two outcomes were possible: either there would be a new revolution that would destroy the hard-liners just as the 1979 revolution had swept away the shah's regime, or the hard-liners were going to snuff out the reform movement.

Revolutions are peculiar things, and it is a rare moment when enough people become willing to fight the institutions of state repression that one becomes possible. The summer of 1999 held that potential in Iran, a potential that had been building since the 1997 election. When Khatami failed to lead the revolution that seemed ready to be unleashed, he doomed the reform movement to defeat.

Of course, it is unfair to blame Khatami entirely for the outcome. While it does seem that this was—in retrospect—the best opportunity for the reformist movement to succeed, there are at least two important qualifiers. First, it just was not clear at the time that the situation had become so polarized that Khatami's preferred gradual approach had become impossible. Nor can we be certain that he would have chosen to lead such a revolution even if he had understood that his only choices were revolutionary victory or defeat. Khatami does not seem to have ever wanted to start a true revolution. He was not a Lenin, a Mao, or a Khomeini. Second, it is unclear if such a revolution would have succeeded even if Khatami had chosen to lead it. This regime had learned from the shah that it had to be willing to resort to massive force to hold power, and it was willing to do so. (This raises the question of the loyalty of the troops who would have been called on to put down the revolt, and with 73 percent of the IRGC voting for Khatami, that too would have been an open question. However, it was widely believed that the regime had assembled Pasdaran divisions that it had determined were loyal and reliable for this critical operation.)

Although a fair number of nonstudents participated in the riots, it was hardly the same level of popular participation as in 1979. Amuzegar observed that "The silent majority wanted the government to honor their basic human rights. They opposed suffocating restrictions on what they eat, drink, wear, watch, listen to, study, write, say or care for. But they shunned renewed instability, riots, bloodshed and loss of life. The Iranian peasantry and an overwhelming majority of the urban proletariat and petite bourgeoisie had, by necessity or choice, become resigned to their fate. They were visibly dissatisfied with their lot and wanted to see it improved. But they did not want it to be violently disturbed once again in the mere hope of something better. They had had their fingers burnt once already."[107] Revolutions are generally conducted by tiny groups of people, but it is an open question whether the students and others who were ready to launch a revolution in the summer of 1999 would have been strong enough to do so, especially if the IRGC remained loyal to the regime.

The conservatives had unquestionably "won" in the summer crisis of 1999, but both sides were rattled by how close they had come to widespread bloodshed. Two weeks afterward, Khatami reportedly told his closest advisers that he wanted to resign the presidency and call for new elections. Although his advisers differed on the subject, the majority convinced him to stay in office.[108] For their part, the conservatives were ready to unleash a massacre, but they had not meant to do so when they had first passed the provisional press law. What's more, they too had doubtless been fearful during the height of the riots that it would turn into a full-scale revolution and that the Pasdaran would defect to the revolutionaries just as the shah's vaunted military had. They had won, but it had been a great gamble in which they might have lost it all had Khatami not folded when he did.

For the rest of the summer and into the fall, both Khatami and Khamene'i made conciliatory gestures toward each other, until the Majles elections rolled around in February 2000.[109] Both sides saw the election as crucial—the hardliners had used the Majles as a weapon against the reform movement, deposing cabinet officials and passing laws against reformist initiatives. The reformists were determined to gain control over it, to take that weapon away from the hard-liners and wield it themselves. But by then, the hard-liners had overcome their temporary fear of having come so close to the brink of revolution. They now understood that Khatami could be bullied and that without his leadership the reformists did not pose an existential challenge to them, so they pressed their advantage. They changed several electoral laws to help their candidates. Recognizing that 'Abdallah Nuri would be a massive vote getter and could easily win the speakership, they arrested him, quickly put him on trial (one of the charges against him was "endorsing relations with the United States and Israel"), and sentenced him to five years in prison.[110] With Nuri out, former President Rafsanjani entered the race, thinking he could recapture his old post of Majles Speaker, but he was now associated with the hard-liners, and when attacked by the reformist press he edged closer to them still.

The Majles election was another ringing public endorsement for the reformists, who swept roughly 73 percent of the seats, while the hard-liners took less than 20 percent. Rafsanjani was probably not even elected, but some post-election shenanigans got him in as the last member of the Tehran delegation—a seat he relinquished because it was clear he would not be Speaker. The defeat of Rafsanjani and a number of other prominent former "pragmatists" who stressed a right-of-center program that envisioned cooperation with the hard-liners further underscored the polarization of Iranian society. Anyone who favored accommodation with the conservatives was hated by the majority of the Iranian people as much as the conservatives themselves.[111]

But none of it mattered. The hard-liners had digested the lesson from the previous summer that Khatami would not lead a revolution and would back down when faced with a choice between doing so or giving in. That gave them the upper hand, and they used it. In the weeks after the crushing electoral victory by the reformists, the security forces began to crack down on dress, gender mingling, music, and other forms of "immodest" behavior. The Council of Guardians summarily deposed a number of newly elected reformist Majles deputies and ordered recounts for others. In March, a newspaper publisher and member of the Tehran Municipal Council named Said Hajjarian, who was also Khatami's closest adviser, was shot in the face at point-blank range by a pair of men on a 1,000 cc motorcycle—a size restricted by law to members of the security services. Hajjarian miraculously survived, but he was not meant to have. His near assassination reportedly had a profound impact on Khatami, reinforcing the lesson he probably had already learned from the previous summer that to continue confronting the hard-liners would lead to a great many people getting killed—likely including his closest friends and family.[112]

The Last Gesture

At that inopportune moment, the United States rolled out its biggest Iran initiative ever. Like Khatami, Washington recognized that the summer 1999 riots had been a setback for the reform movement, but (again like Khatami) the Americans did not understand that they were the beginning of the end. All through the fall Washington had been working to figure out what the United States could do that would make enough of a splash in Tehran to allow the wounded president to demonstrate that there were tangible (if modest, for the moment) benefits to be gained from a rapprochement with the United States. Washington also hoped to be able to help shore up his position if it could demonstrate that his most radical policies had achieved some real successes and that much greater rewards were possible by continuing to pursue them.[113]

In truth, many American officials, myself among them, were beginning to get frustrated with Tehran: the United States had now made nine gestures (liberalizing visas, sending the wrestlers and other cultural exchanges, putting the MEK on the terrorism list, taking Iran off the counternarcotics list, allowing the sale of food and medicine, agreeing to the ILSA waivers, sending Albright to the "six-plus-two" talks on Afghanistan in hope of meeting Kharrazi, the president's Millennium Evening dinner near apology, and the spare parts for the Boeing aircraft). In return, the United States had not gotten very much, especially since the smuggling of Iraqi oil through Iranian waters had resumed in 1999. Nevertheless, we thought it worth making one last grand gesture.[114]

Once again, we went back to Khatami's various informal interlocutors and also consulted with foreign countries that had good relations with the Iranians. They too failed to understand that the fate of the reform movement was already sealed and, out of a certain degree of denial, insisted that a really big American gesture *could* create a breakthrough in Tehran on both domestic politics and U.S.-Iranian relations. Of course, what they wanted Washington to do was to lift all of the sanctions or unfreeze all of Iran's remaining assets in the United States (which the Iranians believed amounted to somewhere in the neighborhood of $35 billion but was probably no more than a fraction of that). This was entirely contrary to U.S. policy and U.S. interests: Iran would get the sanctions completely lifted only when it had demonstrated changed behavior on the issues that mattered to the United States—terrorism, nuclear weapons, and opposition to the peace process—which had prompted the sanctions in the first place. The United States was making a gesture, not giving away the farm. So, in consultation with these various interlocutors, the administration devised what Americans, Iranian interlocutors, and foreign governments that had good relations with Iran all believed was an excellent gesture: Washington would lift the sanctions on foodstuffs and carpets. These were Iran's second and third largest categories of exports, although they were minuscule compared to oil. This would demonstrate a willingness to lift the sanctions on what really mattered to Tehran—the oil—and show some immediate, tangible benefit, while still retaining America's most important bargaining chips.[115]

Moreover, the administration decided to package it with a number of other, smaller gestures, such as an even more apologetic statement on the 1953 coup than the president had given in his Millennium Evening speech. It would all be presented in a major speech that Secretary of State Madeleine Albright (who was widely, but wrongly, accused of being obstructionist on the Iran initiative) would give at the Iranian-American Council, a group that advocated renewed ties between the two countries.

So, on March 17, Albright gave the famous speech. She issued the apology quoted in the introduction to this book. She announced the lifting of the import ban on Iranian foodstuffs and carpets. She said any number of other warm, welcoming things about Iran. And she again called on the Iranian government to begin an official dialogue with the United States, with no preconditions and no demands for a rapid solution to what we acknowledged were extremely complicated problems. The Europeans were ecstatic. Our Iranian interlocutors were impressed and hopeful that it would have a positive impact in Tehran. A number of groups inside Tehran hailed the speech and the partial lifting of the sanctions as a remarkable gesture on the part of the United States, to which Iran should respond positively.[116] Then, ten days later, Khamene'i gave his thoroughly negative response, also quoted in the introduction to this book. The hard-liners were just not interested in a rapprochement.

In fact, the very next month, the hard-line campaign against the reformists began to pick up steam in Tehran. The judiciary began arresting and imprisoning leading journalists on increasingly ridiculous charges—like one prominent publisher who was given a thirty-month sentence for opposing the death penalty. Rafsanjani's Expediency Council ruled that the Majles had no right to investigate state agencies that reported to the Supreme Leader, meaning that there would be no repeat of the investigations into the security services that had followed the "serial murders" in the fall of 1998. It also placed the judiciary, the *bonyad*s, and several other key organizations beyond Parliament's control, effectively freeing their members to do whatever they saw fit without fear that the reformists could take legal or bureaucratic action against them. Khamene'i publicly began to advocate the use of violence to deal with certain sorts of misbehavior. The outgoing, hard-line-dominated Majles finally passed the press law that had been put into provisional form the previous July and immediately closed nineteen newspapers and arrested several dozen more of the best-known reformist journalists.[117]

In July, peaceful demonstrations to commemorate the riots of the year before were furiously assaulted by Hizballahis, and many demonstrators were arrested by the police. Large numbers of nonstudents came to their rescue, but Khatami again failed to back them and instead called for them to go back to their homes and dorm rooms. Once again, without a leader, the reformist protests dwindled quickly. Twenty police officers put on trial for abuses during the previous year's riots were all acquitted—except for one, who was convicted of disobeying an order to attack the student protesters. To cap things off, later that summer the new Majles took office and immediately tabled a new press law that would have nullified the harsh rules just passed. Khamene'i simply ordered that the bill be dropped, and although it provoked a fistfight on the floor of Parliament, it was dropped.[118]

Many in Washington kept hoping that the Albright speech and the partial lifting of the sanctions would have an impact in Tehran. The president himself tried one more gesture, in the hope that he could get something positive that would allow him to follow up and get a process going. Khatami came to New York to address the U.N. General Assembly in September 2000. Clinton made a point of sitting through Khatami's speech—something an American president never does: he arrives, makes his speech, and leaves. There was a vain hope at senior levels that perhaps Khatami and the president might be able to meet and shake hands on the U.N. floor after Khatami's speech, but the Iranians studiously avoided the Americans.[119] With all of the other problems he had going on at home, Khatami did not need to remind the hard-liners of his earlier overtures to the Great Satan.

Reflections on the Clinton Iran Initiative

When I first saw the draft of the Albright speech on Iran, it had a number of problems that needed to be worked out. This was nothing unexpected; every speech usually starts with issues that need to be ironed out, especially from the perspective of the folks responsible for implementing policy, who have different priorities from the speechwriters trying to craft moving prose. However, there were two words in that draft that leapt off the page at me: "unelected hands." The entire sentence read, "Despite the trend towards democracy, control over the military, judiciary, courts and police remains in unelected hands, and the elements of its foreign policy, about which we are most concerned, have not improved." It was in one of the hard-nosed parts of the speech where the secretary of state was reminding the Iranians, the country, and the rest of the world that we had substantial problems lying between us that should not be papered over.

I was certain that the words "unelected hands" would be a red flag in Tehran, as they would call into question Khamene'i's legitimacy. I raised the issue with my boss, the senior director for the Near East and South Asia, Bruce Riedel, and he fully agreed with me. His words were "You better get someone to get State to change it." His point was that the speech had become so important that it was being handled at the highest levels of the government, and even a director at the NSC would be too low to try to get the people at State in charge of the speech to make what would inevitably be seen as a major change. I took all of my changes to one of the most senior people at the NSC and explained why this change in particular was important. My point was that if we were trying to make an overture to Iran (which we were), these two words would effectively kill the overture—either we eliminated these words or there was no point in making the overture. A few hours later, that senior NSC official called me to say that State had taken all of my other changes, but not that one. I then spent fifteen minutes convincing this person why the change was so important and the NSC agreed to take another run at State. This went on for almost forty-eight hours, with State refusing and the NSC pressing. The morning of the speech, I heard back for the last time that "the seventh floor" (the highest leadership, referring to the floor where the secretary, the deputy secretary, and the undersecretaries have their offices) at State had refused to budge, and the White House "had other fish to fry with them."

After the speech and Khamene'i's dreadful response, several of the best-informed Iranian interlocutors told me—entirely unprompted—that the words "unelected hands" had not gone down well in the Supreme Leader's office.[120] In September 2002, Foreign Minister Kharrazi confirmed this in responding to a question about the Clinton initiative: "I regret that Clinton failed to do better to finish the job. They had some efforts and took some positive positions but mixed those positions with some negative elements. They talked about elected and nonelected elements, which has been picked up by the current administration. That was considered an intervention in our internal affairs and backfired in Iran."[121] Several years later, after I had left government again, I had the opportunity to have dinner with an Iranian official. In the course of dinner, the Albright speech came up. He told me that when the speech had been given, he had been one of the people charged with the task of writing an official response. He said that the words "unelected hands" had leapt out at him and his colleagues, but they all—and all of their bosses, including President Khatami—had wanted to give a positive response. He said that they knew it was a major gesture by the United States, and they wanted to show that they understood it and appreciated it. But he said that every time they wrote a draft, it came back from the Supreme Leader's office with orders to make it tougher because of the words "unelected hands," and in the end the Supreme Leader's office simply took over the responsibility itself.

Hearing that story confirmed what was then my sentiment about the Clinton initiative. I felt that we had come very close to making a major breakthrough with Iran and that if only we had done a few things differently—such as eliminating those two words—we might have been able to make it happen. Over the years, however, I have come to the conclusion that I was wrong in this assessment. Any rapprochement that could be nixed by two words in a speech was a rapprochement that was doomed to failure anyway. That is the fundamental lesson of the Clinton initiative with Iran. The Iranians were not ready. Whenever two adversaries try to repair relations, harsh words are inevitable; it is the nature of politics and diplomacy. Thus both sides have to come to the bargaining table ready to shrug off those harsh words. If either is not ready to look past the rhetoric and focus instead on actions, then they are not ready for a rapprochement.

Iran was ruled by a regime in which the lion's share of power—and everything that truly mattered—was in the hands of people who were not ready or interested in improving ties with the United States. There was nothing that Washington could have done to have somehow helped Khatami prevail over the hard-liners and get them out of that controlling position. The mere fact that both the Iranian and American administrations were trying to establish some degree of tenuous contact only provoked the hard-liners and their followers to go after Khatami harder and faster. Nor would it have been possible to somehow have a rapprochement with only one part of the Iranian government, and the weaker part at that. The Iranian polity, as it was constituted in the late 1990s, was not going to be able to agree to détente with the United States. Only Mohammad Khatami could have changed that, and he was simply not willing to do what would have been necessary to make that change. Our effort was worthwhile, but without a leader in Iran ready to lead a revolution, it was doomed to failure.

Although it failed and its failure was probably inevitable, I do not regret having been part of it, nor do I believe that it was a mistake. Quite the contrary. I think it was vital for the United States to have tried. No one knew that in the clutch Khatami would back down. He had seemed so courageous beforehand. He had said all of the right things, and many of the actions we had seen from him—such as shutting off the smuggled Iraqi oil and purging most of the Intelligence Ministry of those associated with terrorism—had suggested that this was someone we should want to see succeed. If nothing else, had we not tried to reach out to Khatami, others would undoubtedly have blamed us for his demise. Many Iranian reformists likely would have added "doing nothing to help Khatami and the reformists who wanted to do everything that the United States had ever asked for" to their long list of grievances against the United States. Many Europeans and others would have chided us for having failed to take advantage of a golden opportunity to change the behavior of the Iranian government, as we had been demanding for years. It would have provided them with a perfect opportunity to trample all over American policy toward Iran. It would have made the United States look utterly cynical in calling for a change in Iranian behavior and then being unwilling to do anything to assist a government that said it wanted to do just that. It would have undermined every aspect of our Iran policy, perhaps fatally. Moreover, because none of the gestures we made was major and most were fully justified on their own merits, I do not see any harm from having made them. Indeed, it is unfortunate that this was all that came of it, but by trying so hard to start a process of rapprochement with the Khatami government, the Clinton administration gave the George W. Bush administration the perfect argument to demand a harder line on Iran from America's allies.

Coming Full Circle

W hen the George W. Bush administration took office in January 2001, it seemed more likely to take a softer line on Iran than a harder one. American oil companies avidly favored lifting the sanctions, and the background of many Bush administration officials in the oil industry (the president included) led many to speculate that they might do so unilaterally. In 1996, when Dick Cheney was still just the chairman of Halliburton, he called U.S. sanctions on Iran "self-defeating" and argued that "There seems to be an assumption that somehow we know what's best for everybody else, and that we are going to use our economic clout to get everybody else to live the way we would like."[1] In his confirmation hearings, Secretary of State Colin Powell argued that "we can see in recent years that there is change happening in Iran. . . . And to the extent that our policies can take into account the serious difficulties we have with the offensive policies but at the same time give encouragement to the people of Iran, that Iranians are not our enemies, that we are trying to make life better for them, we're trying to give them insight into the world that's waiting for them out here, to the extent that we can nuance our policy in that regard, I think it serves our interests and the interests of the region."[2] The new national security advisor, Condoleezza Rice, sounded toughest, writing in *Foreign Affairs* during the election campaign that "All in all, changes in U.S. policy toward Iran would require changes in Iranian behavior," yet this represented little more than a continuation of the existing Clinton administration policy.[3]

Whatever the Bush team's previous ideas, when they took office, Iran policy sunk quickly to the bottom of their list of priorities. By early 2001, Iran had become an extremely thorny issue for the United States to address. As Powell's remarks suggested, it was difficult for anyone outside government—including experts on Iran—to recognize how badly wounded the reform movement already was. Once in office, the Bush administration began to realize that (as the Clinton administration had learned the hard way) a rapprochement with Iran was not in the offing. But having tried so many other approaches to Iran over the years, the United States had few alternatives, except reverting back to the functional but frustrating policy of containment. In addition, many of the Bush administration's senior officials had higher priorities, and they were not interested in devoting the kind of time or resources that would have been necessary to make a major initiative—bellicose or benign—toward so troubled a country as Iran.

Iran was also one of those countries that brought out the deep divisions within the Bush administration that would later become a commonplace in its policy debates. The administration's own "hard-line" faction (mostly clustered in the Office of the Secretary of Defense and the vice president's staff)[4] wanted to overthrow the Iranian government, but the hawks were unwilling to commit the kind of resources or attention that would have been required to do so. As documented in numerous other accounts, they had become fixated on the idea that Iraq was really the key to all of America's problems in the Middle East, and they put their energy and effort into fighting that battle.[5] Nevertheless, they were committed to regime change in Iran just enough to block those from the administration's left wing (mostly at the State Department) from liberalizing the policy.

The outcome was a deadlock that resulted in the administration doing little on Iran during its first year in office. They began a policy review, but it was never concluded. In June 2001, a federal court in Alexandria, Virginia, handed down indictments for fourteen men charged with the terrorist attack on Khobar Towers and detailing Iran's involvement in the operation. This too failed to galvanize U.S. policy in one direction or the other. That August, ILSA came up for renewal and the administration took the compromise position of supporting its renewal, but for only two years rather than five. Congress, as determined in its pursuit of Iran as ever, disregarded the administration's views and renewed it for another five years.[6] By September 11, 2001, Iran policy was officially "still being studied."[7] Perhaps ironically, the Bush administration's Iraq policy was at a similar impasse at that point because the senior officials on either side of that debate cared too passionately about it to compromise, whereas in the case of Iran policy it was undecided because senior officials did not care about it enough to try to break the logjam.

Nor were there developments inside Iran that might have supported one camp or the other within the administration. Khatami easily won reelection as president with 77 percent of the vote in June 2001, but the turnout was down considerably from 1997. Beforehand, Khatami had indicated that he saw no point in running and waited till the last minute to register as a candidate. His supporters were equally unenthusiastic, many of them having lost all faith in him after his betrayal of the July 1999 protests. They still voted for him because he was the only non-hard-liner that the Council of Guardians had approved as a candidate in the election—and in the vain hope that perhaps a new electoral mandate might prod him into action. But they frequently voiced their despair that he—and they—were beaten. In the United States, Iran's election passed with little notice from the Bush administration.[8]

In a further irony, the tragedy of September 11 and the declaration of a war on terror changed almost nothing with regard to Iran, which the State Department's *Patterns of Global Terrorism* continued to describe as "the most active state sponsor of terrorism."[9] In his stirring speech to the nation on September 20, 2001, President Bush warned that the war on terror "will not end until every terrorist group of global reach has been found, stopped and defeated" and that "From this day forward, any nation that continues to harbor or support terrorism will be regarded by the United States as a hostile regime."[10] Afterward, experts inside and outside the government wondered whether this included Iran—after all, Lebanese Hizballah had demonstrated a global reach, and Iran supported a dozen other lethal terrorist groups around the world as well. Very quickly, however, it became clear that Iran was not going to be a target of the war on terrorism, at least not at first. Instead, Iran was going to be an ally.

The Afghan War

Although Madeleine Albright had not been able to meet Foreign Minister Kharrazi under the auspices of the United Nations' "six-plus-two" talks on Afghanistan, other American officials had continued to meet with their Iranian counterparts in this forum. Before 9/11, Iranian-American relations within these meetings were correct and professional but not harmonious. The only topic on the table for these sessions was policy toward Afghanistan, and on this subject (as on so many) the two governments had opposing views on a key issue. The Iranians were among the most important and active supporters of the opposition forces fighting against the Taliban and al-Qa'eda, and they constantly pressured the United States to take a more active role in the fighting too. However, under both the Clinton administration and the new Bush administration, the United States was reluctant to make a major commitment to the war in Afghanistan.

That changed completely as a result of the September 11 attacks. To the surprise of many Americans, the Iranians were remarkably sympathetic after 9/11. There were spontaneous candlelight vigils in Tehran—probably the only ones anywhere in the Muslim Middle East—and the government strongly condemned the attacks. The Iranian officials engaged in the "six-plus-two" talks were also very sympathetic, although there was a certain air of "we warned you about these guys" in their voices, according to American officials. This prompted the Bush administration to send Tehran a message via the Swiss once again, asking it to join the war on terror and provide information on al-Qa'eda and the Taliban. Suddenly, we had something very important in common.[11]

Most of the members of the "six-plus-two" talks (Russia and Pakistan in particular) opposed an American war against Afghanistan, but the Iranians did not. They could not wait for it to start and were so enthusiastic that they just about offered to do the planning. To get away from those countries reluctant to endorse the American military operation and to allow the United States and Iran to cooperate in private, it was decided to create a subgroup that would continue to meet under the auspices of the United Nations but would include only the United States and Iran, bringing in Italy and Germany for political cover. The group started by meeting in Geneva, and even though it would eventually meet in other European cities, it was always referred to as the Geneva Contact Group. In truth, it was nothing but a vehicle for the United States and Iran to meet and discuss Afghanistan. Very quickly the United Nations, the Germans, and the Italians stopped attending all of the sessions, or they would show up for a while and then leave. The Iranians who participated impressed their American and European counterparts considerably. They were professional, thoughtful, constructive, and enormously knowledgeable about Afghanistan and the Taliban.[12]

They also provided considerable assistance to Operation Enduring Freedom. Tehran offered to allow American transport aircraft to stage from airfields in eastern Iran to assist operations in western Afghanistan. It agreed to perform search-and-rescue missions for downed American airmen who bailed out over Iran. The Iranians allowed an American freighter packed with humanitarian supplies to off-load its cargo at their port of Chah Bahar, the fastest route into southwestern Afghanistan and the Taliban stronghold of Qandahar. Although the United States had never completely severed its ties to the Northern Alliance, the major Afghan opposition group fighting the Taliban, we had allowed those ties to attenuate. The Iranians weighed in with the Northern Alliance and helped convince it that Washington was deadly serious and that therefore the Northern Alliance should participate fully in the American effort. The Northern Alliance was made up largely of ethnic Tajiks, while the majority of Afghans are ethnic Pashtuns, and the Iranians also played a role in convincing the Northern Alliance that it should reach out to Pashtun groups to make the war a pan-Afghan effort. When the Muslim holy month of Ramadan loomed on the calendar and the Americans started to worry about whether fighting in Afghanistan during Ramadan would hurt the U.S. image in the Islamic world, the Iranians assured their American counterparts that it would not, and that if it did, they would find ways to help. On at least one occasion, when the United States learned that a key al-Qa'eda leader was fleeing into Iran, the Iranians used the American information to find him and neutralize him.[13]

Indeed, the only real friction between the Americans and Iranians during the war came in mid-October, when, after seven to ten days in which U.S. air power had concentrated on striking Taliban air defense assets and command and control, the Iranians became frustrated at the slow pace of the American campaign. They urged their American counterparts to start striking Taliban field forces and offered to provide information on where those forces were located if the American military lacked it. They were greatly relieved when, just a few days later, the U.S. military's plan moved into its next phase, which concentrated attacks on the Taliban's frontline units.[14]

At the end of November 2001, with the Taliban effectively deposed, the United Nations held a conference on rebuilding Afghanistan in Bonn, Germany. This conference gave birth to the interim government that ultimately took power in Kabul and paved the way for the creation of a permanent government. Behind the scenes, it was the United States and Iran, working together, that pulled all of the strings and made the conference a success. For weeks beforehand, working through the Geneva Group, the two countries laid the groundwork for the event. Although the Iranians (as mostly Shi'ah Persians) had their problems with the Sunni Pashtuns, they were instrumental in bringing in key Pashtun figures, such as the former king, Zahir Shah, and incorporating them into the process. According to Americans who participated in the conference and the backroom negotiations, although the Pakistanis often took the credit, it was the Iranians who generally deserved it.[15]

Of course, there were sources of tension, mostly stemming from the unresolved pathologies of the Iranian government. Iran's Foreign Ministry, Khatami, and Khamene'i were fully committed to the Geneva Group collaboration with the United States. Although Khatami may have still seen this as yet another possible way to develop a relationship with the Americans, by the end of 2001 he had been so marginalized that what he hoped was no longer particularly relevant. Khamene'i (probably with Rafsanjani's encouragement) doubtless saw working with the Americans as a necessary evil. Iran hated the Taliban regime and wanted it destroyed. Moreover, it was very clear from President Bush's September 20 speech that the United States was going to attack Afghanistan regardless of what Iran or any other nation did, so the question became whether it was better to help the Americans—and thus have some ability to see that Iran's interests were not trampled during the war—or oppose them—and risk having the United States take actions that would be detrimental to Iran. Khamene'i's pragmatic decision to work with the Americans and not against them strongly suggests that he no longer felt so insecure that he slavishly adhered to Khomeini's anti-American legacy for fear that doing otherwise would call his legitimacy into question. Nor did he feel as threatened by Khatami and the Americanophile reformists as he once had. Nevertheless, he was still not fully confident in either of these things, so he publicly condemned Operation Enduring Freedom (much to the bemusement of American officials), railing that the war was part of the Americans' drive to "expand their power and domination."[16]

Interestingly, there were other signs that Iran might have been softening its own position toward the United States. A diplomat from the Iranian Mission to the United Nations was permitted to have dinner with a group of American senators in October 2001. Another Iranian official commented to *The Washington Post* about the dinner that "Many things have been done by Iran in a very deliberate and policy-oriented way. . . .We look forward to continuing the positive atmosphere and to seeing some modification of U.S. policy in Iran."[17] Later that month, a majority of deputies from the Majles (then dominated by reformists) called on the government to consider normalizing relations with the United States—something that would have landed them in prison, if not dead, just a few years earlier. In private, Iranian officials confided that there was an increased desire in Tehran to get the American trade sanctions lifted in the hope that this would boost Iran's flagging economy. Apparently, between his greater sense of security and Iran's increasing economic woes, Khamene'i was finally willing to start to explore the possibility of improving relations with the United States in the hope of having the sanctions lifted.[18]

Although Khamene'i was willing to work with the United States on the conduct of the Afghan war, other parts of the Iranian government seemed more ambivalent. In particular, the IRGC and MOIS were very unhappy about the United States conquering Iran's eastern neighbor. This turned into a problem immediately after the fall of Qandahar, when the Iranian intelligence services, seeing a vacuum in Afghanistan, swept in to try to fill it. They made contact with local warlords and attempted to convert them to Iranian assets. They began paying people off for providing information and for being willing to act in Iran's interests. They threatened others to get them to do the same. They began recruiting informers throughout the country. They increased their surveillance of American military, political, and intelligence personnel in Afghanistan. They also greatly increased their own physical presence—and not just in western Afghanistan, where they had traditionally had a degree of influence, but throughout the country. To some extent, this effort was aimed at Pakistan, whose intelligence service had been the principal guardian of the Taliban before 9/11. However, it is also clear that the Pasdaran meant to diminish American influence in Afghanistan while increasing its own.[19]

The happy ending to this story is that the Americans raised it with their Iranian counterparts in Geneva, and within about a month, virtually all of this nefarious intelligence activity stopped. Iran's intelligence services continued to operate in Afghanistan, but they mostly confined themselves to their traditional area of interest around Herat in western Afghanistan, they stopped surveilling American personnel, and they generally toned down their aggressive operations.

This too was a product of Tehran's perception of its own interests and the Bush administration's wisdom in making it a full partner in the Bonn conference. In general, Iran's principal leadership, including Khamene'i, were most frightened that chaos would arise in Afghanistan. That had happened after the Soviet withdrawal in 1989, and it had led to countless problems for Iran, from drug smuggling and the resultant war with the Baluchis to the rise of the Taliban. The Iranians did not want to see a repeat of that. Though it may have been galling to them, they recognized that only the Americans could lead a successful effort to rebuild a stable Afghanistan and that the plan the United States was advocating would, if successful, produce a state that would be a reasonable neighbor for Iran. Consequently, the leadership in Tehran decided that Iran's interests would be best served by helping the Americans to succeed in Afghanistan. It did not want anything to upset that effort or to cause the United States to shift to trying to build a state in Afghanistan that would be hostile to Iran. Hence, when the gung ho types in the Pasdaran threatened to provoke a war with the Americans in Afghanistan, Tehran stepped in to shut them down.[20]

Back to Confrontation

After the war in Afghanistan, the Iranians participating in the Geneva Group showed an interest in expanding their discussions to address other topics of mutual interest to Iran and America, particularly Iraq. The Americans were willing and so held a meeting in early January 2002 that touched on a much broader range of issues. Thus, without really trying, the Bush administration had achieved what the Clinton administration had spent nearly four fruitless years pursuing: it had face-to-face talks with Iranian officials, who were willing to discuss a variety of issues, and there were hints of a willingness to normalize relations on the part of the Iranian government. As one former Clinton administration official noted, "That was our Holy Grail."[21] But the Bush administration did not seem to even realize it. The American diplomats who had been participating in the Geneva Group talks up until early January 2002 had not been under close supervision, and the decision to move beyond the topic of Afghanistan was taken at a fairly low level within the State Department. It did not reflect a formal act of policy by the U.S. government or even that any of the administration's principals were paying attention. Washington was all too busy wrapping up the war in Afghanistan, pursuing al-Qa'eda elsewhere around the globe, and gearing up for the war over going to war with Iraq, the first salvoes of which had just been fired.[22]

So there was little effort to take advantage of what in retrospect might have been a crucial moment in the relationship. Some in the State Department, led by Richard Haass, the director of the Policy Planning Staff, did argue that the United States should stop opposing Iran's accession to the World Trade Organization. Like the Clinton initiative, they saw this not only as a gesture to Iran that might have kicked off a real rapprochement at a time when there were some (admittedly confusing) signals coming from Tehran but also as an action defensible in its own right. The WTO was "a subversive organization," in the words of one of the officials involved, whose regulations regarding political and economic reform could help force the hard-liners to move in the directions they had so far resisted. But the idea went nowhere. No one even among the senior leadership of the State Department was willing to push it. In an administration as deeply divided as that of the second Bush presidency, the principals all felt they needed to save their bureaucratic ammunition for the things they cared about most.[23]

Then everything started to come apart. On January 3, 2002, Israel intercepted a ship, the *Karine A,* in the Red Sea. It was captained by an officer in the Palestinian Authority's navy and carried an arsenal of weaponry and explosives that the Israelis contended had been purchased by another Palestinian tied to the PA and destined for the Palestinian security services in violation of every accord that the PA had ever signed with Israel. It carried Katyusha rockets, mortars, rifles, machine guns, sniper rifles, ammunition, antitank mines, rocket-propelled grenades, and 2.5 tons of explosives. The arms had been manufactured in Iran and loaded onto the ship at Kish Island, Iran. Many of the weapons were still in their factory wrappings, clearly marked as having been produced in Iran. They were also packaged in eighty-three watertight crates attached to buoys so that they could be dumped overboard and picked up by coastal craft without the ship having to put into port to off-load them.[24]

Although many have questioned the Israeli evidence connecting the arms to the PA and suggested that Iran was attempting to smuggle them to Hizballah instead because Syria was restricting its traditional air shipments via Damascus, the U.S. government found the Israeli evidence to be "compelling."[25] In particular, the captain and crew confessed that the weapons had been purchased by members of the PA, had been headed for the Gaza Strip, and were to be collected by other members of the PA.[26] Secretary of State Powell commented in a televised interview that "I can't put it right at [PA Chairman Yasser Arafat] personally, but it is clear from all the information available to us that the Palestinian Authority was involved. And leaders in the Palestinian Authority had to know about this, and there were Palestinian Authority personnel on the ship. . . . It's a pretty big smoking gun."[27]

As far as Washington was concerned, this was unmistakable evidence that whatever Iran's desire to explore improved relations, it had not given up its support for terrorism or its determination to derail a Middle East peace through violence. And that was not all. A number of key al-Qa'eda leaders had fled from the wreckage of Afghanistan into Iran and, unlike in the earlier instances, the Iranians allowed them considerable freedom of action.[28] The U.S. intelligence community apparently had other evidence that Iran was stepping up its support to HAMAS and PIJ to attack the right-wing Israeli government of Ariel Sharon. Reports began to surface that Iran was making greater progress on nuclear weapons than had previously been imagined.[29] As Condi Rice commented, "Iran's direct support of regional and global terrorism, and its aggressive efforts to acquire weapons of mass destruction, belie any good intentions it displayed in the days after the world's worst terrorist attacks in history."[30] This may have been the result of freelancing by hard-line groups within the regime but more likely stemmed from either the ambivalence that Khamene'i and his key supporters felt about improving ties with the United States or the fact that Iran's hard-liners have never shown a great deal of understanding about America (or any other country other than their own, for that matter) and may not have recognized that the one would likely preclude the other.[31]

A bit more than three weeks after the *Karine A* was taken by the Israelis,

President Bush delivered his State of the Union address for 2002. In it he argued that Iran, along with Iraq and North Korea, was part of an "Axis of evil" that threatened the United States and free peoples everywhere. The speechwriters who came up with that line did not have any policy guidance to put Iran in the speech, but in the backs of their minds they may have remembered that the administration was certainly not happy with Iran at that moment. To a certain extent, however, Iran was roadkill: the phrase was not really about Iran. As one administration official described it, Iran was just a "prop" needed to make a point. The speechwriters "had come up with this great line, and they needed a third country to make up an 'Axis.' "[32] In his book *Plan of Attack,* Bob Woodward tells a similar story, that the speechwriters had really been thinking about Iraq and the general connection between states that sponsor terrorism and pursue weapons of mass destruction, and they came up with the phrase, which they—and the president—really liked. But then they needed to fill out the Axis. Some senior administration officials privy to the draft of the speech objected to Iran's inclusion, pointing out that because Iran had something of a democratic movement it should not be lumped in with Saddam Hussein's Iraq and Kim Jong-Il's North Korea.[33] But Iran stayed in because the president believed that "No question about it, North Korea, Iraq and Iran are the biggest threats to peace at the time." Asked afterward how he thought Iranians would feel about the speech, Bush remarked, "I doubt the students and the reformers and the liberators inside Iran were displeased with that. I made the calculation that they would be pleased. . . . Now, I'm confident the leaders didn't like it."[34]

The president was about three quarters right in this calculation. The Iranian-American journalist Afshin Molavi noted that reaction among average Iranians to the speech was very mixed, with some extremely angry about it and others saying that it was an accurate description of their government. A poll of Iranians showed an almost even divide between those who saw the president's speech as positive and those who saw it as negative.[35] However, as Bush predicted, Iran's leadership—the leadership that mattered, that is—did not like it at all. Khamene'i fired back that "the Islamic Republic is proud to be the target of the hate and anger of the world's greatest evil; we never seek to be praised by American officials."[36] Many Iranian reformists also bemoaned the speech, saying that it would help the hard-liners to rally people around the regime.[37] Indeed, even if almost 50 percent of Iranians thought the speech a fair description, it left a slight majority angry—and if the anger of that slight majority had translated into support for the regime, even temporarily, it would have greatly increased the popularity of a group whose candidates were generally polling less than 20 percent of the populace.

The speech had a tangible impact as well. First, the Iranians stopped attending the Geneva talks—"just when they were starting to really get interesting," one senior administration official quipped.[38] Second, the Iranians retaliated with an action that created a headache for the United States in Afghanistan: they freed Gulbuddin Hekmatyar. Hekmatyar was an Afghan Sunni fundamentalist and one of the most anti-American, murderous, and fanatical leaders of the Mujahideen who had fought the Soviets throughout the 1980s. Hekmatyar was a troublemaker and a rabble-rouser, but because he was considered pious, because he was charismatic, and because he had strong ties to Pakistani intelligence, he was a force to be reckoned with in Afghanistan. He had fled to Iran, where he was being held in captivity. The new interim government of Hamid Qarzai did not need a problem like Hekmatyar and so had declined an earlier Iranian offer to have him transferred to Afghan custody. Washington desperately wanted Iran to hold on to him so that he could not make trouble for Qarzai. But in early February, the Iranians released him into Afghanistan. American officials remain convinced that it was payback for the State of the Union address.[39]

As American rhetoric against Iraq heated up in March and April 2002, the Iranians decided to return to the Geneva talks. This forum had proven very useful to them in learning about American plans and intentions toward their eastern neighbor and steering Washington in a direction that was not harmful to their own interests. If the United States was now going to invade their neighbor to the west, they wanted the same insights and influence. However, when the talks resumed, they did so with a different cast of characters. On the Iranian side, the Afghan specialists were supplanted by Tehran's Arabists, as well as more senior political figures. On the American side, Zalmay Khalilzad, the NSC senior director for the Near East and South Asia, was brought in to carry on the Iraq conversations. Khalilzad was far more involved with the administration's Iraq policy, and he was a political appointee who would be certain to carry the White House's political line to the Iranians as well.

When the talks resumed, however, it quickly became clear that they had lost the spirit they had once had. Both sides had now reaffirmed their distrust of each other—Iran through its actions in the *Karine A,* pursuit of WMD, and harboring of al-Qa'eda personnel, the United States through the president's unexpected (and, as far as the Iranians were concerned, unjustified) remarks in the State of the Union address. Moreover, the injection of more politically connected officials into the discussions also bred caution on both sides. Other events added to the tensions. For instance, in July 2002, several thousand students and other supporters of the reformists staged demonstrations in Tehran to commemorate the riots of July 1999—the "almost" revolution. A day later, the Friday prayer leader of Isfahan (the most important clergyman of that major city), Ayatollah Jalaledin Taheri, resigned his post, blasting the hard-line regime for failing to abide by the rule of law, betraying the revolution, and oppressing the Iranian people, among other things. The regime ordered the press not to discuss any of his charges, but President Bush publicly called on them to implement more of the political and economic reforms that the Iranian people so clearly wanted and that Ayatollah Taheri had called for in his letter of resignation. It was actually a rather moderate statement, but, coming from the American president, it naturally drew the ire of the Iranian regime. For-eign Minister Kharrazi told *USA Today*'s Barbara Slavin, "That was another example of intervention in Iranian internal affairs. . . . Iran's society is a vital one, the young generation plays a very important role in Iranian poli-tics today. But this does not mean they would be happy with foreign interven-tion. . . . This reality is very different from the system of government of other countries in the region. The reaction of Americans toward this model was a mistake."[40]

However, because each side needed the help of the other for the impend-ing war with Iraq, the Geneva Group continued to meet and came to a broad, if not necessarily warm, meeting of the minds. In particular, the Iranians came away assured that if the United States attacked (and they were confident that it would), Washington would not stop until Saddam was removed from power and that the administration's intention afterward was to build an independent, democratic Iraq in which its oppressed Shi'ah majority would finally have po-litical power equivalent to its demographic weight. This suited Tehran well. The Iranians still hated and mistrusted Saddam, thanks to their long, painful history with him. Moreover, their own experiences during the Iran-Iraq War, when Iraq's Shi'ah had refused to rise up against Saddam and had fought the Iranian invaders to the death, led them to conclude that it would be very diffi-cult for them to take over the country, or even the Shi'i south, therefore remov-ing any thought of creating an Iranian protectorate over Iraq. What the Americans were proposing therefore actually sounded like the best scenario that Tehran could realistically obtain.

During Operation Iraqi Freedom in March–April 2003, Iran was not as helpful as it had been in the Afghan war, but it certainly was not unhelpful. The IRGC was put on its best behavior and did not create any problems for the U.S.-led coalition. After the war, however, Iran proved to be of considerable assistance to the American reconstruction effort, arguably more helpful than it had been in Afghanistan. Tehran did not do so out of the goodness of its heart. The Iranian leadership, which understood Iraqi society far better than many in the Bush administration, recognized early on that stabilizing Iraq after the fall of Saddam's totalitarian dictatorship and then building a functional pluralistic political system afterward were going to be herculean tasks. They were also precisely what Tehran wanted to see happen in Iraq, because they believed this would ensure that Iraq did not slide into civil war and chaos (which was Iran's greatest fear and first priority) and because doing so would mean the establishment of a Shi'ah-dominated government, which might not be Iran's proxy but was unlikely to be hostile to it either. Given that the Iranians had rather low expectations for postwar Iraq, simply achieving those goals was enough for them.

Consequently, Tehran told its various proxy groups in Iraq not to resist the United States and instead to participate in the U.S.-led process of reconstruction. This was critical because many of the most important Shi'ah groups, such as ad-Dawa and the Supreme Council for the Islamic Revolution in Iraq (SCIRI), as well as key individuals such as famed guerrilla commander 'Abd al-Karim Mahud al-Muhammadawi, had all been supported by Iran in one fashion or another during the 1980s and '90s. In addition, many other Iraqi Shi'ah would likely have looked to Iran as their natural protector in the event of a fight for supremacy. Iran's quiet encouragement of all these groups was critical to their early participation in the U.S.-led process of political and economic reconstruction. Their willingness to stay the course when initial American mistakes created tremendous problems with lawlessness, economic chaos, and the threat of a political collapse was critical in keeping the situation from spiraling out of control. If the Iranians had wanted to cause chaos in Iraq, they could have easily done so in the darkest days after the war, and the United States was fortunate that they did not.

Of course, since it was Iran, it was not as simple as just that. Soon after the end of major combat operations in May 2003, American officials in Iraq began to detect the first Iranian intelligence personnel moving into the country. Over time, this flow began to increase. By early 2004, all of Iran's various intelligence and covert action organizations were represented in Iraq—the IRGC (including its Quds Forces), Hizballah, the MOIS, Lebanese Hizballah, and assorted others. Their mere presence in Iraq alarmed many Americans, particularly those predisposed to see the Iranian bugbear behind every problem. However, American officials and intelligence officers in Iraq stressed a critical fact: the Iranians were in Iraq in strength and were building an intelligence network, but that network was not "operational"—it was not attempting to do anything other than gather information and strengthen itself. In the semichaos of post-Saddam Iraq, there were numerous opportunities for the Iranians to attack (or even surveil) Americans, encourage one Iraqi group to attack another, assassinate Iraqis opposed to their interests, terrorize populations into acquiescing to their wishes, or otherwise add to the violence—both political and random—in the country. But they were studiously avoiding doing so.[41]

Indeed, the only time American or Iraqi officials were able to demonstrate an Iranian "action" inside Iraq came in February 2004, when a group of Iranians was arrested by the Iraqi police in Sunni-controlled Fallujah. The next week, the Iranians staged an attack on the police station that allowed their comrades to escape. Four attackers were killed in the assault, and their papers indicated that one was an Iranian and two others were Lebanese. It is worth noting that this attack was far more skillful than what Coalition forces had seen from the Iraqis themselves. "The attack on the police was unusually bold and sophisticated," *The New York Times* reported, based on the accounts of American military officers, "with the insurgents advancing from four sides, firing heavy machine guns and rocket-propelled grenades. The assault on the police station was coupled with a simultaneous attack on an Iraqi civil defense headquarters about a mile away, intended to hold them in check while the prison break unfolded. In all, the insurgents numbered 30 to 50, operating with heavy firepower in daylight."[42] This single event underscores the point that had the Iranians wanted to cause trouble for the U.S.-led reconstruction of Iraq, they could have made the situation much worse than it already was.

Iran's seemingly inexplicable behavior in Iraq makes considerable sense when viewed as part of the ongoing battles over foreign policy within Iran. Naturally, the reformists pushed for cooperation with the United States, but by 2003–2004 their wishes counted for little in foreign policy debates in Tehran. Khatami mostly mimicked whatever Khamene'i said on an issue, although perhaps without quite the Supreme Leader's conviction. Instead, the critical debate was between the most extreme elements among the Iranian hard-liners—the Pasdaran, some members of the Council of Guardians, and others—on the one hand, and the principal Iranian leadership concentrated in Khamene'i, Rafsanjani, and some emerging figures such as the secretary-general of Iran's Supreme National Security Council, Hasan Ruhani, on the other. It was these principal leaders who had concluded, very pragmatically, that Iran's interests would be best served by seeing the American plan to build a stable, pluralist, and independent Iraq succeed. With more than 100,000 American troops in Iraq, they did not want to provoke an American military operation against Iran. Moreover, their greatest fear was of chaos in Iraq, which they believed would likely spill over into Iran. Given that Iran's economy continued to wither and its populace was increasingly unhappy, they did not need any more instability imported from a chaotic Iraq. Consequently, they saw no reason to try to oppose the Americans and every reason to support the United States, albeit at arm's length.

Typically, IRGC commander Safavi and many of the other firebrands in Tehran had a different view of the situation. They appear to have argued for moving into Iraq in force and using everything at their disposal—money, supplies, promises, threats, assassinations, and large-scale violence—either to secure power for one or more groups loyal to themselves or to build up proxies and drive out Sunni Arabs and Kurds from southern and eastern Iraq to create buffers and protectorates within the country. We do not know their logic, but one of two intertwined reasons seems most likely. Many in Iran feared that the United States intended to create a pro-American puppet regime in Tehran, one that might even serve as the launch pad for an invasion of Iran in the near future. It seems likely that the Iranian extremists shared this view and so may have argued that Iran should get into Iraq and start fighting to undermine the Americans right away to prevent this from happening. Alternatively, it may be that the Iranian extremists simply did not believe that Washington could achieve its goal of creating a stable, pluralistic Iraq. This was a view held by many people throughout the region. In this case, the extremists likely would have maintained that since the United States was bound to fail, it was critical for Iran to put itself into a position to be able to guard its own interests when the Americans did fail, which likely would plunge the country into chaos and civil war. In this defensive version of the scenario, the extremists would have been arguing that it was only prudent for Iran to take prophylactic measures to prevent a worst-case scenario in the future.

Khamene'i, always overly indulgent of his far right because of his insecurity about his legitimacy as *faqih,* appears to have agreed to a compromise. He allowed the intelligence services to deploy to Iraq in force and position themselves to fight a war there if necessary but not to engage in any actual belligerent activities until he ordered them to do so. So the Iranians would recruit assets; reconnoiter the terrain; secure allies; distribute weapons, money, and supplies; establish safe houses and other facilities; set up a logistical and communications network; train their personnel; and even draw up operational plans, but they would not actually be allowed to take action against either the Americans or other Iraqi groups until given permission by Tehran. This was the bureaucratically smart solution, as it kept the security services busy preparing themselves for the need to go active and gave them the sense that the leadership was not ignoring their opinions. It also became Iran's "Plan B." If Tehran determined either that the Americans were attempting to create a puppet government in Iraq (especially one meant to serve as a launching pad for an invasion of Iran) or that the U.S.-led reconstruction effort was going to fail, likely creating the chaos that was Iran's worst nightmare, Tehran would unleash the Iranian intelligence services to protect Iranian interests as best they could. (And they had learned a tremendous amount from their experience in a similar environment in Lebanon in the 1980s and '90s.) Since the intelligence services would have already done much of the preparatory work necessary to build a base for such operations, Iran would be well placed to defend its interests in that scenario as well.

Terrorism and Tehran

As if matters between Iran and the United States were not confusing and contradictory enough, the fall of Baghdad brought new sources of animosity outside of the Iraq conflict. On May 12, 2003, three truck bombs were detonated nearly simultaneously in Western housing complexes in the Saudi capital of Riyadh, killing twenty people, seven of them Americans. Within a few months, U.S. intelligence had solid evidence that al-Qa'eda was behind the attacks and that some of the perpetrators had discussed the operation with superiors located in, of all places, Iran. According to press reporting, the United States had picked up communications between the terrorist cell in Saudi Arabia responsible for the bombings and the roughly half-dozen senior al-Qa'eda personnel inside Iran, including Saif al-Adel, at that time al-Qa'eda's third in command.[43] The great mystery was, why were senior al-Qa'eda personnel being allowed to operate inside Iran—a country that had actively fought them and their Taliban allies for years?

There is a bit more evidence that should be added to the story. These al-Qa'eda leaders apparently were operating in eastern Iran, which is a bit like the Wild West. The government does not have full control over much of eastern Iran and for decades has fought a guerrilla war against the Baluchis who inhabit part of that region. It was not as if these al-Qa'eda leaders had been under lock and key in Evin prison in Tehran and were allowed to make phone calls to set up the attacks. Nevertheless, the Iranian government did know that they were there because the United States had complained about their presence. Therefore, the Iranian leadership must have made a conscious decision not to lock them up. If the Iranians had wanted to do so, they could have, as they demonstrated by quickly apprehending them after the bombings. Given the amount of bad blood between al-Qa'eda and the Iranian government in the past, it seems highly unlikely that Tehran would have opted not to incarcerate these figures because it saw no need to do so. Al-Qa'eda is a savage group that had fought Iran up until just months beforehand, and that alone should have been enough for the Iranians to kill or imprison them. Thus, at some level their freedom had to have been intentional.

The best explanation for Iran's behavior seems to lie in a combination of foreign and domestic policy motives. For a brief period of time after the American invasion of Iraq, some in Iran genuinely worried that the United States intended to move against them next, and the Riyadh attacks fell squarely within that window. There was a certain amount of bluster from a small number of commentators in the United States that Iran ought to be America's next target in the war on terrorism (although just as many said that Iran's ally, Syria, should have that honor). Even Iranians who thought this unlikely may have wanted to hedge their bets and have on hand options to be able to strike back at the United States if at all possible, and the al-Qa'eda leaders might have represented just such an option. An alternative version of this same theory would be that the Iranians actually wanted to see al-Qa'eda make trouble for the United States as a way of heading off such an invasion. In either case, Iran would want to preserve its plausible deniability, and that meant not apprehending these al-Qa'eda personnel. As long as they were running free in the "Wild West" of Iran's eastern marches, Tehran could say that it did not have control over them and so was not responsible for whatever reprehensible activities they conducted. Moreover, by then, with the Afghan war over and the Taliban broken, al-Qa'eda no longer presented the same kind of threat to the Iranians as it once had or as it still did to us—the al-Qa'eda operatives were determined to have their revenge on the United States, and they were not looking to take on Iran at that time.

Domestic political factors probably also played a role. The fears of American aggression—and the desire to head it off by going on the offensive—of the IRGC, MOIS, and other security services probably extended to issues other than just Iran's activities in Iraq. These same groups may have seen real value in enabling (or even encouraging) al-Qa'eda to attack the United States for exactly the reasons described above. Others inside the Iranian government no doubt argued against both the proposed policy of the hard-line extremists and the specific notion of allowing al-Qa'eda leaders to move about freely in Iranian territory. They would likely have argued that harboring al-Qa'eda figures was the surest way for Iran to become the next target in America's war on terrorism and that, given their history of warfare with Iran, these men did not deserve to run free inside their country. Faced with this kind of a divide, Khamene'i, the "tepid liberal turned archconservative," may not have been able to make up his mind. There have been other occasions when Khamene'i has simply chosen not to make a decision, and this is certainly not a problem peculiar to Iran.

Iran's security services retain a limited degree of autonomy, and in any bureaucracy, the opportunity for those with limited autonomy to push the edge of the envelope increases dramatically when no policy directives have been laid out. If you can say that the boss is still considering your idea or hasn't made a decision on it, you have some leeway to advance your idea until he or she specifically says no. That too may have been the case here: faced with strong conflicting arguments, Khamene'i may have chosen not to make a decision on the al-Qa'eda leaders. Allowing them to continue to move around freely—albeit undoubtedly under close surveillance—was the default option, so that was what happened. But since the same security services that were most likely pressing to allow al-Qa'eda a freer hand to attack the United States were also the ones responsible for keeping tabs on the al-Qa'eda leadership, they may have allowed the al-Qa'eda figures a bit more latitude than Khamene'i intended while they waited for a more definitive ruling.

Shortly after the attacks, and after picking up the communications that indicated a link to those in Iran, the United States delivered a message to Tehran via the Swiss—and canceled a meeting of the Geneva Group to add an exclamation point to the message. It demanded that Iran transfer the al-Qa'eda leaders either directly to the Saudis or to third states that would then transfer them to the United States. The Iranians countered with a proposal of their own: they would agree to give up the al-Qa'eda personnel if the United States would hand over the MEK to Iran. Although the MEK was a designated terrorist group under U.S. sanction, when the United States invaded Iraq, American forces did not engage the MEK army, which was still there and still assisting Saddam in controlling the country. Instead, Washington chose to sign a cease-fire with the MEK. Numerous reports surfaced that the American hard-liners in the Pentagon and the office of the vice president demanded such lenient treatment because they hoped to turn the MEK loose on Iran at some point. The Iranians, of course, were anxious to get their hands on their old foes and punish them for both past and recent sins.[44]

The Iranian offer set off yet another round in the interminable debates between the right and left wings of the Bush administration. It sparked a general argument over whether American policy toward Iran should be one of confrontation and regime change or engagement and diplomacy. It threatened to get completely bogged down and lead to no resolution, as so many other, similar debates had. Fortunately, in this case, there were facts and judgments that could be added to the balance. First, the United States had no extradition treaty with Iran, and, of greater importance, Iran had a long record of gross human rights violations. It would have been difficult for the U.S. government to justify sending even terrorists to Iran. Second, the U.S. intelligence community argued that it was highly likely that Iran would not give up the top leaders the United States wanted for fear of risking retaliation by al-Qa'eda itself. Instead, it was expected that it would release to the United States only lower-level figures whose operational and intelligence value was low. Strong arguments can be raised in opposition to all of these points, but all that is relevant here is that they apparently did prove decisive; the United States declined the Iranian offer.[45]

The Iranians had some ground to call the United States hypocritical. While Washington was demanding that they turn the al-Qa'eda personnel they were sheltering over to the United States or to third countries (which in turn would charge them or turn them over to the United States), the U.S. government refused to do the same with the MEK personnel that it was sheltering. In fact, the United States treated the 3,800 members of the MEK who fell into its hands after the invasion of Iraq reasonably well, especially for terrorists who had waged a murderous campaign against the Iranian government for nearly twenty-five years and had pitched in on Saddam's behalf in the bloody suppression of the Iraqi people in 1991. Again, it is hard to image that Washington would have stood for another country treating the MEK as the United States did if its more recent actions had been directed against Americans. Its members were disarmed and their movement was restricted, but they were kept together under surveillance at a camp and treated reasonably well. Then, in late July 2004, the MEK personnel were informed that they would not be charged with any violations of U.S. law and instead would be designated "protected persons." Remarkably, *The New York Times* quoted a senior American official as claiming that "A member of a terrorist organization is not necessarily a terrorist."[46] This too is a standard that Washington has been reluctant to apply to terrorist groups that attack the United States, such as al-Qa'eda, but is less punctilious about when it comes to terrorists attacking other countries.

Iran's Nuclear Challenge

Back in 2002, while the world was transfixed by the drama being played out between Saddam Hussein and the Bush administration, another discovery of potentially equal importance went mostly unnoticed. Ironically, it was the political arm of the MEK (the National Council of Resistance, or NCR) that dropped the bombshell. On August 14, 2002, the NCR announced that its sources had discovered two secret facilities in Iran built to produce fissile material for nuclear weapons. They claimed that Iran had a clandestine gas centrifuge plant at Natanz (to enrich uranium) and a heavy-water production facility at Arak (to extract plutonium). In December 2002, U.S. intelligence sources stated that they had confirmed both the existence of and activities at these two sites.[47] It was no surprise that Iran was interested in enriching uranium—the Clinton administration had convinced the Russians not to sell

Iran a large gas centrifuge facility in the mid-1990s—but it was a surprise that the Iranians had found another way to do so, and entirely in secret. Moreover, since Iran did not have any public plans to build civilian heavy-water reactors, no one had even expected Iran to try to take that route to building a bomb.

Despite the promises the Clinton administration had heard from Khatami's informal interlocutors that the reformists understood the United States' concerns about Iran's nuclear program and would work to accommodate us, Iran's nuclear program had never slowed down. In fact, it had made tremendous progress. Ironically, Khatami's accession had helped make that possible. When the reformists took over the government in 1997, Iran's nuclear program was extensive and a priority for the regime, but it was horribly mismanaged. Led by the incompetent Reza Amrollahi and a team chosen more for their revolutionary credentials than their technical skills, the Iranian nuclear program had stumbled along despite the considerable resources lavished upon it. In addition, before Khatami's election, the United States got much greater traction with its efforts to persuade other countries not to provide assistance to the Iranian nuclear program. During the Clinton administration, Vice President Gore and other senior officials had hammered the Russians and Chinese relentlessly, and although they could not prevent all cooperation, Washington's efforts did help constrain the Iranians. When Khatami took over, he replaced Amrollahi with the efficient Qolam-Reza Aqazadeh-Khoi, who in turn replaced many personnel with true technical experts. In addition, because after Khatami's election there had been so strong an expectation that change in Iran was inevitable and that therefore the threat from Iran had greatly diminished, it became much harder for the United States to convince other countries not to make these highly lucrative sales to Iran.

Two other factors also seem to have influenced the relative surge in Iran's progress on nuclear weapons. First, the country's finances were more limited during the 1990s as a result of lower oil prices, a greater debt burden, and a somewhat greater impact by U.S. sanctions. By 2000, higher oil prices meant greater revenues. In addition, most of the Pakistani cooperation and transfer of materials to Iran occurred in the early and mid-1990s, and it appears that these were not fully digested by the Iranian nuclear program until the late 1990s. For instance, it is one thing to get designs or even samples for a centrifuge plant; it is another to actually have the plant ready and the centrifuges built—and personnel trained to operate them properly. All of this only seems to have borne fruit at the end of the 1990s and the start of the twenty-first century.[48]

Iran was a charter member of the Non-Proliferation Treaty (NPT) in 1970 because the shah had been eager to build a network of nuclear power plants and the United States would sell them only to countries that had signed the treaty. This meant that Iran came under the rules and regulations of the NPT and was monitored by the International Atomic Energy Agency (IAEA). The Iranians had always denied that they had a weapons program, and though Western intelligence agencies had determined that they were lying, the Iranian program was believed to be so rudimentary that it did not require very much to keep it hidden from the IAEA—thereby explaining why no one had found more evidence of Iranian progress. Thus it was a great shock to find that the Iranians were much closer to building nuclear weapons than anyone had imagined—as great a shock as when the world learned after the Gulf War that Iraq had been only six to twenty-four months from having a functional nuclear weapon.

In response to these revelations, the IAEA began a much more intrusive investigation of Iranian nuclear activities. Neither the uranium enrichment facility nor the heavy-water plant constituted incontrovertible proof of a nuclear weapons program because it is possible to use either plutonium or enriched uranium in civilian reactors. However, the fact that these facilities and a great deal of other activity had not been declared to the IAEA made it clear that they were for military purposes; there was no other plausible reason for having concealed them. In addition, Iran's well-known plans to acquire nuclear reactors for civilian purposes (at least ostensibly) did not require either the capability to enrich uranium domestically or to extract plutonium. The Iranians insisted that they were not trying to acquire nuclear weapons, but they could not provide a plausible explanation either for having concealed the plants or for why they needed such capabilities.[49]

At the end of February 2003, the IAEA inspected the Natanz facility[50] and not only confirmed what the intelligence from the NCR had already claimed but made a series of other discoveries as well. It found 160 centrifuges assembled into a pilot program. In another building, a thousand additional centrifuges were being assembled at a facility intended to have 50,000 of them. (That would have been enough to produce fissile material for roughly twenty-five to fifty nuclear weapons per year.) The centrifuges at Natanz were identical to those used by the Pakistanis, and in 2004, A. Q. Khan would admit to having provided extensive support to Iran.[51] The IAEA found traces of enriched uranium hexafluoride (the feedstock used for enrichment) in the centrifuges, indicating that the centrifuges had been used to enrich uranium, which would have violated Iran's Safeguards Agreement with the IAEA, part of its NPT commitments.[52] The fact that Iran had imported centrifuges without notifying the IAEA was a violation of its Safeguards Agreement. The inspectors also found uranium from two different countries. This forced the Iranians to admit that they had acquired nearly two tons of slightly refined uranium (called "yellowcake") from China; uranium hexafluoride and uranium in two other, lesser stages of refinement, from another foreign supplier (Pakistan); and had decided to start mining uranium from their own indigenous sources. The Iranians also admitted to having a laser isotope separation program, which is yet another way to enrich uranium. Finally, the Iranians informed the IAEA that they were building a plant near Isfahan that would convert yellowcake into uranium hexafluoride. Since actually enriching any uranium hexafluoride would have violated their Safeguards Agreement, the Iranians claimed that they had not performed any enrichment or even testing, which not even the IAEA found believable.[53]

Not only were Iran's various explanations for all of this activity unconvincing, they completely contradicted its earlier claims. Nor could the Iranians explain why they needed to produce and enrich uranium domestically when they purportedly had plans only for reactors in which the fuel was to be provided by the Russians and then returned to Russia when it was spent. There was also the inconsistency that Iran's uranium deposits were large enough to make several nuclear weapons but not large enough to fuel even one reactor over its lifetime; thus indigenous production was extremely difficult to square with a peaceful energy program. Altogether, the IAEA found five different areas in which Iran was in violation of its Safeguards Agreement and potentially in violation of the NPT itself, plus a host of other activities that, while not actual violations, were deeply troubling.[54]

Based on this series of disturbing findings, the IAEA issued a set of requests to Iran. It asked the Iranians to answer all of its questions regarding the country's nuclear program, and to do so honestly without all the changes, contradictions, and tall tales they had told the inspectors in February. It also requested that Iran agree to sign the Additional Protocol to the NPT (which had been developed some years before), which would require the Iranians to provide more information when they were going to take any steps on nuclear matters, and to allow surprise inspections of any site that the IAEA wanted to look at. The NPT itself provided for inspections only of declared facilities, which is why the IAEA had never seen the Natanz centrifuge plant before. In addition, it called on Iran to halt its uranium enrichment activities, which had no clear tie to Iran's existing nuclear energy plans.[55] The IAEA warned Iran that if it did not comply with these requests by October 31, it would declare Tehran in violation of the NPT and refer the matter to the U.N. Security Council—with the implicit threat that the Security Council would impose penalties on Iran of some kind.

This galvanized the Europeans into action. Nuclear proliferation, like human rights abuses, is an area that their populations take somewhat seriously. At the very least, the European governments feared that if the IAEA declared Iran in violation of the NPT, it would make it hard for them to maintain high levels of trade with Tehran. The British, French, and Germans organized a diplomatic effort to try to persuade the Iranians to comply with the requests of the IAEA. At no time during these negotiations did the Europeans threaten the Iranians with sanctions. However, they did suggest that if Iran did not comply, they probably would be unable to continue to expand their commercial relations with Iran. They may also have suggested that Iran would likely have difficulty with international financial institutions and with its application to join the WTO. In other words, there were no sticks, but they suggested that the carrots would be smaller, and they actually did back up their words by suspending talks to expand trade with the Iranians until all of the nuclear matters had been cleared up.[56]

This seemed ominous to the Iranians. They had not seen the Europeans actually take any step that would have affected their trade with Iran in recent memory. Moreover, having seen European publics respond more harshly to Iran than their governments had wanted, and knowing that the Americans were again pushing for international sanctions, the Iranians feared that the Europeans would agree to sanctions if the IAEA declared Iran in violation and referred the matter to the Security Council. Of course, Tehran had no intention of stopping its nuclear program and said so endlessly in public. Indeed, in the fall of 2003, it seemed more determined than ever to acquire nuclear weapons as the only sure way to prevent the United States from invading Iran the same way it had Afghanistan and Iraq. Nevertheless, the Iranians did not want to suffer the damage to their economy that multilateral trade sanctions would cause. Consequently, in the fall of 2003, shortly before the deadline, the Iranians agreed to the IAEA's conditions; but they agreed only to the IAEA's conditions, not to the more general American demands that they halt their program altogether and for good. Specifically, Tehran agreed to temporarily halt its uranium enrichment program, but not to do so permanently. It also agreed both to provide more information and to sign the Additional Protocol, which did not prevent Iran either from developing the capability to enrich uranium or even from actually enriching it; the Additional Protocol simply granted the IAEA greater access and ability to keep track of Iran's activities.[57]

At this point, the Iranians had two choices as to how they could proceed in their drive to acquire a nuclear weapon. The first was the "Iraqi route" of hiding what they could, lying, telling only part of the truth, delaying and otherwise hindering inspections, and then giving just enough to avoid negative consequences whenever the international community got mad enough to start considering sanctions or other punitive measures. The other was to pursue a nuclear weapon transparently. Unfortunately, the NPT has proven itself to be a terribly flawed document, largely because it was created in the spirit of the faulty logic of "atoms for peace," which sought to block countries from acquiring nuclear weapons while enabling them to acquire nuclear energy capabilities. The problem is that the capability to do the latter is a tremendous help for a country trying to do the former. A number of unscrupulous states, including Iraq, Libya, and North Korea, have availed themselves of this route. The NPT permits a country to acquire every step in the difficult processes of uranium enrichment and plutonium extraction. All that it prevents is taking actual finished fissile material and loading it into a bomb. The problem for those who would like to prevent proliferation is that once a country has the fissile material, it is virtually impossible to stop it from putting it in a bomb or even knowing whether it has done so if it chooses not to demonstrate the capability. Pakistan (which never signed the NPT) denied that it had manufactured the fissile material, let alone loaded it into weapons, right up until the day in 1998 that it detonated its first nuclear weapon.

For the Iranians, the one problem with the transparent approach was that they feared (and still do) that if all of their nuclear facilities were overt, the United States and/or Israel could mount a military strike against them. However, there was an answer here too, and it came from mixing elements of the clandestine and transparent routes. Iran would take the "transparent" step of declaring a number of facilities capable of developing the entire cycle of processes needed to make fissile material (called the "fuel cycle"). This would provide the cover story for its imports, for the enrichment activities the IAEA would inevitably detect, and for its other nuclear-weapons-related activities. At the same time, it would silently hold out the threat to the United States and Israel that it had other hidden facilities, like Natanz and Arak, so that neither Washington nor Jerusalem could feel certain that if it launched a military strike it would be able to destroy Iran's entire program.

Ultimately, all Iran really had to do was play for time. As long as the IAEA did not declare it in violation of the NPT, the matter was unlikely to be brought before the Security Council. The only thing that Iran was seriously in jeopardy of "violating" within the NPT was its obligation to tell the IAEA what it was doing and allow the IAEA to observe its work. So as long as Iran remained transparent about at least part of the program and was able to keep the IAEA from finding the parts that were to be kept hidden, it would be able to keep working on its capability without risk of sanctions. Since Iran has natural uranium deposits and had opened a uranium mine, once it had the complete fuel cycle it would be entirely self-sufficient. At that point, no one would be able to prevent it from acquiring a nuclear weapon by cutting off the flow of nuclear materials. And once it had the capability to enrich enough uranium to make a bomb, no other state would know whether it had done so.

In keeping with this mixed approach, in June 2004, the Iranians notified the IAEA that they had decided to test their new facility to convert yellowcake into uranium hexafluoride. Again, this was all perfectly legal under the NPT, even though it violated Iran's promises both to the European group and to the IAEA. Of course, even there the Iranians pointed out that they had always said that their suspension was only temporary. At the same time, there were also clues of Iran's continuing efforts to keep other parts of its program hidden. In February and again in June 2004, the IAEA acknowledged finding traces of highly enriched uranium (some nearly weapons grade) at two more facilities in Iran. The Iranians again claimed that the centrifuges on which the traces were found had been imported and that the traces had been left by the previous owner.[58] Although this was a plausible explanation (and was later confirmed by the IAEA), it indicated that Iran was still concealing some things—such as the fact that it had bought centrifuges from some other country, likely Pakistan, although it still refused to say. The United Nations also discovered that Iran had produced polonium 210, a short-lived, unstable element whose only real use is as an initiator for nuclear weapons (although the Iranians claimed it was for nuclear batteries to be used in satellites and deep-space exploration, neither of which they have). The Iranians also continued to dissemble on a range of other issues and delayed the IAEA from conducting several inspections, which seriously hampered its work. In many cases, they were caught in outright lies by the IAEA. As a result, in June 2004, the IAEA Board of Governors adopted a resolution condemning Iran for failing to provide the requisite information, for obstructing inspections, and for not suspending its uranium enrichment process as promised. It did not, however, recommend referring the matter to the Security Council.[59] Like the Iraqis early on, the Iranians had a lot to learn about how to deceive international inspectors—who themselves had become much savvier, having been fooled by the Iraqis in the past. But also like Iraq, U.N. agencies were reluctant to actually declare them in breach of their obligations.[60]

What was most remarkable about all of this was the muted response from the United States. The clock was counting down on the window of opportunity in which the international community could prevent Iran from acquiring nuclear weapons. At some point, it would finish construction on its various sites and acquire all of the equipment and know-how it needed to have an indigenous fuel cycle. Clearly, the best time to stop an Iranian nuclear program was before Iran became self-sufficient. Since the Bush administration and all of its predecessors since Reagan had regarded an Iranian nuclear weapons capability as a nightmare, it was widely expected that the activist Bush administration would go on the offensive on this matter as well. The Israelis were outraged and made their fear and anger known to every American official, former official, and opinion leader they could find. Israel claimed in 2003 that the Iranians might be as little as a year away from having a fully self-sufficient fuel cycle.

Yet, for an administration frequently criticized as overly responsive to Israel's concerns and one so passionately committed to keeping "the worst weapons" out of the hands of "the worst people," the Bush administration was remarkably low key about Iran's nuclear program. While it talked tough, it did little. Ultimately, Washington opted to leave it to the Europeans to handle Iran. Here as well, for an administration that was also frequently criticized as overly "unilateral" in its conduct of foreign policy, this went beyond mere multilateralism to an abdication of American interests to foreign powers that had not exactly shown a great deal of responsibility or attentiveness to American concerns about this issue in the past.[61]

Once again, the principal problem on the American side seems to have been the internal divisions within the Bush administration. Some of the administration's hawks wanted to take a much more aggressive posture on Iranian nuclear activities, just as they did on its flirtation with al-Qa'eda. Indeed, some wanted to try to mount an effort to overthrow the Iranian government via covert action or even launch military strikes against the Iranian facilities. The doves in the administration wanted to try to solve the problem through diplomacy, which mostly meant assisting the European effort. But three other factors intervened. First, after four years of fighting these battles, both sides were weary; however, rather than give in to the other side, they simply deferred the issue altogether. Second, Iraq was a major distraction, not only in the sense of being a drain on the time, attention, and energy of the senior policy makers in Washington, but also because it was soaking up the lion's share of America's military forces, diplomatic capital, and economic assistance funds. There was very little of any of these items left for another major problem such as Iran. And third, Iran was a very difficult conundrum. No one in the administration had a great answer as to how to convince the Iranians to halt their nuclear program, and the result was that the default policy became one of diplomatic pressure on the Europeans to persuade Iran to give up the nuclear program, coupled with some vague but threatening rhetoric.[62]

As far as the Iranians were concerned, their agreement with the Europeans had been intended to prevent a negative report by the IAEA. It is unclear why they believed this, but they did. They may have assumed that the Europeans could somehow sway the IAEA's Board of Governors regardless of what the inspectors themselves might report. The fact that they had gotten such a negative report, and been condemned by the Board of Governors on top of it, negated the deal with the Europeans, in their view. Of greater importance, however, the Iranians appear to have become convinced that they would not suffer real penalties if they reverted to the transparent approach. Apparently, they had heard enough reassurances from the Europeans that they would not be sanctioned to actually believe it. The strange passivity of the United States undoubtedly also persuaded them that America was not looking to start another round of confrontation with Iran. In particular, by mid-2004, Tehran had concluded that the United States was badly bogged down in Iraq and therefore was not to be feared. Indeed, the Iranians may have assumed that since the Americans needed them to continue to be helpful in Iraq, it was unlikely that Washington would pick a fight with them over the nuclear (or terrorism) issue. All of this made Iran bold, and at the end of July 2004, Tehran announced that it had resumed building centrifuges and resumed production of uranium hexafluoride, and that while it had still not started enriching uranium, it fully intended to do so.[63]

Iran's China Model

Something else that may have given Iran's principal leadership the gumption to confront the United States and the world so boldly was a series of further dramatic moves on Iran's domestic political scene. The period following Khatami's pyrrhic reelection in 2001 saw the hard-liners regain almost complete control over the Iranian state, which doubtless gave them considerable confidence in their foreign policy dealings. However, their battle with the reformists had revealed to Tehran's hard-line clerical establishment that it needed to rethink the nature of its relationship with Iran's larger society.

Although the reformists were ever more powerless, Iran was not the same country that it had been before 1997. In 2002, there were student riots to protest a death sentence for apostasy handed down to a popular university professor (a disabled veteran of the Iran-Iraq War, at that) who had suggested that Iranians should think harder about their own vision of Islam and should not accept the words of the mullahs unquestioningly. After several days, Khamene'i ordered Iran's Supreme Court to review the verdict to try to defuse tensions, and they overturned it (it was later reinstated). Meanwhile, forty students who had led the protests were sentenced to everything from fifty lashes to prison time to expulsion.[64] During the summer of 2003, there were more protests, which began in response to government plans to privatize some universities but quickly grew into more general demonstrations against the regime. The protests lasted nearly a week, and the protesters were repeatedly attacked by Hizballahis, Basijis, and other hard-line thugs. Reports put the number arrested at 4,000. What was perhaps most significant about these demonstrations was that the protesters were as angry at Khatami for having betrayed the reformist movement as they were against Khamene'i and other hard-liners.[65] The reformist paper *Tose'eh* observed, "In previous years, the people still had hope in the reformists within the state, but, today, far from having hope in them, their main protests are directed at the reformists."[66] As always, the hard-liners insisted that the attacks had been inspired by the United States, and President Bush's comment that "it's the beginnings of people expressing themselves toward a free Iran, which I think is positive" only enraged them further. The spokesman for the Iranian Ministry of Foreign Affairs complained that this and other mild American statements about the riots constituted "irresponsible intervention in the domestic affairs of the Islamic Republic of Iran."[67]

As worrisome as these protests might sound, they were not a real threat to the regime. "Restive students . . . those who might lead an internal rebellion, remain few and have repeatedly failed to turn their street demonstrations into a broad-based opposition movement," Geneive Abdo, the former *Guardian* Tehran correspondent, wrote at the time. "Simply put, there is no viable alternative on the horizon."[68] The spirit of the reformist political parties had been broken, and without their organizational abilities, it was extremely difficult for the students to turn their protests into a larger revolt.[69] The memory of the brutal repression of the 1999 riots was also an important restraint on the students, as was their inability to mobilize the kind of mass support that they had in 1979 or might have had in 1999 if Khatami had leapt into the fray. The regime was able to handle the 2002 and 2003 protests mostly with irregulars—Hizballahis, Basijis, and the like—coupled with a limited number of LEF and no Pasdars, representing only a fraction of the forces available to it. In addition, while America's popularity continued to rise, many Iranians still bristled at any suggestion that the United States was interfering in Iran's internal affairs, and even Washington's rather subdued statements seemed to provide some evidence for these charges.[70]

Yet the regime recognized that it had serious problems. The increase in oil prices provided a temporary alleviation of popular grievances about the economy, but it still could not solve the problems of education and unemployment that were the core sources of weakness in the Iranian economy. Meanwhile, the populace continued to demand change. The riots may not have threatened the regime, but they certainly did not help it, and the principal leadership appears to have recognized that if the current trend were allowed to continue, it might face real threats at some point in the future. By 2003, 60 percent of Iran's population was under twenty-five years of age, and 70 percent was under thirty. That suggested that the problems could grow worse in the future, not better.[71] In response, the regime consciously adopted what was for it a radically different approach: it would back off on social controls and allow the people to dress and act more as they pleased, while clamping down hard on the political front. The Iranian leaders expected that this, coupled with the temporary boost to Iran's economy from the higher oil prices, would release some of the pressure for real change. They would then use the time this afforded them to fix the Iranian economy in a more permanent fashion, which they believed would allow them to continue to hold power well into the future. In effect, they were (explicitly) taking a page from China's book, at least as they saw it. And like the Chinese, the Iranian leadership hoped to redirect the energy, frustration, and political aspirations of their enormous youth population into social activities and even hedonistic pursuits, making it clear that young people would be allowed to express themselves and enjoy themselves to a much greater extent in this environment than if they chose to be active in the political scene—where the regime would now tolerate no dissent.

This was a brutally and radically pragmatic move by the hard-liners. Iranian social behavior had been one of the most important elements of the revolution to Khomeini and a cherished aspect of his legacy to the old radicals. Nevertheless, it revealed the true nature of the regime in a manner that had never been seen before. The principal leadership was interested in only one thing: maintaining its hold on power. Apparently the hard-liners were willing to betray what had formerly been one of the most important principles of their ideology, that Iranian society should act as a strictly Muslim society (based on their narrow definition of what it means to be a Muslim society). As a result, 2003–2004 witnessed the hitherto unknown spectacle of increasing hard-line dominance in the political realm coupled with decreasing societal restrictions. Veils fell farther and farther back on women's heads. Manteaus (the long coat worn by most women rather than a true chador) got tighter and tighter, and many of them developed slits up to the waist and beyond. Women began wearing more makeup and jewelry in public. Couples could be caught kissing in semipublic spots. Young men and women held hands on the street more frequently and lived together before they were married. The Hizballahis and Basijis stopped raiding parties (or more frequently accepted small bribes when they did so), nor did they confiscate satellite dishes as ruthlessly as they once had. People spoke about whatever they wanted, although they still generally avoided politics in front of "the authorities." However, the forced quality of this sudden blossoming was reflected in accompanying problems such as a massive surge in drug and alcohol addiction and sudden increases in out-of-wedlock pregnancies (always hushed up). All of the energies of Iran's young were being forced into the sphere of social hedonism, and while that provided many with some immediate gratification, it did not address their deeper frustrations with an economy that could not guarantee them a job or a decent living (let alone a prestigious or rewarding career), and a political system that treated them as chattel.[72]

The final proof of this came during the Majles elections of 2004. The Supreme Leader, the judiciary, and the Council of Guardians had made sure that the reformist-dominated Majles had not been able to exercise any real power since it had taken power in 2000. However, the Majles was still problematic because the reformists successfully used it as a bully pulpit to disseminate their positions to the country and the world. As far as the hard-liners were concerned, that had to end. Having repeatedly crushed student protests, and with the reformist political parties thoroughly cowed, the hard-liners also felt confident enough in their position to act brazenly and put an end to the reformists' ability to capitalize on their regular successes in the polls to keep the movement alive within the government.

One month prior to the February elections, the Council of Guardians began disqualifying candidates with abandon. Ultimately, about 2,500 (out of 8,000 who applied) were rejected, nearly all of them members of various reformist organizations. Most outrageous of all, in a move reminiscent of Khamene'i and Rafsanjani's disgraceful activities during the 1992 elections, 87 sitting reformist members of the Parliament were barred from running for reelection. Even Khatami's brother and sister-in-law (who is also Khomeini's granddaughter) were disqualified.[73] A number of cabinet ministers and vice presidents resigned in protest, along with one third of the Majles deputies. More than 1,100 candidates who had been approved withdrew their candidacies to show solidarity with those rejected. Many of the major reformist parties urged their followers to boycott the elections. None of it mattered. The Council did make some token gestures, but nothing that came close to restoring any fairness to the election. The various hard-line thugs harassed and hindered the few reformists left in the pool of candidates, and there were other charges of vote rigging. Not surprisingly, voter turnout barely topped 50 percent, the lowest in any national election since 1979, and the hard-liners "won" 156 out of the 240 seats decided in the first round.[74] Although neither the Americans nor the Europeans raised much more than a whisper in protest, Ayatollah Khamene'i proclaimed, "The losers in this election are the United States, Zionism and the enemies of the Iranian nation."[75]

Déjà Vu

By 2003–2004, Western observers of Iran had the frustrating sense that Washington and Tehran were right back where they had started from so many times before. The hard-liners were firmly in charge in Tehran and were supporting terrorist operations, pursuing nuclear weapons, and advocating violent opposition to a Middle East peace. The U.S. government was worried about Iran's behavior, but not so worried as to make a determined effort to do something about it one way or the other. Washington maintained its sanctions on Iran and continued to urge others not to sell Iran weapons or nuclear-related materials, and to impose sanctions of their own to turn up the economic heat on Tehran. Pragmatists in Iran and doves in America hoped to start a rapprochement, and one poll found that 70 percent of Iranians thought that dialogue with the United States was a good idea. But the two states were simply too far apart on too many fundamental issues—particularly because of the continuing role of the United States in Iran's revolutionary ideology—for anything to come of it.[76]

So many elements of the period from 2001 to 2004 seemed terribly familiar. An American administration that started with little interest in Iran. A flirtation between the two as pragmatists on either side found that there were interests in common. Iran's continuing determination to support terrorism, oppose a Middle East peace with violence, and acquire nuclear weapons—coupled with innate anti-Americanism—wrecking any chances of rapprochement. An American administration forced to confront Iran but facing few attractive options. A president declaring a "get-tough" policy toward Iran that had little substance but still enraged Tehran. Iran's hard-liners cracking down hard on domestic dissent. We have seen this movie several times before, and the ending never seems to get any better.

To be sure, there were also important differences, as there had been in previous iterations. Never before had postrevolutionary Iran been so willing to help the United States as it had in Afghanistan and Iraq. At the very least, this demonstrated a remarkable degree of pragmatism in foreign affairs, well beyond what Iran had demonstrated in the past, if only because it was pragmatism directed at the United States—the one foreign policy issue that had always seemed exempt from practical demands in the minds of Iran's hard-line leadership. Likewise, never before had Iran's hard-liners recognized that they might have to abandon key aspects of Khomeini's legacy to preserve their power as they had in relaxing Iran's social restrictions. On the one hand, this suggested that if they were willing to give up on rigid social rules, perhaps the mullahs might also be willing to give up their anti-Americanism. However, it could equally be the case that giving up the one may only be temporary (until they have solidified their political power and revived Iran's economy) or that giving up on the one will make them even more desperately attached to the latter as the last vestige of Khomeini's legacy. As has been so often the case with Iran over the years, no one could tell—not even the Iranians themselves.

CHAPTER 13

Toward a New Iran Policy

The history of U.S.-Iranian relations holds many lessons for the future conduct of American policy, along with one important warning: there is no easy solution to America's problems with Iran. Iran is a deeply troubled nation torn between the remnants of an impractical ideology and the economic, political, and social problems created by a dysfunctional government. The fact that Iran's ideology and political system have caused the most harm to its own people is small solace for other nations. These problems, coupled with the long, unpleasant history of U.S.-Iranian relations going back over fifty years, make devising any solution to America's differences with Iran complicated and painful. Unfortunately, we have no choice but to brace ourselves and accept the challenge.

Because devising a policy to deal with Iran is so difficult, virtually every American administration since the Iranian Revolution has started off trying to minimize its involvement with Tehran while simultaneously trying to minimize Iran's ability to cause problems for the United States. Virtually every one of those administrations found that ignoring Iran was impossible and over time was forced to become more deeply involved—usually in a negative sense—with the Iranians. As seductive as it might sound to wash our hands of the problem of Iran, history has taught that it is a mistake to do so, and today more than ever.

The United States no longer has the luxury of considering a purely passive approach to Tehran, nor can we simply wait for the Iranians to do something and then devise an ad hoc response. Iran is on the wrong path and marching down it quickly. The great problem that looms before us is Iran's nuclear program. Although our fifteen years of experience misestimating the Iraqi WMD programs should make us wary when trying to ascertain how close Iran might be to acquiring nuclear weapons, there seems to be little doubt that Tehran is determined to do so (or at least to acquire the capability to produce the weapons on short notice, which from a strategic perspective is effectively the same thing) and further along than anyone thought. While the IAEA process has done a reasonable job in exposing Iran's efforts to acquire nuclear weapons, it does not lend itself to stopping the Iranian program. If the Iranian program is to be halted, the United States will have to lead an international effort to do so.

The Trouble with Tehran

Over the past twenty years, the United States has tended to focus on four principal concerns regarding Iran: its support of and participation in international terrorism, its violent opposition to forging a just peace between Arabs and Israelis, its pursuit of weapons of mass destruction (primarily nuclear weapons), and its record of human rights abuses at home. All of these remain issues for the United States. None of them deserves to be dropped or ignored. However, there is also a clear, and increasingly important, hierarchy of U.S. interests, especially since the revelations of 2002–2004. America's greatest problem with Iran today, and likely for some time into the future, is Iran's aggressive pursuit of nuclear weapons. The nuclear issue is the most important both because of the concern that Iran may acquire these weapons fairly soon and because of the impact it could have on the other three issues.

Tehran's drive to acquire nuclear weapons creates two different threats to the vital interests of the United States. The first and most direct is the threat that if Iran acquires a nuclear deterrent it will believe that it is no longer vulnerable to American conventional military retaliation and so can revert to the same aggressive, anti-American foreign policy it pursued in the early 1990s.[1] Iran abandoned this policy in 1996 because Tehran sensed that it had overstepped. The Mykonos verdict, ILSA, the GCC's response to its attempted coup in Bahrain, the international reaction to its successful effort to swing the Israeli election against Shimon Peres via terrorism, and the Khobar Towers attack created the potential for a severe backlash against Iran. In particular, Khobar raised the possibility of a massive American military retaliation. Many Iranians have suggested that they want nuclear weapons so that they never again have to fear such an American retaliation.[2] If that is the case, it could mean that they will see fewer (perhaps no) obstacles to resuming their efforts to drive the United States out of the region with terrorist attacks, subvert or dominate the Gulf states, attack Israel and the conservative Arab states of the region, and forge a new alliance with other radical anti–status quo nations and terrorist groups.

A strong argument can be made that this strategy is most consistent with Khomeini's legacy and most comfortable for his hard-line heirs who are now once again fully in control in Tehran. It is hardly a certainty that Iran would revert to its former, offensive foreign policy, but it certainly cannot be ruled out. During the Cold War, few thought it likely that the Russians would try to invade Western Europe, but the catastrophic consequences if they did so forced NATO to take the risk far more seriously than mere probability would have dictated. So too with the risk that nuclear weapons would embolden Iran to resume its past aggressiveness.

The second problem is the spur of Iranian nuclear development to further proliferation, both in the region and around the world. Because many countries fear that once Iran acquires nuclear weapons it will pursue an aggressive foreign policy, if and when Tehran crosses the nuclear threshold other Middle Eastern countries, particularly Saudi Arabia, might decide to follow suit to deter an Iranian attack, either covert or overt. Those outside the region that are considering whether to acquire nuclear weapons could draw the lesson from the Iranian case (and the North Korean and Pakistani cases as well) that the penalties for developing a nuclear weapon are bearable—and much less than they might have feared.

Proliferation is always worrisome because it increases the number of potentially dangerous states with unquestionably dangerous weapons, but proliferation by itself is not necessarily a *threat*. It becomes a threat only when a state acquiring nuclear weapons is dangerous, aggressive, and difficult to deter. Over the past three or four decades, the United States has been willing to accept a half-dozen or more countries—including India and Pakistan—acquiring nuclear weapons because Washington did not see them as dangerous, nor has Pakistan's accession to the nuclear "club" proved to be much of a spur to other countries, with the mild exception of Iran (whose principal motives were the American and Iraqi threats, not the Pakistani threat). Likewise, France's acquisition of nuclear weapons did not prompt any further proliferation because France was not seen as a threat to any other country. Nor did it require the United States to radically alter its policy to try to deter or contain France once it acquired nuclear weapons. In contrast, one of the strongest justifications for toppling Saddam Hussein's regime was that he was precisely such a dangerous, aggressive, and hard-to-deter leader, who was (mistakenly) believed to be close to acquiring nuclear weapons.[3] Saddam's acquisition of nuclear weapons would have constituted a major spur to further proliferation precisely because he was such a threat to the stability of the Gulf region. However, Saddam was exceptional: few world leaders or national leaderships are as aggressive, risk tolerant, and difficult to deter as he was. Ayatollah Khomeini would have fallen into that same category, but he does not rule Iran any longer.

Thus the greatest problem lies in the present regime acquiring nuclear weapons. This regime has demonstrated that it is aggressive, anti–status quo, anti-American, and willing to employ a host of reprehensible methods (such as terrorism) to try to accomplish its goals. While it may be possible to live with such a regime after it has acquired nuclear weapons, most non-Iranians would prefer not to have to try to do so, if it could be avoided.

The corollary to this argument is that there is an expectation that a new Iranian regime, led by the reformists or otherwise reflecting the actual aspirations of the Iranian people, would not be nearly as threatening.[4] This seems likely, but is hardly a certainty. First of all, there is considerable debate as to whether such a government would even want nuclear weapons. Most Iranians have an outsize impression of their nation's importance and, in the abstract, probably would be proud to have nuclear weapons, regarding them as giving Iran a status they believe it deserves. Likewise, many reformists are former radicals who have reconciled themselves to greater domestic freedom and the need for economic revival but still cling to Khomeini's line on foreign policy; they too would doubtless press for continued acquisition of nuclear weapons even within a reformist-dominated government. However, it seems far more likely that given the priorities of the mainstream reformers on political, economic, and social reform, such a new government could be persuaded to give up its nuclear program in return for economic benefits. This also squares with both the strong push by Khatami and others around him for improved relations with the United States and their private recognition that such an improvement would require them to accommodate Washington on the nuclear issue.[5] For this reason as well, it seems more likely than not that a new government in Tehran would drastically reduce the threat to the United States and its allies even if it were to acquire nuclear weapons.

Of equal or greater importance, it seems highly unlikely that if the reformists somehow took power in Tehran they would pursue an aggressive, anti-American foreign policy. Undoubtedly, some former radicals might argue for such an approach, but the country's need for foreign investment and trade, entry into the WTO and other international economic regimes, and an end to American and other foreign sanctions would likely trump all other considerations. A pragmatic focus on Iran's economic, political, and social needs—one that ruthlessly trumps all other considerations of dogma—has been the hall-mark of the mainstream reformist movement, and while many in a reformist government might continue to dislike the United States, they probably would be unwilling or unable to make such counterproductive emotions the basis of policy, as the hard-liners have since 1979. Weak as the evidence is all around, it does seem likely that if the reformists could somehow take power in Tehran (the biggest "if" of all), then—as Khatami's informal interlocutors told the Clinton administration—they would be willing to make compromises on their nuclear program in return for expanded economic ties. None of this is certain, of course, and so it should temper discussions of American policy toward Iran, but not determine their course.

Iranian involvement in international terrorism is certainly an issue of con-cern as well, but by itself it is not an overriding threat to the United States. Iran has not mounted a terrorist attack against the United States since 1996. Leba-nese Hizballah is a terrorist threat to our Israeli ally but not to the United States; Hizballah has only ever attacked the United States on Tehran's orders.[6] Moreover, since Israel withdrew from Lebanon in 2000, Hizballah too has mostly ceased direct attacks on Israel, and now the greatest problem it causes Israel is through its support to the Palestinian terrorist groups HAMAS and PIJ. The other terrorist groups that Iran supports—including PIJ, HAMAS, the anti-Turkish PKK, and others—are focused on specific targets and have never attacked the United States. Moreover, Iran's response to Khobar Towers is a critical piece of evidence: faced with the threat of American military retalia-tion, Iran backed away from its terrorist operations against the United States. Here as well, the main problem is if the Iranians believe (as Saddam report-edly did) that possession of nuclear weapons would preclude such an Ameri-can retaliation, thereby freeing them to mount a terrorist campaign against the United States without fear of any repercussions. Thus, the real threat from Iranian terrorism is how the Iranian leadership might approach it once it has nuclear weapons.

Whatever Tehran is up to with al-Qa'eda is certainly worrisome but is also almost certainly tactical in nature and temporary in duration. The Iranians have enough stored hatred for al-Qa'eda that it seems unlikely they would forge a strategic alliance with them—unless the United States launched a full-scale assault on Iran, either covertly or militarily, in which case the Iranians would undoubtedly ally with anyone who could hurt us. Getting Tehran to give up the al-Qa'eda personnel in Iran should not be overly difficult, given its will-ingness to swap them for the MEK, but will require our willingness to make such a deal, and so far, Washington has not been willing to do so because administration hawks continue to entertain the notion that the MEK might prove useful in a policy of regime change. At worst, the United States could (and should) lay down a red line that Iran will be held responsible for any al-Qa'eda attack in which U.S. intelligence determines a connection between the attack and those still in Iran. Given Iran's reluctance to provoke an American military strike for its own terrorist attacks, it is likely that it would be even less willing to run such a risk on behalf of al-Qa'eda. Again, the only real question is whether their acquisition of nuclear weapons would prompt the Iranians to disregard the threat of American retaliation.

It will certainly be important to reduce or even eliminate Iranian support for the Palestinian terrorist groups opposing Middle East peace, but to some extent this is dependent on progress on the peace process. The Middle East peace process broke down at the end of the 1990s not because of Iranian opposition but because the Israelis and Palestinians could not overcome their differences. Whether you prefer to blame Yasser Arafat or Ariel Sharon for its collapse, the fact remains that it was largely brought about by factors internal to itself, not by Iranian actions from the outside—damaging and painful though these were. If the United States could eliminate Iranian support for Palestinian terrorist groups overnight, this alone would not revive the peace process. Moreover, even cutting off Iranian support would not strangle PIJ, HAMAS, and Hizballah, all of which could still count on Syrian support. And even without Syria, PIJ and HAMAS would doubtless be able to survive based on nothing but Palestinian animosity to Israel and their ability to buy arms on the international black market and smuggle them into the West Bank and Gaza. Ending Iran's violent opposition to Middle East peace is absolutely necessary to its success and should remain a cause for the United States, but doing so would not be sufficient to see the revival—let alone the conclusion—of comprehensive peace talks. At least until there is a viable new peace process (and arguably even then), Iran's violent opposition to a Middle East peace is not nearly as threatening to the United States as its nuclear ambitions.

Another potential menace to American interests is the possibility that at some point, Iran might choose to actively fight the American reconstruction efforts in Iraq. Because of the extent of Iranian influence and presence in Iraq, this could have devastating consequences. The example of 1980s Lebanon, where the Pasdaran and Hizballah learned their trade, should reinforce our determination to avoid this. Indeed, for as long as the United States remains intensely committed to Iraq's reconstruction, we must consider Iranian support for (or at least no active Iranian opposition to) that effort as a critical fifth issue in U.S.-Iranian relations, along with terrorism, WMD, human rights, and the

Middle East peace process. The skill of the Iranian attack on the Fallujah police station in November 2003 suggests how dangerous a foe Iran could be in Iraq if it chose to be. America's challenges in Iraq are great enough with Iran being mostly supportive of our efforts; if Iran were to turn against us, those problems would increase dramatically, perhaps even insurmountably. Of course, Iraq (and Afghanistan) are two-way streets: Iran needs the United States to stabilize those countries to prevent them from sliding into chaos, so it has every incentive to continue to be supportive of American efforts, as long as those efforts are aimed at building a stable, pluralist, and independent Iraq. As with Iran's flirtation with al-Qa'eda, the greatest danger lies in the United States declaring war on Iran, figuratively or literally, in which case Iran's incentive to avoid problems in Iraq would evaporate.

Last on this list are Iran's human rights violations. Amnesty International, Human Rights Watch, and other organizations continue to document cases of arbitrary arrest, torture, excessive punishments for ridiculous "crimes," summary executions, political killings, the use of other forms of violence against regime dissidents, and other domestic manifestations of state terrorism.[7] This is to be deplored, and the United States should continue to criticize Iran's human rights practices and press the regime to change its ways. However, Iran's human rights abuses do not rise to a level that demands extreme forms of intervention by the United States or the international community. Another compelling argument for war with Iraq in 2003 was the human rights argument—the fact that Saddam was among the worst tyrants of the late twentieth century and that 20,000 to 30,000 Iraqis died each year on average during his reign. Iran does not come close to this level of slaughter. Even the most savage acts of the Iranian regime pale by comparison to Saddam's Anfal campaign against the Kurds, his destruction of the marshes of southern Iraq, and his brutal suppression of the Shi'i-Kurdish intifadah of 1991.[8] In fact, there are many other countries around the world whose human rights records are as bad as or worse than Tehran's is today. The United States should continue to protest against Iran's domestic political and human rights abuses, but this problem falls far short of the threat posed by Tehran's pursuit of nuclear weapons.

A new American policy toward Iran *should* address all of these issues, but it *must* address Iran's pursuit of nuclear weapons. Any policy that does not have a realistic prospect of at least slowing, if not stopping, the Iranian nuclear program should be discarded. In an ideal world, we could devise a policy that would address all of these concerns equally, but this is rarely the case in the real world of foreign policy. If there are trade-offs to be made, they should be made in favor of emphasizing the need to deal with the nuclear program, even at the expense of the other concerns, remembering that one of the greatest dangers inherent in the nuclear program is its potential to exacerbate the other problematic elements of Iranian behavior.

In recent years, experts on Iran and on U.S. foreign affairs have put forward any number of theories regarding how best to tackle this list of problems with Iran. None of them is terribly compelling. All of them have problems with some combination of logic, feasibility, cost, and repercussions. None is indisputably the correct policy for the United States, although some have more problems than others. In particular, because of how troubled the Iranian state is and because of America's long and painful history with Iran, those approaches that offer the quickest, cleanest, and most direct solution to America's problems with Iran are also the least likely to succeed and the most likely to cause more harm than good.

The Case Against Invading Iran

Unless Iran commits some truly egregious act of aggression against the United States on the order of a 9/11-type attack, an invasion of Iran has nothing to recommend it. As a purely military problem, an invasion of Iran would be a daunting task. The easiest way to understand this is by comparison with America's recent invasion of Iraq. The Iranian population is nearly three times as large as that of Iraq, the country's geographic area is four times that of Iraq, and its terrain is awful. Iran's mountain ranges are formidable barriers to movement of combat formations and supplies. Although the Iranian armed forces would collapse in a stand-up fight with U.S. Army and Marine divisions backed up by U.S. air power, they undoubtedly would instead rely on guerrilla tactics against U.S. forces from the start. As American units passed through the mountains en route to Tehran and other major cities in the interior, they would be hit constantly by Iranian insurgents. These ambushes would be coupled with harassing attacks inside Iran's cities and regular strikes against long American supply lines stretching across Iran's barren deserts. The attack on the police station in Fallujah in November 2003 indicates how deadly Iranian guerrillas from the Pasdaran, Hizballah, Basij, and other paramilitary forces could prove to be. In Iran's vast mountain ranges and large cities, these guerrillas could inflict considerable damage on U.S. forces, slowing them by the need to cover supply routes and guard against constant ambushes, and bloodying them for months or years after the initial invasion was completed.

What's more, as in Iraq, once the U.S. forces had prevailed—and they would prevail, just at a higher price than in Iraq—they would be confronted with the same problems of rebuilding a badly mismanaged political and economic system, amid a wildly xenophobic population (much more so than in Iraq) who would undoubtedly be much less enthusiastic about the American invasion than the Iraqis were because of the long tradition of anti-Americanism in Iran. The history of Iranian-American relations suggests that as much as Iranians may want to be rid of their regime (and even though some occasionally express a wish that the United States would invade to rid them of the mullahs), the historical pattern has been for Iranians to rabidly reject any foreign interference in their affairs. Just as Saddam was assured that all of Iran would rise up against the mullahs if he invaded in 1980, only to find that the Iranian people rallied to the government, so too might the United States find the same if the "Great Satan" were ever to invade Iran without a clear and unequivocal provocation.

As difficult as it was to garner international support for the invasion of Iraq, it would likely be many times harder to interest any of our allies in an invasion of Iran unless the Iranians were to commit some unforgivable offense. Saddam Hussein was a genocidal tyrant, a serial aggressor, a dangerous risk taker, and the target of seventeen UNSC resolutions, most of them enacted under Article VII of the U.N. Charter. All of this made it credible for American and foreign audiences—even those who disagreed with Washington about whether to do so—to consider an invasion of Iraq. The Iranian leadership is no one's idea of responsible government, but its sins so far have not been great enough to move foreign populations to consider war. In fact, since the United States has repeatedly failed to convince other nations to enact sanctions against Iran, it is hard to imagine how Washington could get them to join us in a war. And international support would be even more important for a war in Iran than it was for the one in Iraq because the country is so much bigger and the military and political problems are so much more daunting. Indeed, the force requirements for an invasion of Iran would be so great that as long as the United States retains major military and economic commitments to Iraq and Afghanistan, it might be impossible even to consider an invasion of Iran—with or without massive foreign assistance—because the United States would not have the troops or other resources that would be required unless an Iranian provocation made a total mobilization of national resources possible.

It is not just that the costs of an invasion of Iran could be so high as to be prohibitive except in the context of a major Iranian attack on the United States, but that the threat probably does not justify it. This requires a more nuanced discussion of the actual threat presented by Iran's acquisition of nuclear weapons than simply asserting that because Iran might revert to a highly aggressive foreign policy once it has done so, it would be a major threat to the interests of the United States and its allies.

While it is certainly possible that the current regime in Iran would revert to its former aggressive foreign policy once it acquired nuclear weapons, it is far from certain. Therefore, just as American policy must guard against the negative consequences if it were to do so, different responses to that outcome by the United States should be assessed in terms of the likelihood of the threat they are intended to address and the costs they would entail. It would be harder to justify taking an extremely costly action to head off an outcome that had only a 1 percent likelihood of occurring than if that same outcome had a 10 percent likelihood of occurring. In the case of a policy of invading Iran, the exorbitant costs do not appear justified by the likelihood of the threat. An analogy might help. It might be that the best way to keep burglars out of your home would be to surround it with a moat and a ten-foot-tall electrified fence, as well as placing land mines on your front lawn. However, the risk of being burglarized is probably not so great as to justify the outrageous costs and risks of such an approach. Being unwilling to pay for such defenses does not mean either that you discount the threat of burglary or that you will not take other, less costly steps to deal with it, even though you recognize that these steps will undoubtedly be less effective than the moat, electric fence, and land mines. Invading Iran before it has acquired nuclear weapons might be the best way to guarantee that a nuclear-armed Iran would not go on the offensive against the United States and its allies in the region, but its costs could be prohibitive and there are other things that the United States could do instead—albeit of much less efficacy.

The reason that the threat of Iran's acquisition of nuclear weapons probably does not rise to the level of justifying what would be an extremely costly and risky invasion is that Iran's behavior over the past fifteen years suggests that it can probably be deterred from taking the most harmful offensive actions even after it has acquired nuclear weapons. Here as well, the comparison with Saddam's Iraq is useful. Unlike Saddam, there is very little reporting to indicate that Tehran's leaders want a nuclear weapon for the express purpose of embarking on a more aggressive foreign policy. In fact, all of the reporting (and the Iranians discuss this issue in public, another difference from Iraq) indicates that they want nuclear weapons to deter an American—or, to a lesser extent, Israeli or Iraqi—attack.[9] Nor does the current Iranian leadership have a history of reckless behavior. What was so disconcerting about Saddam was that he was a serial aggressor who never seemed to learn from his mistakes: his humiliating confrontation with the shah in 1975 was followed by a confrontation with Syria the next year, which was followed by the invasion of Iran in 1980, then the invasion of Kuwait two years after the end of that war, followed by the decision to fight the United States and thirty other nations for

Kuwait in 1991, then the attempt to assassinate former President Bush in 1993, then the renewed threat to Kuwait in 1994, the attack on the Kurdish city of Irbil in 1996, the eviction of the U.N. inspectors (provoking the Operation Desert Fox strikes) in 1998, and his effort to move a corps of ground troops to the Golan Heights to start a war with Israel in 2000. This was a stunning record of aggressive, risk-taking behavior unrivaled in recent history. To some extent, Iran under Ayatollah Khomeini was the same—refusing to call off the invasion of Iraq despite repeated failures and refusing to back down from the confrontation with the United States in the Gulf. If the ayatollah were still in charge of Iran today, his pattern of similarly aggressive and risk-tolerant leadership (although inspired by very different sources than Saddam's) would make the argument for an invasion far more persuasive in terms of the importance of keeping nuclear weapons out of his hands.

Since his death, however, Iran's leadership has been offensive and, at times, has miscalculated, but it has not been as reckless or difficult to deter as either Saddam or Iran under the ayatollah. Many of Iran's current leaders argued against the invasion of Iraq in 1982–1988, they argued for making peace in 1988, they argued against confronting the United States in the Gulf during 1987–1988, they argued for avoiding further confrontation after Operation Praying Mantis in 1988, and they demonstrated in 1996 that they could be persuaded to change their behavior in part because of the threat of an American military retaliation. None of this makes it certain that Iran could be deterred once it acquired nuclear weapons, but all of it indicates that there is a strong basis for believing it could be. And since nuclear deterrence has proven fairly robust over the years, it suggests that the risk that Iran would adopt a recklessly aggressive foreign policy after acquiring nuclear weapons is probably lower than the virtual certainty that the costs of an invasion would be extremely high.

Nevertheless, just because the threat of Iranian nuclear weapons does not quite justify the extraordinary price of an invasion does not mean that it is not a threat or that it would not justify other actions by the United States that might not be as costly as an invasion but could still require considerable sacrifices. Foreign policy is rarely an all-or-nothing activity—that either a threat is great enough to justify paying any price, including invasion or nuclear strikes, or else it is not a threat at all and therefore does not justify paying any price. Most foreign policy problems fall somewhere in between, and the Iranian nuclear threat still falls toward the higher end of the spectrum.

The Iranians may want nuclear weapons for defensive purposes now and have not proven recklessly aggressive so far, but once in possession of them they might come to see them as enabling offensive actions and act in a more reckless fashion than in the past. To some extent, this is what happened with Pakistan, which originally sought nuclear weapons to deter an Indian attack, but then, once it had them, decided that they were so effective as a deterrent that it could ratchet up its offensive insurgent operations against India in Kashmir—which sparked the Kargil crisis of 2000 and nearly led to an Indo-Pakistani war. This residual risk is why it remains important for the United States to try to deprive this Iranian regime of nuclear weapons, even if the risk is not so great as to justify the potentially astronomically high costs of an invasion.

The Ghost of Kim Roosevelt

Since an invasion of Iran makes no sense except in response to a major, unprovoked Iranian attack on the United States or its allies, a number of commentators and Iran experts have argued for a program employing both covert action and overt public diplomacy to try to topple the Iranian government. In actuality, what they have in mind is fairly different from what the United States did in 1953. Then the United States and Great Britain engineered something much more akin to a military coup d'état, although it certainly was aided by popular elements. Proponents of regime change in Iran this time around recognize that it would be well nigh impossible for Washington to pull off the same: Iran's military units appear mostly loyal to the regime, and they are tightly bound by a web of political controls that would make it extremely difficult for the CIA to penetrate Iran's senior military leadership, let alone encourage them, organize them, and supply them to mount a coup. Instead, those who favor a regime change approach contend that the United States could spark a popular revolution in Iran, possibly assisted by the MEK and other opposition groups.[10]

The basic assumption of this policy is that the Iranian people are desperate to be rid of the clerical regime and that the United States can encourage them and even help them to do so. One of its foremost advocates, Michael Ledeen, who is probably best known for urging the Reagan administration to get involved in the opening to Iran that eventually became the Iran-*contra* scandal, argued before the invasion of Iraq that "Of the four terrorist tyrannies [Iran, Iraq, Saudi Arabia, and Syria], Iran seems the easiest to liberate. The president has eloquently described the circumstances there: The Iranian people have clearly and repeatedly demonstrated their desire to be rid of their self-appointed rulers. They deserve our support just as did the Yugoslavs in their desire to be rid of the Milosevic tyranny. We must support them as we supported the Solidarity free trade union in Poland in their desire to be rid of communist tyranny and as we supported the Filipino people in their desire to be rid of the Marcos tyranny. We know how to do it: broadcasting the truth and funding others who do the same, denouncing the oppression, defending the political prisoners by name, encouraging private American and international organizations to provide money, communications and guidance to the people on the ground. . . . There is every reason to believe the same can be accomplished quite rapidly in Iran, where such a movement already exists."[11]

As a stand-alone policy, this notion is infeasible. It does provide a useful element of a larger approach to Iran, but it is simply not viable or useful as the centerpiece of a new Iran policy. The crucial theory behind it is that the Iranian people are so unhappy with the regime that they would move against it if given the slightest sign by the United States. Certainly, there is considerable evidence—both anecdotal and quantitative—to show that most Iranians are unhappy with the regime. However, it is a giant leap from that to suggesting that they are on the brink of revolution, and that the United States could push them to do so. First, there is equally powerful evidence that as unhappy as the Iranian people may be, they are not on the brink of revolution. In July 1999, they were as close to that point as ever since 1979, but the revolution never happened. It never happened because there was no leader willing and able to lead a revolution, a situation that does not appear to have changed today. What's more, in July 1999—and on numerous occasions since—although groups of students have shown a willingness to mount a true revolution, few other Iranians have. Most of the evidence indicates that Iranians are sick of revolutions and don't want another one. They may not like this regime, but they are not ready to take to the streets to depose it.

The second problem with this approach is its unexplained, but critical, assumption that American support could trigger this revolution-waiting-to-happen. No nation in modern history has caused a popular revolution in another. The Germans came closest in 1917, when they transported Vladimir Lenin in a sealed railroad car across their territory to Russia; however, it would be giving the kaiser's government far too much credit to say that by this action they "caused" the Russian Revolution. It is also true that American actions throughout the Cold War played a role in the fall of the Iron Curtain and the "velvet revolutions" of Eastern Europe. However, in those cases, the role that the United States played was principally giving hope to those inside who wanted to change the system and demonstrating that a better life than what communism offered was possible. The United States can and should play those roles with Iran too, but there is no reason to believe that doing so would spark a revolution anytime soon. It took forty-four years before revolution came to Eastern Europe, and we simply don't have that kind of time with Iran if our goal is to try to forestall an Iranian nuclear capability.

Right now, there are two clocks ticking in Tehran. The first is the clock of regime change. Given the sentiments of the people, it seems likely that there will be further meaningful change in Iran at some point in the future. The second is the clock of Iran's nuclear program. We do not know when the alarm on either of those clocks will go off. History has demonstrated that meaningful change in Iran is likely to take considerable time, lengthened even more by the short-term success that the regime has enjoyed in employing its "China model." Indeed, China too was a country that fifteen years ago seemed ripe for revolution, until the regime figured out how to defuse the pressure coming from China's youth movement for political change. If Iran continues to be successful in doing the same, there is no reason to expect revolutionary change in Iran in the near future. In contrast, the findings of the IAEA suggest that Iran is getting fairly close to having a fully self-contained enrichment process, if not actual weapons. Again, the Iraq experience should make us careful of any estimates of Iranian progress, but at present it does seem likely that the nuclear clock is likely to go off before the regime-change clock. At the very least, the burden of proof must be on the advocates of this policy to prove that it is more likely that regime change could be brought to fruition before Iran's nuclear weapons program becomes self-sufficient for the United States to even consider making this the heart of its policy, rather than merely an adjunct.

This policy proposal also assumes that U.S. involvement in Iran's internal politics would be beneficial to the United States and those we would like to see succeed in Tehran. Such an assumption flies in the face of the last twenty-five years of history. The backing of the United States has generally proven to be the kiss of death for Iranian leaders. Khatami himself is the best proof of this: his effort to reach out to the United States early on in his presidency was a serious mistake that convinced the hard-liners that he opposed the fundamental principles of the revolution upon which their legitimacy was based. Nor would we know who to help or how to do so. The MEK are hated in Iran for their terrorist attacks and their alliance with Saddam (and military operations against Iran during the Iran-Iraq War).[12] The students are clumped in mostly amorphous groups, and there is nothing that would destroy their credibility and legitimacy faster than to have it revealed that they were being supported— covertly or overtly—by the United States.

The Iranian reformist journalist Sa'eed Laylaz once lamented, "Unfortunately the government of the United States usually chooses action that benefits the conservatives. I don't know why, and I can't explain to you how, but every response by the United States on internal Iran issues is to the benefit of the conservatives."[13] In other words, the United States has consistently picked the wrong policy time after time. This is nonsense. Throughout the Clinton administration, the actions that the United States took were those specifically requested by the Iranian reformers themselves. In other words, it is not that the United States keeps picking the wrong policy to help those it favors in Iran, it is that the United States remains such a lightning rod in Iran and anti-Americanism still remains enough of a force that America's mere involvement hurts whomever it is intended to help.

This is the last lesson from Iran's history: the Iranians have a strong streak of xenophobia and fifty years of accumulated anti-Americanism. There is every reason to expect that no matter how much they may idolize and idealize the United States at this moment, if Washington were ever to start fooling around in Iranian politics again, it would almost certainly revive all of the anti-American fervor in an instant. It is conceivable that this is not the case anymore, that Iran has become so pro-American that Iranians would welcome clear American interference in their internal affairs, but there is certainly no evidence of that. Here as well, the burden of proof must lie with the advocates of this policy. Given how much pain the United States has suffered as a result of our past efforts to meddle in Iranian affairs, those recommending we do so again need to have far more compelling evidence that this would be beneficial than merely the longing of Iranian twenty-somethings to be able to shop on Fifth Avenue or Rodeo Drive.

Since the Huyser mission in 1979, it has been American policy to focus on changing Iranian behavior rather than the Iranian regime. A case can be made for the latter. Certainly Iran is an oppressive society, and anecdotal reporting suggests that there are considerable numbers of Iranians who would like to see their government replaced altogether. It is also possible to construe Iranian voting patterns as further support for this: since 1997, whenever the Iranian people have been given any kind of meaningful choice, they have consistently voted for those candidates whose views were farthest from those of the ruling establishment. Indeed, to a great extent, the more extreme in their opposition to the regime a candidate was, the more votes he or she received. Nevertheless, overturning any foreign government is extremely difficult, and overturning Iran's regime would likely prove more difficult than most, especially for the United States, whose involvement in Iranian affairs has provoked the most extreme emotions from Iranians for the past fifty years. For the United States, trying to change the regime in Tehran is not just a lost cause, it would be a mistake. Whenever we have tried, we have ended up worse off than when we started.

Unilateral Concessions[14]

Strangely, where Iran policy is concerned, the far Left and the far Right agree on one thing: faced with the dilemma of the two clocks, the United States should concentrate on accelerating the regime-change clock, rather than slowing the nuclear clock. The hawks, who espouse fomenting a popular revolution, as outlined above, believe that toppling the current regime in Iran can be accelerated by American support—rhetorical and substantive—to what they perceive to be a mass of Iranian revolutionaries straining at the leash to be freed by a signal from Washington. On the other hand, the doves argue that regime change in Iran would be accelerated by opening Iran to outside influences, lashing it firmly to the global economy, and allowing interdependence and globalization to loosen the grip of the reactionary mullahs and tame Iran's bad behavior. This approach assumes that the more the Iranians see benefits from trade and engagement with the rest of the world, the less likely they are to act aggressively. The prescription of this policy is for the United States to unilaterally lift its sanctions on Iran—both the primary sanctions contained in the executive orders and a number of laws, and the secondary sanctions contained in the ILSA—to allow unfettered trade with Iran.[15]

The first problem with this policy is the same as that of the hawkish regime change approach: it fails the test of the two clocks. It is at best unproven that this approach would work, and if it did work, it would likely take a very long time—much longer than it would take Iran to develop nuclear weapons, especially since lifting the sanctions will invariably (just by the signal it would send) improve Iran's access to nuclear-related materials.

Proponents of this plan often point to U.S. policy toward China as an example of how this policy can work. However, the China example actually proves the opposite when applied to Iran. What China demonstrates is that in pursuing this path, the U.S. *removed* much of the pressure for rapid regime change in China. The U.S. opening to China allowed China to boom economically, allowing the government to deflect pressure for political change into the economic sphere—precisely the approach the Iranian hard-liners now hope to follow. The key difference is that the Chinese government with which the United States began this process was not looking to drive the United States out of East Asia and overthrow its allies in the region (except Taiwan, obviously), nor was it the world's worst supporter of terrorism. China had nuclear weapons already, and its possession of them had not turned it into a reckless, aggressive power. Deng Xiaoping was repressive at home but moderate in his foreign policy. Thus it was reasonable, if perhaps ethically questionable, for the United States to adopt a policy that effectively hindered political change in China in the near term because it helped cement the regime's preexisting moderate foreign policy and held out the prospect of helping foment more meaningful political change in the future. The problem is that, simply put, Khamene'i is no Deng. If Khamene'i were as moderate in his foreign policy as Deng, this policy would make sense and there would be no reason for this book.

America's history with Iran also offers other warnings regarding this approach. In practice, this policy would be identical to the failed European policy of Critical Dialogue. It is a policy of all carrots and no sticks. Just as they did with the Critical Dialogue, Iran's hard-liners would undoubtedly pocket all of the carrots and do nothing to change. Indeed, as the China example demonstrates, what this approach does is lock in the current regime—at least in the short and medium terms (after all, there is a case to be made that Chinese politics are changing too, just very slowly). In the case of Iran it is even worse, because the hard-liners have argued for more than a decade that the United States would not be able to maintain the sanctions on Iran because the United States needed Iran more than Iran needed the United States. As Graham Fuller has pointed out, this tends to say as much about the remarkably inflated view of their country held by many Iranians—who see Iran as "the center of the universe"—than it does about their objective understanding of the world.[16] But by reversing course and lifting the sanctions without securing any change in Iranian behavior in return, the United States would be proving the point of the hard-liners.

Over the past fifteen years, the only things that have caused Iran to change its behavior have been the threat of military action by the United States in 1988 and 1996 and the threat of sanctions by the Europeans in 1997 and 2003. The American sanctions have inhibited Iran's freedom of action somewhat, but because Tehran could always turn to Europe (and Russia and Japan) for trade and aid, the American sanctions never forced them to do anything. Far from coaxing Iran to become more responsible, a policy of unilateral concessions is much more likely to convince Tehran's hard-liners that they can continue to pursue their preferred foreign policy of aggressive opposition to the United States and the status quo without suffering any meaningful repercussions.

Counterproliferation

This policy option takes as its inspiration the Israeli strike on Baghdad's Osiraq reactor in 1981. Its central premise is for the United States to mount discrete, but large-scale, air and missile strikes against Iran's nuclear infra-

392 / The Persian Puzzle

structure. In effect, it looks at the other side of the race between the two clocks. It recognizes that, given the nature of Iranian politics and society, the role of anti-Americanism in Iranian ideology, and the history between the two nations, it is probably impossible for the United States to accelerate regime change in Iran—and that trying to do so would likely have exactly the opposite effect. Instead, it looks to slow down the Iranian nuclear clock by obliterating Iran's nuclear infrastructure.

Counterproliferation actually has a surprising amount to recommend it. If the United States could destroy all, or even key elements, of Iran's nuclear program, it probably would not end the program, but it could set it back very considerably. Since the key is to keep nuclear weapons out of the hands of the current regime, such a delay could be all that is necessary. In effect, that is exactly what the Osiraq raid did. It merely set back Saddam's nuclear program, but in doing so, it ensured that Saddam did not have a nuclear weapon in time for either the Iran-Iraq War or the Gulf War, and that was just enough of a delay to prevent him from ever acquiring one. Undoubtedly, there would be a great deal of international animosity toward the United States if it launched unilateral military strikes against Iran, just as there was tremendous international condemnation of Israel for the Osiraq raid. However, unlike an invasion, the United States would not need much international cooperation to conduct the strikes themselves. In addition, there is a consensus that Iran is building nuclear weapons, that it is flouting the NPT by doing so, and that the world probably would be better off if the Iranians did not have them. All of this suggests that while the United States might face a maelstrom of criticism in the short term, over the longer term this would likely dissipate. Indeed, today, the Israeli strike on Osiraq is generally considered an act of tremendous foresight that benefited the entire region, if not the world. If an American raid were equally as bloodless and effective as the Osiraq strike, American counterproliferation attacks might also be looked back upon as the best answer to a hard problem.

Unfortunately, there are also a number of serious complications with this as a policy. First, we almost certainly would pay a price for it. The Iranians would undoubtedly retaliate with terrorist attacks, and because in this case we would have thrown the first punch, they might be so enraged as to be willing to stick out a fight with the United States through many rounds. The Iranians also might choose to retaliate against the United States in Iraq or Afghanistan, not because they had changed their minds about the need for stability in those two countries but purely because these would be excellent venues in which to hurt the U.S. government. Doing so would ultimately hurt Iran more than the

United States, but it would not be the first time that Iran took actions that did so. American counterproliferation strikes against Iran's "peaceful nuclear energy" program could also be the death knell for Iran's reform movement, which continues to be identified in the minds of many Iranians with improved ties to the United States. At the very least, it likely would set the reform movement back even further—and so would affect both clocks, not just the nuclear clock.

Coming on the heels of the invasions of Afghanistan and Iraq, a large, unprovoked military campaign against Iran would likely have severe repercussions throughout the Muslim world. I doubt that the "Arab street" would rise up, as many of my fellow Middle East hands keep predicting incorrectly. However, it would sour diplomatic relations, make it harder for governments of Islamic nations to cooperate with the United States, and likely spur both recruitment and attacks by various Islamist terrorist groups. For many Muslims, the United States launching strikes to disarm Iran would come across as another effort by the Christian United States to prevent a Muslim state from acquiring the same weapons that they believe the Jewish state of Israel already possesses (and about which the United States does nothing).

Still another cost would be the impact on other goals of U.S. policy toward Iran. While counterproliferation properly makes Iran's nuclear program the highest priority, it does nothing to address Iran's support for terrorism or violent opposition to a Middle East peace. In fact, because of all the negative repercussions listed above, counterproliferation could actually undermine America's ability to deal with the other problems posed by Iran. Counterproliferation strikes would encourage both Iranian and other Islamic terrorism; they would likely hinder international cooperation with the United States on terrorism, proliferation, and other regional issues; and they might make it impossible for the Arabs to participate in a new peace process.

Weighed against these costs would be the uncertainty of what we had achieved. By and large, this is the most important problem with the counterproliferation option. With the revelation of Natanz and Arak, the Iranians demonstrated a remarkable capacity to conceal large nuclear facilities. No one knows how many others there may be. Now that the IAEA is aware of the Natanz facility, the Iranians might turn it into a decoy and relocate the real enrichment activities elsewhere. This is precisely what Iraq did after the Osiraq raid, quickly rebuilding it but relocating its nuclear weapons program to several other facilities that were not discovered until U.N. inspectors stumbled upon them after the Gulf War. And destroying several Iranian facilities would probably only convince the regime to redouble its efforts to acquire nuclear weapons in the belief that doing so would deter a future American strike. For these reasons, counterproliferation is likely to have more liabilities than benefits for the foreseeable future.

A counterproliferation option should not be ruled out entirely, because it does have the potential to greatly slow down the Iranian nuclear program at one blow. But it cannot be the centerpiece of America's new Iran policy because the costs would be so high, especially compared to the likelihood that it would actually accomplish its objective. If the United States were able to develop a very solid intelligence profile of the Iranian nuclear program, including high confidence about where (if any) of its secret facilities were located, counterproliferation might be a very sensible option, especially if other approaches had failed and/or there was solid evidence that the Iranians were close to attaining a nuclear weapons capability. Under those circumstances, the costs might well be worth the payoff. Until then, it should be kept on the shelf.

As a sidebar, the United States also should not count on Israel to conduct a counterproliferation strike for us. It is almost certainly the case that Israel would be willing to absorb the diplomatic costs of a strike, would be prepared to deal with Iran's retaliation in the form of either terrorist attacks or missile strikes on Israel, and probably is not overly concerned about Iranian behavior in Iraq. The problem for Israel is much simpler: Iran is too far away. Most of the known Iranian nuclear facilities are around 1,000 miles from Israel. Its Jericho II ballistic missiles could reach these targets, but they lack the payload,[17] accuracy, and numbers to be able to significantly damage (let alone destroy) more than one or two of the large Iranian nuclear facilities, which leaves the matter to the Israeli Air Force. Even assuming that Israeli aircraft were to fly directly to Iran, overflying Jordan and Iraq, the only aircraft in its inventory that could reach Iran's known nuclear sites are its 25 F-15I strike fighters.[18] (Israel would need to set up aerial refueling stations at three to five locations between Israel and the Iranian targets for its roughly 350 F-16s to be able to participate, which would be practically impossible.)[19] Because the F-15Is would have to carry a considerable amount of fuel, they could not carry a great deal of ordnance. Given the size of the various Iranian nuclear facilities, it would not be possible for Israel to destroy all of them in a single raid as it did Osiraq. Nor would it be politically, militarily, or logistically possible for Israel to sustain multiple such strikes over the many days, if not weeks, it would take for its small force of F-15Is to accomplish the job. Thus, at best, Israel might pick out one facility and destroy it, but it would then face the same conundrum as the United States: Would it be able to identify Iran's most important nuclear facility, and even if it were able to do so and destroy it, would that really set back the Iranian program enough to justify the costs to Israel? Since the Iranians have consciously feared just such a strike all along, it seems highly unlikely that such a crucial facility even exists, making the whole exercise pointless. In desperation, Israel might still try this route, but it is unlikely to solve the basic problem.

The Grand Bargain

Another strategy that focuses on slowing the nuclear clock (and other problematic Iranian behavior) in recognition that it will be virtually impossible for the United States to affect the regime-change clock is what is referred to as the "Grand Bargain."[20] The central notion behind the Grand Bargain is that the United States and Iran would negotiate a comprehensive settlement of all their differences. Iran would be persuaded to end its nuclear program, cease supporting terrorism, and refrain from opposing a Middle East peace through violence. In return, the United States would make concessions on issues of concern to Iran, such as Persian Gulf security, unfreezing Iranian assets still held in the United States, and lifting the various sanctions on Iran including ILSA. The logic of the Grand Bargain is that no Iranian could possibly justify making concessions to the United States on any of the issues of concern to Washington unless it simultaneously received very substantial concessions from the United States that it could use to justify its compromises to the Iranian people.

The Grand Bargain has a great deal to recommend it. It would allow both sides to secure what they need and possibly pave the way to a normal relationship. It would allow the United States and Iran to sort out their differences in a cooperative framework, rather than a confrontational contest. Instead of trying to coerce Iran, it is designed to persuade Iran that it should want to do these things because the rewards will be very great. Furthermore, there is an implicit assumption that because Iran would be making this deal of its own free will, it would be more likely to keep its end of the bargain. It also has the great advantage that many Iranian reformers would like to pursue exactly this approach and have told their American contacts so many times.

The problem with the Grand Bargain is that it doesn't work in practice. Every American administration since Reagan has put the Grand Bargain on the table and tried to coax the Iranians into accepting it. In particular, the Grand Bargain was the explicit core of the Clinton initiative. When Clinton administration officials spoke to Khatami's unofficial interlocutors, as well as to various European countries that tried to play a mediating role between Washington and Tehran, the course that they consistently laid out was a process of negotiations that would lead to a comprehensive deal over all of the different problem issues that lay between the two countries—this is where the term "Grand Bargain" came from. The problem that lies at the heart of the Grand Bargain—the problem that the Clinton administration stumbled over, much to its disappointment—is the fundamental problem that lies at the heart of the Iranian-American confrontation.

Whenever American officials are able to talk to Iranians about what it is that they would want from a Grand Bargain, and whenever American citizens are able to talk to Iranian officials about what it is that they would want from a Grand Bargain, one of the foremost things that the Iranians invariably say is "Respect." In my own conversations with Iranians, in and out of government, I have found that it is usually the first of their demands—and they often say it immediately and then have to think hard as to what their other demands might be. "Respect" is an abstract concept that needs to be made tangible if it is going to be part of a deal. So, like good negotiators, the Americans inevitably ask, "What do you mean by 'respect'?" Typically, the Iranians cannot define what respect would be, but they are full of illustrations of disrespectful American behavior that would have to end for Iran to be willing to accept a Grand Bargain. For instance, the Iranians never fail to observe that saying that Iran was part of an "Axis of Evil" was disrespectful. The sanctions are disrespectful. Criticizing the (flagrantly rigged) February 2004 Majles elections for being flagrantly rigged was disrespectful. Any criticism of Iran's internal affairs, such as its kangaroo-court judicial procedures and its arrest of political dissidents on ridiculous charges, is disrespectful. A senator calling Iran the world's worst terrorist state is disrespectful. American newspapers writing articles about problems in the Iranian economy is disrespectful. The State Department stating that Iran supports terrorism rather than acknowledging that Iran is a victim of terrorism (both of which are true) is disrespectful. Claiming that Iran is harboring al-Qa'eda personnel is disrespectful. I have personally heard every one of those statements made by Iranians in response to my question as to what "respect" means to them.

There are two problems inherent in this. First, while it may seem reasonable to require the United States not to do and say these things as part of a rapprochement, it simply is not. Nations, even close allies, criticize each other all the time. It is a founding principle of American foreign policy not to stand silent in the face of repression, and it would be offensive to the American people if their government did not bear witness to oppression and injustice. This was Jimmy Carter's mantra as much as it was Ronald Reagan's. Indeed, the United States' European allies, which have similar beliefs about the importance of speaking out against human rights abuses and political oppression, regularly criticize the United States for retaining capital punishment, which they consider immoral. We do not consider this a sign of disrespect, nor would we expect them not to continue to do so—even though we might prefer that they not. And we certainly would not break diplomatic relations with them because of their criticism of capital punishment.

This gets to the second problem with the Iranian demands: they make it clear that Iran is simply not ready for a meaningful relationship with the United States. Americans don't like the government of the Islamic Republic of Iran and probably won't like it as long as the regime and its various accomplices continue to abuse human rights, prevent the Iranian people from fully participating in governance, refuse to abide by the rule of law, and impose unpopular social codes on their people—let alone support terrorism, violently oppose a Middle East peace, and pursue nuclear weapons. From America's side, our dislike of this regime should not prevent the conclusion of a comprehensive settlement of our differences, but from Iran's side it has and it likely will for quite some time. The Iranians hold up rhetorical terms such as "Axis of Evil" as proof that the United States does not "respect" Iran and therefore there is no basis for a political relationship. But the United States did not like the regime that governed the Soviet Union either, American officials constantly criticized the Soviets for their political and human rights abuses, and President Reagan famously called the USSR the "Evil Empire." None of this meant that we did not respect the Soviet Union—it was hard not to respect a government with ten thousand nuclear weapons—just that we did not like it. Nor were the Soviet leaders any happier with America's criticism than today's Iranian leaders are. (And Washington felt the same way about Russian criticism of racial inequities and income disparities in the United States.) Yet the Soviets, on many occasions, found it in their interest to sit down and reach any number of far-reaching agreements with the United States. Indeed, Mikhail Gorbachev was able to sit down with President Reagan and, despite his "Evil Empire" quip, work out a remarkable set of accords at the end of the Cold War. It did not mean that either country liked the other or respected the other any more or any less, just that both were able to get past the rhetoric and reach mutually beneficial agreements. Iran has not yet shown that it is ready to do so.

As it has for the past fifty years, the United States remains not only Iran's greatest political stumbling block but its greatest psychological stumbling block. The Iranians have so much emotional baggage attached to the United States that they simply cannot move past it. Just as the taking of the embassy in 1979 was more about seeking psychological gratification for twenty-five years of Iranian grievances against the United States (real and imagined), so today any political relationship with the United States remains captive to that same insurmountable sense of grievance. When Iranians talk about getting "respect" from the United States, they are demanding that the United States treat them better than we treat any other nation on earth—that we refrain from all criticism whatsoever, and not just by the administration itself but by the Congress and even the media. We don't treat our closest allies that well. The Iranians still want the United States to beg for forgiveness for 1953 and a host of other "crimes" committed against Iran and to show them a deference that we have never shown to any country since Thomas Jefferson wrote the Declaration of Independence. Whether we should or should not do so for Iran is irrelevant. What matters is that as long as Iranians continue to hold a national grudge, any reconciliation—let alone the kind of comprehensive settlement envisioned by the Grand Bargain—is impossible.

This is the core problem with the Grand Bargain: that it requires the Iranians to deal with the great psychological problem of the United States that has haunted their political discourse for fifty years. Contrary to the suggestion of many who favor unilateral concessions, it is the Iranian government that has consistently rejected engagement with the United States, whereas the U.S. government has been ready for the Grand Bargain for at least fifteen, if not twenty, years. Certainly, one can criticize the second Bush administration for not having been more responsive to Iran after the Afghan War, but what quashed that flirtation was as much Iran's behavior—the *Karine A,* the al-Qa'eda leaders in Iran, and the nuclear revelations—as it was the "Axis of Evil" remark. What's more, there was little to suggest that Iran was any more psychologically ready to have a reasonable relationship with the United States in early 2002 than at any point in the past. Had it not been for the specter of a U.S. invasion of Iraq, the Iranians likely would have ended the Geneva Group conversations altogether because of that phrase, and any rapprochement that can be scuttled by a few words of empty rhetoric is not a serious rapprochement.

These psychological issues regarding America's place in Iran's thinking are important not only in their own right but also for how they play into Iran's domestic politics. Because relations with the United States remain such a hot button for so many Iranians, it is too easy for Tehran's hard-liners to scuttle negotiations with the United States by claiming that those doing so are betraying the country or allowing the Americans to get the best of them. Because it has become so infused in Iran's political discourse that in any dealing with the United States Iran must get the better of the deal (to compensate for fifty years of exaggerated nefarious activities on the part of Washington), it becomes very difficult for Iranian leaders to negotiate publicly with the United States. This is one reason why it has typically been the case that the Iranians insist that Washington "negotiate" by making concessions up front, to which the Iranians can decide whether to respond: the Iranians need to make sure that the American concessions are considered serious enough so that the public will be in no doubt who got the better deal before they give any hint of accepting. This is completely infeasible as a negotiating method, however—no U.S. government would agree to do so. It is one reason why some Iranians have insisted that if negotiations for a Grand Bargain were ever to take place, they would have to be in secret—in the hope that the Iranian side could complete the negotiations and sell the whole package to their populace. However, this too conjures fears on the American side. American officials have been burned too many times in secret negotiations with Iranians—going back to Iran-*contra* and the hostage crisis—to agree to go down that route once more. Thus, as long as Iran's hard-liners can play this card, it will be yet another hindrance to the Grand Bargain.

The men who rule in Tehran today have believed reflexively for fifty years that the U.S. government is evil, that it is the source of all of the problems in the world and the ultimate cause of all of Iran's problems. They defined themselves and led their country once they came to power inspired by the idea that Iran was the champion of goodness and sanctity and that its God-given mission was to combat the forces of evil—led by the United States. In truth, some of them never really believed this. Others likely have ruled their country long enough to understand that its problems are not all the fault of American machinations and that while the United States may be their implacable enemy, it is not necessarily pure evil. However, those who have come to this conclusion are not necessarily in the ascendancy in Tehran. Worse still, the tattered legitimacy of the entire regime—true believers or not—rests upon a revolutionary ideology that does still make this Manichean vision of the world and the cosmic conflict between Iran (Good, Husayn) and the United States (Evil, Yazid) one of its central tenets. Thus, even for the cynical among Tehran's clerical rulers, openly abandoning anti-Americanism holds the potential to call into question their domestic legitimacy, and at a time when the assaults on their positions have been so great that they have had to give up on virtually everything else. Even for the cynics, the great question is whether they can give up on this last strand of Khomeini's legacy too and still command the right to rule. Until a new regime is in power that does not have this same problem of legitimacy, or until this regime decides that it can abandon the last vestiges of Khomeinism, Iran will not be ready politically for a Grand Bargain.

Of course, the United States has not been entirely blameless in terms of the history of repeated failures to start a process that might produce a Grand Bargain. America, too, still has its emotional scars regarding Iran. Many politicians have found it all too easy to score points against an opponent by claiming the opponent was "soft" on Iran, a charge that still causes damage because most Americans continue to see Iran as little more than a nation of hostage-taking terrorists. We have often been slow to recognize that the Iranians have some legitimate reasons to be angry at our behavior toward them in the past, just as we have legitimate reasons to be angry at them. We have been equally unwilling to grant that Iran has legitimate security concerns to go with their legitimate grievances. At times in the past, the United States has posed a threat to Iran (although in most cases this was in response to Iran's own offensive behavior), and Iran lives in a tough neighborhood and must worry about other states as well. Consequently, a Grand Bargain would require a number of compromises on the American side that, for similar political and psychological reasons, we have been unwilling to make so far. But as long as Tehran remains unwilling to come to grips with the chip it has been carrying on its shoulder regarding the United States for the past twenty-five—if not fifty—years, American leaders will have little incentive to try to tackle the list of problems on their own.

Triple Track

None of the policies enumerated above offers a comprehensive and/or realistic solution to America's problems with Iran today. All fail either to create the potential to deal with Iran's nuclear program in a timely fashion or to present a realistic scheme for doing so—and some offer nothing to address the other problematic aspects of Iranian behavior beyond the nuclear threat. Their failings are not the result of foolishness, ideology, or avarice but are inherent in the current challenge of Iran. Iran is a very hard problem.

I believe that there is a better way to tackle the problems of Iran. However, I do not regard this strategy, which I call "Triple Track" because it relies on three reinforcing and overlapping approaches to the problem, as a panacea. It may simply be our least bad option, which is often the best we can get when dealing with problematic states such as Iran, Saddam's Iraq, and North Korea.

There are a number of basic principles that lie behind Triple Track. An effective U.S. policy toward Iran must be flexible. Because of its fragmented political spectrum and the closed nature of its policy-making process (coupled with the considerable ignorance of many of its policy makers), Iran can be extremely unpredictable. Therefore, the United States must be positioned to react to both Tehran's positive and negative moves. This unpredictability, coupled with the basic troubles of Iran, also means that no U.S. policy toward it has a high likelihood of success. Since Iran often axiomatically defines its interests as being the opposite of whatever the United States wants, and since the present leadership seems determined to hew to its nuclear and terrorism policies no matter what the cost, it will be very difficult to do so. Consequently, any American policy toward Iran should have a series of fallback positions to ensure that Washington is never caught flat-footed by the failure of its primary strategy. A new policy toward Iran should incorporate pieces of many of the above strategies—as well as some from the approaches that have served us reasonably well in the past—to enable the United States to deal with the range of problems that Iran poses, the range of potential opportunities available, and the range of different Iranian responses. Last, because even a policy that successfully meets all of these conditions would still run a high risk of failure, a new policy toward Iran must be fully consistent with broader American foreign policy goals and principles. If at some point in the future Iran crosses the nuclear threshold, rendering American policy a failure, the U.S. government will need to be able to say that it remained true to America's values and did not fatally compromise some other foreign policy concern in the name of a desperate gambit to derail Iran's nuclear program without incurring the excessive costs of an invasion.

Track 1: Hold Open the Prospect of the Grand Bargain. If the Iranians can ever get over their psychological and political hurdles regarding the United States, the Grand Bargain would be the best way to handle our mutual problems. Because it is unlikely that the United States would be willing to mount an invasion short of a major Iranian provocation and we lack the intelligence to have high confidence in a strategy of counterproliferation, our best hope is to convince the Iranians to disband their nuclear program and end their support for terrorism because it is in their best interest to do so. The most efficient way that the United States can do this is through a Grand Bargain, no matter how chimerical it may seem at the moment. The United States has nothing to lose by continuing to say that Washington is open to an authoritative dialogue with appropriate officials of the Iranian government regarding our various sources of conflict. If these differences could be resolved through negotiations, it would be infinitely better for both sides.

If and when the Iranians do come to grips with their own emotions regarding the United States and are ready to work out a comprehensive deal, the process itself is likely to be long and excruciating. On the U.S. side alone, there are more than a dozen laws and executive orders imposing various sanctions on Iran. In addition, there are any number of other restrictions on interactions with Iran built into a range of federal regulations. The residue of so many past unsuccessful efforts to engage Iran will also loom over the American side of the negotiations. The U.S. government will also have to decide how to handle the numerous court cases that have been brought by the victims of Iranian terrorism in U.S. courts, who have been awarded millions of dollars' worth of damages by American judges when the Iranians failed to contest these cases (believing them illegal and irrelevant) and so "lost" them by default.

Looking at the Iranian side, the Islamic Republic has typically tried to "negotiate" by demanding that the other side make a series of concessions up front, to which it then can choose whether and to what extent to respond. The Iranians might very well start with the same approach, and it may take a long time to convince them that that is not a negotiation in which we can participate, no matter what their domestic political needs might be. Part of the process will also require Iran's leaders to confront some truths that they have misrepresented to their people, if not themselves. In particular, they frequently claim that the remaining Iranian assets frozen by the United States amount to something in the neighborhood of $30 billion to $40 billion, when in actuality the real number is probably a fraction of that amount. It is also extremely unlikely that the U.S. government would be willing to cut a check to Iran for several billion dollars to settle these claims, and therefore any compensation Iran would receive would likely come in the form of trade or agricultural credits, not hard currency. This would be a bitter pill for many in Tehran.

Of course, the United States would want guarantees that Iran would live up to its promises. Strangely, the nuclear program may then be the easiest part to address. As National Security Advisor Rice once noted, "There is no mystery to voluntary disarmament. Countries that decide to disarm lead inspectors to weapons and production sites, answer questions before they are asked, state publicly and often the intention to disarm and urge their citizens to cooperate. The world knows from examples set by South Africa, Ukraine and Kazakhstan what it looks like when a government decides that it will cooperatively give up its weapons of mass destruction. The critical common elements of these efforts include a high-level political commitment to disarm, national initiatives to dismantle weapons programs, and full cooperation and transparency."[21] Libya can now be added to that list, and the United States should demand that Iran do the same: no games, no lies, no repeatedly revised declarations, no leading inspectors around the country by the nose, no harassing the inspectors—no Iraqi version of inspections.

Much harder would be verifying that Iran has ended its involvement in terrorism and the related problem of its violent opposition to a Middle East peace. In truth, the United States is likely to have considerable intelligence indicating whether or not Iran has ended its support for terrorism but very little that we would be able to use in a court of law (or, more precisely, the court of world opinion)—which could well be necessary if the agreements are codified and Iran chooses to try to skirt the edges. Hizballah should be disarmed and turned into a civilian political party in Lebanon, but that would likely require Syria's blessing too, and Damascus is unlikely to give it except in the context of a Syrian-Israeli peace treaty. Intercepted arms from Tehran—or simply Iranian weapons turning up in the hands of HAMAS, PIJ, and other terrorist groups—should be clear violations of the terms, but the Iranians can always procure weapons from third parties.

Ultimately, because it likely would prove impossible to handle Iranian support for terrorism through inspections or technology control regimes or high-tech gadgets that sniff the air the way it is possible to look for evidence of a nuclear program, determining that the Iranians have fully complied with this aspect of any agreement would require that a Grand Bargain with Iran have escape clauses. The United States would need to be in a position to pay out the benefits to Iran incrementally over a protracted period and to have the process be reversible at Washington's discretion (which would make it even more unpalatable for Iran). To do otherwise, however, would be to run the risk that Iran would agree, collect its benefits up front, and then cheat on its obligations to end terrorism and stop opposing a Middle East peace with violence, knowing how difficult it would be for the United States to prove otherwise. Iran would have to recognize that ending its pursuit of nuclear weapons, terrorism, and violent opposition to a Middle East peace are not onetime affairs but perpetual commitments, and that if it did not live up to those obligations it would lose the benefits of the Grand Bargain.

In return for Iran agreeing to meet these conditions, the United States should be prepared to be fairly generous. We should be ready to lift all of the sanctions on Iran, both those imposed by executive order and those imposed by legislation, as well as to remove all of the different regulations—such as the FBI-mandated fingerprinting of all Iranians who enter the United States. We should be ready to conduct a universal settlement of all claims, including both private U.S. claims against Iran and Iranian claims against the United States, to determine the fate of Iran's frozen assets. The United States should be willing to approve Iran's participation in international economic frameworks such as the WTO, and support its applications for economic assistance from international financial institutions. If Iran enthusiastically and fully abides by its obligations, the United States should even be willing to consider bilateral economic assistance to Iran. The United States should be willing to provide assurances that we will not attack Iran if it does not attack the United States or its allies and should be willing to begin a broader process of regional security discussions, aimed eventually at producing a regional security framework and arms control agreements, similar to the CSCE process in Europe, to address Iran's legitimate security concerns.[22] We should be willing to pledge not to interfere in Iran's internal affairs, if Tehran wants it. The United States should also be ready to establish a contact group including all of Iraq's neighbors to provide a coordinating mechanism and a way for them to provide input into the process of Iraqi reconstruction, and Iran should be invited to participate to address its concerns about the future of Iraq. In addition, once the Iranians begin to think seriously about a Grand Bargain, they may come up with other demands, and we should certainly be willing to consider issues beyond those on this list.

A particularly sensitive question would be whether the United States should be willing to accept an Iranian nuclear energy program as part of the Grand Bargain. Although Iran sits on the second largest natural gas reserves in the world (and natural gas is a perfectly good method of generating power), the Iranians can make a tenuous claim to nuclear energy. The shah wanted it, and other countries with significant petroleum reserves have still developed nuclear energy because this allowed them to export more oil. Consequently, the United States should consider agreeing to allow Iran to purchase properly safeguarded light-water reactors in which the fissile material is supplied by another country (probably Russia), which would also take it back for reprocessing once it is spent.[23] It is still possible to make a nuclear weapon from the fissile material in a light-water reactor, but is harder to do so. It would likely become known if Iran was trying to do so, and therefore Tehran would probably take this step only in the event of a crisis. Nevertheless, the risk could not be eliminated entirely and so should reinforce Washington's determination to see that the terms of the Grand Bargain are paid out only incrementally over time to ensure that Iran always had an incentive to abide by its terms. With the demonstrations of disarmament the United States would want, the difficulty of using properly safeguarded light-water reactors to supply a nuclear weapons program, and the ability to cut off the flow of benefits to Iran (and impose unilateral or even multilateral sanctions against Tehran if it is caught diverting materials to a weapons program), we should be as confident as it is possible to be that Iran would not be able to mount a clandestine program.[24]

Of course, the bottom line remains that since Iran has not shown itself ready to explore this option seriously for the past twenty years, the Grand Bargain cannot be the principal element of a new U.S. policy toward Iran. At some point, the Iranians may be ready to sit down and work out a deal, but we have no idea when that will happen. In the meantime, the nuclear clock is ticking and Iran continues to support terrorist groups. In addition, it would be highly beneficial to the United States to help resurrect an Arab-Israeli peace process soon, and if we are fortunate, this too could happen well before the Iranians are ready to contemplate (let alone conclude) a Grand Bargain. Thus, while there is no harm—and considerable benefit—from leaving the Grand Bargain on the table, making it clear that that is our preferred course of action and regularly reiterating that we are amenable to it at any time, a new Iran policy would have to look to other strategies to deal with Iran's troublesome behavior until the Iranians finally can bring themselves to sit down and work out their differences with the Great Satan.

Track 2: A True Carrot-and-Stick Approach. During the early 1990s, the United States pursued a policy of containment that relied essentially on nothing but punishment to try to coerce Iran into better behavior. During that same period, Europe and Japan pursued a policy of engagement that relied on nothing but rewards that (ostensibly) were meant to persuade Iran to do the same. Both approaches failed in this primary goal, although both enjoyed some modest success in secondary goals—European and Japanese companies did make a fair amount of money off trade with Iran (although much less than was theoretically possible), while the United States was able to constrain Iran's ability to rearm and pursue some of its most aggressive designs. Both failed because they were one-dimensional policies and neither side was willing even to entertain the idea of compromising with the other, which allowed the Iranians to play Europe and Japan off against the United States. As long as the Iranians could convince themselves that the Europeans and Japanese (and Russians and Chinese) would provide them with the aid and trade they needed without the same demands as the Americans, they felt they could withstand the pressure from the United States. It is self-evident that only a multilateral policy that combined the two approaches would have any real chance of success in moving Iran in a positive direction.

Convincing our European and Japanese allies (let alone the Russians and Chinese) to agree to sanctions against Iran in any form would be very difficult. To their credit, the Europeans have shown a greater willingness to threaten sanctions against Iran than ever before for Tehran's refusal to comply with the requests of the IAEA regarding its uranium enrichment and plutonium extraction activities. That is a step in the right direction, but the European nations are still far from being willing to impose the kind of sanctions on Tehran that actually might persuade the Iranians to slow—let alone stop—their nuclear weapons programs. Moving them to that point is going to require the United States to adopt two new approaches to the problem.

The first of these is that the United States must demonstrate a willingness to reward Iran promptly and materially for progress on the nuclear and terrorism issues. The most reasonable objections to America's policies in the 1990s that Europeans and Japanese raised were that the United States expected Iran to give up all of its nefarious activities before Washington would consider making any changes to the sanctions and that it was so obsessed with Iran's bad behavior that it was unwilling to even consider the possibility of rewarding Tehran for moving in a positive direction. The most moderate European and Japanese voices regularly stated that they would be willing to collaborate in a new policy toward Iran, but only if that policy included rewards for progressive actions in addition to punishments for recidivism. That is a perfectly reasonable approach. In fact, it is more than reasonable, it is smart. Moving Iran to give up its support for nuclear weapons and terrorism is going to require both the push of negative incentives such as sanctions and the pull of positive incentives such as loans or liberalized trade.

Our goal should be to present the Iranians with two different paths. If they choose to go down the path of confrontation—stubbornly clinging to their nuclear program, their support for terrorism, and their violent opposition to a Middle East peace—then at each step they will be hit with progressively more painful consequences. If they choose the path of cooperation—by giving up those same patterns of behavior—then at each step they will be rewarded with progressively more advantageous benefits.[25]

The United States, Europe, Japan, and hopefully Russia and China should sit down and draw up a list of "benchmarks," things Iran could do that would be considered either confrontational or cooperative, and assign to each benchmark a corresponding positive or negative incentive proportionate to the step Iran took. This would be simpler than it sounds (although the negotiations over which benefits and penalties to apply for each benchmark would be awful). For instance, if Iran agreed to close down its uranium mines and turn over the extracted yellowcake to the IAEA, the United States and its allies might agree not to block Iran's application to the WTO. Or if Iran agreed to press to disarm Hizballah, the United States and its allies might agree to go forward with a number of predesignated aid projects that Iran had requested. On the other hand, if Iran brought the Natanz uranium enrichment facility online, the United States and its allies might agree to bar all imports from Iran. Likewise, at a lesser level, for every time that Iran tested a Shahab-series missile (including its engine) or that Hizballah attacked into Israel, the United States and its allies might declare a predesignated major Iranian economic project off limits to all of their corporations.

The benchmarks and incentives should also be set up to cover continuous activities (as opposed to onetime actions). Indeed, there is great value in locking in benchmark-incentive pairings for indefinite periods of time to reduce the risk that Iran might try to make a number of moves up front, collect the rewards, and then return to its previous patterns of behavior. For example, for as long as Iran agreed to forgo uranium enrichment activities, the United States would agree to keep issuing ILSA waivers. Alternatively, until Iran agreed to sign the Additional Protocol to the NPT and abide by its conditions, the United States and its allies might agree to suspend all provision of oil-related services to Iran (i.e., European, Japanese, and Russian contracts to develop Iranian oil fields would be suspended).

The complete list of benchmarks and their corresponding incentives should be long; it should include both onetime and ongoing actions; it should address both positive and negative steps Iran could take on nuclear weapons, terrorism, and violent opposition to a Middle East peace; and it should include incentives covering the full range of political, economic, and military affairs. Moreover, both the positive and negative incentives must be graduated and accrue incrementally so that each time Iran takes a further step in the wrong or right direction it would be punished or rewarded immediately and proportionately.

It would be critical to lay out all of these different incentives up front for three reasons. First, Iran needs to see both the whole series of penalties it would suffer if it took the path of confrontation and the whole series of benefits it would gain if it took the path of cooperation. There is a debate going on inside Iran on all of these issues, and it is critical to give those Iranians arguing for the path of cooperation all of the ammunition possible.[26] Laying out very starkly the pleasant future that Iran could expect from choosing the route of cooperation compared to the grim future that it would face if it continued on the route of confrontation is probably the best that any outsider can do to influence that debate. Second, if presented with an imminent Iranian step in the wrong direction, the Europeans and Japanese would be sorely tempted to balk, as they have consistently done in the past. Only if the benchmarks and their consequences were clearly delineated well before Iran approached them would it be likely that our allies would agree to them and that the United States would be able to hold them to their commitments. Last, just as proponents of a Grand Bargain with Iran rightly argue that the Iranians would be able to make concessions only as part of a deal that included the United States making counterbalancing concessions to them, so too is that true of forging a new Iran policy with our allies. The Europeans, Japanese, Russians, and Chinese have steadfastly resisted even the hint of sanctions against Iran for more than a decade; the only way they might be willing to support any theoretical sticks being used against Tehran is if they were presented as part of a comprehensive plan that also included a corresponding set of carrots.

The Second Track should appeal to our allies because it provides for sanctions only in the context of bad Iranian behavior—to which they will have already agreed both that the behavior is bad and what the appropriate punishment should be. Moreover, it cushions the sanctions issue by coupling it with American agreement to reward Iran for good behavior, even small steps in the right direction—something that the United States has never agreed to do in the past. What's more, it leaves the actual imposition of sanctions or benefits in the hands of the Iranians. Since the benchmarks and their corresponding incentives would be defined beforehand, it is the Iranians who would decide which course to take. If they chose the course of confrontation, it would be unmistakable that Iran was flouting the will of the international community and it would relieve the Europeans, Japanese, and others of the need to consciously act to apply sanctions: in effect, the Iranians would be bringing the sanctions upon themselves, having been forewarned. At the same time, if Iran chose cooperation, this too would be unmistakable, Americans would not be able to argue otherwise, and the Europeans would not have to try to persuade the United States to reward Iran since those thresholds would already have been set and the rewards should be automatic.

Although the comprehensive incentive structure of the Second Track should be appealing to our allies because it fits perfectly with their stated goals and previous demands from the United States, that does not mean it would be accepted. Ultimately, it clashes with our allies' paramount desire to make money off Iran regardless of its actions. Consequently, no one should be surprised if the Europeans, Japanese, Russians, and Chinese come up with all kinds of creative excuses as to why they cannot participate in such an approach. In particular, one obvious objection that the United States may hear is that creating such an incentive structure aimed openly at Tehran would trigger Iran's notorious sensitivity to foreign pressure and cause it to dig in its heels on all of its problematic behavior. At one level, this criticism is probably correct. At another, it may also be nothing but an effort to wriggle out of what is an approach fully consistent with the declaratory policies of Europe, Japan, China, and Russia. However, there is an alternative approach available: make the exercise more "theoretical."

My friend Kori Schake, a director for European affairs at the NSC under the second President Bush, likes to tell the story of a French diplomat who responded to an American proposal for a joint policy approach by observing, "That might work in practice, but it will never work in theory." In the event our allies argue that it is too hard to focus the Second Track explicitly and directly on Iran, the United States could propose to move the negative incentives (which, after all, is the part that our allies are squeamish about) into the theoretical realm of the NPT. In fact, this should be done anyway to bolster international nonproliferation efforts beyond the narrow problem of Iran.

Increasingly, members of the international community, including governments, international organizations, and all manner of experts, recognize that the NPT is a deeply flawed document because it is ambiguously phrased and has been interpreted as allowing all activity toward acquisition of a nuclear weapon except actually assembling the device (which is undetectable). As North Korea has done and Iran is trying to do, a country can take every step but the last toward acquiring a nuclear weapon without violating the NPT and then simply withdraw from the treaty at that last moment—or not withdraw, leaving the rest of the world knowing that it is merely "one screwdriver turn" away from having a nuclear weapon yet still technically within the terms of the NPT. Moreover, like so many other international agreements, because there are no penalties for noncompliance built into the NPT, in practice it means that countries that follow this route are never penalized for their actions because all the IAEA can do is declare a nation in violation and then refer the matter to the U.N. Security Council. Yet the Security Council is notorious for being unable to summon the political will to impose sanctions for anything except the most egregious and blatant abuses—Iraq's invasion of Kuwait, Libya's murder of innocents on the Pan Am 103 and UTA 772 flights, and South Africa's policy of apartheid.

The experience of the sanctions against Iraq is extremely important to the Iran case and the more general problem of putting "teeth" into the NPT. After passing the initial sanctions against Iraq in 1990, the United Nations quickly began to tire of enforcing them. The last time the Security Council declared Iraq to be in "material breach" of the cease-fire resolution was in June 1993, despite ever more flagrant Iraqi violations. By the late 1990s, the Security Council was unwilling to consider any punishment for Iraq even after Baghdad announced that it would no longer cooperate with the U.N. arms inspectors. An even greater problem was the unwillingness of the United Nations even to consider penalties against other states violating the sanctions against Iraq. As a result, ever-greater numbers of countries engaged in the smuggling of goods to and from Iraq, purchased Iraqi oil and paid it money outside of the oil-for-food program, and violated the flight ban because there was absolutely no penalty for doing so.

The Bush administration has taken some good first steps toward strengthening international proliferation controls in a way that could be useful to constrain Iran's nuclear program. They made an opening bid in such an effort by calling on the U.N. Security Council to pass a new resolution that would ban the transfer of enrichment and reprocessing equipment and technologies to any state that does not already have them, allowing only states that have signed the Additional Protocol to the NPT to import equipment for civilian nuclear programs, and prohibiting states under investigation by the IAEA from serving on its board of directors. These are all steps in the right direction that would help if they were acted upon, but they fall far short of what is actually needed. Of greatest importance, because the proposed resolution does not include predesignated penalties for violations of the resolution—and penalties to be applied to both the purchaser and the supplier—it falls into the same trap as the Iraq sanctions: over time, it will prove to be unenforceable. Countries will violate it, the Security Council will be unwilling to take action, and the result will be the rapid dissolution of the restrictions.[27]

Ideally, the United States should build such penalties into a new UNSC resolution or reconvene the signatories of the NPT and get them to agree to a revamped document. In practice, neither seems likely: the presence in both venues of nonnuclear states that want the right to acquire such technology and/or a greater commitment on the part of the nuclear states to give up their own weaponry would likely scuttle either effort. In addition, building penalties for violating UNSC resolutions into the resolutions themselves would be a monumental precedent that any number of countries would likely resist, including some of the five permanent members of the Council. At the very least, these kinds of problems could drag out either effort until long after Iran crossed the nuclear threshold.

In that case, the United States should do the next best thing: convene a conference to produce a new "convention on nuclear proliferation" including the G7 nations, Russia, China, India, Ukraine, Belarus, Kazakhstan, Pakistan, and any other E.U. states that could be persuaded to join.[28] This group should first announce that it will henceforth take a strict interpretation of the NPT as forbidding even civilian nuclear activities that could be related to weapons acquisition (a perfectly defensible interpretation of the treaty's language),[29] and that the burden of proof in this matter must rest with the country in question. Then this group should take all of the negative benchmarks for Iran and turn them into more generic statements to which they would bind themselves in a joint agreement. So, for example, what was originally envisioned in the Second Track as a benchmark regarding Iran's unwillingness to close its uranium-mining facilities would be recast as a general statement regarding any nation that engaged in uranium mining. The same types of penalties would then be applied, and all of the members of the group would agree to impose those penalties automatically based either on credible evidence provided by a member of the group or on a statement from the IAEA.

There are several issues related both to Iran and to the general problems with the NPT that this convention would have to address. First among them is that the convention must prohibit any signatory to the NPT from withdrawing from it and severely sanction those that do by forbidding all commercial interaction with any country that does withdraw from it. The convention should proscribe all use by any country (including the members of the group) of nuclear reactors employing plutonium or highly enriched uranium. These are not economically optimal systems to begin with, and they are much more useful for weapons development than for power generation. However, part of the problem is Japan's large-scale reliance on plutonium reactors for a variety of idiosyncratic reasons. Both the current IAEA director, Mohamed ElBaradei, and the last IAEA director, Hans Blix, have suggested that a key step to slowing nuclear proliferation is to ban all use of plutonium and HEU reactors, and this proposed nonproliferation convention should not only adopt that proposal but, again, impose sanctions on states that do not comply.[30]

In addition, to avoid the problem that was most responsible for the erosion of the containment of Iraq in the 1990s, the members would pledge to impose sanctions and other penalties on any other country (including members of the group) that violated another series of actions regarding the provision of nuclear-related materials to any other country, regardless of whether it was a signatory of the NPT or not. For instance, the sale of a plutonium reactor should trigger sanctions on both the purchasing country and the selling country. If proliferation is to be curbed, both the purchasers and the suppliers need to have strong disincentives to prevent them from doing so. Moreover, because Iran in particular has repeatedly demonstrated a willingness to endure extreme hardships in pursuit of goals it considers vital, slowing Tehran's program will require convincing those countries who have been helping it— Pakistan, China, and Russia—not to do so.[31]

Is such a convention possible? Absolutely. Its provisions would fall well within the declaratory policy of all of these states except Pakistan, whose inclusion in the group (a de facto recognition of its membership in the nuclear "club") ought to be enough to convince it to go along with such provisions and exorcise the ghost of A. Q. Khan's global nuclear proliferation racket. Of course, just because it is possible does not mean that it is assured. Again, because so many of these countries have repeatedly demonstrated a willingness to put avarice ahead of security—and because many of them cynically believe that even if Iran acquires nuclear weapons, it will be America's problem to keep them in check—there is no guarantee that they won't resist what is self-evidently in the interests of the entire world for the sake of making money. Still, the United States would have some powerful leverage on its side to persuade these states to participate in full. Many of the publics in these countries could be mobilized to compel their governments (which are usually much more deeply intertwined with their business communities, for both good and bad reasons) to join the effort. Likewise, numerous international and national nongovernmental peace and antiproliferation organizations would likely be highly supportive of such an effort. Convening such a convention and convincing it to put teeth into nuclear nonproliferation would be an uphill struggle, but it is hardly a lost cause and it could be the best way to address Iran's nuclear program.

Track 3: Preparing for a New Containment Regime. While there is real reason to hope that a true carrot-and-stick approach would move Iran in a progressive direction, the United States should not assume that it will. We must have a fallback option in the event that Iran remains incapable of coming to a Grand Bargain and steadfastly refuses a system of inducements and punishments designed to persuade it to become a more responsible member of the international community and discontinue its nuclear program. Of necessity, that fallback option would have to be a revised version of containment. If the First and Second Tracks fail, the United States would be left with nothing but containment, one of the usual reasons that Washington has adopted containment in the past. Nevertheless, if at all possible, this containment regime should be different from the version employed in the early 1990s. It may be able to reap some benefits from even the partial successes of the Second Track, and it can be blended with elements of some of the other policy proposals—which are not feasible as stand-alone policies but could be useful adjuncts to a policy of containment.

To a certain extent, the negative inducements of the Second Track (in other words, the "sticks") create the first elements of such a revised containment regime. In fact, they create the basis for a far more effective containment regime against Iran than the United States mounted unilaterally during the 1990s. That is one of the advantages of this approach—just as the positive inducements (the "carrots") of Track 2 could become a path toward a Grand Bargain if the Iranians are ready for a more cooperative relationship, so the negative incentives lay the basis for a more robust, multilateral containment regime if Tehran persists in its preference for an aggressive, anti–status quo policy. To a certain extent, as part of the Second Track carrot-and-stick approach, the United States would be making a deal with Europe, Japan, and hopefully Russia and China as well. We would agree to progressively reward Iran, including by lifting all of the sanctions, if Iran agrees to cease its problematic patterns of behavior, and they would agree to multilateral sanctions and a containment regime in the event that Iran refused to do so. If Iran did refuse to do so, it would find itself enmeshed in exactly the kind of multilateral sanctions regime that it successfully avoided before 1997.

The problem arises if our allies snub us too. Despite how self-evidently beneficial it would be for our allies to join us in a structured carrot-and-stick approach to Tehran, we should not assume they will. All have demonstrated a frustrating willingness to walk away from their strategic principles in the name of continuing to make money from commercial relations with Iran. Thus, the Second Track might fail not because Iran is not responsive to the incentive structures but because the Europeans, Japanese, Russians, and Chinese refused to create one.

In this case, the key question the United States will face is whether to attempt to impose some of the various provisions of the Second Track unilaterally. Here, the provisions against Iran itself are essentially beside the point—the United States certainly could repeal the Clinton administration's last gesture to Iran and again ban imports of Iranian carpets and foodstuffs—but these are mostly insignificant compared to its oil exports and its desire for American imports. The fact remains that the United States is basically doing everything it can to squeeze Iran through direct sanctions. The bigger question would be whether the United States wanted to impose some of the sanctions envisioned in the Second Track against those countries helping Iran's nuclear program—in other words, more secondary sanctions such as the ILSA. In this respect, the United States could announce that it will impose trade sanctions on foreign nations that provide Iran with nuclear-related materials—or that engage in the sale of plutonium or HEU reactors or related technology in general—as the Clinton administration did with Russia in 1997–1998 and threatened to do to China in 2000. As another example, Washington could decide that unless the Europeans were willing to sign on to a multilateral effort aimed either specifically at Iran or against proliferators in general, it would no longer award any ILSA waivers (which would be appropriate, given that the European Union's promise was to be more aggressive in combating both terrorism and proliferation). Other such secondary sanctions could certainly be envisioned.

Whether the United States should take this path is not a straightforward matter and is almost impossible to answer beforehand. At that point, the United States will be playing a very weak hand against Iran. Throughout the 1990s, Washington attempted to change Iran's behavior through unilateral sanctions and was largely unsuccessful. At a future date, if confronted with the failure of the First and Second Tracks, with Iran getting ever closer to having a fully self-contained fuel cycle, it may prove even harder to do so. At that point, we will need to ask ourselves how willing we are to damage our relations with our primary trading partners to try to keep nuclear weapons out of Iran's hands. One important consideration will be our assessment of how close Iran is to acquiring a self-contained fuel cycle when we are forced to confront this decision. If there is still time to head off an Iranian weapons capability, it certainly would be more worthwhile to try to exert additional pressure on our allies than if Iran was on the cusp of becoming self-sufficient. The willingness of the Europeans, Japanese, Chinese, and Russians to take other actions against Iran will also play a role in such calculations. It is conceivable that they might take actions unilaterally—as they did with the mild but significant step of suspending trade expansion talks with Tehran in 2003—and in this case, secondary sanctions would likely be inappropriate. Finally, Iran's own internal dynamics should also weigh in this decision. If Iran shows increasing signs of pragmatism (or if the reformists are somehow able to resurrect themselves), we may want to show forbearance in the expectation that a pragmatic Iran is more likely to be deterrable—and might even opt to discontinue its nuclear program on its own in hope of improving its international standing. On the other hand, while the willingness of the United States to take such steps unilaterally would undoubtedly further infuriate our allies, it could help persuade them that they should participate in the process envisioned in the Second Track—which would be more effective and consistent with their own policies—than face a trade war with the United States if we were forced to fall back on the Third Track without any allied support.

Beyond the question of sanctions, the United States could announce a policy of seizing any plane or ship believed to be carrying nuclear-related material to Tehran that American military forces are able to intercept. Such a policy would face some serious legal challenges but would be consistent with the Bush administration's own Proliferation Security Initiative, which proposed that the United States and its allies take precisely such steps to curb proliferation.[32] The United States should also look for other ways to physically interdict nuclear-related shipments to Iran. In addition, it should lay out a set of red lines for the use of force in hope of curbing some of Tehran's more egregious behavior. As noted above, one of those must be that in the event of any act of terrorism committed by al-Qa'eda personnel in communication with those inside Iran, the United States would hold Tehran responsible.

In the military realm, the United States may need to reconfigure its forces in the Persian Gulf (which have mostly been focused on containing, then invading, and then rebuilding Iraq) to better deal with Iran. This would include the need to interdict contraband being shipped to Iran, the ability to deal with renewed Iranian aggression, and forces in place to execute a counterproliferation option if the intelligence ever became available to do so. Indeed, as part of the Third Track, the United States should make a major intelligence effort—akin to the increase in our efforts against al-Qa'eda after 9/11—to gather information regarding Iran's nuclear program in the hope of developing a viable counterproliferation strike option. If the First and Second Tracks fail, then, as part of a new containment regime as the final fallback position in the Third Track, the United States should take a much harder look at a counter-proliferation campaign and work much harder to try to make such an operation plausible. Again, there are likely to be strong diplomatic and military ratio-nales arguing against this strategy, but they may be less compelling if we have already failed to entice either the Iranians to bargain away their program or our allies to set up a multilateral incentive structure to convince Iran to do so.

Of course, one of the residual arguments against a counterproliferation strike is likely to be concern that Iran might retaliate by destabilizing Iraq. This raises another element of a Third Track containment strategy: the need to keep Iran on the right side in Iraq. Here it might be useful to pick up the idea of a contact group of neighboring states, specifically as a forum to give the Ira-nians a greater say in Iraq's reconstruction activities. If nothing else, it should reassure Tehran that the process of reconstruction envisioned by the United States and the new Iraqi authorities would not be inimical to Tehran's interests.

Finally, the United States should stick to its principles regarding Iran in all other respects. After the disgraceful rigging of the 2004 Majles elections, the relative quiet of the Bush administration—which issued nothing but a per-functory condemnation from the State Department spokesman—was equally disgraceful. It is likely that the administration did so because the president's previous statements (from the inflammatory "Axis of Evil" to his much more moderate comments afterward) only seemed to enrage the hard-liners in Tehran. While this logic stems from good intentions, it flies in the face of U.S.-Iranian history. For the past twenty-five years, the United States has had zero success trying to influence Iranian domestic politics. As noted earlier, our mere involvement invariably hurts whoever we try to help no matter what it is we do. Under these circumstances, it is vital that the United States maintain a consistent position advocating democratization, rule of law, religious toler-ance, and respect for human rights in Iran. Remaining true to our convictions is actually a lot more useful to our foreign policy than experts and diplomats usually credit, and they are critical to who we are. If we cannot help those in Iran we would like to see succeed, then at the very least we need to remain true to the values that the whole world admires in the United States.

It is here that those who advocate a policy of regime change by pressing for a popular revolution illustrate a valuable kernel of truth. Throughout all the years of the Cold War, it was important that the United States stood like a lighthouse on the other side of the Iron Curtain, reminding the peoples of Eastern Europe that there was a free world out there that believed in very different values and whose citizens enjoyed a much better life. As long as that beacon existed, it made Eastern Europeans—even if only in the deepest recesses of their subconscious—yearn for the end of communism. So too should the United States continue to play that role for Iran. We cannot help the Iranian people directly because of our long, painful history and their psychological scars, but we can play an indirect role, as a reminder of what Iran might be if it were willing to move in a different direction. It seems altogether appropriate that the ultimate irony of U.S.-Iranian relations twenty-five years after the taking of the U.S. Embassy in Tehran is that the best thing we can do for Iran may be to remain true to ourselves.

Living with a Nuclear Iran

Because Iran is so willing to make enormous sacrifices in pursuit of its goals, and because our allies have so often shown themselves unwilling to make any sacrifices to exert real pressure on Tehran, even a multifaceted policy such as Triple Track could fail to prevent Iran from acquiring a nuclear weapons capability. In that case, we may find ourselves forced to live with a nuclear-armed Iran. That will not be easy, but it is not necessarily impossible either.[33]

Our history with Iran suggests that this regime probably can be deterred, either from using its nuclear arsenal or from taking other aggressive actions in the belief that its nuclear arsenal will itself deter countermoves by the United States or other states. Although willing to tolerate very high costs when core interests are threatened, key members of this regime—including Khamene'i and Rafsanjani—have also demonstrated that they will concede in the face of heavy damage and are often unwilling to suffer more modest damage when their core interests are not threatened. Ultimately, this group is not Khomeini, although there are certainly wild-eyed extremists such as IRGC Commander Safavi and Council of Guardians Secretary-General Jannati in influential positions from which they could no doubt argue for such radical approaches. Although deterring a nuclear-armed Iran does seem possible, it is not guaranteed, and it will not happen by itself. The United States will have to make a considerable investment to make it work, probably similar to our efforts to deal with North Korea for the past fifty years. If we are willing to make that effort, then deterrence can become the cornerstone of a new strategy for containment of Iran.

A key input into a regime to contain and deter a nuclear Iran will be whether Iran chooses to openly cross the nuclear weapons threshold. Some states, such as India and China, proclaimed their new nuclear status to the entire world by detonating nuclear devices. Other states, such as Pakistan until 1998, chose not to do so. Instead, they quietly let it be known to their adversaries that they had the proverbial "bomb in the basement." South Africa did the same, and it is widely believed that Israel and North Korea have as well. Openly crossing the nuclear weapons threshold (what is normally referred to as "transparent proliferation" because the state is not trying to hide it) is more useful in terms of its prestige and its utility as a clear deterrent—no potential adversary can miscalculate what it faces in taking on a country that has tested a nuclear weapon. On the other hand, overtly crossing the nuclear threshold can also trigger international diplomatic opprobrium and economic sanctions. Pakistan chose covert (or "opaque") proliferation and stuck to it until the 1998 Indian nuclear test in large part because Islamabad did not want to incur such sanctions, especially from the United States.

Iran would face the same set of pressures. On the one hand, for a nation as obsessed about its status in the world and in the eyes of others as Iran, Tehran will undoubtedly want to enjoy the prestige of being an avowed (if not accepted) member of the nuclear "club." Given how paranoid many of its leaders are regarding a possible American (or Israeli or Pakistani) attack, they doubtless will want to proclaim their new deterrent so that there can be no doubt in the minds of Washington, Jerusalem, or Islamabad that Tehran is now their equal. On the other hand, the Iranians will likely fear that crossing the nuclear threshold would be a step too far for the Europeans and cause them to finally agree to sanctions against Iran. Tehran's efforts to keep the program quiet so far, and its willingness to accept (temporarily) the E.U. conditions in September 2003, all indicate its ongoing concern about European or possibly even U.N. sanctions.

Even after Iran acquired a nuclear weapons capability (whether that meant possessing actual weapons or merely the capability to put the weapons together on short notice), the United States would do well to try to put in place, or keep in place, many of the steps envisioned in the Triple Track approach. This effort would be greatly helped by a consensus among the United States, Europe, Japan, Russia, and China that Iran had acquired nuclear weapons. In turn, this would be best helped by Iran openly crossing the nuclear weapons threshold—which is precisely the disincentive for Iran to do so. Once Iran has acquired nuclear weapons, the United States might be able to coax our allies into agreeing to put teeth into the NPT if they have not already done so. It would do little for the Iranian problem, but it should help dampen the ardor for other states (such as Saudi Arabia or Iraq) to pursue nuclear weapons in response. In addition, a modified version of Triple Track in terms of convincing our allies to apply multilateral sanctions against Iran while simultaneously holding out the prospect of a Grand Bargain might succeed over the long term. Libya gave up its nuclear program in response to sustained multilateral sanctions, and South Africa gave up its nuclear weapons. Especially if there is a change of regime at some point in Iran, it is not impossible that Tehran might decide to trade away even actual weapons in return for getting comprehensive sanctions lifted.

Some of the more collaborative aspects of Triple Track would also be worth pursuing even after Iran has crossed the nuclear threshold. In particular, it would be even more important to involve Tehran in a Persian Gulf security framework similar to Europe's CSCE. Whereas before Iran acquired nuclear weapons the purpose of this enterprise would be to try to address Iran's legitimate security concerns through dialogue, confidence-building measures, and (eventually) arms control to eliminate Iran's strategic impetus for nuclear weapons, afterward it would be to try to work out diplomatic "rules of the road" for all of the states of the region to avoid unintended provocations, crises, and the like. Once Iran has nuclear weapons, difficult as it may be, we are going to have to find a way to live with them and reassure the Iranians enough about our intentions and actions that they do not react aggressively out of fear while also making very clear to them the consequences of going on the offensive themselves.

Depressing as it may be, even after Iran crosses the nuclear threshold it is just not certain that we could count on our allies joining us in a multilateral effort to punish and contain Iran. Again, the justification would be self-evident: Iran will need to be dissuaded or prevented from reverting to an aggressive foreign policy, and other states considering whether to pursue nuclear weapons need to believe that Iran paid an unacceptable cost for having done so. Given the remarkable perfidy of our allies regarding Iran in the past—and our own willingness to embrace Pakistan despite its crossing the nuclear weapons threshold when it suddenly became convenient for us to do so after 9/11—we cannot assume that they will be willing to join us even then. Some will undoubtedly argue that there would be no point once Iran has crossed the nuclear threshold, while others will continue to propound the theme that "now it is more important than ever that the West expand economic relations with Tehran to moderate its behavior." The fact that this has been their response to every single Iranian action—good, bad, or indifferent—and has only encouraged Iran to pursue its problematic behavior will no doubt be lost on them.

In that case, there would still be unilateral actions that the United States could take that would have a meaningful impact on the strategic balance of the region. In fact, these are steps that the United States should take regardless of what our European and Asian allies may do. For instance, in these circumstances, the deployment of American ballistic missile defenses would become extremely useful. For this reason, those who advocate the development of antiballistic missile defenses are not entirely misguided. Although the prospect that such defenses could shelter the continental United States from a large-scale Russian (or future Chinese) attack are probably slim, and so probably would not justify their costs, in a regional environment, such defenses become extremely important. Iran's own missile force is still quite small and not terribly potent, and likely will remain so for quite some time. Moreover, ABM systems such as Israel's Arrow have shown a surprising degree of capability to intercept shorter-range ballistic missiles. Deploying even marginally capable ABM systems could be very useful in reassuring our regional allies—and hopefully convincing them that it is unnecessary to incur the diplomatic and economic costs of acquiring nuclear weapons of their own. Moreover, even weak ballistic missile defenses could complicate Tehran's strategic planning, possibly making it more reticent to embark on aggressive foreign adventures. For all of these reasons, a commitment to developing theater ballistic missile defenses is a worthwhile component of American strategic planning to deal with a nuclear Iran.

Other unilateral actions that the United States could take would again be identical to steps envisioned as part of Triple Track. In particular, the United States should lay down clear red lines regarding Iranian actions that would trigger the use of American force. At the very least, these should include Iran's use of force against any American allies, terrorist attacks against Americans or American allies, and transfer of nuclear arms to terrorists.

The threat that Iran might give nuclear weapons to terrorists tends to receive far too much attention, but it cannot be dismissed. Iran has possessed chemical and biological weapons since the end of the Iran-Iraq War, and if it had wanted to, it could have provided these to any of the different Hizballahs it has spawned; to HAMAS, PIJ, or any other Palestinian rejectionist group; or to any of a half-dozen other groups. Tehran has never done so. It has never done so because it has never believed that these groups required such weapons and because it feared that if their use were ever traced back to Tehran, the retaliation it would suffer would outweigh any gains from the attack itself. In the past, Iran's skilled intelligence operatives have been able to maintain some degree of plausible deniability for at least some time after many of their terrorist attacks. But in the aftermath of a nuclear terrorist attack, the victim—and its allies—are probably not going to be too concerned about how good the evidence linking it to Tehran was. Moreover, so unforgivable a crime would not have a statute of limitations. If Iran's hand were discovered behind it—and in every case in the past, Iran's hand was eventually proven—Tehran would have hell to pay. Thus it is hard to imagine why Tehran would want to give nuclear weapons to a terrorist group except in extreme circumstances when the regime itself was threatened by outside attack and this was the only means at its disposal to stave off the *coup de grâce*. Iranians' support for terrorism has been entirely instrumental—they are not nihilists like the Japanese Aum Shinrikyo, nor do they simply want to kill huge numbers of their enemies as al-Qa'eda does. In virtually every scenario imaginable, Iran's need for nuclear deterrence—or even nuclear blackmail if it were feeling offensively inclined—would be better served by having a nuclear force deliverable by its own ballistic missiles, which is precisely the route Iran seems to be pursuing. From Tehran's own perspective, giving nuclear weapons even to its most faithful servants, such as Lebanese Hizballah, would make no sense.

Still, the consequences of their doing so would be so catastrophic that the United States should take some actions to reinforce what are likely to be Tehran's natural inclinations not to do so. There are really only two steps that could be taken, but they should suffice. First, as part of the red lines that the United States laid down, Washington should emphasize that any transfer of nuclear technology to any terrorist group would be met with an immediate American response and that under those circumstances the U.S. government would be forced to consider employment of all capabilities within the American arsenal to neutralize this threat. Second, the United States should pursue the massive augmentation of its intelligence gathering against Iran already envisioned in Triple Track. The Iranians need to feel that the United States is watching their every move and that if they so much as debate giving nuclear weapons to terrorists, the U.S. intelligence community would find out about it.

Iran is already a high priority for American intelligence agencies, but it needs to be moved up several more notches. In the world of intelligence, there is always more that can be done. Before 9/11, terrorism (and al-Qa'eda specifically) was one of the intelligence community's highest priorities, but after the attacks, CIA and other agencies increased their efforts against al-Qa'eda by orders of magnitude. It goes without saying that the United States needs more Farsi speakers among its intelligence officers, but of equal importance, although less understood, the United States needs the kind of intelligence officers who might actually be able to penetrate the Iranian government. In particular, because the United States has no embassy in Tehran and Iranian diplomats are largely forbidden to speak to American officials, the U.S. intelligence community needs to make a major effort to recruit case officers willing to work in the much more dangerous and demanding capacity of "nonofficial cover." This means they go out pretending to be businessmen and -women and other occupations not formally linked to the U.S. government. It also means that they do not have a diplomatic passport to protect them if they are ever exposed, which is why it is considered such dangerous work. But the days when American spies could attend cocktail parties and troll for potential agents among the foreign diplomats gathered at these occasions are long gone, especially in the case of the Iranians. We must do a better job of penetrating the Iranian regime to be able to monitor Iran's nuclear-related activities, and that means adapting our intelligence services to the demands of their state and society.

Another question that will bear heavily on the ability of the United States to construct an effective new containment of a nuclear-armed Iran is how Iran's neighbors and other interested countries will respond. In particular, the response of the GCC states will be important in gauging what may be possible. From Washington's perspective, only a determination on the part of the GCC to balance against Iran in cooperation with the United States would be a good outcome. In this case, the United States could call on the Gulf states to help lobby the Europeans and Asians to join in multilateral sanctions against Iran and probably could also beef up the American naval presence in the Gulf as a way of underlining and enforcing its red lines to Tehran. Neither of the other two imaginable options would serve American interests. On a variety of occasions, some or all of the GCC states have chosen to bend to Tehran's wishes in the hope of not provoking Iran—a strategy that many of them have pursued at different times in the past. If they were to decide to respond to an Iranian nuclear weapons capability with a policy of accommodation, it could make it hard for the United States to convince other countries to enact sanctions against Iran or to beef up its own forces in the Gulf region. Finally, they might look to balance off Iran by developing a nuclear capability of their own. Saudi Arabia is best positioned to do so, given Riyadh's long-standing support for the Pakistani nuclear program, which undoubtedly was motivated by precisely the fear that Iran or Iraq would acquire nuclear weapons and the Saudis would then want to be able to counter them without having to increase their reliance on the United States—already a painful domestic political issue. The UAE, Qatar, and Kuwait also have the kind of financial resources that would sorely tempt a North Korea or Pakistan to sell them one or more nuclear weapons, if any of them was inclined to do so. Obviously, such a scenario is the ultimate proliferation nightmare.

There are three other countries at least that would be obvious concerns if Iran were to cross the nuclear threshold. Israel would be highly agitated, but undoubtedly would resign itself to pursuing a policy of deterrence. Jerusalem would likely send a message to Tehran that if it did not try anything, neither would Israel. And the Iranians would probably be comfortable with that as well. The United States might help by formalizing its relationship with Israel in an alliance treaty. Nevertheless, the Israelis would fear that rather than a more moderate government taking power in Tehran, at some point they might face an even more radical regime—one that looked more like the old Khomeini regime and so might be more willing to take greater risks to try to damage Israel for purely ideological reasons. To guard against that, Israel might try to find covert methods to aid Iranian opposition groups, although it is highly unlikely that even if it could it would have any impact on Iranian politics. Turkey certainly would not be happy about a nuclear-armed Iran, but it would probably be reassured by an explicit American reminder to Iran that the United States was adamantly committed to the security of its NATO allies.

Iraq would be in the most difficult position. A new Iraqi government, struggling to establish itself, knit its fractious society together, and build a stable economy in the midst of ongoing violence would feel both threatened and completely unable to cope with a nuclear-armed Iran. The obvious solution to its problem would be for Washington to add a red line that any Iranian attack on Iraq would trigger the use of force by the United States, and retain a military force in Iraq to serve as a trip wire if not an outright deterrent to Iranian attack. If this is possible, it would likely go a long way toward assuaging Iraqi fears. Unfortunately, this might not be a viable approach. Depending on Iraqi public sentiment and the further course of the reconstruction, by the time Iran crosses the nuclear threshold, Baghdad may be desperate to minimize the U.S. presence and its reliance on Washington for any sort of security. In these circumstances, the best the United States is likely to do is to send private messages to Tehran warning it that the United States would respond to any Iranian use of force against Iraq, while warning Iraq that the United States would be forced to impose sanctions on Baghdad if it attempted to solve this problem by acquiring nuclear weapons of its own. Just as Iran and Iraq are perplexing problems in their own right, any time they intersect the dilemmas just become that much worse.

The Persian Puzzle

How to handle Iran and, in particular, its pursuit of nuclear weapons is a problem from Hell. There simply is no school solution. The current regime in Tehran is determined to resist all foreign pressure to acquire these weapons and, when it has done so, may revert to an aggressive, anti–status quo foreign policy that would destabilize the Middle East and threaten the vital interests of the United States and its allies. There is reason to believe that a different government in Tehran—one more reflective of the will of the Iranian people—would be willing to discontinue or reorient the program to make it much less threatening. However, there seems to be little likelihood that such a new government will take power soon and effectively nothing that the United States could do to change that. In fact, anything that the United States did would probably just make the situation worse. This conundrum is even more frustrating because it derives largely from the psychological and political taboos that have calcified around the idea of the United States in Iran's collective psyche over the past fifty years. They are a product of American mistakes made twenty-five or fifty years ago, embellished and exaggerated to grandiose proportions by the Iranian imagination. We may not like it, but those ideas define the reality.

The two clocks keep ticking and our ability to influence either is not great, but our history suggests that there is little hope of affecting the clock of regime change in Tehran. If it happens, it will happen of its own volition, on its own schedule. There is no question that slowing the nuclear clock will also be difficult. But it is not impossible. There are still ways to do so. A great deal rests on our allies in Europe and Japan, China, and Russia. If they are willing to take the Iranian nuclear threat seriously and put international security and stability ahead of their crass economic gains, there is real reason to hope that Iran could be convinced that a nuclear weapons capability just isn't worth it.

In a fundamental way, the problem of Iran embodies the new realities of the post–Cold War world. The United States is an extraordinarily powerful nation, but not an omnipotent one. There are problems that we simply cannot handle by ourselves. The problem of Iran today is one of them. There are actions we could take toward Iran entirely on our own that might help the problem, but they are unlikely to solve it. The potential solutions lie only in the hope of collective action by all of the leading nations of the world. Multilateralism often gets a bad rap in Washington. This is a problem that demands it.

Nevertheless, the Iran problem also illustrates the central role of the United States in the post–Cold War world. No other nation places global security and stability ahead of its economic interests, which is not to say that the United States is entirely selfless. It is merely to say that because the United States is the principal benefactor of the current international order, we also have the greatest interest in its preservation—or at least in preventing sudden, violent challenges to that order. Consequently, when there is a threat to international security and stability posed by a nation such as Iran, it is the United States that must lead a multilateral effort to address it. The key, however, is to craft an approach that can both solve the problem and preserve the interests of all of the states we hope will join in the effort. No country other than the United States can put together such an effort, but the United States cannot pursue such an effort alone. If we do not lead, others will not follow; but neither will they follow if we try to lead them in a direction they do not like. Indeed, one of the great challenges of the post–Cold War world is for the United States to find solutions to labyrinthine problems like that of Iran in the wilderness of interests that emerged when the simple struggle between East and West collapsed on that day in November 1989 when the Cold War ended and the world suddenly became a much more complicated place again.

That is the last element of the Persian puzzle. We must sort through the myriad pieces of our own relationship with this troubled and troubling nation, while also sorting out our equally difficult relations with the rest of the world. For this reason, perhaps more than the invasion of Iraq, the war on terror, or any of the other conflicts we have waged since the fall of the Berlin Wall, the problem of Iran may be the ultimate test of America's leadership in the new era that is dawning. How we handle the problem of Iran will tell us a great deal about whether we are up to its challenges.

Author's Note

Every observer of Iran has a story about the moment that he or she had an epiphany about just how different Iran is from any other country in the world. My own came in 1989, when I was a junior military analyst in the Central Intelligence Agency's Iran-Iraq Branch. At that time, my then mentor, Steve Ward, and I set out to write a paper on the likely course of Iranian military rearmament. The year before, the Iranians had suffered a devastating series of defeats at the hands of the Iraqi Army that forced Tehran to make peace with Saddam Hussein. After the war, the Iranians announced that they planned to rebuild their armed forces quickly so that they would never be defenseless again. Steve and I assumed that the Iranians would make a major effort to purchase tanks, artillery, armored personnel carriers, ground attack aircraft, helicopters, and everything else they needed to reconstitute their shattered ground forces. We assumed that after the events of 1988, Iran's highest priority would be to eliminate the potential for Iraq to employ its superiority on the ground to blackmail Tehran or seize Iran's oil-rich Khuzestan province—one of Saddam's initial goals when he attacked in 1980.

Instead, when we began piecing together the evidence of what the Iranians were up to, two things struck us: first, the Iranians really weren't making much of an effort at rearmament at all. In fact, they were engaging in prolonged and bizarre negotiations with a whole variety of arms manufacturers over rather minor issues that dragged out the whole process. They certainly were not acting the way that any other nation facing a serious threat would act. Second, they were buying mostly weaponry intended for naval warfare: antiship missiles, medium-range strike aircraft, fixed surface-to-air missiles, and the like. In other words, they were not arming to defend themselves against Iraq—the state that had invaded their country and just obliterated their armies—they were arming to defend themselves against us, the United States. That was when I first truly understood that Iran was a very different country from most others and that it was a country obsessed with the United States of America.

In some ways, I have been trying to write this book ever since. For the last sixteen years, Iran has always been one of the countries I have worked on—at the CIA, the National Defense University, the National Security Council, and several Washington think tanks, now including the Saban Center at Brookings. Iran was always the most fascinating of all of the countries I followed. However, throughout that time there seemed to be a pattern: I would start work on a project on Iranian-American relations only to have Iraq (the other country I always had responsibility for) do something stupid or aggressive or both, forcing me to shelve the Iran project and deal with the Iraq crisis *du jour*.

In 1998, I was happily cochairing a project requested by the Joint Staff at the Pentagon to look at the political and military implications of Iran obtaining a nuclear weapon when I got a phone call from Sandy Berger, President Clinton's national security adviser, asking me to come back to the NSC to work on—what else?—Iraq. While I was at the NSC, Iran was also part of my portfolio, and I was part of the effort by the Clinton administration to reach out to the new Khatami government in Iran in the hope of starting a process of rapprochement. But I still found myself spending three quarters of my time dealing with matters related to Iraq and our efforts to shore up the sagging multinational containment regime. It happened to me again in 2002, after I had left government with the rest of the Clinton administration and had taken on the job of director of national security studies at the Council on Foreign Relations. I was again planning to write a monograph on U.S.-Iranian relations when Jon Karp, my editor at Random House, out of the blue sent me an e-mail asking whether I was interested in writing a book on Iraq. Everyone I knew and respected, including my sagacious boss, Les Gelb, told me I was crazy not to put aside the Iran book and instead get back to work on Iraq.

So now I have finally gotten to write it.

A couple of caveats are in order. I have never been to Iran. I have tried on at least three occasions during my time out of government, but I have never made it there. On two previous occasions I was warned not even to apply for a visa by Iranians connected to the government. This past year I tried again and was encouraged by Iranians who no doubt thought that they could get me a visa, but my request simply went nowhere. I will leave it up to the reader to decide which aspect of my background the Iranian government objected to.

I regret not having been able to travel to Iran for many reasons, not least of which is that it is always helpful to see people in their own context and to meet the much broader range of people that can be encountered only in a foreign country itself. However, while this is deeply regrettable, I do not see it as a calamitous gap. Even with foreign countries in which I have spent considerable time, I am always cautious to remember that my own experiences there are only those of one person and so are an unreliable sample. It is always best to count one's own observations as simply one data point and not to privilege them above others. I have always found that it is much better to listen to the views and experiences of a wide range of people to create a more "statistically significant" and, hopefully, unbiased portrait of the country. In this case, I do not have my own experiences to draw upon, and that has forced me to listen even more carefully to those who have spent time in Iran—Iranians, Americans, and others. I will say only that I have tried to be as objective and unbiased a listener as possible during my sixteen years following Iran, but every reader will have to be his or her own judge of how successful I have been.

I also do not speak any Farsi (Persian). The dribs and drabs of Arabic I have left after a decade of neglect provide some meager insight into the principal Iranian tongue, but that is the extent of it. It certainly might have been helpful to know Farsi to be able to read some of the more obscure books and articles written by Iranians about their country and its relationship to the world that are not translated into English. It is also true that knowing a language often provides insight into some of the subtler aspects of a nation's culture and society—and Iran is nothing but subtlety. I am certain that I have missed at least some, and possibly many, of those nuances in thinking about Iran. Fortunately, there is a vast literature on Iran in English written by Iranians and foreigners upon which I have been able to rely over the years. I have also leaned heavily on the advice and comments of a number of fluent Persian speakers and residents or frequent visitors to Iran to help me catch these subtle mistakes wherever possible.

This is not a book on Iranian history per se. My principal goal is to discuss U.S.-Iranian relations, how they have been shaped by their history, and ultimately how best to treat them in the years ahead. For that purpose, I believe that my own experiences working on Iran within the U.S. government for much of the past sixteen years grant me both knowledge and perspectives that provide me with useful insights even though I cannot read any of the Iranian newspapers that are not regularly translated into English. I have seen Iran policy through the eyes of America's intelligence and defense communities, and I have participated in the making of that policy at the White House itself. I hope those experiences have lent me a somewhat different perspective from that of most authors who write about Iran—a perspective that will be helpful in understanding the tangled relations between our two countries.

Acknowledgments

It is typically the case that the author's long-suffering spouse receives her due only at the very end of the acknowledgments. My wonderful wife, Andrea, put up with enough in the writing of this book that I think she deserves to come first in the long list of those who helped make it possible. Especially for the final six months of writing, Andrea had to deal with a newborn infant, selling our old house and buying a new one, a nightmarish move, assorted other misadventures, and the demands of her own extremely hectic career—all effectively without a husband. The fact that we survived without a divorce is testimony to her forbearance; the fact that I finished what proved to be a bear of a book to write is testimony to her love and support. She is the love of my life, and I am grateful to have her and our wonderful son, Aidan, each and every day.

I was once again fortunate to be able to count on the work of some extremely able research assistants. In particular, my senior research associate, Garner Gollatz, was invaluable to the writing of this book from start to finish. On more than one occasion, Garner was a lifesaver. His tireless efforts and his quick, competent work, as well as his great sensitivity to Middle Eastern cultures and politics, meant that I could count on him to shoulder much of what turned out to be a herculean task. Garner was very ably assisted by some of the best young researchers I have ever had the privilege of working with: Lucie-Kay Desthuis-Francis, Andrew Horesch, Ashley Goodrich-Mahoney, Janessa Karawan, Anna Johnson, Ari Varon, and Airella Viehe never ceased to amaze me with their ability to doggedly run topics to ground, synthesize vast amounts of data, and piece together arcane statistics. They all have my sincerest thanks. The library staff at Brookings—David Bair, Sarah Chilton, Eric Eisinger, John Grunwell, and especially Laura Mooney—also have my gratitude. From tracking down obscure texts to fending off the demands of other libraries, they could not have been more helpful.

A number of people were exceedingly generous with their time and their great stores of wisdom. Shaul Bakhash lavished his staggering knowledge of Iranian politics and society upon me, working to help me with everything from the right interpretation of the Iranian Constitution to the broad causes of the revolution. Daniel Byman played his usual role as my alter ego, providing invaluable criticism on every aspect of the book as well as steering me nimbly through the wilderness of mirrors of international terrorism. Bruce Riedel helped me to understand any number of key moments in American decision making and shared with me at least a dozen truly brilliant insights into the U.S.-Iranian relationship that he has been working on since he first got pulled onto the Iran Task Force at the CIA in December 1978. As always, Steve Ward kept me honest, remembered things that I had forgotten, explained things that I could not understand, and was more generous than I had any reason to expect in working with me on both substance and presentation. Although he is now a close friend, he has never ceased to be a wonderful mentor. Judith Yaphe granted me large doses of her broad knowledge of Iran and the Persian Gulf, her long experience in the U.S. intelligence community, and her irascible sense of humor—which was a welcome boost at many a difficult moment. I owe Judi lunch, a vacation, and much else for her help on this book. Jim Steinberg proved to me over and over again why he is one of the few generalists who is a true specialist on every aspect of international relations, sharpening my analysis not only of Iran but also of the connections between U.S-Iranian relations and America's larger foreign policy objectives. Jim's comments constantly amazed me because they were so damn smart and so damn obvious once he said them—but neither I nor anyone else would have seen them had he not.

Four other great scholars of Iran and U.S.-Iranian relations—Mark Gasiorowski, Daniel Brumberg, Ray Takeyh, and Gary Sick—read major chunks of the manuscript and provided all manner of superb comments, large and small. Their knowledge helped me to correct numerous egregious errors and their insight enriched every facet of this book. Michael Levi provided me with some wonderful guidance on Iran and the NPT, as did Jim Placke and Gal Luft on aspects of Iran's oil industry and Ted Koppel on the American media and the hostage crisis. Ted also has my thanks, along with my good friend Bart Aronson, for playing the role of "intelligent nonexpert" in reading much of the manuscript to help me understand what readers who had not spent their entire lives poring over the Friday sermons from Qom would want to see in a book about U.S.-Iranian relations. If this book is at all enjoyable to read, they deserve the credit.

And, of course, any remaining mistakes or poor analysis are mine alone.

This book was reviewed by two of my former employers, the Central Intelligence Agency and the National Security Council, in keeping with the requirements of my security clearance agreements. Rod Soubers at the NSC and David and Paul (who must remain last-nameless) at CIA shepherded the manuscript through the clearance process while making it as painless as it could have been.

Martin Indyk, my boss at the Saban Center for Middle East Policy at the Brookings Institution, has my gratitude, not just for hiring me to be his deputy—which has been a most rewarding assignment—but for giving me the opportunity to write this book. Haim Saban, our great benefactor, has also earned more than a few thanks for everything that he has done for me and for the center. Haim and Martin deserve recognition for having the vision to see the need for an institution like the Saban Center, at which someone like me could write a book like this. It is impossible to mention the Saban Center without mentioning Ellen McHugh, our dynamo of an assistant director for administration, who makes the trains run on time and who helped me in more ways than she can imagine. Ellen gets a short mention here, but she has a very big place in my heart.

At Brookings itself, I would like to thank Strobe Talbott and Jim Steinberg. Strobe was gracious enough not only to hire me but to write a wonderful foreword to this book. Strobe has always been a pleasure to work for. Likewise, Jim Steinberg has been nothing but generous to me—with his time, his insight, and his advice—since I first joined the Foreign Policy Studies staff, and he bent over backward on more than one occasion to help me write this book. Ona Dosunmu, Jim's able deputy, always makes me smile whenever I think of her. She is one of those people who makes an organization better than it otherwise would be through her intelligence, her patience, and her determination to work things out, and I benefited from all of those qualities at various points during the writing of this book. Bob Faherty of the Brookings Press also has my great gratitude for his efforts on my behalf. He made working out the details for this book easy and painless when they might have been nothing of the kind.

Random House again proved to me that it could work miracles. Jonathan Jao did superb work editing the manuscript and helping to cut back and tighten a painfully long text. He was a great addition to the team that put this book together. Steve Messina was his usual remarkable and meticulous self, bringing to his work (and thus mine) the patience and care of a fine craftsman. Also at Random House, many thanks to my superstar publicist, Sally Marvin; Victoria Wong, who designed the book; Richard Elman, who oversaw the production process; editorial assistant Jillian Quint; my invaluable copy editors, Lynn Anderson, Fred Chase, and Carol Shookhoff; and proofreaders Bill Molesky, Rose Ann Ferrick, and Beth Thomas.

Since my wife got top billing, I will give the final place of honor to my remarkable editor, Jonathan Karp. This book is another example of why he is worth his weight in gold to me and, I hope, to Random House. Although I have been trying to write a book about Iran for sixteen years, it was Jon who convinced me that now was the time to do so. He has an uncanny ability to know what people are going to want to know about. He is also a tremendous editor and an incredible advocate. I doubt anyone could have pulled the kind of rabbits out of Random House's hat for me that Jon did routinely and with nothing but grace. I constantly marvel at my good luck that one day he picked up a copy of *Foreign Affairs* and saw my name on the cover.

Notes

Introduction: The Persistence of Memory

1. Robin Wright, *The Last Great Revolution* (New York: Alfred A. Knopf, 2000), p. 29.

Chapter 1: From Persepolis to the Pahlavis

1. For a superb discussion of this and other aspects of Iranian culture as they apply to Iranian foreign policy, see Graham E. Fuller, *"The Center of the Universe": The Geopolitics of Iran* (Boulder, Colo.: Westview, 1991).
2. Elaine Sciolino, *Persian Mirrors: The Elusive Face of Iran* (New York: Free Press, 2000), p. 26.
3. Ervand Abrahamian, *Iran Between Two Revolutions* (Princeton, N.J.: Princeton University Press, 1988), p. 11; Barry Rubin, *Paved with Good Intentions* (New York: Free Press, 2000), pp. 6–7.
4. Abrahamian, *Iran Between Two Revolutions*, pp. 11–36.
5. Elton L. Daniel, *The History of Iran* (Westport, Conn.: Greenwood Press, 2001), pp. 3, 26–28; Firoozeh Kashani-Sabet, "Cultures of Iranianness: The Evolving Polemic of Iranian Nationalism," in Nikki R. Keddie and Rudi Matthee, eds., *Iran and the Surrounding World: Interactions in Culture and Cultural Politics* (Seattle: University of Washington Press, 2002), p. 163; Nikki R. Keddie, *Modern Iran: Roots and Results of Revolution,* rev. and updated (New Haven, Conn.: Yale University Press, 2003), p. 2; Helen Chapin Metz, *Iran: A Country Study* (Washington, D.C.: U.S. Government Printing Office, 1989), pp. 31–33.
6. Daniel, *The History of Iran,* pp. 29–30; Stephen Kinzer, *All the Shah's Men: An American Coup and the Roots of Middle East Terror* (Hoboken, N.J.: John Wiley & Sons, 2003), p. 19. There are still several tens of thousands of Zoroastrians in Iran today.
7. Daniel, *The History of Iran,* p. 37; John A Garraty and Peter Gay, *The Columbia History of the World* (New York: Harper and Row, 1981), pp. 154, 163; Metz, *Iran,* p. 34.
8. Daniel, *The History of Iran,* pp. 41–45; Garraty and Gay, *Columbia History,* pp. 163–167; Metz, *Iran,* pp. 34–36.
9. Garraty and Gay, *Columbia History,* pp. 169–170; Daniel, *The History of Iran,* pp. 47–50.
10. Theodore Ayrault Dodge, *Alexander* (New York: Da Capo, 1996); J. F. C. Fuller, *A Military History of the Western World,* vol. 1: *From the Earliest Times to the Battle of Lepanto* (New York: Da Capo, 1987); Garraty and Gay, *Columbia History,* pp. 180–181; Metz, *Iran,* p. 37.

11. Daniel, *The History of Iran,* pp. 51–65.

12. Ibid., pp. 64–68; Garraty and Gay, *Columbia History,* pp. 259–272.

13. Daniel, *The History of Iran,* pp. 64–68; Metz, *Iran,* pp. 41–42.

14. Keddie, *Modern Iran,* p. 19.

15. Daniel, *The History of Iran,* pp. 83–93; Michael M. J. Fischer, *Iran: From Religious Dispute to Revolution* (Madison, Wis.: University of Wisconsin Press, 1980), pp. 28–30; Keddie, *Modern Iran,* pp. 10–11.

16. My thanks to professors Shaul Bakhash and Daniel Brumberg for explaining these various concepts.

17. Abrahamian, *Iran Between Two Revolutions,* pp. 36–38; Daniel, *The History of Iran,* pp. 97–102; Keddie, *Modern Iran,* p. 37.

18. Daniel, *The History of Iran,* p. 98.

19. Ibid., pp. 102–103; Keddie, *Modern Iran,* p. 38; Chris Paine and Erica Schoenberger, "Iranian Nationalism and the Great Powers, 1872–1954," *MERIP Reports* 37 (May 1975), p. 3.

20. Alvin Cottrell, "Iran's Armed Forces Under the Pahlavi Dynasty," in George Lenczowski, ed., *Iran Under the Pahlavis* (Stanford, Calif.: Hoover Institution Press, 1978), p. 389; Daniel, *The History of Iran,* p. 103; Paine and Schoenberger, "Iranian Nationalism and the Great Powers," p. 3.

21. William E. Griffith, "Iran's Foreign Policy in the Pahlavi Era," in George Lenczowski, ed., *Iran Under the Pahlavis* (Stanford, Calif.: Hoover Institution Press, 1978), p. 366.

22. James A. Bill, *The Eagle and the Lion: The Tragedy of American-Iranian Relations* (New Haven, Conn.: Yale University Press, 1988), p. 4; Daniel, *The History of Iran,* pp. 103–104; Paine and Schoenberger, "Iranian Nationalism and the Great Powers," p. 3.

23. Keddie, *Modern Iran,* pp. 38–39, 50–51.

24. Daniel, *The History of Iran,* pp. 110–111, 113–114; Keddie, *Modern Iran,* p. 56.

25. Abrahamian, *Iran Between Two Revolutions,* pp. 56–57; Keddie, *Modern Iran,* p. 53.

26. Abrahamian, *Iran Between Two Revolutions,* pp. 56–57.

27. Mark J. Gasiorowski, *U.S. Foreign Policy and the Shah: Building a Client State in Iran* (Ithaca, N.Y.: Cornell University Press, 1991).

28. Said Arjomand, *The Turban for the Crown: The Islamic Revolution in Iran* (New York: Oxford University Press, 1988), pp. 32–33; Gasiorowski, *U.S. Foreign Policy and the Shah,* pp. 32–34; Keddie, *Modern Iran,* pp. 35, 42, 52, 58.

29. Daniel, *The History of Iran,* pp. 104–106, 110–114, 115–117; Keddie, *Modern Iran,* pp. 35, 50; Paine and Schoenberger, "Iranian Nationalism and the Great Powers," p. 4.

30. Paine and Schoenberger, "Iranian Nationalism and the Great Powers," p. 4.

31. Abrahamian, *Iran Between Two Revolutions,* p. 55; Bill, *The Eagle and the Lion,* p. 4; Daniel, *The History of Iran,* p. 114; Keddie, *Modern Iran,* pp. 54–56; Paine and Schoenberger, "Iranian Nationalism and the Great Powers," p. 4.

32. Abrahamian, *Iran Between Two Revolutions,* pp. 53–54; Gasiorowski, *U.S. Foreign Policy and the Shah,* p. 34; Keddie, *Modern Iran,* p. 30.

33. Abrahamian, *Iran Between Two Revolutions,* p. 73; Daniel, *The History of Iran,* pp. 116–117; Gasiorowski, *U.S. Foreign Policy and the Shah,* p. 35; Keddie, *Modern Iran,* pp. 61–62; Roy Mottahedeh, *The Mantle of the Prophet: Religion and Politics in Iran* (New York: Pantheon, 1985), pp. 215–218; Paine and Schoenberger, "Iranian Nationalism and the Great Powers," p. 4.

34. Michael A. Palmer, *Guardians of the Gulf: A History of America's Expanding Role in the Persian Gulf, 1833–1992* (New York: Free Press, 1992), pp. 6–7.

35. Yonah Alexander and Allan Nanes, eds., *The United States and Iran: A Documentary History* (Frederick, Md.: University Publications of America, 1980), pp. 2–3.

36. Palmer, *Guardians of the Gulf,* p. 7.

37. Rubin, *Paved with Good Intentions,* p. 4.

38. Bill, *The Eagle and the Lion,* p. 57; Daniel, *The History of Iran,* pp. 118–119; Keddie, *Modern Iran,* p. 65; Paine and Schoenberger, "Iranian Nationalism and the Great Powers," p. 8.

39. Arjomand, *The Turban for the Crown,* p. 33.

40. Paine and Schoenberger, "Iranian Nationalism and the Great Powers," p. 6.

41. Abrahamian, *Iran Between Two Revolutions*, p. 81; Keddie, *Modern Iran*, pp. 66–67.

42. Daniel, *The History of Iran*, pp. 119–124; Keddie, *Modern Iran*, pp. 67–71; Rubin, *Paved with Good Intentions*, p. 4.

43. Abrahamian, *Iran Between Two Revolutions*, p. 81; Arjomand, *The Turban for the Crown*, p. 33; Daniel, *The History of Iran*, p. 120; Keddie, *Modern Iran*, p. 59; Paine and Schoenberger, "Iranian Nationalism and the Great Powers," p. 6; Rouhollah K. Ramazani, "Iran's 'White Revolution': A Study in Political Development," *International Journal of Middle East Studies*, 5, no. 2 (April 1974), p. 127; Roger M. Savory, "Social Development in Iran During the Pahlavi Era," in Lenczowski, *Iran Under the Pahlavis*, p. 88.

44. Daniel, *The History of Iran*, pp. 119–124; Keddie, *Modern Iran*, pp. 67–71; Mottahedeh, *The Mantle of the Prophet*, p. 53; Rubin, *Paved with Good Intentions*, p. 8; author's correspondence with Shaul Bakhash, July 12, 2004.

45. Bill, *The Eagle and the Lion*, p. 4; Rubin, *Paved with Good Intentions*, pp. 8–9; Keddie, *Modern Iran*, pp. 69–70; Paine and Schoenberger, "Iranian Nationalism and the Great Powers," pp. 6–7.

46. Arjomand, *The Turban for the Crown*, pp. 48–49; Daniel, *The History of Iran*, pp. 125–126; Paine and Schoenberger, "Iranian Nationalism and the Great Powers," p. 7; Rubin, *Paved with Good Intentions*, p. 9.

47. Abrahamian, *Iran Between Two Revolutions*, pp. 81–118; Ali M. Ansari, *Modern Iran Since 1921: The Pahlavis and After* (London: Longman, 2003), pp. 21–22; Arjomand, *The Turban for the Crown*, pp. 36–58; Gasiorowski, *U.S. Foreign Policy and the Shah*, pp. 35–37; Keddie, *Modern Iran*, pp. 67–71; Paine and Schoenberger, "Iranian Nationalism and the Great Powers," pp. 6–7.

48. Cottrell, "Iran's Armed Forces Under the Pahlavi Dynasty," p. 390; Daniel, *The History of Iran*, pp. 126–127; Paine and Schoenberger, "Iranian Nationalism and the Great Powers," p. 7. Rubin, *Paved with Good Intentions*, pp. 10–11; Amir Taheri, *Nest of Spies: America's Journey to Disaster in Iran* (New York: St. Martin's Griffin, 1999), pp. 10–11.

49. Alexander and Nanes, *The United States and Iran*, pp. 10–14; also Keddie, *Modern Iran*, p. 71.

50. Abrahamian, *Iran Between Two Revolutions*, pp. 81–118; Ansari, *Modern Iran Since 1921*, pp. 21–22; Arjomand, *The Turban for the Crown*, pp. 36–58; Gasiorowski, *U.S. Foreign Policy and the Shah*, pp. 35–37; Keddie, *Modern Iran*, pp. 67–71; Paine and Schoenberger, "Iranian Nationalism and the Great Powers," pp. 6–7; Taheri, *Nest of Spies*, pp. 10–11.

51. For a concurring view, see Griffith, "Iran's Foreign Policy in the Pahlavi Era," p. 367.

52. Bill, *The Eagle and the Lion*, p. 57; Paine and Schoenberger, "Iranian Nationalism and the Great Powers," p. 8; Daniel Yergin, *The Prize: The Epic Quest for Oil, Money, and Power* (New York: Touchstone, 1991), pp. 11, 142–143.

53. It is often suggested that the British invasion of Iraq was intended to defend India from the Turks. At most, this was a secondary concern. India was very distant from Iraq, and the Turks had no real naval capability in the Indian Ocean. But Iran's vital oil fields were just across the border.

54. Bill, *The Eagle and the Lion*, pp. 4, 58; Daniel, *The History of Iran*, pp. 127–129; Keddie, *Modern Iran*, pp. 23, 73–76; Paine and Schoenberger, p. 9; Savory, "Social Development in Iran During the Pahlavi Era," p. 88.

55. Bill, *The Eagle and the Lion*, pp. 4, 58; Daniel, *The History of Iran*, pp. 127–129; Keddie, *Modern Iran*, pp. 73–76; Paine and Schoenberger, "Iranian Nationalism and the Great Powers," p. 9.

56. Abrahamian, *Iran Between Two Revolutions*, pp. 81–118; Ansari, *Modern Iran Since 1921*, pp. 21–23; Arjomand, *The Turban for the Crown*, pp. 36–58; Daniel, *The History of Iran*, pp. 129–131; L. P. Elwell-Sutton, "Reza Shah the Great: Founder of the Pahlavi Dynasty," in Lenczowski, *Iran Under the Pahlavis*, pp. 12–15; Gasiorowski, *U.S. Foreign Policy and the Shah*, pp. 35–37; Keddie, *Modern Iran*, pp. 67–71, 76–79; Paine and Schoenberger, "Iranian Nationalism and the Great Powers," pp. 6–7, 9–10.

57. Bill, *The Eagle and the Lion*, pp. 4, 58; Daniel, *The History of Iran*, pp. 127–131; Keddie, *Modern Iran*, pp. 73–76; Paine and Schoenberger, "Iranian Nationalism and the Great Powers," pp. 9–10.

Chapter 2: Reza the Great

1. For a brief, sympathetic biography of Reza Shah, see Elwell-Sutton, "Reza Shah the Great," "Founder of the Pahlavi Dynasty," in Lenczowski, *Iran Under the Pahlavis*, pp. 1–50. On the growth of the Cossack Brigade to a division, see Cottrell, "Iran's Armed Forces Under the Pahlavi Dynasty," p. 390; Keddie, *Modern Iran*, p. 57.

2. Ansari, *Modern Iran Since 1921*, pp. 20–21; Daniel, *The History of Iran*, pp. 131–135; Elwell-Sutton, "Reza Shah the Great," pp. 17–27; Paine and Schoenberger, "Iranian Nationalism and the Great Powers," pp. 10–11.

3. The role of the British government in Reza Khan's coup remains unclear. However, the participation of British officials on the ground in Persia is unquestionable and is reflected in their documents and statements at the time. British officials probably helped arm and supply the Cossack Division, and may have provided additional pay for them as well. These officials, particularly General Ironside, the commander of British forces in Persia, appear to have actively encouraged Reza Khan's ambitions in the belief that the protectorate they had hoped to achieve in 1919 was doomed to failure, and therefore a strongman who could keep the peace and keep the country together (so that they could keep pumping oil) was the best they could hope for. See Abrahamian, *Iran Between Two Revolutions*, p. 117; Ansari, *Modern Iran Since 1921*, pp. 26–27; Keddie, *Modern Iran*, pp. 80–81; Kinzer, *All the Shah's Men*, p. 42; Paine and Schoenberger, "Iranian Nationalism and the Great Powers," p. 11. For a confused sort of dissent that is much less of a dissent than the author seems to intend, see Elwell-Sutton, "Reza Shah the Great," pp. 15–16.

4. Abrahamian, *Iran Between Two Revolutions*, p. 120; Arjomand, *The Turban for the Crown*, p. 62; Daniel, *The History of Iran*, pp. 131–135; Kashani-Sabet, "Cultures of Iranianness," p. 169; Keddie, *Modern Iran*, p. 85; Paine and Schoenberger, "Iranian Nationalism and the Great Powers," pp. 10–11; Elwell-Sutton, "Reza Shah the Great," pp. 17–27. For a dissenting view, see Ansari, *Modern Iran Since 1921*, p. 39.

5. Ansari, *Modern Iran Since 1921*, p. 25; Houchang Chehabi, "Staging the Emperor's New Clothes: Dress Codes and Nation-Building Under Reza Shah," *Iranian Studies* 26 (1993), p. 225; Daniel, *The History of Iran*, p. 136; Kashani-Sabet, "Cultures of Iranianness," pp. 170–172; Keddie, *Modern Iran*, p. 81; Kinzer, *All the Shah's Men*, pp. 42–43; Ramazani, "Iran's 'White Revolution,' " p. 128.

6. Ansari, *Modern Iran Since 1921*, p. 62; Arjomand, *The Turban for the Crown*, p. 67; Charles Issawi, "The Iranian Economy 1925–1975: Fifty Years of Economic Development," in Lenczowski, *Iran Under the Pahlavis*, pp. 129–130; Keddie, *Modern Iran*, pp. 85–87.

7. Keddie, *Modern Iran*, pp. 85–87.

8. Abrahamian, *Iran Between Two Revolutions*, pp. 143–144; Elwell-Sutton, "Reza Shah the Great," pp. 41–44; Griffith, "Iran's Foreign Policy in the Pahlavi Era," p. 367; Ramazani, "Iran's 'White Revolution,' " p. 128.

9. Abrahamian, *Iran Between Two Revolutions*, p. 118; Bill, *The Eagle and the Lion*, p. 58; Daniel, *The History of Iran*, p. 133; Keddie, *Modern Iran*, p. 81; Paine and Schoenberger, "Iranian Nationalism and the Great Powers," p. 10; Taheri, *Nest of Spies*, p. 12.

10. Arthur L. Millspaugh, *Americans in Persia* (Washington, D.C.: Brookings Institution, 1946), p. 23.

11. Ibid., p. 26, n. 7.

12. Abrahamian, *Iran Between Two Revolutions*, p. 131; Alexander and Nanes, *The United States and Iran*, pp. 35–44; Ansari, *Modern Iran Since 1921*, p. 34; Arjomand, *The Turban for the Crown*, p. 65; Daniel, *The History of Iran*, p. 141; Ferydoon Firoozi, "Income Distribution and Taxation Laws of Iran," *International Journal of Middle East Studies* 9, no. 1 (January 1978), p. 77; Griffith, "Iran's Foreign Policy in the Pahlavi Era," p. 370; Keddie, *Modern Iran*, p. 83; Millspaugh, *Americans in Persia*, pp. 21–26; Rubin, *Paved with Good Intentions*, p. 13; Paine and Schoenberger, "Iranian Nationalism and the Great Powers," pp. 14–15; Taheri, *Nest of Spies*, pp. 12–14.

13. Bill, *The Eagle and the Lion*, pp. 60–61; Daniel, *The History of Iran*, p. 140; Paine and Schoenberger, "Iranian Nationalism and the Great Powers," pp. 12–13; Robert B. Stobaugh, "The Evo-

lution of Iranian Oil Policy, 1925–1975," in Lenczowski, *Iran Under the Pahlavis*, pp. 203–206; Yergin, *The Prize*, pp. 269–271.

14. Ansari, *Modern Iran Since 1921*, pp. 65–66; Daniel, *The History of Iran*, p. 3.

15. Alexander and Nanes, *The United States and Iran*, pp. 62–69.

16. Mottahedeh, *The Mantle of the Prophet*, p. 60.

17. Ansari, *Modern Iran Since 1921*, pp. 49–51; Cottrell, "Iran's Armed Forces Under the Pahlavi Dynasty," pp. 391–392; Elwell-Sutton, "Reza Shah the Great," pp. 20–27; Griffith, "Iran's Foreign Policy in the Pahlavi Era," p. 370; Keddie, *Modern Iran*, pp. 82–85; Mottahedeh, *The Mantle of the Prophet*, p. 60; Paine and Schoenberger, "Iranian Nationalism and the Great Powers," p. 11.

18. Abrahamian, *Iran Between Two Revolutions*, pp. 131–133, 136; Ansari, *Modern Iran Since 1921*, pp. 42–48; Arjomand, *The Turban for the Crown*, p. 61; Cottrell, "Iran's Armed Forces Under the Pahlavi Dynasty," pp. 391–392; Daniel, *The History of Iran*, pp. 135–137; Elwell-Sutton, "Reza Shah the Great," pp. 19–20; Paine and Schoenberger, "Iranian Nationalism and the Great Powers," p. 15; Savory, "Social Development in Iran During the Pahlavi Era," p. 95.

19. On Reza Shah's reforms, see Abrahamian, *Iran Between Two Revolutions*, pp. 136–137, 144; Ansari, *Modern Iran Since 1921*, pp. 51–71; Arjomand, *The Turban for the Crown*, pp. 65–68, 82; Daniel, *The History of Iran*, p. 137; Wilhelm Eilers, "Educational and Cultural Development in Iran During the Pahlavi Era," in Lenczowski, ed., *Iran Under the Pahlavis*, pp. 303–331; Fischer, *Iran*, pp. 108–109; Gasiorowski, *U.S. Foreign Policy and the Shah*, pp. 40–42; Issawi, "The Iranian Economy," pp. 131–133; Keddie, *Modern Iran*, pp. 29, 88–104; Savory, "Social Development in Iran During the Pahlavi Era," pp. 90–99.

20. Arjomand, *The Turban for the Crown*, p. 67; Issawi, "The Iranian Economy," pp. 131–133; Keddie, *Modern Iran*, pp. 9–94.

21. Arjomand, *The Turban for the Crown*, p. 65.

22. Abrahamian, *Iran Between Two Revolutions*, pp. 136–137.

23. Ansari, *Modern Iran Since 1921*, p. 62; James A. Bill, "Modernization and Reform from Above: The Case of Iran," *The Journal of Politics*, 32, no. 1 (February 1970), p. 30; Fischer, *Iran*, pp. 108–109; Gasiorowski, *U.S. Foreign Policy and the Shah*, p. 40.

24. Keddie, *Modern Iran*, pp. 88–104.

25. Ansari, *Modern Iran Since 1921*, p. 63; Gasiorowski, *U.S. Foreign Policy and the Shah*, pp. 40–42.

26. Arjomand, *The Turban for the Crown*, pp. 66–68; Savory, "Social Development in Iran During the Pahlavi Era," pp. 90–99.

27. Kinzer, *All the Shah's Men*, pp. 43–44.

28. Abrahamian, *Iran Between Two Revolutions*, pp. 162–163; Arjomand, *The Turban for the Crown*, pp. 63–64; Issawi, "The Iranian Economy," pp. 131–133; Keddie, *Modern Iran*, pp. 88, 90–91, 94–97, 99; Paine and Schoenberger, p. 15; Rubin, *Paved with Good Intentions*, p. 15.

29. Abrahamian, *Iran Between Two Revolutions*, pp. 138–142, 154–155; Arjomand, *The Turban for the Crown*, pp. 64–65; Gasiorowski, *U.S. Foreign Policy and the Shah*, p. 39; Kinzer, *All the Shah's Men*, p. 44; Paine and Schoenberger, "Iranian Nationalism and the Great Powers," p. 15; Rubin, *Paved with Good Intentions*, p. 15.

30. Quoted in Gasiorowski, *U.S. Foreign Policy and the Shah*, p. 39.

31. Abrahamian, *Iran Between Two Revolutions*, pp. 137, 141–142, 150; Kinzer, *All the Shah's Men*, p. 44.

32. Daniel, *The History of Iran*, p. 139; Gasiorowski, *U.S. Foreign Policy and the Shah*, p. 39.

33. Arjomand, *The Turban for the Crown*, p. 82; Eilers, "Educational and Cultural Development in Iran During the Pahlavi Era," pp. 305–306, 313–314; Keddie, *Modern Iran*, pp. 88–97.

34. Abrahamian, *Iran Between Two Revolutions*, pp. 151–153; Arjomand, *The Turban for the Crown*, p. 69; Keddie, *Modern Iran*, pp. 88–97, 99; Robin Wright, *In the Name of God: The Khomeini Decade* (New York: Simon & Schuster, 1989), pp. 43–44.

35. Ansari, *Modern Iran Since 1921*, pp. 65–66; Daniel, *The History of Iran*, p. 3; Elwell-Sutton, "Reza Shah the Great," p. 48; Griffith, "Iran's Foreign Policy in the Pahlavi Era," p. 371;

Kashani-Sabet, "Cultures of Iranianness," p. 176; Keddie, *Modern Iran,* p. 109; Taheri, *Nest of Spies,* p. 15.

36. Bill, *The Eagle and the Lion,* p. 18; Daniel, *The History of Iran,* p. 141; Elwell-Sutton, "Reza Shah the Great," pp. 48–49; Gasiorowski, *U.S. Foreign Policy and the Shah,* p. 43; Griffith, "Iran's Foreign Policy in the Pahlavi Era," p. 371; Keddie, *Modern Iran,* pp. 101, 105; Paine and Schoenberger, "Iranian Nationalism and the Great Powers," pp. 15–16; Rubin, *Paved with Good Intentions,* p. 18; Taheri, *Nest of Spies,* pp. 15–16.

37. Habib Ladjevardi, "The Origins of U.S. Support for an Autocratic Iran," *International Journal of Middle East Studies* 15, no. 2 (May 1983), p. 225. Also see Gasiorowski, *U.S. Foreign Policy and the Shah,* p. 43.

38. Ladjevardi, "The Origins of U.S. Support for an Autocratic Iran," p. 225.

Chapter 3: The Ugly Americans

1. Palmer, *Guardians of the Gulf,* p. 24.

2. Walter S. Dunn, *The Soviet Economy and the Red Army, 1930–1945* (Westport, Conn.: Praeger, 1995), p. 69.

3. Ibid., pp. 83–86; David M. Glantz and Jonathan House, *When Titans Clashed: How the Red Army Stopped Hitler* (Lawrence, Kans.: University of Kansas Press, 1995), p. 150; Richard Overy, *Why the Allies Won* (New York: Norton, 1995), p. 214.

4. Glantz and House, *When Titans Clashed,* p. 150.

5. Dunn, *The Soviet Economy and the Red Army,* pp. 80, 87; Gerhard Weinberg, *A World At Arms: A Global History of World War II* (Cambridge, U.K.: Cambridge University Press, 1994), p. 284.

6. Bill, *The Eagle and the Lion,* pp. 18, 30; Daniel, *The History of Iran,* p. 144; Paine and Schoenberger, "Iranian Nationalism and the Great Powers," p. 16; Palmer, *Guardians of the Gulf,* p. 24; Rubin, *Paved with Good Intentions,* p. 19; Taheri, *Nest of Spies,* pp. 16–18.

7. See Alexander and Nanes, *The United States and Iran,* pp. 130–133.

8. Ansari, *Modern Iran Since 1921,* p. 85; Bill, *The Eagle and the Lion,* pp. 46–48.

9. Of course, there is reason to believe that some economic considerations also played a role in American thinking—albeit certainly not an exclusive or even primary role. The American Standard-Vacuum oil company (which later became Mobil) began pressing the government of Iran for an oil concession in 1943. However, this move actually backfired by prompting the Russians to do the same in northern Iran. The Iranian Majles, led by Mohammad Mosaddeq, responded by passing an oil bill in 1944 that prohibited the government from granting any oil concessions without legislative ratification. (Bill, *The Eagle and the Lion,* pp. 28–29; Daniel, *The History of Iran,* p. 145; Paine and Schoenberger, "Iranian Nationalism and the Great Powers," p. 19.)

10. Bill, *The Eagle and the Lion,* p. 19; Rubin, *Paved with Good Intentions,* p. 22.

11. Quoted in Bill, *The Eagle and the Lion,* p. 49.

12. The text of the Tehran Conference Declaration is available at www.yale.edu/lawweb/avalon/wwii/tehran.htm. Also see Daniel, *The History of Iran,* p. 145; Paine and Schoenberger, "Iranian Nationalism and the Great Powers," p. 18; Palmer, *Guardians of the Gulf,* p. 25; Rubin, *Paved with Good Intentions,* p. 23.

13. United States Department of Commerce, Bureau of Foreign and Domestic Commerce, Office of Business Economics, *A Supplement to the Survey of Current Business: Foreign Aid, 1940–1951* (Washington, D.C.: U.S. Government Printing Office, 1952). See also Vail Motter, *The Persian Corridor and Aid to Russia* (Washington, D.C.: Center of Military History, 1952), pp. 436–459.

14. Bill, *The Eagle and the Lion,* pp. 20, 41; Paine and Schoenberger, "Iranian Nationalism and the Great Powers," pp. 18–19.

15. Alexander and Nanes, *The United States and Iran,* pp. 108–122; Bill, *The Eagle and the Lion,* pp. 20, 25; Gasiorowski, *U.S. Foreign Policy and the Shah,* p. 50; Keddie, *Modern Iran,* pp. 107–108; Millspaugh, *Americans in Persia,* pp. 46–71; Paine and Schoenberger, "Iranian Na-

tionalism and the Great Powers," pp. 17–19; Rubin, *Paved with Good Intentions,* p. 22; Taheri, *Nest of Spies,* pp. 17–18.

16. Keddie, *Modern Iran,* pp. 106, 108; Paine and Schoenberger, "Iranian Nationalism and the Great Powers," p. 17; Rubin, *Paved with Good Intentions,* p. 19.

17. See the correspondence reprinted in Alexander and Nanes, *The United States and Iran,* pp. 85–90.

18. Ansari, *Modern Iran Since 1921,* p. 85; Rubin, *Paved with Good Intentions,* pp. 20–21; Paine and Schoenberger, "Iranian Nationalism and the Great Powers," p. 17.

19. Ansari, *Modern Iran Since 1921,* pp. 77–78; Gasiorowski, *U.S. Foreign Policy and the Shah,* p. 44. For confirmation of Soviet direction of the Tudeh from declassified Soviet documents, see Christian F. Ostermann, "New Evidence on the Iran Crisis, 1945–46," *Cold War International History Project Bulletin* 12–13 (Fall–Winter 2001), pp. 311–314; and Natalia I. Yegorova, "The 'Iran Crisis' of 1945–46: A View from the Russian Archives," Working Paper no. 15, Cold War International History Project, Washington, D.C., May 1996, pp. 4–5.

20. Ansari, *Modern Iran Since 1921,* pp. 86–93; Mehrdad R. Izady, *The Kurds: A Concise Handbook* (Washington, D.C.: Crane Russak, 1992), pp. 65–66; David McDowall, *A Modern History of the Kurds* (London: I. B. Tauris, 1997), pp. 231–240; Edgar O'Ballance, *The Kurdish Struggle* (New York: St. Martin's Press, 1996), pp. 21–26; Rubin, *Paved with Good Intentions,* pp. 19, 24–25.

21. Gasiorowski, *U.S. Foreign Policy and the Shah,* pp. 45–46; Rubin, *Paved with Good Intentions,* pp. 24–25.

22. The text is reproduced in Alexander and Nanes, *The United States and Iran,* p. 143.

23. Bill, *The Eagle and the Lion,* p. 34; Yegorova, "The 'Iran Crisis' of 1945–46," pp. 7–14.

24. The Azeris announced that autonomy meant that they would keep most of their own taxes, run their internal affairs themselves, implement a broad policy of land reform, and teach the Azeri language in schools, among other things. (Keddie, *Modern Iran,* p. 111.)

25. Bill, *The Eagle and the Lion,* p. 34; Daniel, *The History of Iran,* p. 146; Gasiorowski, *U.S. Foreign Policy and the Shah,* p. 46; Izady, *The Kurds,* pp. 65–66; Keddie, *Modern Iran,* p. 111; McDowall, *A Modern History of the Kurds,* pp. 240–243; O'Ballance, *The Kurdish Struggle,* pp. 27–30; Paine and Schoenberger, "Iranian Nationalism and the Great Powers," pp. 20–21; Palmer, *Guardians of the Gulf,* p. 30.

26. Dean Acheson, *Present at the Creation: My Years at the State Department* (New York: W. W. Norton, 1969), pp. 196–198; Bill, *The Eagle and the Lion,* pp. 31–37; Paine and Schoenberger, "Iranian Nationalism and the Great Powers," pp. 20–21; Taheri, *Nest of Spies,* pp. 19–20.

27. A *New York Times* reporter estimated the Tudeh would receive 40 percent of the vote in truly free national elections. (Gasiorowski, *U.S. Foreign Policy and the Shah,* p. 44.) On Soviet direction of the Tudeh, see Yegorova, "The 'Iran Crisis' of 1945–46," pp. 4–5.

28. Bill, *The Eagle and the Lion,* pp. 31–34; Rubin, *Paved with Good Intentions,* pp. 24–25.

29. Daniel, *The History of Iran,* p. 146; Palmer, *Guardians of the Gulf,* pp. 30–33. Palmer is particularly good in establishing that the Soviets continued to reinforce their position in Iran *after* the withdrawal announcement.

30. Acheson, *Present at the Creation,* pp. 197–198; Bill, *The Eagle and the Lion,* pp. 32–33, 37–38; Gasiorowski, *U.S. Foreign Policy and the Shah,* p. 51.

31. Bill, *The Eagle and the Lion,* p. 31; Gasiorowski, *U.S. Foreign Policy and the Shah,* pp. 46–47; Ladjevardi, "The Origins of U.S. Support for an Autocratic Iran," p. 231; Paine and Schoenberger, "Iranian Nationalism and the Great Powers," p. 21; Rubin, *Paved with Good Intentions,* p. 33; Taheri, *Nest of Spies,* pp. 19–20; Yegorova, "The 'Iran Crisis' of 1945–46," pp. 19–20.

32. Bill, *The Eagle and the Lion,* p. 36; Gasiorowski, *U.S. Foreign Policy and the Shah,* p. 47; Izady, *The Kurds,* pp. 65–66; McDowall, *A Modern History of the Kurds,* pp. 243–246; O'Ballance, *The Kurdish Struggle,* pp. 30–35.

33. President Truman apparently was mistaken in remembering having sent an "ultimatum" to Stalin demanding that the Russians withdraw in March. All of the available documentary evidence, as well as the recollections of senior American officials who would have participated in the drafting and delivery of such an ultimatum, indicates that this claim is erroneous. See James A. Thorpe,

"Truman's Ultimatum to Stalin on the 1946 Azerbaijan Crisis: The Making of a Myth," *The Journal of Politics,* vol. 40, no. 1 (February 1978), pp. 188–195.

34. Ostermann, "New Evidence on the Iran Crisis," pp. 309–311; Yegorova, "The 'Iran Crisis' of 1945–46," pp. 2–4, 7.

35. My contention that the American military threat played an important (but not necessarily exclusive) role in resolving the Soviet Withdrawal Crisis runs contrary to the view of a number of eminent scholars of both Russia and Iran. This group contends that the American role was largely irrelevant and that all the Russians wanted was the oil concession. They explain the Soviet moves as follows: initially, the Russians believed that the best way to secure the oil concession was to keep their troops in Iran; however, when it later became clear that the only way to get the oil concession was actually to pull their troops out, they did so. I disagree with this argument for several reasons. First, I find it hard to ascribe to mere coincidence that America would alert its military forces and several weeks later the Russians would pull out of a country they had eyed for centuries. Second, some of the documents declassified from the Soviet archives demonstrate that, initially, the Russians had hoped to mobilize large-scale political support to secure the secession of Azerbaijan (and likely Kurdistan). This suggests that they did have greater ambitions than merely the oil concession, although they may have scaled them back upon recognizing it would be difficult to accomplish this objective. (Yegorova, "The 'Iran Crisis' of 1945–46," pp. 2–3.)

Third, and of greatest importance, as long as the Russians were willing to keep their troops in Iran they could have done whatever they wanted to with the oil—a point that Natalia Yegorova acknowledges, noting, "It is hard to believe that Soviet leaders, having such a powerful army, could sincerely believe in the possibility of Iranian aggression." (Yegorova, "The 'Iran Crisis' of 1945–46," p. 18.) And she is right: the Iranians certainly could not have evicted the Russians if Stalin had wanted to stay—and his conduct in Eastern Europe suggested that unhappy public opinion was not the kind of thing that made him change his mind. Under those circumstances, Russia could have done whatever it wanted to in terms of oil development. Indeed, as one of the declassified documents states, Russian engineers suggested it would be necessary to retain Soviet troops in Iran—or even to annex the territory—in order to properly exploit the fields. Keeping their troops in Iran ensured that they could exploit the oil fields, while the route they eventually took was far less certain, as evidenced by the fact that it failed. So the critical question that is unanswered by the alternative theory is "If all the Russians wanted was the oil, why did they not simply stay and annex the territory?" In the absence of dispositive evidence from the Soviet archives, the most simple and logical answer to that question is that they were afraid that if they did so it would trigger a war with the United States, and so they opted for the less certain, but less risky (in terms of provoking a war with the United States) course of action of striking a deal with Qavam and then trying to bolster Qavam's position to make the deal stick.

36. Ladjevardi, "The Origins of U.S. Support for an Autocratic Iran," pp. 231–233.

37. Daniel, *The History of Iran,* pp. 146–147.

38. Ansari, *Modern Iran Since 1921,* pp. 96–100; Bill, *The Eagle and the Lion,* pp. 34–35; Ladjevardi, "The Origins of U.S. Support for an Autocratic Iran," pp. 231–233.

39. See Malcolm Byrne and Mark J. Gasiorowski, eds., *Mohammad Mosaddeq and the 1953 Coup in Iran* (Syracuse, N.Y.: Syracuse University Press, 2004), pp. 208–210, and Palmer, *Guardians of the Gulf,* pp. 34–35. Palmer notes that the American Joint Chiefs of Staff argued throughout the crisis that the United States should write off northern Iran to Russia and suggests that, given the USSR's extensive and effective intelligence-gathering apparatus, it may well have been the case that Stalin was aware of this assessment and so may have thought he was pushing on an open door in Iran. (Palmer, *Guardians of the Gulf,* p. 31.)

40. Abrahamian, *Iran Between Two Revolutions,* p. 11; Keddie, *Modern Iran,* pp. 109–118; Rubin, *Paved with Good Intentions,* pp. 36–37.

41. Acheson, *Present at the Creation,* p. 198. Also see Rubin, *Paved with Good Intentions,* p. 36.

42. Ladjevardi, "The Origins of U.S. Support for an Autocratic Iran," p. 230; Stephen McFarland, "A Peripheral View of the Origins of the Cold War: The Crisis in Iran, 1941–47," *Diplomatic History* (Fall 1980), p. 333.

43. See the memorandum by the assistant secretary of state for Near Eastern, South Asian, and African affairs (McGhee) to the secretary of state, November 17, 1949 (prior to the shah's December visit to the United States), in Alexander and Nanes, *The United States and Iran*, pp. 201–202. Also see Gasiorowski, *U.S. Foreign Policy and the Shah*, p. 55; Rubin, *Paved with Good Intentions*, pp. 38–39.

44. Gasiorowski, *U.S. Foreign Policy and the Shah*, pp. 52–55.

45. Bill, *The Eagle and the Lion*, pp. 39–41; Cottrell, "Iran's Armed Forces Under the Pahlavi Dynasty," p. 397; Rubin, *Paved with Good Intentions*, pp. 36–37.

46. Quoted in Rubin, *Paved with Good Intentions*, p. 50.

47. Ladjevardi, "The Origins of U.S. Support for an Autocratic Iran," p. 230; McFarland, "A Peripheral View of the Origins of the Cold War," p. 333.

48. Ladjevardi, "The Origins of U.S. Support for an Autocratic Iran," pp. 231–233.

49. Kinzer, *All the Shah's Men*, pp. 50–52.

50. Paine and Schoenberger, "Iranian Nationalism and the Great Powers," p. 14.

51. Bill, *The Eagle and the Lion*, p. 51; Kinzer, *All the Shah's Men*, p. 52.

52. Abrahamian, *Iran Between Two Revolutions*, pp. 240–244.

53. Ibid., pp. 245–247.

54. Ibid., pp. 249–250; Bill, *The Eagle and the Lion*, p. 51; Daniel, *The History of Iran*, p. 148; Gasiorowski, *U.S. Foreign Policy and the Shah*, pp. 48–49; Rubin, *Paved with Good Intentions*, p. 40.

55. Bill, *The Eagle and the Lion*, p. 63.

56. Ansari, *Modern Iran Since 1921*, pp. 107–108; Daniel, *The History of Iran*, pp. 154–155; Gasiorowski, *U.S. Foreign Policy and the Shah*, p. 59; Rubin, *Paved with Good Intentions*, pp. 42–43.

57. Quoted in Kinzer, *All the Shah's Men*, p. 96.

58. Ibid., p. 109.

59. Abrahamian, *Iran Between Two Revolutions*, pp. 252–259; Bill, *The Eagle and the Lion*, pp. 51, 54; Daniel, *The History of Iran*, pp. 148–149; Mark J. Gasiorowski, "The 1953 Coup d'Etat in Iran," *International Journal of Middle East Studies* 19, no. 3 (August 1987), p. 262.

60. Ansari, *Modern Iran Since 1921*, pp. 113–114; Fakhreddin Azimi, "Unseating Mosaddeq: The Configuration and Role of Domestic Forces," in Byrne and Gasiorowski, *Mohammad Mosaddeq and the 1953 Coup in Iran*, pp. 55–56; Gasiorowski, *U.S. Foreign Policy and the Shah*, pp. 57–58; Kinzer, *All the Shah's Men*, pp. 75–76.

61. Abrahamian, *Iran Between Two Revolutions*, p. 261; Gasiorowski, *U.S. Foreign Policy and the Shah*, p. 49; Kinzer, *All the Shah's Men*, pp. 69–70.

62. Abrahamian, *Iran Between Two Revolutions*, pp. 317–319.

63. Ansari, *Modern Iran Since 1921*, p. 110; William Roger Louis, "Britain and the Overthrow of the Mosaddeq Government," in Byrne and Gasiorowski, *Mohammad Mosaddeq and the 1953 Coup in Iran*, pp. 129–130.

64. Robert B. Stobaugh, "The Evolution of Iranian Oil Policy, 1925–1975," in Lenczowski, ed., *Iran Under the Pahlavis*, pp. 206–207.

65. Gasiorowski, *U.S. Foreign Policy and the Shah*, p. 62.

66. Bill, *The Eagle and the Lion*, pp. 61–63; Kinzer, *All the Shah's Men*, p. 68; Paine and Schoenberger, "Iranian Nationalism and the Great Powers," p. 22; Rubin, *Paved with Good Intentions*, p. 12.

67. Kinzer, *All the Shah's Men*, p. 69.

68. Bill, *The Eagle and the Lion*, pp. 75–77; Gasiorowski, *U.S. Foreign Policy and the Shah*, p. 82; Gasiorowski, "The 1953 Coup d'Etat Against Mosaddeq," in Byrne and Gasiorowski, *Mohammad Mosaddeq and the 1953 Coup in Iran*, pp. 229–230; Kinzer, *All the Shah's Men*, pp. 86–92; Louis, "Britain and the Overthrow of the Mosaddeq Government," pp. 151–153; Rubin, *Paved with Good Intentions*, pp. 43–45.

69. Gasiorowski, *U.S. Foreign Policy and the Shah*, p. 56. Also see Malcolm Byrne, "The Road to Intervention: Factors Influencing U.S. Policy Toward Iran, 1945–1953," in Byrne and Gasiorowski, *Mohammad Mosaddeq and the 1953 Coup in Iran*, p. 214.

70. Byrne, "The Road to Intervention," pp. 201–203, 214; Gasiorowski, *U.S. Foreign Policy and the Shah*, p. 56; Rubin, *Paved with Good Intentions*, pp. 46–47; Taheri, *Nest of Spies*, p. 27.

71. Kinzer, *All the Shah's Men*, p. 78; Rubin, *Paved with Good Intentions*, pp. 47–49. Documents found in the AIOC offices in Tehran after the nationalization showed that the previous prime minister, Hassan Ali Mansur, had "begged AIOC to allow him to remain in office, promising in return to appoint a new finance minister more agreeable to the company." These documents demonstrated the company's interference throughout the Iranian regime, including having forced from office Iranian ministers and Majles deputies who opposed it. (Kinzer, p. 97.)

72. Kinzer, *All the Shah's Men*, p. 73; Rubin, *Paved with Good Intentions*, p. 48.

73. Bill, *The Eagle and the Lion*, pp. 65–66; Daniel, *The History of Iran*, p. 149; Gasiorowski, *U.S. Foreign Policy and the Shah*, pp. 49–50; Keddie, *Modern Iran*, p. 124; Kinzer, *All the Shah's Men*, pp. 76–80; Rubin, *Paved with Good Intentions*, pp. 51–52.

74. Kinzer, *All the Shah's Men*, p. 112; Louis, "Britain and the Overthrow of the Mosaddeq Government," pp. 133–134.

75. Kinzer, *All the Shah's Men*, p. 111.

76. Mary Ann Heiss, "The International Boycott of Iranian Oil and the Anti-Mosaddeq Coup of 1953," in Byrne and Gasorowski, *Mohammad Mosaddeq and the 1953 Coup in Iran*, pp. 178–189; Stobaugh, "The Evolution of Iranian Oil Policy," p. 210.

77. Daniel, *The History of Iran*, p. 151; Kinzer, *All the Shah's Men*, pp. 94, 145; Rubin, *Paved with Good Intentions*, p. 65.

78. Bill, *The Eagle and the Lion*, pp. 75–77; Kinzer, *All the Shah's Men*, pp. 97–99; Rubin, *Paved with Good Intentions*, pp. 64, 27–29.

79. Kinzer, *All the Shah's Men*, pp. 112–113; Taheri, *Nest of Spies*, p. 29.

80. Kinzer, *All the Shah's Men*, p. 93.

81. Ibid., p. 113.

82. "The American Ambassador at Tehran to the Iranian Minister for Foreign Affairs Stressing United States Nonintervention, May 26, 1951," reprinted in Alexander and Nanes, *The United States and Iran*, pp. 215–218.

83. Bill, *The Eagle and the Lion*, pp. 75–77.

84. Ansari, *Modern Iran Since 1921*, p. 107; Bill, *The Eagle and the Lion*, p. 53; Daniel, *The History of Iran*, pp. 18–19.

85. Bill, *The Eagle and the Lion*, p. 55; Kinzer, *All the Shah's Men*, pp. 102–103; Mottahedeh, *The Mantle of the Prophet*, pp. 127–128.

86. Mottahedeh, *The Mantle of the Prophet*, p. 120. On Mosaddeq's academic work and its relationship to his approach to politics, see ibid., pp. 118–121, 128–130.

87. Yergin, *The Prize*, p. 460.

88. Bill, *The Eagle and the Lion*, p. 84. Also see Ansari, *Modern Iran Since 1921*, p. 107, and Kinzer, *All the Shah's Men*, pp. 56, 59–61, 105.

89. Daniel, *The History of Iran*, p. 150; Kinzer, *All the Shah's Men*, pp. 117–129; Paine and Schoenberger, "Iranian Nationalism and the Great Powers," p. 24.

90. Ansari, *Modern Iran Since 1921*, p. 115; Bill, *The Eagle and the Lion*, pp. 75–77; Kinzer, *All the Shah's Men*, pp. 97, 131; Rubin, *Paved with Good Intentions*, p. 77.

91. Gasiorowski, *U.S. Foreign Policy and the Shah*, p. 68; Heiss, "The International Boycott of Iranian Oil," pp. 184–190; Rubin, *Paved with Good Intentions*, pp. 63–72.

92. According to Gasiorowski, in the late 1940s the CIA had begun a covert action program in Iran aimed at defeating Soviet efforts to build support for the Tudeh and guard against a possible Soviet invasion. These operations developed a network of stay-behind agents among the Qashqa'i and other tribes who would mount an insurgency in the rear area of Soviet invasion forces, planned escape routes for American and Iranian personnel in the event of a Soviet assault, monitored the Soviet presence in Iran, and waged a propaganda war against the Tudeh and the Russians by planting anti-Communist articles and cartoons in newspapers, subsidizing books and leaflets critical of the USSR and the Tudeh, and starting anti-Soviet rumors. In addition, some CIA operations used Iran and its deeply diverse population to recruit and mount espionage and

subversion missions into the USSR by using Iranian Azeris, Armenians, and members of other ethnic groups that spanned the border between Iran and Russia. None of these operations was intended to influence Iranian domestic politics except to discredit the Tudeh. (Gasiorowski, "The 1953 Coup d'Etat in Iran," p. 267; Gasiorowski, *U.S. Foreign Policy and the Shah,* pp. 54, 69.)

93. Gasiorowski, *U.S. Foreign Policy and the Shah,* pp. 69–71; James Risen, "Secrets of History," *New York Times,* April 16, 2000, p. A1. Gasiorowski implies that either Kermit Roosevelt, the head of Near East Operations at the CIA, or another operations officer, Donald Wilber, undertook these operations on their own because they clearly ran against the Truman administration's policy of trying to support Mosaddeq and the nationalists. When interviewed by Gasiorowski, Roosevelt claimed he could not remember who had given the order to undertake such actions at variance with stated U.S. policy. I concur with Gasiorowski that it seems unlikely that Roosevelt would not be able to remember who had given so momentous an order, and therefore it seems likely that he was dissembling.

94. Stobaugh, "The Evolution of Iranian Oil Policy," p. 212.

95. Kinzer, *All the Shah's Men,* p. 136. Also see Heiss, "The International Boycott of Iranian Oil," pp. 190–193, who demonstrates that the economic effects of the British embargo were not as catastrophic as once believed, although they did impose hardships on the Iranian people.

96. Azimi, "Unseating Mosaddeq," pp. 55–58; Gasiorowski, "The 1953 Coup d'Etat in Iran," p. 265; Homa Katouzian, "Mosaddeq's Government in Iranian History: Arbitrary Rule, Democracy, and the 1953 Coup," in Byrne and Gasiorowski, *Mohammad Mosaddeq and the 1953 Coup in Iran,* p. 11; Rubin, *Paved with Good Intentions,* p. 76.

97. What Mosaddeq actually did and how he justified it remain something of a mystery to this day. Shaul Bakhash provided the following analysis: The relevant articles of the 1906 Constitution are the following:

• Article 5: The members elected to represent Tehran shall, so soon as they meet, have the right to constitute the Assembly, and to begin their discussions and deliberations. During the period preceding the arrival of the provincial delegates, their decisions shall depend on their validity and due execution on the majority [by which they are carried].

• Article 6: On the opening of the debates, at least two thirds of the members of the Assembly shall be present, and, when the vote is taken, at least three quarters. A majority shall be obtained only when more than half of those present record their votes.

The Constitution says nothing about authority for the prime minister or anyone else to suspend the elections. A quorum should be necessary to convene the Majles, and it seems to say that two thirds of the members constitute a quorum. Obviously, 79 out of 136 is short of two thirds. It is possible that Mosaddeq claimed the right to convene the Majles on the basis of Article 5, because the Tehran deputies had been elected, and with the added rationale that more than 50 percent of the deputies had been elected. But here again, he seems to have stretched the law. (Shaul Bakhash, personal correspondence with the author, July 20, 2004.)

98. Abrahamian, *Iran Between Two Revolutions,* p. 269; Azimi, "Unseating Mosaddeq," pp. 51–52; Daniel, *The History of Iran,* p. 151; Kinzer, *All the Shah's Men,* pp. 136–137.

99. Ansari, *Modern Iran Since 1921,* pp. 118–119; Bill, *The Eagle and the Lion,* p. 66; Azimi, "Unseating Mosaddeq," pp. 52–54; Gasiorowski, "The 1953 Coup d'Etat in Iran," p. 265; Kinzer, *All the Shah's Men,* pp. 134–141; Louis, "Britain and the Overthrow of the Mosaddeq Government," pp. 141–145; Rubin, *Paved with Good Intentions,* pp. 72–73.

100. Gasiorowski, "The 1953 Coup d'Etat in Iran," p. 265; Kinzer, *All the Shah's Men,* pp. 134–141.

101. Abrahamian, *Iran Between Two Revolutions,* p. 273; Ansari, *Modern Iran Since 1921,* pp. 118–119; Bill, *The Eagle and the Lion,* p. 66; Rubin, *Paved with Good Intentions,* pp. 72–73.

102. Abrahamian, *Iran Between Two Revolutions,* p. 273.

103. Azimi, "Unseating Mosaddeq," pp. 58–59; Gasiorowski, "The 1953 Coup d'Etat in Iran," p. 269; Mottahedeh, *The Mantle of the Prophet,* pp. 131–132.

104. Abrahamian, *Iran Between Two Revolutions,* p. 273; Gasiorowski, "The 1953 Coup d'Etat in Iran," p. 266; Gasiorowski, *U.S. Foreign Policy and the Shah,* pp. 65–66; Rubin, *Paved with Good Inten-*

tions, pp. 74–75. For a concurring view, see Mark J. Gasiorowski, "Conclusion: Why Did Mosaddeq Fall?," in Byrne and Gasiorowski, *Mohammad Mosaddeq and the 1953 Coup in Iran,* p. 269.

105. Bill, *The Eagle and the Lion,* p. 66; Daniel, *The History of Iran,* p. 152; Kinzer, *All the Shah's Men,* p. 147; Louis, "Britain and the Overthrow of the Mosaddeq Government," p. 170.

106. Bill, *The Eagle and the Lion,* p. 85.

107. Gasiorowski, *U.S. Foreign Policy and the Shah,* p. 72; Gasiorowski, "The 1953 Coup d'Etat Against Mosaddeq," pp. 227–228; Risen, "Secrets of History"; Rubin, *Paved with Good Intentions,* p. 77. The CIA station chief in Tehran, Roger Goiran, did not support the British scheme and was later replaced by Allen Dulles with a more enthusiastic participant. Gasiorowski, "The 1953 Coup d'Etat Against Mosaddeq," p. 231; Kinzer, *All the Shah's Men,* p. 164.

108. Rubin, *Paved with Good Intentions,* p. 77.

109. Ansari, *Modern Iran Since 1921,* pp. 120–121; Azimi, "Unseating Mosaddeq," pp. 71–73; Bill, *The Eagle and the Lion,* pp. 66–67, 80; Rubin, *Paved with Good Intentions,* pp. 62, 66; Stobaugh, "The Evolution of Iranian Oil Policy," pp. 209–210. On the debate within the Tudeh and the decision not to openly support Mosaddeq, see Abrahamian, *Iran Between Two Revolutions,* pp. 321–323.

110. Rubin, *Paved with Good Intentions,* p. 57. Also see Bill, *The Eagle and the Lion,* pp. 79, 85.

111. It is worth noting that the Iran experts at both the CIA and the State Department did not share the administration's fears of a Communist takeover. Bill, *The Eagle and the Lion,* p. 93; Gasiorowski, "The 1953 Coup d'Etat in Iran," p. 276.

112. Kinzer, *All the Shah's Men,* pp. 156–160, 205–206; Rubin, *Paved with Good Intentions,* p. 78. Some authors have suggested that a key motive for the United States was the possibility of securing a piece of Iran's oil pie for American companies. However, the best work on this issue demonstrates that it is a red herring: the Eisenhower administration's motives effectively all fell within the broad anti-Communist rubric. In particular, Mark Gasiorowski and Mostafa Zahrani both point out that because of the global oil glut, none of the American countries expressed an interest in securing an Iranian concession during the crisis, and when the Truman administration made its final bid at mediation, it had to offer tremendous incentives to the U.S. oil companies to get them to participate *and they still refused.* All of this suggests that oil was not a principal motive of the 1953 coup. See Gasiorowski, "The 1953 Coup d'Etat in Iran," pp. 275–276; Mostafa Zahrani, "The Coup That Changed the Middle East: Mossadeq v. the CIA in Retrospect," *World Policy Journal* 19, no. 2 (Summer 2002), p. 96.

113. Technically, the operation was known as "TP/AJAX" (Byrne and Gasiorowski, *Mohammad Mosaddeq and the 1953 Coup in Iran,* p. xiv), and some authors have continued to use that as the full name. However, "TP" is simply a CIA digraph that indicates which country the operation or source is being employed in. Any CIA action in Iran, from the most benign to the most "active," would have had the "TP" digraph before its actual code name, and CIA officers generally do not include these digraphs when they discuss their activities. Thus, "TP/AJAX" would simply have been "Ajax" in Agency parlance. For instance, Richard Helms, the ultimate Agency insider, also refers to the operation simply as "AJAX." See Richard Helms, *A Look over My Shoulder: A Life in the Central Intelligence Agency* (New York: Random House, 2003), pp. 182, 187.

114. Daniel, *The History of Iran,* p. 153; Gasiorowski, *U.S. Foreign Policy and the Shah,* p. 75; Gasiorowski, "The 1953 Coup d'Etat Against Mosaddeq," pp. 233–243; Kinzer, *All the Shah's Men,* pp. 5–8; Risen, "Secrets of History."

115. Azimi, "Unseating Mosaddeq," pp. 30–31, 78–82; Gasiorowski, "The 1953 Coup d'Etat in Iran," p. 265; Gasiorowski, *U.S. Foreign Policy and the Shah,* pp. 72–73.

116. Gasiorowski, *U.S. Foreign Policy and the Shah,* p. 76, n. 43.

117. Cited in Kinzer, *All the Shah's Men,* p. 6.

118. Rubin, *Paved with Good Intentions,* p. 81.

119. Gasiorowski, "The 1953 Coup d'Etat Against Mosaddeq," pp. 257–258.

120. Ansari, *Modern Iran Since 1921,* p. 122; Azimi, "Unseating Mosaddeq," pp. 58–69; Bill, *The Eagle and the Lion,* p. 66; Daniel, *The History of Iran,* p. 151; Gasiorowski, "The 1953 Coup d'Etat in Iran," p. 265; Gasiorowski, *U.S. Foreign Policy and the Shah,* pp. 65–66; Gasiorowski,

"The 1953 Coup d'Etat Against Mosaddeq," pp. 230–233; Katouzian, "Mosaddeq's Government in Iranian History," pp. 13–15; Kinzer, *All the Shah's Men*, pp. 117, 159; Stobaugh, "The Evolution of Iranian Oil Policy," p. 212.

121. Abrahamian, *Iran Between Two Revolutions*, pp. 276–277; Azimi, "Unseating Mosaddeq," pp. 82–84; Gasiorowski, "The 1953 Coup d'Etat Against Mosaddeq," p. 244; Katouzian, "Mosaddeq's Government in Iranian History," p. 17; Rubin, *Paved with Good Intentions*, pp. 80–81.

122. Azimi, "Unseating Mosaddeq," pp. 83–84; Katouzian, "Mosaddeq's Government in Iranian History," p. 18.

123. Abrahamian, *Iran Between Two Revolutions*, pp. 273–274; Daniel, *The History of Iran*, p. 152; Gasiorowski, *U.S. Foreign Policy and the Shah*, p. 75; Kinzer, *All the Shah's Men*, p. 165; Rubin, *Paved with Good Intentions*, pp. 81–82.

124. Abrahamian, *Iran Between Two Revolutions*, p. 274.

125. Rubin, *Paved with Good Intentions*, pp. 81–82; Kinzer, *All the Shah's Men*, p. 165.

126. Daniel, *The History of Iran*, p. 153; Gasiorowski, "The 1953 Coup d'Etat in Iran," p. 266; Kinzer, *All the Shah's Men*, pp. 162–163; Risen, "Secrets of History."

127. Ansari, *Modern Iran Since 1921*, pp. 123–125; Bill, *The Eagle and the Lion*, pp. 90–91; Rubin, *Paved with Good Intentions*, pp. 83–86; Daniel, *The History of Iran*, pp. 153–154; Gasiorowski, "The 1953 Coup d'Etat Against Mosaddeq," pp. 248–256; Kinzer, *All the Shah's Men*, pp. 5–8, 167–192; Risen, "Secrets of History." For those interested in more details about the coup, Kinzer's *All the Shah's Men* offers a good, highly readable account. However, the new volume edited by Byrne and Gasiorowski, *Mohammad Mosaddeq and the 1953 Coup in Iran*, is without question the most expert and insightful treatment of events.

128. Zahrani, "The Coup That Changed the Middle East," p. 93.

129. Ansari, *Modern Iran Since 1921*, pp. 115–116; Bill, *The Eagle and the Lion*, pp. 5, 127–129; Daniel, *The History of Iran*, p. 154; Gasiorowski, "Conclusion," p. 261.

130. Mark J. Gasiorowski's concluding essay in the volume he edited with Malcolm Byrne is a superb treatment of all of the different questions surrounding Mosaddeq's fall. See *Mohammad Mosaddeq and the 1953 Coup in Iran*, pp. 261–277.

131. Rubin, *Paved with Good Intentions*, p. 89.

132. Abrahamian, *Iran Between Two Revolutions*, pp. 275–276; Azimi, "Unseating Mosaddeq," pp. 28–29; Daniel, *The History of Iran*, pp. 155–156; Gasiorowski, "The 1953 Coup d'Etat in Iran," p. 277; Gasiorowski, "The 1953 Coup d'Etat Against Mosaddeq," pp. 233–246; Gasiorowski, "Conclusion," pp. 264–268; Kinzer, *All the Shah's Men*, pp. 178, 211; Rubin, *Paved with Good Intentions*, p. 89.

133. Gasiorowski, "The 1953 Coup d'Etat Against Mosaddeq," p. 259. Also see Kinzer, *All the Shah's Men*, p. 211; Taheri, *Nest of Spies*, pp. 36–37.

134. Katouzian, "Mosaddeq's Government in Iranian History," pp. 16–17.

135. Ansari, *Modern Iran Since 1921*, p. 107.

136. Kinzer, *All the Shah's Men*, pp. 74–75; Ramazani, "Iran's 'White Revolution,' " p. 129; Savory, "Social Development in Iran During the Pahlavi Era," p. 102; Zahrani, "The Coup That Changed the Middle East," p. 94.

137. For Mosaddeq making this claim, see Rubin, *Paved with Good Intentions*, p. 68.

138. Ramazani, "Iran's 'White Revolution,' " p. 129.

139. Ibid.; Savory, "Social Development in Iran During the Pahlavi Era," p. 102.

Chapter 4: The Last Shah

1. Quoted in Ansari, *Modern Iran Since 1921*, p. 125.

2. Kinzer, *All the Shah's Men*, p. 184.

3. Ansari, *Modern Iran Since 1921*, pp. 123–125; Bill, *The Eagle and the Lion*, pp. 90–91; Rubin, *Paved with Good Intentions*, pp. 83–86; Daniel, *The History of Iran*, pp. 153–154; Kinzer, *All the Shah's Men*, pp. 5–8, 167–192.

4. Bill, *The Eagle and the Lion*, pp. 100–101; Rubin, *Paved with Good Intentions*, p. 92.

5. Bill, *The Eagle and the Lion*, pp. 98, 100; Gasiorowski, *U.S. Foreign Policy and the Shah*, p. 86.

6. Rubin, *Paved with Good Intentions*, pp. 90–93.

7. Bill, *The Eagle and the Lion*, p. 99; Gasiorowski, *U.S. Foreign Policy and the Shah*, p. 88.

8. Rubin, *Paved with Good Intentions*, p. 93.

9. Ansari, *Modern Iran Since 1921*, pp. 135–137; Bill, *The Eagle and the Lion*, p. 98; Gasiorowski, "The 1953 Coup d'Etat Against Mosaddeq," pp. 257–258; Gasiorowski, *U.S. Foreign Policy and the Shah*, pp. 117–120; Keddie, *Modern Iran*, p. 136; Ashraf Pahlavi, *Faces in a Mirror: Memoirs from Exile* (Englewood Cliffs, N.J.: Prentice-Hall, 1980), p. 150.

10. Bill, *The Eagle and the Lion*, pp. 98, 100.

11. Keddie, *Modern Iran*, p. 139; Savory, "Social Development in Iran During the Pahlavi Era," pp. 102–103.

12. Savory, "Social Development in Iran During the Pahlavi Era," p. 103.

13. Ansari, *Modern Iran Since 1921*, pp. 126–127; Rubin, *Paved with Good Intentions*, pp. 91, 98–101; Savory, "Social Development in Iran During the Pahlavi Era," pp. 102–103.

14. Keddie, *Modern Iran*, pp. 136–137; Rubin, *Paved with Good Intentions*, pp. 95–96; Daniel, *The History of Iran*, p. 156; Yergin, *The Prize*, pp. 475–477.

15. Bill, *The Eagle and the Lion*, pp. 107–109, 112; Rubin, *Paved with Good Intentions*, p. 96.

16. Bill, *The Eagle and the Lion*, p. 67; Gasiorowski, "The 1953 Coup d'Etat Against Mosaddeq," pp. 257–258; Gasiorowski, *U.S. Foreign Policy and the Shah*, p. 91; Rubin, *Paved with Good Intentions*, pp. 87, 94–96.

17. Ansari, *Modern Iran Since 1921*, p. 136; Bill, *The Eagle and the Lion*, pp. 117–118; Cottrell, "Iran's Armed Forces Under the Pahlavi Dynasty," p. 399; Griffith, "Iran's Foreign Policy in the Pahlavi Era," p. 374; Rubin, *Paved with Good Intentions*, p. 97.

18. Ansari, *Modern Iran Since 1921*, p. 136; Rubin, *Paved with Good Intentions*, p. 100.

19. Rubin, *Paved with Good Intentions*, p. 100.

20. Gasiorowski, "The 1953 Coup d'Etat Against Mosaddeq," pp. 257–258.

21. Gasiorowski, *U.S. Foreign Policy and the Shah*, pp. 95–96.

22. Ansari, *Modern Iran Since 1921*, p. 135; Rubin, *Paved with Good Intentions*, pp. 97, 101.

23. Gasiorowski, *U.S. Foreign Policy and the Shah*, p. 119.

24. Bill, *The Eagle and the Lion*, pp. 128–130; Rubin, *Paved with Good Intentions*, p. 100.

25. Bill, *The Eagle and the Lion*, pp. 114–115; Young, "Iran in Continuing Crisis," pp. 291–292.

26. Abrahamian, *Iran Between Two Revolutions*, p. 420.

27. Ibid.; Ansari, *Modern Iran Since 1921*, pp. 138, 142–143; Gasiorowski, *U.S. Foreign Policy and the Shah*, pp. 172–174.

28. Bill, *The Eagle and the Lion*, pp. 117–118.

29. Rubin, *Paved with Good Intentions*, pp. 101–102.

30. Ansari, *Modern Iran Since 1921*, p. 147; Bill, *The Eagle and the Lion*, pp. 117–118; Cottrell, "Iran's Armed Forces Under the Pahlavi Dynasty," p. 398; Griffith, "Iran's Foreign Policy in the Pahlavi Era," pp. 374–375; Rubin, *Paved with Good Intentions*, p. 103.

31. Bill, *The Eagle and the Lion*, pp. 125–126; Gasiorowski, *U.S. Foreign Policy and the Shah*, pp. 96–97.

32. Gasiorowski, *U.S. Foreign Policy and the Shah*, pp. 96–97; Rubin, *Paved with Good Intentions*, p. 102.

33. Ansari, *Modern Iran Since 1921*, p. 138; Gasiorowski, *U.S. Foreign Policy and the Shah*, p. 175.

34. Gasiorowski, *U.S. Foreign Policy and the Shah*, p. 181; Rubin, *Paved with Good Intentions*, pp. 108–109; Taheri, *Nest of Spies*, p. 52.

35. The text is available in Alexander and Nanes, *The United States and Iran*, pp. 306–307. Also see Bill, *The Eagle and the Lion*, p. 119, and Cottrell, "Iran's Armed Forces Under the Pahlavi Dynasty," p. 398.

36. Abrahamian, *Iran Between Two Revolutions*, pp. 421–422; Alexander and Nanes, *The United States and Iran*, pp. 315–316; Ansari, *Modern Iran Since 1921*, pp. 145–146; Gasiorowski, *U.S. Foreign Policy and the Shah*, pp. 177–180; Young, "Iran in Continuing Crisis," pp. 275–276; Rubin, *Paved with Good Intentions*, p. 103.

37. Bill, *The Eagle and the Lion,* p. 150.

38. Ibid.

39. Ibid., pp. 132–133; Rubin, *Paved with Good Intentions,* p. 107; Taheri, *Nest of Spies,* p. 51.

40. Rubin, *Paved with Good Intentions,* p. 105. Also, Alexander and Nanes, *The United States and Iran,* pp. 335–349; Daniel, *The History of Iran,* p. 157; Gasiorowski, *U.S. Foreign Policy and the Shah,* p. 98; Keddie, *Modern Iran,* pp. 143–144.

41. See the documents in Alexander and Nanes, *The United States and Iran,* pp. 317–320.

42. Griffith, "Iran's Foreign Policy in the Pahlavi Era," p. 375; Rubin, *Paved with Good Intentions,* p. 108.

43. Abrahamian, *Iran Between Two Revolutions,* pp. 422–423. Also see Taheri, *Nest of Spies,* pp. 51–52.

44. Abrahamian, *Iran Between Two Revolutions,* pp. 422–423; Ansari, *Modern Iran Since 1921,* p. 153; Bill, *The Eagle and the Lion,* pp. 135–136, 142–144; Ramazani, "Iran's 'White Revolution,' " p. 130; Taheri, *Nest of Spies,* pp. 51–53.

45. Mottahedeh, *The Mantle of the Prophet,* p. 308.

46. Ansari, *Modern Iran Since 1921,* pp. 151–152; Eric Hooglund, "Iran's Agricultural Inheritance," *MERIP Reports* 99 (September 1981), p. 15; Keddie, *Modern Iran,* p. 139; Rubin, *Paved with Good Intentions,* pp. 98–101, 106–107; Young, "Iran in Continuing Crisis," p. 283.

47. Abrahamian, *Iran Between Two Revolutions,* p. 423; Ansari, *Modern Iran Since 1921,* p. 153; Bill, *The Eagle and the Lion,* pp. 142–144; Daniel, *The History of Iran,* p. 157; Keddie, *Modern Iran,* pp. 150–151.

48. Gasiorowski, *U.S. Foreign Policy and the Shah,* p. 102.

49. Ibid., pp. 106–109.

50. Ibid., p. 113; Rubin, *Paved with Good Intentions,* pp. 107–108.

51. Gasiorowski, *U.S. Foreign Policy and the Shah,* p. 112.

52. Ibid., pp. 120, 124.

53. Arjomand, *The Turban for the Crown,* p. 85; Shaul Bakhash, *Reign of the Ayatollahs: Iran and Islamic Revolution,* rev. ed. (New York: Basic Books, 1990), pp. 24–25; Gasiorowski, *U.S. Foreign Policy and the Shah,* p. 182.

54. Ansari, *Modern Iran Since 1921,* pp. 153–157.

55. Bill, *The Eagle and the Lion,* pp. 145–146; Keddie, *Modern Iran,* p. 152.

56. Abrahamian, *Iran Between Two Revolutions,* p. 423; Ansari, *Modern Iran Since 1921,* p. 157; Bill, *The Eagle and the Lion,* pp. 135–140, 146–148; Daniel, *The History of Iran,* p. 157; Keddie, *Modern Iran,* pp. 144–145.

57. Bill, *The Eagle and the Lion,* p. 142.

58. Keddie, *Modern Iran,* p. 139; Savory, "Social Development in Iran During the Pahlavi Era," pp. 102–103.

59. Even the shah's good friend Henry Kissinger remarked, "As time went on and I got to know the Shah better, I realized that he was not by nature a domineering personality. Indeed, he was rather shy and withdrawn. I could never escape the impression that he was a gentle, even sentimental man who had schooled himself in the maxim that the ruler must be aloof and hard, but had never succeeded in making it come naturally." Kissinger, *White House Years,* p. 1259. Also see Ambassador Sullivan's assessment of the shah that he suffered from "a fateful sort of indecision and an absence of conviction in crisis." (William H. Sullivan, *Mission to Iran* [New York: W. W. Norton, 1981], pp. 56–57.)

60. For concurring views, see Abrahamian, *Iran Between Two Revolutions,* p. 424; Ansari, *Modern Iran Since 1921,* pp. 157–158; Arjomand, *The Turban for the Crown,* pp. 72–73.

61. Abrahamian, *Iran Between Two Revolutions,* p. 424.

62. Eventually, five other programs would be added in the 1970s; however, these were never really followed up as the White Revolution had mostly run its course as a dynamic agent of change by then.

63. Fred Halliday, "Iran: The Economic Contradictions," *MERIP Reports* 69 (July–August 1978), pp. 13–14.

64. Bill, "Modernization and Reform from Above," pp. 31–32; Bill, *The Eagle and the Lion,* p. 151;

Savory, "Social Development in Iran During the Pahlavi Era," pp. 109–121. The last three points were not added until 1967 and were implemented least of all.

65. Arjomand, *The Turban for the Crown*, p. 73; Bakhash, *The Reign of the Ayatollahs*, pp. 27–28.

66. Arjomand, *The Turban for the Crown*, p. 73; Ansari, *Modern Iran Since 1921*, pp. 142–143; Bill, *The Eagle and the Lion*, p. 148; Daniel, *The History of Iran*, p. 157.

67. Bill, "Modernization and Reform from Above," p. 36.

68. Bakhash, *The Reign of the Ayatollahs*, pp. 27–28; Bill, *The Eagle and the Lion*, p. 152; Daniel, *The History of Iran*, p. 157; Keddie, *Modern Iran*, pp. 146–147; Rubin, *Paved with Good Intentions*, p. 109.

69. Quoted in Wright, *In the Name of God*, p. 50.

70. Mottale, *Iran*, p. 6.

71. Ibid.

72. Quoted in Wright, *In the Name of God*, p. 51.

73. Abrahamian, *Iran Between Two Revolutions*, pp. 424–426; Ansari, *Modern Iran Since 1921*, p. 161; Bill, *The Eagle and the Lion*, pp. 147–152; Fischer, *Iran*, p. 124; Rubin, *Paved with Good Intentions*, p. 109; Wright, *In the Name of God*, p. 51.

74. Bill, *The Eagle and the Lion*, pp. 149–150; Savory, "Social Development in Iran During the Pahlavi Era," pp. 105–110.

75. Alexander and Nanes, *The United States and Iran*, pp. 349–353; Rubin, *Paved with Good Intentions*, pp. 110–113.

76. Rubin, *Paved with Good Intentions*, p. 113.

77. See Gasiorowski, *U.S. Foreign Policy and the Shah*, pp. 102–103.

78. For a similar view, see Rubin, *Paved with Good Intentions*, p. 115.

79. Arjomand, *The Turban for the Crown*, p. 73; Bill, *The Eagle and the Lion*, p. 151; Savory, "Social Development in Iran During the Pahlavi Era," pp. 109–121.

80. *Iran: Country Statistical Yearbook (1372)*, Statistical Center of Iran, 1994, p. 436.

81. Savory, "Social Development in Iran During the Pahlavi Era," p. 114.

82. Ibid., p. 122; Robert E. Looney, *Economic Origins of the Iranian Revolution* (Elmsford, N.Y.: Pergamon, 1988), p. 75. This is in constant rials.

83. Hooglund, "Iran's Agricultural Inheritance," p. 15. Hooglund's article is outstanding in covering the failings of land reform during the White Revolution.

84. Ibid., p. 16; United Nations, *Demographic Yearbook; Special Topic: Marriage and Divorce Statistics* (New York: Statistical Office of the United Nations, Department of Economic and Social Affairs, 1969), p. 326.

85. Gasiorowski, *U.S. Foreign Policy and the Shah*, p. 132; Hooglund, "Iran's Agricultural Inheritance," p. 16; Keddie, *Modern Iran*, pp. 152–153.

86. Ansari, *Modern Iran Since 1921*, pp. 157–160; Arjomand, *The Turban for the Crown*, p. 73.

87. Ansari, *Modern Iran Since 1921*, pp. 157–160; Hooglund, "Iran's Agricultural Inheritance," p. 16.

88. Hooglund, "Iran's Agricultural Inheritance," p. 18; Keddie, *Modern Iran*, p. 155. Also see Gasiorowski, *U.S. Foreign Policy and the Shah*, p. 132; Keddie, *Modern Iran*, pp. 152–153.

89. Keddie, *Modern Iran*, pp. 157–159.

90. Halliday, "Iran: The Economic Contradictions," p. 13.

91. Ibid., p. 14. On Iranian educational practices, see Eilers, "Educational and Cultural Developments in Iran During the Pahlavi Era," pp. 306–309.

92. Daniel, *The History of Iran*, p. 14; Mohsen Nazari, "Characteristics of Labor Force Developments in Iran During Four Decades, 1956–1996: Trends and Consequences," *Political and Economic Ettela'at*, no. 11–12 (August–September 1998), available at www.irvl.net/characteristics_of_labor_force.htm, accessed June 23, 2004.

93. Bill, *The Eagle and the Lion*, p. 168.

94. Ibid., p. 151.

95. Ibid., pp. 153–156; Taheri, *Nest of Spies*, p. 53.

96. Bill, *The Eagle and the Lion*, pp. 156–157.

97. For a concurring opinion from another former U.S. government official, see Gary Sick, *All Fall Down: America's Fateful Encounter with Iran* (London: I. B. Tauris, 1985), pp. 10–11. While I was director for Persian Gulf affairs at the National Security Council during the 1990s, one of the issues on my watch was a similar status of forces agreement with the United Arab Emirates. American legal advisers would not budge on the question of immunity for American military personnel ashore in the UAE for port call (Dubayy has the only port in the Persian Gulf capable of handling a *Nimitz*-class aircraft carrier), and the Emiratis—in part because of the Iranian experience—refused to concede the point.

98. Rubin, *Paved with Good Intentions*, p. 110.

99. Ansari, *Modern Iran Since 1921*, pp. 161–162; Bakhash, *The Reign of the Ayatollahs*, pp. 33–35; Bill, *The Eagle and the Lion*, pp. 156–157.

100. Quoted in Ansari, *Modern Iran Since 1921*, p. 162.

101. Bakhash, *The Reign of the Ayatollahs*, pp. 33–35; Rubin, *Paved with Good Intentions*, p. 114.

102. Rubin, *Paved with Good Intentions*, p. 114.

103. Gasiorowski, *U.S. Foreign Policy and the Shah*, p. 120, n. 67.

104. Ibid., p. 99; Rubin, *Paved with Good Intentions*, pp. 117–118.

105. Author's interview with Shaul Bakhash, June 21, 2004.

106. For similar views, see Gasiorowski, *U.S. Foreign Policy and the Shah*, p. 99; Rubin, *Paved with Good Intentions*, p. 115.

107. Rubin, *Paved with Good Intentions*, p. 96.

108. Gasiorowski, *U.S. Foreign Policy and the Shah*, pp. 102–103.

109. Bill, *The Eagle and the Lion*, pp. 177–180; Rubin, *Paved with Good Intentions*, p. 119.

110. Rubin, *Paved with Good Intentions*, pp. 119–122.

111. Gasiorowski, *U.S. Foreign Policy and the Shah*, p. 112.

112. Bill, *The Eagle and the Lion*, pp. 172–173, 177; Cottrell, "Iran's Armed Forces Under the Pahlavi Dynasty," p. 398; Gasiorowski, *U.S. Foreign Policy and the Shah*, p. 125; Griffith, "Iran's Foreign Policy in the Pahlavi Era," pp. 374–375; Rubin, *Paved with Good Intentions*, p. 118.

113. Alan Heston, Robert Summers, and Bettina Aten, "Penn World Table," Version 6.1, Center for International Comparisons at the University of Pennsylvania (CICUP), October 2002, available at pwt.econ.upenn.edu/php_site/pwt61_form.php, accessed June 23, 2004.

114. Ansari, *Modern Iran Since 1921*, pp. 166–167.

115. Rubin, *Paved with Good Intentions*, p. 122.

116. Bill, *The Eagle and the Lion*, p. 3.

117. For instance, see Bill, "Modernization and Reform from Above," pp. 19–40, which notes that the White Revolution was an effort to mobilize traditional classes (i.e., the peasantry) in support of the monarchy against the intelligentsia. Regardless of the accuracy of this analysis, Bill is very careful not to predict that this will fail. Instead, he simply notes that it has never really been employed as a method of modernization and therefore faces challenges.

118. Bill, *The Eagle and the Lion*, pp. 170–171; Rubin, *Paved with Good Intentions*, p. 128.

119. Ansari, *Modern Iran Since 1921*, p. 177; Cottrell, "Iran's Armed Forces Under the Pahlavi Dynasty," pp. 399–400; Griffith, "Iran's Foreign Policy in the Pahlavi Era," p. 376; Taheri, *Nest of Spies*, pp. 53–54.

120. Bill, *The Eagle and the Lion*, p. 168; Eilers, "Educational and Cultural Developments in Iran During the Pahlavi Era," pp. 306–309; Rubin, *Paved with Good Intentions*, p. 113.

121. Fischer, *Iran*, pp. 109–135.

122. Bill, *The Eagle and the Lion*, pp. 161–163.

123. Abrahamian, *Iran Between Two Revolutions*, pp. 489–491; Daniel, *The History of Iran*, p. 161; Keddie, *Modern Iran*, pp. 220–222.

124. Daniel, *The History of Iran*, p. 161; Keddie, *Modern Iran*, pp. 219–220.

Chapter 5: Come the Revolution

1. For a similar critique, see Cyrus Vance, *Hard Choices: Critical Years in America's Foreign Policy* (New York: Simon & Schuster, 1983), pp. 24–29.
2. Ansari, *Modern Iran Since 1921,* pp. 176–177.
3. Bill, *The Eagle and the Lion,* p. 203; Gasiorowski, *U.S. Foreign Policy and the Shah,* p. 100; Henry Kissinger, *White House Years* (Boston: Little, Brown, 1979), pp. 1260–1265; Palmer, *Guardians of the Gulf,* pp. 86–88; Rubin, *Paved with Good Intentions,* pp. 124–126.
4. Kissinger, *White House Years,* p. 1261. See also Bill, *The Eagle and the Lion,* p. 203.
5. Their relationship was so close—and the shah benefited so greatly from Nixon's presidency— that there have been widespread allegations that the shah funneled considerable money to Nixon's reelection campaign in 1972. Whether this is true or the Nixon administration knew about it (certainly not impossible given its other sordid activities—such as the Watergate break-ins—during that election) is unproven at this time. See Bill, *The Eagle and the Lion,* p. 212.
6. Ansari, *Modern Iran Since 1921,* p. 178.
7. The quote is repeated in both Sick, *All Fall Down,* p. 14, and Walter Isaacson, *Kissinger: A Biography* (New York: Touchstone, 1992), p. 563.
8. Sick, *All Fall Down,* p. 15. Also see Bill, *The Eagle and the Lion,* pp. 200–201; Rubin, *Paved with Good Intentions,* p. 134; Taheri, *Nest of Spies,* pp. 57–58. In the third part of his memoirs, Kissinger maintains that no such formal policy decision was ever made. (Henry Kissinger, *Years of Renewal* [New York: Touchstone, 1991], pp. 582–583.) I believe that Secretary Kissinger has misremembered this issue. First, in the initial volume of his memoirs he does note that Nixon "added a proviso that in the future Iranian requests should not be second-guessed." (Kissinger, *White House Years,* p. 1264.) Moreover, a July 25, 1972, memorandum from Kissinger to the secretaries of state and defense stated, "The President also reiterated that, in general, decisions on the acquisition of military equipment should be left primarily to the government of Iran. If the Government of Iran has decided to buy certain equipment, the purchase of US equipment should be encouraged tactfully where appropriate, and technical advice on the capabilities of the equipment in question should be provided." (A copy of this memorandum was found in the U.S. Embassy in Tehran and publicly released by the government of Iran. A scanned photograph of the memo can be found at the Web site of the Iran Documentation Project of the National Security Archive at www.gwu.edu/~nsarchiv/NSAEBB/NSAEBB21/03-01.htm, accessed June 30, 2004.) Likewise, a staff report by the Senate Foreign Relations Committee also found that the Nixon administration had issued explicit guidance that "effectively exempted Iran from arms sales review processes in the State and Defense Departments." (Senate Foreign Relations Committee, Subcommittee on Multinational Corporations, *Multinational Corporations and United States Foreign Policy: Grumman Sale of F-14s to Iran,* 94th Congress, 2nd Session, August and September 1976, pp. 176–177.) Even if Kissinger were right that there was no explicit policy pronouncement— and the evidence seems rather categorical that he is not correct—the point is still irrelevant as for all intents and purposes that is still what happened: during the Nixon and Ford administrations the shah was not denied any weapon he desired.
9. Ansari, *Modern Iran Since 1921,* p. 176; Bill, *The Eagle and the Lion,* p. 199; John C. Campbell, "Oil Power in the Middle East," *Foreign Affairs* 56, no. 1 (October 1977), pp. 93–94; Griffith, "Iran's Foreign Policy in the Pahlavi Era," p. 378; Palmer, *Guardians of the Gulf,* pp. 90–91; Taheri, *Nest of Spies,* pp. 58–66; Sepehr Zabih, "Iran's Policy Toward the Persian Gulf," *International Journal of Middle East Studies* 7, no. 3 (July 1976), pp. 345–358.
10. Bill, *The Eagle and the Lion,* p. 199; Cottrell, "Iran's Armed Forces Under the Pahlavi Dynasty," in Lenczowski, *Iran Under the Pahlavis,* pp. 407–413; Griffith, "Iran's Foreign Policy in the Pahlavi Era," p. 380; Kissinger, *White House Years,* pp. 1261–1262; Leslie M. Pryor, "Arms and the Shah," *Foreign Policy* 31 (Summer 1978), pp. 61–62; Ann Tibbits Schulz, *Buying Security: Iran Under the Monarchy* (Boulder, Colo.: Westview, 1989), pp. 17–22.
11. Ansari, *Modern Iran Since 1921,* pp. 176–177; Bill, *The Eagle and the Lion,* p. 198; Griffith,

"Iran's Foreign Policy in the Pahlavi Era," p. 378; Pryor, "Arms and the Shah," p. 60; Rubin, *Paved with Good Intentions*, p. 133.

12. Palmer, *Guardians of the Gulf*, p. 90.

13. Taheri, *Nest of Spies*, p. 65.

14. Bill, *The Eagle and the Lion*, pp. 205–208; Cottrell, "Iran's Armed Forces Under the Pahlavi Dynasty," pp. 414–416; Izady, *The Kurds*, pp. 68–69; Kissinger, *Years of Renewal*, pp. 576–596; McDowall, *A Modern History of the Kurds*, pp. 330–340; O'Ballance, *The Kurdish Struggle*, pp. 93–101; Rubin, *Paved with Good Intentions*, pp. 134, 138.

15. Gasiorowski, *U.S. Foreign Policy and the Shah*, p. 100; Precht, "The Iranian Revolution 25 Years Later," *The Middle East Journal* 58, no. 1 (Winter 2004), pp. 15–16; Taheri, *Nest of Spies*, pp. 77–79; Vance, *Hard Choices*, pp. 315–316.

16. For a concurring analysis, see Taheri, *Nest of Spies*, pp. 66–67.

17. Yergin, *The Prize*, pp. 522–525.

18. Ibid., p. 567.

19. Ibid., p. 582. Also see Rubin, *Paved with Good Intentions*, p. 131.

20. Gasiorowski, *U.S. Foreign Policy and the Shah*, pp. 102–103.

21. Rubin, *Paved with Good Intentions*, pp. 131, 139–140.

22. Yergin, *The Prize*, pp. 605–609, 614.

23. Griffith, "Iran's Foreign Policy in the Pahlavi Era," p. 379.

24. Ibid.; Isaacson, *Kissinger*, pp. 563–564; Yergin, *The Prize*, p. 626.

25. Quoted in Yergin, *The Prize*, p. 626.

26. Quoted in Isaacson, *Kissinger*, p. 564.

27. Office of Technology Assessment, Congress of the United States, *U.S. Oil Import Vulnerability: The Technical Replacement Capability* (Washington, D.C.: U.S. Government Printing Office, 1991), p. 39.

28. Wikipedia, "1973 Oil Crisis," available at en.wikipedia.org/wiki/1973_energy_crisis, accessed June 27, 2004.

29. Gasiorowski, *U.S. Foreign Policy and the Shah*, pp. 102–103.

30. Ansari, *Modern Iran Since 1921*, pp. 184–185; Bill, *The Eagle and the Lion*, p. 202; Keddie, *Modern Iran*, pp. 162–163; Rubin, *Paved with Good Intentions*, p. 132; author's personal correspondence with Shaul Bakhash, July 29, 2004.

31. Author's interview, June 21, 2004.

32. Schulz, *Buying Security*, pp. 134–135.

33. Bill, *The Eagle and the Lion*, p. 202. Also see Schulz, *Buying Security*, pp. 131–150.

34. Bill, *The Eagle and the Lion*, p. 170; Rubin, *Paved with Good Intentions*, p. 130; Taheri, *Nest of Spies*, pp. 58–59.

35. See, for instance, Isaacson, *Kissinger*, pp. 563–565.

36. Pryor, "Arms and the Shah," p. 57.

37. Bill, *The Eagle and the Lion*, pp. 202, 226; Rubin, *Paved with Good Intentions*, p. 158.

38. Bill, *The Eagle and the Lion*, pp. 204–208; Daniel, *The History of Iran*, pp. 164–165; Rubin, *Paved with Good Intentions*, p. 138.

39. Bill, *The Eagle and the Lion*, pp. 209–210; Rubin, *Paved with Good Intentions*, pp. 133, 163–165.

40. The cable was found by Iranian students in the U.S. Embassy and released by the Iranian government after the revolution in "Daneshjuyan-e Mosalman-e Payru-ye Khatt-e Emam" ("Muslim Students Following the Line of the Imam"), "Asnad-e Laneh-ye Jasusi" ("The Nest of Spies Documents"), "Rabetin-e khub-e Amrika" ("America's Good Contacts" or "America's Good Intermediaries"), in English and Farsi, vol. 17, pp. 74–89. For a parallel opinion on the dangers of American arms sales to Iran, see Pryor, "Arms and the Shah," pp. 56–71.

41. Robert Looney argues that Iran's strategy of growth—a "technocratic" approach focusing on industrialization that benefited the upper classes and concentrated income—was a mistake. Instead, he contends that Iran should have adopted a "reformist" strategy that focused on greater income distribution and small-scale, labor-intensive industry that would have reduced unemploy-

ment and underemployment, plus more modest growth driven by the consumer goods industry. This would also have allowed for a greater diversification of exports. Also, the low productivity of the Iranian industrial sector meant that Iranian manufactured goods were not competitive on international markets, requiring ever more government investment to keep them afloat. (Looney, *Economic Origins of the Iranian Revolution*, pp. 258–260.)

42. Rubin, *Paved with Good Intentions*, p. 142; author's correspondence with Shaul Bakhash, July 29, 2004.

43. Hooglund, "Iran's Agricultural Inheritance," p. 17.

44. Bakhash, *Reign of the Ayatollahs*, p. 11; Halliday, "Iran: The Economic Contradictions," p. 17; Hooglund, "Iran's Agricultural Inheritance," pp. 17–18; Looney, *Economic Origins of the Iranian Revolution*, p. 4; Rubin, *Paved with Good Intentions*, p. 142. Hooglund's article is, without doubt, the definitive work on the destruction of Iranian agriculture before the revolution.

45. Abrahamian, *Iran Between Two Revolutions*, p. 497.

46. Ibid., p. 447.

47. Looney, *Economic Origins of the Iranian Revolution*, p. 4; Rubin, *Paved with Good Intentions*, p. 269.

48. Cited in Rubin, *Paved with Good Intentions*, p. 144.

49. EconStats, "Iran," available at www.econstats.com/global/air.xls, accessed June 27, 2004.

50. Looney, *Economic Origins of the Iranian Revolution*, pp. 3–5. Also see Abrahamian, *Iran Between Two Revolutions*, p. 497; Schulz, *Buying Security*, p. 76.

51. Abrahamian, *Iran Between Two Revolutions*, pp. 498–499; Bakhash, *Reign of the Ayatollahs*, p. 13; Fischer, *Iran*, p. 128; Schulz, *Buying Security*, p. 77.

52. Rubin, *Paved with Good Intentions*, p. 143; Statistical Center of Iran, "Population with 10 Years of Age and Over, Sorted by Sex and Activity (1956–1997)," available at www.iranworld.com/Indicators/isc-t099.asp, accessed June 30, 2004.

53. Fischer, *Iran*, p. viii.

54. Bill, *The Eagle and the Lion*, pp. 216–217; Rubin, *Paved with Good Intentions*, p. 267.

55. Looney, *Economic Origins of the Iranian Revolution*, p. 4; World Bank, *World Tables: 1976* (Baltimore: Johns Hopkins University Press, 1976), pp. 124–125.

56. Halliday, "Iran: The Economic Contradictions," p. 14.

57. Ibid., pp. 14–16; Keddie, *Modern Iran*, pp. 157–161.

58. Charles Kurzman, *The Unthinkable Revolution in Iran* (Cambridge, Mass.: Harvard University Press, 2004), p. 81.

59. Arjomand, *The Turban for the Crown*, p. 70.

60. Rubin, *Paved with Good Intentions*, pp. 159–160.

61. Ibid., p. 143.

62. Parvin Merat Amini, "A Single Party State in Iran, 1975–78," *Middle Eastern Studies* 38, no. 1 (January 2002), pp. 133–135.

63. Firoozi, "Income Distribution and Taxation Laws of Iran," pp. 73–87.

64. Ansari, *Modern Iran Since 1921*, pp. 192–193. Also see Halliday, "Iran: The Economic Contradictions," pp. 16–17.

65. Ryszard Kapuściński, *Shah of Shahs*, trans. William R. Brand and Katarzyna Mroczkowska-Brand (New York: Vintage, 1992), pp. 56–57.

66. Looney, *Economic Origins of the Iranian Revolution*, p. 261.

67. Abrahamian, *Iran Between Two Revolutions*, pp. 442–445; Bakhash, *The Reign of the Ayatollahs*, p. 191; Rubin, *Paved with Good Intentions*, pp. 266, 268.

68. Halliday, "Iran: The Economic Contradictions," p. 14.

69. Looney, *Economic Origins of the Iranian Revolution*, pp. 3–5.

70. Eilers, "Educational and Cultural Developments in Iran During the Pahlavi Era," p. 313; Rubin, *Paved with Good Intentions*, p. 145.

71. Mottahedeh, *The Mantle of the Prophet*, p. 333.

72. Ibid., p. 316.

73. Keddie, *Modern Iran*, p. 218.

74. Ansari, *Modern Iran Since 1921*, p. 179; Arjomand, *The Turban for the Crown*, p. 108; Bakhash, *The Reign of the Ayatollahs*, pp. 10–11.

75. Bakhash, *The Reign of the Ayatollahs*, p. 11.

76. Abrahamian, *Iran Between Two Revolutions*, pp. 441–442; Amini, "A Single Party State in Iran," pp. 131–169; Bakhash, *The Reign of the Ayatollahs*, p. 11; Bill, *The Eagle and the Lion*, p. 196; Shaul Bakhash interview, June 21, 2004.

77. Bill, *The Eagle and the Lion*, p. 186; Gasiorowski, *U.S. Foreign Policy and the Shah*, p. 194; Rubin, *Paved with Good Intentions*, pp. 176–180.

78. Quoted in Abrahamian, *Iran Between Two Revolutions*, pp. 441–442.

79. Ansari, *Modern Iran Since 1921*, pp. 168–175; Bill, *The Eagle and the Lion*, pp. 168, 183–185; Afshin Molavi, *Persian Pilgrimages: Journeys Across Iran* (New York: W. W. Norton, 2002), p. 23; Taheri, *Nest of Spies*, pp. 56–57; Geoffrey Wawro, "Letter from Iran," *Naval War College Review* 55, no. 1 (Winter 2002).

80. Ansari, *Modern Iran Since 1921*, pp. 184–185; Bakhash, *The Reign of the Ayatollahs*, pp. 10–11; Halliday, "Iran: The Economic Contradictions," p. 9; Hooglund, "Iran's Agricultural Inheritance," p. 17; Keddie, *Modern Iran*, pp. 162–163; Rubin, *Paved with Good Intentions*, p. 132.

81. Keddie, *Modern Iran*, pp. 134–135.

82. Kurzman, *The Unthinkable Revolution in Iran*, pp. 37–38; Mottahedeh, *The Mantle of the Prophet*, pp. 345–351.

83. Arjomand, *The Turban for the Crown*, pp. 91–94; Bill, *The Eagle and the Lion*, p. 218; Fischer, *Iran*, pp. 184–185; Keddie, *Modern Iran*, p. 226; Mottahedeh, *The Mantle of the Prophet*, pp. 269–356, esp. 345–356.

84. Bill, *The Eagle and the Lion*, pp. 187–190, 217; Keddie, *Modern Iran*, pp. 222–224; Looney, *Economic Origins of the Iranian Revolution*, p. 5.

85. Arjomand, *The Turban for the Crown*, p. 83; Rubin, *Paved with Good Intentions*, pp. 266, 276–277.

86. Fischer, *Iran*, p. 127.

87. Arjomand, *The Turban for the Crown*, pp. 92–93.

88. Keddie, *Modern Iran*, pp. 229–230.

89. Abrahamian, *Iran Between Two Revolutions*, pp. 511–512.

90. Bakhash, *The Reign of the Ayatollahs*, p. 13; Daniel, *The History of Iran*, p. 165; Gasiorowski, *U.S. Foreign Policy and the Shah*, p. 134; Keddie, *Modern Iran*, p. 217; Looney, *Economic Origins of the Iranian Revolution*, pp. 3–5, 262; Rubin, *Paved with Good Intentions*, pp. 131, 171, 270.

91. Vance, *Hard Choices*, p. 317.

92. Bill, *The Eagle and the Lion*, pp. 227–228; Daniel, *The History of Iran*, p. 167; Rubin, *Paved with Good Intentions*, pp. 190–192, 196; Vance, *Hard Choices*, p. 323.

93. Taheri, *Nest of Spies*, p. 90.

94. Precht, "The Iranian Revolution 25 Years Later," p. 11; Taheri, *Nest of Spies*, pp. 88–89.

95. Bill, *The Eagle and the Lion*, pp. 219–220.

96. For concurring views, see Arjomand, *The Turban for the Crown*, p. 108; Keddie, *Modern Iran*, pp. 214–215; Precht, "The Iranian Revolution 25 Years Later," p. 11; Taheri, *Nest of Spies*, pp. 88–89. Bill argues that Carter had nothing to do with the shah's lighter hand in early 1977 and that it was entirely about paving the way for his son. I find this unconvincing for several reasons. First, there is no evidence that the shah actually believed this at the time. Second, Bill is alone in arguing this point, and the vast majority of Iran experts are convinced that even the shah's liberalization efforts in 1976 were driven by the American presidential election. Third, the timing is much too coincidental, with the shah showing the greatest restraint during the period between Carter's election in November 1976 and his own trip to Washington a year later. Finally, the fact that he began to crack down again immediately after he was assured that Carter was not going to act on his human rights rhetoric where Iran was concerned strongly supports the theory that he eased up only for fear of Carter's likely behavior in the first place. Precht points out that "The Shah had been terribly concerned about Carter's ascension to the presidency even before he was

nominated, fearing he would be another Kennedy who would force him down a liberal path."
Precht, "The Iranian Revolution 25 Years Later," p. 11.

97. Arjomand, *The Turban for the Crown*, p. 108; William O. Beeman, "Images of the Great Satan: Representations of the United States in the Iranian Revolution," in Nikki R. Keddie, ed., *Religion and Politics in Iran: Shi'ism from Quietism to Revolution* (New Haven, Conn.: Yale University Press, 1983), pp. 214–215; Bill, *The Eagle and the Lion*, pp. 221–223.

98. Zbigniew Brzezinski, *Power and Principle: Memoirs of the National Security Adviser, 1977–1981,* rev. ed. (New York: Farrar, Straus and Giroux, 1985), pp. 357–358; Rubin, *Paved with Good Intentions,* pp. 190–192; Sullivan, *Mission to Iran,* p. 20; Taheri, *Nest of Spies,* pp. 89–90; Vance, *Hard Choices,* pp. 314–316.

99. Bill, *The Eagle and the Lion,* pp. 254, 401–402; Sullivan, *Mission to Iran,* pp. 21–22, 99.

100. Bill, *The Eagle and the Lion,* p. 231; Sullivan, *Mission to Iran,* pp. 20, 117–120, 122; Vance, *Hard Choices,* pp. 322–323.

101. Bill, *The Eagle and the Lion,* p. 228; Rubin, *Paved with Good Intentions,* p. 196; Sick, *All Fall Down,* pp. 24–25; Vance, *Hard Choices,* pp. 317–319.

102. Bill, *The Eagle and the Lion,* pp. 228–229; Rubin, *Paved with Good Intentions,* pp. 197–198; Sick, *All Fall Down,* pp. 26–27; Vance, *Hard Choices,* pp. 319–321.

103. Arjomand, *The Turban for the Crown,* pp. 108–109, 130; Bakhash, *The Reign of the Ayatollahs,* p. 14; Bill, *The Eagle and the Lion,* pp. 225, 228; Fischer, *Iran,* p. 192; Keddie, *Modern Iran,* pp. 214–216; Kurzman, *The Unthinkable Revolution in Iran,* pp. 17–22; Rubin, *Paved with Good Intentions,* p. 196; Sick, *All Fall Down,* pp. 24–25.

104. Arjomand, *The Turban for the Crown,* p. 108.

105. Bakhash, *The Reign of the Ayatollahs,* p. 11; Fischer, *Iran,* p. 189.

106. Kurzman, *The Unthinkable Revolution in Iran,* pp. 25–29.

107. Bill, *The Eagle and the Lion,* p. 232; Rubin, *Paved with Good Intentions,* pp. 200–201; Sick, *All Fall Down,* pp. 28–29.

108. Sick, *All Fall Down,* pp. 31–32.

109. Kurzman, *The Unthinkable Revolution in Iran,* pp. 20–21.

110. Bakhash, *The Reign of the Ayatollahs,* p. 12; Fischer, *Iran,* p. 193.

111. Kurzman, *The Unthinkable Revolution in Iran,* p. 29.

112. Sick, *All Fall Down,* p. 30.

113. AmConsul Shiraz, "Official Support for the Shah and Anti-American Sentiment," October 30, 1978, original classification confidential, declassified and available at www.gwu.edu/%7Ensarchiv/NSAEBB/NSAEBB78/propaganda%20137.pdf, accessed July 10, 2004; Beeman, "Images of the Great Satan," pp. 214–215; Bill, *The Eagle and the Lion,* p. 228; Keddie, *Modern Iran,* pp. 214–215; Rubin, *Paved with Good Intentions,* p. 196; Sick, *All Fall Down,* pp. 24–25.

114. Harold H. Saunders, "The Crisis Begins," in Warren Christopher and Paul H. Kreisberg, eds., *American Hostages in Iran: The Conduct of a Crisis* (New Haven, Conn.: Yale University Press, 1985), p. 54.

115. Taheri, *Nest of Spies,* p. 74. Also see Beeman, "Images of the Great Satan," p. 204.

116. Taheri, *Nest of Spies,* p. 83.

117. Beeman, "Images of the Great Satan," pp. 204–205; Bill, *The Eagle and the Lion,* pp. 5, 211–213; Daniel, *The History of Iran,* p. 165; Rubin, *Paved with Good Intentions,* pp. 136–137; Schulz, *Buying Security,* p. 135; Taheri, *Nest of Spies,* pp. 73–75, 81–82.

118. Taheri, *Nest of Spies,* pp. 84–85.

119. Quoted in ibid., p. 86.

120. Quoted in Rubin, *Paved with Good Intentions,* p. 261.

121. R. K. Ramazani, "Iran's Foreign Policy: Contending Orientations," in R. K. Ramazani, ed., *Iran's Revolution: The Search for Consensus* (Bloomington, Ind.: Indiana University Press, 1990), p. 49.

122. Beeman, "Images of the Great Satan," pp. 206–211.

123. Azar Nafisi, *Reading Lolita in Tehran* (New York: Random House, 2004), p. 126.

124. Brad Hanson, "The 'Westoxication' of Iran: Depictions and Reactions of Behrangi, al-e Ahmad,

and Shariati," *International Journal of Middle East Studies* 15, no. 1 (February 1983), pp. 1–23; Mottahedeh, *The Mantle of the Prophet*, p. 296.

125. Bill, *The Eagle and the Lion*, p. 214.

126. Ibid., pp. 190–191; Taheri, *Nest of Spies*, pp. 82–83.

127. Abrahamian, *Iran Between Two Revolutions*, p. 505; Bill, *The Eagle and the Lion*, pp. 234–235; Daniel, *The History of Iran*, p. 166; Keddie, *Modern Iran*, p. 225; Kurzman, *The Unthinkable Revolution in Iran*, p. 37; Wright, *In the Name of God*, p. 57.

128. Abrahamian, *Iran Between Two Revolutions*, p. 506.

129. Abrahamian, "Iran: The Political Crisis Intensifies," pp. 4–5; Abrahamian, *Iran Between Two Revolutions*, pp. 505–558; Bakhash, *The Reign of the Ayatollahs*, pp. 14–18; Bill, *The Eagle and the Lion*, pp. 235–236, 239–240; Daniel, *The History of Iran*, pp. 166–173; Fischer, *Iran*, pp. 194–213; Keddie, *Modern Iran*, pp. 225–239; Kurzman, *The Unthinkable Revolution in Iran*, pp. 35–124; Rubin, *Paved with Good Intentions*, pp. 206–239; Sick, *All Fall Down*, pp. 22–46.

130. Abrahamian, *Iran Between Two Revolutions*, pp. 509–510; Kurzman, *The Unthinkable Revolution in Iran*, pp. 51–53.

131. Abrahamian, "Iran: The Political Crisis Intensifies," p. 3; Abrahamian, *Iran Between Two Revolutions*, pp. 505–558; Bakhash, *The Reign of the Ayatollahs*, pp. 14–18; Bill, *The Eagle and the Lion*, pp. 235–236, 239–240; Daniel, *The History of Iran*, pp. 166–173; Fischer, *Iran*, pp. 194–213; Keddie, *Modern Iran*, pp. 225–239; Kurzman, *The Unthinkable Revolution in Iran*, pp. 61–62; Precht, "The Iranian Revolution 25 Years Later," p. 12; Rubin, *Paved with Good Intentions*, pp. 206–239. It is worth noting that, according to Precht, a SAVAK contact of the CIA had claimed that SAVAK was in fact responsible for the fire.

132. Abrahamian, "Iran: The Political Crisis Intensifies," p. 3; Abrahamian, *Iran Between Two Revolutions*, p. 515.

133. Abrahamian, *Iran Between Two Revolutions*, pp. 515–516; Bakhash, *The Reign of the Ayatollahs*, pp. 15–16; Daniel, *The History of Iran*, p. 169; Kurzman, *The Unthinkable Revolution in Iran*, p. 75; Precht, "The Iranian Revolution 25 Years Later," pp. 12–13.

134. Arjomand, *The Turban for the Crown*, pp. 114–115.

135. Precht, "The Iranian Revolution 25 Years Later," p. 13; Sick, *All Fall Down*, pp. 50–54.

136. Brzezinski, *Power and Principle*, p. 358; Sick, *All Fall Down*, p. 65.

137. Bill, *The Eagle and the Lion*, pp. 258, 401–402; Brzezinski, *Power and Principle*, pp. 358–359; Precht, "The Iranian Revolution 25 Years Later," pp. 9–10; Rubin, *Paved with Good Intentions*, pp. 180–185; Sick, *All Fall Down*, pp. 3–4, 41–42, 63–66; Taheri, *Nest of Spies*, pp. 95–97; Howard Teicher and Gayle R. Teicher, *Twin Pillars to Desert Storm: America's Flawed Vision in the Middle East from Nixon to Bush* (New York: William Morrow, 1993), pp. 33–34; Vance, *Hard Choices*, pp. 324–326.

138. Precht, "The Iranian Revolution 25 Years Later," p. 13. Brzezinski notes that he did not consider Iran a crisis until early November and until then was preoccupied with SALT II, U.S.-China negotiations, and the unfolding Nicaraguan revolution. (Brzezinski, *Power and Principle*, p. 358.)

139. Bill, *The Eagle and the Lion*, p. 238; Daniel, *The History of Iran*, p. 169.

140. Brzezinski, *Power and Principle*, pp. 363–365, 374; Sick, *All Fall Down*, p. 74; Sullivan, *Mission to Iran*, pp. 170–172, 178–179; Vance, *Hard Choices*, pp. 327–329. A common version of American policy toward Iran at the climax of the revolution was that the Carter administration was deeply divided and that these divisions paralyzed U.S. policy (which in turn helped paralyze the shah). This is untrue. There *were* strong differences within the administration beginning to emerge in November–December 1978, and some of the debates between Vance and Brzezinski were very pointed. However, they were of little consequence initially since, in the end, all of the principals agreed on the course of action the United States needed to take—although different actors stressed different options in the conditional courses of action the United States urged on the shah. The real differences did not emerge until after the shah's departure. Indeed, even in pointing up the differences, Brzezinski stresses the crucial point that the shah had all the encouragement he should have needed to have taken "the tougher line" had he been willing to do so. (Brzezinski, pp. 355–356.)

141. Sick, *All Fall Down,* p. 74.
142. Gary Sick notes that Ambassador Sullivan's readout from the meeting with the shah "provided no indication that the shah had any doubt about the accuracy or authoritative nature of the message, which would have been odd in any event, since Sullivan had a fully coordinated policy cable from Washington confirming its key elements."
143. Brzezinski, *Power and Principle,* p. 365.
144. Ibid., p. 367; Sick, *All Fall Down,* p. 88.
145. Sick has a similar interpretation of events. See Sick, *All Fall Down,* p. 171.
146. There is an alternative version of events that may also have been part of the shah's thinking, given how confused and contradictory his thinking seems to have been at this time. Throughout the crisis, Mohammad Reza Shah had suggested to all kinds of people that he suspected the CIA and British intelligence were behind the popular unrest. (See, e.g., Sick, *All Fall Down,* p. 88.) Thus, he may have wanted explicit "instructions" from Washington as to what he was supposed to do in order to get the Western powers to stop making trouble for him. In this version, the shah may have seen the popular unrest as simply a form of blackmail on the part of Washington and London, and the question was simply what he had to do to get them to turn down the pressure. I ultimately think this unlikely, because other statements made by the shah—such as his retort to the American businessman on November 14—demonstrate that he understood (1) that the opposition was independent and (2) that the United States was on his side.
147. Brzezinski, *Power and Principle,* p. 375.
148. Kurzman, *The Unthinkable Revolution in Iran,* p. 77; Sick, *All Fall Down,* p. 99.
149. Bill, *The Eagle and the Lion,* pp. 255–256.
150. Abrahamian, *Iran Between Two Revolutions,* p. 523; Arjomand, *The Turban for the Crown,* p. 134; Richard Cottam, "Inside Revolutionary Iran," in Ramazani, *Iran's Revolution,* p. 3; Fischer, *Iran,* pp. 203–204; Kurzman, *The Unthinkable Revolution in Iran,* pp. 121–122; Sick, *All Fall Down,* p. 122.
151. Kurzman, *The Unthinkable Revolution in Iran,* pp. 121–122.
152. Brzezinski, *Power and Principle,* p. 375; Sick, *All Fall Down,* p. 126; Vance, *Hard Choices,* pp. 329–334.
153. Sick, *All Fall Down,* p. 126.
154. Charles Kurzman's new book does a terrific job of considering various generalized theories of revolution and demonstrating that none of them fully explains the Iranian Revolution. See Kurzman, *The Unthinkable Revolution in Iran.*
155. Bill, *The Eagle and the Lion,* pp. 401–404; Rubin, *Paved with Good Intentions,* pp. 180–185; Sick, *All Fall Down,* pp. 32, 66.
156. Bill, *The Eagle and the Lion,* pp. 258, 401–403; Brzezinski, *Power and Principle,* pp. 357–369; Sick, *All Fall Down,* pp. 3–4, 63–64; Taheri, *Nest of Spies,* pp. 93–96.
157. Full disclosure: I have been a friend of Stan Turner's for nearly twenty years, since I was a student of his at Yale. That said, I honestly believe that my judgment about him is unaffected by my affection for him. If I believed that Turner had been to blame for our misread of developments in Iran, I would have found a gentle way to make the point. For instance, see my treatment of Henry Kissinger's role in the development of America's Iran policy on pages 101–110. Kissinger is a close friend of members of my family and a man for whom I also have great respect for his intellectual and diplomatic achievements. However, I believe that the policy he and President Nixon adopted toward Iran was a terrible mistake, and while I have tried to convey my criticism in a respectful manner, I have not pulled my punch for the sake of that friendship.
158. For example, see David B. Ottaway, "U.S.-Saudi Relations Show Signs of Stress," *The Washington Post,* April 21, 2004, p. A16. The piece discusses how Gina Abercrombie-Winstanley, the intrepid U.S. consul general in Jiddah, Saudi Arabia (and, in the interest of full disclosure, a good friend of mine), insists on meeting with Saudi opposition figures despite efforts by the government to intimidate and otherwise prevent her from doing so.
159. Sick, *All Fall Down,* pp. 41–42. Also see the description by Ambassador Sullivan to his famous

cable titled "Thinking the Unthinkable," which effectively was the first time someone had "made the call." Sullivan, *Mission to Iran*, pp. 202–203.

160. For an excellent critique of the theory that the United States might somehow have prevented the fall of the shah, see Arjomand, *The Turban for the Crown*, pp. 132–133.

161. For instance, Kissinger, *White House Years*, p. 1260.

162. Those American officials with access to this information have insisted that the CIA had absolutely no involvement with SAVAK's internal security functions. For example, Ambassador Sullivan has written, "That liaison, it should be stressed, had never involved official United States complicity in the political-police aspects of SAVAK behavior or in the use of torture, arbitrary arrest, or murder, as many critics have alleged." (Sullivan, *Mission to Iran*, p. 97.) The one possible exception I have come across is Amir Taheri's claim that the United States provided SAVAK with wiretapping equipment that helped it track (and ultimately kill) a leader of the Mujahideen-e Khalq. However, Taheri's source for this is an unnamed former SAVAK official. See Taheri, *Nest of Spies*, pp. 82, 285, n. 26.

163. Taheri, *Nest of Spies*, p. 97.

164. Again, Kissinger has a good account of the benefits. Kissinger, *White House Years*, pp. 1261–1264.

Chapter 6: America Held Hostage

1. Arjomand, *The Turban for the Crown*, p. 104.

2. Kurzman, *The Unthinkable Revolution in Iran*, p. viii.

3. Bakhash, *The Reign of the Ayatollahs*, pp. 55–64; Bill, *The Eagle and the Lion*, p. 261.

4. Author's correspondence with Shaul Bakhash, July 29, 2004.

5. Arjomand, *The Turban for the Crown*, p. 117.

6. Interview with senior U.S. government official, July 1, 2004.

7. Bakhash, *The Reign of the Ayatollahs*, pp. 55–64; Bill, *The Eagle and the Lion*, pp. 261–262; Daniel, *The History of Iran*, p. 185.

8. Ansari, *Modern Iran Since 1921*, p. 219.

9. Sick, *All Fall Down*, p. 219.

10. Fischer, *Iran*, p. xxv.

11. Ansari, *Modern Iran Since 1921*, p. 201; Kurzman, *The Unthinkable Revolution in Iran*, p. 66. Much of Khomeini's thought ran counter to traditional Shi'i orthodoxy. For instance, as a means of criticizing the shah, he claimed that Islam invalidated hereditary succession, when this is the basis of the most fundamental concept in Shi'ah Islam, the blood succession from Muhammad to Ali to Husayn and on down through the twelve imams. (Daniel, *The History of Iran*, p. 180.)

12. Kurzman, *The Unthinkable Revolution in Iran*, pp. 44–49; Rubin, *Paved with Good Intentions*, p. 211.

13. Kurzman, *The Unthinkable Revolution in Iran*, p. 142. Also see pp. 143–154.

14. Abrahamian, *Iran Between Two Revolutions*, pp. 531–533; Wright, *In the Name of God*, p. 59.

15. Molavi, *Persian Pilgrimages*, p. 74.

16. Taheri, *Nest of Spies*, p. 83.

17. Beeman, "Images of the Great Satan," p. 216.

18. Quoted in Rubin, *Paved with Good Intentions*, p. 277.

19. Brzezinski, *Power and Principle*, pp. 376–382.

20. Arjomand, *The Turban for the Crown*, pp. 131–132; Bill, *The Eagle and the Lion*, pp. 253–256; Brzezinski, *Power and Principle*, pp. 382–393; Kurzman, *The Unthinkable Revolution in Iran*, pp. 160–161; Rubin, *Paved with Good Intentions*, pp. 226–227; Sepehr Zabih, *The Iranian Military in Revolution and War* (London: Routledge, 1988), pp. 43–54, 93–111.

21. Sick, *All Fall Down*, p. 187.

22. General Robert E. Huyser, *Mission to Tehran* (New York: Harper and Row, 1986), pp. 289–290; Sick, *All Fall Down*, p. 138.

23. Huyser, *Mission to Tehran*, p. 18.

24. See ibid., pp. 25–285.
25. Kurzman, *The Unthinkable Revolution in Iran*, pp. 160–161; Rubin, *Paved with Good Intentions*, p. 227; Tim Wells, *444 Days: The Hostages Remember* (New York: Harcourt Brace Jovanovich, 1985), p. 8.
26. Sick, *All Fall Down*, p. 187.
27. Bakhash, *The Reign of the Ayatollahs*, pp. 64–65; Bill, *The Eagle and the Lion*, pp. 263–265.
28. Bakhash, *The Reign of the Ayatollahs*, pp. 56–57; Daniel, *The History of Iran*, pp. 186–187; Wright, *In the Name of God*, pp. 67–68.
29. Bakhash, *The Reign of the Ayatollahs*, p. 63; Bill, *The Eagle and the Lion*, p. 273; Wilfried Buchta, *Who Rules Iran? The Structure of Power in the Islamic Republic* (Washington, D.C.: Washington Institute for Near East Policy and the Konrad Adenauer Stiftung, 2000), p. 67; Daniel, *The History of Iran*, pp. 185–186; Kenneth Katzman, *The Warriors of Islam: Iran's Revolutionary Guard* (Boulder, Colo.: Westview, 1993), pp. 7–19, 23–37; Wright, *In the Name of God*, p. 69.
30. Daniel, *The History of Iran*, p. 186; Keddie, *Modern Iran*, p. 246; Suzanne Maloney, "Agents or Obstacles? Parastatal Foundations and Challenges for Iranian Development," in Parvin Alizadeh, ed., *The Economy of Iran: Dilemmas of an Islamic State* (London: I. B. Tauris, 2000), pp. 145–176.
31. Nafisi, *Reading Lolita in Tehran*, p. 96. Also Bakhash, *The Reign of the Ayatollahs*, p. 62.
32. Wright, *In the Name of God*, pp. 68–69.
33. Bakhash, *The Reign of the Ayatollahs*, pp. 59–60, 111. See also Daniel, *The History of Iran*, pp. 186–187.
34. Bakhash, *The Reign of the Ayatollahs*, p. 73; Keddie, *Modern Iran*, pp. 243–246.
35. Bakhash, *The Reign of the Ayatollahs*, p. 73; Daniel, *The History of Iran*, p. 188.
36. Bakhash, *The Reign of the Ayatollahs*, pp. 74–88; Daniel Brumberg, *Reinventing Khomeini: The Struggle for Reform in Iran* (Chicago: University of Chicago Press, 2001), pp. 105–111; Daniel, *The History of Iran*, pp. 189–190; Keddie, *Modern Iran*, p. 247.
37. Rubin, *Paved with Good Intentions*, pp. 280–281; Admiral Stansfield Turner, *Terrorism and Democracy* (Boston: Houghton Mifflin, 1991), pp. 21–24; Wright, *In the Name of God*, p. 63.
38. Actually, the students apparently were disappointed that the African Americans at the embassy did not feel any solidarity with them. One student asked communications officer Charles Jones (an African American), "Why aren't any of the blacks sympathetic to the cause of the Iranian people?" To which Jones replied, "Look, I'm an American. I'm a foreign service officer. What you guys are doing is illegal. There is no way I could ever be sympathetic to a terrorist action. The color of my skin doesn't change the fact that you are a terrorist." (Wells, *444 Days*, p. 90.)
39. On the beatings and interrogations of the hostages, see Wells, *444 Days*, pp. 50–113.
40. Daniel, *The History of Iran*, p. 190; Rubin, *Paved with Good Intentions*, pp. 280–281; Wells, *444 Days*, pp. 33–479; Wright, *In the Name of God*, p. 63.
41. There are a number of Americans who believe that the shah's admittance into the United States was simply a pretext to take over the embassy and that had that not happened, the students would have found another excuse to do so. (See, e.g., Saunders, "The Crisis Begins," pp. 58–59.) While it is certainly possible that other groups would have done so without the shah having been admitted to the United States—the leftists had not had that as a reason when they attacked in February—and even that this group might have found another reason to do so, I am willing to accept the claim of Ebtekar (and her husband) that it was the shah's admittance that provided the spark to get the ringleaders to form the "Students Following the Imam's Line" and take over the embassy. To disbelieve her without any evidence to the contrary is to indulge in conspiracy theories of our own. Again, this is not to suggest that others, including Khomeini, did not have ulterior motives as discussed in the text, just that the students were all so naive that I am willing to believe they did act as a result of this specific event.
42. Massoumeh Ebtekar as told to Fred A. Reed, *Takeover in Tehran: The Inside Story of the 1979 U.S. Embassy Capture* (Vancouver, Canada: Talon Books, 2000), p. 58.
43. Scott MacLeod, "Radicals Reborn: Iran's Student Heroes Have Had a Rough and Surprising Passage," *Time*, November 15, 1999; Rubin, *Paved with Good Intentions*, pp. 252–253, 267; Zahrani, "The Coup That Changed the Middle East," p. 98.

44. Ebtekar, *Takeover in Tehran*, p. 50.
45. Ibid., p. 44.
46. Ibid., p. 69.
47. Wells, *444 Days*, pp. 28–29.
48. Ebtekar, *Takeover in Tehran*, p. 26.
49. Sick also believes (and so there may have been intelligence available at the time indicating) that Khomeini was aware and that the students did not know that Khomeini was, in fact, aware of their plans. (Sick, *All Fall Down*, p. 197.) For other experts who also believe that Khomeini was aware of the preparations to take the embassy, see Arjomand, *The Turban for the Crown*, p. 102; Daniel, *The History of Iran*, p. 192. Wright argues that Khomeini did not know of the planning beforehand but immediately recognized the action as beneficial to his goals when it happened. See Wright, *In the Name of God*, p. 80.
50. This is the view of Khomeini's biographer Baqer Moin, who claims that Khomeini was surprised by the embassy takeover and took "several days" to determine whether it was popular before deciding to support it. (Baqer Moin, *Khomeini, Life of the Ayatollah* [London: I. B. Tauris, 1999], pp. 226–227.) On this tendency in Khomeini, see Daniel, *The History of Iran*, p. 191; Sick, *All Fall Down*, p. 205.
51. Wells, *444 Days*, pp. 75–77.
52. For a concurring opinion that Khomeini's foreknowledge is irrelevant and what matters is that he condoned it afterward, see Houghton, *U.S. Foreign Policy and the Iran Hostage Crisis*, pp. 55–56.
53. Ramazani, "Iran's Foreign Policy," p. 53.
54. Rubin, *Paved with Good Intentions*, pp. 252–253, 267; Sick, "Military Options and Constraints," p. 149; Robert Snyder, "Explaining the Iranian Revolution's Hostility Toward the United States," *Journal of South Asian and Middle Eastern Studies* 17, no. 3 (Spring 1994), p. 19.
55. Ebtekar, *Takeover in Tehran*, p. 77; Sick, "Military Options and Constraints," p. 149. Moin also claims that Khomeini believed that a clash with the United States was inevitable and that admitting the shah might have been the start of the American counterrevolution. (Moin, *Khomeini*, p. 220.)
56. Cottam, "Inside Revolutionary Iran," pp. 3–4; Wright, *In the Name of God*, p. 92.
57. Bakhash, *The Reign of the Ayatollahs*, p. 230; Central Intelligence Agency, *World Factbook 1989* (Washington, D.C.: U.S. Government Printing Office, 1989); Fischer, *Iran*, p. 224.
58. Bakhash, *The Reign of the Ayatollahs*, p. 237; Javier Estrada, Helge Ole Bergesen, Arild Moe, and Anne Kristin Sydnes, *Natural Gas in Europe: Markets, Organization and Politics* (London: Pinter Publishers, 1988), p. 175; U.S. Department of Energy, "Natural Gas Prices," available at www.eia.doe.gov/emeu/mer/pdf/pages/sec9_17.pdf, accessed August 7, 2004.
59. See, for instance, Ansari, *Modern Iran Since 1921*, p. 227; Keddie, *Modern Iran*, p. 248.
60. Ebtekar, *Takeover in Tehran*, p. 75; Keddie, *Modern Iran*, p. 249.
61. Daniel, *The History of Iran*, p. 192; Ramazani, "Iran's Foreign Policy," p. 53; Harold H. Saunders, "Diplomacy and Pressure, November 1979–May 1980," in Christopher and Kreisberg, *American Hostages in Iran*, pp. 115–116; Sick, "Military Options and Constraints," p. 149; Turner, *Terrorism and Democracy*, pp. 35–36.
62. It is reprinted in Ebtekar, *Takeover in Tehran*, p. 244.
63. Bakhash, *The Reign of the Ayatollahs*, pp. 69–70; Bill, *The Eagle and the Lion*, pp. 270, 280–282; Keddie, *Modern Iran*, p. 249; Rubin, *Paved with Good Intentions*, p. 285; Wright, *In the Name of God*, p. 67.
64. Ebtekar, *Takeover in Tehran*, p. 998.
65. Precht, "The Iranian Revolution 25 Years Later," p. 29. Also see Brzezinski, *Power and Principle*, p. 473.
66. Brzezinski, *Power and Principle*, p. 474.
67. Saunders, "The Crisis Begins," p. 57; Vance, *Hard Choices*, p. 368.
68. Saunders, "The Crisis Begins," pp. 53–57; Turner, *Terrorism and Democracy*, p. 24; Vance, *Hard Choices*, p. 370.
69. Brzezinski never shied from the fact that he believed ardently that the shah should be granted

asylum in the United States from beginning to end of the crisis. (Brzezinski, *Power and Principle*, p. 472.) Turner also believed that the shah should be admitted for the same reasons but apparently was never consulted about the decision. (Turner, *Terrorism and Democracy*, pp. 24–25.) That the DCI would not have been consulted on such a decision speaks well to the problems within the Carter administration.

70. Saunders, "The Crisis Begins," p. 59.
71. Precht, "The Iranian Revolution 25 Years Later," pp. 27–29; Saunders, "The Crisis Begins," pp. 54–57; Wells, *444 Days*, pp. 18–27.
72. Saunders, then assistant secretary of state for Near Eastern affairs, has a good discussion of this question in his essay in Christopher and Kreisberg's *American Hostages in Iran*. (See Saunders, "The Crisis Begins," pp. 54–57.) Saunders makes a reasonable case for why so many Americans were present. Nevertheless, I disagree. The United States has faced other similar situations since, and I believe we could have reduced the staff of the embassy by perhaps as much as half—at least temporarily, until it was clear that there would be no reaction to the shah's admittance—without compromising the various functions that Saunders describes. It would not have avoided the hostage crisis altogether, and here Saunders is absolutely right to point out that there was a well-acknowledged risk but one that was thought to be worth taking; however, it would have meant that a couple of dozen fewer Americans would have had to suffer through the trauma of their imprisonment. Turner notes that even after the February attack on the embassy no contingency plans had been drawn up against the possibility of a repeat performance. (Turner, *Terrorism and Democracy*, p. 29.)
73. Saunders, "The Crisis Begins," p. 47.
74. Precht, "The Iranian Revolution 25 Years Later," p. 30; Wells, *444 Days*, pp. 17–18.
75. Saunders, "The Crisis Begins," p. 49.
76. For a concurring view, see Keddie, *Modern Iran*, p. 249.
77. Saunders, "The Crisis Begins," p. 51.
78. Brzezinski, *Power and Principle*, p. 482; Sick, "Military Options and Constraints," pp. 144–145. Many of the Carter administration participants refer to the air strikes contemplated against Iranian air bases and oil facilities as "punitive." Although in practice they might have turned out to be merely punitive, in the context in which they were being discussed they were clearly intended as coercive strikes—they were meant to coerce the Iranians into letting the hostages go, not simply punishing them for having taken the hostages.
79. Jimmy Carter, *Keeping Faith: Memoirs of a President* (Fayetteville, Ark.: University of Arkansas Press, 1995), p. 468; Saunders, "The Crisis Begins," p. 50; Sick, "Military Options and Constraints," p. 145; Turner, *Terrorism and Democracy*, p. 34.
80. Sick, "Military Options and Constraints," p. 145.
81. Sick, *All Fall Down*, p. 287; Sick, "Military Options and Constraints," pp. 145–146; Turner, *Terrorism and Democracy*, pp. 36, 56.
82. Turner, *Terrorism and Democracy*, p. 32.
83. Ibid., p. 77.
84. Ibid.
85. Ibid., pp. 76–78.
86. Warren Christopher, *Chances of a Lifetime* (New York: Scribner's, 2001), pp. 97–98; Saunders, "Diplomacy and Pressure," pp. 95–96; Vance, *Hard Choices*, pp. 376–383.
87. Brzezinski, *Power and Principle*, p. 479; Saunders, "Diplomacy and Pressure," pp. 93–94; Sick, *All Fall Down*, p. 227; Turner, *Terrorism and Democracy*, p. 37.
88. Saunders, "Diplomacy and Pressure," p. 81.
89. Brzezinski, *Power and Principle*, p. 479; Saunders, "Diplomacy and Pressure," pp. 93–94; Turner, *Terrorism and Democracy*, p. 49.
90. Bakhash, *The Reign of the Ayatollahs*, p. 114; Brzezinski, *Power and Principle*, p. 479; Robert Carswell and Richard J. Davis, "Crafting the Financial Settlement," in Christopher and Kreisberg, *American Hostages in Iran*, p. 205; Saunders, "The Crisis Begins," p. 71; Saunders, "Diplomacy and Pressure," pp. 93–94; Turner, *Terrorism and Democracy*, p. 52; Vance, *Hard Choices*, p. 378.

91. Brzezinski, *Power and Principle,* p. 480; Saunders, "Diplomacy and Pressure," pp. 97–98; Sick, *All Fall Down,* p. 245.

92. Saunders, "Diplomacy and Pressure," pp. 115–134.

93. Brzezinski, *Power and Principle,* p. 485; Saunders, "Diplomacy and Pressure," p. 102. Former DCI Robert Gates has written that the CIA learned soon after the seizure of the hostages that the Soviet general staff had begun to draw up plans to occupy northern Iran in the event of an American military intervention. Moscow even began to improve the readiness of its forces opposite Iran and conducted exercises simulating an invasion of Iran. (Robert M. Gates, *From the Shadows* [New York: Simon & Schuster, 1996], p. 130.)

94. Saunders, "Diplomacy and Pressure," pp. 97–143; Sick, *All Fall Down,* pp. 287, 293; Sick, "Military Options and Constraints," pp. 153–154; Vance, *Hard Choices,* pp. 399–400.

95. Daniel, *The History of Iran,* p. 195.

96. Bill, *The Eagle and the Lion,* pp. 283–288.

97. Bakhash, *The Reign of the Ayatollahs,* p. 114.

98. Saunders, "Diplomacy and Pressure," pp. 96, 105.

99. Ibid., pp. 105–106.

100. Ibid., pp. 140–141; Sick, "Military Options and Constraints," pp. 153–154.

101. Bakhash, *The Reign of the Ayatollahs,* pp. 105–107; Daniel, *The History of Iran,* p. 199.

102. Daniel, *The History of Iran,* p. 199.

103. Bakhash, *The Reign of the Ayatollahs,* p. 107.

104. Ibid., pp. 108–109; Daniel, *The History of Iran,* p. 200.

105. Brzezinski, *Power and Principle,* p. 488.

106. For authoritative and dispassionate accounts of both the planning and the execution of the mission, see Paul B. Ryan, *The Iranian Rescue Mission: Why It Failed* (Annapolis, Md.: Naval Institute Press, 1985); Sick, *All Fall Down,* pp. 280–302; Turner, *Terrorism and Democracy,* pp. 99–131.

107. Gates, *From the Shadows,* pp. 153–155; Turner, *Terrorism and Democracy,* pp. 115–124.

108. Brzezinski, *Power and Principle,* p. 500.

109. Turner, *Terrorism and Democracy,* p. 147.

110. Christopher, *Chances of a Lifetime,* pp. 108–112.

111. Quoted in Houghton (who apparently has the transcript of the interview), *U.S. Foreign Policy and the Iran Hostage Crisis,* p. 143.

112. Teicher and Teicher, *Twin Pillars to Desert Storm,* pp. 86–87; author's correspondence with Bruce O. Riedel, July 27, 2004. On the impact of the hostage crisis on Carter's popularity, see Houghton, *U.S. Foreign Policy and the Iran Hostage Crisis,* pp. 3–4.

113. Bakhash, *The Reign of the Ayatollahs,* p. 150; Sick, "Military Options and Constraints," p. 170. There is also the lingering issue of the "October surprise." This has two variations. First, all through the fall of 1980, the Republican Party charged that the Carter administration was going to provide Iran with a huge amount of weapons and ammunition in return for Tehran releasing the hostages right before the election. This was absolutely false and is well documented by the various memoirs and histories of the hostage crisis. (Although in light of later developments, it is ironic that it would be the Reagan campaign claiming that the Carter administration had intended to trade arms for hostages.) The second variant is that the Reagan campaign made contact with the Iranian regime prior to the election and requested that the Iranians delay releasing the hostages until after Reagan took office in return for a promise of arms shipments. A congressional investigation of these charges found that there was no evidence of any such contacts and that many key sources who made such claims had been lying or exaggerating.

114. Daniel, *The History of Iran,* p. 201.

115. Bakhash, *The Reign of the Ayatollahs,* p. 149.

116. Christopher, *Chances of a Lifetime,* pp. 112–123; Daniel, *The History of Iran,* p. 201; Turner, *Terrorism and Democracy,* pp. 151–154.

117. "October Surprise," *Wikipedia,* available at en.wikipedia.org/wiki/October_Surprise, accessed July 10, 2004.

118. Haynes Johnson, "Hostages to the Past," *The Washington Post,* July 9, 1991.

119. Saunders, "The Crisis Begins," p. 48.
120. Turner, *Terrorism and Democracy*, pp. 5–18, 37; Vance, *Hard Choices*, p. 380.
121. Houghton, *U.S. Foreign Policy and the Iran Hostage Crisis*, pp. 6–7.
122. Bakhash, *The Reign of the Ayatollahs*, p. 230.
123. Author's conversation with Ted Koppel, July 11, 2004.

Chapter 7: At War with the World

1. Quoted in Wright, *In the Name of God*, p. 108. On the Iranian leadership's notion of the export of the revolution, see Saskia Gieling, *Religion and War in Revolutionary Iran* (London: I. B. Tauris, 1999), pp. 44–54.
2. Anthony Cordesman and Abraham Wagner, *The Lessons of Modern War*, vol. 2, *The Iran-Iraq War* (Boulder, Colo.: Westview, 1990), pp. 24–25; Dilip Hiro, *The Longest War: The Iran-Iraq Military Conflict* (New York: Routledge, 1991), p. 28; Wright, *In the Name of God*, p. 82.
3. Gieling, *Religion and War in Revolutionary Iran*, pp. 14–16; Hiro, *The Longest War*, pp. 35–36; Gary Sick, "Trial by Error: Reflections on the Iran-Iraq War," in *Iran's Revolution: The Search for Consensus*, R. K. Ramazani, ed. (Bloomington, Ind.: Indiana University Press, 1990), p. 106.
4. Bakhash, *The Reign of the Ayatollahs*, p. 127; John Bulloch and Harvey Morris, *The Gulf War* (London: Methuen, 1989), pp. 20–23, 27; Cordesman and Wagner, *The Lessons of Modern War*, vol. 2, pp. 29–30; Charles Tripp, *A History of Iraq* (Cambridge, U.K.: Cambridge University Press, 2000), pp. 230–231.
5. Cordesman and Wagner, *The Lessons of Modern War*, vol. 2, p. 13; Pryor, "Arms and the Shah," p. 59.
6. Bulloch and Morris, *The Gulf War*, pp. 23–25; Cordesman and Wagner, *The Lessons of Modern War*, vol. 2, pp. 25–26; Gieling, *Religion and War in Revolutionary Iran*, pp. 12–13, 17; Hiro, *The Longest War*, p. 36; Wright, *In the Name of God*, p. 83.
7. Bakhash, *The Reign of the Ayatollahs*, pp. 125, 127; Bulloch and Morris, *The Gulf War*, pp. 31–32; Shahram Chubin, "Reflections on the Gulf War," *Survival* 28, no. 4 (July–August 1986), p. 308; Cordesman and Wagner, *The Lessons of Modern War*, vol. 2, pp. 13–14, 22–23, 28, 31–32; Gieling, *Religion and War in Revolutionary Iran*, pp. 12–13, 15–17; Hiro, *The Longest War*, pp. 36–38; Bruce W. Jentleson, *With Friends Like These: Reagan, Bush, and Saddam, 1982–1990* (New York: W. W. Norton, 1994), p. 41; Keddie, *Modern Iran*, p. 251; Phebe Marr, "The Iran-Iraq War: The View from Iraq," in Christopher C. Joyner, ed., *The Persian Gulf War: Lessons for Strategy, Law, and Diplomacy* (Westport, Conn.: Greenwood Press, 1990), pp. 59–74; Gary Sick, "Iran's Foreign Policy: A Revolution in Transition," in Nikki R. Keddie and Rudi Matthee, eds., *Iran and the Surrounding World* (Seattle: University of Washington Press, 2002), pp. 359–360; Sick, "Trial by Error," p. 109; Taheri, *Nest of Spies*, pp. 139–140; Teicher and Teicher, *Twin Pillars to Desert Storm*, pp. 65–66, 102; Tripp, *A History of Iraq*, pp. 232–234.
8. Author's interviews with former senior Iraqi military officers, November 1998, June 1999, and September 1999.
9. Bakhash, *The Reign of the Ayatollahs*, pp. 113, 127; Cordesman and Wagner, *The Lessons of Modern War*, vol. 2, pp. 57–67; Cottrell, "Iran's Armed Forces Under the Pahlavi Dynasty," pp. 419–422; Mark J. Roberts, *Khomeini's Incorporation of the Iranian Military*, McNair Paper 48 (Washington, D.C.: National Defense University, 1996), pp. 36–50; Wright, *In the Name of God*, p. 84; Zabih, *The Iranian Military in Revolution and War*, pp. 115–161; author's interviews with former senior Iraqi military officers, November 1998, June 1999, and September 1999.
10. For a more detailed account of the military conduct of the Iran-Iraq War, see Kenneth M. Pollack, *Arabs at War: Military Effectiveness, 1948–1991* (Lincoln, Neb.: University of Nebraska Press, 2002), pp. 183–235.
11. Author's interview with former Iraqi senior military officer, November 1998.
12. Pollack, *Arabs at War*, pp. 183–193.
13. Ansari, *Modern Iran Since 1921*, p. 235.
14. An important element in Iraq's glacial advance was its tactical doctrine. As they had learned

against the Kurds, Iraqi units relied on overwhelming firepower as their method of attack. Iraqi armored and mechanized formations would not advance until the area in front of them had been saturated with tank and artillery fire. They would then advance a short distance and dig in to wait for the next round of bombardment. On those occasions when they encountered Iranian resistance—no matter how light—Iraq's armor would halt, bring up engineers to build defensive positions, and then lay down a massive barrage of fire from tanks, mortars, artillery, multiple-rocket launchers, FROG rockets, air strikes, and anything else available. When the Iranian position was a smoldering ruin, they would resume their advance, only to halt again at the next sign of resistance. Likewise, when Iraqi maneuver units began to approach the maximum range of their artillery support, they would stop, dig in, and wait for the artillery to redeploy before they would resume creeping forward. In the central Zagros, Iraqi infantry units even added volleys of Sagger ATGMs to their barrages against Iranian roadblocks, which often were undefended. In a few instances, notably outside of Dezful during the first week of the war, Iraqi forces did employ a sort of flanking attack; the Iranians lacked the troops to form a continuous front line, and after several days' bombardment, Iraqi forces would take up a position on one of the Iranian wings—threatening to outflank the Iranian lines but not actually conducting a flanking attack—which would cause the outgunned Iranians to pull back. Pollack, *Arabs at War,* pp. 187–188.

15. Cordesman and Wagner, *The Lessons of Modern War,* vol. 2, pp. 92–93; R. D. McLaurin, *Military Operations in the Gulf War: The Battle of Khorramshahr* (Aberdeen Proving Grounds, Md.: U.S. Army Human Engineering Laboratory, July 1982); Edgar O'Ballance, *The Gulf War* (London: Brassey's, 1988), pp. 37–39; Pollack, *Arabs at War,* pp. 187–190.

16. Hiro, *The Longest War,* pp. 46–47; Pollack, *Arabs at War,* pp. 187–193; Tripp, *A History of Iraq,* pp. 233–234.

17. Hiro, *The Longest War,* pp. 46–47; O'Ballance, *The Gulf War,* p. 49.

18. Bakhash, *The Reign of the Ayatollahs,* pp. 135–136.

19. Cordesman and Wagner, *The Lessons of Modern War,* vol. 2, p. 35; Gieling, *Religion and War in Revolutionary Iran,* pp. 19–20.

20. Author's interviews with former senior Iraqi military officers, June 1999 and September 1999.

21. Pollack, *Arabs at War,* pp. 193–195.

22. Bakhash, *The Reign of the Ayatollahs,* pp. 144, 151–162; Daniel, *The History of Iran,* pp. 204–205.

23. Bakhash, *The Reign of the Ayatollahs,* p. 219; Daniel, *The History of Iran,* pp. 205–206; Wright, *In the Name of God,* pp. 98–100.

24. Bakhash, *The Reign of the Ayatollahs,* pp. 219–220; Bill, *The Eagle and the Lion,* p. 271; Wright, *In the Name of God,* pp. 98–101.

25. Bakhash, *The Reign of the Ayatollahs,* p. 221.

26. Arjomand, *The Turban for the Crown,* p. 154; Daniel, *The History of Iran,* p. 206; Wright, *In the Name of God,* p. 101.

27. Gieling, *Religion and War in Revolutionary Iran,* pp. 20–21; William F. Hickman, "How the Iranian Military Expelled the Iraqis," *The Brookings Review* 1, no. 3 (Spring 1983), pp. 19–23; Ed McCaul, "Interview: Iranian Tank Commander," *Military History* 21, no. 1 (April 2004), pp. 47–48; Pollack, *Arabs at War,* pp. 199–203.

28. Hickman, "How the Iranian Military Expelled the Iraqis," pp. 19–23; Pollack, *Arabs at War,* pp. 195–199.

29. Actually, Saddam had had a role in provoking the Israeli invasion of Lebanon because he foolishly convinced himself that if Israel were to invade Lebanon, then the ferociously anti-Israel mullahs would themselves agree to end the Iran-Iraq War and join forces to fight Israel. See Jentleson, *With Friends Like These,* pp. 52–53; Hiro, *The Longest War,* p. 63; Kenneth M. Pollack, *The Threatening Storm: The Case for Invading Iraq* (New York: Random House, 2002), p. 18; Ze'ev Schiff and Ehud Ya'ari, *Israel's Lebanon War,* trans. Ira Friedman (New York: Simon & Schuster, 1984), pp. 99–100; Teicher and Teicher, *Twin Pillars to Desert Storm,* pp. 195–196.

30. Daniel, *The History of Iran,* p. 210; Gieling, *Religion and War in Revolutionary Iran,* p. 21.

31. Bakhash, *The Reign of the Ayatollahs,* pp. 232–234; Daniel, *The History of Iran,* p. 210; Gieling, *Religion and War in Revolutionary Iran,* p. 21; Katzman, *The Warriors of Islam,* pp. 131–132;

Sick, "Trial by Error," p. 112. On Khomeini's conception of the war as a jihad, see Gieling, *Religion and War in Revolutionary Iran*, pp. 44–54.

32. Wright, *In the Name of God*, p. 88.

33. Pollack, *Arabs at War*, p. 203.

34. Ibid., pp. 203–204.

35. Ibid., pp. 204–205.

36. Daniel, *The History of Iran*, p. 210; Hiro, *The Longest War*, p. 91.

37. Pollack, *Arabs at War*, pp. 205–213.

38. Historically, this has been a terrible strategy. It almost never works and often results in disaster, as the Germans found when they tried it against the French at Verdun in 1916.

39. Cordesman and Wagner, *The Lessons of Modern War*, vol. 2, pp. 152–156.

40. Ibid., pp. 99, 157–159, 205–206, 229–231; Dilip Hiro, "Chronicle of the Gulf War," *MERIP Middle East Report*, 125–126, July–September 1984, p. 13; O'Ballance, *The Gulf War*, pp. 42–45, 126–127, 153–154, 169–170, 181–182; Pollack, *Arabs at War*, pp. 214–215.

41. Frederick W. Axelgard, "Iraq and the War with Iran," *Current History*, February 1987, p. 58; Cordesman and Wagner, *The Lessons of Modern War*, vol. 2, pp. 170–175, 191–199, 205–206, 208–213, 229–231, 235–237, 242–244, 271–274, 282–290, 310–313; Hiro, "Chronicle of the Gulf War," pp. 12–13; Eric Hooglund, "The Gulf War and the Islamic Republic," *MERIP Middle East Report*, 125–126, July–September 1984, p. 36; O'Ballance, *The Gulf War*, pp. 55–56, 108–109, 122–125, 128–129, 154–156, 170–172, 182–185; Pollack, *Arabs at War*, p. 215; Marion Farouk-Sluglett and Peter Sluglett, *Iraq Since 1958: From Revolution to Dictatorship* (London: Kegan Paul International, 1987), p. 260.

42. Axelgard, "Iraq and the War with Iran," p. 58; Cordesman and Wagner, *The Lessons of Modern War*, vol. 2, pp. 170–175, 191–199, 205–206, 208–213, 229–231, 235–237, 242–244, 271–274, 282–290, 310–313; Hiro, "Chronicle of the Gulf War," p. 13; Hooglund, "The Gulf War and the Islamic Republic," p. 36; O'Ballance, *The Gulf War*, pp. 55–56, 108–109, 122–125, 128–129, 154–156, 170–172, 182–185; Pollack, *Arabs at War*, p. 216.

43. Cordesman and Wagner, *The Lessons of Modern War*, vol. 2, pp. 90–92, 133–135, 170, 186.

44. Central Intelligence Agency, "Iran-Iraq: Chemical Warfare Continues, November 1986," declassified and released as part of the U.S. Department of Defense GulfLink project, available at www.gulflink.osd.mil/muhammadiyat/muhammidiyat_refs/n59en018/970409_cia_95224_95224_01.html, accessed July 11, 2004; Cordesman and Wagner, *The Lessons of Modern War*, vol. 2, pp. 122–517; Aaron Danis, "Iraqi Army Operations and Doctrine," *Military Intelligence*, April–June 1991, p. 10; McLaurin, *Military Operations in the Gulf War*, p. 29; O'Ballance, *The Gulf War*, pp. 149–150, 164, 179.

45. See Maziar Behrooz, "Trends in the Foreign Policy of the Islamic Republic of Iran, 1979–1988," in Nikki R. Keddie and Mark J. Gasiorowski, eds., *Neither East nor West: Iran, the Soviet Union, and the United States* (New Haven, Conn.: Yale University Press, 1990), pp. 13–35.

46. Bakhash, *The Reign of the Ayatollahs*, p. 235; Katzman, *The Warriors of Islam*, p. 99; Wright, *In the Name of God*, pp. 26–27.

47. Michael Dunn, "In the Name of God: Iran's Shi'ite International," *Defense and Foreign Affairs*, August 1985, p. 34.

48. Wright, *In the Name of God*, p. 111.

49. Dunn, "In the Name of God," p. 34; Katzman, *The Warriors of Islam*, pp. 98–99.

50. Bakhash, *The Reign of the Ayatollahs*, p. 235; Katzman, *The Warriors of Islam*, p. 99; Wright, *In the Name of God*, pp. 111–112.

51. Dunn, "In the Name of God," p. 34.

52. Ansari, *Modern Iran Since 1921*, p. 238.

53. Katzman, *The Warriors of Islam*, pp. 99–100.

54. Jentleson, *With Friends Like These*, pp. 52–53; Hiro, *The Longest War*, p. 63; Schiff and Ya'ari, *Israel's Lebanon War*, pp. 99–100.

55. On Israel's goals (i.e., those of Sharon and, to a lesser extent, Begin), see Schiff and Ya'ari, *Israel's Lebanon War*, pp. 31–108.

56. George Shultz, *Turmoil and Triumph* (New York: Charles Scribner's Sons, 1993), pp. 46–84, 103; Teicher and Teicher, *Twin Pillars to Desert Storm*, pp. 116–122, 151–152, 166–169, 171–172, 195–200, 208–211; Caspar Weinberger, *Fighting for Peace* (New York: Warner Books, 1990), pp. 142–150.

57. Daniel L. Byman, *Deadly Connections: States That Sponsor Terrorism* (Cambridge, U.K.: Cambridge University Press, forthcoming); Katzman, *The Warriors of Islam*, p. 71. Byman notes that the Iranians had wanted to send 10,000 Pasdars to Lebanon in 1980 to fight Israel, but at that point they were rebuffed by the Syrians.

58. Bakhash, *The Reign of the Ayatollahs*, p. 63; Bill, *The Eagle and the Lion*, p. 273; Buchta, *Who Rules Iran?*, p. 67; Daniel, *The History of Iran*, pp. 185–186; Katzman, *The Warriors of Islam*, pp. 7–19, 23–37; Wright, *In the Name of God*, p. 69.

59. Judith Palmer Harik, *Hezbollah: The Changing Face of Terrorism* (London: I. B. Tauris, 2004), pp. 39–40, 55; Katzman, *The Warriors of Islam*, p. 96; Amal Saad-Ghorayeb, *Hizb'ullah: Politics, Religion* (London: Pluto Press, 2002), pp. 10–13, 71–72; Sick, "Trial by Error," p. 112.

60. Hiro, *The Longest War*, p. 96; Katzman, *The Warriors of Islam*, p. 71.

61. Byman, *Deadly Connections;* Harik, *Hezbollah*, pp. 22–23; Hiro, *The Longest War*, pp. 109–110; Saad-Ghorayeb, *Hizb'ullah*, pp. 15, 95–97.

62. Saad-Ghorayeb, *Hizb'ullah*, p. 14.

63. Harik, *Hezbollah*, pp. 16–19; Saad-Ghorayeb, *Hizb'ullah*, pp. 34–38, 64–68, 71–72; Robin Wright, "Shiite Muslims Capture Center Stage in Lebanon," *The Christian Science Monitor*, October 5, 1984, p. 1.

64. On the anti-Americanism/anti-Westernism of Hizballah, see Saad-Ghorayeb, *Hizb'ullah*, pp. 88–111.

65. The best account of these various events remains Schiff and Ya'ari, *Israel's Lebanon War*, pp. 247–285. On the American thinking, see Teicher and Teicher, *Twin Pillars to Desert Storm*, pp. 213–216.

66. Harik, *Hezbollah*, pp. 36–37; Hiro, *The Longest War*, p. 101; Shultz, *Turmoil and Triumph*, pp. 101–114; Teicher and Teicher, *Twin Pillars to Desert Storm*, pp. 216–221; Weinberger, *Fighting for Peace*, pp. 151–154.

67. Hiro, *The Longest War*, pp. 96–98; Shultz, *Turmoil and Triumph*, pp. 196–216; Teicher and Teicher, *Twin Pillars to Desert Storm*, pp. 225–230; Weinberger, *Fighting for Peace*, pp. 154–155.

68. Hiro, *The Longest War*, p. 101; Teicher and Teicher, *Twin Pillars to Desert Storm*, pp. 227–230.

69. Shultz, *Turmoil and Triumph*, pp. 220–227; Teicher and Teicher, *Twin Pillars to Desert Storm*, pp. 231–254; Turner, *Terrorism and Democracy*, pp. 162–165; Weinberger, *Fighting for Peace*, pp. 157–160.

70. Daniel Benjamin and Steven Simon, *The Age of Sacred Terror* (New York: Random House, 2002), pp. 223–224; Byman, *Deadly Connections;* Central Intelligence Agency, "Memorandum for the DCI: Iranian Support for International Terrorism," November 22, 1986, declassified June 1999, available at www.foia.cia.gov, accessed July 22, 2004, pp. 2–5; Dunn, "In the Name of God," p. 34; Richard Harwood, "The Riddle of Islamic Jihad," *The Washington Post*, September 21, 1984, p. A27; Kenneth Katzman, "Terrorism: Middle Eastern Groups and State Sponsors, 1998," Congressional Research Service, August 27, 1998, pp. 5–6; Augustus Richard Norton, "Hizballah: From Radicalism to Pragmatism?," *Middle East Policy* 5, no. 4 (January 1998), p. 147; David Ottaway, "Baalbek Seen as Staging Area for Terrorism," *The Washington Post*, January 9, 1984, p. A1; Robert Parry, "U.S. Intelligence Seen Identifying Beirut Terrorists," Associated Press, October 4, 1984; Weinberger, *Fighting for Peace*, p. 356.

71. Alvin H. Bernstein, "Iran's Low-Intensity War Against the United States," *Orbis* 30, no. 1 (Spring 1986), pp. 149–167; Byman, *Deadly Connections;* Magnus Ranstorp, *Hizb'allah in Lebanon* (London: Macmillan, 1997), p. 70; Hala Jaber, *Hezbollah* (New York: Columbia University Press, 1997), pp. 82, 117; Teicher and Teicher, *Twin Pillars to Desert Storm*, pp. 256–257; Turner, *Terrorism and Democracy*, pp. 165–166. Jaber claims that Syria and Iran helped with logistics and planning but did not specify the target of the attack. For statements by Hizballah leaders, see Saad-Ghorayeb, *Hizb'ullah*, pp. 95–98, 219, n. 98. Mohsen Rafiq-Dust, the first

commander of the IRGC contingent in Lebanon, admitted in 1988 that Iran had trained the suicide bombers but then insisted that they had not ordered the attacks. (Wright, *In the Name of God,* pp. 119–120.) Rafiq-Dust's statements should be taken as a clear sign that at the very least, the Iranians trained the bombers, but given that Rafiq-Dust does have a strong incentive to deny responsibility for the attack itself, we should not assume that this constitutes the sum total of Iran's involvement.

72. Byman, *Deadly Connections;* Jaber, *Hezbollah,* pp. 105–117.

73. Additional information came after the fact. On September 20, 1984, another truck bomb exploded at the new U.S. Embassy in Christian East Beirut. Again, Islamic Jihad took credit. Immediately after that attack, American photo interpreters realized that a mockup of the embassy's defenses and obstacle system had been built at the Shaykh Abdallah barracks, the home of the Pasdaran in Lebanon. Thus, whether Islamic Jihad was another name for a part of Hizballah or not, it clearly was connected to Hizballah and, more important, to Iran. (Turner, *Terrorism and Democracy,* pp. 170–178, esp. 177.)

74. Teicher and Teicher, *Twin Pillars to Desert Storm,* pp. 262–268; Turner, *Terrorism and Democracy,* p. 166. Weinberger's version of events is available in Weinberger, *Fighting for Peace,* pp. 161–162. Weinberger cites authors David Martin and John Walcott as confirming his version of events. However, they do exactly the opposite, concurring with the Teichers and Turner that Reagan *did* give the order to execute the retaliatory strike. (David C. Martin and John Walcott, *Best Laid Plans* [New York: Harper & Row, 1988], pp. 138–139.)

75. Harik, *Hezbollah,* p. 37; Hiro, *The Longest War,* pp. 106–107.

76. Shultz, *Turmoil and Triumph,* p. 229; also see p. 228, n. 5, regarding problems with the operation itself.

77. Harik, *Hezbollah,* p. 37; Hiro, *The Longest War,* pp. 106–108; Shultz, *Turmoil and Triumph,* pp. 227–231; Teicher and Teicher, *Twin Pillars to Desert Storm,* pp. 278–286, 289–293; Weinberger, *Fighting for Peace,* pp. 166–169.

78. For some concurring opinions by U.S. policy makers of the time, see Shultz, *Turmoil and Triumph,* p. 231; Teicher and Teicher, *Twin Pillars to Desert Storm,* pp. 293, 303.

79. See, for instance, Eric Hooglund, "The Policy of the Reagan Administration Toward Iran," in Keddie and Gasiorowski, *Neither East nor West,* p. 181.

80. Shultz, *Turmoil and Triumph,* p. 237. Also see Teicher and Teicher, *Twin Pillars to Desert Storm,* pp. 206–207.

81. Conspiracy theorists have long claimed that the United States colluded with Iraq on its invasion of Iran and that Brzezinski traveled to Baghdad in September 1980 to give Saddam the "green light." This is utterly untrue. Any number of American officials who were responsible for policy toward Iran and Iraq at the time have attested to this—and they have no particular reason to conceal such involvement if it were the case. See, e.g., Gary Sick, *October Surprise* (New York: Times Books, 1992), pp. 106–107; Teicher and Teicher, *Twin Pillars to Desert Storm,* pp. 59–70. In a letter to *The Wall Street Journal* dated June 18, 1991, Brzezinski wrote, "It is also false to suggest that the Carter administration in any fashion whatsoever, directly or indirectly, encouraged Iraq to undertake a military adventure against Iran." Moreover, Gary Sick has stated, "I was with Zbig almost constantly in the hours after we learned of the Iraqi attack, and I can assure you that he was quite surprised and was trying to understand the implications, just as I was. At a minimum, it was a superb acting job, when there was no real reason to pretend. However, Zbig made no secret of the fact that he saw the Iraqi attack as a potentially positive development that would put pressure on Iran to release the hostages. In MidEast conspiracy theories, if an action benefits a particular actor, it is obvious that it was planned or encouraged by that actor. His favorable attitude toward the Iraqi invasion of Iran has probably guaranteed that he will always be tagged with it. I have interviewed Zbig at length about this. He has denied the entire story absolutely and unequivocally—including an important letter to the WSJ that apparently went by unnoticed. If he HAD engineered such an attack, Zbig would not be one to shrink from taking credit for what could be perceived as a massive strategic ploy on the geo-strategic chess board." Gary Sick,

e-mail correspondence with the author, July 12, 2004. Finally, Deputy Secretary of State Warren Christopher warned Baghdad on September 28 that the United States "could not condone" the seizure of Iran's oil-producing Khuzestan province. (Sick, *October Surprise*, pp. 106–107.)

82. Shultz, *Turmoil and Triumph*, pp. 235–237; Wright, *In the Name of God*, p. 133.

83. For an official American memorandum regarding the "tilt" toward Iraq, see Micholas A. Veliotes and Jonathan Howe, "Iran-Iraq War: Analysis of Possible U.S. Shift from Position of Strict Neutrality," memorandum for Mr. Eagleburger, U.S. Department of State, October 7, 1983.

84. Shultz, *Turmoil and Triumph*, pp. 235–237; Teicher and Teicher, *Twin Pillars to Desert Storm*, pp. 274–278.

85. Jentleson, *With Friends Like These*, pp. 52–53.

86. Ibid., p. 33; Jeffrey T. Richelson, *The U.S. Intelligence Community*, 4th ed. (Boulder, Colo.: Westview, 1999), p. 352; Teicher and Teicher, *Twin Pillars to Desert Storm*, pp. 274–278, 286–288.

87. Said K. Aburish, *Saddam Hussein: The Politics of Revenge* (New York: Bloomsbury, 2000), p. 228; Rick Francona, *Ally to Adversary: An Eyewitness Account of Iraq's Fall from Grace* (Annapolis: U.S. Naval Institute Press, 1999), pp. 5–6; Jentleson, *With Friends Like These*, pp. 42–55; Richelson, *The U.S. Intelligence Community*, p. 352; Teicher and Teicher, *Twin Pillars to Desert Storm*, pp. 329–330.

88. Jentleson, *With Friends Like These*, pp. 48–49; Shultz, *Turmoil and Triumph*, pp. 238–244; Teicher and Teicher, *Twin Pillars to Desert Storm*, pp. 304–305.

89. Byman, *Deadly Connections;* Ranstorp, *Hizb'allah in Lebanon*, pp. 90–91; Turner, *Terrorism and Democracy*, p. 162; Wright, *In the Name of God*, pp. 115–116.

90. Shultz, *Turmoil and Triumph*, p. 644; Teicher and Teicher, *Twin Pillars to Desert Storm*, pp. 281–282; Wright, *In the Name of God*, pp. 121–122.

91. Shultz, *Turmoil and Triumph*, pp. 651, 653.

92. Bakhash, *The Reign of the Ayatollahs*, pp. 258–259; Harik, *Hezbollah*, pp. 37–38; Katzman, *The Warriors of Islam*, pp. 136–137; Shultz, *Turmoil and Triumph*, pp. 653–667; Teicher and Teicher, *Twin Pillars to Desert Storm*, pp. 334–336; *Tower Commission Report*, p. B-13; Turner, *Terrorism and Democracy*, pp. 188–198; Wright, *In the Name of God*, pp. 130–131.

93. *Tower Commission Report*, p. B-3.

94. Bakhash, *The Reign of the Ayatollahs*, pp. 241–243; Wright, *In the Name of God*, p. 133.

95. Behrooz, "Trends in the Foreign Policy of the Islamic Republic of Iran," pp. 20–26; Daniel, *The History of Iran*, p. 214; Wright, *In the Name of God*, pp. 134–139.

96. Turner, *Terrorism and Democracy*, p. 207.

97. Gates, *From the Shadows*, p. 397.

98. See Robert C. McFarlane with Zofia Smardz, *Special Trust* (New York: Cadell & Davies, 1994), pp. 6–7, 21–23; Shultz, *Turmoil and Triumph*, pp. 784–785, 794; Teicher and Teicher, *Twin Pillars to Desert Storm*, p. 362; *Tower Commission Report*, pp. B-15–16; Weinberger, *Fighting for Peace*, pp. 353–354, 356–357, 366, 368–373.

99. Shultz, *Turmoil and Triumph*, p. 794.

100. This summary of events is drawn from Gates, *From the Shadows*, pp. 395–403; Peter Kornbluh and Malcolm Byrne, *The Iran-Contra Scandal: The Declassified History* (New York: W. W. Norton, 1993), entire; McFarlane, *Special Trust*, pp. 17–108; President's Special Review Board ("The Tower Commission"), *Report of the President's Special Review Board* (Washington, D.C.: U.S. Government Printing Office, 1987), entire; Shultz, *Turmoil and Triumph*, pp. 783–807; Turner, *Terrorism and Democracy*, pp. 207–214; U.S. Congress, House of Representatives Select Committee to Investigate Covert Arms Transactions with Iran and Senate Select Committee on Secret Military Assistance to Iran and the Nicaraguan Opposition, *Report of the Congressional Committees Investigating the Iran-Contra Affair; with Supplemental, Minority, and Additional Views* (Washington, D.C.: U.S. Government Printing Office, 1987), entire.

101. Quoted in Wright, *In the Name of God*, p. 134.

102. Behrooz, "Trends in the Foreign Policy of the Islamic Republic of Iran," p. 26.

103. Scheherezade Faramarzi, "Khomeini Contains Dissent over Arms Deal with Washington," Associated Press, December 6, 1986; Charles P. Wallace, "Khomeini Blasts Aides for Secret Talks with U.S.," *Los Angeles Times,* November 21, 1986, p. 1.

104. Charles J. Hanley, " 'Iran Scandal' in Washington, 'U.S. Scandal' in Tehran," Associated Press, November 27, 1986; David B. Ottaway, "Khomeini Attempts to Minimize Political Fallout in Parliament," *The Washington Post,* November 23, 1986, p. A17.

105. See, for instance, Shultz, *Turmoil and Triumph,* pp. 783–859, esp. 790–791; Weinberger, *Fighting for Peace,* pp. 422–423; author's interview with Sandra Charles, July 23, 2004.

Chapter 8: The Imam's Legacy

1. Sick, "Trial by Error," p. 114.

2. Political Deputy of the General Command Post, War Studies and Research, *Battle of Faw* (Tehran: 1988), in Persian, translated in FBIS-NES-94-076-S, April 20, 1994, pp. 28–49; Captain Michael E. Bigelow, "The Faw Peninsula: A Battle Analysis," *Military Intelligence,* April–June 1991, pp. 15–16; Cordesman and Wagner, *The Lessons of Modern War,* vol. 2, pp. 219–221; Hiro, *The Longest War,* pp. 167–168; O'Ballance, *The Gulf War,* pp. 173–174; Pollack, *Arabs at War,* pp. 217–218; Zabih, *The Iranian Military in Revolution and War,* pp. 190–192.

3. Axelgard, "Iraq and the War with Iran," p. 58; Political Deputy of the General Command Post, War Studies and Research, *Battle of Faw,* pp. 49–51; Bigelow, "The Faw Peninsula," pp. 16–17; Cordesman and Wagner, *The Lessons of Modern War,* vol. 2, pp. 222–224; Hiro, *The Longest War,* pp. 166–170; O'Ballance, *The Gulf War,* pp. 173–179; Pollack, *Arabs at War,* pp. 217–218.

4. Katzman, *The Warriors of Islam,* p. 129; Sick, "Trial by Error," p. 115.

5. Cordesman and Wagner, *The Lessons of Modern War,* vol. 2, pp. 245–246.

6. Ibid., pp. 247–250; Hiro, *The Longest War,* pp. 180–181; O'Ballance, *The Gulf War,* pp. 194–195; Pollack, *Arabs at War,* pp. 221–223; Zabih, *The Iranian Military in Revolution and War,* pp. 196–199.

7. Cordesman and Wagner, *The Lessons of Modern War,* vol. 2, pp. 250–254; Hiro, *The Longest War,* pp. 181–184; O'Ballance, *The Gulf War,* pp. 195–196; Pollack, *Arabs at War,* pp. 223–224; Zabih, *The Iranian Military in Revolution and War,* pp. 196–199.

8. Cordesman and Wagner, *The Lessons of Modern War,* vol. 2, pp. 229–230; Richard Johns and Lucy Kellaway, "Iraq Hits Hormuz Strait Oil Terminal," *Financial Times,* November 26, 1986, p. 1; Paul Lewis, "War on Oil Tankers Heats Up in the Persian Gulf," *The New York Times,* May 18, 1986, p. 1; Palmer, *Guardians of the Gulf,* pp. 120–121.

9. Central Intelligence Agency, "Iran–Gulf States: Prospects for Expanded Conflict," May 17, 1986, declassified September 1999, available at www.foia.cia.gov, accessed July 22, 2004, pp. 24–25; Cordesman and Wagner, *The Lessons of Modern War,* vol. 2, pp. 230–231, 255–256, 271–280; Lewis, "War on Oil Tankers Heats Up in the Persian Gulf," p. 1; Palmer, *Guardians of the Gulf,* pp. 120–123.

10. Cordesman and Wagner, *The Lessons of Modern War,* vol. 2, p. 255; David Hirst, "Iran Warns Gulf States over Oil," *The Guardian,* August 23, 1986, p. 1.

11. Cordesman and Wagner, *The Lessons of Modern War,* vol. 2, pp. 271–280.

12. Ibid., pp. 271–280, 282–285; Palmer, *Guardians of the Gulf,* pp. 122–127; Janice Gross Stein, "The Wrong Strategy in the Right Place: The United States in the Gulf," *International Security* 13, no. 3 (Winter 1988–1989), pp. 148–161; author's interview with Sandra Charles, July 23, 2004.

13. Katzman, *The Warriors of Islam,* pp. 133–134.

14. Cordesman and Wagner, *The Lessons of Modern War,* vol. 2, pp. 282–290.

15. Ibid., pp. 288–290; Central Intelligence Agency, "Iranian Reaction to Recent Military Setbacks," April 21, 1988, declassified September 1999, available at www.foia.cia.gov, accessed on July 22, 2004, pp. 2–3; Weinberger, *Fighting for Peace,* p. 413.

16. Wright, *In the Name of God,* p. 167.

17. Weinberger, *Fighting for Peace,* pp. 387–394.

18. Ibid., p. 394.

19. Ibid., pp. 389–392.

20. Author's interview with Sandra Charles, July 23, 2004; author's interview with senior U.S. official, July 10, 2003.

21. Palmer, *Guardians of the Gulf,* pp. 131–132, 135–136; Stein, "The Wrong Strategy in the Right Place," pp. 150–161.

22. Cordesman and Wagner, *The Lessons of Modern War,* vol. 2, pp. 318–320; Palmer, *Guardians of the Gulf,* p. 133; Weinberger, *Fighting for Peace,* pp. 414–416.

23. Central Intelligence Agency, "Persian Gulf: Bolder Iranian Actions," September 30, 1987, declassified September 1999, available at www.foia.cia.gov, accessed July 22, 2004, p. 16.

24. Cordesman and Wagner, *The Lessons of Modern War,* vol. 2, pp. 328–331; Palmer, *Guardians of the Gulf,* pp. 133–134.

25. Central Intelligence Agency, "Iranian Reaction to Recent Military Setbacks," pp. 3–4.

26. Pollack, *Arabs at War,* p. 224.

27. Bakhash, *The Reign of the Ayatollahs,* p. 273.

28. Cordesman and Wagner, *The Lessons of Modern War,* vol. 2, pp. 363–368; Palmer, *Guardians of the Gulf,* p. 138; Pollack, *Arabs at War,* p. 229; Pollack, *The Threatening Storm,* pp. 23–24.

29. Central Intelligence Agency, "Subject: Iran-Iraq Frontline," June 23, 1988, declassified and released as part of the U.S. Department of Defense GulfLink project, available at www.dtic.mil:80/Gulflink/indexpages/intelligence documents, accessed November 10, 1996; " 'Fourth Part' of Saddam's al-Faw Meeting," in FBIS-NES-93-081, April 29, 1993, pp. 30–31, 34; "Saddam al-Faw Anniversary Address; Part II," in FBIS-NES-93-075, April 21, 1993, pp. 23–24; and author's interviews with General Bernard Trainor.

30. " 'Fourth Part' of Saddam's al-Faw Meeting," pp. 27–41; "Saddam's al-Faw Anniversary Address; Part II," pp. 23–24.

31. David Crist, "Operation Earnest Will: The United States in the Persian Gulf, 1986–1989" (Ph.D. dissertation, Florida State University, 1998); Palmer, *Guardians of the Gulf,* pp. 138–144.

32. There was one exception: the attack on Mehran in June was a comparatively small affair that employed fewer forces than any of Iraq's other offensives in 1988.

33. David Black, "Last Call for Flight 655," *The Independent,* July 3, 1989, p. 17; Palmer, *Guardians of the Gulf,* pp. 145–148; Wright, *In the Name of God,* pp. 186–187.

34. The United States later apologized and paid $20,000 reparations to the families for each of the victims.

35. Youssef M. Ibrahim, "The Downing of Flight 655," *The New York Times,* July 5, 1988, p. A9. See also Ansari, *Modern Iran Since 1921,* pp. 238–239; Stephen Engleberg, Michael R. Gordon, and Bernard E. Trainor, "Downing of Flight 655: Questions Keep Coming," *The New York Times,* July 11, 1988, p. A1; John Morocco et al., "Iranian Airbus Shootdown," *Aviation Week and Space Technology* 129, no. 2 (July 11, 1988), p. 16.

36. Ansari, *Modern Iran Since 1921,* pp. 239–241.

37. Ibid., pp. 238–239; Daniel, *The History of Iran,* p. 216.

38. Palmer, *Guardians of the Gulf,* p. 145.

39. Bakhash, *The Reign of the Ayatollahs,* p. 274; Wright, *In the Name of God,* p. 188.

40. Daniel, *The History of Iran,* pp. 216–217; Wright, *In the Name of God,* p. 190. On the religious elements of Khomeini's acceptance of a cease-fire, see Gieling, *Religion and War in Revolutionary Iran,* pp. 168–171.

41. Quoted in Wright, *In the Name of God,* pp. 190–191.

42. For those looking for a detailed taxonomy of the Iranian state and its multifarious power centers, there is no more comprehensive source (at least for the moment) than Buchta, *Who Rules Iran?*

43. Brumberg, *Reinventing Khomeini,* pp. 126–133.

44. Ibid., pp. 133–134; Mehdi Moslem, *Factional Politics in Post-Khomeini Iran* (Syracuse, N.Y.: Syracuse University Press, 2002), pp. 71–78.

45. Moslem, *Factional Politics in Post-Khomeini Iran,* p. 75.

46. Ansari, *Modern Iran Since 1921,* p. 240; Bakhash, *The Reign of the Ayatollahs,* pp. 251–253; Brumberg, *Reinventing Khomeini,* pp. 135–137; Daniel, *The History of Iran,* pp. 224–225; Keddie, *Modern Iran,* p. 260; David Menashri, *Revolution at a Crossroads: Iran's Domestic Politics*

and Regional Ambitions (Washington, D.C.: Washington Institute for Near East Policy, 1997), p. 8; Moslem, *Factional Politics in Post-Khomeini Iran,* pp. 73–75.

47. Gieling, *Religion and War in Revolutionary Iran,* p. 32.
48. Central Intelligence Agency, "Iran's Economy: A Survey of its Decline," July 1991, declassified November 1999, available at www.foia.cia.gov, accessed July 22, 2004, p. iii.
49. Ansari, *Modern Iran Since 1921,* p. 241; Daniel, *The History of Iran,* p. 228; Kanovsky, *Iran's Economic Morass,* p. 12; Keddie, *Modern Iran,* p. 264; Wright, *In the Name of God,* pp. 26, 208.
50. Cordesman and Wagner, *The Lessons of Modern War,* vol. 2, p. 3.
51. Bakhash, *The Reign of the Ayatollahs,* pp. 278–279; Keddie, *Modern Iran,* p. 260; David Menashri, "Iran," in Ami Ayalon, Barbara Newson, and Haim Shaked, eds., *Middle East Contemporary Survey,* vol. 12 (Oxford, U.K.: Westview, 1988), pp. 479–481. *Note:* Hereafter, all references to David Menashri entries in the annual *Middle East Contemporary Survey* will include only the author's last name, *MECS,* the year of publication, and the page numbers.
52. Behrooz, "Trends in the Foreign Policy of the Islamic Republic of Iran," pp. 30–31; Brumberg, *Reinventing Khomeini,* pp. 143–146; Menashri, *MECS,* 1988, pp. 473–476; Wright, *In the Name of God,* pp. 29–193.
53. Quoted in Wright, *In the Name of God,* p. 195.
54. Ibid.
55. Ramazani, "Challenges for US Policy," in Ramazani, *Iran's Revolution,* p. 133; Wright, *In the Name of God,* p. 197.
56. Quoted in Wright, *In the Name of God,* p. 198.
57. I take no position on the question of whether *The Satanic Verses* is blasphemous or should be considered offensive to Muslims. I have not read the book, and I am not a Muslim. I have read enough about the controversy to know that the most sophisticated criticisms of the book relate to rather esoteric aspects of Quranic history and historiography that I simply lack the knowledge to be able to judge. What's more, I recognize that oftentimes who or how something is said is as important as what is actually being said when deciding whether something is offensive to a group of people. Nevertheless, my own personal values do not condone the killing of a person for saying *anything,* even something that is truly offensive. As an example, I believe Adolf Hitler deserved to die for the 11 million to 12 million Jews, Gypsies, Communists, homosexuals, and others who died in the Holocaust. But I do not believe he deserved death for having written unforgivably offensive things about all of these groups in *Mein Kampf.*
58. Quoted in Wright, *In the Name of God,* p. 199. Also see Daniel, *The History of Iran,* pp. 226–229; Ramazani, "Challenges for US Policy," p. 134.
59. Bakhash, *The Reign of the Ayatollahs,* p. 280; Wright, *In the Name of God,* pp. 195–196.
60. Quoted in Ramazani, "Challenges for US Policy," p. 135.
61. "Khomeini Issues Message to Religious Authorities," Tehran Radio, in FBIS-NESA, February 23, 1989, pp. 44–48.
62. Menashri, *MECS,* 1988, p. 493.
63. Quoted in Bakhash, *The Reign of the Ayatollahs,* p. 282.
64. Bakhash, *The Reign of the Ayatollahs,* pp. 282–283; Wright, *In the Name of God,* p. 201. In addition, it had been Montazeri's son-in-law Mehdi Hashemi who had apparently leaked the Iran-*contra* affair and McFarlane's trip to Tehran to the Lebanese journal *ash-Shiraa,* and this too had rankled Khomeini.
65. Menashri, *MECS,* 1988, p. 494.
66. Daniel, *The History of Iran,* p. 224; Menashri, *MECS,* 1988, p. 472.
67. Bakhash, *The Reign of the Ayatollahs,* pp. 284–285; Brumberg, *Reinventing Khomeini,* pp. 147–149; Daniel, *The History of Iran,* pp. 220–222; Keddie, *Modern Iran,* pp. 260–261; Menashri, *MECS,* 1989, pp. 345–350; Menashri, *Revolution at a Crossroads,* p. 17; Moslem, *Factional Politics in Post-Khomeini Iran,* pp. 78–81.
68. On the succession debate, see Moslem, *Factional Politics in Post-Khomeini Iran,* pp. 84–87.
69. Daniel, *The History of Iran,* pp. 223–234; Keddie, *Modern Iran,* p. 262.
70. Out of eighty candidates who applied to run for the presidency, the Council of Guardians rejected

all but two: Rafsanjani and 'Abbas Sheybani, who was a former agriculture minister but still a virtual unknown. He had also run in Iran's first presidential elections in 1980, where he had come in third, with 2.8 percent of the vote—against Bani Sadr's 91 percent. Not surprisingly, Rafsanjani won, with 94.5 percent of the vote. Menashri, *MECS,* 1989, pp. 353–355, 369, n. 58.

71. For concurring views, see Stephen C. Fairbanks, "A New Era for Iran?," *Middle East Policy* 5, no. 3 (September 1997), p. 54; Menashri, *MECS,* 1989, pp. 352–353.

Chapter 9: Collision Course

1. Giandomenico Picco, *Man Without a Gun* (New York: Random House, 1999), pp. 99–263.

2. Author's interviews with Rand Beers, July 28, 2004; Sandra Charles, July 23, 2004; Richard Haass, July 23, 2004; and Bruce O. Riedel, August 1, 2004.

3. Author's interviews with Sandra Charles, July 23, 2004; Richard Haass, July 23, 2004; and Bruce O. Riedel, August 1, 2004.

4. Ofra Bengio, "Baghdad Between Shi'a and Kurds," Policy Focus no. 18, Washington Institute for Near East Policy, February 1992, p. 26, n. 44; Andrew and Patrick Cockburn, *Out of the Ashes: The Resurrection of Saddam Hussein* (New York: HarperCollins, 1999), pp. 12–13.

5. James A. Baker III, *The Politics of Diplomacy* (New York: G.P. Putnam's Sons, 1995), p. 439. Also see George Bush and Brent Scowcroft, *A World Transformed* (New York: Alfred A. Knopf, 1998), p. 433; author's interviews with Sandra Charles, July 23, 2004; Richard Haass, July 23, 2004; and Bruce O. Riedel, August 1, 2004.

6. Central Intelligence Agency, "Iraq: Implications of Insurrection and Prospects for Saddam's Survival," March 16, 1991, declassified January 2001, available at www.foia.cia.gov, accessed July 22, 2004, p. 4.

7. Nora Boustany, "The Hostage Labyrinth—Many Complex Deals Lie Behind Any Release," *The Washington Post,* March 18, 2004; author's interviews with Sandra Charles, July 23, 2004; Richard Haass, July 23, 2004; Bruce O. Riedel, August 1, 2004; and former senior administration official, July 10, 2004.

8. Author's interview with former senior administration official, July 10, 2004.

9. Menashri, *MECS,* 1989, pp. 354–355.

10. Ibid., pp. 356–357.

11. Ibid., pp. 350, 359–362; Moslem, *Factional Politics in Post-Khomeini Iran,* pp. 149–151.

12. Ramazani, "Challenges for US Policy," p. 134.

13. Moslem, *Factional Politics in Post-Khomeini Iran,* pp. 224–226.

14. Menashri, *Revolution at a Crossroads,* pp. 29–30.

15. Menashri, *MECS,* 1992, pp. 357–358; Menashri, *MECS,* 1992, p. 408.

16. The earliest use of the term I have found is in Ramazani, "Iran's Foreign Policy" (1990), p. 59.

17. For discussions of this problem—and the ultimate need to continue to use broad terms like "radical" and "pragmatist" even while recognizing that they are not fully accurate—see Buchta, *Who Rules Iran?,* pp. 11–20; Menashri, *MECS,* 1990, pp. 400–401; Moslem, *Factional Politics in Post-Khomeini Iran,* pp. 90–141.

18. On this phenomenon, see Brumberg, *Reinventing Khomeini,* pp. 137–161, 181–184.

19. Menashri, *MECS,* 1990, p. 363.

20. Menashri, *MECS,* 1989, pp. 364–365; Menashri, *MECS,* 1990, p. 363; Menashri, *Revolution at a Crossroads,* pp. 73–74.

21. Menashri, *MECS,* 1990, p. 362.

22. Ibid., p. 363.

23. Menashri, *MECS,* 1989, pp. 364–365; Menashri, *MECS,* 1990, p. 363.

24. Central Intelligence Agency, "Iran Under Rafsanjani: Seeking a New Role in the World Community?," October 1991, declassified (no date), available at www.foia.cia.gov, accessed July 22, 2004, pp. 15, 19–21.

25. Ibid., p. iii.

26. Menashri, *MECS,* 1992, pp. 397–398.

27. Ibid., pp. 419–420; Menashri, *Revolution at a Crossroads,* p. 80.

28. Central Intelligence Agency, "Iran Under Rafsanjani," pp. 14, 20; Menashri, *Revolution at a Crossroads,* pp. 80–82; Norton, "Hizballah," p. 147.

29. Iran may have had something to do with the destruction of Pan Am flight 103 over Lockerbie, Scotland, in December 1989. Although today it is widely believed that Libya alone was responsible for this attack, at the time many suspected Iranian involvement. While an analyst at the CIA, I was told by friends who worked counterterrorism issues that there was evidence linking the attack to Iran. It was said at the time that, for the Iranians, this was a retaliation for the shoot-down of Iran Air flight 655 in 1988 and that they had asked the Libyans—who had much greater capabilities to conduct this kind of mission and a similar desire stemming from the 1986 U.S. bombing of Tripoli—to conduct the actual operation. The Iranians were said to have provided supplies, funding, and a payoff to the Libyans for making the "hit." After I started work on my Ph.D. in 1992 and moved into a part-time status with the Agency, I no longer received regular reports on this. When I returned to full-time government service in 1995 with the National Security Council, the FBI had decided that the Libyans had acted alone. Although I have no evidence that this is the case, I have since heard from friends still in the intelligence community that they believe the FBI acted peremptorily in determining that Libya alone had been responsible for the attack and that, in the murky world of terrorism, there was still reason to believe that the Iranians had also played a significant role.

30. For concurring views, see Benjamin and Simon, *The Age of Sacred Terror,* p. 224; Central Intelligence Agency, "Iran Under Rafsanjani," pp. 19–21.

31. Robert S. Greenberger, "Arab Nightmare: Sudan's Links to Iran Cause Growing Worry over Islamic Terrorism," *The Wall Street Journal,* August 18, 1993, p. A1; Menashri, *MECS,* 1992, pp. 398, 421, 431–435; Marguerite Michaels, "Is Sudan Terrorism's New Best Friend?," *Time,* August 30, 1993, p. 30.

32. See, for example, "Mubarak on Terrorism; Iran, Washington Talks; Hala'ib Triangle," reported by the BBC, May 13, 1993; Walid M. Abdel-Nasser, "Three Regional Spheres in Iran's Foreign Policy," Strategic Papers no. 38 (Cairo: Al-Ahram Center for Political and Strategic Studies, 1996), p. 19; "Egyptian-Sudanese Security Meetings Resumed in Cairo," *al-Wasat,* August 11–17, 1997, in FBIS-NES-97-224, August 13, 1997; "Wanted Terrorist Leaders Still in Sudan," *al-Ahram,* May 28, 1996, in FBIS-TOT-96-018-L, July 19, 1996; "Al-Ahram Looks at al-Turabi Regime, Terrorism," *Al-Ahram,* March 20, 1996, in FBIS-TOT-96-013-L, June 7, 1996; "Cairo Serves Notice, Our Patience with Khartoum Is Running Out," *The Middle East Mirror,* July 7, 1995; "Something Is Being Cooked Up Against the Regime in Sudan," *The Middle East Mirror,* June 29, 1995, pp. 14–17; "Egypt Puts Sudan in the Dock over Attempt on Mubarak's Life," *The Middle East Mirror,* June 27, 1995, pp. 11–13; "Al-Ahram Criticises Muslim Organization and Sudanese Policy on Hala'ib," BBC, August 7, 1992.

33. Richard A. Clarke, *Against All Enemies: Inside America's War on Terror* (New York: Free Press, 2004), pp. 102–103; Central Intelligence Agency, "Iran: Roots of Growing Activism Against Israel," *National Intelligence Daily,* September 29, 1989, declassified June 1999, available at www.foia.cia.gov, accessed July 22, 2004, pp. 12–13; Svante E. Cornell, "Iran and the Caucasus," *Middle East Policy* 5, no. 4 (January 1998); Menashri, *MECS,* 1992, pp. 421–422; Menashri, *Revolution at a Crossroads,* pp. 81–82.

34. Joseph Kostiner, "The Search for Gulf Security: The Politics of Collective Defense," in Ami Ayalon, ed., *Middle East Contemporary Survey,* vol. 16 (Boulder, Colo.: Westview, 1992), p. 236; Menashri, *MECS,* 1992, pp. 422–425.

35. Michael Eisenstadt, *Iranian Military Power: Capabilities and Intentions* (Washington, D.C.: Washington Institute for Near East Policy, 1997), p. 78; United States Department of State, *Patterns of Global Terrorism* (Washington, D.C.: U.S. Department of State, 1993), p. 22.

36. On Iran's conventional military rearmament, see Anthony Cordesman, *Iran and Iraq: The Threat from the Northern Gulf* (Boulder, Colo.: Westview, 1994), pp. 25–28, 35–42; Eisenstadt, *Iranian Military Power,* pp. 35–64; Kenneth M. Pollack, "The Regional Military Balance," in Richard D.

Sokolsky, ed., *The United States and the Persian Gulf* (Washington, D.C.: National Defense University Press, 2003), pp. 72–76.

37. Anthony Cordesman, "The Military Balance in the Middle East—IX," Center for Strategic and International Studies, December 28, 1998, pp. 11–19.

38. Eisenstadt, *Iranian Military Power,* p. 11.

39. Bill, *The Eagle and the Lion,* pp. 204–208; Daniel, *The History of Iran,* pp. 164–165; Rubin, *Paved with Good Intentions,* p. 138.

40. Cordesman, *Iran and Iraq,* pp. 104–105, Gary Sick, "Rethinking Dual Containment," *Survival* 40, no. 1 (Spring 1998), pp. 16–18.

41. Cordesman, *Iran and Iraq,* pp. 103–104, 105–108; Eisenstadt, *Iranian Military Power,* pp. 9–12; Joint Atomic Energy Intelligence Committee, "Iran's Nuclear Program: Building a Weapons Capability," February 1993, declassified (no date), available at www.foia.cia.gov, accessed July 22, 2004. Bizarrely, only the title—and thus the existence—of this assessment has been released. However, the title is enough to make the point.

42. Eisenstadt, *Iranian Military Power,* pp. 10–11; Ray Takeyh, "Iran's Nuclear Calculations," *World Policy Journal* (Summer 2003).

43. Author's interviews with Mark R. Parris, July 21, 2004; Bruce O. Riedel, August 1, 2004; and former senior administration official, July 2004.

44. Warren Christopher, *In the Stream of History: Shaping Foreign Policy for a New Era* (Stanford, Calif.: Stanford University Press, 1998), pp. 74–81; Warren Christopher, "Building Peace in the Middle East," address at Columbia University, September 20, 1993, reprinted in Christopher, *In the Stream of History,* pp. 81–90; Warren Christopher, "Maintaining the Momentum for Peace in the Middle East," reprinted in Christopher, *In the Stream of History,* pp. 195–202; Martin Indyk, "Back to the Bazaar," *Foreign Affairs* 81, no. 1, January–February 2002, pp. 76–77; Dennis Ross, *The Missing Peace* (New York: Farrar, Straus and Giroux, 2004), pp. 98–121.

45. Christopher, *In the Stream of History,* pp. 74–81; Thomas W. Lippman, "Iranian President to Visit U.N.," *The Washington Post,* June 28, 1998, p. A25.

46. Full disclosure: Martin Indyk is my immediate boss at the Saban Center for Middle East Policy at the Brookings Institution.

47. Martin Indyk, "The Clinton Administration's Approach to the Middle East," speech given at the Soref Symposium of the Washington Institute for Near East Policy, May 18, 1993, available at www.washingtoninstitute.org/pubs/soref/indyk.htm, accessed July 24, 2004.

48. On the development of the policy of containment toward Iraq, see Pollack, *The Threatening Storm,* pp. 58–70.

49. Indyk, "The Clinton Administration's Approach to the Middle East."

50. Hooman Estelami, "The Evolution of Iran's Reactive Measures to US Economic Sanctions," *The Journal of Business in Developing Nations* 2 (1998), p. 5.

51. Commission of the European Communities, European Council in Edinburgh, December 11–12, 1992.

52. Charles Lane, "Germany's New Ostpolitik: Changing Iran," *Foreign Affairs* 74, no. 6 (November–December 1995), pp. 77–89.

53. "Iranian Gets Life for Killing Shah's Last Premier," Reuters, December 6, 1994.

54. "Danish Politicians Boycott Visiting Iranian Minister," Agence France-Presse, February 9, 1995, p. 1.

55. Lane, "Germany's New Ostpolitik," pp. 79–80.

56. See Christopher, "Building Peace in the Middle East," p. 449.

57. Anthony Lake, "Confronting Backlash States," *Foreign Affairs* 73, no. 2 (March–April 1994).

58. Christopher, "Maintaining the Momentum for Peace in the Middle East," p. 201.

59. "Argentine Judge Hears Testimony of Detainee Linked with Buenos Aires Bombing," *BBC Summary of World Broadcasts,* January 12, 1995; Ian Brodie, Michael Theodoulou, and Hazhir Teimourian, "CIA Confirms Tehran's Role in Bombing of Jewish Targets," *The Times,* August 12, 1994; James Brooke, "Argentines Suspect Iranian Hand in Bombing; Death Toll Hits 80," *The*

New York Times, July 26, 1994, p. A3; James Brooke, "Iranian in Argentine Blast: Tinker, Refugee, Liar, Spy?," *The New York Times,* July 29, 1994, p. A2; Byman, *Deadly Connections;* Clarke, *Against All Enemies,* p. 103; Katherine Ellison, "Argentina, Iran on Verge of Severing Diplomatic Relations," Knight Ridder/Tribune News Service, May 20, 1998; "Judge Finds Iranian Link to Bombing, Reports Say," Associated Press, August 8, 1994; Katzman, "Terrorism," p. 6; Sebastian Rotella, "South America: Trail Heats Up in '94 Bombing," *Los Angeles Times,* December 6, 1997, p. A2; U.S. Department of State, *Patterns of Global Terrorism, 1994,* p. 21, available at dosfan.lib.uic.edu/ERC/arms/PGT_report/1994PGT.html, accessed July 25, 2004; U.S. Department of State, *Patterns of Global Terrorism, 2003,* available at www.state.gov/s/ct/rls/pgtrpt/2003/c12108.htm, accessed July 23, 2004.

60. U.S. Department of State, *Patterns of Global Terrorism, 1993* (Washington, D.C.: U.S. Department of State, Office of the Secretary of State, Office of the Coordinator for Counterterrorism, April 1994), p. 1.

61. Martin Kramer, "Rallying Around Islam," in Ami Ayalon, ed., *MECS,* vol. 17 (Boulder, Colo.: Westview, 1993), p. 115; Joshua Teitelbaum, "Saudi Arabia," in Ayalon, *MECS,* 1993, p. 588.

62. Ofra Bengio, "Iraq," in Ayalon, *MECS,* 1993, p. 403.

63. Barry Rubin, "The United States and the Middle East," in Bruce Maddy-Weitzman, ed., *MECS,* vol. 19 (Boulder, Colo.: Westview, 1995), pp. 35–36.

64. To this day, Iran's involvement in the Mubarak assassination attempt is unclear. For a sample of claims that Iran provided some degree of assistance, see Ami Ayalon, "Egypt," in Maddy-Weitzman, *MECS,* 1995, pp. 272–273; "Cairo Radio Reports Anti-Sudan UN Resolution, Envoy's Reaction," Cairo Arab Republic of Egypt Radio Network, in Arabic, February 1, 1996, in FBIS-NES-96-042, March 4, 1996; "Sudan: Villain or Scapegoat?" *The Middle East Mirror,* June 30, 1995, pp. 15–20; "Something Is Being Cooked Up Against the Regime in Sudan," *The Middle East Mirror,* June 29, 1995, pp. 14–17; "Egypt Puts Sudan in the Dock over Attempt on Mubarak's Life," *The Middle East Mirror,* June 27, 1995, pp. 11–13; "Mubarak's Advisor Accuses Iran of Assassination Attempt," Agence France-Presse, September 4, 1996; author's interviews with Western military officers, Egyptian foreign ministry officials, Egyptian civilian defense experts, and former Egyptian senior military officers, September–December 1997.

65. Nadeya Sayed Ali Mohammed, "Political Reform in Bahrain: The Price of Stability," *Middle East Intelligence Bulletin* 4, no. 9 (September 2002); Bruce Maddy-Weitzman, "Inter-Arab Relations," in Maddy-Weitzman, *MECS,* 1995, p. 80; Joshua Teitelbaum, "Saudi Arabia," in Maddy-Weitzman, *MECS,* 1995, pp. 238–243.

66. For a sample of the voluminous reporting on these problems, see David Briscoe, "U.S. Asserts China-Iran Nuclear Deal Off, Chinese Call It Suspended," Associated Press, September 29, 1995; John M. Broder, "Despite a Secret Pact by Gore in '95, Russian Arms Sales to Iran Go On," *The New York Times,* October 13, 2000, p. A1; Ann Devroy, "Clinton, Yeltsin Open Summit, Smoothing Over a Few Bumps," *The Washington Post,* September 28, 1994, p. A15; Steven Erlanger, "U.S. Telling Russia to Bar Aid to Iran by Arms Experts," *The New York Times,* August 22, 1997, p. A3; Steven Erlanger, "U.S. Says Chinese Will Stop Sending Missiles to Iran," *The New York Times,* October 18, 1997, p. A1; Steven Erlanger, "U.S. Gets Russia's Firm Vow to Halt Missile Aid to Iran," *The New York Times,* January 16, 1998, p. A8; Steven Erlanger, "U.S. Imposes Curbs on 9 Russian Concerns," *The New York Times,* July 16, 1998, p. A10; Barton Gellman and John Pomfret, "U.S. Action Stymied China Sale to Iran; Chemical Involved Can Be Used to Enrich Uranium," *The Washington Post,* March 13, 1998, p. A1; Michael R. Gordon and Eric Schmitt, "Iran Nearly Got a Missile Alloy from Russians," *The New York Times,* April 25, 1998, p. A1; "Gore, Russian Premier Hold First Meeting of Joint U.S.-Russian Commission," Agence France-Presse, September 1, 1993; Steven Greenhouse, "Russia and China Pressed Not to Sell A-Plants to Iran," *The New York Times,* January 25, 1995, p. A6; Fred Hiatt, "Russian Agency Disputes U.S. on Iranian A-Arms; Moscow Sees No Need to Bar Reactor Sale," *The Washington Post,* March 24, 1995, p. A28; Fred Hiatt, "Gore, Chernomyrdin Sign Deal to Find Oil; No Accord on Iranian A-Plant Issue," *The Washington Post,* July 1, 1995, p. A24; John Lancaster, "U.S. Waives Proliferation Penalties on China; Beijing Vows to Stop Exporting Missile Parts," *The*

Washington Post, November 22, 2000, p. A20; Thomas W. Lippman, "U.S. and Russia Sign Economic, Technical Pacts; Internationalizing Space Station, Aiding Nuclear Safety Are Aims," *The Washington Post,* September 3, 1993, p. A28; Thomas W. Lippman, "U.S. Confirms China Missile Sale to Iran," *The Washington Post,* May 31, 1997, p. A15; Thomas W. Lippman, "Gore Lauds Russia's Policy Curbing Arms for Iran; U.S. Pledges to Help Build Safeguards Against Illicit Transfers of High-Tech Weapons," *The Washington Post,* March 12, 1998, p. A9; Steven Mufson, "Chinese Nuclear Officials See No Reason to Change Plans to Sell Reactor to Iran," *The Washington Post,* May 18, 1995, p. A22; Barry Schweid, "U.S. to Punish Chinese for Chemical Weapons Shipments to Iran," Associated Press, May 22, 1997; Elaine Sciolino, "U.S. May Threaten China with Sanctions for Reported Arms Sales," *The New York Times,* July 20, 1993, p. A3; Elaine Sciolino, "U.S. and Chinese Resolve Dispute on Missile Sales," *The New York Times,* October 5, 1994, p. A1; Elaine Sciolino, "Beijing Rebuffs U.S. on Halting Iran Atom Deal," *The New York Times,* April 18, 1995, p. A1; R. Jeffrey Smith, "China May Cancel Proposed Sale of Nuclear Facility to Iran," *The Washington Post,* November 6, 1996, p. A9; R. Jeffrey Smith, "China's Pledge to End Iran Nuclear Aid Yields U.S. Help; Clinton Says He'll Allow U.S. Exports of Technology; Scrutiny and Debate Are Expected," *The Washington Post,* October 30, 1997, p. A15; Patrick E. Tyler, "Russian's Links to Iran Offer a Case Study in Arms Leaks," *The New York Times,* May 10, 2000, p. A6; Daniel Williams, "U.S., Russia Trade Gibes over Iran; Kremlin Vows 'Tough' Reply to American Sanctions, Threats," *The Washington Post,* January 15, 1999, p. A23. Also see Robert O. Freedman, "Russian-Iranian Relations in the 1990s," *MERIA Journal,* vol. 4, no. 2 (June 2000).

67. Barton Gellman, "Likud Leader Hammers Rabin, PLO; Premier-Hopeful Netanyahu Claims Ascendancy of Israeli Opposition," *The Washington Post,* September 9, 1995, p. A22; Youssef M. Ibrahim, "Israel Accusing Muslim Militants in Recent Bombings in the West," *The New York Times,* July 28, 1994, p. A10; David Makovsky, "Labor's Leading Duo Looks to Win the Battle and the War," *The Jerusalem Post,* July 28, 1995, p. 11; "Prime Minister Rabin Comments on Explosion, Attacks 'Extremist Islamic Terrorism,' " IDF Radio, Tel Aviv, in Hebrew, July 19, 1994, *BBC Summary of World Broadcasts,* July 20, 1994; Lally Weymouth, "It's Peace or a New Wave of Terrorism, Says Rabin," *The Washington Post,* June 21, 1995, p. A21; author's interviews with Mark R. Parris, July 21, 2004; and Bruce O. Riedel, August 1, 2004.

68. "Clinton Administration Bans Conoco Deal with Iran," National Public Radio, March 15, 1995.

69. Lane, "Germany's New Ostpolitik," pp. 77–78.

70. D'Amato's legislation closely followed a plan set forth in late 1994 by AIPAC in a document called "Comprehensive US Sanctions Against Iran: A Plan for Action."

71. Clarke, *Against All Enemies,* p. 103; author's interviews with senior administration official, July 1, 2004; Mark R. Parris, July 21, 2004; and Bruce O. Riedel, August 1, 2004.

72. Hossein Alikhani, *Sanctioning Iran: Anatomy of a Failed Policy* (London: I. B. Tauris, 2000), pp. 182–183; Agis Salpukas, "Conoco's Deal in Iran Faces Broad Hurdle," *The New York Times,* March 14, 1995; Elaine Sciolino, "Iranian Leader Says U.S. Move on Oil Deal Wrecked Chance to Improve Ties," *The New York Times,* May 16, 1995.

73. "Burned by Loss of Conoco Deal, Iran Says U.S. Betrays Free Trade," *The New York Times,* March 20, 1995, p. D2.

74. Author's interviews with senior administration official, July 1, 2004, and with former senior administration official, July 2004.

75. Alikhani, *Sanctioning Iran,* p. 182.

76. The text of the executive order, Number 12957, is available at frwebgate.access.gpo.gov/cgi-bin/getdoc.cgi?dbname=1995_register&docid=fr17mr95-136.pdf.

77. Alikhani, *Sanctioning Iran,* pp. 182–183; Reuel Marc Gerecht (writing as "Edward Shirley"), "Not Fanatics, and Not Friends," *The Atlantic Monthly,* December 1993, p. 3; David E. Sanger, "The Iran Exception; U.S. Will Deal with Other Old Foes but Still Sees Teheran as an Outlaw," *The New York Times,* March 15, 1995; author's interviews with senior administration official, July 1, 2004; Mark R. Parris, July 21, 2004; and Bruce O. Riedel, August 1, 2004.

78. Alikhani, *Sanctioning Iran,* pp. 190–191.

79. The text of the executive order, no. 12959, is available at www.ustreas.gov/offices/enforcement/ofac/legal/eo/12959.pdf. In August 1997, the administration issued yet another executive order (no. 13059, available at frwebgate.access.gpo.gov/cgi-bin/getdoc.cgi?dbname=1997_register&docid=fr21au97-142.pdf), which consolidated and clarified the various other executive orders and eliminated several small loopholes that had been discovered in the original orders.

80. Lane, "Germany's New Ostpolitik," p. 78.

81. Clarke, *Against All Enemies*, pp. 103–104; James Risen, "Gingrich Wants Funds for Covert Action Against Iran," *Los Angeles Times*, December 10, 1995, p. 1; David Rogers, "Gingrich Wants Funds Set Aside for Iran Action," *The Wall Street Journal*, October 27, 1995, p. 1.

82. Author's interview with former senior administration official, July 2004.

83. Author's interviews with former Bush and Clinton administration officials, June–July 2004.

84. Risen, "Gingrich Wants Funds for Covert Action Against Iran," p. 1; author's interviews with former Bush and Clinton administration officials, June–July 2004.

85. Seymour Hersh, "Saddam's Best Friend," *The New Yorker*, April 5, 1999, p. 37.

86. "White House Agrees to Covert-Action Plan for Iran," Agence France-Presse, December 22, 1995, p. 1; Clarke, *Against All Enemies*, pp. 102–103; Jim Lobe, "U.S.-Iran: Republicans Push Confrontation with Iran," Inter Press Service, December 22, 1995, p. 1.

87. Tim Weiner, "U.S. Plan to Change Iran Leaders Is an Open Secret Before It Begins," *The New York Times*, January 26, 1996, p. 1.

88. Ibid.

89. "Iran's Islamic Militants Threaten to Strike US Interests," Agence France-Presse, January 2, 1996, p. 1.

90. "Iran Urges UN to React to US Undercover Action Plan," Agence France-Presse, December 28, 1995, p. 1.

91. Weiner, "U.S. Plan to Change Iran Leaders Is an Open Secret Before It Begins," p. 1.

92. Ibid.

93. Russell Baker, "Button Up Your Overt Coat," *The New York Times*, August 6, 1983, p. 21. Baker naturally meant this as a satiric jibe, directed at the time at President Reagan's effort to topple the Sandinista government in Nicaragua, which had been exposed publicly but which the administration continued to argue for in public. With all due respect to Baker, a wonderful writer and thinker, he was unfair to the Reagan administration. Overtly publicizing a nominally covert operation can still have the desired effect—it is often much harder to do so, because it is a form of attack on the country and often causes the population to rally around the government. However, it can be successful, and arguably was so in the Nicaraguan case: it was not the skill or popularity of the *contras* that the CIA was aiding in Nicaragua that convinced the Sandinistas to hold fair elections—that resulted in their electoral defeat—it was the relentless American pressure and the fact that Washington was willing even to entertain mining Nicaragua's harbors. Now, there is more to the story than just this, including the fact that the Sandinistas thought they would actually win the election, but there is a strong case to be made that they went to the polls to try to get the United States to call off its overt covert action campaign.

94. "Iranian President Says Those Who Live by the Sword, Die by the Sword," Voice of the Islamic Republic of Iran, in Persian, November 5, 1995, in *BBC Summary of World Broadcasts*, November 5, 1995.

95. "Iran's Majlis Speaker Says the West Has Not Expressed Regret over Muslim Deaths," Vision of the Islamic Republic of Iran Network, Tehran, in Persian, November 5, 1995, in *BBC Summary of World Broadcasts*, November 5, 1995.

Chapter 10: To the Brink

1. Meir Litvak, "The Palestine Islamic Jihad: Background Information," February 26, 2003, International Policy Institute for Counter-Terrorism at the Interdisciplinary Center Herzliya, available at www.ict.org, accessed July 20, 2004; also see Katzman, "Terrorism," p. 8. PIJ also has a relationship with Damascus, where it was (and still is) headquartered. The Syrians try to keep con-

trol over PIJ so that it doesn't mount attacks detrimental to Syrian interests, but because Syria's agenda and Iran's often diverge, they are not always able to do so. The February 1996 suicide attacks came literally while Syrian negotiators were meeting with Israelis and making reasonable progress; in other words, there was no reason for Syria to condone the attacks (let alone order them), and every reason for Iran, which opposed Syria's effort to make peace with Israel, to do so. Indeed, the attacks had the effect of terminating that round of Syrian-Israeli negotiations.

2. Barton Gellman, "Israel Finds Challenge Impossible to Ignore; Hezbollah, Election Pressure Push Jerusalem to Send Message to Syria," *The Washington Post,* April 12, 1996, p. A31; Barton Gellman and John Lancaster, "The Undoing of Israel's 'Security Zone,' " *The Washington Post,* April 21, 1996, p. A1; Joel Greenberg, "An Attack on Israel Brings Woe to Peres," *The New York Times,* April 10, 1996; Joel Greenberg, "Iran's Party of God Puts Deep Roots in Lebanon," *The New York Times,* April 12, 1996; "Hezbollah Makes Threat," *The Washington Post,* March 22, 1996, p. A31; "Israeli Soldier Killed in Bombing in Lebanon," *The New York Times,* March 21, 1996; "Israel and Militants Trade Fire in Lebanon," *The New York Times,* April 1, 1996; John Lancaster, "Israel Attacks Hezbollah Sites in Lebanon," *The Washington Post,* April 12, 1996, p. A27; Serge Schmemann, "Israeli Aircraft Strike Guerrillas in Beirut Suburbs," *The New York Times,* April 12, 1996, p. A1; Serge Schmemann, "Giving War a Chance," *The New York Times,* April 14, 1996.

3. Ross, *The Missing Peace,* p. 250. It is highly unlikely that Shara would simply have lied when he assured the United States that Syria would stop the Hizballah attacks. That just isn't Syria's modus operandi. It invariably denies its support to Hizballah, and if it doesn't want to stop a Hizballah operation, it simply responds that it has no ability to prevent the legitimate resistance of the Lebanese people to Zionist occupation. Shara would not have said that Syria would stop the fighting if he had not meant to do so.

4. Byman, *Deadly Connections;* Gary C. Gambill, "The Balance of Terror: War by Other Means in the Contemporary Middle East," *Journal of Palestine Studies* 28, no. 1 (Autumn 1998), p. 63; Gellman and Lancaster, "The Undoing of Israel's 'Security Zone,' " p. A1; Human Rights Watch, "Israel/Lebanon: 'Operation Grapes of Wrath,' " 9, no. 8 (September 1997), pp. 15, 17; Jaber, *Hezbollah,* p. 199; Douglas Jehl, "Lebanon Fighters Gain Stature, but for How Long?" *The New York Times,* April 21, 1996; Schmemann, "Israeli Aircraft Strike Guerrillas in Beirut Suburbs," p. A1; Serge Schmemann, "Israel and Militants Trade Blows as Fighting Spreads in Lebanon," *The New York Times,* April 13, 1996; Serge Schmemann, "Israel and Guerrillas Joined Again in Deadly Dance," *The New York Times,* April 14, 1996.

5. Byman, *Deadly Connections;* Warren Christopher, "Fighting Terrorism: Challenges for Peacemakers," address to the Soref Symposium of the Washington Institute for Near East Policy, May 21, 1996, reprinted in Christopher, *In the Stream of History,* p. 448; Eisenstadt, *Iranian Military Power,* p. 74; Katzman, "Terrorism," p. 7.

6. "Hezbollah Rocket Attacks Slam Northern Israel, Peres under Fire," Agence France-Presse, April 9, 1996; Dianna Cahn, "Israel Shuns Hamas Pitch for Deal to Halt Attacks," Associated Press, March 1, 1996; Barton Gellman, "Bombings Imperil Peres Premiership," *The Washington Post,* March 4, 1996, p. A1; Dan Perry, "Peres Blames Defeat on Colleagues, Terrorists—and Makeup," Associated Press, July 4, 1996.

7. Comment to the author at the time. Quoted with permission of Ambassador Indyk.

8. Gerald Ford might have argued that his was the first. As noted in chapter 5, Iran's determination to drive up the price of oil was a major element of the economic recession of the mid-1970s, which was one cause of his defeat by Jimmy Carter.

9. Bruce Maddy-Weitzman and Joshua Teitelbaum, "Inter-Arab Relations," in Bruce Maddy-Weitzman, ed., *Middle East Contemporary Survey,* vol. 20 (Boulder, Colo.: Westview, 1996), p. 89; Joshua Teitelbaum, "Bahrain," in Maddy-Weitzman, *MECS,* 1996, p. 256.

10. "Bahrain Coup Suspects Say They Trained in Iran," *The New York Times,* June 6, 1996; "Bahrain Holds 44 It Says Are Tied to Pro-Iran Plot," *The New York Times,* June 5, 1996; Clarke, *Against All Enemies,* p. 112; Maddy-Weitzman and Teitelbaum, "Inter-Arab Relations," p. 89; Shawn L.

Twing, "Iran, Bahrain Will Exchange Envoys," *Washington Report on Middle East Affairs,* January–February 1998, p. 38.

11. "Bahrain Coup Suspects Say They Trained in Iran."

12. Teitelbaum, "Bahrain," p. 256.

13. The best unclassified sources at present are Byman, *Deadly Connections;* Clarke, *Against All Enemies,* pp. 112–131; and the Grand Jury indictment against thirteen members of Saudi Hizbollah filed by the U.S. government in Alexandria, Virginia. The indictment in particular provides an excellent overview of the operational elements of the attack and is available at news.findlaw.com/cnn/docs/khobar/khobarindict61901.pdf, accessed July 26, 2004. The 9/11 Commission also found that the evidence of Iran behind the Khobar Towers bombing was "strong." See *Report of the 9/11 Commission: Final Report of the National Commission on Terrorist Attacks Upon the United States* (Washington, D.C.: U.S. Government Printing Office, 2004), p. 60.

14. Clarke, *Against All Enemies,* p. 114; author's interviews with Bruce O. Riedel, August 1, 2004; Mark R. Parris, July 21, 2004; and former senior Clinton administration official, July 2004.

15. On this point, see Ross, *The Missing Peace,* pp. 256–258.

16. Clarke, *Against All Enemies,* p. 118. For the record, I was an NSC staffer at this time but was too junior to be included in this particular meeting.

17. Clarke, *Against All Enemies,* pp. 116–121; author's interviews with Bruce O. Riedel, August 1, 2004; Mark R. Parris, July 21, 2004; and former senior Clinton administration official, July 2004.

18. Ibid.

19. Ibid.

20. Teicher and Teicher, *Twin Pillars to Desert Storm,* pp. 50–51.

21. Cockburn and Cockburn, *Out of the Ashes,* pp. 40–41; Pollack, *The Threatening Storm,* p. 187.

22. Clarke tells a similar version; see Clarke, *Against All Enemies,* pp. 116–121.

23. Clarke, *Against All Enemies,* pp. 116–121; author's interviews with Bruce O. Riedel, August 1, 2004; Mark R. Parris, July 21, 2004; and former senior Clinton administration official, July 2004. Clarke has a slightly different version of events, probably owing to our different positions at the NSC: at the time he was already a senior counterterrorism official, while I was still a junior Middle East staffer.

24. Clarke, *Against All Enemies,* p. 117.

25. Pollack, *The Threatening Storm,* pp. 82–84.

26. "Iran Fails to Withdraw Death Sentence or Promise Rushdie's Safety," Associated Press, June 22, 1995, p. 1; Michael Sheridan, "Norway Steps Up Rushdie Campaign," *The Independent,* July 4, 1995, p. 1.

27. "Iran Rejects as 'Baseless' German Murder Probe," Agence France-Presse, December 12, 1995, p. 1.

28. "France Mulling New Moves Against Iran," United Press International, March 7, 1996, p. 1; Daniel Williams, "EU Ministers Urge Iran to Condemn Terrorism," *The Washington Post,* March 11, 1996, p. 1.

29. Peter Bild, "Germany Investigating Iranian Minister," United Press International, December 10, 1995, p. 1.

30. Christopher, "Fighting Terrorism," p. 449; Clarke, *Against All Enemies,* p. 111; Ely Karmon, "Why Tehran Starts and Stops Terrorism," *Middle East Quarterly* 5, no. 4 (December 1998); "Iran 'Pickle' Cargo Had Mortar Launcher," United Press International, May 2, 1996.

31. The text of the bill is available in a number of locations on the Web. See, e.g., www.fas.org/irp/congress/1996_cr/h960618b.htm, accessed July 22, 2004.

32. Alikhani, *Sanctioning Iran,* pp. 289–296.

33. Clinton's critics often charge that he signed ILSA purely for political reasons. However, this does not square with the timing. Although the State Department bureaucracy remained adamantly opposed, the White House began to signal a willingness to accept the bill in November 1995—not coincidentally, right after Rabin's assassination and well before it was clear that the bill would pass with such overwhelming margins. In the end, the White House worked with D'Amato to re-

structure the bill (and even tone it down somewhat) so that they could more enthusiastically support it. Moreover, in 1997, Congress also overwhelmingly passed the Iran Missile Proliferation Sanctions Act by margins of 90–4 and 392–22, but Clinton vetoed that bill on policy grounds. That bill also had more than adequate support to override the president's veto, at least in theory, but the White House chose to veto it anyway. See, e.g., Alikhani, *Sanctioning Iran,* pp. 289–308, 332–333.

34. Alikhani, *Sanctioning Iran,* pp. 320–328; Jahangir Amuzegar, "Adjusting to Sanctions," *Foreign Affairs* 76, no. 3 (May–June 1997); Kenneth Katzman, "The Iran-Libya Sanctions Act (ILSA)," Congressional Research Service, CRS Report for Congress, July 31, 2003.

35. "Statement of Alan Larson, Assistant Secretary, Bureau of Economic and Business Affairs, Department of State" and "Statement of David Welch, Acting Assistant Secretary, Bureau of Near East Affairs, Department of State" in "Iran-Libya Sanctions Act—One Year Later," Hearing Before the Committee on International Relations, United States House of Representatives, 105th Congress, 1st Session, July 23, 1997, pp. 9–15.

36. Katzman, "The Iran-Libya Sanctions Act," pp. 5–6.

37. See, for instance, Ambrose Evans-Pritchard, "U.S. Hawks Urge Massive Strike on Iran: Clinton Advised to End Gulf Threat by Friendship or by Force," *The Sunday Telegraph* via *The Ottawa Citizen,* April 20, 1997, p. A5; Michael S. Lelyveld, "Ex-Presidential Advisers Press for Limited Business with Iran," *Journal of Commerce,* April 21, 1997, p. 1A; Thomas W. Lippman and Bradley Graham, "U.S. Mulls Possible Response to Iran in Saudi Bombing," *The Washington Post,* December 22, 1996, p. A30; Amos Perlmutter, "Tracing the Terror Trail Back to Iran," *The Washington Times,* June 23, 1997, p. A13; Eric Rosenberg, "Options Against Iran Readied for Clinton," *The Times Union* (Albany, N.Y.), April 27, 1997, p. F1; Michael E. Ruane, "Retaliations for Terrorism: Do They Deter or Prompt Attacks?," *The Philadelphia Inquirer,* August 8, 1996, p. A14; "Tensions Rise as Washington and Tehran Trade Accusations," Agence France-Presse, August 4, 1996.

38. See, for instance, Lippman and Graham, "U.S. Mulls Possible Response to Iran in Saudi Bombing," p. A30; Rosenberg, "Options Against Iran Readied for Clinton," p. F1.

39. Amuzegar, "Adjusting to Sanctions," pp. 31–33; Amuzegar, "Iran's Economy and the U.S. Sanctions," pp. 185–193; Eisenstadt, *Iranian Military Power,* pp. 93–94; Sick, "Rethinking Dual Containment," pp. 12–17.

40. Amuzegar, "Iran's Economy and the U.S. Sanctions," pp. 192–193.

41. Ibid.

42. "Iran Warns Germany over Kurdish Murder Trial," Agence France-Presse, August 29, 1996, p.1.

43. "Iranian Reassures Germans: No Death Threats Against Prosecutors," Agence France-Presse, December 26, 1996, p. 1.

44. Tehran IRNA, "Interior Minister: Mykonos Trial 'A Zionist Plot,' " April 16, 1997, available at www.salamiran.org/Media/IRNA/970416.html#HLN10, accessed July 27, 2004.

45. Tehran IRNA, "Official Warns of German Coordination with U.S. Designs Against Iran," April 16, 1997, available at www.salamiran.org/Media/IRNA/970416.html#HLN10, accessed July 27, 2004.

46. Dan Eldar, "Western Europe, Russia and the Middle East," in Bruce Maddy-Weitzman, ed., *Middle East Contemporary Survey,* vol. 21 (Boulder, Colo.: Westview, 1997), p. 49.

47. Ibid., pp. 49–51.

48. The broad contours of this operation were revealed in Clarke, *Against All Enemies,* pp. 120–121; and Barbara Slavin, "Officials 'Outed' Iran's Spies in 1997," *USA Today,* March 29, 2004. The details remain classified.

49. Sick, "Iran's Foreign Policy," p. 357; Teitelbaum, "Saudi Arabia," pp. 618–619; Esther Webman, "The Dynamics of Retreat and Change in Political Islam," in Bruce Maddy-Weitzman, ed., *Middle East Contemporary Survey,* vol. 21 (Boulder, Colo.: Westview, 1997), pp. 160–161.

50. On the containment of Iraq and what it did and did not accomplish, see Pollack, *The Threatening Storm,* pp. 74–108, 211–242; Kenneth M. Pollack, "Spies, Lies, and Weapons: What Went Wrong?" *The Atlantic Monthly* 293, no. 1 (January–February 2004). The fact that containment of

Iraq had succeeded in convincing Saddam to eradicate most of his remaining WMD programs at some point after 1996 (as we learned after Operation Iraqi Freedom) does not mitigate the fact that the containment of Iraq was failing badly because more and more countries, led by the French and the Russians, were violating the UNSC resolutions themselves and refusing to enforce those that Iraq and others violated. They had no interest in strengthening the sanctions even after the United States deployed 250,000 troops to the region in late 2002. France, Russia, and Germany did suddenly (and undoubtedly temporarily) reverse themselves partially and show interest in a revived inspection regime at that point. However, they still refused to do anything to make that interest permanent or to address the erosion of the sanctions and restore the ability to use limited military operations to coerce Iraqi compliance with the UN resolutions, which had always been the most important aspects of the containment of Iraq.

51. I argued this at the time. See Kenneth M. Pollack, "What if Iran Was Behind al-Khobar? Planning for a US Response," Policy Watch no. 243 (Washington, D.C.: Washington Institute for Near East Policy, April 16, 1997).

52. See chapter 9, note 28, above.

53. For a powerful case that the ash-Shifa plant was a valid target, see Benjamin and Simon, *The Age of Sacred Terror,* pp. 353–365.

Chapter 11: The Ecstasy and the Agony

1. Anoushirivan Ehteshami, *After Khomeini: The Iranian Second Republic* (London: Routledge, 1995), p. 117.

2. Amuzegar, "Iran's Economy and the U.S. Sanctions," pp. 188–190; Jahangir Amuzegar, "Khatami and the Iranian Economy at Mid-Term," *The Middle East Journal* 53, no. 4 (Autumn 1999).

3. Amuzegar, "Iran's Economy and the U.S. Sanctions," pp. 191–192.

4. Kanovsky, "Iran's Sick Economy: Prospects for Change Under Khatami," in Patrick Clawson, ed., *Iran Under Khatami* (Washington, D.C.: Washington Institute for Near East Policy, 1998), p. 59; Neil MacFarquhar, "Backlash of Intolerance Stirring Fear in Iran," *The New York Times,* September 20, 1996.

5. Fred S. Eldin, "On the Road: Coping in Islamic Iran," *Middle East Quarterly,* June 1997.

6. Kanovsky, "Iran's Sick Economy," pp. 57–58.

7. Central Intelligence Agency, *World Factbook 1997* (Washington, D.C.: U.S. Government Printing Office, 1997).

8. Kanovsky, "Iran's Sick Economy," pp. 60–62. There are two excellent works on the *bonyad*s in English at present: Jerrold Green, "Parastatal Economic Organizations and Stability in Iran: The Role of the Bonyads," draft manuscript, RAND, February 1999; and Maloney, "Agents or Obstacles?," pp. 145–176.

9. Eldin, "On the Road."

10. Amuzegar, "Iran's Economy and the U.S. Sanctions," pp. 190–192; Amuzegar, "Khatami and the Iranian Economy at Mid-Term"; Menashri, *MECS,* 1997, p. 355.

11. Amuzegar, "Iran's Economy and the U.S. Sanctions," pp. 189–190.

12. *Economist* Intelligence Unit, "Iran," May 7, 1997; "Iran Extends Voting Hours for Presidential Elections," CNN.com, available at www.cnn.com/WORLD/9705/23/iran.elex.day.wrap/, accessed July 30, 2004.

13. U.S. Bureau of the Census, *Current Population Reports,* Series P25-1130, "Population Projections of the United States by Age, Sex, Race, and Hispanic Origin: 1995 to 2050," Population Division, U.S. Bureau of the Census.

14. On the importance of Iranian youth to the reform movement, see Gasiorowski, "The Power Struggle in Iran," p. 23.

15. MacFarquhar, "Backlash of Intolerance Stirring Fear in Iran."

16. For those looking for a better sense of how the changes in Iranian society led to broad disenchantment with the behavioral codes of the old regime and helped bring Khatami to power, four superb

recent books by journalists well acquainted with Iran stand out as eloquent and engaging depictions of this process: Geneive Abdo and Jonathan Lyons, *Answering Only to God: Faith and Freedom in Twenty-first-Century Iran* (New York: Henry Holt, 2003); Molavi, *Persian Pilgrimages;* Sciolino, *Persian Mirrors;* Wright, *The Last Great Revolution.*

17. John Daniszewski, "Landslide Election in Iran; A Mullah with Open Mind, Khatami Won by Dint of Character," *Los Angeles Times,* May 25, 1997, p. A10; Stephen Kinzer, "Voice for Change Makes Iran Vote a Real Race," *The New York Times,* May 23, 1997, p. A1.

18. Wright, *The Last Great Revolution,* p. 25.

19. Daniel, *The History of Iran,* pp. 237–238; Keddie, *Modern Iran,* p. 269; Kinzer, "Voice for Change Makes Iran Vote a Real Race," p. A1; Wright, *The Last Great Revolution,* pp. 25–26.

20. Barbara Demick, "Moderate Wins Iranian Presidency," *The Philadelphia Inquirer,* May 25, 1997, p. A1.

21. Brumberg, *Reinventing Khomeini,* pp. 186–190; Gasiorowski, "The Power Struggle in Iran," pp. 22–24.

22. Anwar Faruqi, "Thousands Rally for Iranian Candidate in Test for Ruling Clergy," Associated Press, May 21, 1997.

23. Mehrdad Balali, "Iranian Voters Clamor for Change," Agence France-Presse, May 23, 1997.

24. Ibid.

25. Ibid.

26. "Khatami Receives Hero's Welcome at Polling Station," Agence France-Presse, May 23, 1997.

27. Balali, "Iranian Voters Clamor for Change."

28. For excellent scholarly work on the shifting factional struggles in Iran, see Brumberg, *Reinventing Khomeini,* pp. 152–229; Gasiorowski, "The Power Struggle in Iran," pp. 24–28; Moslem, *Factional Politics in Post-Khomeini Iran,* pp. 186–251.

29. Daniel, *The History of Iran,* pp. 237–238; Keddie, *Modern Iran,* p. 269; Wright, *The Last Great Revolution,* pp. 25–26.

30. Gasiorowski, "The Power Struggle in Iran," p. 23.

31. "Presidential Candidate Khatami on Law and Order, Economy, Foreign Policy," Vision of the Islamic Republic of Iran Network 1, Tehran, in Persian, May 10, 1997, in *BBC Summary of World Broadcasts,* May 13, 1997.

32. Martin Regg Cohn, "Iran Election Mixes Prayers and Platitudes; Religion Dominates the Race Between 'Reform and Establishment' Parties," *The Toronto Star,* May 17, 1997, p. D5.

33. Ibid.; Demick, "Moderate Wins Iranian Presidency," p. A1; Kinzer, "Voice for Change Makes Iran Vote a Real Race," p. A1.

34. "Cleric Declared Iran's President in Election," Associated Press, May 25, 1997; Daniel, *The History of Iran,* p. 238; Demick, "Moderate Wins Iranian Presidency," p. A1.

35. Stephen Kinzer, "Moderate Leader Is Elected in Iran by a Wide Margin," *The New York Times,* May 25, 1997; Sciolino, *Persian Mirrors,* p. 77.

36. Ibid.

37. Institute for Democracy and Electoral Assistance, "Voter Turnout Since 1945: Islamic Republic of Iran," available on the web at www.idea.int/vt/country_view.cfm, accessed July 30, 2004; Gasiorowski, "The Power Struggle in Iran," p. 24; Kinzer, "Moderate Leader Is Elected in Iran by a Wide Margin"; Menashri, *MECS,* 1997, p. 344.

38. Quoted in Menashri, *MECS,* 1997, p. 344.

39. Daniel, *The History of Iran,* p. 238; Fairbanks, "A New Era for Iran?," p. 54; Keddie, *Modern Iran,* p. 269.

40. Steven Erlanger, "Iran Vote May Bring Pressure for a Change in U.S. Policy," *The New York Times,* May 26, 1997; Kinzer, "Moderate Leader Is Elected in Iran by a Wide Margin"; Alison Mitchell, "Clinton Sees Hope in the Election of Moderate as President of Iran," *The New York Times,* May 30, 1997.

41. Erlanger, "Iran Vote May Bring Pressure for a Change in U.S. Policy"; Mitchell, "Clinton Sees Hope in the Election of Moderate as President of Iran."

42. Fairbanks, "A New Era for Iran?," pp. 52–53; Gasiorowski, "The Power Struggle in Iran," p. 28; Christopher Hines, "Iran Elects New Moderate President in Shock to Conservatives," Agence France-Presse, May 24, 1997; Menashri, *MECS*, 1997, pp. 355–358.

43. Daniel, *The History of Iran*, pp. 239–240; Menashri, *MECS*, 1997, pp. 350–352, 56–57; "Political Skirmishing in Tehran," *The New York Times*, August 16, 1997; Afshin Valinejad, "Iranian Parliament Approves Moderate President's Cabinet Nominees," Associated Press, August 20, 1997.

44. Menashri, *MECS*, 1997, p. 352.

45. Dorranie Kianouche, "Iranian Factions Squabble over Khatami's New Cabinet," Agence France-Presse, August 9, 1997.

46. Buchta, *Who Rules Iran?*, p. 125.

47. On the changes to Iran's security services, see Kenneth M. Pollack, "Iran: Shaking Up the High Command," Policy Watch No. 269, Washington Institute for Near East Policy, October 1, 1997. On the battles over the Intelligence Ministry, see also Kianouche, "Iranian Factions Squabble over Khatami's New Cabinet."

48. "Khatami Says USA Holds Key to Future Relations with Iran," Vision of the Islamic Republic of Iran Network 1, Tehran, in Persian, May 27, 1997, *BBC Summary of World Broadcasts*, May 29, 1997.

49. Menashri, *MECS*, 1997, p. 362.

50. "Transcript of Interview with Iranian President Mohammad Khatami," CNN.com, January 7, 1998. The full text of the interview is available at www.cnn.com/WORLD/9801/07/iran/interview.html, accessed July 30, 2004.

51. Menashri, *MECS*, 1997, p. 366.

52. For a concurring view, see Gasiorowski, "The Power Struggle in Iran," p. 29.

53. Menashri, *MECS*, 1997, p. 363.

54. Ibid., pp. 363–364.

55. Ibid.

56. "Transcript of Interview with Iranian President Mohammad Khatami."

57. See "Israeli Paper Publishes Interview with Vice-President Ebtekar," *BBC Summary of World Broadcasts*, February 3, 1998.

58. Elaine Sciolino, "Pleased Yet Wary, U.S. Offers Gestures of Support for Iran," *The New York Times*, March 26, 1998, p. A1.

59. Katzman, "Iran," p. 20; Robin Wright, "In Shift, U.S. Makes Quiet Overtures to Iran Following Election Upset," *Los Angeles Times*, July 9, 1997; author's interviews with Bruce O. Riedel, August 1, 2004, and former senior Clinton administration officials, June and July 2004.

60. Madeleine Albright, *Madam Secretary* (New York: Miramax Books, 2003), p. 320; author's interviews with Bruce O. Riedel, August 1, 2004, and former senior Clinton administration officials, June and July 2004.

61. Sciolino, "Pleased Yet Wary, U.S. Offers Gestures of Support for Iran," p. A1.

62. Norman Kempster, "U.S. Designates 30 Groups as Terrorists," *Los Angeles Times*, October 9, 1997, p. A16.

63. Daniel, *The History of Iran*, p. 245; Katzman, "Iran," p. 21; United States Department of State, "Mujahidin-e Khalq," *Patterns of Global Terrorism, 2003*, available at www.state.gov/s/ct/rls/pgtrpt/2003/c12108.htm, accessed July 23, 2004.

64. "Reps. Support Iran Opposition Group," Associated Press, October 28, 1997.

65. Kempster, "U.S. Designates 30 Groups as Terrorists," p. A16.

66. Kenneth J. Cooper, "U.S., Iranian Wrestlers Break Diplomatic Ground in Tourney," *The Washington Post*, February 20, 1998, p. A2.

67. Of course, these efforts were not without their problems. In particular, because the U.S. government had spent nearly two decades in a state of aggressive confrontation with Iran, a great many laws and regulations were on the books mandating certain actions against Iran and prohibiting others. One of these was that Iranians—alone among all of the people of the world, including Iraqis and North Koreans—were uniformly fingerprinted when they came to America, no matter how old or how young. The FBI had started the practice in the hope that the finger-

prints collected would create a database that could be consulted after terrorist attacks in hope of finding a match and demonstrating Iranian complicity. Over the years, the FBI had built up a database of hundreds of thousands of Iranian fingerprints but had never been able to find a match at any terrorism attack site. The Iranians complained loudly about this practice—and the fact that they were the only nationality so treated. Another gesture we tried to make was to have the fingerprinting requirement lifted or simply narrowed to people of a certain age (i.e., exempting children or the very old). The FBI, under Louis Freeh, who had a tempestuous relationship with the Clinton administration, refused, and because of the president's political problems with the Congress, the White House was reluctant to force him to do so. At times, the foreign policy team did try to have certain important Iranian groups exempted from the fingerprinting requirement. On one occasion, National Security Advisor Sandy Berger and Secretary Albright raised the matter with Attorney General Janet Reno, who agreed that the Iranian delegation was both so important and so innocuous that the fingerprinting requirement should be waived for them. But somewhere along the way, that message was discarded: when the group arrived at Kennedy Airport in New York, they were all duly fingerprinted, much to their anger and our embarrassment.

68. Barbara Crossette, "Albright, in Overture to Iran, Seeks a 'Road Map' to Amity," *The New York Times,* June 18, 1998. See also Albright, *Madam Secretary,* p. 320; Katzman, "Iran," p. 21.

69. Albright, *Madam Secretary,* pp. 322–323; Laura Myers, "Albright, Minister Meet," Associated Press, September 21, 1998.

70. Katzman, "Iran," p. 21; Steven Mufson and Thomas W. Lippman, "State Dept. Slightly Softens View of Iran," *The Washington Post,* May 1, 1999, p. A10.

71. The White House, Office of the Press Secretary, "Remarks at Millennium Evening: The Perils of Indifference: Lessons Learned from a Violent Century," released April 12, 1999. The full text is available at clinton6.nara.gov/1999/04/1999-04-12-remarks-at-millennium-lecture.html, accessed August 1, 2004.

72. Katzman, "Iran," p. 22.

73. Ibid., p. 23; John Lancaster, "Boeing Can Provide Parts to Iran Airline," *The Washington Post,* December 4, 1999, p. A16.

74. "Clinton Reaches Out to Iran in 1996 Bomb Attack," Reuters, September 29, 1999; Katzman, "Iran," p. 22; John Lancaster and Robert Suro, "Clinton Reaches Out to Iran," *The Washington Post,* September 29, 1999, p. A2; author's interviews with Bruce O. Riedel, August 1, 2004, and senior former Clinton administration officials, June and July 2004.

75. Ibid.

76. Sherine Bahaa, "Attack on Khatami," *Al-Ahram Weekly On-line,* July 30–August 5, 1998, available at weekly.ahram.org.eg/1998/388/re5.htm, accessed August 1, 2004, p. 1; Brumberg, *Reinventing Khomeini,* p. 241; Buchta, *Who Rules Iran?,* pp. 140–141; Daniel, *The History of Iran,* pp. 241–242; Gasiorowski, "The Power Struggle in Iran," pp. 28–29; Moslem, *Factional Politics in Post-Khomeini Iran,* pp. 259–260.

77. Moslem, *Factional Politics in Post-Khomeini Iran,* p. 262.

78. Bahaa, "Attack on Khatami," pp. 1–2; Brumberg, *Reinventing Khomeini,* p. 241; Buchta, *Who Rules Iran?,* p. 143; Daniel, *The History of Iran,* pp. 241–242; Gasiorowski, "The Power Struggle in Iran," p. 30; "Iran's Guards Chief Blasts Liberalization, Critics," Reuters, April 29, 1998; Douglas Jehl, "Iran Closes a Leading Newspaper and Arrests Top Editors," *The New York Times,* September 18, 1998; Moslem, *Factional Politics in Post-Khomeini Iran,* pp. 262–263.

79. Buchta, *Who Rules Iran?,* pp. 142–143; Daniel, *The History of Iran,* p. 244; Gasiorowski, "The Power Struggle in Iran," p. 30; Keddie, *Modern Iran,* p. 275.

80. Bahaa, "Attack on Khatami," pp. 1–2; Buchta, *Who Rules Iran?,* pp. 140–141; Daniel, *The History of Iran,* p. 244; Keddie, *Modern Iran,* p. 274; Moslem, *Factional Politics in Post-Khomeini Iran,* pp. 260–261.

81. Buchta, *Who Rules Iran?,* p. 144; Gasiorowski, "The Power Struggle in Iran," p. 30.

82. Moslem, *Factional Politics in Post-Khomeini Iran,* p. 262.

83. Gasiorowski, "The Power Struggle in Iran," p. 30; Keddie, *Modern Iran,* p. 275.

84. Buchta, *Who Rules Iran?*, pp. 144–145.
85. Ibid., pp. 152–153.
86. Ibid., pp. 142–143.
87. Moslem, *Factional Politics in Post-Khomeini Iran*, pp. 263–264.
88. Buchta, *Who Rules Iran?*, pp. 146–148; Jehl, "Iran Closes a Leading Newspaper and Arrests Top Editors."
89. Jehl, "Iran Closes a Leading Newspaper and Arrests Top Editors."
90. For a description of many of these attacks, see Buchta, *Who Rules Iran?*, pp. 176–178.
91. Buchta, *Who Rules Iran?*, pp. 156–159, 176; Keddie, *Modern Iran*, p. 275; Moslem, *Factional Politics in Post-Khomeini Iran*, p. 264.
92. Buchta, *Who Rules Iran?*, pp. 156–169; Daniel, *The History of Iran*, pp. 242–243; Gasiorowski, "The Power Struggle in Iran," p. 31; Moslem, *Factional Politics in Post-Khomeini Iran*, pp. 264–265.
93. Buchta, *Who Rules Iran?*, pp. 159–169; Gasiorowski, "The Power Struggle in Iran," p. 31.
94. Buchta, *Who Rules Iran?*, pp. 168–170; Daniel, *The History of Iran*, p. 244.
95. "By Popular Demand: Iranian Elections, 1997–2001," PBS *Frontline:* "Terror and Tehran," available at www.pbs.org/wgbh/pages/frontline/shows/tehran/inside/elections.html, accessed July 30, 2004; Buchta, *Who Rules Iran?*, pp. 178–182; Daniel, *The History of Iran*, p. 241; Keddie, *Modern Iran*, p. 276.
96. Brumberg, *Reinventing Khomeini*, p. 243; Daniel, *The History of Iran*, p. 255; Gasiorowski, "The Power Struggle in Iran," p. 31.
97. Abdo, "Days of Rage in Tehran," p. 78; Amuzegar, "Iran's Future," p. 86; Brumberg, *Reinventing Khomeini*, p. 243; Buchta, *Who Rules Iran?*, pp. 187–188; Daniel, *The History of Iran*, pp. 245–247; Gasiorowski, "The Power Struggle in Iran," p. 32; Keddie, *Modern Iran*, pp. 276–277.
98. Amuzegar, "Iran's Future," pp. 90–91.
99. Abdo, "Days of Rage in Tehran," pp. 78–84; Amuzegar, "Iran's Future," pp. 87–89; Brumberg, *Reinventing Khomeini*, p. 243; Buchta, *Who Rules Iran?*, p. 188.
100. Buchta, *Who Rules Iran?*, pp. 189–190.
101. Amuzegar, "Iran's Future," pp. 90–91, 96–97; Brumberg, *Reinventing Khomeini*, pp. 243–244; Buchta, *Who Rules Iran?*, pp. 189–190; Gasiorowski, "The Power Struggle in Iran," p. 32; Keddie, *Modern Iran*, pp. 276–277.
102. Amuzegar, "Iran's Future," pp. 90–91, 96–97; Brumberg, *Reinventing Khomeini*, pp. 243–244; Daniel, *The History of Iran*, pp. 245–247; Gasiorowski, "The Power Struggle in Iran," p. 32; Keddie, *Modern Iran*, pp. 276–277.
103. Buchta, *Who Rules Iran?*, p. 189.
104. Amuzegar, "Iran's Future," pp. 92–93; Daniel, *The History of Iran*, pp. 245–247; Gasiorowski, "The Power Struggle in Iran," p. 32; Keddie, *Modern Iran*, pp. 276–277.
105. Amuzegar, "Iran's Future," p. 96.
106. Ibid., pp. 92–93; Gasiorowski, "The Power Struggle in Iran," p. 32.
107. Amuzegar, "Iran's Future," p. 96.
108. Buchta, *Who Rules Iran?*, p. 190.
109. John F. Burns, "Top Leader in Iran Tries to Calm Rage of Its Hard-Liners," *The New York Times*, October 2, 1999; Gasiorowski, "The Power Struggle in Iran," p. 32.
110. Brumberg, *Reinventing Khomeini*, pp. 244–245; Buchta, *Who Rules Iran?*, p. 194; Gasiorowski, "The Power Struggle in Iran," p. 33.
111. Brumberg, *Reinventing Khomeini*, pp. 244–245, 251–252; Gasiorowski, "The Power Struggle in Iran," pp. 33–34; Suzanne Maloney, "Elections in Iran: A New Majlis and a Mandate for Reform," *Middle East Policy* 7, no. 3 (June 2000), pp. 59–66.
112. Afshin Valinejad, "Iran Reform Leader Shot in Tehran," Associated Press, March 13, 2000.
113. See also Puneet Talwar, "Iran in the Balance," *Foreign Affairs* 80, no. 4 (July–August 2001). Talwar, a highly regarded staffer on the Senate Foreign Relations Committee, was on rotation as a member of the State Department's Policy Planning Staff for the last year of the Clinton administration.

114. In November 1999, the United States renewed the sanctions on Iran, as it was required to do by law every six months, and reported publicly to the Congress that it was doing so. For some reason, this was picked up in Tehran and by a number of ignorant academics in the United States and Europe and taken as a reversal of the Iran initiative and a slap at Khatami. It was nothing of the sort. The executive branch is required by law to renew sanctions enacted under the International Emergency Economic Powers Act every six months or else the sanctions lapse. We had renewed the sanctions every May and November since they were first enacted. Failing to renew the sanctions would have been the same as lifting them, and we had made it clear to the Iranians—and the rest of the world—that we would lift the sanctions only if Iran demonstrated that it had given up its support for terrorism, abandoned its pursuit of nuclear weapons, and stopped opposing the Middle East peace process. Since, despite whatever nice things Khatami had said and done since coming to office, he had clearly not done any of those things, it was idiotic to suggest that the United States should have lifted sanctions in November 1999, let alone that renewing them as we did every six months amounted to some kind of change in our policy.

115. In fact, the idea had been around among Iran experts inside the government and out for some time. In September 1999, Foreign Minister Kharrazi spoke to a number of people on the margins of the U.N. General Assembly, including several Americans. He was asked how Iran would respond if the United States dropped sanctions on carpets and foodstuffs, and his carefully thought out answer was that Iran would "respond positively." This helped determine what the grand gesture in the Albright speech would be. The story is also recounted in Talwar, "Iran in the Balance," op. cit.

116. Kaveh Basmenji, "Beating Swords into Pistachios," *Middle East Times,* March 20, 2000; Ali Akbar Dareini, "Iran Lawmaker Likes U.S. Gesture," Associated Press, March 27, 2000; Talwar, "Iran in the Balance."

117. Gasiorowski, "The Power Struggle in Iran," pp. 33–35.

118. Ibid., pp. 34–36.

119. See also Albright, *Madam Secretary,* p. 325.

120. Secretary Albright notes the same in her memoirs. (Ibid., p. 324.)

121. Barbara Slavin, "Q&A with Foreign Minister Kamal Kharrazi," *USA Today,* September 18, 2002.

Chapter 12: Coming Full Circle

1. John Ward Anderson, "Iran Throwing Off Its Isolation; U.S. Remains Dubious After Decades of Mutual Distrust," *The Washington Post,* March 31, 2001, p. A18.

2. "Confirmation Hearings of General Colin Powell to Be Secretary of State," Senate Foreign Relations Committee, January 17, 2001.

3. Rice, "Campaign 2000: Promoting the National Interest."

4. I purposely refrain from using the term "neoconservatives" because I think at this point that it has come to mean a certain set of ideas that are not actually consistent across the group of people to whom it is applied. It is painting with too broad a brush and therefore blurring what are often important distinctions in the views of different people within this camp. There are a lot of different neocons with a wide range of views. In many ways, neoconservatism is more of a paradigm than a catechism, and so adherents to it often vary widely in what they believe on any specific issue.

5. Clarke, *Against All Enemies,* pp. 30–35; Nicholas Lemann, "The Iraq Factor: Will the New Bush Team's Old Memories Shape Its Foreign Policy?" *The New Yorker,* January 22, 2001; Nicholas Lemann, "The Next World Order," *The New Yorker,* April 1, 2002; Nicholas Lemann, "The War on What? The White House and the Debate About Whom to Fight Next," *The New Yorker,* September 9, 2002; Nicholas Lemann, "Real Reasons," *The New Yorker,* September 22, 2003; James Mann, *The Rise of the Vulcans* (New York: Penguin, 2004); Pollack, *The Threatening Storm,* pp. 105–108; Ron Suskind, *The Price of Loyalty: George W. Bush, the White House, and the Education of Paul O'Neill* (New York: Simon & Schuster, 2004); Bob Woodward, *Plan of Attack* (New York: Simon & Schuster, 2004), pp. 9–23.

6. Christophe de Roquefeuil, "Divided US Policymakers Await Outcome of Iranian Election," Agence France-Presse, June 8, 2001; Alison Mitchell, "Senate Extends Sanctions on Libya and Iran," *The New York Times,* July 26, 2001.

7. Author's interviews with Richard N. Haass, July 23, 2004; Bruce O. Riedel, August 1, 2004; and senior administration official, July 28, 2004.

8. Bellaigue, "Iran's Last Chance for Reform," pp. 71–72; "By Popular Demand: Iranian Elections, 1997–2001"; Cameron W. Barr, "In Iran, Hopes Rise Among the Reformers," *The Christian Science Monitor,* June 11, 2001.

9. United States Department of State, *Patterns of Global Terrorism, 2001.*

10. The text of the president's speech can be found at www.cnn.com/2001/US/09/20/gen.bush. transcript/, accessed August 1, 2004.

11. Alan Sipress and Steven Mufson, "U.S. Explores Recruiting Iran into New Coalition," *The Washington Post,* September 25, 2001, p. A1; author's interviews with former Bush administration officials, July 10 and July 23, 2004, and with senior administration officials, July 1, July 28, and August 2, 2004.

12. "Excerpt: U.S., Iran Discussing Afghanistan, Iraq, Other Issues of Mutual Interest," U.S. Department of State, Press Release, May 13, 2003; Alan Sipress, "Bush's Speech Shuts Door on Tenuous Opening to Iran," *The Washington Post,* February 4, 2002, p. A10; Barbara Slavin, "Iran, U.S. Holding Talks in Geneva," *USA Today,* May 11, 2003; author's interviews with former Bush administration officials, July 10 and July 23, 2004, and with senior administration officials, July 1, July 28, and August 2, 2004.

13. Ali Akbar Dareini, "U.S. Food Aid for Afghanistan to Be Delivered Through Iran," Associated Press, October 18, 2001; Steven Mufson and Marc Kaufman, "Longtime Foes U.S., Iran Explore Improved Relations," *The Washington Post,* October 29, 2001, p. A9; Sipress, "Bush's Speech Shuts Door on Tenuous Opening to Iran," p. A10; author's interviews with former Bush administration officials, July 10 and July 23, 2004, and with senior administration officials, July 1, July 28, and August 2, 2004.

14. Author's interview with senior administration official, July 28, 2004.

15. "Excerpt: U.S., Iran Discussing Afghanistan, Iraq, Other Issues of Mutual Interest"; Sipress, "Bush's Speech Shuts Door on Tenuous Opening to Iran," p. A10; author's interviews with former Bush administration officials, July 10 and July 23, 2004, and with senior administration officials, July 28 and August 2, 2004.

16. "Chronology: U.S.-Iran Relations, 1906–2002," PBS *Frontline:* "Terror and Tehran," available at www.pbs.org/wgbh/pages/frontline/shows/tehran/etc/cron.html, accessed August 1, 2004.

17. Mufson and Kaufman, "Longtime Foes U.S., Iran Explore Improved Relations," p. A9.

18. Ibid.; Sipress, "Bush's Speech Shuts Door on Tenuous Opening to Iran," p. A10; Slavin, "Iran, U.S. Holding Talks in Geneva."

19. Sally Buzbee, "A Warning for Iran: Bush Says Don't Help al-Qaida, Don't Interfere in Afghanistan," Associated Press, January 10, 2002; Kathy Gannon, "U.S. Fears Iranian Interference in Afghanistan; Aid Agencies Fan Out to Starving Afghans," Associated Press, January 18, 2002; Charles J. Hanley, "American Detention of Iranian General, Others May Set Off Violence, Afghan Says," Associated Press, March 9, 2002; Anthony Shadid and John Donnelly, "Fighting Terror: The Struggle for Influence; Iranian Arms, Goods Flood Afghan Region," *The Boston Globe,* January 25, 2002; Sipress, "Bush's Speech Shuts Door on Tenuous Opening to Iran," p. A10; Amy Waldman, "After Mixup, Americans Free 12 Afghans Suspected of Being Iranian Agents," *The New York Times,* March 21, 2002; author's interviews with former Bush administration officials, July 10 and July 23, 2004, and with senior administration officials, July 28 and August 2, 2004.

20. Amy Waldman, "12 Iranians Turned Over to Americans," *The New York Times,* March 9, 2002; author's interviews with former Bush administration officials, July 10 and July 23, 2004, and with senior administration official, July 28, 2004.

21. Author's interview with Bruce O. Riedel, August 1, 2004.

22. Sipress, "Bush's Speech Shuts Door on Tenuous Opening to Iran," p. A10; author's interviews

with former Bush administration officials, July 10 and July 23, 2004, and with senior administration officials, July 28 and August 1, 2004.

23. Sipress, "Bush's Speech Shuts Door on Tenuous Opening to Iran," p. A10; author's interviews with Richard N. Haass, July 23, 2004; former Bush administration officials, July 10 and July 23, 2004; and senior administration officials, July 28 and August 1, 2004.

24. James Bennet, "Seized Arms Would Have Vastly Extended Arafat Arsenal," *The New York Times,* January 12, 2002, p. A5; Sipress, "Bush's Speech Shuts Door on Tenuous Opening to Iran," p. A10; Steve Weizman, "Israelis Say Palestinians Forming Strategic Alliance with Iran, Palestinians Deny Allegation," Associated Press, January 14, 2002.

25. Nicholas Blanford, "Palestinian Ties to Iran, Hizbullah Look Firmer," *The Christian Science Monitor,* January 18, 2002, p. 8. On arguments questioning the Israeli version of evidence, see Brian Whitaker, "The Strange Affair of Karine A," *The Guardian,* January 21, 2002.

26. Bennet, "Seized Arms Would Have Vastly Extended Arafat Arsenal," p. A5; Michael Kelly, "It All Points to Arafat," *The Washington Post,* January 9, 2002.

27. "Powell Says Arafat Needs to Acknowledge Karine A Incident," U.S. Department of State, International Information Programs Press Release, January 25, 2002.

28. Matt Kelley, "Iran Has Allowed Taliban, al-Qaida Members to Escape, Rumsfeld Says," Associated Press, February 3, 2002; Eli J. Lake, "U.S., Iran in Talks over al-Qaida Suspects," United Press International, May 8, 2003; for the Iranian response, see Afshin Valinejad, "Iran Denies Giving Refuge to al-Qaida or Taliban, Admits It Can't Fully Control Borders," Associated Press, February 5, 2002.

29. See, e.g., Seymour M. Hersh, "The Iran Game: How Will Tehran's Nuclear Ambitions Affect Our Budding Partnership?," *The New Yorker,* December 3, 2001, p. 42.

30. Sipress, "Bush's Speech Shuts Door on Tenuous Opening to Iran," p. A10.

31. Author's interviews with former Bush administration officials, July 10 and July 23, 2004, and with senior administration officials, July 1, July 28, and August 2, 2004. Of course, the Iranians are not alone in such "cognitive dissonance." The Carter administration does not seem to have recognized beforehand that the Russians found Washington's scathing criticism of their human rights policy incompatible with moving forward with the SALT II negotiations.

32. Author's interviews with former Bush administration official, July 2004, and senior administration official, July 28, 2004.

33. Woodward, *Plan of Attack,* pp. 86–88.

34. Quoted in ibid, p. 88.

35. See the interview with Molavi on National Public Radio, "Analysis: Politics and Reform in Iran," *Talk of the Nation,* January 22, 2003. The transcript is available at www.npr.org/programs/totn/transcripts/2003/jan/030122.conan.html, accessed August 3, 2004.

36. Nazila Fathi, "Bush's 'Evil' Label Rejected by Angry Iranian Leaders," *The New York Times,* February 1, 2002.

37. Neil MacFarquhar, "Iran: Bush's Comments Bolster Old Guard in Tehran," *The New York Times,* February 8, 2002.

38. Author's interview with senior administration official, August 1, 2004.

39. B. Raman, "Iran: An Osirak in the Offing," Paper No. 700, South Asia Analysis Group, May 29, 2003; Neil MacFarquhar, "Warlords: Tehran Shuts Offices of Afghan Hard-Liner as Calls to Expel Him Increase," *The New York Times,* February 11, 2002; author's interviews with former Bush administration official, July 10, 2004, and with senior administration officials, July 28 and August 1, 2004.

40. Slavin, "Q&A with Foreign Minister Kamal Kharrazi."

41. Farah Stockman, "Unease Builds with Rise of Iran," *The Boston Globe,* August 4, 2004, p. A1; author's interviews with American and British military and political personnel in Iraq, November 2003.

42. Dexter Filkins, "25 Slain and 40 Wounded in Iraq as Raid on Police Frees Prisoners," *The New York Times,* February 15, 2004, p. A1.

43. "Iran Admits Holding al Qaeda Operatives," CNN.com, May 25, 2003; Douglas Jehl and Eric

Schmitt, "Havens: U.S. Suggests a Qaeda Cell in Iran Directed Saudi Bombings," *The New York Times,* May 21, 2003; Steven R. Weisman, "The Attack: Bush Condemns Saudi Blasts; 7 Americans Are Dead," *The New York Times,* May 14, 2003.

44. Douglas Jehl, "Iran Said to Hold Qaeda's No. 3, but to Resist Giving Him Up," *The New York Times,* August 2, 2003; Eli Lake, "U.S., Iran Had Talks on Prisoner Deal," *The New York Sun,* December 15, 2003.

45. Lake, "U.S., Iran Had Talks on Prisoner Deal." See also "Iran: We've Got Qaeda Bigs," CBSNews.com, July 23, 2003, available at www.cbsnews.com/stories/2003/07/07/world/printable561909.shtml, accessed August 5, 2004. On the emergence of the broader policy debate on Iran, see Steven R. Weisman, "U.S. Demands That Iran Turn Over Qaeda Agents and Join Saudi Inquiry," *The New York Times,* May 26, 2003.

46. Douglas Jehl, "U.S. Sees No Basis to Prosecute Iranian Opposition 'Terror' Group Being Held in Iraq," *The New York Times,* July 27, 2004.

47. Michael Eisenstadt, "Iran's Nuclear Program: Gathering Dust or Gaining Steam?" Policy Watch no. 707, Washington Institute for Near East Policy, February 2003; Nuclear Weapons—2002 Developments," GlobalSecurity.org, available at www.globalsecurity.org/wmd/world/iran/nuke2002.htm, accessed August 5, 2004.

48. "A. Q. Khan and Iran," GlobalSecurity.org, available at www.globalsecurity.org/wmd/world/iran/khan-iran.htm, accessed August 5, 2004.

49. Seth Carus, "Iran and Weapons of Mass Destruction," prepublication copy prepared for the American Jewish Committee Annual Meeting, May 3, 2000, pp. 2–4; Gary Milhollin, "The Mullahs and the Bomb," *The New York Times,* October 23, 2003; "Nuclear Weapons—2004 Developments," GlobalSecurity.org, available at www.globalsecurity.org/wmd/world/iran/nuke2004.htm, accessed August 5, 2004; "Nuclear Weapons—2003 Developments," GlobalSecurity.org, available at www.globalsecurity.org/wmd/world/iran/nuke2003.htm, accessed August 5, 2004; "Nuclear Weapons—2002 Developments."

50. Production of heavy water is not covered under the IAEA's mandate, even though it could be part of a program to build nuclear weapons relying on plutonium.

51. George Jahn, "UN Finds Secret Iran Nuclear Documents," Associated Press, February 12, 2004; David E. Sanger and William J. Broad, "Iran Admits That It Has Plans for a Newer Centrifuge," *The New York Times,* February 13, 2004; David E. Sanger, "In Face of Report, Iran Acknowledges Buying Nuclear Components," *The New York Times,* February 23, 2004.

52. As part of signing on to the NPT, each country is required to have a Safeguard Agreement with the IAEA that describes procedures for handling nuclear materials, notification of changes in the country's nuclear program, and other basic functions. It is unclear legally whether violation of the Safeguard Agreement constitutes a violation of the NPT itself, another problem with the NPT.

53. International Atomic Energy Agency, Report by the Director General, "Implementation of the NPT Safeguards Agreement in the Islamic Republic of Iran," GOV/2003/40, June 6, 2003. Also see Joby Warrick and Glenn Kessler, "Iran's Nuclear Program Speeds Ahead," *The Washington Post,* March 10, 2003, p. A1. Note that Warrick and Kessler claim that the Natanz facility was designed to house 5,000 centrifuges, while the actual IAEA report says 50,000. (See IAEA, "Implementation of the NPT Safeguards Agreement in the Islamic Republic of Iran," p. 6.)

54. International Atomic Energy Agency, Report by the Director General, "Implementation of the NPT Safeguards Agreement in the Islamic Republic of Iran," GOV/2003/40, June 6, 2003; Warrick and Kessler, "Iran's Nuclear Program Speeds Ahead."

55. International Atomic Energy Agency, "Implementation of the NPT Safeguards Agreement in the Islamic Republic of Iran," p. 7; "Iran's Nuclear Deal," *The NewsHour with Jim Lehrer,* October 21, 2003, the transcript of which is available at www.nci.org/03NCI/10/Irans-Nuclear-Deal.htm, accessed July 19, 2004. The IAEA has no grounds to demand that any country halt uranium enrichment activity, since such activity is permissible under the NPT—although it must be reported to the IAEA. Thus the IAEA did not demand that Iran end its uranium enrichment program. In fact, according to nuclear proliferation expert Michael Levi, the IAEA seems to have

merely been making a technical request: it needed to conduct environmental sampling and did not want the Iranians enriching uranium because doing so would contaminate its tests. However, this request got confused with the American demand (and European admonition) that Iran cease enrichment because doing so was part of Iran's nuclear weapons program. In many minds, these two things became conflated, and it appeared that the IAEA too was demanding that Iran end its enrichment activities, rather than just temporarily suspend them. (Author's correspondence with Michael Levi, August 6, 2004.)

56. Michael Levi, "Nuclear Reaction: Why Won't the IAEA Get Tough with Iran?" *The New Republic,* September 5, 2003; Valerie Lincy, "Nonproliferation: Unexpected Momentum After Iraq," *Iraq Watch* 3, no. 2 (Spring 2004), Wisconsin Project on Nuclear Arms Control.

57. Louis Charbonneau, "Iran to Accept Tougher Nuke Checks," Reuters, November 8, 2003; Joby Warrick and Glenn Kessler, "Iran Had Secret Nuclear Program, UN Agency Says," *The Washington Post,* November 11, 2003, p. A1.

58. Board of Governors of the International Atomic Energy Agency, "Implementation of the NPT Safeguards Agreement in the Islamic Republic of Iran: Resolution Adopted by the Board on 18 June 2004," GOV/2004/49, June 18, 2004; Esther Pan and Sharon Otterman, "Iran: Curtailing the Nuclear Program," Council on Foreign Relations, May 13, 2004, available at www.cfr. org/background/iran_curtail.php?print=1, accessed May 14, 2004; "Weapons Uranium Found in Iran," Agence France-Presse via Yahoo! News, March 12, 2004, available at au.news.yahoo. com/030826/2/lfr0.html, accessed August 6, 2004.

59. International Atomic Energy Agency, "Implementation of the NPT Safeguards Agreement in the Islamic Republic of Iran: Resolution Adopted by the Board on 18 June 2004"; "Iran's Continuing Pursuit of Weapons of Mass Destruction: Testimony by Under Secretary of State for Arms Control and International Security John R. Bolton," House International Relations Committee, Subcommittee on the Middle East and Central Asia, June 24, 2004; Karl Vick, "Another Nuclear Program Found in Iran," *The Washington Post,* February 24, 2004, p. A1.

60. There is a widespread popular perception that Iraq disbanded all of its WMD programs after the 1991 Persian Gulf War. This is absolutely false. The fact that the United States has not found a sizable WMD program in Iraq is not evidence that one never existed after the Gulf War or that Iraq did not succeed in hiding elements of it till the very end. For an account of what the Iraqis did and did not do, see Pollack, "Spies, Lies, and Weapons."

61. "Iran's Continuing Pursuit of Weapons of Mass Destruction"; Richard L. Armitage, Deputy Secretary of State, "Iran and U.S. Policy: Testimony Before the Senate Foreign Relations Committee," October 28, 2003.

62. Author's interviews with senior administration official, July 1, 2004, and former Bush administration official, July 10, 2004.

63. "Iran Won't Give Up Nuclear Program," Associated Press, August 1, 2004; Mark Landler, "Iran Threatens to Restart Nuclear Work," *The New York Times,* June 17, 2004, p. A10; Stefan Smith, "Iran Admits Resuming Centrifuge Assembly; European Powers Report 'No Progress' in Talks," Agence France-Presse, August 6, 2004.

64. Jim Muir, "Iran to Review Academic's Verdict," BBC News, November 25, 2002, available at news.bbc.co.uk/1/low/world/middle_east/2511941.stm, accessed August 5, 2004.

65. "4,000 Arrests in Iran Reform Protests," CBSNEWS.com, June 28, 2003, available at www. cbsnews.com/stories/2003/06/12/world/main558295.shtml, accessed August 5, 2004.

66. Quoted in "Iranian Press Takes Sides Over Unrest," BBC News, June 14, 2003, available at news.bbc.co.uk/go/r/fr/-/1/hi/world/middle_east/2989974.stm, accessed May 24, 2004.

67. "Iran Unrest," *The NewsHour with Jim Lehrer,* June 18, 2003. The transcript is available at www.pbs.org/newshour/bb/middle_east/jan-june03/iran_6-18.html, accessed August 5, 2004.

68. Genieve Abdo, "Stay Out of Iran," *The Washington Post,* June 22, 2003, p. B7.

69. See the remarks of Shaul Bakhash and Daniel Brumberg in "Iran Unrest."

70. Jim Muir, "Iranian Protests Fail to Bring Change," BBC News, June 22, 2003, available at news.bbc.co.uk/go/pr/fr/-/2/hi/middle_east/3011132.stm, accessed May 24, 2004.

71. Karl Vick, "The Appearance of Change in Iran," *The Washington Post,* January 15, 2004, p. A1.

72. See, e.g., Pooneh Ghoddoosi, "Postcards from Iran: Tehran Party," BBC News, February 13, 2004, available at news.bbc.co.uk/go/pr/fr/-/1/hi/world/middle_east/3486779.stm, accessed May 24, 2004; Nicholas D. Kristof, "Those Sexy Iranians," *The New York Times,* May 8, 2004, p. A29; Nicholas Kristof, "Velvet Hand, Iron Glove," *The New York Times,* May 15, 2004; Rozita Lotfi, "Iranian Postcards: Wrapped in Red Tape," BBC News, February 13, 2004, available at news.bbc.co.uk/go/pr/fr/-/1/hi/world/middle_east/3487249.stm, accessed May 24, 2004; Vick, "The Appearance of Change in Iran"; Karl Vick, "Sorry, Wrong Chador," *The Washington Post,* July 19, 2004, p. C1.

73. Ali Akbar Dareini, "Khatami Acknowledges Deadlock, Minister Says Polls Will Be Illegitimate," Associated Press, January 31, 2004; Nazila Fathi, "The Education of an Iranian Reformer," *The New York Times,* February 19, 2004; Jefferson Morley, "Reformists Take Debate to Iranian Press," *The Washington Post,* January 15, 2004.

74. Ali Akbar Dareini, "Iranian Cabinet Ministers, Others Resign," Associated Press, January 21, 2004; Nazila Fathi, "One-Third of Iranian Parliament Quits in Protest," *The New York Times,* February 2, 2004, p. A1; Nazila Fathi, "Low Turnout May Aid the Hard-Liners," *The New York Times,* February 20, 2004; Neil MacFarquhar, "Iran Chides Critics as Hard-Liners Make Gains," *The New York Times,* February 23, 2004.

75. MacFarquhar, "Iran Chides Critics as Hard-Liners Make Gains." The White House issued a written statement that read simply, "I am very disappointed in the recently disputed parliamentary elections in Iran. The disqualification of some 2,400 candidates by the unelected Guardian Council deprived many Iranians of the opportunity to freely choose their representatives. I join many in Iran and around the world in condemning the Iranian regime's efforts to stifle freedom of speech—including the closing of two leading reformist newspapers—in the run-up to the election. Such measures undermine the rule of law and are clear attempts to deny the Iranian people's desire to freely choose their leaders. The United States supports the Iranian people's aspirations to live in freedom, enjoy their God-given rights, and determine their own destiny." The White House, Office of the Press Secretary, "Statement by the President," February 24, 2004.

76. "The Modern Face of Iran," BBC News, November 2, 2002, available at news.bbc.co.uk/1/low/programmes/from_our_own_correspondent/2383267.stm, accessed May 24, 2004.

Chapter 13: Toward a New Iran Policy

1. For a concurring assessment, see Michael Eisenstadt, "Living with a Nuclear Iran?" *Survival* 41, no. 3 (Autumn 1999), pp. 124–148.

2. International Crisis Group, "Dealing with Iran's Nuclear Program," October 27, 2003, pp. 11–15; Ray Takeyh, "Iranian Options: Pragmatic Mullas and America's Interests," *The National Interest,* Fall 2003, pp. 49–56; Ray Takeyh, "Iran's Nuclear Calculations," *World Policy Journal,* Summer 2003, pp. 21–26.

3. This was the central argument of my book *The Threatening Storm.*

4. On Iran's domestic debate over nuclear weapons, see Farideh Farhi, "To Have or Not to Have? Iran's Domestic Debate on Nuclear Weapons," in Geoffrey Kemp, ed., *Iran's Nuclear Weapons Options: Issues and Analysis* (Washington, D.C.: Nixon Center, 2001), pp. 35–53; International Crisis Group, "Dealing with Iran's Nuclear Program," pp. 15–20; Takeyh, "Iranian Options," pp. 49–53; Takeyh, "Iran's Nuclear Calculations," pp. 23–26.

5. Some Washington hard-liners have cited public statements by Khatami and other reformers that sound notoriously similar to the rantings of the Iranian hard-liners to argue that there is no real difference among Tehran's political leadership on the issue of nuclear weapons. However, these claims need to be taken with more than a few grains of salt. Khatami's early public statements regarding nuclear weapons categorically disavowed any desire to have them, and were different both from what the hard-liners were then saying and from his tone today. Moreover, since the July 1999 riots, virtually all of Khatami's public statements have sounded suspiciously like those of the hard-liners—not just his comments on nuclear power. It seems much more likely that he was

speaking his mind at first (as he did on every issue) but was thereafter forced to toe Khamene'i's line.

6. For an excellent discussion of the extent of the threat from Hizballah and what the United States should do about it, see Daniel L. Byman, "Should Hezbollah Be Next?," *Foreign Affairs* 82, no. 6 (November–December 2003).

7. "Iran," Amnesty International, available at web.amnesty.org/library/eng-irn/index, accessed August 5, 2004; "Iran, 2004," Human Rights Watch, available at hrw.org/doc/?t=mideast&c=iran, accessed August 5, 2004. See also U.S. State Department, "Country Reports on Human Rights Practices—2003: Iran," available at www.state.gov/g/drl/rls/hrrpt/2003/27927.htm, accessed August 5, 2004.

8. On Iraqi human rights violations, see Pollack, *The Threatening Storm,* pp. 20, 48–52, 122–125.

9. Takeyh, "Iran's Nuclear Calculations," pp. 23–26.

10. See, for instance, Robert Dreyfuss and Laura Rozen, "Still Dreaming of Tehran," *The Nation,* April 12, 2004; Lisa Hoffman, "Is Iran Next?," Scripps Howard News Service, May 27, 2003; Charles Krauthammer, "Axis of Evil, Part Two," *The Washington Post,* July 23, 2004, p. A29; Michael Ledeen, "The War Won't End in Baghdad," *The Wall Street Journal,* September 4, 2002; Michael Ledeen, "The Peace Trap," *National Review Online,* August 27, 2003, available at www.nationalreview.com/ledeen/ledeen082703.asp, accessed August 6, 2004.

11. Ledeen, "The War Won't End in Baghdad."

12. On the MEK, see Mahan Abedin, "First-Hand View of the Mojahedin-e Khalq," Ocnus.Net, July 16, 2004, available at www.ocnus.net/artman/publish/printer_12914.shtml, accessed July 20, 2004; Eldin, "On the Road"; International Crisis Group, "Iran: Discontent and Disarray," ICG Middle East Briefing, October 15, 2003, pp. 9–10.

13. Quoted in Ray Takeyh, "Iran at a Crossroads," *Middle East Journal* 57, no. 1 (Winter 2003), p. 54.

14. Proponents of this approach tend to refer to it by some variation on the term "engagement," but that is very misleading. Most of the different policy options are amenable to engagement with Iran, and that is not the key to this policy option. However, referring to this option as "unilateral concessions," which is simply an objective description of it, highlights its flaws immediately; hence its proponents prefer not to use that term.

15. For versions of this position, see Lee H. Hamilton, James Schlesinger, and Brent Scowcroft, "Thinking Beyond the Stalemate in U.S.-Iranian Relations, vol. I—Policy Review," Atlantic Council, Policy Paper, May 2001; Brent Scowcroft, "An Opening to Iran," *The Washington Post,* May 11, 2001; Takeyh, "Iran at a Crossroads," p. 55.

16. Fuller, *"The Center of the Universe."*

17. Unless they are armed with nuclear weapons, which is unimaginable except if the existence of the state were at stake because the Iranians were threatening to launch a WMD strike against Israel.

18. This would be a reach for the F-15Is, which have a maximum combat range of just under 800 miles. However, as the Israelis demonstrated in the Osiraq raid, they are willing to take risks—such as cutting down on the amount of loiter time available at the target—to reach important targets at great distances. I assume that they would be willing to do so again with the F-15Is. It might be possible for the Israelis to refuel the F-15Is once somewhere over eastern Jordan or western Iraq, or they might simply go with a much reduced payload.

19. Although it would be theoretically possible for Israeli F-16Cs to participate in such strikes, in practical terms it would be impossible. The F-16C has a maximum range of more than 2,000 miles, which means it could fly to a target 1,000 miles away and return; however, that is its *ferry* range, not its tactical range. An F-16C can fly to a target 1,000 miles away only if it is carrying nothing but fuel—not terribly useful if you actually want to bomb anything. In addition, the aircraft would have virtually no loiter time over the target to locate it, deal with any air defenses, set up a proper attack, and wait for other aircraft to strike. Finally, to reach this range, the F-16C has to fly at a very high altitude, which is the best way for it to be observed and attacked by enemy

air defenses. This is why an F-16C's combat range is only 350 miles. Thus, even these aircraft would require refueling, probably several times, to get from Israel to the Iranian nuclear sites.

20. For commentators advocating a Grand Bargain, see Geoffrey Kemp, "U.S. and Iran: The Nuclear Dilemma: Next Steps," Nixon Center, 2004, pp. 38–40; Nicholas D. Kristof, "Nuts with Nukes," *The New York Times,* May 19, 2004; Ray Takeyh, "Iran Would Give Up Nukes for the Right Deal," *International Herald Tribune,* October 23, 2003.

21. Condoleezza Rice, "Why We Know Iraq Is Lying," *The New York Times,* January 23, 2003.

22. For a fuller description of the utility and possible mechanics of such regional security frameworks, see Kenneth M. Pollack, "Securing the Gulf," *Foreign Affairs* 82, no. 4 (July–August 2003).

23. For a more in-depth discussion of what these safeguards should consist of, see Robert J. Einhorn and Gary Samore, "Ending Russian Assistance to Iran's Nuclear Bomb," *Survival* 44, no. 2 (Summer 2002), pp. 65–67.

24. On this, see Graham Allison, "How to Stop Nuclear Terror," *Foreign Affairs* 83, no. 1 (January–February 2004); Kemp, "U.S. and Iran," pp. 35–36; Einhorn and Samore, "Ending Russian Assistance to Iran's Nuclear Bomb," pp. 64–67. Einhorn and Samore make this argument about light-water reactors, specifically the Bushehr light-water reactor, which the United States has opposed to date not out of concerns about it but that it will continue to serve as a cover for additional illegal sales unrelated to Bushehr. Their arguments can be generalized to other light-water reactors as well.

25. For an early, similar approach, see Shahram Chubin and Jerrold Green, "Engaging Iran," *Survival* 40, no. 1 (Spring 1998), pp. 5–32.

26. See, e.g., Takeyh, "Iran Would Give Up Nukes for the Right Deal."

27. "President Announces New Measures to Counter the Threat of WMD," Remarks by the President on Weapons of Mass Destruction Proliferation, White House Office of the Press Secretary, released February 11, 2004. See also Dana Milbank and Peter Slevin, "Bush Details Plan to Curb Nuclear Arms," *The Washington Post,* February 12, 2004, p. A1.

28. Other states, such as North Korea and Israel, whose status is more ambiguous and whose presence would likely be unhelpful in any event, should not be invited to participate. This conference would be intended not to revise the NPT, but to organize a framework outside of it, intended to enforce it by mutual agreement of the participating states. Consequently, it would not require reopening the NPT itself and obtaining the signatories of all of the current member states.

29. For a legal opinion in support of this, see Eldon V. C. Greenberg, "The NPT and Plutonium," Nuclear Control Institute, 1993, available at www.nci.org/03NCI/12/NPTandPlutonium.pdf, accessed August 12, 2004.

30. Mohamed ElBaradei, "Nuclear Proliferation: Global Security in a Rapidly Changing World," Keynote Address to the Carnegie International Non-Proliferation Conference, Washington, D.C., June 21, 2004; Melanie Sully, "Blix Calls for International Treaty to Ban Production of WMDs," Voice of America News, June 30, 2004, transcript available at www.nci.org/04nci/06/VOANews.htm, accessed August 11, 2004. Also see Paul Leventhal, "Iranian Proliferation: Implications for Terrorists," Testimony Before the House Committee on International Relations, Subcommittee on the Middle East and Central Asia, Hearing on "Iranian Proliferation: Implications for Terrorists, Their State Sponsors and U.S. Countermeasures," June 24, 2004, available at www.nci.org/04nci/07/Iran-testimony.htm, accessed August 12, 2004; Henry Sokolski, "That Iranian Nuclear Headache," *National Review Online,* January 22, 2004, available at www.npec-web.org, accessed January 22, 2004.

31. In an ideal world, the same conference, or a parallel one, could do the same for ballistic missile proliferation. The Wassenar Agreement on conventional arms sales included similar provisions banning ballistic missile and related technology transfer but lacked the automatic sanctioning mechanisms that are crucial for such an arrangement to have any real persuasive power.

32. Tom Raum, "Bush Calls on Europe to Overcome Differences and Unite Against Terrorism," Associated Press, May 31, 2003.

33. For two excellent discussions of issues related to a nuclear-armed Iran, see Eisenstadt, "Living with a Nuclear Iran?," pp. 124–148; and Kori N. Schake and Judith S. Yaphe, "The Strategic Implications of a Nuclear-Armed Iran," McNair Paper No. 64 (Washington, D.C.: National Defense University, 2001).

Selected Bibliography

Government Documents

AmConsul Shiraz, "Official Support for the Shah and Anti-American Sentiment," October 30, 1978, original classification confidential, declassified and available at www.gwu.edu/%7Ensarchiv/NSAEBB/NSAEBB78/propaganda&20137.pdf, accessed July 10, 2004.

Bolton, John R. "Iran's Continuing Pursuit of Weapons of Mass Destruction: Testimony by Under Secretary of State for Arms Control and International Security John R. Bolton." House International Relations Committee, Subcommittee on the Middle East and Central Asia. June 24, 2004.

Central Intelligence Agency. "Iran-Gulf States: Prospects for Expanded Conflict," May 17, 1986, declassified September 1999. Available at www.foia.cia.gov, accessed July 22, 2004.

———. "Iran-Iraq: Chemical Warfare Continues," November 1986, declassified and released as part of the U.S. Department of Defense GulfLink project. Available at www.gulflink.osd.mil/muhammadiyat/muhammidiyat_refs/n59en018/970409_cia_95224_95224_01.html, accessed July 11, 2004.

———. "Iran's Economy: A Survey of Its Decline," July 1991, declassified November 1999. Available at www.foia.cia.gov, accessed July 22, 2004.

———. "Iran: Roots of Growing Activism Against Israel." *National Intelligence Daily,* September 29, 1989, declassified June 1999. Available at www.foia.cia.gov, accessed July 22, 2004.

———. "Iran Under Rafsanjani: Seeking a New Role in the World Community?" October 1991, declassified (no date). Available at www.foia.cia.gov, accessed July 22, 2004.

———. "Iranian Reaction to Recent Military Setbacks," April 21, 1988, declassified September 1999. Available at www.foia.cia.gov, accessed July 22, 2004.

———. "Iraq: Implications of Insurrection and Prospects for Saddam's Survival," March 16, 1991, declassified January 2001. Available at www.foia.cia.gov, accessed July 22, 2004.

———. "Memorandum for the DCI: Iranian Support for International Terrorism," November 22, 1986, declassified June 1999. Available at www.foia.cia.gov, accessed July 22, 2004.

———. "Persian Gulf: Bolder Iranian Actions," September 30, 1987, declassified September 1999. Available at www.foia.cia.gov, accessed July 22, 2004.

———. "Response to National Security Review—10: U.S. Policy Toward the Persian Gulf," March 3, 1989, declassified July 2001. Available at www.foia.cia.gov, accessed July 22, 2004.

————. "Russia-Iran: Planning Nuclear Power Cooperation," March 19, 1992, declassified June 2001. Available at www.foia.cia.gov, accessed July 22, 2004.

————. "Subject: Iran-Iraq Frontline," June 23, 1988, declassified and released as part of the U.S. Department of Defense GulfLink project. Available at www.dtic.mil:80/Gulflink/indexpages/intelligence_documents, accessed November 10, 1996.

————. "Unclassified Report to Congress on the Acquisition of Technology Relating to Weapons of Mass Destruction and Advanced Conventional Munitions, 1 January through 30 June 2003." July 2003.

————. *World Factbook 1989*. Washington, D.C.: U.S. Government Printing Office, 1989.

————. *World Factbook 1997*. Washington, D.C.: U.S. Government Printing Office, 1997.

" 'Fourth Part' of Saddam's al-Faw Meeting." In FBIS-NES-93-081, April 29, 1993.

Joint Atomic Energy Intelligence Committee. "Iran's Nuclear Program: Building a Weapons Capability," February 1993, declassified (no date). Available at www.foia.cia.gov, accessed July 22, 2004.

Katzman, Kenneth. "Iran: Arms and Weapons of Mass Destruction Suppliers." Congressional Research Service, January 3, 2003.

————. "The Iran-Libya Sanctions Act (ILSA)." Congressional Research Service, CRS Report for Congress, July 31, 2003.

————. "Terrorism: Middle Eastern Groups and State Sponsors, 1998." Congressional Research Service, August 27, 1998.

Leventhal, Paul. "Iranian Proliferation: Implications for Terrorists." Testimony before the House Committee on International Relations, Subcommittee on the Middle East and Central Asia, Hearing on "Iranian Proliferation: Implications for Terrorists, Their State Sponsors and U.S. Countermeasures," June 24, 2004. Available at www.nci.org/04nci/07/Iran-testimony.htm, accessed August 12, 2004.

Office of Technology Assessment, Congress of the United States. "U.S. Oil Import Vulnerability: The Technical Replacement Capability." Washington, D.C.: U.S. Government Printing Office, 1991.

President's Special Review Board ("The Tower Commission"). *Report of the President's Special Review Board*. Washington, D.C.: U.S. Government Printing Office, 1987.

Report of the 9/11 Commission: Final Report of the National Commission on Terrorist Attacks Upon the United States. Washington, D.C.: U.S. Government Printing Office, 2004.

"Saddam al-Faw Anniversary Address, Part II." In FBIS-NES-93-075, April 21, 1993, pp. 23–24.

Senate Foreign Relations Committee. "Confirmation Hearings of General Colin Powell to Be Secretary of State," January 17, 2001.

————. "Iran and U.S. Policy: Testimony before the Senate Foreign Relations Committee" by Richard L. Armitage, Deputy Secretary of State, October 28, 2003.

————, Subcommittee on Multinational Corporations. *Multinational Corporations and United States Foreign Policy: Grumman Sale of F-14s to Iran*. 94th Congress, 2nd Session, August and September 1976.

"Statement of Alan Larson, Assistant Secretary, Bureau of Economic and Business Affairs, Department of State," and "Statement of David Welch, Acting Assistant Secretary, Bureau of Near East Affairs, Department of State," in "Iran-Libya Sanctions Act—One Year Later," Hearing Before the Committee on International Relations, United States House of Representatives, 105th Congress, 1st Session, July 23, 1997, pp. 9–15.

U.S. Bureau of the Census. *Current Population Reports*, Series P25-1130, "Population Projections of the United States by Age, Sex, Race, and Hispanic Origin: 1995 to 2050." Population Division, U.S. Bureau of the Census.

U.S. Congress, House of Representatives Select Committee to Investigate Covert Arms Transactions with Iran and Senate Select Committee on Secret Military Assistance to Iran and the Nicaraguan Opposition. *Report of the Congressional Committees Investigating the Iran-Contra Affair; with Supplemental, Minority, and Additional Views*. Washington, D.C.: U.S. Government Printing Office, 1987.

U.S. Department of Commerce, Bureau of Foreign and Domestic Commerce, Office of Business Economics. *A Supplement to the Survey of Current Business: Foreign Aid, 1940–1951.* Washington, D.C.: U.S. Government Printing Office, 1952.

U.S. Department of Energy. "Natural Gas Prices." Available at www.eia.doe.gov/emeu/mer/pdf/pages/sec9_17.pdf, accessed August 7, 2004.

U.S. Department of State. "Country Reports on Human Rights Practices—2003: Iran." Available at www.state.gov/g/drl/rls/hrrpt/2003/27927.htm, accessed August 5, 2004.

———. "Excerpt: U.S., Iran Discussing Afghanistan, Iraq, Other Issues of Mutual Interest." Press Release, May 13, 2003.

———. "Mujahidin-e Khalq," *Patterns of Global Terrorism, 2003.* Available at www.state.gov/s/ct/rls/pgtrpt/2003/c12108.htm, accessed July 23, 2004.

———. *Patterns of Global Terrorism.* Washington, D.C.: U.S. Department of State, 1993.

———. *Patterns of Global Terrorism, 1994.* Available at dosfan.lib.uic.edu/ERC/arms/PGT_report/1994PGT.html, accessed July 25, 2004.

———. *Patterns of Global Terrorism, 2003.* Available at www.state.gov/s/ct/rls/pgtrpt/2003/c12108.htm, accessed July 23, 2004.

———. "Powell Says Arafat Needs to Acknowledge Karine A Incident." International Information Programs Press Release, January 25, 2002.

U.S. Department of State, Division of Public Studies. "U.S. Public Opinion on Iran." November 10, 1952, declassified May 29, 1992.

Veliotes, Nicholas A., and Jonathan Howe. "Iran-Iraq War: Analysis of Possible U.S. Shift from Position of Strict Neutrality." Memorandum for Mr. Eagleburger, U.S. Department of State, October 7, 1983.

White House, Office of the Press Secretary. "President Announces New Measures to Counter the Threat of WMD," Remarks by the President on Weapons of Mass Destruction Proliferation. Released February 11, 2004.

White House, Office of the Press Secretary. "Remarks at Millennium Evening: The Perils of Indifference: Lessons Learned from a Violent Century." Released April 12, 1999. Full text is available at clinton6.nara.gov/1999/04/1999-04-12-remarks-at-millennium-lecture.html, accessed August 1, 2004.

Books

Abdo, Geneive, and Jonathan Lyons. *Answering Only to God: Faith and Freedom in Twenty-first-Century Iran.* New York: Henry Holt, 2003.

Abrahamian, Ervand. *Iran Between Two Revolutions.* Princeton, N.J.: Princeton University Press, 1982.

Aburish, Said K. *Saddam Hussein: The Politics of Revenge.* New York: Bloomsbury, 2000.

Acheson, Dean. *Present at the Creation: My Years at the State Department.* New York: W. W. Norton, 1969.

Albright, Madeleine. *Madam Secretary.* New York: Miramax Books, 2003.

Alexander, Yonah, and Allan Nanes, eds. *The United States and Iran: A Documentary History.* Frederick, Md.: University Publications of America, 1980.

Alikhani, Hossein. *Sanctioning Iran: Anatomy of a Failed Policy.* London: I. B. Tauris, 2000.

Amuzegar, Jahangir. *Iran's Economy Under the Islamic Republic.* London: I. B. Tauris, 1993.

Ansari, Ali M. *Modern Iran Since 1921: The Pahlavis and After.* London: Longman, 2003.

Arjomand, Said. *The Turban for the Crown: The Islamic Revolution in Iran.* New York: Oxford University Press, 1988.

Baker, James A., III. *The Politics of Diplomacy.* New York: G.P. Putnam's Sons, 1995.

Bakhash, Shaul. *The Reign of the Ayatollahs: Iran and the Islamic Revolution,* rev. ed. New York: Basic Books, 1990.

Benjamin, Daniel, and Steven Simon. *The Age of Sacred Terror.* New York: Random House, 2002.

Bergquist, Major Ronald E. *The Role of Airpower in the Iran-Iraq War.* Maxwell Air Force Base, Ala.: Air University Press, 1988.

Bill, James A. *The Eagle and the Lion: The Tragedy of American-Iranian Relations.* New Haven, Conn.: Yale University Press, 1988.

Brumberg, Daniel. *Reinventing Khomeini: The Struggle for Reform in Iran.* Chicago: University of Chicago Press, 2001.

Brzezinski, Zbigniew. *Power and Principle: Memoirs of the National Security Adviser, 1977–1981,* rev. ed. New York: Farrar, Straus and Giroux, 1985.

Buchta, Wilfried. *Who Rules Iran? The Structure of Power in the Islamic Republic.* Washington, D.C.: Washington Institute for Near East Policy and the Konrad Adenauer Stiftung, 2000.

Bulloch, John, and Harvey Morris. *The Gulf War.* London: Methuen, 1989.

Bush, George, and Brent Scowcroft. *A World Transformed.* New York: Alfred A. Knopf, 1998.

Byman, Daniel L. *Deadly Connections: States That Sponsor Terrorism.* Cambridge, U.K.: Cambridge University Press, forthcoming.

———, Shahram Chubin, Anoushiravan Ehteshami, and Jerrold Green. *Iran's Security Policy in the Post-Revolutionary Era.* Santa Monica, Calif.: RAND, 2001.

Byrne, Malcolm, and Mark J. Gasiorowski, eds. *Mohammad Mosaddeq and the 1953 Coup in Iran.* Syracuse, N.Y.: Syracuse University Press, 2004.

Carter, Jimmy. *Keeping Faith: Memoirs of a President.* Fayetteville, Ark.: University of Arkansas Press, 1995.

Christopher, Warren. *Chances of a Lifetime.* New York: Scribner's, 2001.

———. *In the Stream of History: Shaping Foreign Policy for a New Era.* Stanford, Calif.: Stanford University Press, 1998.

———, and Paul H. Kreisberg, eds. *American Hostages in Iran: The Conduct of a Crisis.* New Haven, Conn.: Yale University Press, 1985.

Chubin, Shahram. *Iran's National Security Policy: Capabilities, Intentions, and Impact.* Washington, D.C.: Carnegie Endowment, 1994.

Clarke, Richard A. *Against All Enemies: Inside America's War on Terror.* New York: Free Press, 2004.

Cockburn, Andrew and Patrick. *Out of the Ashes: The Resurrection of Saddam Hussein.* New York: HarperCollins, 1999.

Cordesman, Anthony. *Iran and Iraq: The Threat from the Northern Gulf.* Boulder, Colo.: Westview, 1994.

———, and Abraham Wagner. *The Lessons of Modern War,* vol. 2: *The Iran-Iraq War.* Boulder, Colo.: Westview, 1990.

Crowe, Admiral William J., Jr. *In the Line of Fire.* New York: Simon & Schuster, 1993.

Daniel, Elton L. *The History of Iran.* Westport, Conn.: Greenwood Press, 2001.

Dodge, Theodore Ayrault. *Alexander.* New York: Da Capo, 1996.

Dunn, Walter S. *The Soviet Economy and the Red Army, 1930–1945.* Westport, Conn.: Praeger, 1995.

Ebtekar, Massoumeh, as told to Fred A. Reed. *Takeover in Tehran: The Inside Story of the 1979 U.S. Embassy Capture.* Vancouver, Canada: Talon Books, 2000.

Ehteshami, Anoushiravan. *After Khomeini: The Iranian Second Republic.* London: Routledge, 1995.

Eisenstadt, Michael. *Iranian Military Power: Capabilities and Intentions.* Washington, D.C.: Washington Institute for Near East Policy, 1997.

Estrada, Javier, Helge Ole Bergesen, Arild Moe, and Anne Kristin Sydnes. *Natural Gas in Europe: Markets, Organization and Politics.* London: Pinter Publishers, 1988.

Farouk-Sluglett, Marion, and Peter Sluglett. *Iraq Since 1958: From Revolution to Dictatorship.* London: Kegan Paul International, 1987.

Fischer, Michael M. J. *Iran: From Religious Dispute to Revolution.* Madison, Wis.: University of Wisconsin Press, 1980.

Francona, Rick. *Ally to Adversary: An Eyewitness Account of Iraq's Fall from Grace.* Annapolis, Md.: U.S. Naval Institute Press, 1999.

Fuller, Graham E. *"The Center of the Universe": The Geopolitics of Iran.* Boulder, Colo.: Westview, 1991.

Fuller, J. F. C. *A Military History of the Western World,* vol. 1: *From the Earliest Times to the Battle of Lepanto.* New York: Da Capo, 1987.

Garraty, John A., and Peter Gay, eds. *The Columbia History of the World*. New York: Harper and Row, 1981.

Gasiorowski, Mark J. *U.S. Foreign Policy and the Shah: Building a Client State in Iran*. Ithaca, N.Y.: Cornell University Press, 1991.

Gates, Robert M. *From the Shadows*. New York: Simon & Schuster, 1996.

Gerecht, Reuel Marc (writing as "Edward Shirley"). *Know Thine Enemy: A Spy's Journey into Revolutionary Iran*. Boulder, Colo.: Westview, 1999.

Gieling, Saskia. *Religion and War in Revolutionary Iran*. London: I. B. Tauris, 1999.

Glantz, David M., and Jonathan House. *When Titans Clashed: How the Red Army Stopped Hitler*. Lawrence, Kans.: University of Kansas Press, 1995.

Green, Jerrold D. *Parastatal Economic Organizations and Stability in Iran: The Role of Bonyads*. Santa Monica, Calif.: RAND, 1997.

———. *Revolution in Iran: The Politics of Countermobilization*. Westport, Conn.: Praeger, 1982.

Grummon, Stephen R. *The Iran-Iraq War: Islam Embattled*. The Washington Papers no. 92. New York: Praeger, 1982.

Harik, Judith Palmer. *Hezbollah: The Changing Face of Terrorism*. London: I. B. Tauris, 2004.

Harrison, Mark. *Accounting for War: Soviet Production, Employment, and Defence Burden, 1940–45*. Cambridge, U.K.: Cambridge University Press, 1996.

Hashim, Ahmed. *The Crisis of the Iranian State*. Adelphi Paper no. 296. London: IISS, 1995.

Helms, Richard. *A Look over My Shoulder: A Life in the Central Intelligence Agency*. New York: Random House, 2003.

Hiro, Dilip. *Lebanon: Fire and Embers*. New York: St. Martin's Press, 1992.

———. *The Longest War: The Iran-Iraq Military Conflict*. New York: Routledge, 1991.

Houghton, David Patrick. *U.S. Foreign Policy and the Iran Hostage Crisis*. Cambridge, U.K.: Cambridge University Press, 2001.

Huyser, General Robert E. *Mission to Tehran*. New York: Harper and Row, 1986.

Isaacson, Walter. *Kissinger: A Biography*. New York: Touchstone, 1992.

Izady, Mehrdad R. *The Kurds: A Concise Handbook*. Washington, D.C.: Crane Russak, 1992.

Jaber, Hala. *Hezbollah*. New York: Columbia University Press, 1997.

Jentleson, Bruce W. *With Friends Like These: Reagan, Bush, and Saddam, 1982–1990*. New York: W. W. Norton & Company, 1994.

Kanovsky, Eliyahu. *Iran's Economic Morass: Mismanagement and Decline Under the Islamic Republic*. Washington, D.C.: Washington Institute for Near East Policy, 1997.

Kapuściński, Ryszard. *Shah of Shahs*, trans. William R. Brand and Katarzyna Mroczkowska-Brand. New York: Vintage Books, 1992.

Karsh, Efraim. *The Iran-Iraq War: A Military Analysis*. Adelphi Paper no. 220. London: IISS, 1987.

———, and Inari Rautsi. *Saddam Hussein: A Political Biography*. New York: Free Press, 1991.

Katzman, Kenneth. *The Warriors of Islam: Iran's Revolutionary Guard*. Boulder, Colo.: Westview, 1993.

Keddie, Nikki R. *Modern Iran: Roots and Results of Revolution*, rev. and updated ed. New Haven, Conn.: Yale University Press, 2003.

———, ed. *Religion and Politics in Iran: Shi'ism from Quietism to Revolution*. New Haven, Conn.: Yale University Press, 1983.

———, and Rudi Matthee, eds. *Iran and the Surrounding World: Interactions in Culture and Cultural Politics*. Seattle: University of Washington Press, 2002.

Kemp, Geoffrey, ed. *Iran's Nuclear Weapons Options: Issues and Analysis*. Washington, D.C.: Nixon Center, 2001.

Kinzer, Stephen. *All the Shah's Men: An American Coup and the Roots of Middle East Terror*. Hoboken, N.J.: John Wiley & Sons, 2003.

Kissinger, Henry. *White House Years*. Boston: Little, Brown, 1979.

———. *Years of Renewal*. New York: Touchstone, 1999.

Kornbluh, Peter, and Malcolm Byrne. *The Iran-Contra Scandal: The Declassified History*. New York: W. W. Norton, 1993.

Kuniholm, Bruce. *The Origins of the Cold War in the Near East: Great Power Conflict and Diplomacy in Iran, Turkey and Greece.* Princeton, N.J.: Princeton University Press, 1980.

Kuppersmith, Major Douglas A., USAF. *The Failure of Third World Air Power: Iraq and the War with Iran.* Maxwell Air Force Base, Ala.: Air University Press, 1993.

Kurzman, Charles. *The Unthinkable Revolution in Iran.* Cambridge, Mass.: Harvard University Press, 2004.

Lenczowski, George, ed. *Iran Under the Pahlavis.* Stanford, Calif.: Hoover Institution Press, 1978.

Litwak, Robert S. *Rogue States and U.S. Foreign Policy.* Washington, D.C.: Woodrow Wilson Center, 2000.

Looney, Robert E. *Economic Origins of the Iranian Revolution.* Elmsford, N.Y.: Pergamon, 1982.

Mann, James. *The Rise of the Vulcans.* New York: Penguin, 2004.

Marr, Phebe. *The Modern History of Iraq.* 2nd ed. Boulder, Colo.: Westview, 2004.

Martin, David C., and John Walcott. *Best Laid Plans.* New York: Harper & Row, 1988.

Martin, Vanessa. *Creating an Islamic State: Khomeini and the Making of a New Iran.* London: I. B. Tauris, 2000.

McDowall, David. *A Modern History of the Kurds.* London: I. B. Tauris, 1997.

McFarlane, Robert C., with Zofia Smardz. *Special Trust.* New York: Cadell & Davies, 1994.

McLaurin, R. D. *Military Operations in the Gulf War: The Battle of Khorramshahr.* Aberdeen Proving Grounds, Md.: U.S. Army Human Engineering Laboratory, July 1982.

Menashri, David. *A Decade of War and Revolution.* New York: Holmes and Meier, 1990.

———. *Revolution at a Crossroads: Iran's Domestic Politics and Regional Ambitions.* Washington, D.C.: Washington Institute for Near East Policy, 1997.

Metz, Helen Chapin. *Iran: A Country Study.* Washington, D.C.: U.S. Government Printing Office, 1989.

Millspaugh, Arthur C. *Americans in Persia.* Washington, D.C.: Brookings Institution, 1946.

Moin, Baqer. *Khomeini: Life of the Ayatollah.* London: I. B. Tauris, 1999.

Molavi, Afshin. *Persian Pilgrimages: Journeys Across Iran.* New York: W. W. Norton, 2002.

Moslem, Mehdi. *Factional Politics in Post-Khomeini Iran.* Syracuse, N.Y.: Syracuse University Press, 2002.

Mottahedeh, Roy. *The Mantle of the Prophet: Religion and Politics in Iran.* New York: Pantheon, 1985.

Mottale, Morris M. *Iran: The Political Sociology of the Islamic Revolution.* Lanham, Md.: University Press of America, 1995.

Motter, Vail. *The Persian Corridor and Aid to Russia.* Washington, D.C.: Center of Military History, 1952.

Nafisi, Azar. *Reading Lolita in Tehran.* New York: Random House, 2004.

O'Ballance, Edgar. *The Gulf War.* London: Brassey's, 1988.

———. *The Kurdish Struggle.* New York: St. Martin's Press, 1996.

Overy, Richard. *Why the Allies Won.* New York: Norton, 1995.

Pahlavi, Ashraf. *Faces in a Mirror: Memoirs from Exile.* Englewood Cliffs, N.J.: Prentice-Hall, 1980.

Pahlavi, Mohammed Reza. Shah of Iran. *Answer to History.* New York: Stein and Day, 1980.

———. *Mission for My Country.* New York: McGraw-Hill, 1960.

———. *Shahanshah of Iran on Oil: Tehran Agreement: Background and Perspectives.* London: Transorient, 1971.

Palmer, Michael A. *Guardians of the Gulf: A History of America's Expanding Role in the Persian Gulf, 1833–1992.* New York: Free Press, 1992.

Parsons, Anthony. *The Pride and the Fall: Iran 1974–79.* London: Jonathan Cape, 1984.

Pelletiere, Stephen. *The Iran-Iraq War.* New York: Praeger, 1992.

——— and Douglas V. Johnson. *Lessons Learned: The Iran-Iraq War.* Carlisle Barracks, Pa.: Strategic Studies Institute, U.S. Army War College, 1990.

Picco, Giandomenico. *Man Without a Gun.* New York: Random House, 1999.

Pollack, Kenneth M. *Arabs at War: Military Effectiveness, 1948–1991.* Lincoln, Neb.: University of Nebraska Press, 2002.

———. *The Threatening Storm: The Case for Invading Iraq.* New York: Random House, 2002.

President's Special Review Board ("The Tower Commission"). *Report of the President's Special Review Board.* Washington, D.C.: U.S. Government Printing Office, 1987.

Rajaee, Farhad. *Iranian Perspectives on the Iran-Iraq War.* Gainesville: University Press of Florida, 1997.

———, ed. *The Iran-Iraq War.* Gainesville: University Press of Florida, 1993.

Ramazani, R. K., ed. *Iran's Revolution: The Search for Consensus.* Bloomington, Ind.: Indiana University Press, 1990.

Ranstorp, Magnus. *Hizb'allah in Lebanon.* London: Macmillan, 1997.

Richelson, Jeffrey T. *The U.S. Intelligence Community,* 4th ed. Boulder, Colo.: Westview, 1999.

Roberts, Mark J. *Khomeini's Incorporation of the Iranian Military.* McNair Paper 48. Washington, D.C.: National Defense University, 1996.

Roosevelt, Kermit. *Countercoup: The Struggle for Control of Iran.* New York: McGraw-Hill, 1979.

Ross, Dennis. *The Missing Peace.* New York: Farrar, Straus and Giroux, 2004.

Rubin, Barry. *Paved with Good Intentions: The American Experience and Iran.* New York: Penguin, 1981.

Ryan, Paul B. *The Iranian Rescue Mission: Why It Failed.* Annapolis, Md.: Naval Institute Press, 1985.

Saad-Ghorayeb, Amal. *Hizb'ullah: Politics, Religion.* London: Pluto Press, 2002.

Schake, Kori N., and Judith S. Yaphe. *The Strategic Implications of a Nuclear Armed Iran.* McNair Paper 64. Washington, D.C.: National Defense University, 2001.

Schiff, Ze'ev, and Ehud Ya'ari. *Israel's Lebanon War,* trans. Ina Friedman. New York: Simon & Schuster, 1984.

Schulz, Ann Tibbits. *Buying Security: Iran Under the Monarchy.* Boulder, Colo.: Westview, 1989.

Sciolino, Elaine. *Persian Mirrors: The Elusive Face of Iran.* New York: Free Press, 2000.

Shultz, George P. *Turmoil and Triumph.* New York: Charles Scribner's Sons, 1993.

Sick, Gary. *All Fall Down: America's Fateful Encounter with Iran.* London: I. B. Tauris, 1985.

———. *October Surprise.* New York: Times Books, 1992, paperback.

Sokolsky, Richard D., ed. *The United States and the Persian Gulf.* Washington, D.C.: National Defense University Press, 2003.

Sullivan, William H. *Mission to Iran.* New York: W. W. Norton, 1981.

Suskind, Ron. *The Price of Loyalty: George W. Bush, the White House, and the Education of Paul O'Neill.* New York: Simon & Schuster, 2004.

Taheri, Amir. *Nest of Spies: America's Journey to Disaster in Iran.* New York: Pantheon, 1988.

Tahir-Kheli, Shirin, and Shaheen Ayubi, eds. *The Iran-Iraq War: New Weapons, Old Conflicts.* New York: Praeger, 1983.

Tanter, Raymond. *Rogue Regimes: Terrorism and Proliferation.* New York: St. Martin's Griffin, 1999.

Teicher, Howard, and Gayle R. Teicher. *Twin Pillars to Desert Storm: America's Flawed Vision in the Middle East from Nixon to Bush.* New York: William Morrow, 1993.

Tripp, Charles. *A History of Iraq.* Cambridge, U.K.: Cambridge University Press, 2000.

Turner, Admiral Stansfield. *Terrorism and Democracy.* Boston: Houghton Mifflin, 1991.

Vance, Cyrus. *Hard Choices: Critical Years in America's Foreign Policy.* New York: Simon & Schuster, 1983.

Weinberg, Gerhard. *A World at Arms: A Global History of World War II.* Cambridge, U.K.: Cambridge University Press, 1994.

Weinberger, Caspar. *Fighting for Peace.* New York: Warner Books, 1990.

Wells, Tim. *444 Days: The Hostages Remember.* New York: Harcourt Brace Jovanovich, 1985.

Woodward, Bob. *Plan of Attack.* New York: Simon & Schuster, 2004.

World Bank. *World Tables: 1976.* Baltimore: Johns Hopkins University Press, 1976.

Wright, Robin. *In the Name of God: The Khomeini Decade.* New York: Simon & Schuster, 1989.

———. *The Last Great Revolution: Turmoil and Transformation in Iran.* New York: Alfred A. Knopf, 2000.

Yergin, Daniel. *The Prize: The Epic Quest for Oil, Money, and Power.* New York: Touchstone, 1991.

Zabih, Sepehr. *The Iranian Military in Revolution and War.* London: Routledge, 1988.

Articles and Book Chapters

Abdel-Nasser, Walid M. "Three Regional Spheres in Iran's Foreign Policy." Strategic Papers no. 38. Cairo: Al-Ahram Center for Political and Strategic Studies, 1996.

Abdo, Genieve. "Days of Rage in Tehran." *Middle East Policy* 7, no. 1 (October 1999): 78–86.

———. "Letter from Tehran." *The Washington Quarterly* 23, no. 1 (Winter 2000): 55–64.

———. "Stay Out of Iran." *The Washington Post*, June 22, 2003, p. B7.

Abedin, Mahan. "First-Hand View of the Mojahedin-e Khalq." Ocnus.Net, July 16, 2004. Available at www.ocnus.net/artman/publish/printer_12914.shtml, accessed July 20, 2004.

Abrahamian, Ervand. "Iran: The Political Challenge." *MERIP Reports* 69 (July–August 1978): 3–8.

———. "Iran: The Political Crisis Intensifies." *MERIP Reports* 71 (October 1978): 3–4, 6.

"Al-Ahram Criticises Muslim Organization and Sudanese Policy on Hala'ib." BBC, August 7, 1992.

"Al-Ahram Looks at al-Turabi Regime, Terrorism." *Al-Ahram*, March 20, 1996. In FBIS-TOT-96-013-L, June 7, 1996.

Allison, Graham. "How to Stop Nuclear Terror." *Foreign Affairs* 83, no. 1 (January–February 2004).

Amini, Parvin Merat. "A Single Party State in Iran, 1975–78: The Rastakhiz Party—the Final Attempt by the Shah to Consolidate His Political Base." *Middle Eastern Studies* 38, no. 1 (January 2002): 131–169.

Amnesty International. "Iran." Available at web.amnesty.org/library/eng-irn/index, accessed August 5, 2004.

Amuzegar, Jahangir. "Adjusting to Sanctions." *Foreign Affairs* 76, no. 3 (May–June 1997): 31–42.

———. "Iran's Economy and the U.S. Sanctions." *The Middle East Journal* 51, no. 2 (Spring 1997): 185–200.

———. "Iran's Future: Civil Society or Civil Unrest." *Middle East Policy* 7, no. 1 (October 1999): 86–101.

———. "Khatami and the Iranian Economy at Mid-Term." *The Middle East Journal* 53, no. 4 (Autumn 1999).

Anderson, John Ward. "Iran Throwing Off Its Isolation; U.S. Remains Dubious After Decades of Mutual Distrust." *The Washington Post*, March 31, 2001, p. A18.

Antal, Major John F. "The Iraqi Army Forged in the Other Gulf War." *Military Review*, February 1991.

"Argentine Judge Hears Testimony of Detainee Linked with Buenos Aires Bombing." *BBC Summary of World Broadcasts*, January 12, 1995.

Atkeson, Major General Edward B. "Iraq's Arsenal: Tool of Ambition." *Army*, March 1991.

Axelgard, Frederick W. "Iraq and the War with Iran." *Current History*, February 1987.

Ayalon, Ami. "Egypt." In *Middle East Contemporary Survey*, vol. 19, ed. Bruce Maddy-Weitzman. Boulder, Colo.: Westview, 1995.

Azimi, Fakhreddin. "Unseating Mosaddeq: The Configuration and Role of Domestic Forces." In *Mohammad Mosaddeq and the 1953 Coup in Iran*, ed. Malcolm Byrne and Mark J. Gasiorowski. Syracuse, N.Y.: Syracuse University Press, 2004, pp. 27–101.

Bahaa, Sherine. "Attack on Khatami." *Al-Ahram Weekly On-line*, July 30–August 5, 1998. Available at weekly.ahram.org.eg/1998/388/re5.htm, accessed August 1, 2004.

"Bahrain Coup Suspects Say They Trained in Iran." *The New York Times*, June 6, 1996.

"Bahrain Holds 44 It Says Are Tied to Pro-Iran Plot." *The New York Times*, June 5, 1996.

Baker, Russell. "Button Up Your Overt Coat." *The New York Times*, August 6, 1983, p. 21.

Balali, Mehrdad. "Iranian Voters Clamor for Change." Agence France-Presse, May 23, 1997.

Banuazizi, Ali. "Faltering Legitimacy: The Ruling Clerics and Civil Society in Contemporary Iran." *International Journal of Politics, Culture and Society* 4, no. 4 (1995).

———. "Iran's Revolutionary Impasse: Political Factionalism and Societal Resistance." *Middle East Report* 24, no. 191 (November–December 1994).

Barlow, Robin. "Economic Growth in the Middle East, 1950–1972." *International Journal of Middle East Studies* 14, no. 2 (May 1982): 129–157.

Barr, Cameron W. "In Iran, Hopes Rise Among the Reformers." *The Christian Science Monitor*, June 11, 2001.

Basmenji, Kaveh. "Beating Swords into Pistachios." *Middle East Times,* March 20, 2000.

Beeman, William O. "Images of the Great Satan: Representations of the United States in the Iranian Revolution." In *Religion and Politics in Iran: Shi'ism from Quietism to Revolution,* ed. Nikki R. Keddie. New Haven, Conn.: Yale University Press, 1983, pp. 191–217.

Behrooz, Maziar. "Trends in the Foreign Policy of the Islamic Republic of Iran, 1979–1988." In *Neither East nor West: Iran, the Soviet Union, and the United States,* ed. Nikki R. Keddie and Mark J. Gasiorowski. New Haven, Conn.: Yale University Press, 1990, pp. 13–35.

Bellaigue, Christopher de. "Iran's Last Chance for Reform." *The Washington Quarterly* 24, no. 4 (Autumn 2001): 71–80.

Bengio, Ofra. "Iraq." In *Middle East Contemporary Survey,* vol. 17, ed. Ami Ayalon. Boulder, Colo.: Westview, 1993.

Bennet, James. "Seized Arms Would Have Vastly Extended Arafat Arsenal." *The New York Times,* January 12, 2002, p. A5.

Bernstein, Alvin H. "Iran's Low-Intensity War Against the United States." *Orbis* 30, no. 1 (Spring 1986): 149–167.

Bigelow, Captain Michael E. "The Faw Peninsula: A Battle Analysis." *Military Intelligence,* April–June 1991.

Bild, Peter. "Germany Investigating Iranian Minister." United Press International, December 10, 1995, p. 1.

Bill, James A. "Modernization and Reform from Above: The Case of Iran." *The Journal of Politics* 32, no. 1 (February 1970): 19–40.

———. "The U.S. Overture to Iran, 1985–1986: An Analysis." In *Neither East nor West: Iran, the Soviet Union, and the United States,* ed. Nikki R. Keddie and Mark J. Gasiorowski. New Haven, Conn.: Yale University Press, 1990: 166–179.

Black, David. "Last Call for Flight 655." *The Independent,* July 3, 1989, p. 17.

Blanford, Nicholas. "Palestinian Ties to Iran, Hizbullah Look Firmer." *The Christian Science Monitor,* January 18, 2002, p. 8.

Boustany, Nora. "The Hostage Labyrinth—Many Complex Deals Lie Behind Any Release." *The Washington Post,* March 18, 2004.

Briscoe, David. "U.S. Asserts China-Iran Nuclear Deal Off, Chinese Call It Suspended." Associated Press, September 29, 1995.

Broder, John M. "Despite a Secret Pact by Gore in '95, Russian Arms Sales to Iran Go On." *The New York Times,* October 13, 2000, p. A1.

Brodie, Ian, Michael Theodoulou, and Hazhir Teimourian. "CIA Confirms Tehran's Role in Bombing of Jewish Targets." *The Times,* August 12, 1994.

Brooke, James. "Argentines Suspect Iranian Hand in Bombing; Death Toll Hits 80." *The New York Times,* July 26, 1994, p. A3.

———. "Iranian in Argentine Blast: Tinker, Refugee, Liar, Spy?" *The New York Times,* July 29, 1994, p. A2.

Burgess, Capt. William H., III. "Special Operations in the Iran-Iraq War." *Special Warfare,* Winter 1989: 16–29.

"Burned by Loss of Conoco Deal, Iran Says U.S. Betrays Free Trade." *The New York Times,* March 20, 1995, p. D2.

Burns, John F. "Top Leader in Iran Tries to Calm Rage of Its Hard-Liners." *The New York Times,* October 2, 1999.

Buzbee, Sally. "A Warning for Iran: Bush Says Don't Help Al-Qaida, Don't Interfere in Afghanistan." Associated Press, January 10, 2002.

Byman, Daniel L. "Should Hezbollah Be Next?" *Foreign Affairs* 82, no. 6 (November–December 2003).

Byrne, Malcolm. "The Road to Intervention: Factors Influencing U.S. Policy Toward Iran, 1945–1953." In *Mohammad Mosaddeq and the 1953 Coup in Iran,* ed. Malcolm Byrne and Mark J. Gasiorowski. Syracuse, N.Y.: Syracuse University Press, 2004, pp. 201–226.

Cahn, Dianna. "Israel Shuns Hamas Pitch for Deal to Halt Attacks." Associated Press, March 1, 1996.

"Cairo Radio Reports Anti-Sudan UN Resolution, Envoy's Reaction." Cairo Arab Republic of Egypt Radio Network, in Arabic, February 1, 1996. In FBIS-NES-96–042, March 4, 1996.

"Cairo Serves Notice, Our Patience with Khartoum Is Running Out." *The Middle East Mirror,* July 7, 1995.

Campbell, John C. "Oil Power in the Middle East." *Foreign Affairs* 56, no. 1 (October 1977): 89–110.

Carswell, Robert, and Richard J. Davis. "Crafting the Financial Settlement." In *American Hostages in Iran: The Conduct of a Crisis,* ed. Warren Christopher and Paul H. Kreisberg. New Haven, Conn.: Yale University Press, 1985, pp. 201–234.

CBSNEWS.com. "4,000 Arrests in Iran Reform Protests." June 28, 2003. Available at www.cbsnews.com/stories/2003/06/12/world/main558295.shtml, accessed August 5, 2004.

———. "Iran: We've Got Qaeda Bigs." July 23, 2003. Available at www.cbsnews.com/stories/2003/07/07/world/printable561909.shtml, accessed August 5, 2004.

Charbonneau, Louis. "Iran to Accept Tougher Nuke Checks." Reuters, November 8, 2003.

Chehabi, Houchang. "Staging the Emperor's New Clothes: Dress Codes and Nation-Building Under Reza Shah." *Iranian Studies* 26 (1993).

Chubin, Shahram. "Iran's Security in the 1980s." *International Security* 2, no. 3 (Winter 1978): 51–80.

———. "Reflections on the Gulf War." *Survival* 28, no. 4 (July–August 1986).

———, and Jerrold Green. "Engaging Iran." *Survival* 40, no. 1 (Spring 1998): 5–32.

"Clinton Administration Bans Conoco Deal with Iran." National Public Radio, March 15, 1995.

"Clinton Reaches Out to Iran in 1996 Bomb Attack." Reuters, September 29, 1999.

CNN.com. "Iran Admits Holding al Qaeda Operatives." May 25, 2003.

———. "Iran Extends Voting Hours for Presidential Elections." Available at www.cnn.com/WORLD/9705/23/iran.elex.day.wrap/, accessed July 30, 2004.

———. "Transcript of Interview with Iranian President Mohammad Khatami." January 7, 1998. Full text available at www.cnn.com/WORLD/9801/07/iran/interview.html, accessed July 30, 2004.

Cohn, Martin Regg. "Iran Election Mixes Prayers and Platitudes; Religion Dominates the Race Between 'Reform and Establishment' Parties." *The Toronto Star,* May 17, 1997, p. D5.

Cooper, Kenneth J. "U.S., Iranian Wrestlers Break Diplomatic Ground in Tourney." *The Washington Post,* February 20, 1998, p. A2.

Cordesman, Anthony. "The Military Balance in the Middle East—IX." Center for Strategic and International Studies, December 28, 1998, pp. 11–19.

Cornell, Svante E. "Iran and the Caucasus." *Middle East Policy* 5, no. 4 (January 1998).

Cottam, Richard. "Inside Revolutionary Iran." In *Iran's Revolution: The Search for Consensus,* ed. R. K. Ramazani. Bloomington, Ind.: Indiana University Press, 1990, pp. 3–26.

Cottrell, Alvin. "Iran's Armed Forces Under the Pahlavi Dynasty." In *Iran Under the Pahlavis,* ed. George Lenczowski. Stanford, Calif.: Hoover Institution Press, 1978, pp. 389–431.

Crossette, Barbara. "Albright, in Overture to Iran, Seeks a 'Road Map' to Amity." *The New York Times,* June 18, 1998.

Dadkhah, Kamran M. "The Inflationary Process of the Iranian Economy, 1970–1980." *International Journal of Middle East Studies* 17, no. 3 (August 1985): 365–381.

Danis, Aaron. "Iraqi Army Operations and Doctrine." *Military Intelligence,* April–June 1991.

"Danish Politicians Boycott Visiting Iranian Minister." Agence France-Presse, February 9, 1995, p. 1.

Daniszewski, John. "Landslide Election in Iran; A Mullah with Open Mind, Khatami Won by Dint of Character." *Los Angeles Times,* May 25, 1997, p. A10.

———. "Twenty Years After Revolution, Iran Has Hope." *Los Angeles Times,* February 11, 1999.

Dareini, Ali Akbar. "Iran Lawmaker Likes U.S. Gesture." Associated Press, March 27, 2000.

———. "Iranian Cabinet Ministers, Others Resign." Associated Press, January 21, 2004.

———. "Khatami Acknowledges Deadlock, Minister Says Polls Will Be Illegitimate." Associated Press, January 31, 2004.

———. "U.S. Food Aid for Afghanistan to Be Delivered Through Iran." Associated Press, October 18, 2001.

Demick, Barbara. "Moderate Wins Iranian Presidency." *The Philadelphia Inquirer,* May 25, 1997, p. A1.

Devroy, Ann. "Clinton, Yeltsin Open Summit, Smoothing Over a Few Bumps." *The Washington Post,* September 28, 1994, p. A15.

Dreyfuss, Robert, and Laura Rozen. "Still Dreaming of Tehran." *The Nation,* April 12, 2004.

Dunn, Michael. "In the Name of God: Iran's Shi'ite International." *Defense and Foreign Affairs,* August 1985, p. 34.

"Egypt Puts Sudan in the Dock over Attempt on Mubarak's Life." *The Middle East Mirror,* June 27, 1995, pp. 11–13.

"Egyptian-Sudanese Security Meetings Resumed in Cairo." *al-Wasat,* August 11–17, 1997. In FBIS-NES-97-224, August 13, 1997.

Eilers, Wilhelm. "Educational and Cultural Development in Iran During the Pahlavi Era." In *Iran Under the Pahlavis,* ed. George Lenczowski. Stanford, Calif.: Hoover Institution Press, 1978, pp. 303–331.

Einhorn, Robert J., and Gary Samore. "Ending Russian Assistance to Iran's Nuclear Bomb." *Survival* 44, no. 2 (Summer 2002): 51–70.

Eisenstadt, Michael. "Iran's Nuclear Program: Gathering Dust or Gaining Steam?" PolicyWatch no. 707, Washington Institute for Near East Policy, February 2003.

————. "Living with a Nuclear Iran?" *Survival* 41, no. 3 (Autumn 1999): 124–148.

Eldar, Dan. "Western Europe, Russia and the Middle East." In *Middle East Contemporary Survey,* vol. 21, ed. Bruce Maddy-Weitzman. Boulder, Colo.: Westview, 1997, pp. 39–70.

Eldin, Fred S. "On the Road: Coping in Islamic Iran." *Middle East Quarterly,* June 1997.

Ellison, Katherine. "Argentina, Iran on Verge of Severing Diplomatic Relations." Knight Ridder/Tribune News Service, May 20, 1998.

Elwell-Sutton, L. P. "Reza Shah the Great: Founder of the Pahlavi Dynasty." In *Iran Under the Pahlavis,* ed. George Lenczowski. Stanford, Calif.: Hoover Institution Press, 1978.

Engleberg, Stephen, Michael R. Gordon, and Bernard E. Trainor. "Downing of Flight 655: Questions Keep Coming." *The New York Times,* July 11, 1988, p. A1.

Erlanger, Steven. "Iran Vote May Bring Pressure for a Change in U.S. Policy." *The New York Times,* May 26, 1997.

————. "U.S. Gets Russia's Firm Vow to Halt Missile Aid to Iran." *The New York Times,* January 16, 1998, p. A8.

————. "U.S. Imposes Curbs on 9 Russian Concerns." *The New York Times,* July 16, 1998, p. A10.

————. "U.S. Says Chinese Will Stop Sending Missiles to Iran." *The New York Times,* October 18, 1997, p. A1.

————. "U.S. Telling Russia to Bar Aid to Iran by Arms Experts." *The New York Times,* August 22, 1997, p. A3.

Estelami, Hooman. "The Evolution of Iran's Reactive Measures to US Economic Sanctions." *The Journal of Business in Developing Nations* 2 (1998).

Evans-Pritchard, Ambrose. "U.S. Hawks Urge Massive Strike on Iran: Clinton Advised to End Gulf Threat by Friendship or by Force." *The Sunday Telegraph* via *The Ottawa Citizen,* April 20, 1997, p. A5.

Fairbanks, Stephen C. "A New Era for Iran?" *Middle East Policy* 5, no. 3 (September 1997): 51–57.

————. "Theocracy vs. Democracy: Iran Considers Political Parties." *The Middle East Journal* 52, no. 1 (Winter 1998): 17–32.

Faramarzi, Scheherezade. "Khomeini Contains Dissent over Arms Deal with Washington." Associated Press, December 6, 1986.

Farhi, Farideh. "To Have or Not to Have? Iran's Domestic Debate on Nuclear Weapons." In *Iran's Nuclear Weapons Options: Issues and Analysis,* ed. Geoffrey Kemp. Washington, D.C.: Nixon Center, 2001, pp. 35–53.

Faruqi, Anwar. "Thousands Rally for Iranian Candidate in Test for Ruling Clergy." Associated Press, May 21, 1997.

Fathi, Nazila. "Bush's 'Evil' Label Rejected by Angry Iranian Leaders." *The New York Times,* February 1, 2002.

————. "The Education of an Iranian Reformer." *The New York Times,* February 19, 2004.

————. "Low Turnout May Aid the Hard-Liners." *The New York Times,* February 20, 2004.

———. "One-Third of Iranian Parliament Quits in Protest." *The New York Times,* February 2, 2004, p. A1.

Filkins, Dexter. "25 Slain and 40 Wounded in Iraq as Raid on Police Frees Prisoners." *The New York Times,* February 15, 2004, p. A1.

Firoozi, Ferydoon. "Income Distribution and Taxation Laws of Iran." *International Journal of Middle East Studies* 9, no. 1 (January 1978): 73–87.

———. "The Iranian Budgets: 1964–1970." *International Journal of Middle East Studies* 5, no. 3 (June 1974): 328–343.

"France Mulling New Moves Against Iran." United Press International, March 7, 1996, p. 1.

Freedman, Robert O. "Russian-Iranian Relations in the 1990s." *MERIA Journal* 4, no. 2 (June 2000).

Gambill, Gary C. "The Balance of Terror: War by Other Means in the Contemporary Middle East." *Journal of Palestine Studies* 28, no. 1 (Autumn 1998).

Gannon, Kathy. "U.S. Fears Iranian Interference in Afghanistan; Aid Agencies Fan Out to Starving Afghans." Associated Press, January 18, 2002.

Gasiorowski, Mark J. "The 1953 Coup d'Etat Against Mosaddeq." In *Mohammad Mosaddeq and the 1953 Coup in Iran,* ed. Malcolm Byrne and Mark J. Gasiorowski. Syracuse, N.Y.: Syracuse University Press, 2004, pp. 227–260.

———. "The 1953 Coup d'Etat in Iran." *International Journal of Middle East Studies* 19, no. 3 (August 1987): 261–286.

———. "The Power Struggle in Iran." *Middle East Policy* 7, no. 4 (October 2000): 22–40.

Gellman, Barton. "Bombings Imperil Peres Premiership." *The Washington Post,* March 4, 1996, p. A1.

———. "Israel Finds Challenge Impossible to Ignore; Hezbollah, Election Pressure Push Jerusalem to Send Message to Syria." *The Washington Post,* April 12, 1996, p. A31.

———. "Likud Leader Hammers Rabin, PLO; Premier-Hopeful Netanyahu Claims Ascendancy of Israeli Opposition." *The Washington Post,* September 9, 1995, p. A22.

———, and John Lancaster. "The Undoing of Israel's 'Security Zone.' " *The Washington Post,* April 21, 1996, p. A1.

———, and John Pomfret. "U.S. Action Stymied China Sale to Iran. Chemical Involved Can Be Used to Enrich Uranium." *The Washington Post,* March 13, 1998, p. A1.

Gerecht, Reuel Marc (writing as "Edward G. Shirley"). "Not Fanatics, and Not Friends." *The Atlantic,* December 1993.

" 'Get Rid of the Shah' Was the Cry Throughout the Country." *MERIP Reports* 75–76, *Iran in Revolution* (March–April 1979): 13–16.

Ghareeb, Edmund. "The Forgotten War." *American-Arab Affairs* 5 (Summer 1983).

Ghoddoosi, Pooneh. "Postcards from Iran: Tehran Party." BBC News, February 13, 2004. Available at news.bbc.co.uk/go/pr/fr/-/1/hi/world/middle_east/3486779.stm, accessed May 24, 2004.

Gordon, Michael R., and Eric Schmitt. "Iran Nearly Got a Missile Alloy from Russians." *The New York Times,* April 25, 1998, p. A1.

"Gore, Russian Premier Hold First Meeting of Joint U.S.-Russian Commission." Agence France-Presse, September 1, 1993.

Green, Jerrold. "Parastatal Economic Organizations and Stability in Iran: The Role of the Bonyads." Draft manuscript, RAND, February 1999.

Greenberg, Joel. "An Attack on Israel Brings Woe to Peres." *The New York Times,* April 10, 1996.

———. "Iran's Party of God Puts Deep Roots in Lebanon." *The New York Times,* April 12, 1996.

Greenberger, Robert S. "Arab Nightmare: Sudan's Links to Iran Cause Growing Worry over Islamic Terrorism." *The Wall Street Journal,* August 18, 1993, p. A1.

Greenhouse, Steven. "Russia and China Pressed Not to Sell A-Plants to Iran." *The New York Times,* January 25, 1995, p. A6.

Griffith, William E. "Iran's Foreign Policy in the Pahlavi Era." In *Iran Under the Pahlavis,* ed. George Lenczowski. Stanford, Calif.: Hoover Institution Press, 1978, pp. 365–388.

Halliday, Fred. "Iran: The Economic Contradictions." *MERIP Reports* 69, July–August 1978: 1–18, 23.

Hamilton, Lee H., James Schlesinger, and Brent Scowcroft. "Thinking Beyond the Stalemate in U.S.-Iranian Relations, vol. I—Policy Review." Atlantic Council, Policy Paper, May 2001.

Hanley, Charles J. "American Detention of Iranian General, Others May Set Off Violence, Afghan Says." Associated Press, March 9, 2002.

———. " 'Iran Scandal' in Washington, 'U.S. Scandal' in Tehran." Associated Press, November 27, 1986.

Hanson, Brad. "The 'Westoxication' of Iran: Depictions and Reactions of Behrangi, al-e Ahmad, and Shariati." *International Journal of Middle East Studies* 15, no. 1 (February 1983): 1–23.

Harwood, Richard. "The Riddle of Islamic Jihad: Who and What Is It? Does It Even Exist? And Where Will the Bombers Strike Next?" *The Washington Post,* September 21, 1984, p. A27.

Heiss, Mary Ann. "The International Boycott of Iranian Oil and the Anti-Mosaddeq Coup of 1953." In *Mohammad Mosaddeq and the 1953 Coup in Iran,* ed. Malcolm Byrne and Mark J. Gasiorowski. Syracuse, N.Y.: Syracuse University Press, 2004, pp. 178–200.

Hersh, Seymour M. "The Iran Game: How Will Tehran's Nuclear Ambitions Affect Our Budding Partnership?" *The New Yorker,* December 3, 2001, p. 42.

———. "Saddam's Best Friend." *The New Yorker,* April 5, 1999.

"Hezbollah Makes Threat." *The Washington Post,* March 22, 1996, p. A31.

"Hezbollah Rocket Attacks Slam Northern Israel, Peres Under Fire." Agence France-Presse, April 9, 1996.

Hiatt, Fred. "Gore, Chernomyrdin Sign Deal to Find Oil. No Accord on Iranian A-Plant Issue." *The Washington Post,* July 1, 1995, p. A24.

———. "Russian Agency Disputes U.S. on Iranian A-Arms. Moscow Sees No Need to Bar Reactor Sale." *The Washington Post,* March 24, 1995, p. A28.

Hickman, William F. "How the Iranian Military Expelled the Iraqis." *The Brookings Review* 1, no. 3 (Spring 1983): 19–23.

Hines, Christopher. "Iran Elects New Moderate President in Shock to Conservatives." Agence France-Presse, May 24, 1997.

Hiro, Dilip. "Chronicle of the Gulf War." *MERIP Middle East Report* 125–126, July–September 1984.

Hirst, David. "Iran Warns Gulf States over Oil." *The Guardian,* August 23 1986, p. 1.

Hoffman, Lisa. "Is Iran Next?" Scripps Howard News Service, May 27, 2003.

Hooglund, Eric. "The Gulf War and the Islamic Republic." *MERIP Middle East Report* 125–126, July–September 1984.

———. "Iran's Agricultural Inheritance." *MERIP Reports* 99 (September 1981): 15–19.

———. "The Policy of the Reagan Administration Toward Iran." In *Neither East nor West: Iran, the Soviet Union, and the United States,* ed. Nikki R. Keddie and Mark J. Gasiorowski. New Haven, Conn.: Yale University Press, 1990, pp. 180–200.

Human Rights Watch. "Israel/Lebanon: 'Operation Grapes of Wrath,' " 9, no. 8 (September 1997).

Ibrahim, Youssef M. "The Downing of Flight 655." *The New York Times,* July 5, 1988, p. A9.

———. "Israel Accusing Muslim Militants in Recent Bombings in the West." *The New York Times,* July 28, 1994, p. A10.

Indyk, Martin. "Back to the Bazaar." *Foreign Affairs* 81, no. 1 (January–February 2002): 76–77.

Institute for Democracy and Electoral Assistance. "Voter Turnout Since 1945: Islamic Republic of Iran." Available at www.idea.int/vt/country_view.cfm, accessed July 30, 2004.

International Crisis Group. "Dealing with Iran's Nuclear Program." October 27, 2003, pp. 11–15.

———. "Iran: Discontent and Disarray." ICG Middle East Briefing, October 15, 2003.

"Iran Fails to Withdraw Death Sentence or Promise Rushdie's Safety." Associated Press, June 22, 1995, p. 1.

"Iran 'Pickle' Cargo Had Mortar Launcher." United Press International, May 2, 1996.

"Iran Rejects as 'Baseless' German Murder Probe." Agence France-Presse, December 12, 1995, p. 1.

"Iran Unrest." *The NewsHour with Jim Lehrer,* June 18, 2003. Transcript available at www.pbs.org/newshour/bb/middle_east/jan-june03/iran_6-18.html, accessed August 5, 2004.

"Iran Urges UN to React to US Undercover Action Plan." Agence France-Presse, December 28, 1995, p. 1.

"Iran Warns Germany over Kurdish Murder Trial." Agence France-Presse, August 29, 1996, p. 1.

"Iran Won't Give Up Nuclear Program." Associated Press, August 1, 2004.

"Iranian Gets Life for Killing Shah's Last Premier." Reuters, December 6, 1994.

"Iranian President Says Those Who Live by the Sword, Die by the Sword." Voice of the Islamic Republic of Iran, in Persian, November 5, 1995, in *BBC Summary of World Broadcasts,* November 5, 1995.

"Iranian Press Takes Sides over Unrest." BBC News, June 14, 2003. Available at news.bbc.co.uk/go/r/fr/-/1/hi/world/middle_east/2989974.stm, accessed May 24, 2004.

"Iranian Reassures Germans: No Death Threats Against Prosecutors." Agence France-Presse, December 26, 1996, p. 1.

"Iran's Guards Chief Blasts Liberalization, Critics." Reuters, April 29, 1998.

"Iran's Islamic Militants Threaten to Strike US Interests." Agence France-Presse, January 2, 1996, p. 1.

"Iran's Majlis Speaker Says the West Has Not Expressed Regret over Muslim Deaths." Vision of the Islamic Republic of Iran Network, Tehran, in Persian, November 5, 1995, in *BBC Summary of World Broadcasts,* November 5, 1995.

"Iraq's Army: Lessons from the War with Iran." *The Economist,* January 12, 1991.

"Israel and Militants Trade Fire in Lebanon." *The New York Times,* April 1, 1996.

"Israeli Paper Publishes Interview with Vice-President Ebtekar." *BBC Summary of World Broadcasts,* February 3, 1998.

"Israeli Soldier Killed in Bombing in Lebanon." *The New York Times,* March 21, 1996.

Issawi, Charles. "The Iranian Economy 1925–1975: Fifty Years of Economic Development." In *Iran Under the Pahlavis,* ed. George Lenczowski. Stanford, Calif.: Hoover Institution Press, 1978.

Jahn, George. "UN Finds Secret Iran Nuclear Documents." Associated Press, February 12, 2004.

Jawdat, Nameer Ali. "Reflections on the Gulf War." *Arab-American Affairs* 5 (Summer 1983).

Jehl, Douglas. "Iran Closes a Leading Newspaper and Arrests Top Editors." *The New York Times,* September 18, 1998.

———. "Iran Said to Hold Qaeda's No. 3, but to Resist Giving Him Up." *The New York Times,* August 2, 2003.

———. "Lebanon Fighters Gain Stature, but for How Long?" *The New York Times,* April 21, 1996.

———. "U.S. Sees No Basis to Prosecute Iranian Opposition 'Terror' Group Being Held in Iraq." *The New York Times,* July 27, 2004.

———, and Eric Schmitt. "Havens: U.S. Suggests a Qaeda Cell in Iran Directed Saudi Bombings." *The New York Times,* May 21, 2003.

Johns, Richard, and Lucy Kellaway. "Iraq Hits Hormuz Strait Oil Terminal." *Financial Times,* November 26, 1986, p. 1.

Johnson, Haynes. "Hostages to the Past." *The Washington Post,* July 9, 1991.

"Judge Finds Iranian Link to Bombing, Reports Say." Associated Press, August 8, 1994.

Jupa, Richard, and James Dingemann. "The Republican Guards: Loyal, Aggressive, Able." *Army,* March 1991.

Kanovsky, Eliyahu. "Iran's Sick Economy: Prospects for Change Under Khatami." In *Iran Under Khatami,* ed. Patrick Clawson. Washington, D.C.: Washington Institute for Near East Policy, 1998.

Karmon, Ely. "Why Tehran Starts and Stops Terrorism." *Middle East Quarterly* 5, no. 4 (December 1998).

Kashani-Sabet, Firoozeh. "Cultures of Iranianness: The Evolving Polemic of Iranian Nationalism." In *Iran and the Surrounding World: Interactions in Culture and Cultural Politics,* ed. Nikki R. Keddie and Rudi Matthee. Seattle: University of Washington Press, 2002, pp. 162–181.

———. "Fragile Frontiers: The Diminishing Domains of Qajar Iran." *International Journal of Middle East Studies* 29, no. 2 (May 1997): 205–234.

Katouzian, Homa. "The Aridisolatic Society: A Model of Long-Term Social and Economic Development in Iran." *International Journal of Middle East Studies* 15, no. 2 (May 1983): 259–281.

——. "Mosaddeq's Government in Iranian History: Arbitrary Rule, Democracy, and the 1953 Coup." In *Mohammad Mosaddeq and the 1953 Coup in Iran*, ed. Malcolm Byrne and Mark J. Gasiorowski. Syracuse, N.Y.: Syracuse University Press, 2004, pp. 1–26.

Kelley, Matt. "Iran Has Allowed Taliban, al-Qaida Members to Escape, Rumsfeld Says." Associated Press, February 3, 2002.

Kelly, Michael. "It All Points to Arafat." *The Washington Post*, January 9, 2002.

Kemp, Geoffrey. "U.S. and Iran: The Nuclear Dilemma: Next Steps." Washington, D.C.: Nixon Center, 2004.

Kempster, Norman. "U.S. Designates 30 Groups as Terrorists." *Los Angeles Times*, October 9, 1997, p. A16.

Kennedy, Edward M. "The Persian Gulf: Arms Race or Arms Control." *Foreign Affairs* 54, no. 1 (October 1975): 14–35.

"Khatami Receives Hero's Welcome at Polling Station." Agence France-Presse, May 23, 1997.

"Khatami Says USA Holds Key to Future Relations with Iran." Vision of the Islamic Republic of Iran Network 1, Tehran, in Persian, May 27, 1997, *BBC Summary of World Broadcasts*, May 29, 1997.

"Khomeini Issues Message to Religious Authorities." Tehran Radio. In FBIS-NESA, February 23, 1989, pp. 44–48.

Kianouche, Dorranie. "Iranian Factions Squabble over Khatami's New Cabinet." Agence France-Presse, August 9, 1997.

Kinzer, Stephen. "Moderate Leader Is Elected in Iran by a Wide Margin." *The New York Times*, May 25, 1997.

——. "Voice for Change Makes Iran Vote a Real Race." *The New York Times*, May 23, 1997, p. A1.

Kostiner, Joseph. "The Search for Gulf Security: The Politics of Collective Defense." In *Middle East Contemporary Survey*, vol. 16, ed. Ami Ayalon. Boulder, Colo.: Westview, 1992.

Kramer, Martin. "Rallying Around Islam." In *Middle East Contemporary Survey*, vol. 17, ed. Ami Ayalon. Boulder, Colo.: Westview, 1993.

Krauthammer, Charles. "Axis of Evil, Part Two." *The Washington Post*, July 23, 2004, p. A29.

Kristof, Nicholas D. "Nuts with Nukes." *The New York Times*, May 19, 2004.

——. "Those Sexy Iranians." *The New York Times*, May 8, 2004, p. A29.

——. "Velvet Hand, Iron Glove." *The New York Times*, May 15, 2004.

Ladjevardi, Habib. "The Origins of U.S. Support for an Autocratic Iran." *International Journal of Middle East Studies* 15, no. 2 (May 1983): 225–239.

Lake, Anthony. "Confronting Backlash States." *Foreign Affairs* 73, no. 2 (March–April 1994).

Lake, Eli. "U.S., Iran Had Talks on Prisoner Deal." *The New York Sun*, December 15, 2003.

——. "U.S., Iran in Talks over al-Qaida Suspects." United Press International, May 8, 2003.

Lancaster, John. "Boeing Can Provide Parts to Iran Airline." *The Washington Post*, December 4, 1999, p. A16.

——. "Israel Attacks Hezbollah Sites in Lebanon." *The Washington Post*, April 12, 1996, p. A27.

——. "U.S. Waives Proliferation Penalties on China. Beijing Vows to Stop Exporting Missile Parts." *The Washington Post*, November 22, 2000, p. A20.

——, and Robert Suro, "Clinton Reaches Out to Iran." *The Washington Post*, September 29, 1999, p. A2.

Landler, Mark. "Iran Threatens to Restart Nuclear Work." *The New York Times*, June 17, 2004, p. A10.

Lane, Charles. "Germany's New Ostpolitik: Changing Iran." *Foreign Affairs* 74, no. 6 (November–December 1995), pp. 77–89.

Ledeen, Michael. "The Peace Trap." *National Review Online*, August 27, 2003. Available at www.nationalreview.com/ledeen/ledeen082703.asp, accessed August 6, 2004.

——. "The War Won't End in Baghdad." *The Wall Street Journal*, September 4, 2002.

Lelyveld, Michael S. "Ex-Presidential Advisers Press for Limited Business with Iran." *Journal of Commerce*, April 21, 1997, p. 1A.

Lemann, Nicholas. "The Iraq Factor: Will the New Bush Team's Old Memories Shape Its Foreign Policy?" *The New Yorker*, January 22, 2001.

———. "The Next World Order." *The New Yorker,* April 1, 2002.

———. "Real Reasons." *The New Yorker,* September 22, 2003.

———. "The War on What? The White House and the Debate About Whom to Fight Next." *The New Yorker,* September 9, 2002.

Levi, Michael. "Nuclear Reaction: Why Won't the IAEA Get Tough with Iran?" *The New Republic,* September 5, 2003.

Levy, Walter J. "Issues in International Oil Policy." *Foreign Affairs,* April 1957, pp. 454–469.

———. "Oil Power." *Foreign Affairs,* July 1971, pp. 652–668.

Lewis, Paul. "War on Oil Tankers Heats Up in the Persian Gulf." *The New York Times,* May 18, 1986, p. 1.

Lilienthal, David E. "Enterprise in Iran: An Experiment in Economic Development." *Foreign Affairs,* October 1959, pp. 132–139.

Lincy, Valerie. "Nonproliferation: Unexpected Momentum After Iraq." *Iraq Watch* 3, no. 2 (Spring 2004), Wisconsin Project on Nuclear Arms Control.

Lippman, Thomas W. "Gore Lauds Russia's Policy Curbing Arms for Iran. U.S. Pledges to Help Build Safeguards Against Illicit Transfers of High-Tech Weapons." *The Washington Post,* March 12, 1998, p. A9.

———. "Iranian President to Visit U.N." *The Washington Post,* June 28, 1998, p. A25.

———. "U.S. and Russia Sign Economic, Technical Pacts. Internationalizing Space Station, Aiding Nuclear Safety Are Aims." *The Washington Post,* September 3, 1993, p. A28.

———. "U.S. Confirms China Missile Sale to Iran." *The Washington Post,* May 31, 1997, p. A15.

———, and Bradley Graham. "U.S. Mulls Possible Response to Iran in Saudi Bombing." *The Washington Post,* December 22, 1996, p. A30.

Litvak, Meir. "Iran." In *Middle East Contemporary Survey,* vol. 24, ed. Bruce Maddy-Weitzman. Oxford, U.K.: Westview, 2000, pp. 206–244.

———. "The Palestine Islamic Jihad: Background Information." International Policy Institute for Counter-Terrorism at the Interdisciplinary Center Herzliya, February 26, 2003. Available at www.ict.org, accessed on July 20, 2004.

Lobe, Jim. "U.S.-Iran: Republicans Push Confrontation with Iran." Inter Press Service, December 22, 1995, p. 1.

Lotfi, Rozita. "Iranian Postcards: Wrapped in Red Tape." BBC News, February 13, 2004. Available at news.bbc.co.uk/go/pr/fr/-/1/hi/world/middle_east/3487249.stm, accessed May 24, 2004.

Louis, William Roger. "Britain and the Overthrow of the Mosaddeq Government." In *Mohammad Mosaddeq and the 1953 Coup in Iran,* ed. Malcolm Byrne and Mark J. Gasiorowski. Syracuse, N.Y.: Syracuse University Press, 2004, pp. 126–177.

MacFarquhar, Neil. "Backlash of Intolerance Stirring Fear in Iran." *The New York Times,* September 20, 1996.

———. "Iran: Bush's Comments Bolster Old Guard in Tehran." *The New York Times,* February 8, 2002.

———. "Iran Chides Critics as Hard-Liners Make Gains." *The New York Times,* February 23, 2004.

———. "Warlords: Tehran Shuts Offices of Afghan Hard-Liner as Calls to Expel Him Increase." *The New York Times,* February 11, 2002.

MacLeod, Scott. "Radicals Reborn: Iran's Student Heroes Have Had a Rough and Surprising Passage." *Time,* November 15, 1999.

Maddy-Weitzman, Bruce. "Inter-Arab Relations." In *Middle East Contemporary Survey,* vol. 19, ed. Bruce Maddy-Weitzman. Boulder, Colo.: Westview, 1995.

———, and Joshua Teitelbaum. "Inter-Arab Relations." In *Middle East Contemporary Survey,* vol. 20, ed. Bruce Maddy-Weitzman. Boulder, Colo.: Westview, 1996, pp. 66–102.

Makovsky, David. "Labor's Leading Duo Looks to Win the Battle and the War." *The Jerusalem Post,* July 28, 1995, p. 11.

Maloney, Suzanne. "Agents or Obstacles? Parastatal Foundations and Challenges for Iranian Development." In *The Economy of Iran: Dilemmas of an Islamic State,* ed. Parvin Alizadeh. London: I. B. Tauris, 2000, pp. 145–176.

———. "Elections in Iran: A New Majlis and a Mandate for Reform." *Middle East Policy* 7, no. 3 (June 2000): 59–66.

Marr, Phebe. "The Iran-Iraq War: The View from Iraq." In *The Persian Gulf War: Lessons for Strategy, Law, and Diplomacy,* ed. Christopher C. Joyner. Westport, Conn.: Greenwood Press, 1990, pp. 59–74.

McCaul, Ed. "Interview: Iranian Tank Commander." *Military History* 21, no. 1 (April 2004): 44–49.

McFarland, Stephen. "A Peripheral View of the Origins of the Cold War: The Crisis in Iran, 1941–47." *Diplomatic History,* Fall 1980.

McLaurin, R. D. *Military Operations in the Gulf War: The Battle of Khorramshahr.* Aberdeen, Md.: U.S. Army Human Engineering Lab, 1982.

McNaugher, Thomas L. "The Iran-Iraq War: Slouching Toward Catastrophe?" *Middle East Review,* Summer 1987, pp. 5–16.

Menashri, David. "Iran." In *Middle East Contemporary Survey,* vol. 12, ed. Ami Ayalon, Barbara Newson, and Haim Shaked. Oxford, U.K.: Westview, 1988, pp. 469–499.

———. "Iran." In *Middle East Contemporary Survey,* vol. 13, ed. Ami Ayalon and Barbara Newson. Oxford, U.K.: Westview, 1989, pp. 333–371.

———. "Iran." In *Middle East Contemporary Survey,* vol. 14, ed. Ami Ayalon and Barbara Newson. Oxford, U.K.: Westview, 1990, pp. 350–375.

———. "Iran." In *Middle East Contemporary Survey,* vol. 16, ed. Ami Ayalon and Barbara Newson. Oxford, U.K.: Westview, 1992, pp. 395–466.

———. "Iran." In *Middle East Contemporary Survey,* vol. 17, ed. Ami Ayalon. Oxford, U.K.: Westview, 1993, pp. 317–363.

———. "Iran." In *Middle East Contemporary Survey,* vol. 18, ed. Ami Ayalon and Bruce Maddy-Weitzman. Oxford, U.K.: Westview, 1994, pp. 291–319.

———. "Iran." In *Middle East Contemporary Survey,* vol. 19, ed. Bruce Maddy-Weitzman. Oxford, U.K.: Westview, 1995, pp. 280–308.

———. "Iran." In *Middle East Contemporary Survey,* vol. 20, ed. Bruce Maddy-Weitzman. Oxford, U.K.: Westview, 1996, pp. 295–322.

———. "Iran." In *Middle East Contemporary Survey,* vol. 21, ed. Bruce Maddy-Weitzman. Oxford, U.K.: Westview, 1997, pp. 341–371.

———. "Iran." In *Middle East Contemporary Survey,* vol. 22, ed. Bruce Maddy-Weitzman. Oxford, U.K.: Westview, 1998, pp. 255–279.

———. "Iran." In *Middle East Contemporary Survey,* vol. 23, ed. Bruce Maddy-Weitzman. Oxford, U.K.: Westview, 1999, pp. 231–262.

Michaels, Marguerite. "Is Sudan Terrorism's New Best Friend?" *Time,* August 30, 1993, p. 30.

Milbank, Dana, and Peter Slevin. "Bush Details Plan to Curb Nuclear Arms." *The Washington Post,* February 12, 2004, p. A1.

Milhollin, Gary. "The Mullahs and the Bomb." *The New York Times,* October 23, 2003.

Mitchell, Alison. "Clinton Sees Hope in the Election of Moderate as President of Iran." *The New York Times,* May 30, 1997.

———. "Senate Extends Sanctions on Libya and Iran." *The New York Times,* July 26, 2001.

"The Modern Face of Iran." BBC News, November 2, 2002. Available at news.bbc.co.uk/1/low/programmes/from_our_own_correspondent/2383267.stm, accessed May 24, 2004.

Mohammadi-Nejad, Hassan. "The Iranian Parliamentary Elections of 1975." *International Journal of Middle East Studies* 8, no. 1 (January 1977): 103–116.

Mohammed, Nadeya Sayed Ali. "Political Reform in Bahrain: The Price of Stability." *Middle East Intelligence Bulletin* 4, no. 9 (September 2002).

Morley, Jefferson. "Reformists Take Debate to Iranian Press." *The Washington Post,* January 15, 2004.

Morocco, John, et al. "Iranian Airbus Shootdown." *Aviation Week and Space Technology* 129, no. 2 (July 11, 1988): 16.

"Mubarak on Terrorism; Iran, Washington Talks; Hala'ib Triangle." Reported by the BBC, May 13, 1993.

"Mubarak's Advisor Accuses Iran of Assassination Attempt." Agence France-Presse, September 4, 1996.

Mufson, Steven. "Chinese Nuclear Officials See No Reason to Change Plans to Sell Reactor to Iran." *The Washington Post,* May 18, 1995, p. A22.

―――, and Marc Kaufman. "Longtime Foes U.S., Iran Explore Improved Relations." *The Washington Post,* October 29, 2001, p. A9.

Muir, Jim. "Iran to Review Academic's Verdict." BBC News, November 25, 2002. Available at news.bbc.co.uk/1/low/world/middle_east/2511941.stm, accessed August 5, 2004.

―――. "Iranian Protests Fail to Bring Change." BBC News, June 22, 2003. Available at news.bbc.co.uk/go/pr/fr/-/2/hi/middle_east/3011132.stm, accessed May 24, 2004.

Myers, Laura. "Albright, Minister Meet." Associated Press, September 21, 1998.

Nazari, Mohsen. "Characteristics of Labor Force Developments in Iran During Four Decades 1956–1996: Trends and Consequences." *Political and Economic Ettela'at,* no. 11/12 (August–September 1998). Available at www.irvl.net/characteristics_of_labor_force.htm, accessed June 23, 2004.

Norton, Augustus Richard. "Hizballah: From Radicalism to Pragmatism?" *Middle East Policy* 5, no. 4 (January 1998).

Ostermann, Christian F. "New Evidence on the Iran Crisis 1945–46." *Cold War International History Project Bulletin* 12–13 (Fall–Winter 2001): 309–314.

Ottaway, David B. "Baalbek Seen as Staging Area for Terrorism." *The Washington Post,* January 9, 1984, p. A1.

―――. "Khomeini Attempts to Minimize Political Fallout in Parliament." *The Washington Post,* November 23, 1986, p. A17.

―――. "U.S.-Saudi Relations Show Signs of Stress." *The Washington Post,* April 21, 2004, p. A16.

Paine, Chris, and Erica Schoenberger. "Iranian Nationalism and the Great Powers, 1872–1954." *MERIP Reports* 37 (May 1975): 3–28.

Painter, David S. "The United States, Great Britain and Mossadegh." Institute for the Study of Diplomacy, School of Foreign Service, Georgetown University, Washington, D.C., 1993.

Pan, Esther, and Sharon Otterman. "Iran: Curtailing the Nuclear Program." The Council on Foreign Relations, May 13, 2004. Available at www.cfr.org/background/iran_curtail.php?print=1, accessed May 14, 2004.

Parry, Robert. "U.S. Intelligence Seen Identifying Beirut Terrorists." Associated Press, October 4, 1984.

Pechatnov, Vladimir. "The Big Three After World War II: New Documents on Soviet Thinking About Post-War Relations with the United States and Great Britain." Working Paper no. 13, Cold War International History Project, Washington, D.C., May 1995.

Perkovich, George. "Bush's Nuclear Revolution." *Foreign Affairs* 82, no. 2 (March–April 2003): 2–8.

Perlmutter, Amos. "Tracing the Terror Trail Back to Iran." *The Washington Times,* June 23, 1997, p. A13.

Perry, Dan. "Peres Blames Defeat on Colleagues, Terrorists—and Makeup." Associated Press, July 4, 1996.

Pesaran, M. H. "The System of Dependent Capitalism in Pre- and Post-Revolutionary Iran." *International Journal of Middle East Studies* 14, no. 4 (November 1982): 501–522.

Political Deputy of the General Command Post, War Studies and Research. *Battle of Faw* (in Persian). Tehran, 1992. Translated in FBIS-NES-94-076-S, April 20, 1994. [Note: In the front of this document, FBIS indicates it was published in 1982—which is impossible, given that the battle took place in February 1986. However, on the final page, it indicates that it was published in 1988.]

"Political Skirmishing in Tehran." *The New York Times,* August 16, 1997.

Pollack, Kenneth M. "Iran: Shaking Up the High Command." Policy Watch no. 269. Washington Institute for Near East Policy, October 1, 1997.

―――. "The Regional Military Balance. In *The United States and the Persian Gulf,* ed. Richard D. Sokolsky. Washington, D.C.: National Defense University Press, 2003.

———. "Spies, Lies, and Weapons: What Went Wrong?" *The Atlantic Monthly* 293, no. 1 (January–February 2004).

———. "What If Iran Was Behind al-Khobar? Planning for a US Response." Policy Watch no. 243. Washington Institute for Near East Policy, April 16, 1997.

Precht, Henry. "The Iranian Revolution 25 Years Later: An Oral History with Henry Precht, Then State Department Desk Officer." *The Middle East Journal* 58, no. 1 (Winter 2004): 9–31.

"Presidential Candidate Khatami on Law and Order, Economy, Foreign Policy." Vision of the Islamic Republic of Iran Network 1, Tehran, in Persian, May 10, 1997, in *BBC Summary of World Broadcasts*, May 13, 1997.

"Prime Minister Rabin Comments on Explosion, Attacks 'Extremist Islamic Terrorism.' " IDF Radio, Tel Aviv, in Hebrew, July 19, 1994, *BBC Summary of World Broadcasts*, July 20, 1994.

Pryor, Leslie M. "Arms and the Shah." *Foreign Policy* 31 (Summer 1978): 56–71.

Raman, B. "Iran: An Osirak in the Offing." Paper No. 700, South Asia Analysis Group, May 29, 2003.

Ramazani, Rouhollah K. "Challenges for US Policy." In *Iran's Revolution: The Search for Consensus*, ed. R. K. Ramazani. Bloomington, Ind.: Indiana University Press, 1990, pp. 125–140.

———. "Iran's Foreign Policy: Contending Orientations." In *Iran's Revolution: The Search for Consensus*, ed. R. K. Ramazani. Bloomington, Ind.: Indiana University Press, 1990, pp. 48–68.

———. "Iran's 'White Revolution': A Study in Political Development." *International Journal of Middle East Studies* 5, no. 2 (April 1974): 124–139.

Raum, Tom. "Bush Calls on Europe to Overcome Differences and Unite Against Terrorism." Associated Press, May 31, 2003.

"Reps. Support Iran Opposition Group." Associated Press, October 28, 1997.

Rice, Condoleezza. "Campaign 2000: Promoting the National Interest." *Foreign Affairs* 79, no. 1 (January–February 2000).

Richards, Helmut. "America's Shah, Shahanshah's Iran." *MERIP Reports* 40 (September 1975): 3–22, 24, 26.

———. "Land Reform and Agribusiness in Iran." *MERIP Reports* 43 (December 1975): 3–18, 24.

Risen, James. "CIA Tried, with Little Success, to Use U.S. Press in Coup." *The New York Times*, April 16, 2000, p. A14.

———. "Gingrich Wants Funds for Covert Action Against Iran." *Los Angeles Times*, December 10, 1995, p. 1.

———. "Oh, What a Fine Plot We Hatched. (And Here's What to Do the Next Time)." *The New York Times*, June 18, 2000, Section 4, p. 7.

———. "Secrets of History: The CIA in Iran—A Special Report: How a Plot Convulsed Iran in '53 (and in '79)." *The New York Times*, April 16, 2000, p. A1.

Rogers, David. "Gingrich Wants Funds Set Aside for Iran Action." *The Wall Street Journal*, October 27, 1995, p. 1.

Roquefeuil, Christophe de. "Divided US Policymakers Await Outcome of Iranian Election." Agence France-Presse, June 8, 2001.

Rosenberg, Eric. "Options Against Iran Readied for Clinton." *The Times Union* (Albany, N.Y.), April 27, 1997, p. F1.

Rotella, Sebastian. "South America: Trail Heats Up in '94 Bombing." *Los Angeles Times*, December 6, 1997, p. A2.

Rottman, Gordon L. "Saddam's Juggernaut or Armed Horde? The Origins of the Iraqi Army." *International Defense Review*, November 1990, pp. 1240–1242.

Roy, Olivier. "The Crisis of Religious Legitimacy in Iran." *The Middle East Journal* 53, no. 2 (Spring 1999): 201–217.

Ruane, Michael E. "Retaliations for Terrorism: Do They Deter or Prompt Attacks?" *The Philadelphia Inquirer*, August 8, 1996, p. A14.

Rubin, Barry. "The United States and the Middle East." In *Middle East Contemporary Survey*, vol. 19, ed. Bruce Maddy-Weitzman. Boulder, Colo.: Westview, 1995, pp. 27–39.

"Salman Rushdie Condemns EU Ambassadors' Return to Iran." Agence France-Presse, May 6, 1997, p. 1.

Salpukas, Agis. "Conoco's Deal in Iran Faces Broad Hurdle." *The New York Times,* March 14, 1995.

Samii, A. William "Iran's Guardian Council as an Obstacle to Democracy." *The Middle East Journal* 55, no. 4 (Autumn 2001): 643–662.

Sanger, David E. "In Face of Report, Iran Acknowledges Buying Nuclear Components." *The New York Times,* February 23, 2004.

———. "The Iran Exception; U.S. Will Deal with Other Old Foes but Still Sees Teheran as an Outlaw." *The New York Times,* March 15, 1995.

———, and William J. Broad. "Iran Admits That It Has Plans for a Newer Centrifuge." *The New York Times,* February 13, 2004.

Saunders, Harold H. "The Crisis Begins." In *American Hostages in Iran: The Conduct of a Crisis,* ed. Warren Christopher and Paul H. Kreisberg. New Haven, Conn.: Yale University Press, 1985, pp. 35–71.

———. "Diplomacy and Pressure, November 1979–May 1980." In *American Hostages in Iran: The Conduct of a Crisis,* ed. Warren Christopher and Paul H. Kreisberg. New Haven, Conn.: Yale University Press, 1985, pp. 72–144.

Savory, Roger M. "Social Development in Iran During the Pahlavi Era." In *Iran Under the Pahlavis,* ed. George Lenczowski. Stanford, Calif.: Hoover Institution Press, 1978, pp. 85–127.

Schmemann, Serge. "Giving War a Chance." *The New York Times,* April 14, 1996.

———. "Israel and Guerrillas Joined Again in Deadly Dance." *The New York Times,* April 14, 1996.

———. "Israel and Militants Trade Blows as Fighting Spreads in Lebanon." *The New York Times,* April 13, 1996.

———. "Israeli Aircraft Strike Guerrillas in Beirut Suburbs." *The New York Times,* April 12, 1996, p. A1.

Schweid, Barry. "U.S. to Punish Chinese for Chemical Weapons Shipments to Iran." Associated Press, May 22, 1997.

Sciolino, Elaine. "Beijing Rebuffs U.S. on Halting Iran Atom Deal." *The New York Times,* April 18, 1995, p. A1.

———. "Iranian Leader Says U.S. Move on Oil Deal Wrecked Chance to Improve Ties." *The New York Times,* May 16, 1995.

———. "Pleased Yet Wary, U.S. Offers Gestures of Support for Iran." *The New York Times,* March 26, 1998, p. A1.

———. "U.S. and Chinese Resolve Dispute on Missile Sales." *The New York Times,* October 5, 1994, p. A1.

———. "U.S. May Threaten China with Sanctions for Reported Arms Sales." *The New York Times,* July 20, 1993, p. A3.

Scowcroft, Brent. "An Opening to Iran." *The Washington Post,* May 11, 2001.

Segal, David. "The Iran-Iraq War: A Military Analysis." *Foreign Affairs,* Summer 1988.

Shadid, Anthony, and John Donnelly. "Fighting Terror: The Struggle for Influence; Iranian Arms, Goods Flood Afghan Region." *The Boston Globe,* January 25, 2002.

Sheridan, Michael. "Norway Steps Up Rushdie Campaign." *The Independent,* July 4, 1995, p. 1.

Sick, Gary. "Iran's Foreign Policy: A Revolution in Transition." In *Iran and the Surrounding World,* ed. Nikki R. Keddie and Rudi Matthee. Seattle: University of Washington Press, 2002, pp. 355–374.

———. "Military Options and Constraints." In *American Hostages in Iran: The Conduct of a Crisis,* ed. Warren Christopher and Paul H. Kreisberg. New Haven, Conn.: Yale University Press, 1985, pp. 144–172.

———. "Rethinking Dual Containment." *Survival* 40, no. 1 (Spring 1998): 5–32.

———. "Trial by Error: Reflections on the Iran-Iraq War." In *Iran's Revolution: The Search for Consensus,* ed. R. K. Ramazani. Bloomington: Indiana University Press, 1990, pp. 104–124.

Sipress, Alan. "Bush's Speech Shuts Door on Tenuous Opening to Iran." *The Washington Post,* February 4, 2002, p. A10.

———, and Steven Mufson. "U.S. Explores Recruiting Iran into New Coalition." *The Washington Post,* September 25, 2001, p. A1.

Slavin, Barbara. "Iran, U.S. Holding Talks in Geneva." *USA Today,* May 11, 2003.

————. "Officials 'Outed' Iran's Spies in 1997." *USA Today,* March 29, 2004.

————. "Q&A with Foreign Minister Kamal Kharrazi." *USA Today,* September 18, 2002.

Smith, R. Jeffrey. "China May Cancel Proposed Sale of Nuclear Facility to Iran." *The Washington Post,* November 6, 1996, p. A9.

————. "China's Pledge to End Iran Nuclear Aid Yields U.S. Help. Clinton Says He'll Allow U.S. Exports of Technology. Scrutiny and Debate Are Expected." *The Washington Post,* October 30, 1997, p. A15.

Smith, Stefan. "Iran Admits Resuming Centrifuge Assembly; European Powers Report 'No Progress' in Talks." Agence France-Presse, August 6, 2004.

Snyder, Robert. "Explaining the Iranian Revolution's Hostility Toward the United States." *Journal of South Asian and Middle Eastern Studies* 17, no. 3 (Spring 1994).

Sokolski, Henry. "That Iranian Nuclear Headache," *National Review Online,* January 22, 2004. Available at www.npec-web.org, accessed January 22, 2004.

"Something Is Being Cooked Up Against the Regime in Sudan." *The Middle East Mirror,* June 29, 1995, pp. 14–17.

Staudenmaier, William O. "The Iran-Iraq War." In *The Lessons of Recent Wars in the Third World,* ed. Robert Harkavy and Stephanie Neuman. Lexington, Mass.: Lexington Books, 1986.

————. "A Strategic Analysis of the Gulf War." Carlisle Barracks, Pa.: Strategic Studies Institute, U.S. Army War College, 1982.

Stein, Janice Gross. "The Wrong Strategy in the Right Place: The United States in the Gulf." *International Security* 13, no. 3 (Winter 1988–1989).

Stobaugh, Robert B. "The Evolution of Iranian Oil Policy, 1925–1975." In *Iran Under the Pahlavis,* ed. George Lenczowski. Stanford, Calif.: Hoover Institution Press, 1978, pp. 201–252.

Stockman, Farah. "Unease Builds with Rise of Iran." *The Boston Globe,* August 4, 2004, p. A1.

"Sudan: Villain or Scapegoat?" *The Middle East Mirror,* June 30, 1995, pp. 15–20.

Sully, Melanie. "Blix Calls for International Treaty to Ban Production of WMDs." Voice of America News, June 30, 2004. Transcript available at www.nci.org/04nci/06/VOANews.htm, accessed August 11, 2004.

Takeyh, Ray. "God's Will: Iranian Democracy and the Islamic Context." *Middle East Policy* 7, no. 4 (October 2000): 41–49.

————. "Iran at a Crossorads." *Middle East Journal* 57, no. 1 (Winter 2003).

————. "Iran Would Give Up Nukes for the Right Deal." *International Herald Tribune,* October 23, 2003.

————. "Iranian Options: Pragmatic Mullas and America's Interests." *The National Interest,* Fall 2003, pp. 49–56.

————. "Iran's Nuclear Calculations." *World Policy Journal,* Summer 2003, pp. 21–28.

Talwar, Puneet. "Iran in the Balance." *Foreign Affairs* 80, no. 4 (July–August 2001).

"A Tangled History with Iran." *The New York Times,* April 18, 2000, p. A24.

Tehran IRNA. "Interior Minister: Mykonos Trial 'A Zionist Plot.' " April 16, 1997. Available at www.salamiran.org/Media/IRNA/970416.html#HLN10, accessed July 27, 2004.

————. "Official Warns of German Coordination with U.S. Designs Against Iran." April 16, 1997. Available at www.salamiran.org/Media/IRNA/970416.html#HLN10, accessed July 27, 2004.

Teitelbaum, Joshua. "Bahrain." In *Middle East Contemporary Survey,* vol. 20, ed. Bruce Maddy-Weitzman. Boulder, Colo.: Westview, 1996, pp. 250–259.

————. "Saudi Arabia." In *Middle East Contemporary Survey,* vol. 17, ed. Ami Ayalon. Boulder, Colo.: Westview, 1993.

————. "Saudi Arabia." In *Middle East Contemporary Survey,* vol. 19, ed. Bruce Maddy-Weitzman. Boulder, Colo.: Westview, 1995, pp. 238–243.

"Tensions Rise as Washington and Tehran Trade Accusations." Agence France-Presse, August 4, 1996.

Thorpe, James A. "Truman's Ultimatum to Stalin on the 1946 Azerbaijan Crisis: The Making of a Myth." *The Journal of Politics* 40, no. 1 (February 1978): 188–195.

Trainor, Lt. General Bernard. "Iraqi Offensive: Victory Goes Beyond Battlefield." *The New York Times,* April 20, 1988.

Turner, Arthur Campbell. "Nationalism and Religion: Iran and Iraq at War." In *The Regionalization of Warfare*, ed. James Brown and William P. Snyder. New Brunswick, N.J.: Transaction Books, 1990.

Twing, Shawn L. "Iran, Bahrain Will Exchange Envoys." *Washington Report on Middle East Affairs*, January–February 1998, p. 38.

Tyler, Patrick E. "Russian's Links to Iran Offer a Case Study in Arms Leaks." *The New York Times*, May 10, 2000, p. A6.

Valinejad, Afshin. "Iran Denies Giving Refuge to al-Qaida or Taliban, Admits It Can't Fully Control Borders." Associated Press, February 5, 2002.

———. "Iran Reform Leader Shot in Tehran." Associated Press, March 13, 2000.

———. "Iranian Parliament Approves Moderate President's Cabinet Nominees." Associated Press, August 20, 1997.

Vick, Karl. "Another Nuclear Program Found in Iran." *The Washington Post*, February 24, 2004, p. A1.

———. "The Appearance of Change in Iran." *The Washington Post*, January 15, 2004, p. A1.

———. "Sorry, Wrong Chador." *The Washington Post*, July 19, 2004, p. C1.

Viorst, Milton. "Iraq at War." *Foreign Affairs*, Winter 1986–1987.

Wagner, John S. "Iraq: A Combat Assessment." In *Fighting Armies: Antagonists in the Middle East*, ed. Richard Gabriel. Westport, Conn.: Greenwood, 1983.

Waldman, Amy. "After Mixup, Americans Free 12 Afghans Suspected of Being Iranian Agents." *The New York Times*, March 21, 2002.

Wallace, Charles P. "Khomeini Blasts Aides for Secret Talks with U.S." *Los Angeles Times*, November 21, 1986, p. 1.

"Wanted Terrorist Leaders Still in Sudan." *al-Ahram*, May 28, 1996. In FBIS-TOT-96-018-L, July 19, 1996.

Warrick, Joby, and Glenn Kessler. "Iran Had Secret Nuclear Program, UN Agency Says." *The Washington Post*, November 11, 2003, p. A1.

———. "Iran's Nuclear Program Speeds Ahead." *The Washington Post*, March 10, 2003, p. A1.

Wawro, Geoffrey. "Letter from Iran." *Naval War College Review* 55, no. 1 (Winter 2002).

"Weapons Uranium Found in Iran." Agence France-Presse via Yahoo! News, March 12, 2004. Available at au.news.yahoo.com/030826/2/lfr0.html, accessed August 6, 2004.

Webman, Esther. "The Dynamics of Retreat and Change in Political Islam." In *Middle East Contemporary Survey*, vol. 21, ed. Bruce Maddy-Weitzman. Boulder, Colo.: Westview, 1997.

Weiner, Tim. "U.S. Plan to Change Iran Leaders Is an Open Secret Before It Begins." *The New York Times*, January 26, 1996, p. 1.

Weisman, Steven R. "The Attack: Bush Condemns Saudi Blasts; 7 Americans Are Dead." *The New York Times*, May 14, 2003.

———. "Israelis Say Palestinians Forming Strategic Alliance with Iran, Palestinians Deny Allegation." Associated Press, January 14, 2002.

———. "U.S. Demands That Iran Turn Over Qaeda Agents and Join Saudi Inquiry." *The New York Times*, May 26, 2003.

Wells, Matthew C. "Thermidor in the Islamic Republic of Iran: The Rise of Muhammad Khatami." *British Journal of Middle Eastern Studies* 26, no. 1 (May 1999): 27–39.

Weymouth, Lally. "It's Peace or a New Wave of Terrorism, Says Rabin." *The Washington Post*, June 21, 1995, p. A21.

Whitaker, Brian. "The Strange Affair of Karine A." *The Guardian*, January 21, 2002.

"White House Agrees to Covert-Action Plan for Iran." Agence France-Presse, December 22, 1995, p. 1.

Wikipedia. "1973 Oil Crisis." Available at en.wikipedia.org/wiki/1973_energy_crisis, accessed June 27, 2004.

———. "October Surprise." Available at en.wikipedia.org/wiki/October_Surprise, accessed July 10, 2004.

Williams, Daniel. "EU Ministers Urge Iran to Condemn Terrorism." *The Washington Post*, March 11, 1996, p. 1.

———. "U.S., Russia Trade Gibes over Iran. Kremlin Vows 'Tough' Reply to American Sanctions, Threats." *The Washington Post,* January 15, 1999, p. A23.

Wright, Robin. "In Shift, U.S. Makes Quiet Overtures to Iran Following Election Upset." *Los Angeles Times,* July 9, 1997.

———. "Shiite Muslims Capture Center Stage in Lebanon." *The Christian Science Monitor,* October 5, 1984, p. 1.

Yegorova, Natalia I. "The 'Iran Crisis' of 1945–46: A View from the Russian Archives." Working Paper no. 15, Cold War International History Project, Washington, D.C., May 1996.

Young, T. Cuyler. "Iran in Continuing Crisis." *Foreign Affairs,* January 1962, pp. 275–292.

Zabih, Sepehr. "Iran's Policy Toward the Persian Gulf." *International Journal of Middle East Studies* 7, no. 3 (July 1976): 345–358.

Zahrani, Mostafa. "The Coup That Changed the Middle East: Mossadeq v. the CIA in Retrospect." *World Policy Journal* 19, no. 2 (Summer 2002): 93–99.

Miscellaneous

Bengio, Ofra. "Baghdad Between Shi'a and Kurds." Policy Focus No. 18, Washington Institute for Near East Policy, February 1992.

Carus, Seth. "Iran and Weapons of Mass Destruction." Pre-publication copy prepared for the American Jewish Committee Annual Meeting, May 3, 2000.

Christopher, Warren. "Fighting Terrorism: Challenges for Peacemakers." Address to the Soref Symposium of the Washington Institute for Near East Policy, May 21, 1996, reprinted in Warren Christopher, *In the Stream of History: Shaping Foreign Policy for a New Era.* Stanford, Calif.: Stanford University Press, 1998, p. 448.

Crist, David. "Operation Earnest Will: The United States in the Persian Gulf, 1986–1989." Ph.D. dissertation, Florida State University, 1998.

EconStats. "Iran." Available at www.econstats.com/global/air.xls, accessed June 27, 2004.

ElBaradei, Mohamed. "Nuclear Proliferation: Global Security in a Rapidly Changing World." Keynote Address to the Carnegie International Non-Proliferation Conference, Washington, D.C., June 21, 2004.

GlobalSecurity.org. "A. Q. Khan and Iran." Available at www.globalsecurity.org/wmd/world/iran/khan-iran.htm, accessed August 5, 2004.

———. "Nuclear Weapons–2002 Developments." Available at www.globalsecurity.org/wmd/world/iran/nuke2002.htm, accessed August 5, 2004.

———. "Nuclear Weapons–2003 Developments." Available at www.globalsecurity.org/wmd/world/iran/nuke2003.htm, accessed August 5, 2004.

———. "Nuclear Weapons–2004 Developments." Available at www.globalsecurity.org/wmd/world/iran/nuke2004.htm, accessed August 5, 2004.

Greenberg, Eldon V. C. "The NPT and Plutonium." Nuclear Control Institute, 1993. Available at www.nci.org/03NCI/12/NPTandPlutonium.pdf, accessed August 12, 2004.

Heston, Alan, Robert Summers, and Bettina Aten. Penn World Table Version 6.1. Center for International Comparisons at the University of Pennsylvania (CICUP), October 2002. Available at pwt.econ.upenn.edu/php_site/pwt61_form.php, accessed June 23, 2004.

Human Rights Watch. "Iran, 2004." Available at hrw.org/doc/?t=mideast&c=iran, accessed August 5, 2004.

Indyk, Martin. "The Clinton Administration's Approach to the Middle East." Speech given at the Soref Symposium of the Washington Institute for Near East Policy, May 18, 1993. Available at www.washingtoninstitute.org/pubs/soref/indyk.htm, accessed July 24, 2004.

International Atomic Energy Agency. Report by the Director General, "Implementation of the NPT Safeguards Agreement in the Islamic Republic of Iran." GOV/2003/40, June 6, 2003.

———. Board of Governors. "Implementation of the NPT Safeguards Agreement in the Islamic Republic of Iran: Resolution Adopted by the Board on 18 June 2004." GOV/2004/49, June 18, 2004.

National Public Radio. "Analysis: Politics and Reform in Iran." *Talk of the Nation,* interview with Molavi, January 22, 2003. Transcript available at www.npr.org/programs/totn/transcripts/2003/jan/030122.conan.html, accessed August 3, 2004.

NewsHour with Jim Lehrer. "Iran's Nuclear Deal," October 21, 2003. Transcript available at www.nci.org/03NCI/10/Irans-Nuclear-Deal.htm, accessed July 19, 2004.

PBS *Frontline.* "Terror and Tehran." "Chronology: U.S.-Iran Relations, 1906–2002." Available at www.pbs.org/wgbh/pages/frontline/shows/tehran/etc/cron.html, accessed August 1, 2004.

Statistical Center of Iran. "Population with 10 Years of Age and Over, Sorted by Sex and Activity (1956–1997)." Available at www.iranworld.com/Indicators/isc-t099.asp, accessed June 30, 2004.

Index

KENNETH M. POLLACK is director of research at the Saban
Center for Middle East Policy at the Brookings Institution.
From 1995 to 1996 and from 1999 to 2001, he served as
director for Gulf affairs at the National Security Council,
where he was the principal working-level official responsible
for implementation of U.S. policy toward Iran. Prior to his
time in the Clinton administration, he spent seven years in
the CIA as a Persian Gulf military analyst. He is the author
of *The Threatening Storm* and *Arabs at War*. He lives in
Washington, D.C.

ABOUT THE TYPE

This book was set in Times Roman, designed by Stanley Morison specifically for *The Times* of London. The typeface was introduced in the newspaper in 1932. Times Roman has had its greatest success in the United States as a book and commercial typeface, rather than one used in newspapers.